Law for Professionals

Kai Jacob • Dierk Schindler •
Roger Strathausen • Bernhard Waltl
Editors

Liquid Legal – Humanization and the Law

Springer

liquid legal institute

Editors
Kai Jacob
Liquid Legal Intsitute
Wiesloch, Germany

Dierk Schindler
Liquid Legal Institute
Ottobrunn, Germany

Roger Strathausen
Liquid Legal Institute
Málaga, Spain

Bernhard Waltl
Liquid Legal Institute
Munich, Germany

ISSN 2662-141X ISSN 2662-1428 (electronic)
Law for Professionals
ISBN 978-3-031-14239-0 ISBN 978-3-031-14240-6 (eBook)
https://doi.org/10.1007/978-3-031-14240-6

This Springer imprint is published by the registered company Springer Nature Switzerland AG
The registered company address is: Gewerbestrasse 11, 6330 Cham, Switzerland

Foreword: Humanizing The Legal Function—What It Means and Why It Matters

> When people have points of reference that are humanizing, that demystifies difference.—Laverne Cox

The speed, scale, and effects of change are challenging the limits of human adaptability. The pandemic has accelerated and intensified an already perfect storm of socioeconomic factors that include: digital transformation, technological advances, big data, social/political fragmentation, and climate change. These and other convergent forces are transforming our lives, business, society, and the planet. Then came the pandemic.

Covid-19 has accelerated change and exposed the fragility of human networks—individual, social, business, supply chain, societal, and environmental. It has ravaged physical and emotional health, elevated uncertainty, upended routine, limited human contact, and elevated isolation. The pandemic has been a painful reminder that life is not a solitary pursuit and interpersonal contact is essential to feeling—and being—human.

The pandemic has intensified the daily battle of subsistence for hundreds of millions of our fellow humans. For the more fortunate, it has provided an opportunity to reflect, reboot, and rebalance their lives. What is our purpose? Where do we live and work? How do we achieve balance that fulfills life's purpose?

The search for purpose has contributed to "The Great Resignation." A record number of American workers have voluntarily left their jobs. There are many reasons, of course, and a lack of purpose—especially among Millennials and Gen Z's—tops the list. The younger generations tend to view life more holistically and do not compartmentalize work/life/family the way their parents did. Purpose is not confined to a paycheck; it is also a voice, a team, an opportunity to collaborate, learn, grow, experiment, understand the *why* of work, and contribute to the common good. This is stakeholder capitalism applied to the individual.

The pandemic has also contributed to dramatic demographic shifts produced by technological advances that support remote working, especially in knowledge-based industries. People are moving to where they want to live, not where their job is. They are also moving across industries. Digital transformation has accelerated dramatically during Covid-19, further blurring demarcation lines that once separated industries. Skilled workers, especially those that possess agile minds, are learners-for-life, possess advanced "people skills" (EQ), and can "connect the dots," have more choices than ever before. Many have migrated to work that provides an elevated sense of purpose, not necessarily accompanied by a bigger paycheck. Purpose, balance, and understanding "the why" of work are elements of "individual stakeholder capitalism."

It is no coincidence that stakeholder capitalism and the individual version of it are converging. Business sustainability—and profit—is promoted by a clearly articulated, widely embraced statement of purpose and mission that commits to doing well by doing good. The key ingredients are: a humane approach not only to the workforce but also customers, communities, society, and the environment; providing value and an outstanding end-to-end customer experience; contributing to the communities business operates in and impacts; committing to diversity, equity, and inclusion (DEI) as well as environmental, social, and governance (ESG) sustainability and ethical impact; and creating a culture that respects the individual and advances the collective good.

The 2019 Business Roundtable Statement, signed by 181 CEO's of leading companies, is a blueprint for the "Modern Standard For Corporate Responsibility." It taps into the vein of the common good, injecting purpose; diversity, equity, and inclusion; sustainability; social responsibility; and governance into business. This prescription for corporate health positively impacts a wide group of stakeholders, enabling business to do well by doing good. It has proven to be a magnet for talent, customers, and investors—a corporate virtuous circle.

"We Have Forgotten What Law Is *For*"

How has the legal function responded to individual and societal needs during this time of change, crisis, and suffering? Ralph S. Tyler, Jr., a Harvard constitutional law professor, gives it a failing grade in a recent New York Times Opinion piece. "Something has gone badly wrong: It is unclear, in America in 2022, what the point of law is, what higher ends it should strive to attain. We have forgotten what law is *for*."

What's missing from law today, Tyler argues, is an emphasis on the common good, a core precept of American legal tradition whose roots trace back to the nation's founding. The "general welfare," Tyler notes, appears in both the preamble to the Constitution and its text. He maintains the common good has been replaced by intractable, competing ideologies and factionalism. Even the Supreme Court, in his view, has succumbed to these social, political, ideological, and economic societal fissures.

There is ample evidence to support the contention that we *have* forgotten what law is for. Big Law may be celebrating its 2021 record profits, but the rule of law is on the precipice; a small fraction of the population can afford legal services even when they are desperately needed; and self-regulation has conflated legal practice with the business of delivering accessible, affordable, efficient, and fit for purpose legal services, products, and assistance.

These issues are not endemic to the US legal system. The challenges and solutions to law's global malaise share more in common than their jurisdictional practice differences. The digital legal function is a profession subsumed within a global industry and should be owned, operated, and regulated as such. Law should follow the lead of business by crafting and collectively pledging to adopt a "Modern Standard For Legal Responsibility." The cornerstone of the document should be a commitment to forge a more humane legal function, one that is committed not only to insure the well-being of its workforce but also its clients/customers, society, and the environment.

What steps can be taken to humanize law—to make it more accessible, relatable, humane, and less arcane, remote, and forbidding? Here is a starter list.

1. Law is about human interaction—preserving social order and advancing cohesion. People are the essence of law's purpose. A legal system that is accessible and affordable only to a small segment of the population cannot foster respect for the rule of law, nor can it promote a willingness to compromise, a key ingredient of the common good.
2. Modern societies rely upon law to resolve conflict, maintain order, protect and defend rights, and enforce responsibilities. Law is the societal cement that binds cracks and supports the common good. Law must itself be humane and set an example for humanity; its core purpose is to create a framework for orderly, peaceful human co-existence.
3. Law is a function, part of a larger societal whole. The legal function's purpose is derived from and proscribed by that larger societal whole, not internally. Many in the legal industry have lost sight of that.
4. A humane, compassionate, equitable, and diverse legal function is essential to building public trust, compromise, and advancing the common good. Law must reclaim its humanity internally—within its ecosystem—and externally—in its interaction with customers/clients and society at large.
5. There are a legion of ways that the legal function can better align itself internally and with those for whom its purpose is to serve. Here is a representative sampling of ways that law can advance alignment and promote the common good. The crux is humanizing the legal function's purpose and applying it to everyone and everything it impacts—and should touch.
   (a) creating a culture and environment that is welcoming to a diverse workforce
   (b) creating a legal culture whose purpose is to serve people and to solve problems
   (c) building a legal function whose diversity more closely resembles the society it serves and the complexities of its challenges
   (d) stressing the importance of and honing people skills throughout one's career
   (e) focusing on well-being, upskilling, learning for life, and other characteristics to meet the needs of a digitally transforming society
   (f) jettisoning the antiquated "lawyers and 'non-lawyers'" mindset and replacing it with a team approach to problem-solving that does not relegate non-licensed attorneys or younger generations to a lesser status

(g) using language that is clear, concise, and designed to "speak the language of individuals, business, and society"—not "legalese." The goal of language is to communicate and create community. Legal language has the opposite effect

(h) Reimagining legal education and training so that it is more affordable, flexible, people-oriented, accountable, outcome-driven, diverse (student body and faculty) and produces graduates that not only know the rudiments of doctrinal law and can "think like a lawyer" but also possess an understanding of the marketplace and the needs of the clients/customers and society they serve.

(i) Legal regulation must be humanized. Crispin Passmore, a legal regulatory authority and friend explains how: "If we are to humanize law, we need to make it accessible and relevant, ensuring that it evolves with the society and economy it serves. Only independent, genuinely public interest regulation can do that."

(j) The legal function's purpose must be clearly articulated and adopted throughout its ecosystem. It *is* a "legal mosaic" and must function as an integrated whole with a clear sense of purpose, compassion, and clarity.

(k) Courts must be humanized, because the judicial process is skewed against individuals. A 2020 Pew Charitable Trusts report highlighted the desperate need for reform. It found that at least four million Americans are sued over consumer debt each year. More than 90% lack counsel, and in excess of 70% of cases result in default judgments against the defendant. When individuals have a legal right to assert, they are, likewise, highly unlikely to retain counsel. This is not a humane, equitable, or sustainable legal system.

(l) The legal function can learn a great deal from the digital transformation of business; it need not reinvent the wheel. Law should focus less on "innovation" and more on alignment within its ecosystem and with society at large. Business has created a roadmap that can be adapted—and followed—by the legal function.

(m) Knowledge, skills, and judgment are core elements of the legal function. Technology, data, process, and other tools enable people to leverage and scale legal delivery—to make it more predictive, proactive, accessible, affordable, and fast. But without empathy, collaboration, and humanity, the legal function cannot earn the trust and respect of its workforce or those it serves. That's why humanization is the lynchpin of law's ability to restore public trust and a return to the common good.

Conclusion

The legal industry has been largely dismissive of "soft skills" and "humanizing law." One of the paradoxes of our time is that the ascendency of automation, artificial intelligence, blockchain, Big Data, and other technological platforms has elevated, not diminished, the importance of humanity. It is not only what distinguishes us from machines but it also enables us to apply our humanity *to* machines. The legal function will play an important role in this process but must first take a hard look at itself.

The article was first published in: Mark A. Cohen, idem nomen, in Forbes, 02.15.2022, www.forbes.com/sites/markcohen1/2022/02/15/humanizing-the-legal-function-what-it-means-and-why-it-matters/.

Mark A. Cohen is a global thought leader and innovator in the legal industry. He is the CEO of Legal Mosaic; Executive Chairman of the Digital Legal Exchange, a unique global non-profit comprised of leading multinationals focused on the legal function's digital transformation; regular Forbes Contributor; Economist contributor; and Singapore Academy of Law (SAL) Distinguished Scholar. Mark has held numerous positions as Distinguished Fellow/Scholar at prestigious law and business schools including Georgetown, Northwestern, IE, and Bucerius. He is a sought-after keynote speaker who has spoken to leading multinationals, Bar Associations, academic institutions, and Governments around the world.

Mark has focused on "the business of law" since the turn of the Millennium. Prior to that, he was an internationally recognized civil trial lawyer, serving stints as a decorated Assistant United States Attorney, BigLaw partner, national boutique founder, outside General Counsel, and Federally-Appointed Receiver of an international aviation parts business. He was also a co-founder of Clearspire, a globally acclaimed pioneer law firm/legal services company that reimagined the delivery of legal services from the customer perspective.

Legal Mosaic

Digital Legal Exchange

Mark A. Cohen

Foreword

AI and automation have without a doubt transformed the ways we live our lives, in the workforce and beyond. As technologies continue to advance, a number of challenges have arisen regarding the quality, utility, and adoption of these tools. These challenges are particularly acute in areas that require deep domain expertise, one being the legal profession.

A central theme that intersects all of these challenges will revolve around the human capabilities to embrace the far-reaching technological changes spreading across private and public sectors alike. Legal professionals find themselves aspiring to comprehend and embrace these changes with the intention to shape this transformation, and to enhance their abilities to make legal services more accessible to the general public. After all, the legal profession shapes society in important ways: by making laws that sustain social order while promoting equal access to fairness and justice, by interpreting laws to guide daily activities based on evolving social tenets, and by adjudicating disputes among different stakeholders.

One might argue that the legal profession had successfully embraced and adapted to the coming of new technologies over the past century. As a young practicing lawyer who started shortly after the dawn of the new millennium, I quickly embraced technologies such as document comparison via redlining and contract review using electronic data rooms as they rolled out of Skadden Arp's IT department. There was no reminiscence of the long days and longer nights spent in the windowless conference rooms trying to copy contract clauses by hand. There was no questioning of the accuracy of computer redlining versus the human eyes, or the speed of gaining access to an electronic data room versus a physical data room located hundreds of miles away. Those technologies were clearly better than their predecessors, and they did not require much contribution or involvement from the lawyers, if any at all.

That, unfortunately, is not the case for automation and AI technologies which enable AI completing contract review and legal research across thousands of documents within minutes, and smart contracts written in computer code stored on a blockchain executing themselves upon legally relevant events and actions. Deep understanding of the legal concepts and their interpretative nuances across a diverse range of legal specializations are a crucial part to not only the widespread adoption of these technologies, but also their initial development.

Very few legal professionals understand the secret of success of the modern-day AI: it requires a large amount of training data to be able to perform a task that surpasses human accuracy. In M&A contract review, for example, an effective AI tool would need to learn from tens of thousands, or even hundreds of thousands, example legal clauses across a large variety of contracts to be able to accurately predict the existence of a type of legal clause in new and different contracts. Even with ample training data, an effective AI product would rely heavily on legal professionals to quality check the results and correct the predictions. The only group of people who can create the training data or perform quality checks are highly skilled legal professionals, but many are oblivious of the fact that their contributions are required to advance the quality of the AI.

Law by definition is a social construct that cannot be automated by machines. It is a concept of justice and fairness that will always require human judgement and social consensus. Accordingly, legal transformation does not follow the playbook of the Industrial Revolution. Unlike Henry Ford, who did not need to consult with a specialist of horse anatomy to design the Model T, or horsemen who could be replaced by newly trained car drivers, a technologist or AI scientist needs the expertise of the practicing lawyers to usher in a new era of legal transformation.

In 2018, I started the search for an "accurate" AI tool that could extract relevant legal clauses accurately within minutes. Many tools promised great results—yet many failed experiments ensued. When hype outpaces progress, motivation for contribution dissipates; expectation quickly turns into distrust. I, too, made the mistake of demanding others to meet my hyped expectation without knowing that the key to success laid in the hands of legal professionals like me. That is why I started a non-profit organization called *The Atticus Project*, the curator of CUAD, an open-sourced high quality training dataset of legal contracts with 13,000+ annotations crowd-sourced under the supervision of experienced lawyers.

A successful legal transformation depends on creating a human-centric strategy that motivates legal professionals to take part. Its success depends on our ability to design systems and workflows that make the human lawyers' experience more rewarding than before. Existing AI tools, at its infancy, require lawyers to strain themselves by meeting the demands of two parallel workflows. New generations of lawyers are being rewarded for work done manually via memos in Microsoft Word with impeccably formatted executive summaries, yet the AI tools largely learn from csv files that are not suitable for human consumption. Many AI tools have a steep learning curve that requires hours or even weeks to learn, yet clients are willing to pay for the time spent formatting a Word document instead of learning a new technology. Creating structural changes where lawyers in all practices are rewarded both economically and professionally to learn new technologies is an essential first step toward an AI-enhanced legal transformation.

The human-centric strategy also requires the AI industry to do its part. There needs to be ongoing dialogues between the legal professionals and the technologists to understand the human challenges in performing their daily tasks and work together to design effective tools to tackle them. Many solutions are desperately needed to facilitate legal contribution, such as labeling tools that are easy to use, and tools that can reformat existing legal work products in Word into training datasets in csv digestible by AI models.

Parallel structural changes are needed in the AI industry to reward the technologists and scientists both economically and professionally to design tools that facilitate the creation of training data by the legal professionals instead of mere advancement of AI algorithms.

This book contains multiple examples demonstrating how this human-centric transformation is possible in practice. It takes time for new technology to ripen to the point that it can be widely adopted. To get there, we need a lot of perseverance, patience, and dialogue on the part of both the legal professionals and the technologists. Human-centric AI and automation tools have the potential of fulfilling the vision of equal access to justice and fairness by everyone at a time when needed. That vision should be enough motivation for all of us to participate in the transformation.

Wei Chen is the General Counsel of Infoblox, the leader in next generation DNS management and security. Wei has over 20 years of legal experience advising businesses of all sizes on corporate governance, strategic transactions, compliance, commercial contracts, intellectual property, operations and legal innovations. Prior to joining Infoblox, Wei served as the SVP and Associate General Counsel, Strategic Transactions, at Salesforce, Inc. and the Assistant General Counsel at Sun Microsystems.

Wei founded The Atticus Project, a non-profit organization and the curator of CUAD, an open-sourced high quality AI training dataset of legal contracts with 13,000+ annotations crowd-sourced under the supervision of experienced lawyers. As part of The Atticus Project, Wei has mobilized over 50 experienced lawyers to create rich learning materials and provide hands-on legal training to nearly 100 law students and volunteers around the world.

Wei is a member of the Advisory Board of the Berkeley Center for Law and Business and a frequent lecturer on the topics of AI innovations in Legal, including at various legal conferences hosted by TechGC and Transaction Advisors

(continued)

Institute, as well as law schools such as Berkeley, Columbia and Stanford.

Wei started her legal career at Skadden Arps and then at Cooley. Wei is a sub-4-hour marathoner and an active volunteer in her community and local schools.

Wei Chen

Foreword: Preserving the Rule of Law in the Digital Era—The Responsibility of Lawyers

What is the purpose of the Law? Why does it matter?
Ne cives ad arma veniant—to avoid that citizens resort to weapons to settle their controversies—is the Latin expression which is taught in Italy to students in their first year at Law schools to explain what is the Law. Even in today's world, in which the objectives pursued by lawyers in the performance of their daily tasks are much broader and more complex than in ancient Rome, it keeps true that a system of rules to which all forms of powers are ultimately subject—the legal system—remains the minimum and essential condition for a society to thrive, where the relationship between men (and women) is not determined by their strength and violence. Those thinking that these are abstract reflections should look no further than at Afghanistan[1] to see how the abrupt fall of a legal system has a profound impact on the life of each citizen and how relationships among them are then regulated by violence and more recently, in February 2022, at the launch of a war of aggression, in violation of international law, by Russia against Ukraine, which obliged millions of people to seek refuge in the neighboring countries. And those believing this does not concern us, as we live in Western democracies, may want to remember that 2021 was inaugurated by a handful of people storming one of the most ancient Parliaments of the world,[2] because they contested the validity of the outcome of an electoral contest, and ultimately the rules underpinning it.

What is the role of lawyers today? Let me offer three considerations. The first is that law is an inherently human phenomenon: not only it is made ***by*** men and women, but (even in those systems where the source of law is believed to be otherwise) it is always made ***for*** men and women: primarily for those who are going to be subject to it, but also for those who are called to interpret it, apply it, and adjudicate on its basis, namely lawyers, legislators, judges. The Law should always be serving men and women, and not vice versa, and it is the responsibility of

[1] In April 2021, President Joe Biden announced the withdrawal of the U.S. military forces from Afghanistan and by the end of July 2021, the withdrawal was nearly completed. On 15 August 2021, the Taliban announced they had entered the presidential palace and taken control of the capital. See https://www.cfr.org/global-conflict-tracker/conflict/war-afghanistan.

[2] https://www.britannica.com/event/United-States-Capitol-attack-of-2021.

those who draft, apply, and interpret the law to keep this in mind. The second consideration is that, whatever the specific task they are accomplishing, lawyers—and more generally all those involved with the application of the individual rules which emerge from a legal system—are part of a collective endeavor that goes beyond the assignments and concerns which keeps them busy on a day-to-day basis. Each application of a rule of law is at the same time evidence of the continued effectiveness of the legal system, and a testimony to its validity. The third consideration is the logical extension of the first two: the Rule of Law (and its preservation) is at the core of what the Law is today, and what the ultimate objective of lawyers is or should be. Indeed, men and women need to be subject to the (Rule of) Law to preserve their freedom from an abusive exercise of Power. To achieve this objective, the law cannot be applied mechanically, but interests have to be considered and weighted to ensure that the concrete application of the Law respects and preserves those features which characterize our legal system as a liberal democracy: human rights, the independence of the judiciary, the separation of Powers, and the accountability of the holders of Power. Accessibility and transparency of the law are essential elements in ensuring this.

How can the role of the lawyers, i.e. producing, applying, interpreting, and adjudicating the law to preserve the fundamental legal features of our society, remain the same in an environment that is, from many perspectives, profoundly changing? Digital transformation is probably the biggest qualitative change in our lives in this century, one which impacts on many fields of expertise, including the legal profession. These challenges are also generational opportunities: a transversal red thread in the way different fields of expertise are impacted revolves around digitalization, new technologies, and human capability to embrace the deep and far-reaching changes spreading across the private and public sectors alike. All these factors significantly impact the already complex reality of the legal profession.

This book has the great merit of attempting to provide an answer to the question of how to organize the legal knowledge and the legal practice (the two being inherently and inevitably intertwined in a knowledge-based profession such as that of lawyers) in the face of the challenges posed by modern times and especially by a digitally fast evolving world. Lawyers of the last generation have struggled with the issue of finding and retaining information. Thanks to the tools of digitalization, one of the challenges of lawyers of our and next generations is to effectively deal with an overabundance of information, which needs to be systematized, structured, and shared in an efficient manner. Digital tools can convert our human experience into a multitude of data points which can be analyzed from a quantitative point of view, therefore having an impact on a traditionally qualitative branch of knowledge such as law: "how well do I know" gradually moves toward a more quantitative approach, "how much do I know," and the latter impacts on, and improves, the quality of the knowledge too.

On the other hand, technological developments do not only impact the efficiency and effectiveness of the way lawyers work, but also pose ethical questions on the legitimacy of our legal system, therefore ultimately on its validity: is the ultimate purpose of Law being served in a society where the Rule of Law does not apply to a

Power which has moved (at least in part) somewhere else than where it used to reside (i.e., in human beings) in a world where our existences become a collection of data points with a market tag and price at the mercy of artificial intelligences? There is a say in French, "*il faut remettre l'Eglise au milieu du village*"—the Church needs to be put back at the center of the village. The center and the objective of the legal profession, as argued above, cannot be anything else than the human being. This is why it is absolutely essential, going forward, to find the soft spot, where the Rule of Law and digital and technological development support each other in preserving, protecting, and further expanding human freedom while ensuring the respect of fundamental rights.

At this juncture, where digitalization and datafication trends have the potential to either help or hinder our legal orders, the responsibility of lawyers is to stand up for fair data governance and ethics. One objective should be to protect privacy and preserve the essence of the fundamental rights of individual subjects, while making use of digitalization to improve the accessibility of lawyers and citizens to information. Another objective, especially for lawyers working in the public sector, should be to make good use of digitalization and datafication to foster easier access to justice, more accountability, and better citizen's understanding—and consequently potential support—for the way in which the holders of power take political and policy decisions.

Indeed, legal professionals find themselves at a crossroad: either to cultivate a sense of distance to the current technological and artificial intelligence-driven challenges, or to rise to the challenge and embrace them proactively, with the intention to shape the deep transformation already under way. Motivating lawyers in all walks of their practice to augment their toolboxes with new technologies, while at the same time retaining their long-standing practice of being the guardian of the rule of law, is of crucial importance.

This book contains multiple examples demonstrating how this fusion is possible in practice. Growing a sense of opportunity to humanize the law while embracing the possibilities new technologies offer will keep lawyers busy, but also equip them for the years (and challenges) to come. Defining the map of the territory and articulating the need for a structural mindset adjustment and sustained technological transition in the practice of law is only the first step. Becoming proactive actors of the transformation should be the key motivation and vision guiding lawyers in their delivery of benefits to their clients and to society.

While lawyers have not traditionally been perceived as leaders in technology, at this stage they can contribute in a unique way, by combining their in-depth knowledge of the various legal fields of expertise, their extensive analytical skills, and their presence in almost all domains of life with the capacity to draw benefits from augmenting their toolboxes with new technologies. The practices of the law where digitalization can provide very useful support to lawyers cover an extensive list of activities, e.g. rationalizing due diligence procedures for checking contracts, detecting processes and "operations optimizing artificial intelligence" to eliminate or delegate manual and repetitive legal tasks, attending online court hearings which give wider access to justice, or using design thinking and visualization approaches to strengthen client and solution orientation.

What is the real legal challenge for the legal profession dealing with digitalization? On this journey, the legal profession might find that the real challenge lies potentially more in the mobilization of the leadership appetite for change rather than the technological hurdles. Thus, I would like to encourage legal departments in both the public and private sectors to evolve their ecosystems toward an ever more humanized practice of the law (diversity and inclusion to move away from groupthink can help in this respect) to counterbalance an ever more digitally and technologically augmented world. Indeed, making the best use of the digital support for the legal practice should not transform the application of the law into a mechanical activity, as the application, interpretation, and adjudication of the law need to remain the prerogative of human beings. **When venturing into the realm of digitalization and artificial intelligence, lawyers and legal departments should strive to ensure that their input remains essential in the value chain for defining the future.** They need to be active to keep playing a key role as the guardians of the law, and for the benefit of society, while making the best use of digital technology, to better serve men and women.

The key to the future for lawyers and legal departments lies in winning this challenge: in respecting and valuing the essential role of the human mind in ensuring the respect for the Rule of Law, and in making the best use of the support of digital tools and artificial intelligence, to enable better understanding of data, more precision in quantitative assessments and, for public authorities, more transparent accessibility for citizens of decisions affecting them, increasing, as a consequence, the accountability of the Power toward men and women.

Prof. Dr. Chiara Zilioli is the General Counsel of the European Central Bank. The views contained in this foreword are solely the ones of the author in her personal capacity and do not necessarily coincide with the position of, or cannot be attributed to, the European Central Bank.

Chiara Zilioli has dedicated her entire working life to the European integration project. In 1989, she joined the Legal Service of the Council of Ministers in Brussels, moving to the Legal Service of the European Monetary Institute in 1995 and subsequently to the ECB as a Head of Division in Legal Services in 1998. She was appointed Director General of the ECB's Legal Services in 2013.

She holds an LL.M. from Harvard Law School and a PhD from the European University Institute. She lectures at the Institute for Law and Finance at Goethe University Frankfurt, where she was appointed Professor of Law in 2016, and at the European College of Parma, Parma University. She has published numerous articles and four books. She is a member of the Parma Bar Association.

(continued)

Professor Zilioli has been married to Dr Andreas Fabritius for 33 years; they have four wonderful children.

Institute for Law and Finance, Goethe University Frankfurt Frankfurt, Germany

European College of Parma, Parma University
Parma, Italy

Parma Bar Association

Chiara Zilioli

Frankfurt, Germany February 2022

Preface: While the Cannons Thunder!

Six years have passed since we called for the transformation of the legal profession with our first Springer book compendium *"Transforming Legal into a Business Savvy, Information Enabled and Performance Driven Industry."*

For four years, since the foundation of our Liquid Legal Institute e.V., we gather an ever-growing number of members, followers, and friends. We organize exchanges, setup platforms to collaborate, and share insights and work results with our members and our network.

Two years ago, our second Springer book compendium *"Towards a Common Legal Platform"* has been published. Motivated by winning a Gaia-X competition funded by the German government with our concept of a Common Legal Platform (project name "DIKE—Digitales Ökosystem Recht"), we have taken concrete steps toward the realization and implementation of a Digital Legal Ecosystem following the CLP principles in 2021. Yes, the topic is alive and evolving!

We focus on connecting people to promote exchange, co-opetition, and the realization of innovative ideas. To ensure effective cooperation, it was and continues to be important to define the rules of the game from the very beginning.

At the Liquid Legal Institute,

- we maintain an amicable atmosphere
- we don't give much about titles or hierarchies and
- we put humans at the center

Those who know us well describe us as a "Doocracy": we roll up our sleeves and get things done—together. We want to talk less and do more!

To sum up the mental spirit of the LLI: *"Humans first—everything else second."* Professional exchanges are most interesting when people with different backgrounds, experiences, and perspectives work together. We are deeply committed to diversity, a commitment we manifested in our Diversity Guide and our Diversity Code.

When the pandemic sent people into home offices, when some of them worried about their professional future and forced them to meet each other only in virtual space, we asked ourselves: What is happening to us as humans? How does this profound change in day-to-day business life affect the way we work, feel, and behave?

And regarding the general working conditions in the legal industry, we asked: What is the human cost of our professional pursuit for greater efficiency and effectiveness?

Consequently, right at the beginning of the pandemic, we doubled down on the question of how the mental and physical health of our colleagues in the legal market is faring. The results of our *"Lawyer Well-Being Study"*[3] had been alarming. It was time to invite diverse perspectives on why that is, discussing the root causes, and—as important—on what can be done? Thus, we have just published a booklet on lawyer well-being as a reference point and source of inspiration for our network.[4]

More broadly, with the 7-dimensional transformation method described in our *"LIQUIFY"*-booklet, we provided a concept for how the legal professional can adapt to the changing environment and approach the digital transformation in a self-determined way. And as we finalize this book, we have just launched the Corporate Digital Responsibility (CDR) initiative at the LLI which aims to provide a "values compass for lawyers" in the digital age, also to secure our role as a trusted organ of the judiciary.

Finally, we also dare to look into the future and try to find answers on how a legal department will look like in 2030, or how the law will be applied in companies in 2030. Will there still be legal departments in 2030? Maybe all companies need is the legal function, but not necessarily a legal department. Maybe the "legal" product will be a mixture of legal services and tools, both provided externally? And the future task of the "CLO" (Chief Legal Officer)—quite similar to that of his or her CIO and CTO colleagues—may be to ensure the proper operation of the services and tools with the help of (Legal) Engineers, (Legal) Data Scientists, and (Legal) Designers and the many more new roles that emerge in the legal ecosystem.

All these considerations culminate in the question: What is the role of humans in the (legal) future?

Our answer might not surprise you: Together with the Liquid Legal Institute, we are designing the future of the legal market! Our goal is to provide to the individual the inspiration and guidance he or she needs to achieve his or her dreams of self-realization.

We had set ourselves the goal of completing this third Liquid Legal Compendium by 2022. We hope you enjoy our characteristic "*bridges*" or "*drops*" with which we highlight connections and lines of thought between the articles and stimulate mind jumps.

Since February 24, 2022, rockets have been hitting Kiev, Kharkiv, Mariupol, and many other places in Ukraine—the unimaginable has happened. President Putin has declared a war of aggression on his peaceful neighbor and is sending his soldiers to the battlefield. The images that reach us make us realize of how important "humanization" is in the world.

---

[3] Whitepaper report published by the Liquid Legal Institute. Freely available at https://www.liquid-legal-institute.com/wp-content/uploads/2021/01/LLI-LawyerWellBeing-Survey-Findings-1.pdf.

[4] https://www.liquid-legal-institute.com/library/.

Before Continuing to Read This Book, Please Reflect on the Following

Abraham Maslow, the child of Jewish-Ukrainian immigrants who was born over 100 years ago in Brooklyn, New York, is considered the founding father of humanistic psychology. He vividly describes people's pursuit of self-realization as steps in a pyramid of needs:

Once a person has satisfied his or her basic (level 1) and security needs (level 2), he or she will spend time for social purposes (level 3). If people still have time, they will use it for individual purposes (step 4) or dedicate it to self-realization (step 5), i.e. they will unfold their talents, potentials, and creativity, develop their personality and abilities, shape their life and its purpose.

Our thinking was directed to the ultimate level of self-realization—all needs on the lower levels seemed to be guaranteed for many of us. Mankind, or homo deus (as Harari[5] would describe it), approaches perfection—yet suddenly, the house of cards we have built is under attack and a growing number of fellow humans are again struggling for nourishment and security.

We don't know what the future holds for us—but we do know that, as Homo sapiens, we have a skill that has served us well for the last 200,000 years: We can achieve amazing results as an organized team—as humans.

We hope you enjoy reading this book—this time edited by a team of four: We have realized that with informatics an important area in the new legal world had been underrepresented in our editorial team, and so we on-boarded Dr. Bernhard Waltl as a co-editor. As a computer scientist and Head of Legal Operations at the BMW Group, he brings new aspects and ideas to the team.

[5] Harari, Y. N. (2017). *Homo deus: eine Geschichte von Morgen*. CH Beck.

Acknowledgements

"*What it means to be human is learned first and foremost in the family*"

Of all living creatures, humans need the longest time to be able to live independently. While a young foal takes its first steps on shaky legs immediately after birth, even a 5-year-old child will not be able to cope without the help and protection of its family. Community is a deep-rooted desire, a source of support, and encouragement for us—because we want to help each other, encourage each other, and drive each other forward.

I dedicate this book to my wonderful parents Helga (née Pospichal) and Tilman Jacob. It was wonderful to meet you and our relatives for the big family celebration in Winterberg!

Kai – Wiesloch, May 2022

"*First, we meet as human beings—and then we work together.*"

The above has been my mantra throughout my career. Seeing colleagues primarily as fellow humans means to base one's ethics on human values, human capabilities, and on the distinctly human ability to shape one's own life. Embracing the diversity of human individuals lies at the heart of creativity, well-being, and the performance of teams. We owe it to each other. And with the challenges ahead, we need it more than ever.

This book is for the two most special human beings in my life, *Christina*, my north star, and *Emily Joy*, my sunshine.

Dierk – Munich/Stuttgart, June 2022

"*I always want to be free.*" (K., in Franz Kafka, The Castle)

As humans, I believe, we all feel like the protagonist in Franz Kafka's novel *The Castle*: We want to be free. Yet freedom is not *for free*. Freedom always comes at a price—the willingness to sacrifice personal desires for the greater good. Or, as the great German philosopher Friedrich Hegel put it in the nineteenth century: A*s individuals and as a society, we must give rules to ourselves*. Freedom and responsibility are linked inseparably. This linkage between freedom and responsibility, the human aspect of the law, is exactly what is being explored in this third Liquid Legal edition "Humanization & The Law."

I dedicate this volume to my long-term mentor and friend, Don Hernandez († 2022).

Roger – Málaga, June 2022

"Collaboration is the key to success."

I am a firm believer that we can only be successful as humans and as a society if we work together. This requires that—whenever we meet—we firstly meet as humans. Everything else comes afterwards. Technology can help us shift the boundaries and make distance in time and space irrelevant, but ultimately, we are meeting human beings. We need to stay humble and critically reflect our role as humans in a digitalized world. For us and all the generations to come!

Bernhard – Munich, June 2022

The Editors are extremely grateful to Evgeny Ioffe for his project management support! Without his continuous and diligent effort to connect editors, authors, and the publisher, this book could not have appeared in its current form. Great work, Evgeny—Thank You!

The Editors – June 2022

"Humanization & The Law": A Call to Action for the Digital Age

Are We Humane?

The first homo sapiens appeared about 300,000 years ago in Africa. Relying on their erect posture, their fine manual motor skills, and their complex brains, they began making heavy use of tools and developed language to organize large societies.

Today, as a species, we humans are clearly the rulers of the world—for better or worse. Almost eight billion people populate the Earth, and while our lives, measured by gross national product and life expectancy, have improved for all countries in the past 200 years,[6] manmade pollution, climate change, and the food industry make one wonder if the same can be said for other species inhabiting the Earth, and for the planet as a whole.

Humanity thus carries a double meaning. It may simply and neutrally refer to a collective of humans, but it may also specifically refer to ethics, virtues, and altruistic behavior derived from the human condition. Simply put, the question is: *Are we humans actually humane?*

A similar question arises around the usage of the word *Humanization*. To portray and endow the world with human characteristics or attributes—*is that a good thing, or is it a bad thing?* Does *Humanization* primarily suggest acts of charity and kindness to fellow beings, or does it bring to mind environmental destruction and the alienation of other life forms from their natural state of existence?

As the lever of technology is accelerating and growing stronger in all areas of business, the answer to that question is of pressing importance. First, to keep the focus on continuously exploring what a given innovation may mean for humanity. Second, to prioritize the co-development of the framework required to humanize such innovation.

At the Liquid Legal Institute, we believe that it is time to take stock of the forms, the meanings and the effects of *Humanization* as the digital transformation disrupts business and technology—and thereby the Law.

[6] That gross national product and life expectancy have improved in the past 200 years is true also for poorer countries, even though to a lesser degree than for richer countries; see Hans Rosling, 200 Countries, 200 Years, 4 Minutes, https://www.youtube.com/watch?v=jbkSRLYSojo.

We are convinced that *the Law* plays a fundamental role in enabling, promoting, and safeguarding Humanization in business, technology, and society at large. (In this context, we adopt the broadest possible interpretation of "the Law," in order to include all personas that are part of the modern legal ecosystem as it undergoes a transformation itself.)

Why? Because as internationalization increases and legal regulations become more complex, and as artificial intelligence outperforms human decision-making, we want to understand if *Humanization* can help us become more humane in three social areas that today, at the beginning of the third millennium, are more interlinked than at any other time in human history.

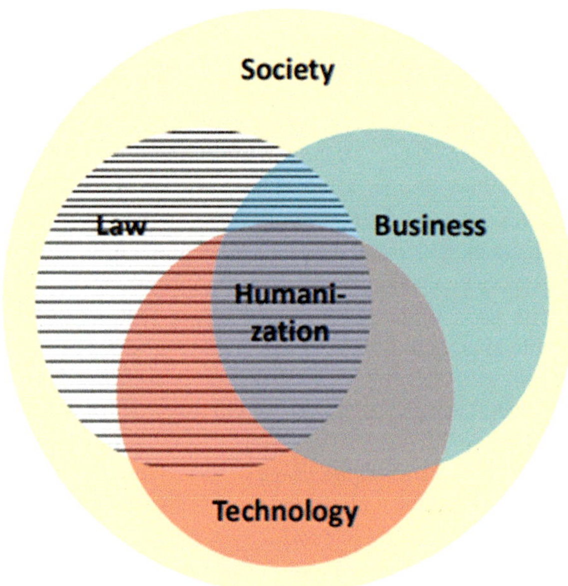

Humanization in Law

In the history of Law, *humanism* refers to the pan-European efforts of the sixteenth and seventeenth centuries to make Roman law philologically accessible, and no longer interpret it merely with the theological methods of scholasticism. However, the term *humanism* is also used to describe the striving for a more humane design of law, i.e., its *Humanization,*[7] notably in penal law, but of course also in many other legal areas such as family and labor law. For example, it took Germany almost 100 years, from 1872 until 1969, to de-criminalize homosexuality among men. It

[7] See Eric Hilgendorf, *Humanismus und Recht—Humanistisches Recht?*.

took US lawmakers until 1920 to grant women the right to vote, and it took the UN until 1989 to define the *Convention on the Rights of the Child* which has since been ratified by most, but not all countries in the world. On August 26, 2020, the *Commission on Unalienable Rights,*[8] initiated by US Secretary of State Mike Pompeo, released its final report to the general public, distinguishing, for example, *unalienable human rights* from *positive rights* within a particular country, and thus causing a debate among human rights activists about the report's alleged conservative or even reactionary character.

- How can *the Law* become more humane?
- Besides ethical reasons, are there also economic and technological drivers that make *Humanization* in law reasonable and desirable?
- Which effects, in turn, does *Humanization in Law* have on society at large?

Humanization in Business

The times in which TSR (total shareholder return) served as the sole measurement of a corporation's business performance appear to be over.[9] The mechanistic mindset that largely ignored social aspects, and the linear thinking of cause and effect that informed the static structure of large organizations, are things of the past. They are being replaced with the awareness that dynamic interactions between employees create unforeseeable effects and that complex companies cannot be fully controlled from the top or center. NGOs and non-profit organizations are on the rise, and agility, self-organized teams and holistic thinking are now part of corporate culture. Executives begin to take corporate social responsibility (CSR) seriously and to focus on environmental, social, and governance (ESG) issues. New regulations force companies to ensure that human rights standards are being followed along the whole value chain, even before raw materials arrive at their factories. And while most older employees to a large degree feel disengaged at work, distrust their companies, and primarily work for pay, the new generation of millennials entering the job market are more interested in meaningful tasks than in financial rewards and are more prepared to leave a company they do not trust.

Humanization also directly affects business in the legal industry. Diversity and inclusion are no longer buzzwords but concrete corporate criteria for selecting vendors, and inhouse legal departments are checking whether the law firms they engage are adhering to these requirements.

[8] See https://en.wikipedia.org/wiki/Commission_on_Unalienable_Rights.

[9] See, for example, The Boston Consulting Group, *The Humanization of the Corporation*, https://www.bcg.com/publications/2018/humanization-corporation.

- How does Humanization change the *business of legal*?
- Does a *humane* working culture have positive effects on recruiting talent and finding clients?
- Can law firms and inhouse legal departments afford to pursue goals that are neither legal nor financial, but simply *humane*?

Humanization in Technology

The Massachusetts Institute of Technology (MIT) argues that digitalization is less about technology than about changing the conditions under which people interact and do business with each other. At the same time, machines are becoming more and more humanlike—not only in their cognitive abilities, through artificial intelligence, but also in their appearance. We design human avatars in virtual reality games, we speak to Siri, Alexa, and Cortana on our mobile phones as if they were real people, and when we look at Sophia,[10] the first social humanoid robot, we actually see a human face that can smile or appear angry. By investigating how best to support US army combat veterans suffering from post-trauma stress disorder, an insurance company discovered that the veterans preferred talking to a chatbot rather than a human person—because they felt less judged.[11]

- Will machines become better therapists and lawyers—maybe even judges—than humans?
- Do digitalization, social media, and virtual worlds require more regulation to prevent them from replacing reality and authentic human experience?
- At some point, will robots, in turn, require human rights, e.g. the right not to be turned off?

The Humanization trends in law, business, and technology described above are, of course, in flux; they support, influence, and also contradict each other. And in one way or another, they affect all the topics and projects that members of the LLI are currently engaged in via the "5 +1" working groups (digitalization, standardization, education, methodologies, material law, and the Common Legal Platform):
Leadership, Design Thinking, Change Management, User Experience, Diversity and Inclusion, Lawyer Well-Being, Legal Inhouse Processes and KPIs, Robotic Process Automation, CLM Vendor Selection, Remote Legal Teams, eSignature, Future of Legal Education, Standard NDA and SPA, and Legal Agile Toolkit.

---

[10] See https://en.wikipedia.org/wiki/Sophia_(robot).

[11] See https://www.wired.com/story/virtual-therapists-help-veterans-open-up-about-ptsd/.

Contents

About the Editors

Kai Jacob is the founder and co-chair of the Liquid Legal Institute, a think tank for the transformation of the legal market based in Munich. He is also a partner in Legal Operations & Transformation Services (LOTS) at KPMG Law since 2021.

Kai is involved in various projects and initiatives concerning agile working in the legal department, the health of the legal profession, and the future of legal managed services. He publishes regularly on these and other topics in professional journals (AnwaltSpiegel, Going Digital, Business Law Magazine), publications (LIQUIFY, CLM, Lawyer Well-being), and in the series of publications he co-founded, Liquid Legal (at Springer Verlag). Prior to joining KPMG Law, Kai was a partner at Deloitte Legal and previously spent many years at SAP SE. Kai Jacob was admitted to the bar in 2004 and studied law in Marburg, Göttingen, and Osnabrück.

Dierk Schindler is one of the co-founders of the Liquid Legal Institute e.V. He serves as Co-CEO, together with Kai Jacob and Bernhard Waltl. He is a co-author and co-editor of numerous publications on innovation and transformation in the legal profession, most notably the two previous volumes of the book-series "Liquid Legal" (Springer) in 2017 and 2020.

In 2019, Dierk joined Robert BOSCH GmbH as their Vice President Corporate Legal Services, Mobility Solutions, Supply Chain and Logistics. In his role, he drives the adoption of digitally supported Agile practices and, jointly with the leadership team, the digital transformation of the legal team. Prior to BOSCH, Dierk has spent 14 years with NetApp Inc., where he built the EMEA Legal Team, established the Deal Management function, and implemented the Global Legal Shared Services Team.

Dierk's teams have been awarded IACCM "Global Innovation Awards" in 2014 and 2015. He teaches at the Management Center Innsbruck (MCI) on Innovation Management, Digital Business Law, and Compliance. Dierk is a certified lawyer, took his doctorate degree from Augsburg University, Germany, and his Master of International Law from Lund University, Sweden.

Roger Strathausen is a business consultant, author, and lecturer with expertise in legal operations, learning, and leadership whose clients are chiefly multinational companies. He took his Ph.D. from Stanford University in 1996 and was an employee at SAP and an executive at Accenture. In 2015, he published his book "Leading When You Are Not the Boss" (Apress, New York), and in 2017 and 2020, he co-edited two contributed volumes on the digital transformation of the legal industry, called "Liquid Legal" and "Towards a Common Legal Platform" (Springer, Heidelberg). He is a co-founder of the Liquid Legal Institute and serves as a vice chair of the supervisory board.

Bernhard Waltl has been an academic researcher and designs, develops, and evaluates technology and methods transforming the future of law. In 2017, he was invited from the Stanford University CodeX: Center for Legal Informatics where he conducted research on text mining and artificial intelligence in the legal domain. He is part of an international network of leading researchers from computer science, informatics, and legal science, and organizes scientific workshops at relevant conferences. He successfully had many projects with industry partners on text mining for the legal domain and also consulting projects for governments on algorithmic-decision-making.

"The Missing Piece"

Why Humanism Must Dominate the Digital Transformation of Legal Work

Dierk Schindler

Contents

Abstract

Too often, digital transformation of legal work comes across as a quest to cure imperfection, as a technocratic pursuit of effectiveness and efficiency aiming to eradicate wasted effort and deficiencies. While leaders and their visions certainly phrase it differently—centering around "better service for the client", "more focus on high value work", or "higher impact of the legal department"—their companions on the team do feel uneasy, because the underlying message still seems to be to "fix something". And where there is something to fix, something

---

Dierk Schindler is Co-founder and co-CEO of the Liquid Legal Institute e.V., Vice President Corporate Legal Services, Mobility Solutions, Supply Chain and Logistics at Robert BOSCH GmbH.

D. Schindler (✉)
Ottobrunn, Germany
e-mail: d.schindler@liquid-legal-institute.org

K. Jacob et al. (eds.), *Liquid Legal – Humanization and the Law*, Law for Professionals, https://doi.org/10.1007/978-3-031-14240-6_1

must be broken. And if technology or digital means are the fix—well, it is probably then the human part that must be "broken" or "deficient"?!

Strange enough, no modern leader in legal services will sign off on the above—including myself! We all genuinely believe that our digital transformation agenda will help both, the team, as well as the client, to benefit from the new opportunities that legal technology and new methodologies bring about. Yes, of course this is our goal—yet, let's face it: If we read the fine print of our strategies, if we listen to the tone of our presentations and the stories on our vision (specifically the version for executive management), we will find that they are mainly about getting more done with less, about improving the ROI of the legal department, and about broadening and accelerating the delivery of the legal services. More, better, faster!

So, what are we missing? A simple test reveals the missing piece: it is the human factor, or even more boldly, the focus on the human being. How would our story change if we purposely refocused and rephrased our vision and strategy so that it is truly humanistic and centers around the human being and the specific needs as represented by each key stakeholder (the client, executive management, the team as a whole, and the individual on the team)? We will also establish that there is no trade-off in the sense that humanism comes at the expense of optimizing the economics or the impact of a legal team. To the contrary, they are complementary and mutually supportive.

We will then put our findings into the context of current trends around professional work relations in high-skill markets such as the legal market: Relationships between employers and workers change radically; talent becomes an ever scarcer resource; and the strain of an increased density and variety of work demands (combined with the effects of the pandemic) take their toll on the human being. Inevitably the question arises: Can we—even economically—afford to "miss a piece", i.e., the human factor?

Data—the famous new oil—drives businesses in the digital age. Yet, it also drives business functions and enables informed decision making. For lawyers, is digitalization then the choice between Dr. Jekyll and Mr. Hyde?—We will lay out that data literacy is fundamental and that a humanistic approach to data is crucial. Data and metrics are not a goal in themselves. We must keep focus on what we are ultimately aiming for, and, even more importantly, we must lead on our data journey with clear values.

Finally, we will turn to the question which methodologies are predestined to support a humanistic approach to the digital transformation of legal work. We need a strong culture, based on trust and transparency. This is why Agile practices, supported by a "digital-first" agenda, and embedded in the principles of DevOps offer a perfect basis for modern legal teams.

1 Introduction

Our world is ruled by the pursuit of perfection. Good is not good enough. It only serves as the reference point to define the gap to what ideally would be possible, what would be better. And even perfection is a moving target, as technological and scientific advancements keep pushing out the boundaries of what is possible. Current society negates the finiteness of natural resources, as well as the limitations of the human being.[1]

It seems that technology and digital means are mainly designed to augment the human being and to overcome the limitations that humans have. We humans are missing certain elements, we are limited in many ways and technology is the double-edged sword that helps us to bridge such gaps and that, at the same time, constantly points out our human shortcomings. The theme of our times is that we are not perfect and that this needs to be addressed.

This rather fatalistic line of thought raises sweet memories to one of my favorite childhood books. In his novel *"The Missing Piece"*, Shel Silverstein wonderfully captures the sweet and painful temptation to go onto the quest for perfection and the surprising ambiguity of its outcome.[2] A happy circular creature—back then I baptized it "Pelle"—realizes that he is missing a wedge-shaped piece to make it a perfect circle. While generally content, Pelle does feel the urge to become complete and embarks on the adventure to find the missing piece.

He happily wanders the world, singing a beautiful song about his search. Due to the little dent, caused by the missing piece, Pelle is bumping along rather slowly, at his individual pace. This gives him the time to meet other creatures, to experience the wide variety of nature and to enjoy the four seasons. Pelle also masters adventures, like overcoming huge walls or climbing out of big holes.

However, his quest for the missing piece, for perfection, seems to find a tragic ending. Pelle does find a matching piece—but it wants to stay on its own ("I am myself – not anyone's missing piece"). Many other great pieces, he meets, are too small, too large, too square, or too sharp. But Pelle is resilient and keeps going until he finally finds it: the missing piece—his missing piece, which makes him all round and seemingly perfect!

As the new, perfectly "whole" Pelle rolls on, he initially experiences the joy of perfection. He is faster than ever before and roars on his way home.—Yet, he is too fast to stop and talk to the worm he had met . . . too fast for the butterfly to land on him . . . too fast to experience the beauty of nature. The upside being, however, that Pelle may now sing his happy song uninterrupted and all the time! But soon, he

[1] Harald Welzer, in his book *"Obituary to myself"* (original title in German: *"Nachruf auf mich Selbst"), fischer, Frankfurt am Main, 2021*, examines the root cause and effects of the contemporary culture of growth and belief in technology as the savior to the existential challenges of mankind; see p. 26 f.

[2] Silverstein (1978).

realizes that his speed and the frequency of rotation makes him all dizzy so that he confuses the lyrics and ultimately loses his ability to sing at all. He is just superfast.

Finally, Pelle stops, gently puts down the missing piece and wishes farewell. He then happily bumps along again at his natural, imperfect speed, ready to meet the worm and the butterfly again, all receptive for what's around him and in best shape to sing his song.

> *"Oh, I'm lookin' for my missin' piece*
>
> *I'm lookin' for my missin' piece*
>
> *Hi-dee-ho, here I go*
>
> *lookin' for my missin' piece."*[3]

Where are we, the modern lawyers, on our journey through digital transformation, on our quest for perfection? Unconsciously believing that we must find or create the missing pieces to fulfil our ambition of more, better, faster? Already using some pieces that we have found to go ever faster and maybe not realizing that they are not really fitting or that we are undervaluing or even sacrificing our distinctly human skills?

2 The Missing Piece

2.1 Do More with Less! . . . or Rather: Do Less with More?

The fact that lawyers have been laggards in embracing digital transformation, as well as in systematically modernizing the interpretation of our role in business, has put our profession on the backfoot. Initially, the strongest challenges to transform are therefore being made from the outside. Our internal clients request an ever more and faster adaptability to constantly changing business environments. Our CFOs challenge our "bills", i.e., the budget and its distribution. For law firms, our clients challenge the billable hour plus the rates, demanding alternative fee arrangements, the passing on of economic benefits from automation—or they even turn to alternative service providers for certain parts of the work, altogether.[4]

2.1.1 The Defense Battle

The transformation of legal work (including the digital element of it) typically starts as a defense battle. As our added value and our ability to use the funds well has been

[3] Silverstein (1978), p. 7.

[4] Richard Susskind and Mark Cohen have been among the strongest constructive challengers of our profession. Susskind (2017), p. xix and, together with Susskind (2015), p. 67; as to Mark Cohen, see his various blogs under https://www.legalmosaic.com/.

put into question, we are focused on proving two things: *First*, that we also use digital means to the extent "reasonable" to become more efficient. *Second*, that we use our resources responsibly to deliver top-notch service and to add value. Thus, digital means are often predominantly deployed to tick one (or several) of the following three boxes:

- To serve as a visible *"catch up"* to the digitization across the company,
- To support an *efficiency-play* to get certain things done faster and with less resources, or
- To provide *means of gathering data* to prove the legal innovation case.

KPMG Law in its current *"Global Legal Benchmarking Report 2021"* proves the point.[5] When being asked about the strongest drivers for technology investment, the top three aspects that General Counsels named were:

1. Optimizing resourcing (88%)
2. Increasing quality (84%)
3. Increasing value delivered to the business (59%)

"Lowering cost" (45%) is ranked number five and "being part of corporate digital strategy" number eight (37%). The only reason among the top ten that has a faint human aspect to it is number seven: "providing inhouse knowledge" (37%).

2.1.2 Economics Over People?

If the above reflects the motivation that then sets the agenda of digital transformation of a legal department, one should not blame the human beings that are being exposed to such an agenda (i.e., the team) to read two things between the lines: *First*, no matter how hard we have worked, there is something broken in our service delivery that needs to be fixed and technology is the savior. *Second*, this is about efficiency (i.e., budget) and effectiveness (i.e., better ROI)—not about me as a person and my needs.

In essence, digital transformation of legal work seems to be predominantly a quest to cure imperfection, a pursuit of effectiveness and efficiency aiming to eradicate wasted effort and deficiencies. The implied message is that there is a missing piece in the people dominated legal function, that must be filled by technology. The human being is seemingly not good enough.

I readily admit that probably every leader in the legal profession—including myself—would strongly and genuinely oppose that conclusion. Our vision statements do have "people" as an element and our strategies do include items like developing new skills etc. However, the issue at hand is not the intent of the sender, but the interpretation of the recipient. If the driving force to embrace technology is the list above, everything else comes second. If the human dimension is about skills

[5] KPMG Law, Recht auf Fortschritt, Der IX. Rechtabteilungsreport von KPMG Law 2021/22, p. 72.

and talent, it is about the economic value of the employee, and not about the employee as a human being.

If we want to avoid our employees reading from our vision and strategy "do more with less", we must be deliberate and explicit about it and dare to state:

Our digital transformation is also about doing less with more. Legal technology (of course alongside new methodologies) is the lever for a more humane workplace.

2.2 What Is the Missing Piece?

It is the human factor and the fact that it must have center stage in a modern legal team. Humanism[6] must dominate the digital transformation of legal work.

Instead of embracing the human being in its entirety, however, we tend to look at the "worker" or the "employee" and thus solely at a person's economic function in the value chain. Skills, hours spend on tasks, or billable hours etc. are nothing but an x-ray to assess the ROI of our people investment and how it can be optimized. And technology has become the primary lever to pull.

2.2.1 The Trend Is Not Our Friend

Again, the statement is blunt and heavily boiled down, but it is urgent that we realize the massive blind spot our approach tends to carry, especially as we are putting more and more pressure on executing against such strategies. The *KPMG* study also shows that, while in the past legal departments have followed an insourcing strategy, the focus is now shifting towards efficiency gains. The lawyers per billion € revenue ratio has dropped 4% between 2019 and 2021, while it had been growing constantly since 2005.[7] Growth in demand will not be reflected in people growth. Consequently, if we drive efficiency with a non-human-centric strategy, there is a very high risk of "accidentally" squeezing the human beings that we expect to execute on it. In the course of this article, I will underpin the thesis that this would inevitably lead us onto the slippery slope of short-term economic gains at the expense of long-term sustainability.

---

[6]In full respect of the breadth and depth of science around the term, for the sake of clarity in laying out my theses I am using the term "humanism" in this context as represented by the International Humanist and Ethical Union (https://en.wikipedia.org/wiki/International_Humanist_and_Ethical_Union) as their "Minimum Statement on Humanism" and as summarized by Andrew Copson in *"What is Humanism?"*, a contribution to *"The Wiley Blackwell Handbook of Humanism"*, 2015, that he edited with A. C. Grayling, New York, John Wiley & Sons. pp. 5–6: ***"Humanism is a democratic and ethical life stance, which affirms that human beings have the right and responsibility to give meaning and shape to their own lives. It stands for the building of a more humane society through an ethic based on human and other natural values in the spirit of reason and free inquiry through human capabilities. It is not theistic, and it does not accept supernatural views of reality."***

[7]KPMG, Law, Recht auf Fortschritt, Der IX. Rechtabteilungsreport von KPMG Law 2021/22, p. 78.

The question arises, what exactly would change if we took a human centric approach? Are we talking about "sacrificing" part of the (economic) outcome of the digital transformation? Are we trading the desired maximized impact with the happiness of our folks?—Let's start with a simple experiment and revisit the above listed top three reasons for investing in legal technology and let's add a human dimension:

1. Optimizing resourcing (88%)
2. Increasing quality (84%)
3. Increasing value delivered to the business (59%)

Optimizing Resourcing What if we said: We want to dedicate the *talent of our team* to the most interesting and value creating work for our clients. To achieve that, we want to be deliberate about how to get the various types of work done and will implement the most effective and efficient way for it with a focus on leveraging technology. We thereby want to *liberate our team* from shallow work, e.g., repetitive, and simple tasks, we want to *avoid overloading our team* and we ultimately aim to *reduce the workload.*

Quality What if we said: To provide top-quality services for our clients, we want to focus on optimizing the outcome for our clients and thereby our positive impact on *client happiness* (as reflected in analysis of client feedback, net promoter score, and/or client retention) and the business at large. This is the overarching and joint goal with our clients. *Leveraging distinctly human skills* like creativity, problem-solving and interpersonal relationships will be our key focus. We will *invest in learning opportunities* internally and externally for our team and will *personally engage with our clients* to for mutual feedback geared towards the joint success for the company.

Value Delivered What if we said: We will base our service delivery on a *deep understanding of our clients' needs* and measure ourselves against it. We will seek *continuous interpersonal connection* to maintain the seamless mutual understanding of the respective priorities and to *create a positive and trusting working atmosphere.* We will make room for *managing the workload* together by fair prioritization and the mutual willingness to *reduce unnecessary burden.*

2.2.2 Human Traits: Human Needs—Human Skills

Underpinning our strategy with the human dimension is much more engaging, but what is it exactly that we have weaved into the above by our rough "translation" into humanistic language? – *First*, it is explicit reference to distinct and exclusive *human traits*: interpersonal relationships, creativity and problem solving. In simple terms the message is: We need you because you are human—and we need you where your valuable human strength can be leveraged best! – *Second*, it is explicit reference to the *human needs*, specifically in a transformative world. The message is: We are aware of the human boundaries and want to protect your (and your client's) wellbeing; technology will be there to support you and the client—not the other way round. – *Third*, we deliver more value by a smart orchestration of various ways of rendering our services and by making room for distinctly *human skills* and interpersonal interaction on the most critical and most interesting parts of our work.

A humanistic approach to digital transformation will be a paradigm shift. The—mostly unwanted—implied notion of overcoming human limitations will be replaced by explicitly embracing the unique upside of the "human factor". Unconscious pressure to cope with increasing expectations and workload will give way to conscious respect for the natural boundaries of humanity. Work life will follow the basic rules of human life and thereby invite the human beings to do their unique magic in the job, supported by legal technology.

> *"Oh my, now that*
>
> *it was complete*
>
> *it could not sing at all.*[8]"

3 A Humanistic View on Transformation

3.1 Transformation + Innovation ≠ Progress

3.1.1 Transformation

Transformation, at a corporate level, relates at its core to adapting a corporation to a changed—and nowadays constantly changing—business context, aiming to improve its chances for long-term business success.[9] It serves as an enabler to introduce and leverage innovation potentially at all levels of the business to strengthen its competitiveness. So far so good and no surprise: We need to innovate to transform, we need to transform to stay competitive, and the legal team is part of the game.

3.1.2 Innovation

We should bear in mind, however, that in business theory the concept of innovation fundamentally serves as a filter for the huge sea of ideas and inventions by adding the criteria of a positive economic impact for the company.[10] According to Schumpeter, there are four basic types of innovation (incremental, disruptive, architectural and radical) and there are eight fields of innovation (product, technology, business model, organizational, process, go-to-market, network and customer retention). There is a lot of cool stuff, but to pass the test it must create business benefit. Again, so far so good, and very useful: Any business function (including legal)

---

[8] Silverstein (1978), p. 84.

[9] For a broader definition and context about the term "transformation" see https://de.wikipedia.org/wiki/Transformation_(Betriebswirtschaft).

[10] As originally introduced by Schumpeter in his book Schumpeter (1939).

should be rigorous in its selection of new ideas. There must be clear answer to questions like "what is the issue we are trying to resolve?" and "how are we helping the company to become more successful?" in terms of business success.

Yet, once again, we are missing the human factor. Transformation plus innovation does not equal a better outcome for the human beings involved, be it employees, leaders, or clients. If innovation as defined above is what you are looking for, this is what you get. It will follow the rule of business benefit—period. There will be no overarching purpose that would include benefits for the human beings involved, let alone society at large. In that sense, automating certain legal processes and streamlining the remaining work with all sorts of software applications, thereby eliminating the need for part of the human lawyers, is innovation, maybe even (part of) transformation. It is faster and cheaper in the long run. But does this already amount to progress?

3.1.3 Progress

As stated above, this is not about making the case for "either / or", i.e. a tradeoff between what's good for the economics versus what's good for the people. It is about taking innovation one step further so that it includes not only scientific and business intelligence, but also social intelligence. Social intelligence must be connected to a normative purpose and this when you don't just get innovation, but progress. Innovation is about new stuff that works in—or for—business. Progress is about improving current state and, thus, requires a justification why things got better and for whom. For the sceptics, *Harald Welzer*, in his book *"Obituary to Myself"*, makes a great point when he reminds us that fundamental progress in history has been tied to social intelligence, rather than scientific or business intelligence. The dramatic decrease of victims from violence has not been caused by the dramatic improvement of weapons and warfare technology—but by introducing the monopoly of the state on the use of force. [11]

Building on that example one might think that it is up to the state to adjust the legal boundaries of the market economy to make business more humane. While there might be a place for the regulatory framework to support, I believe that adding and prioritizing the social—or better human—dimension to "digital transformation" and thereby enforcing a holistic normative reference has a business logic, as well, and thus is not dependent on the regulator to interfere. Pursuing a humane workplace saves leaders to (potentially only inadvertently) sacrificing humanism for the sake of business benefits. This is particularly important for the so called "supporting functions" (like legal) that tend to have less voting power when business strategy is being set, as long as we remain in the boundaries of legality. We must not buy into pure positivism related to the mere law of business, i.e., that transformation and innovation simply take their toll on human beings. Our true leadership challenge is to realize innovative business benefits in a humanistic way.

[11] As to the aspect of progress and the example provided see Welzer (2021), p. 26.

To get courageous innovators on our teams, we must talk progress instead of innovation and we must call out a purpose that includes the unique power of the human being, as well as the human limitations.

3.2 The Missing Piece Is the Cornerstone to Success

3.2.1 People Have a Choice . . .

. . . and they will choose. According to a recent study by *Bain & Company Inc.*, 25% of American workers (across all industries) changed companies between February 2020 and February 2021—the biggest reshuffling on record. 58% of American workers feel that the pandemic has forced them to rethink their work-life-balance.[12] Law firms in Germany have just announced yet another increase of salaries for entry-level associates, now trending up to €155,000 p.a.[13] Next to the "traditional" lawyer roles, new job profiles are on the rise: since 2019, the average ratio of Legal Operations employees on legal inhouse teams has increased by 500%, and the average ratio of legal tech or digitalization employees on legal teams by 300%.[14] Given the fact that there are still no systematic options to study specifically for such roles, recruiting needs to tap into the existing pool of talent—and a hot market gets even hotter.

As the talent pool is limited while the choice is high and further increasing, our primary goal must be to retain and develop existing talent by pursuing a human centric strategy, executed at a human friendly workplace. The same strategy will also be a decisive selling point to new talent, as information about "what really happens" at a given legal team or a given provider of legal services travels fast in times of social media.

3.2.2 Purpose

Successful organizations are driven by a purpose. As so often, it is instructive to look at the extreme. What drives so called "exponential organizations", i.e., companies that scale way beyond most businesses around them (e.g., Airbnb, Google)? *Salim Ismael*, in his great book *"Exponential Organizations"*, has identified the Massive Transformation Purpose (MTP) as the crucial element. What is it, and what is it not? It has nothing to do with the strategy or even the mission. It is, however, the aspirational, visionary moonshot! *"The most important outcome of a proper MTP is that it generates a cultural movement."*[15]

---

[12] Schwedel et al. (2022), p., at https://www.bain.com/contentassets/d620202718c146359acb05c02d9060db/bain-report_the-working-future.pdf.

[13] See https://www.juve.de/karriere/155-000-euro-willkie-prescht-mit-neuem-einstiegsgehalt-vor/.

[14] KPMG Law, Recht auf Fortschritt, Der IX. Rechtabteilungsreport von KPMG Law 2021/22, p. 35.

[15] Ismael (2014), p. 55.

If a corporation has set out an MTP, it mainly intends to spark its human capacity, the people, by creating a strong culture based on an inspiring purpose. It is a center point of a strong vision. How could it then ever make sense that a (digital) transformation effort in any department would (inadvertently) ignore that? Why would we solely talk "business" and "technology", i.e., *innovation* and *transformation*, when we pursue *massive progress* driven by the people based on their diverse talent?

In a disrupted and rapidly changing business environment, human traits are more required than ever. We urgently need creative thinking, proactive risk and opportunity management, and ultimately a well-connected human network that dynamically teams to master a given challenge, that form a diverse, collective brain across the business that keeps or corrects the course of the business.[16]

3.2.3 The Exponential Factor and the Limiting Factor

Today, human beings are both, the exponential factor, and the limiting factor. Therefore, digital transformation must address both elements: leveraging legal technology and digital assets to allow humans to deploy their talent where the impact is the greatest, as well as to create and maintain an environment that fosters and protects the personal well-being of the individual. The legal profession already faces a distinct and severe crisis around mental health. Severe, given the alarming numbers that studies have surfaced and, distinct, admitting that our professions sticks out at the wrong end of the spectrum.[17]

In times of ambiguity, we need confident human beings. Our goal must be to liberate their capacity and to unfold their unique human talents while respecting the natural human limitations. Thus, deprioritizing humanism in transformational times is even worse than having a blind spot because it means putting the fundamental lever to sustainable and long-term success at risk. Human beings ultimately form and represent the culture, and it is the culture that carries the purpose, maybe even an MTP. Technology or innovation must not be the goal, but the means to a purpose dominated by humanism, so that we do not just transform, but create real progress.

If, instead, we make humanism a core part of our vision, mission and strategy, our fellow employees will feel respected, safe, and inspired. Instead of selling them why change pain and digital transformation is worth it for the sake of long-term business success, we invite them to be the core, the crucial, and the exponential force to success. Respecting the human limitations—including the requirements for human well-being in the workplace—will not hinder us but keep us honest. It will keep us honest, in the sense that our strategy is truly about making best and sustainable use of the limited but special force: the unique human skills, the human factor!

---

[16] See Strathausen (2017), p. 9 ff.

[17] On the crisis in Well-Being and Personal Health, see *"The Silent Epidemic"*, LLI Drop, Editions Weblaw, Zurich, 2021 and the LLI Whitepaper *"Lawyer Well-Being – Personal Health of Legal Professionals in Times of Disruption"*, both by Kai Jacob, Jutta Löwe, Diane Manz, Dierk Schindler, Roger Strathausen, Bernhard Waltl Editions Weblaw, Zurich, 2022.

"Aha", it thought.

"So that's how it is!

So it stopped rolling,

and it set the piece down gently

and slowly rolled away . . ."[18]

4 Information Enablement & New Methodologies

4.1 A Humanistic Approach to Data and Information

4.1.1 Why Lawyers Are Data Sceptics

It is widely accepted that data and data science are key to advance businesses and the economy at large, as well as for research. The potential benefits for human beings are huge, as data opens new insights and new areas of business. The progress of mankind in the last decades is based on scientific methods and the use of data in virtually every aspect of our life. However, some areas are harder to conquer for (or with) data than others and, certainly, the legal profession is one of the harder ones.

Lawyers are trained to weigh primarily the quality of an argument—not the quantity. Making a case or judging on it is based on assessing facts and weighing arguments in light of the law. The quantitative element typically comes second. It might lead to an aggravation of a case, i.e., higher penalties, fines or damages, but it does not decide the matter itself. This approach is engrained in a lawyer's mind. The use of data gives us new perspectives and a chance to find ways to successfully react to new challenges.

So, as we see the business world transform around data, calling it the "new oil", and as we see our function being pulled into management approaches thar are based on data and pushed towards data analytics, we feel uneasy. Yet, it gives us the opportunity to understand much better how we organize ourselves and to understand what makes a legal department effective and efficient.

4.1.2 Data Becomes Paramount: Embrace the Enemy You Cannot Fight

As corporations create new digital business models, lawyers increasingly work on matters that are based on data or in which data is even the key asset. Understanding data therefore drives business decisions and risk assessments. Data, and all the possible aspects of it, becomes part of the lawyer's file and data literacy is needed to get the job done. Once adopted, the success of this approach is stunning. We see

[18] Silverstein (1978), pp. 85–89.

data changing our lives at incredible speed and this happens also in the legal field, specifically since the use of Legal Tech is becoming the new normal.

> The discussion on KPIs and metrics in Legal Departments has just started. We need to lead it actively so we can lead transformation, avoid external control, and be aligned with internal (enterprise-wide) objectives including their financial metrics. To do so, we have to enter territory quite unknown to most lawyers. We need to leave the argument behind and develop trust in numbers.[19]

Next to the business dimension of data, adapting to the changing business environments and client demands also requires a deeper and better understanding of our working reality. Therefore, we must information-enable our teams and lead them to embrace being information-enabled and data-driven. Information-enablement requires data on all aspects of the content of our work (the professional legal dimension), but also on all aspects of the genesis of our work, e.g.:

- volumes of work and effort required,
- load distribution by client, type of work, field of law, and by sub-team etc.,
- trends in the complexion of our work,
- the work-mix in DevOps-terms (business work, development work, operational work, unplanned work)[20]

As corporations digitalize, legal is no longer granted the "get-out-of-digitalization-free"-card and this change can be used to our advantage. Modern Legal Departments work ever more closely connected to their clients so that their (digital) working processes often even have direct interfaces. Certain data is even being shared or made part of a holistic digital process flow, plus, speed and efficiency are being improved in lockstep.

As Legal Departments digitize their own work and digitalize their working environment, a diverse amount of data at mass scale is being created—if we like it or not. If designed and implemented well, the new digital means can provide a plethora of what may then be called "effortless data" i.e., data that is generated merely because we work with digital means, rather than based on whipping the team to fill out the infamous Excel-sheets just for the sake of tracking.

Yet again, a humanistic approach to a data-driven, information-enabled team must not only find a human-oriented way of getting to the data, but—even more importantly—a humanistic way of leveraging the data.

---

[19] Ebersoll et al. (2021), p. 7.

[20] *"Rethinking Legal Work"*, published jointly with Jason Padman in 2020 in Rethinking: Law, Vol. 4, 2020, p. 7.

4.1.3 The Choice Between Dr. Jekyll and Mr. Hyde? – We Must Obtain Data Literacy

The use of data in a legal department, a data-driven approach to our work will depend on the acceptance by the people working there. Any implementation will fail if it is only used as a management tool without the team members supporting it. Even worse, this might even slow down a successful team. Therefore, it is essential to convince the team that such data is not meant to limit the responsibility or the freedom of each person, but rather intended to be a tool to help the whole organization to continue their journey towards a better way of getting the work done.

However, we face the actual dilemma that data can be used for the better or for the worse: the tool itself is neutral and only as good as the hand using it. A humanized approach is essential for the success of a legal team and at the same time depends solely on the people using the tool and on their intentions. Therefore, it is a prerequisite to have clear guidelines and boundaries for the use of data, and to communicate them clearly and openly, from the very beginning of the data journey. Such framework will likely go even beyond—or will at least be more specific than—the mere regulatory framework (e.g. labor laws and data privacy laws). We must avoid a "spotlight effect" on the team. *"(A) Potential outcome may be an explicit agreement within the team, but even more importantly between the team and its manager. There should be clear do's and don'ts."*[21]

To make sense, we must obtain data literacy. Is it data—or metrics—or OKR's—or KPI's?—If we jump into the data-lake unprepared, there is a real risk of drowning. We hold on to a grid of random metrics—and they turn out to be incomplete. We grab the lifebelt of "standard" KPI's—and they turn out to be irrelevant for our clients and full of holes that our teams or CxO-peers point out to us.

As we embark on the journey towards data and metrics and beyond, we must expect to have to work through the hype cycle[22] until we come out on stable ground. To get there, we must stay laser-focused on our key stakeholders that we approach with our insights and each data-analysis should pass a dual test:

(1) ***Is this data analysis relevant*** for them?
(2) Is this data analysis relevant ***for them***?

While analyzing the data we must think about how we want to achieve covering both aspects? Should we use the same approach as other departments, or can we add specific value by injecting our unique perspective to it? How can we build on quantitative data and add qualitive insights to the discussion and thereby use the best of both worlds? As to our key-stakeholders, we should initially focus on the following four:

- Our client
- Management (line and peers)

[21] Ebersoll et al. (2021), p. 31.

[22] See https://en.wikipedia.org/wiki/Gartner_hype_cycle.

- Our team as a whole
- The individual on our team

Data—and then what? What does a qualitative approach to data mean? This now puts our focus onto the question of how we get from data to information, and form information to decision. The most important first step is to be very clear about what lens we take in analyzing the data. First, we need to understand the pathway from data to insights and from insights to knowledge. Second, we must connect our analysis to the value chain of a Legal services team:

Resources → Work → Output → Outcome → Impact

For each of these categories there will be data points available that can serve as metrics, based on which we can lead fruitful discussions to obtain informed insights into our work and service delivery.[23]

4.1.4 Humanizing the Use of Data and Metrics

As legal professionals, part of our training is how to embed ethics into our work. In a digitalized Legal Department, data will be paramount. You could do a lot with it and pursue many avenues. It is important to avoid overstretching the team with the efforts inevitably needed to structure and analyze the data. Additionally, we must fight the temptation of overwhelming the stakeholders with random data and make sure that we rather offer targeted insights. Finally, we must make ethical (and legal) choices around what to measure, what to analyze, how to derive conclusions, and how to involve the team in all of this—including how to protect the legitimate interests of the individual.

In short—we must carefully consider the human dimension in generating, analyzing, and using the data. Data and metrics are not a goal in themselves. We must keep focus on what we are ultimately aiming for—the vision and mission and the operational goals of the Legal Department. Even more importantly, we must lead on our data journey with clear values.

1. First, *people cannot be reduced to data points*—and we absolutely must avoid the impression that this is what's happening.
2. Second, we all know that data can be a powerful lever in discussions. Therefore, we must *democratize it and provide full access* to operational data to everyone on the team!
3. Third, the mere fact that we now have *data must not lure the leadership approach away from self-empowered teams* back towards "command and control" based on data.

To achieve this goal, we need a clear and common understanding of our "Why" (i.e., why do we leverage data) of our methods of analysis (i.e., how do we move from data to metrics to insights and to decisions), and a crystal-clear commitment towards the team on the borders we will not cross (e.g., individualized monitoring).

[23] Ebersoll et al. (2021), p. 20.

With data comes transparency which in turn requires trust, i.e., a safe environment for the individuals on the team.[24] We must put the human interaction into the middle of it all. The "new legal" is not about running applications, but first and foremost about human beings that interact, at an ever-increasing frequency and in rapidly changing business environments.

4.2 New Methodologies for New Legal Work

We want to work with data so that we can constantly gain insights. We want to keep sharing wins and failures to continuously improve. We consider the rapidly growing options for automation a key success factor to thrive. Therefore, we need a strong culture, based on trust and transparency. Against that background, Agile practices, supported by a "digital-first" agenda, and embedded in the principles of DevOps, offer a perfect basis for modern legal teams.

4.2.1 Why DevOps[25]

DevOps is the answer to two crucial questions in transformational times:

1. How do you manage a stable, but adaptable co-existence of operational business work with continuous development work?
2. How do you plan if planning must include the unplannable?

In DevOps, the below principles have been identified to master that exact challenge.

- Focus on all business value streams (related to Systems Thinking [26]),
- Shorten and amplify feedback loops, and
- Maintain a 'growth mindset' [27]—it is OK that mistakes happen.

What is the origin of that logic, you may ask? In the well-known novel on DevOps by Gene Kim, *"The Phoenix Project"*, [28] the mentor of the main character and CIO of the company (Erik Reid), continues to force Steve Masters to learn from looking at a production line in a factory. As he observes the line running smoothly, then starting to slow down or even collapsing and coming to a halt, Steve Masters realizes, first, that a production line is basically the combination of several value

[24] Please find a more elaborate discussion of this aspect in my chapter: The New Legal Agil – and it has a New DNA, in *"Liquid Legal, Towards a Common Legal Platform"*, Kai Jacob, Roger Strathausen, Dierk Schindler (Eds.), Springer, Cham, 2020, p. 205 ff.

[25] This part on DevOps is an extract from a more extensive article called *"Rethinking Legal Work"*, that I have published jointly with Jason Padman in 2020 in the magazine REthinking:Law, Vol. 4, 2020, Stefan Breidenbach, Dierk Schindler (Eds.), pp. 4–10.

[26] https://opensource.com/article/18/3/how-apply-systems-thinking-devops.

[27] https://en.wikipedia.org/wiki/Carol_Dweck.

[28] https://itrevolution.com/book/the-phoenix-project/.

streams. It only moves as fast as its slowest element—i.e., you must focus on all value streams.—Second, the unforeseeable will happen, be it an overflow of demand leading to a shortage in resources, or a slowdown in production due to an unplanned event (lack of workers, a broken machine etc.) causing a jam in incoming work (raw material) and lack of finished product. Whatever happens and whenever it occurs, leveraging the feedback loop overall to react quickly and effectively is key to limiting the negative impact.—Finally, perfectionism and leaning too heavily on experts will create bottlenecks and thus inevitably a slowdown of the production line.

Understanding the various types of work we do, their different dynamics and requirements and their varying impact on the capacity of the team, will put legal teams in the position to actively manage load, to effectively prioritize work and to deliver on all areas of demand. Times when "project work must give way to business work" all the time, when project work "simply comes on top of a full day job", and the frustration associated with it will belong to the past.

A growth mindset that allows for speed and scale while accepting a tolerable risk of mistakes is crucial. Those that have some experience in Agile or Scum may have herd of the term *"Kaizen"* [29] which is a Japanese word often used that has similar meaning to a growth mindset.

If we embrace looking at the provisioning of legal services as ultimately a production process, plus if we then accept the underlying principles to keep it running smoothly, it is evident that we as legal professionals must approach our work with a new mindset, plus, we must not slip into a purely mechanical and factory-type of view, but we must maintain a humanistic approach.

4.2.2 Why Agile?

Like DevOps, Agile also has its origins in IT. It is a methodology that was created in 2001 by a group of developers wanted to deliver products in a way that would lead to more value for the customer. The IT world was moving ever faster, with customer needs changing more rapidly than the software could be built using traditional ways of working. The 'Agile Manifesto' that was the result of this rethink focused on a series of values and principles, like trust, empowerment, and transparency, that would support teams in delivering value to the customer in rapidly changing environments.

Translating the key principles of Agile into a more generic language immediately reveals their potential for business functions beyond IT. They can be summarized, as follows [30]:

[29] https://en.wikipedia.org/wiki/Kaizen.

[30] More detail around the adoption of Agile practices into the world of professional legal services can be found in "The New Legal is Agile, and it has a New DNA", by the author, in "Liquid Legal – towards a Common Legal Platform", Kai Jacob, Dierk Schindler, Roger Strathausen (Eds.), Cham (Switzerland), 2020.

- **Focus on producing results**—to make the product tangible early and continuously.
- **Embrace changing requirements**—to adapt to reality throughout the project.
- **Interact with your client**—to constantly work as one team.
- **Let the team self-organize**—to always find the best way to deliver the next set of results.
- **Make sure the team self-reflects regularly**—to improve continuously.

As the question arises which of the many Agile practices are the right ones to leverage for a specific team or for addressing a specific situation, the first important step is to fully understand the specific challenge by answering the question: "What is the issue you are trying to resolve?"

Two main principles should then be the guideposts for the journey into adopting Agile practices: The first one is that the large and ever-growing offering of Agile should be regarded as a supermarket. There is a wealth of options, but one will never need and buy everything! It is of paramount importance to know what you want to achieve—then select what you need for that—and finally to focus on such ingredients. The second guidepost is that there is no "right or wrong way" of adopting Agile. Of course, there are proven principles and mechanics that one should stick to when marching into an Agile practice. Therefore, engaging an Agile coach is of fundamental value. At the same time, we are looking at a relatively young and evolving methodology—and, moreover, for legal we are adapting it to an entirely new context. Feel empowered to make it Yours and to keep adapting it with Your teams!

A solid selection that the author has adopted in practice repeatedly is the combination of *"Scrum"* and *"Kanban"*, both supported by a fully digital environment. The power of Scrum is that it radically prioritizes individuals and interactions over fixed processes and limiting tools. A highly structured and very targeted set of events (daily's), based on a setup of small, cross-functional units (squads) will create a new and highly adaptable neural system between individuals and across the organization. *"Kanban"* [31] goes back to the 1940s, when Toyota switched its production from a long-term planning-model (push) to a demand-driven (pull) model. The term "Kanban" speaks volumes, as it originates from the Japanese language and means "sign" or "signal". Visualizing work by adopting a digital Kanban board will display the flow—and when it slows down; it will show overload and available capacity; it will provide relevant status information to any stakeholder on demand, to just name the main advantages.

Altogether, "Scrum" and "Kanban" empower teams to self-organize and to adapt based on their collective insights—rather than waiting for "the manager" to deep-dive, analyze, understand, plan, decide and take a top-down decision. A strong team culture that rests on the proven pillars of Scrum and Kanban provides exactly that

[31] For a good overview on Kanban, see https://kanbanize.com/de/kanban-ressourcen/kanban-erste-schritte/was-ist-kanban/.

strong but flexible foundation for legal professional teams to thrive. Continuous change is a given. Empowered teams can constantly tap into their wealth of professional diversity to master the challenges. Transparency reduces surprises to a realistic minimum while it enables every team member to be proactive, leveraging daily insights. The high level of fact-based communication and personal interconnection will over time create the solid foundation of trust that makes a team more than the sum of its individual members.

Practices like "Scrum" and "Kanban" which are an integral component of both, the Agile and DevOps frameworks, offer a great toolset to thrive in such transformational times. They enable legal to unlock the full potential of teams and their diverse set of members, to react quickly and to team according to task. However, to scale effectively and efficiently, maintain stability in all areas, and to preserve a healthy work environment for the individuals, legal must integrate planned and unplanned work and thereby make the dynamic reality of ongoing change part of the routine.

> ... (W)hen we're trapped in a system that prevents us from succeeding, our job becomes thankless, reinforces a feeling of powerlessness, and we feel that we are trapped in a system that preordains failure. ... We know that DevOps principles and patterns are what allow us to turn this downward spiral into a virtuous spiral, through a combination of cultural norms, architecture, and technical practices. [32]

4.2.3 Liquify Legal: Seven Dimensions for the Transformation of Modern Legal Teams

Jointly with my fellow co-founders of the Liquid Legal Institute, we have developed *"Liquify Legal"*, a methodology to approach the transformation of legal teams, so that continued progress is the outcome.[33] Structured in seven dimensions, "Liquify Legal" aims to support a new approach of legal teams to their work and to serving their clients. While we use the term steps,—we believe that there is neither a hard-coded order, nor a straight line from "start to finish". We consider it rather an evolutionary process that may commence at any dimension and will likely be revisited, will have different emphasis points at different times, and that will be developed further over time. As you read the outline of the approach below, you will notice how it underpins the thesis of this chapter:

> *Humanism must dominate the digital transformation of legal work.*

---

[32] from the afterword of *"The Phoenix Project"*, by Gene Kim, Kevin Behr and George Spafford, Portland, 2016, p. 344.

[33] *"Liquify Legal, The Transformation Method of the Liquid Legal Institute e.V. in 7 Steps"*, Kai Jacob, Dierk Schindler, Roger Strathausen, B. Waltl, Editions Weblaw, Zurich, 2021.

Dimension 1: "Lift Your Head"

Lift your head in English not only has a literal meaning, but also a metaphorical one. It expresses self-confidence, and self-confidence is something we feel many legal departments have too little of when it comes to the business side of their work. More literally when we lift our heads, we can see farther, and the ability to see what is happening in the distance was essential to our ancestors' survival in finding food and avoiding danger.

Lifting our heads is easier said than done. It often happens to us that we get lost in mundane activities, that the sheer amount of work forces us to bury our heads deep in various issues. As a result, we lose track of what is going on around us, and we may even lose sight of why we are doing all this work in the first place and what we really want to accomplish in the long run.

To envision the future may not be an urgent task—but it is certainly an important one! Our visions provide us with meaning and purpose, they motivate us to keep going and they tell us where, in what direction, we need to go.

Dimension 2: "Information-Enable Your Services"

We want to have a clear understanding of what is in our portfolio. Which services do our teams deliver to whom, when, how, how often—and why? Which services are really needed, i.e., how do measure success in terms of customer satisfaction and business relevance?

Only when you have the information to answer these questions, you can build up knowledge to take the right decisions, e.g., determining which services to continue or discontinue, which to change, and which new services to add to your portfolio.—In case you are currently missing such information, this may have several different reasons: It might not exist. Maybe it exists, but you don't know where. Maybe you know where, but don't know how to retrieve it. And maybe you even get to the information, but not fast enough or in a format that hinders us from connecting it with other information and draw the right conclusions.

We must crack the code to get to relevant information with acceptable effort, so that we are in a position to lead our team and to develop our services based on facts and enlightening insights.

Dimension 3: "Quadruple Your Speed"

In a fast paced and rapidly evolving business environment, we must be adaptable, and we must be capable of adapting quickly. Three things will support that ability:

First, we need to be open to continuous learning. This is not about a meta-level ambition. First and foremost, it very pragmatically refers to frequent interactions with our internal experts, to frequent feedback from our customers, and to regular exchanges with peers in our internal and external networks. Second, we need to be methodical in analyzing our work, by distinguishing between work types, as well as applying DevOps principles for analysis and to derive options for optimization. The necessary insights depend on a solid data base that can be analyzed and discussed. Third, we need to harness the information available to us. We must let it flow freely and easily across the team, *using a digital Agile First approach*.

Dimension 4: "Usher-In AI"

Pushing the digital frontier within legal teams so that it includes AI requires an algorithmic mindset, known as computational thinking. This means a combination of (i) a technical understanding of what AI can do, as well as (ii) a business understanding of what is relevant and should be done.

Legal departments need both, a mandate, and management support to close the so-called "knowing-doing gap". Teams that want to use AI must feel empowered to act as intermediaries between IT and the business. AI will not work with 100% accuracy (by the way, neither do humans), but AI can work 24/7 and thus process large volumes of documents much faster than humans. So, the point is to carefully identify those use cases where machines, AI, can help us. *We want to understand how the cooperation between humans and trained algorithms can be designed in such a way that humans can perform their tasks more efficiently and without errors and thus emerge as the big winners.*

Dimension 5: "Inspire Your Ecosystem"

Transformation is not an end in itself. It needs a vision and thus an overarching goal. We need to be clear about who the stakeholders of our transformation are, what their different interests are, and how we can win them over as supporters.

The client should be at the center. This is as much right as it is wrong! Of course, the result of our work must reach our client "in time" and "in quality". However, we must respect the legitimate expectations of our team, the needs of the individuals, the human beings on our team, and we must keep an eye on the interests of our functional leadership. *The strategy must make sense to all stakeholders, by creating tangible value that is measurable and clearly communicated.*

Dimension 6: "Face Your Fears"

Humanization or "humanizing" is the necessary practical counterpart to digitalization. Many companies and executives ignore or even suppress employees' fears of digitization, which then jeopardizes transformation projects. Transformation projects fail if the affected employees are not turned into participants, if the digital solutions introduced do not bring them any real benefit, or if the interfaces are not designed to be user-friendly.

The empirically proven, declining mental health of lawyers as a professional group and the resulting negative consequences for society, companies, and the affected individuals themselves make targeted well-being-programs both, *a mandate given by humanism, and a benefit demanded by the business clients.*

Dimension 7: "Yearn for Excellence"

Desire is part of human nature. It relates to the innate ability of imagining things differently than they actually are—and to realize such imagination. In formal legal education at university, as well as in large parts of professional development, such desire is funneled on acquiring knowledge. Traditional legal skills primarily include research, document review, drafting, abstract thinking, and reasoning. In essence, most of legal training focuses on subsuming a particular case under a general rule of law.

As business reality and the expectation on the role of lawyers change, lawyers increasingly need to acquire business-relevant, practical skills that encompass and support their work, especially interpersonal and communication skills, but also skills required for working with non-lawyers, leading cross-functional and geographically dispersed legal teams.

Yet, there is another domain that is equally important and of particular relevance for lawyers: Values. Lawyers are sworn and intrinsically motivated to protect the law as a representation of societal values that culminate in the ideal of justice. *Yearning for excellence for the human lawyer includes the desire to promote and to protect values.* Any optimization by digitalization must respect that and ideally create a net-positive in that regard.

5 Conclusion

> We have modified our environment so radically that we must now modify ourselves in order to exist in this new environment. We can no longer live in the old one. Progress imposes not only new possibilities for the future but new restrictions.[34]

Norbert Wiener, the originator of cybernetics, points us into the right direction. The modification of our environment is radical. In the context of this chapter, let's use the digital transformation as a reference point for such radical and continuous change. There is no turning back, no "stop"—we must adapt to the new environments that we have created and that we keep creating for ourselves.

This, however, does not make us human beings mere passengers on the train of digital revolution. To the contrary: This is when humanism must interject and dominate the agenda! Yes, we may and should follow the desire to innovate, to keep creating new ideas, and to pursue innovation—new possibilities! But, at the same time, we must yearn for excellence in humanizing the process and its outcomes—up to the point of identifying and implementing new restrictions.

Striking that balance is a distinctly human ability, driven by creativity and guided by human values. The outcome is far superior to "new" and "innovative": It is progress—transformational progress!

[34] Wiener (1954), p. 46.

Liquid Legal Waves to Other Chapters, Written by the Editors

Dierk reminds us to rethink both, our vision and mission as well as our communication about the drivers behind digital transformation. *Liam*, *John* and *Joyce* build on those findings as they define the key elements of *"The Elevated Workplace"*.

Emma and *Madeleine* make the case for an even more profound approach to a humanization-based company. They introduce *"Patagonia"*, the prototype of a humanized company, and tackle the question if that can work for a law firm. Should we let our lawyers go surfing?

It often occurs to us that the biggest challenge (maybe even threat) to lawyers might actually be – lawyers. Or, as *Barbara* puts it in the following chapter *"Of Mice and Lawyers"*: Hell is *just* lawyers! How can we reconcile the contradicting phenomena of an overcrowded legal profession, an ever-fiercer war for talent, and growing issues around access-to-justice?

References

Ebersoll M, Obst J, Querfurth J, Schichl P, Schindler D, Schreyvogel M, Stoeckl N, Waltl B (2021) Data-driven legal departments – an introduction into metrics and KPIs. LLI Whitepaper, Editions Weblaw, Zurich, p 7

Ismael S (2014) Exponential organizations. Diversion Books, New York, p 55

Schumpeter JA (1939) Business cycles: a theoretical, historical, and statistical analysis of the capitalist process. McGraw-Hill Book Company, New York

Schwedel A, Root J, Allen J, Hazan J, Almquist E, Devlin T (2022) The working future: more human, not less. Bain & Company Inc

Silverstein S (1978) The missing piece, 1st edn. HarperCollins Publishers

Strathausen R (2017) *Masters of ambiguity: how legal can lead the business.* In: Liquid legal, transforming legal into a business savvy, information enabled and performance driven industry. Springer, Cham. p 9 ff

Susskind D (2015) *The future of the professions*. Oxford University Press, London p, p 67

Susskind D (2017) Tomorrows lawyers, 2nd edn. Oxford University Press, London, p xix

Welzer H (2021) Nachruf auf mich selbst, (Obituary to myself – title as translated by the author), S. Fischer, Frankfurt/Main, p 26

Wiener N (1954) The human use of human beings: cybernetics and society, 2nd edn. Houghton Mifflin, p 46

Dierk Schindler is one of the co-founders of the Liquid Legal Institute e.V. (www.liquid-legal-institute.com) and serves as Co-CEO, together with Kai Jacob and Bernhard Waltl. He is co-author and co-editor of numerous publications on innovation and transformation in the legal profession, most notably the two previous volumes of the book-series "Liquid Legal" (Springer) in 2017 and 2020.

In 2019, Dierk joined Robert BOSCH GmbH as their Vice President Corporate Legal Services, Mobility Solutions, Supply Chain and Logistics. In his role he drives the adoption of digitally supported Agile practices and, jointly with the leadership team, the digital transformation of the legal team. Prior to BOSCH, Dierk has spent 14 years with NetApp Inc., where he built the EMEA Legal Team, established the Deal Management function, and implemented the Global Legal Shared Services Team.

Dierk's teams have been awarded IACCM "Global Innovation Awards" in 2014 and 2015. He teaches at the Management Center Innsbruck (MCI) on Innovation Management, Digital Business Law, and Compliance. Dierk is a certified lawyer, took his doctorate degree from Augsburg University, Germany, and his Master of International Law from Lund University, Sweden.

Of Mice and Lawyers. Learning from Calhoun's Rodent Utopia

Barbara Chomicka

Contents

Abstract

There is good data available to demonstrate that before starting law school, law students are healthier than the general population, both physically and mentally. They drink less than other young people, use fewer substances, suffer less from depression, and start school with a good sense of self and values. Then something goes astray for many of them. Today, according to some reports, lawyers have the highest rate of depression of any occupational group. The results of one study showed that more than one in five practicing attorneys are problem drinkers and 75 per cent of attorneys skipped the survey section on drug use as if it wasn't there. Lawyers, as individuals and as a profession, seem to experience a *behavioral sink*.

Barbara Chomicka is Director, Contract Solutions at Turner and Townsend.

'Of mice and men' is a novella written by John Steinbeck. Published in 1937, it narrates the experiences of two displaced migrant ranch workers, who move from place to place in California in search of new job opportunities during the Great Depression in the United States.

B. Chomicka (✉)
New York, NY, USA
e-mail: barbara.chomicka@turntown.com

K. Jacob et al. (eds.), *Liquid Legal – Humanization and the Law*, Law for Professionals, https://doi.org/10.1007/978-3-031-14240-6_2

Behavioral sink is a term coined by ethologist John Calhoun to describe a collapse in behavior that can result from overcrowding. The term and concept originate in a series of experiments in overpopulation that Calhoun conducted on rats and mice from the 1940s onwards. Calhoun's work, and his utopian mouse community, Universe 25, became an animal model of societal collapse, and a touchstone of urban sociology and psychology in general. According to Calhoun's findings, no matter how sophisticated we consider ourselves to be, once the number of individuals capable of filling roles significantly exceeds the number of roles available, the disruption of social organization will follow. Individuals under these circumstances will be out of touch with reality to the point of being incapable even of alienation. Their most complex behaviors will become fragmented. The creation and application of ideas appropriate for life in a post-industrial digital society will be thwarted.

This chapter considers the humanization of the law from the perspective of the increasingly crowded legal profession. Looking at the coping mechanisms of Calhoun's mice in the face of crisis suggests another way of 'humanizing' the legal profession.

1 Introduction

It is a good moment to engage in a discussion about the humanization of the law.

The progress of technology affects the quantity of work available: technologies turn physical goods, knowledge and experiences into data that can be easily replicated, shared, and stored. Today, a very small number of highly skilled people can create products and services that deliver significant consumer value with minimum employment levels. The current Covid-19 pandemic has led to a further demand shock that could mean that the economy simply no longer retains the need for the labor of some workers. The very nature of whatever work is left shifts from autonomy and competence towards commoditized, standardized, semi-automated tasks. The amount of social interaction at work has also decreased rapidly. As noted by the futurist Martin Ford, 'people usually say they want a human element to their interactions, but Covid-19 has changed that' (Thomas 2020).

One of the professions particularly concerned about its future under these conditions is the legal profession.

Following a recent survey in which nearly 60 per cent of young lawyers declared that they are so discouraged in their work that they are thinking about changing career, William Vogeler (2019), a practicing attorney, who has written about court cases in virtually every jurisdiction in the United States, titled one of his articles 'Two-thirds of lawyers want out of the profession'. In the article, he suggests that the misery is not linked to money or prestige. 'It is mostly about autonomy and mastery', he wrote, 'so if you feel trapped in your job, you don't have to quit the law. Maybe it's time to change the way you practice'. Paula Davis (2020), who writes about lawyers, stress resilience, burnout, and well-being at work, supports this view: 'autonomy, belonging and competence are most strongly correlated with motivation and well-being'. In essence, a meaningful legal job is the fundamental prerequisite for lawyers' happiness at work.

However, these meaningful legal jobs are currently in short supply. According to the American Bar Association (2020), over the past two decades the legal profession has become more than twice as competitive for lawyers. A combination of technological progress, the Covid -19 pandemic and the ever-increasing number of new entrants to the profession has resulted in significant professional overpopulation. There are far more lawyers today than there are meaningful traditional legal roles.

People are not compulsorily enlisted in the legal profession as they are in military service; the crowding in the legal profession is therefore voluntary.

One of the most prominent analyses of the effects of voluntary crowding comes from a behavioral study of captive mice conducted by ethologist John B. Calhoun at a rural facility in Poolesville, Maryland, United States. Within the giant box, known as Universe 25, several pairs of mice bred a sizable population. Once the size of the population crossed a certain threshold, heaven turned into hell. Calhoun designed several mouse environments before he got to the 25th try, with thoroughly consistent results: overpopulation led to pathological behavior that escalated beyond any possibility of control.

Calhoun's studies confirmed the grim hypothesis that overpopulation generates a breakdown in social functions (Calhoun 1962). The dissolution of social organization—the *behavioral sink*—leads to the death of the establishment. The death of the establishment leads to *spiritual death*—to the loss of capacity of the species to engage in behaviors essential to the survival of the species. *Spiritual death* leads to physical death. That, in turn, inevitably leads to the species' extinction. Calhoun consistently found that the animals that were better able to handle high numbers of social interactions fared comparatively well. *High social velocity* mice were the winners in hell.

The *high social velocity* lawyers, or the *integrative lawyers*, to use the term promoted by J. Kim Wright (2016), an attorney, publisher, and editor of CuttingEdgeLaw.com, are 'the harbingers of a new cultural consciousness'. *Integrative lawyers*, according to Wright, 'explore and draw upon many disciplines and wisdom traditions, such as philosophy, science, psychology, and spirituality'.

What exactly do *high social velocity* lawyers do at work? For example, Robert, an independently practicing South African commercial attorney, who lives in one of the world's most unequal societies, wanted to do something about people's vulnerability when they sign contracts, especially people who are poor and illiterate. He developed and promoted legally binding illustrated contracts—'comic contracts'—as a way for illiterate people to independently understand contracts, as a guide to behavior and to improve the relationship between contracting parties. Amanda, an attorney, lecturer, and non-profit director, runs the Centre for Integrative Law, a consultancy for emergent thinking in the practice of law. The Centre has pioneered many initiatives, including training the first fifty lawyers in the Collaborative Divorce methodology and introducing more than a hundred lawyers to Neuro-literacy (neuroscientific learnings for improved lawyering) for Lawyers. In 2016 she launched Women Leading in Law (WOLELA), a national network of women lawyers that supports individual women lawyers. Diane, an attorney and a civil mediator, currently serving her third term as a Hearing Member on the Indiana Workers' Compensation Board, hears all the workers' compensation cases in the Indianapolis district. In addition to her numerous accolades, she created and co-chaired a Diversity Committee at Hamilton Southeastern Schools and co-created a civilian military support program during the conflict in Iraq, known as Support Our Troops. She is also a Reiki Master and is trained in Matrix Energetics and other holistic healing practices (Lawyers as Changemakers n.d.).

As for other lawyers, Mark Cohen (2015), chief executive officer of Legalmosaic, advised that 'just being a lawyer' doesn't often cut it anymore."

2 The Mice

Universe 25 was designed to cater for the well-being of its rodent residents and increase their lifespan. It took the form of a tank, 101 inches (2.6 m) square, enclosed by walls 54 inches (1.4 m) high. The first 37 inches (0.9 m) of wall was structured so that the mice could climb up, but they were prevented from escaping by 17 inches (0.4 m) of bare wall above. Each wall had sixteen 'stairwells' attached to it. Four horizontal corridors opened off each stairwell, each leading to four nesting boxes. That means there were 256 boxes in total, each capable of housing fifteen mice. The enclosure capacity was then 3840 mice.

There was plenty of clean water, food, and nesting material. The Universe was cleaned every four to eight weeks. There were no predators. The mice were a disease-free elite selected from the National Institute of Health's breeding colony. Heaven. Four breeding pairs of mice were moved in on day one. After 104 days they started to reproduce. The population increased exponentially, doubling every 55 days.

After day 315, however, population growth slowed. More than 600 mice now lived in the Universe, constantly rubbing shoulders on their way up and down the stairwells to eat, drink, and sleep. Mice found themselves in a world that was more crowded every day, and there were far more mice than meaningful social roles. With more and more peers challenging them, male mice found it difficult and stressful to defend their territory, so they abandoned the activity altogether. Normal social discourse within the mouse community broke down, and with it the ability of the mice to form social bonds.

The mice congregated in large groups in the middle of the enclosure, their withdrawal occasionally interrupted by waves of violence. The victims of these random attacks were becoming attackers themselves. Left on their own in nests and subject to invasion, nursing females attacked their own young. Procreation plummeted, infant abandonment and mortality soared. Lone females retreated to isolated nesting boxes. Some males and females, a group Calhoun termed *the beautiful ones*, never sought sex and never attacked their peers—they just ate, slept and groomed. Elsewhere, cannibalism, pan-sexualism, and violence became endemic. The mice were not nice. When the population started declining, *the beautiful ones* were spared from violence and death, but had completely lost touch with social behaviors, including having sex or caring for their young. The *behavioral sink*, the shared hopelessness, drew in pathological behavior and its effects were exacerbated. The mouse society had collapsed.

On day 560, a little more than eighteen months into the experiment, the population peaked at 2200 mice and its growth ceased. A few mice survived until day 600, after which there were few pregnancies and no surviving young. The population had ceased to regenerate itself, taking the path to extinction. Even when the population dropped back to the size of the early days of the Universe, the downfall was already unstoppable. The mice had lost the ability to socialize and come together to mate. In a way, they had ceased to be mice long before their physical death. The *spiritual death* ruined their soul and their society as thoroughly as the subsequent death of the physical body. The last rodent in Universe 25 died on the 1588th day of the experiment.

Calhoun saw the fate of the mouse population as a metaphor for the potential fate of humans. He feared that humankind could lurch toward a similar fate if cities became overcrowded and the population swelled beyond the capacity of the job market.

This apocalyptic worldview associated with overpopulation was widespread in postwar society, when Calhoun conducted his experiments. Conservationists like Fairfield Osborn, author of the bestselling books *Our plundered planet* (1948) *The limits of the earth* (1953), and *Our crowded planet* (1962), were sounding the alarm over soaring population levels, promoting a belief that unless humankind drastically reduced its consumption and limited its population, global ecosystems would be ravaged. Ecologists specializing in the planet's carrying capacity and population control, such as William Vogt, author of the bestselling book *Road to survival* (1948), argued that affluence is our biggest problem. If we continued to take more than the Earth could give, he said, the unavoidable result would be devastation on a global scale. In 1968, Paul Ehrlich and his wife, Anne Ehrlich (who was uncredited), published *The population bomb*, a best-selling alarmist book predicting worldwide famine in the 1970s and 1980s due to overpopulation, as well as other major societal upheavals, and advocating immediate action to limit population growth. The issue reached its mainstream peak in 1972, with the report of the Rockefeller Commission on US Population, which recommended that population growth should be slowed, or even reversed.

But Calhoun's conclusions from his experiments were different. Osborn, Vogt, Ehrlich, and many other thought leaders of the time were arguing that population growth would cause our demise by exhausting our natural resources, leading to starvation and conflict. In Calhoun's mouse civilization there was no scarcity of food and water; the only thing that was in short supply was the ability to fulfil a meaningful social role. His main finding was that overpopulation itself could destroy a society before famine even got a chance.

In Universe 25, hell was other mice.

3 The Lawyers

The population of lawyers consists of professionals who have completed a degree at an accredited law school and passed the bar examination. The United States of America hosts the largest population of lawyers in the world—over 1.3 million, according to the American Bar Association (2020). Clifford Winston (2012), senior fellow in economic studies, suggests that American society spends approximately $200 billion annually on lawyers.

The growth in the population of the legal profession has slowed in recent years, according to the ABA National Lawyer Population Survey (2020), a tally of lawyers by every state bar association and licensing agency. However, since the professional associations were established, the number of lawyers has grown faster than the nation's population. Since 2010, the number of lawyers increased by 10.4 per cent, while the population of the United States grew 6.3 per cent over the same period, according to the U.S. Census Bureau (2020). Over time, the ratio of lawyers to the general population has become less and less favorable for lawyers. More and more lawyers find themselves entering a professional world that is more and more crowded, and there are increasingly far more lawyers than meaningful legal jobs. With more and more peers challenging their territory, lawyers find it difficult and stressful to defend it, and some abandon the activity altogether. According to the ABA Profile of the Legal Profession (2020), 80 per cent of female lawyers of color have left, or have considered leaving, the profession.

Nationwide, in the United States there are roughly four lawyers for every 1000 residents.[1] They are not evenly distributed among the 50 states, though, or even within the states. Despite the large nationwide number of lawyers, large swathes of the United States have few lawyers or no lawyers. There are more than 3100 counties and county equivalents in the United States, and 54 of them have no lawyers. Another 182 have only one or two lawyers. There are therefore several legal deserts in the United States—large areas where residents must travel far to find a lawyer for routine matters like drawing up a will, handling a divorce or disputing a traffic violation. One could argue that this, 'the greatest country in the world', according to a solid majority of US Republicans and Conservatives, has, instead of a lawyer population problem, a *fair lawyer distribution problem.* American lawyers congregate in large groups in big cities. In New York City, there are 14 lawyers for every 1000 residents.

[1] To compare this figure with other established professions: there were 116,000 licensed architects in the United States at the start of 2020. That means that nationwide, the figure is 0.3 architect per 1000 people. Statistically, then, there are 13 times more lawyers than architects per 1000 residents.

The *fair lawyer distribution problem* is not only geographical, but also economic. Throughout the United States, millions of people on low incomes have no access to affordable lawyers, even for life-altering civil matters such as child custody disputes or home foreclosures, where legal representation really matters (Amato 2015), and this 'justice gap' is vast. According to the World Justice Project's latest Rule of Law Index (2021), which gathers primary data on people's practical experience of the law in 102 countries globally, the United States ranks 65th for the accessibility and affordability of its civil justice, the same ranking as Botswana, Pakistan and Uzbekistan, not far behind Moldova and Nigeria. In most service industries, such an epic imbalance of supply and demand would entice more entrepreneurs. But not the American legal services market. There's no shortage of lawyers to bridge the justice gap, though—in the last four years, less than 60 per cent of law school graduates have found full-time jobs requiring a bar qualification.

Many lawyers who have a job obsess about the competition, about their compensation, about their clients and their demands, and the fear of losing their clients. The resulting mental health distress is significant. Recent studies show that lawyers struggle with mental health issues, alcohol, and substance misuse at levels substantially higher than the general population and other highly educated professionals. Among nearly 13,000 US lawyers surveyed by ABA and the Hazelden Betty Ford Foundation, 21 per cent were considered to be problem drinkers (Krill et al. 2016). This is more than triple the proportion of problem drinkers in the general population (6 per cent) and nearly double the rate for other highly educated professionals (12 per cent). 28 per cent of lawyers struggle with depression and 19 per cent have symptoms of anxiety. These issues have major professional consequences. Studies show that between 25 and 30 per cent of lawyers facing disciplinary charges suffer from some type of addiction or mental illness (ABA 2020).

Everyday experiences of lawyers in the workplace are also worrying: 75 per cent of female lawyers (and 8 per cent of their male equivalents) had experienced demeaning comments, stories, and jokes. 82 per cent of female lawyers (but no male lawyers) had been mistaken for a lower-level employee. There is reliable data showing that a significant segment of the bar routinely and patently pads bills and defrauds clients (Bogus 1996). A lot of recent writing on this situation focuses on the profession's silence in the face of open and endemic fraud as evidence of 'the death of the legal profession'. Or, rather, a *behavioral sink,* as Calhoun would put it.

To paraphrase Judge Leon Higginbotham (1980), the crisis among legal professionals arises not because lawyers misunderstand Blackstone or the Bluebook, the Uniform Commercial Code or the Federal Rules of Evidence; there are just too many lawyers for the amount of traditional legal work currently available in society. The overpopulation in the profession, and the resulting shortage of meaningful roles, destroys both lawyers' souls and the legal profession itself.

In the United States, hell is other lawyers.

4 "Guys Like us Got Nothing to Look Ahead to"[2]

How many 'too many' lawyers are there in the United States? The answer, provided by Stephen Magee (1992b), a professor of finance and economics, is '40 per cent too many'.

Magee mapped the relationship between economic growth rates and the population of lawyers in various countries. The 'Magee curve' indicates that lawyers bring economic benefits to a country up to a certain point—by enforcing contracts, prosecuting criminals and so forth. According to Magee (1992a), beyond the optimal number of lawyers, the effects of their work are negative. By Magee's estimate, 'on average, each excess lawyer knocks $1 million off US gross domestic product every year'. He acknowledged that the number of lawyers in society is just 'a proxy for the level of legal activity', but he concluded that it is the best one available. One could wonder: why don't the laws of supply and demand operate to keep the number of lawyers in society at, or near, the optimal level? Magee says the US market for legal services has imperfections, in part due to lawyers' own contrivance. Most notably, he says, lawyers use their domination of Congress and state legislatures to create new demands for their skills. Magee relies in part on the 'collective action' theories of Mancur Olson (1971), an economist and political scientist, to suggest that lawyers organize themselves in legislative bodies and bar associations to engage in 'rent seeking'—a term used in economics for engaging in or involving the manipulation of public policy or economic conditions as a strategy for increasing profits (Majaski 2021).

Understandably, Magee's framing of the issue has been controversial. According to the most direct rebuttal, by Charles Epp (Epp 1992), a political scientist, there is no viable explanation that 'supports Mr. Magee's case that our large legal profession saps the economy'. 'How could Mr. Magee draw those conclusions, while we found no such effects?' asks Epp. Magee is also challenged for his failure to account for the fact that lawyers create both benefits and costs. According to Ronan Gilson, a professor at Stanford Law School, 'Lawyers produce social goods, like civil rights and social justice: to that extent, measures of GNP [gross national product] growth ignore a critical aspect of social welfare' (Andrews 1994).

The belief promoted by Magee that limiting the size of the legal profession would help to reinvigorate the profession, and consequently the quality of life in society, is fairly prevalent. In 1991, American Vice-President Dan Quayle, head of the President's Council on Competitiveness, when proposing a 50-point agenda for limiting lawsuits, noted: 'Let's ask ourselves: does America really need 70 per cent of the world's lawyers? (…) Is it healthy for our economy to have eighteen million new lawsuits coursing through the system annually?' (Mencimer 2006). Scholars who study the court system have called Quayle's numbers into question, but the relationship between a sufficient quantity of legal work for lawyers, the well-being of society and a sound economy remains important.

[2]John Steinbeck, 'Of mice and men'.

Population control in the legal profession, though, is a very complex issue. Lawyers are a highly institutionalized workforce. According to Ryan Nunn (2018), licensing requirements have already constrained the supply. The licensing of lawyers in the United States is very restrictive, prohibiting businesses from selling legal services unless they are owned and managed by lawyers. Not surprisingly, the definition of the practice of law by the lawyers' professional associations is extensive, and includes any potentially 'legal' services, such as the sale of standard-form wills. Lawyers' professional associations also enjoy a monopoly on law school accreditation. Since the profession controls the accrediting of law schools, why does it accredit so many new law schools, allow existing schools to increase dramatically in size, or permit schools to reduce their traditionally high attrition rate through grade inflation? If law schools cannot be controlled, why not lower the pass rate for bar examinations?

Limiting the number of qualified lawyers would raise both the cost of becoming a lawyer and legal fees. Magee (1992a) believed that the latter would be more than offset by a reduction in 'costly and inefficient make-work litigation by "excess" lawyers scrambling for income'. However, the 'exclusivity' of professional membership inevitably leads to special protection for elites (in the United States these are usually white and wealthy). If we look at the ABA survey (2020), it is clear that the surge in numbers of law adepts is associated with greater participation by women and minorities. From 1950 to 1970, only 3 per cent of all lawyers in the United States were women. This percentage has increased gradually since then—it was 8 per cent in 1980, 27 per cent in 2000 and over 37 per cent in 2020. According to the ABA National Lawyer Population Survey, the percentage of US lawyers who are men and women of color—Hispanic, African American, Asian, Native American, and mixed race—has grown slowly over the past decade. Collectively, the number of lawyers of color grew less than 3 percentage points in the past 10 years, from 11.4 per cent of all lawyers in 2010 to 14.1 per cent of all lawyers in 2020.

The favoritism currently shown by courts towards wealthy Americans, and its hostility toward the interests of underrepresented groups, is, at least in part, a product of the makeup of the legal profession and the judiciary. In the United States, the federal bench has long been dominated by a white male elite. There have been periods during which the Supreme Court has robustly protected the American people, including the most vulnerable. As noted by Root and Berger (2019), if one looks at the entirety of American legal history, however, the court has more frequently served to check social progress rather than advance it. For example, in the 1800s, the Supreme Court benefited white landowners and businesspeople by ruling that African Americans were not American citizens and by upholding 'separate but equal' racial segregation and discrimination (Sullivan 2015). Between 1905 and 1918, the Supreme Court struck down important labor laws, including those establishing humane work hours and banning child labor (Hammer v. Dagenhart 1918; Lochner v. New York 1905). Later, it upheld a Virginia law permitting the sterilization of people with disabilities and the criminalization of same-sex relationships (Buck v. Bell 1927; Korematsu v. United States 1944; Bowers v. Hardwick 1986). More recently, the Supreme Court sided with powerful corporations by prohibiting workers and consumers from bringing class action lawsuits and by allowing the wealthy to drown out the voices of everyday Americans through corporate financial contributions.[3]

One way to address the current bias starts with the ethnic and gender diversity of people who do 'legal' work. Having individuals in power who look like or share characteristics with the broader population furthers the perceived legitimacy of the courts and their decisions. According to Judge Harry Edwards (2002), it is 'inevitable that judges' different professional and life experiences have some bearing on how they confront various problems that come before them'. Any profession that is to have a future in a modern society must sustain itself by means other than limited access and a high financial threshold to entry. The humanization of the law must involve broadening access to the profession and improving access to justice.

In parallel with proposals for the control of the population of lawyers, there is strong advocacy for the deregulation of entry to the profession and the removal of barriers that prevent individuals and firms from providing legal services without satisfying occupational licensing or other regulatory requirements. The widely accepted justification for licensing lawyers is that consumers don't have the knowledge to distinguish competent from incompetent lawyers until it is too late (Winston 2012). In the United States this argument is debatable. In the United States, lawyers are today judged by their reputation and licensing requirements, and customers of the legal industry do not enjoy the benefits of warranties, industry-sponsored voluntary disclosure, third-party disclosure, or even government-mandated disclosure. The American Bar Association has vigorously opposed third-party ratings of law schools, lawyers, and law firms (Winston 2012).

Along with lowering the price of legal services and bringing it closer to the cost of providing them, deregulation could accelerate the adoption of cost-cutting technologies, as well as the introduction of new services. The potential benefits of new technologies can already be seen, as clients have started to perform many tasks traditionally undertaken by lawyers. Winston (2012) estimated that the annual gain in 'economic welfare'—the difference between consumer benefits and lawyers' losses resulting from the elimination of inflated prices for legal services—would be at least $10 billion. This would also help to address the 'justice gap'—the reality that some litigants cannot afford lawyers, yet do not qualify for legal aid or don't have lawyers assigned to them because of diminishing public budgets.

There is strong opposition to such deregulation, based on what economists call 'distributional' grounds: who wins and who loses. The number of people who would lose if the legal industry was deregulated is substantial: as evidenced in the statistics provided above, potentially over 1.3 million lawyers—four per 1000 American people. According to current licensing requirements, a lawyer, before becoming employed, unemployed, or under-employed, must complete a degree at an accredited law school and pass a state bar examination at huge cost, both direct and indirect, and

[3] See, for example, AT&T Mobility v. Concepcion (2011); Citizens United v. Federal Election Commission (2010).

this cost should not be underestimated. The conclusions of a new survey by the ABA Young Lawyers Division and the ABA Media Relations and Strategic Communications Division are rather frightening: many new lawyers are postponing major life decisions like marriage, having children, and buying a home, or rejecting them outright, because they are carrying heavy student loan debts. Nearly half of lawyers (48 per cent) who responded to the ABA survey said they have postponed or decided not to have children because of their debts. More than 1 in 4 (29 per cent) said they have postponed or decided not to get married because of their debts. More than half (56 per cent) said they have postponed or decided not to buy a house because of their debts. Some said they cannot afford rent and have moved in with their parents to save money. More than half (58 per cent) said they postponed or decided not to take a vacation because of their debts. Career-wise, roughly one-third (37 per cent) said they chose a job that pays more instead of a job they really wanted. One in 6 (17 per cent) said they chose a job that qualifies for loan forgiveness instead of a job they really wanted. The median cumulative debt (for law school, undergraduate and other education expenses) at law school graduation among those who completed the survey was $160,000. More than 40 per cent reported that their current debt is higher than the debt they had when they graduated from law school.

Lawyers, recent law school graduates and current law students would presumably object to any deregulation that would allow new legal service providers to enter the profession at a time that many (highly indebted) lawyers are unemployed. It should also be noted that any fundamental change in regulatory policy would have to go through state legislatures or courts, whose sentiments are likely to be aligned with incumbents. The overpopulation in the law profession is therefore here to stay.

5 Conclusions. Hell Is *Just* Lawyers

Following repeated failures to create a 'heaven' for the mouse population, later in his career Calhoun built universes that minimized the ill-effects of overcrowding and maximized opportunities for creativity. Humans, he argued, were positive animals, and creativity and urban design could solve our problems. He cited creativity and art as giving people the ability to create distance between others to cope with overcrowding.

This 'creativity', in the legal profession, may take many forms.

Today, law is intersecting with business and technology as never before. In the process, what it means to be a lawyer is being redefined. The practice of law, by moving towards becoming an interdisciplinary one, is offering new opportunities for lawyers. Even though technology is increasingly substituting legal products for what were once legal services, it also brings new opportunities for lawyers. The global legal market has plenty of room for new, innovative models of legal and interdisciplinary service delivery. What seems to stand in the way of professional success is lawyers being *just* lawyers.

Cohen (2015), in his article titled 'Why are Lawyers so unpopular and stressed?', compared the reality of the professional work of many lawyers to the aimless existence of the bookkeeper in Dickens' *A tale of two cities*. He pointed to professional expectations, and the need for their recalibration, as the source of most of the challenges faced by legal professionals today: unemployment, burnout, and substance abuse. 'Delivering more value, speaking plainly, being more transparent, embracing innovation, responding to the needs of the marketplace, providing affordable service for all who need it, focusing on delivering solutions, utilizing tools available to deliver legal services more efficiently and collaboratively', he says, 'would go a long way towards making lawyers more popular and happier'.

A recalibration from being *just* a lawyer to becoming a *high social velocity* lawyer entails a lot of work. Robert, Amanda and Diane created their own success, by thinking creatively about what it means to be a lawyer, what it means to practice law, where lawyers' skillset might prove particularly valuable, where is the need, and how one can help others by putting one's legal skillset to the test.

When asked what the American Bar Association is doing to help combat mental health and substance abuse—the *behavioral sink*—Linda Klein, its president, said the ABA's requirement for continuing professional development and education 'recommends that lawyers be required to take one credit of programming every three years that focuses on mental health or substance abuse disorders'. She added that 'by requiring lawyers to attend such programs periodically, the hope is that these concerns will be reduced.' It is possible that if this one credit, to be completed triennially, instead of focusing on mental health or substance abuse disorders focused on creativity training, the results might be more promising.

6 Post Scriptum

The author of this chapter originally trained as an architect and practices a creative exercise popular among members of this professional group—psychogeography. Psychogeography is the practice of aimlessly walking the city, which not only allows architects to deal with work stress and explore the city—its by-product is a renewed energy and passion for urban design, i.e., enthusiasm for one's work. Today, 'work' for the author is contract solutions, following a change of career in her mid-thirties, when the architectural design services market started feeling too crowded. It is not unusual for architects to switch fields in mid-career—the myth of the architectural profession is all encompassing. One of the architects the author most admires—Daniel Libeskind—started his practice when he was 44. He originally trained as a virtuoso musician and historian.

Liquid Legal Waves to Other Chapters, Written by the Editors

"Hell is just lawyers"—a monument of a statement by Barbara! Matthias explores how to approach *"entry-level professionals and the digital transformation of legal services"* posing the challenge that traditional experiential training on lower-level tasks vanishes thanks to technology. Is that the opportunity to invite new skills beyond the traditional legal hard skills?

In his chapter *"The Elevated Customer Experience"*, Stephen proposes an even broader view on the job-to-be-done by lawyers. Stephen argues that focusing merely on customer satisfaction would miss the emotional and experiential component, the true meeting of the minds between lawyer and client.

In the following chapter *"Women as Game Changer in the Legal Industry"*, Bruno offers yet another dimension to the "behavioral sink" that glooms in a self-centered, overcrowded legal market: the continued lack of diversity. While the power of diversity is legend, well-analyzed and proven, the legal market still lags behind fixing that structural issue.

References

Amato T (2015) Put lawyers where they're needed. New York Times, 17 June. https://www.nytimes.com/2015/06/17/opinion/put-lawyers-where-theyre-needed.html

American Bar Association (2020) ABA Profile of the legal profession 2020. https://www.americanbar.org/content/dam/aba/administrative/news/2020/07/potlp2020.pdf

Andrews JH (1994) Do too many lawyers spoil the economy? Christian Science Monitor, 15 February. https://www.csmonitor.com/1994/0215/15081.html

AT&T Mobility v. Concepcion, 563 U.S. 333 (2011). https://www.law.cornell.edu/supremecourt/text/09-893

Bogus C (1996) The death of an honorable profession. Indiana Law J 71(4):911–947. http://ilj.law.indiana.edu/articles/71/71_4_Bogus.pdf

Bowers v. Hardwick, 478 U.S. 186 (1986). https://www.oyez.org/cases/1985/85-140

Buck v. Bell, 274 U.S. 200 (1927). https://www.oyez.org/cases/1900-1940/274us200

Calhoun JB (1962) Population density and social pathology. Sci Am 206(2):139–149

U.S. Census Bureau (2020) State Population Totals and Components of Change: 2010-2019. https://www.census.gov/data/tables/time-series/demo/popest/2010s-state-total.html

Citizens United v. Federal Election Commission, 558 U.S. 310 (2010). https://www.oyez.org/cases/2008/08-205

Cohen MA (2015) Legalmosaic: why are lawyers so unpopular and stressed? Bloomberg Law, Sept. 30. https://news.bloomberglaw.com/business-and-practice/why-are-lawyers-so-unpopular-and-stressed/

Davis P (2020) Money doesn't lead to happiness in law – here is what does. Forbes, October 8. https://www.forbes.com/sites/pauladavislaack/2020/10/08/money-doesnt-lead-to-happiness-in-law%2D%2Dhere-is-what-does/?sh=4e4cfc534c81

Edwards HT (2002) Race and the judiciary. Yale Law Policy Rev 20(2):325–330. https://digitalcommons.law.yale.edu/cgi/viewcontent.cgi?referer=https://www.google.com/&httpsredir=1&article=1439&context=ylpr

Epp CR (1992) Let's not kill all the lawyers. Wall St. Journal, 9 July:A13

Hammer v. Dagenhart, 247 U.S. 251 (1918). https://www.oyez.org/cases/1900-1940/247us251

Higginbotham LA Jr (1980) In the matter of color: race and the American legal process: the colonial period, 4th edn. Oxford University Press, Oxford

Korematsu v. United States, 323 U.S. 214 (1944). https://www.law.cornell.edu/supremecourt/text/323/214

Krill PR, Johnson R, Albert L (2016) The prevalence of substance use and other mental health concerns among American Attorneys. J Addict Med 10(1):46–52. https://journals.lww.com/journaladdictionmedicine/Fulltext/2016/02000/The_Prevalence_of_Substance_Use_and_Other_Mental.8.aspx

Lawyers as Changemakers (n.d.) Rob de Rooy: comic contracts. https://lawyersaschangemakers.com/rob-de-rooy-comic-contracts/

Lochner v. New York, 198 U.S. 45 (1905). https://www.oyez.org/cases/1900-1940/198us45

Magee SP (1992a) The optimum number of lawyers: a reply to Epp. Law Soc Enq 17(4):667–693. https://www.cambridge.org/core/journals/law-and-social-inquiry/article/abs/optimum-number-of-lawyers-a-reply-to-epp/B40D7615EB95D49E29E2D435282BCAB0

Magee SP (1992b) The optimum number of lawyers: cross-national estimates. (University of Texas at Austin, February 1992; presented at the universities of Chicago, Texas, and Wisconsin, and at the White House)

Majaski C (2021) Rent Seeking, Investopiedia, December 03. https://www.investopedia.com/terms/r/rentseeking.asp#:~:text=Rent%20seeking%20is%20an%20economic,potentially%20manipulative%20use%20of%20resources

Mencimer S (2006) Blocking the courthouse door: how the republican party and its corporate allies are taking away your right to sue. Free Press

Nunn R (2018) How occupational licensing matters for wages and careers. Brookings, 15 Mar. https://www.brookings.edu/research/how-occupational-licensing-matters-for-wages-and-careers/

Olson M (1971) [1965] The logic of collective action: public goods and the theory of groups. Rev. edn. Harvard University Press, Cambridge

Root D, Berger S (2019) Structural reforms to the federal judiciary restoring independence and fairness to the courts. American Progress, 8 May. https://www.americanprogress.org/issues/courts/reports/2019/05/08/469504/structural-reforms-federal-judiciary/

Sullivan CC (2015) 13 worst Supreme Court decisions of all time. FindLaw, 14 October. https://blogs.findlaw.com/supreme_court/2015/10/13-worst-supreme-court-decisions-of-all-time.html

Thomas Z (2020) Coronavirus: will Covid-19 speed up the use of robots to replace human workers? BBC News, 19 April. https://www.bbc.co.uk/news/technology-52340651

Vogeler W (2019) Two-thirds of lawyers want out of the profession. FindLaw,14 May. https://www.findlaw.com/legalblogs/greedy-associates/two-thirds-of-lawyers-want-out-of-the-profession/

Winston C (2012) Deregulate the lawyers. Brookings, 30 April. https://www.brookings.edu/opinions/deregulate-the-lawyers/

World Justice Project (2021) WJP rule of law index. https://worldjusticeproject.org/rule-of-law-index/

Wright JK (2016) Lawyers as changemakers: the global integrative law movement. American Bar Association. https://www.americanbar.org/products/inv/book/262994059/

Barbara Chomicka is a creative thinker and problem solver, named among the most inspirational women in contract and commercial by World Commerce and Contracting. A registered architect and certified project, contact and commercial manager, she has been combining the design and management disciplines for over 20 years, optimizing the delivery of projects. She has received two doctorate degrees from British universities and has produced a body of published work endorsed by the leading global professional associations.

Her professional, academic and voluntary work has been recognized with APM Herbert Walton Award, Women in Construction Project Manager of the Year Award and Communitas Making the Difference Award. Her approach to life exemplifies her belief that everything we face is a project—a collaborative enterprise requiring the right methods to resolve it. In her thought-provoking writing and presentations, she promotes a 360-degree duty of care inside and outside of work.

Women as a Game Changer in the Legal Industry: Relevance of Diversity and Inclusion

Bruno Mascello

Contents

Bruno Mascello is an attorney at law, Professor of business law and legal management at the University of St. Gallen (HSG) and Director at the Executive School of Management, Technology and Law of the University of St. Gallen (ES-HSG).

B. Mascello (✉)
Executive School of Management, Technology and Law of the University of St.Gallen (ES-HSG), St.Gallen, Switzerland
e-mail: bruno.mascello@unisg.ch

K. Jacob et al. (eds.), *Liquid Legal – Humanization and the Law*, Law for Professionals, https://doi.org/10.1007/978-3-031-14240-6_3

Abstract

A bigger variety, in particular gender diversity, improves the working environment, delivers a higher and qualitative better output, and leads to a higher satisfaction of employees, employers, and customers. One may expect that an employer would automatically strive for more diversity to achieve these positive results. However, the legal market like most other industries, still lacks sufficient representation of women at top management levels, be it as partners in law firms or as general counsel in legal departments. The legal industry often claims this is due to lack of qualitative good and available talent. However, it is not (anymore) a pipeline issue but a structural problem which prevents diversity on all levels. Going forward, the legal industry can no longer afford to deliberately waste these precious resources. To the contrary, opening the working environment at all levels to a diverse team may position an employer at least as an early adopter of diversity in the legal industry. This will open the race to become the most attractive employer and win the best talent in the market. In the long run, an employer can secure the required human resources in a sustainable way.

1 Introduction

This article provides an overall analysis as to why we see fewer women than men in leadership roles in the legal industry, both as equity partners in law firms and as general counsel in legal departments. For the sake of simplicity, the focus here is on gender diversity since everybody is exposed to this topic somehow. However, it goes without saying that this analysis also applies to other underrepresented groups. Further, this also extends to new generations, which do not fit into the traditional understanding of how the legal industry works, e.g. when asking for a better work-life-balance (generation Y) or a meaningful job with a purpose and a social and environmental impact (generation Z). "Millennials are the new women. They do not fit." (Quote attributed to Riccardo Zezza; Leistner 2019, p. 664). In a nutshell, it is all about the willingness to adapt to change in the market to become and stay attractive as an employer, and to win and retain new and promising talents—or, about wasting precious resources and losing them forever.

2 Terminology

2.1 Diversity

"Using diversity as an overarching term, we contend that it has three distinctive types: separation, variety, or disparity." (Harrison and Klein 2007). It refers to the composition and distribution of people in a group or social unit according to certain criteria. This is regularly based on socio-demographic attributes such as nationality, race or ethnicity, gender, age, sexual orientation, health or disability, and education.

2.2 Equity

Equity means that, from a moral point of view, to achieve diversity is simply "the right thing to do" in order to provide equal opportunities to qualified individuals regardless of their background. In the legal profession in particular, diversity also serves the higher purpose of giving credibility to the perception that the legal system is fair and equitable (Holcomb 2021). The irony is that the profession leading the struggle for diversity has failed to set an example in its own workplaces (Rhode 2018, p. 871). Actually, according to the American Bar Association (ABA), only two professions have less diversity than law: natural sciences and dentistry (Rhode and Buford Ricca 2015, p. 2483).

2.3 Inclusion

If variety is only the first step in creating diversity in a workplace and only reflects a static composition of one group, then inclusion goes one step further. It also uncovers the potentials and added values needed to realize the benefits and profits expected by establishing diversity. Inclusion ensures that diversity is "lived", i.e. that the uniqueness of the individual is guaranteed, that people work together in diverse teams and that different perspectives are accepted and can be brought in equally. Therefore, to unleash the desired potential of diversity, management efforts also need to promote a climate of inclusion to really attain positive outcomes. Companies should move beyond the simple focus on solely increasing diverse representation, and rather start developing policies and practices that also foster a climate of inclusion which ensures access, acceptance, and advancement (Mor Barak et al. 2016; McKinsey and Company 2020b). Further, being genuinely valued and respected involves more than just feeling included. It also requires having the power to change the agenda and influence the work (Ely and Thomas 2020).

2.4 Measurement

There are four maturity levels to show what an organization has achieved in terms of diversity and inclusion: step 1 ("we commit") shows a clear intention to increase the ratio of female managers; step 2 ("we act") takes specific measures in recruitment and building an inclusive mindset; step 3 ("we promote") puts a specific focus on the promotion process; and step 4 ("we advance") has achieved the final goal of diversity and inclusion. Let us examine Switzerland as an example to show the current status and how difficult it is to advance along this path: the majority of the companies surveyed in Switzerland reached level 1; however, so far only 20, 11 and 5% have achieved levels 2, 3 and 4 respectively (University of St.Gallen 2020, Gender Maturity Compass).

3 Consequences and Impact

3.1 Leadership and Management

Companies with more women in senior positions are not only more profitable, but also more socially responsible, and provide a safer and higher-quality customer experience. The company's long-term strategies seem to change after the appointment of female executives as follows: (1) cognitions shift and companies become more open to change and less risk-seeking, i.e. organizations increasingly embrace transformation while seeking to reduce the risks associated with it. (2) As a direct result of this, they shift their focus from a knowledge-buying strategy focused on mergers & acquisitions (M&A) towards a knowledge-building strategy focused on internal research & development (R&D), i.e. a collaborative approach. (3) The impact on the decision-making process is greater when women are well integrated into the top management team (TMT). This also depends on whether the woman is the only woman, and is one of many new appointments (Post et al. 2020, 2021). Besides the value-enhancing effect, the diversity of board resources and the number of women in boardrooms also affect the company's corporate social responsibility (CSR) ratings, and thus also influences the corporate reputation; CSR ratings mediate the relationship between the number of women on the board and corporate reputation (Bear et al. 2010).

3.2 General Disadvantages

Diversity entails more effort, causes uncomfortable tensions, communication mistakes and coordination problems, and requires a lot of time to manage associated productivity losses. It creates group conflict through prejudice, mistrust, stereotyping and misunderstanding, and this leads to dissatisfaction and ultimately to employee resignations. All these disadvantages do not really come as a surprise and are understandable. However, they should not obscure the many advantages arising from diversity. Of course, one may feel more comfortable and at ease working with people who share one's own background, thoughts, and culture. But enriching the employee pool is key to boosting the joint intellectual potential (Rock and Grant 2016).

3.3 Benefits in General

Fostering a culture of equality is important. Much more important for companies, however, are the many direct advantages and benefits which are associated with diversity, such as (Boston Consulting Group 2019; Dezsö and Gaddis Ross 2012; Ely and Thomas 2020; Phillips 2014; Fernando and Fonseka 2018):

- Higher problem-solving competence, better decision-making, and improved solutions due to a broader perspective and a better customer understanding.
- Higher performance and productivity, higher-quality work, and a more creative and increased innovation competence since such teams avoid group thinking.
- Broader recruiting and talent pool, allowing a better exploitation of talent and the use of the existing potential of individuals. It is a business imperative to have a broad talent base.
- Positive impact on team satisfaction, engagement, and motivation of employees, which in turn not only leads to higher satisfaction, but also to improved health and reduced sick days.
- Better management of demographic change, and securing important knowledge retention and transfer in the company.

Working in diverse teams challenges your brain, sharpens your performance, and keeps the individual members competitive, which makes teams smarter and more innovative. Such teams focus more on facts and process the information more carefully, constantly reexamine the facts, and remain objective. They also encourage greater scrutiny of each member's actions, thus keeping the cognitive resources sharp and vigilant (Rock and Grant 2016).

3.4 Economic Benefits

Research shows that firms with more women in senior positions are more profitable and have financial returns above their industry average, i.e. higher return on equity and higher net income growth (Post et al. 2020, 2021). It confirms the link between diversity and financial performance (McKinsey & Company 2020b, 2018, 2015). For example, a company with at least one woman on its top management team can generate one percent more economic value, and it also enjoys superior accounting performance and delivers more innovation (Deszö and Gaddis Ross 2012, p. 1084). Furthermore, a recent analysis of the top 100 stock-listed companies in Germany reveals a 2% higher share price, higher Ebit and more innovation for companies with diverse top management teams (Boston Consulting Group 2019). However, there is also research that does not confirm a link between diversity and financial results (Ely and Thomas 2020).

3.5 Causality and Correlation

When it comes to providing a "business case" which directly links diversity to economic benefits, the criticism is often that such research lacks robust findings and rigorous systematic evidence, and that at most, it may show a correlation only and not causality. Not all research finds strong performance benefits from diversity or a causality between diversity and profitability. Simply increasing the numbers of underrepresented people in the workforce, but then letting business continue as usual, does not do the trick. What matters is how an organization harnesses diversity, and whether it is willing to reshape its power structures, and to create and promote an inclusive corporate culture. Diverse teams can realize performance benefits when the team members are willing to reflect, discuss and learn from the differences. This means that a company's activity must go beyond solely establishing diversity and extend to and cover inclusion as well. If poorly managed, simply implementing diversity may even worsen the situation (Ely and Thomas 2020; see also Rhode 2018, p. 892).

4 Relevance for the Legal Industry

4.1 Lawyers as Complex Problem Solvers

Customers of legal service providers are facing complex challenges and are forced to take a diverse approach to solving these problems, and consequently demand diverse talent. It might be interesting for legal service providers to learn that a diverse group of intelligent problem solvers outperforms a team comprised of the best-performing agents. The reason for this is that problem solvers with nearly identical perspectives and the same heuristics are expected to communicate easily with each other. However, they risk confirmation bias and homogeneous thinking. Therefore, the relatively greater ability of the highest-ability problem solvers is more than offset by their lack of problem-solving diversity and the lack of diversity in heuristics. This result has direct implications for lawyers and law firms that are considered problem-solving organizations. If they still prefer to hire people with similar perspectives simply to reduce communication cost, they should at least make sure they acquire and maintain teams with a diversity of heuristics (Hong and Page 2004). For customers, this outcome means that, if they are interested in receiving the best advice when solving tricky problems, they should request their legal service providers to work in diverse teams.

4.2 Litigation

Litigation represents a further practical use case for lawyers. Defense-side trial teams composed of male and female lawyers tend to significantly outperform a trial team with only male lawyers, winning more often, making fewer decision errors, and underpricing settlement offers far less frequently, resulting in a stunning $2.6 million average reduction in defendant liability. For plaintiffs, the benefits of mixed male and female trial teams were no less striking (Henderson 2019).

4.3 ESG and Procurement

Customers face increased pressure to explain their efforts related to equal treatment, social and environmental responsibility, and sustainability (Environmental, Social, Governance, ESG) to shareholders, investors and employees. Customers are not only under increasing scrutiny of various stakeholders and new laws are implemented (e.g., new EU legislation on due diligence), but customers are also facing real claims and litigation cases if they disregard ESG principles and related issues like ethics, poverty, exploitation, and pollution. Law firms may intuitively perceive this as a new field of practice which promises new revenues where they can offer consulting in legal and compliance questions, investigations, and litigation. There is nothing wrong with this. However, there is also a flip side to it which law firms need to keep in mind as well. Since companies are forced to analyze their entire value chain thoroughly, they will also request full compliance with these principles from their suppliers such as law firms. Therefore, law firms and legal departments must be prepared to operate in an increasingly diverse society with customers demanding such standards. If they cannot effectively recruit and retain diverse groups, they may potentially risk suffering competition disadvantages. (Rhode 2018, pp. 891 and 894).

4.4 Profitability

There is some research which shows that law firms with more diversity realize a kind of diversity dividend and enjoy higher than average partner compensation. This result indicates that such firms have a higher leverage, higher gross revenue, lower geographic concentration, more non-equity partners, and fewer equity partners. The most likely explanation provided by the authors is that this is due to the benefits that flow from the diversity of cognition which include information, education, feelings, and life experiences, and that such diversity overlaps with the diversity of identity, such as race, gender, age, sexual orientation, and physical abilities (Nath and Parker 2021). In this context, it is also interesting to mention a different analysis which observed that there is a significant negative correlation between the number of female partners and the profit and revenue per partner, and that there is a significant correlation between the percentages of partners and associates who were female (Adams and Engel 2015, p. 1242 ff.).

5 Diversity in the Legal Industry

5.1 Pipeline Issue 1: Attractivity of Attending Law School

Women do not need to be encouraged anymore, either to study in general, or specifically to study law. If we look, for example, at the distribution of students at universities in Switzerland by gender, we see that for several years now, more women than men have been studying law (Statista 2021b). In 2020/21, over 60% of the students who are studying law in Switzerland are women (Statista 2021c). In the European Union and the OECD, the average is even higher (OECD 2020). In 2020, about 30% each of 25–64 year-old men and women had a university degree (Statista 2021a). In the U.S. as well, gender diversity in law schools has changed dramatically over the last 60 years, from a national average of 3% female law students in 1950 to 46% in 2014 (Adams and Engel 2015, p. 1248).

As a positive interim result, it can be concluded that this pipeline is well filled and that on this level there is no need for action in terms of improving gender diversity. To study law is attractive for women, and even more women than men graduate from university and law school.

5.2 Pipeline Issue 2: Attractivity of Working as a Lawyer

The second step addresses the question as to how attractive it is for women to start working as a lawyer after law school. In the U.S., like in law schools, the same dramatic change and subsequently continued growth can be observed for law firms: from zero female partners in 1955, close to 5% in 1975 and up to 29% in 2005 (Adams and Engel 2015, p. 1248). Today, approximately 36% of the lawyers and 47% of the associates are women, however, only 24% of the partners and just 19–21% of the equity partners are women (American Bar Association (ABA) 2020; The National Association of Women Lawyers (NAWL) 2020). Corporate law and Fortune 500 show a similar picture when it comes to assessing the ratio of female general counsel (Rhode and Buford Ricca 2015, p. 2485 f.).

In the U.K., women in law firms represent on average 61% of the trainees, 59% of the associates and 27% of the partners, and the city firms even score below that (Chambers 2018/19).

In Germany, we see a similar distribution curve: 10% of equity partners are women, 25% are non-equity partners, and 35% are counsel and associated partners (Lucke and Mader 2021). The same can be observed in legal departments of the top 150 German companies according to revenue: 16% of general counsel are women (26% in SMEs and 2% in big companies), 27% at the second management level, 45% among the associates and 89% among the secretaries and assistants. In the same global survey 2 years later (2021), the numbers changed to 30% for the first management level and 25% for the second, and to 41% for associates (KPMG 2019/2020, 2021).

And in Switzerland it looks similar: in January 2021, the share of female associates in the 15 largest law firms was around half (spread: 34–60.9%), and at partner level the figure was 13.6% (spread: 5.6–30.4%) (Buschor 2021).

The good news is that it is attractive for women to start working as a lawyer and that law firms and legal departments are doing a good job at the entry level. They do not seem to face any challenges when it comes to recruiting associates. At the beginning, the pipeline of female associates is filled with close to 50%. Women are ambitious and want to advance. As a result, at the entry level to business after law school, there is no need to complain about gender diversity either. The bad news, however, comes later with development, promotion, and retention. We can see that the gender gap is much wider in law firms than in other industries. Women are well represented up to equity partner level, but thereafter, the ratio drops sharply at post-associate levels, and attrition increases. Women are ambitious when starting to work and they want promotion to the next level, but they seem less excited or face barriers to becoming a partner (McKinsey & Company 2017; for Australia see The Law Society of New South Wales 2018).

6 Reasons Why Women Are Leaving the Profession

The legal industry regularly refers to the war for talent. However, looking at the numbers above, one must admit that there is a very big resource and talent pool available, but employers do not seem able or willing to retain it. Therefore, it is legitimate to ask why even more female lawyers leave the profession, in particular law firms.

One could refer to the easy explanation that women, due to family priorities, miss the "rush hour" in life (aged 30–40), during which time careers are also built. However, such an argument falls short. Some top reasons for leaving are rather that women expect to spend less time at their law firms, feel forced to make significant trade-offs between career and personal lives, and have difficulty balancing work and family due to structural circumstances. Further, women are not convinced by law firms' statements of commitment to gender diversity; most law firms track gender diversity metrics, but few set targets (McKinsey & Company 2017, p. 5 ff.). A new survey of the American Bar Association (ABA) studied the reasons why experienced women leave the profession and concluded that the female lawyers liked the constant challenges and intellectual stimulation of practicing law. However, women mentioned in particular the following reasons for changing law firms, moving to in-house counsel jobs, or leaving the profession: not being recognized or rewarded, the existence of an unfair compensation system, pay disparities, hyper-competitiveness and a bullying atmosphere that erode collegiality, sexist and racist behavior, the credit and promotion system, a lack of challenging and fulfilling work, social isolation as a result of increasing billable hour requirements, and an unequal distribution of assignments in firms resulting in fewer billed hours and less credit for women. It is important to mention that the decision to leave is not simply long hours or family reasons and unpredictable schedules, but rather a complex picture of a cumulative effect and a combination of all the factors, which slowly leads to the decision to leave ("death by a thousand cuts") (Sterling and Chanow 2021); Liebenberg and Scharf 2019; Rhode 2018, p. 873). It is not the work but the toxic work culture and work environment which drives women out of a company.

As if this were not enough, a recent ABA report further showed an additional impact on women lawyers caused by Covid-19. Lawyers felt overwhelmed by the pressure of their work and experienced high levels of stress, particularly experienced women with young children (aged 5 or younger) and lawyers of color. Women reported increased disruption to work due to personal obligations and increased responsibilities. They worried about employer support, client access, developing business and advancement, and meeting billable hour requirements. It is interesting, however, that only 17% of those surveyed thought it very or extremely important to lower their required billable hours or workload (American Bar Association 2021; Robert 2021). Further factors which led women to downshifting their careers or leaving the workforce in these unprecedented times were the lack of flexibility at work, feeling that they needed to be available at all hours, the additional housework and caregiving burdens which had mostly fallen to mothers, and the worry that their performance was being negatively judged because of caregiving responsibilities during the pandemic (McKinsey & Company 2020a, p. 13; Deloitte 2021).

Considering the above-mentioned reasons for leaving the traditional legal profession, it might be interesting to see whether other companies, in particular the alternative legal service providers, will benefit and become more attractive to female talent by offering them a new home base, in particular for those with caregiving responsibilities who are not looking for a career or stable position in a law firm (anymore), don't need the prestige of a top law firm or company, and would prefer more flexibility, lower hour commitment and remote work options.

7 An Attempt to Explain This Result

The underrepresentation of women in the legal profession is definitively not a pipeline issue or a lack of available talent: women constitute half of the students in law school and of the associates in law firms, and they are not only well-trained and talented, but also ambitious and enthusiastic about the practice of law. It is not the lack of education and recruitment that are the problem, but the subsequent development and advancement which are burdened by three challenges, in particular. The most common explanation for the current outcome is underperformance, which is measured by traditional merit standards. This approach still leaves the focus on "fixing women" and how to make them fit into an existing structure. Further, stereotypes and workplace structures hinder to change and open the existing setup to diversity (for further comments see Mascello 2021).

8 Measures

On the one hand, there is some self-responsibility to be considered. Each woman is responsible for herself and can increase her chances of success, if she is clear about her goals, seeks challenging assignments, solicits frequent feedback, develops relationships with influential mentors and builds mentoring relationships, seeks formal leadership training and coaching, cultivates a reputation for effectiveness, sets priorities and manages time, and pays attention to unconscious biases and exclusionary networks that could impact careers (Rhodes 2018, p. 894 ff.). On the other hand, organizations are also, if not even more, responsible for building strategies and measures to help the legal profession to eliminate biases and enhance diversity. Instead of looking to equality we should try to achieve equal opportunities. This includes ensuring equal access to professional opportunities, which needs to come from the top (for further measures including quotas see Mascello 2021). See in particular the initiative started by general Counsel (General Counsel for Diversity and Inclusion 2021).

9 Conclusion and Final Remarks

What could be shown is that the situation today is obviously not at all a pipeline issue as often claimed by law firms and sometimes legal departments; the pipeline is more than packed with enough resources and top talents that are ready to be exploited immediately. And neither the recruitment nor the employment market lacks sufficient and adequate availability. Therefore, one may raise legitimate questions of why the legal industry does not seem to care about further exploiting this pool of resource and is still deeply relaxed about this situation, and why it can still afford such a waste and consumption of easily available and excellent human resources and talent.

Lawyers are considered knowledge workers and the production of knowledge not only requires highly skilled human capital, which is relatively rare and correspondingly expensive, but the related business model is also quite labor-intensive. Moreover, a large part of the knowledge is created in the heads of the individual employees and is also stored there as experience and insights, or so-called tacit or implicit knowledge. However, a company has a compelling need and interest in making this knowledge accessible and usable to the entire company, and in preserving it for the future in a formal, verbalized, and codified form, as so-called explicit knowledge. Otherwise, a company runs the risk of also losing precious corporate knowledge when losing the knowledge carriers. This reflects a key challenge that each knowledge management system wants to master.

The legal industry can be proud of the progress and achievements made over the last decades when it comes to establishing diversity. However, there is still sufficient room to improve an area mainly driven by human interactions. The legal industry should have a genuine interest in fostering diversity, equity, and inclusion. "Homogeneity isn't better; it's just easier." (Ely and Thomas 2020).

Liquid Legal Waves to Other Chapters, Written by the Editors

What it means to be exposed to a working environment that discourages or even prevents diversity sometimes remains abstract to those not personally affected. *Roger* brings the issue of diversity to life in his fictitious chapter *"Who are you…? - A Story About a Gay Humanist Working at a Law Firm"*.

How do we tackle the diversity issue systematically? *Duc* provides a bold answer in his chapter: by *"Injecting Humanity (Back) Into Talent Development"*! Lawyers must be trained at the intersection of law, business and interpersonal relationships to enable them to provide legal services that are not only correct, but useful to clients.

A commitment at all levels to a diverse team may position an employer at least as an early adopter of diversity in the legal industry. *Martina* expands the view on diversity in perspectives, as companies increasingly recognize the need to take people's and societies' interests as a guiding principle in their digital transformation. Corporations are taking on *"Corporate Digital Responsibility"* and lawyers should take an active role in this.

References

Adams ES, Engel SP (2015) Gender diversity and disparity in the legal profession: an empirical analysis of the gender profile in national law firms and law schools. Buffalo Law Rev 63(5): 1211–1261

American Bar Association (ABA) (2020) 2020 ABA Model Diversity Survey. https://www.americanbar.org/groups/diversity/DiversityCommission/model-diversity-survey/

American Bar Association (ABA) (2021) Practicing Law in the Pandemic and Moving Forward: Results and Best Practices from a Nationwide Survey of the Legal Profession. https://www.americanbar.org/content/dam/aba/administrative/digital-engagement/practice-forward/practice-forward-survey.pdf

Bear S, Rahman N, Post C (2010) The impact of board diversity and gender composition on corporate social responsibility and firm reputation. J Bus Ethics 97(2010):207–221

Boston Consulting Group (2019). Boarding Call: How Diversity Moves Companies Forward – BCG Gender Diversity Index Germany

Buschor D (2021) Anwältinnen & Partnerinnen in den grössten Schweizer Anwaltskanzleien, 1.4.2021. https://www.vista.blog/anwaeltinnen-partnerinnen-in-den-groessten-schweizer-anwaltskanzleien

Chambers (2018/19) Law Firm Diversity 2018/19. https://www.chambersstudent.co.uk/where-to-start/newsletter/law-firm-diversity-201819

Deloitte (2021) Women@Work, a Global Outlook. https://www2.deloitte.com/global/en/pages/about-deloitte/articles/women-at-work-global-outlook.html

Dezsö CL, Gaddis Ross D (2012) Does female representation in top management improve firm performance? A panel data investigation. Strategic Manage J 33:1072–1089

Ely RJ, Thomas DA (2020) Getting Serious About Diversity: Enough Already with the Business Case. Harvard Business Review

Fernando SSN, Fonseka A (2018) The influence of board diversity on firm performance. Sri Lankan J Manage 23(2):99–129

General Counsel for Diversity and Inclusion (2021). https://www.gcdandi.com/

Harrison DA, Klein KJ (2007) What's the difference? Diversity constructs as a separation, variety, or disparity in organizations. The Academy of Management Review

Henderson B (2019) American law firms in transition: trends, threats, and strategies (book review) (110), 18 August 2019, with reference to Randall Kiser. https://www.legalevolution.org/2019/08/american-law-firms-in-transition-book-review-110/

Holcomb L (2021) Why Gender Diversity in the Legal Profession Matters, 8 March 2021. https://www.jdsupra.com/legalnews/why-gender-diversity-in-the-legal-3189811/

Hong L, Page SE (2004) Groups of diverse problem solvers can outperform groups of high-ability problem solvers. PNAS 101(46):16385–16389. https://pubmed.ncbi.nlm.nih.gov/15534225/

KPMG (2019/2020) Rechtsabteilungsreport

KPMG (2021) Rechtsabteilungsreport

Leistner M (2019) The importance of diversity – and how it will change the practice of law forever and for the better (with help from technology). In: DeStefano M, Dobrauz G (eds) New suits – appetite for disruption in the legal world. Staempli Verlag, Berne

Liebenberg RD, Scharf SA (2019) Walking out the door – the facts, figures, and future of experienced women lawyers in private practice, ABA 2019. https://www.americanbar.org/groups/diversity/women/initiatives_awards/long-term-careers-for-women/walking-out-the-door/

Lokshin B, Boone C (2020) What changes after women enter top management teams? A gender-based model of strategic renewal. Acadamy of Management Journal, 19.11.2020

Lucke K, Mader L (2021) Diversity als Erfolgsfaktor in der Praxis – Diversity-Studie mit Top-100-Kanzleien in Deutschland. Deutscher Anwaltspiegel, 9/28.4.2021, 13–15 https://www.deutscheranwaltspiegel.de/anwaltspiegel/diversity/diversity-als-erfolgsfaktor-in-der-praxis-25162/

Mascello B (2021) How the legal industry is wasting talent – despite diversity policies women still lack representation at top level. In: Mascello B (ed) Beiträge zu aktuellen Themen an der Schnittstelle zwischen Recht und Betriebswirtschaft VII, vol 11. Schulthess Verlag, Zürich

McKinsey & Company (2015) Why Diversity Matters. https://www.mckinsey.com/business-functions/organization/our-insights/why-diversity-matters

McKinsey & Company (2017) Women in Law Firms. https://www.mckinsey.com/featured-insights/gender-equality/women-in-law-firms

McKinsey & Company (2018) Delivering Through Diversity. https://www.mckinsey.com/~/media/mckinsey/business%20functions/organization/our%20insights/delivering%20through%20diversity/delivering-through-diversity_full-report.ashx

McKinsey & Company (2020a) Women in the Workplace (report on corporate America). https://wiw-report.s3.amazonaws.com/Women_in_the_Workplace_2020.pdf

McKinsey & Company (2020b) Diversity Wins: How Inclusion Matters. https://www.mckinsey.com/featured-insights/diversity-and-inclusion/diversity-wins-how-inclusion-matters

Mor Barak ME, Lizano EL, Kim A, Duan L, Rhee MK, Hsiao HY, Brimhall KC (2016) The promise of diversity management for climate of inclusion: a state-of-the-art review and meta-analysis. Human Serv Organ Manage Leadership Gov 40(4):305–333

Nath Y, Parker E (2021) Nothing not to like: diversity and law firm profitability, 27 June 2021. https://www.legalevolution.org/2021/06/nothing-not-to-like-diversity-and-law-firm-profitability-238/#

OECD (2020) Education at a Glance. https://www.oecd.org/education/education-at-a-glance/

Phillips KW (2014) How Diversity Works, Scientific American, October 2014. file:///Q:/ES/Law/01%20Bruno%20Mascello/08a_Referate%20und%20Artikel/Liquid%20Legal_2021_Women/Literatur%20weitere/Phillips_How%20Diversity%20Works_2014.pdf
Post C, Lokshin B, Boone C (2020) What changes after women enter top management teams? A gender-based model of strategic renewal. Acad Manag J, 19.11.2020
Post C, Lokshin B, Boone C (2021) Adding women to the C-suite changes how companies think. Harv Bus Rev 6(4):2021. https://hbr.org/2021/04/research-adding-women-to-the-c-suite-changes-how-companies-think
Rhode DL (2018) Diversity and gender equity in legal practice. Univ Cincinnati Law Rev 82(3): 871–899
Rhode DL, Buford Ricca L (2015) Diversity in the legal profession: perspectives from managing partners and general counsel. Fordham Law Rev 83(5):2483–2507
Robert A (2021) How should the legal profession navigate a post-COVID-19 world? ABA Journal, 26.4.2021 https://www.abajournal.com/web/article/abas-practice-forward-group-explores-effect-of-covid-19-future-of-profession-in-new-survey
Rock D, Grant H (2016) Why diverse teams are smarter. Harv Bus Rev 4(11):2016
Statista (2021a) Bildungsstand der Wohnbevölkerung in der Schweiz nach Geschlecht im Jahr 2020
Statista (2021b) Verteilung der Studierenden an Universitäten in der Schweiz nach Geschlecht vom Winter- bzw. Herbstsemester 2009/2010 bis 2020/2021
Statista (2021c) Verteilung der Studierenden an Universitäten in der Schweiz nach Geschlecht und Fachbereichsgruppen im Winter- bzw. Herbstsemester 2020/2021
Sterling J, Chanow L (2021) In their own words: experienced women lawyers explain why they are leaving their law firms and the profession. https://www.americanbar.org/content/dam/aba/administrative/women/intheirownwords-f-4-19-21-final.pdf
The Law Society of New South Wales (2018) Diversity and Inclusion in the Legal Profession: The Business Case. https://www.lawsociety.com.au/sites/default/files/2018-03/DIC%20business%20case_0.pdf
The National Association of Women Lawyers (NAWL) (2020) 2020 Survey Report on the Promotion and Retention of Women in Law Firms. https://www.nawl.org/p/cm/ld/fid=2019
University of St.Gallen (2020) Advance & HSG Gender Intelligence Report 2020

Bruno Mascello is adjunct (titular) professor of business law and legal management at the University of St. Gallen (HSG) and Director at the Executive School of Management, Technology and Law of the University of St. Gallen (ES-HSG). He lectures at both the Executive School and the University of St.Gallen, is a keynote speaker at conferences and researches and publishes about various topics at the intersection of law and management.

Before joining the University of St.Gallen he served at an international insurance group in various leading management positions of the worldwide legal function (i.a., as Chief Operations Officer Group Legal/Compliance; Regional General Counsel), after having worked first as a senior attorney in law firms focused on international corporate and business law.

Bruno Mascello studied law at the faculty of law (lic.iur./masters of laws), earned a Ph.D. (Dr.iur.) and completed an Executive MBA at the University of St.Gallen. He holds an LL. M. in Comparative Jurisprudence from New York University School of Law. He is a qualified lawyer, admitted to the Swiss Bar and runs a private practice providing legal and legal management consulting services.

Corporate Digital Responsibility: Stimulating Human-Centric Innovation and Building Trust in the Digital World

Martina Seidl

Contents

Abstract

Accelerated by the COVID-19 pandemic, the influence of digitalization on daily life and our dependence on digital technology have continued to increase rapidly. Mobile working, digital classrooms, online shopping, video streaming, contactless payments, virtual parties, fitness apps, COVID-19 alert apps, digital vaccination certificates and e-health services. Not only is data digital, but our lives themselves have become largely digital.

Martina Seidl is Group Chief Legal & Compliance Officer for Giesecke+Devrient (G+D).

M. Seidl (✉)
München, Germany
e-mail: martina.seidl@gi-de.com

K. Jacob et al. (eds.), *Liquid Legal – Humanization and the Law*, Law for Professionals, https://doi.org/10.1007/978-3-031-14240-6_4

At the same time, the expanding use of digital technologies by corporations is leading to public discussions that go beyond data privacy and security issues. Other aspects of concern range from surveillance, transparency, profiling, manipulation of opinion and behaviors, automated decision making, bias, discrimination by algorithmic systems, to autonomous systems and existential risk from AI.

Yet, as Prof. Melvin Kranzberg stated in his six laws of technology (Kranzberg, M. (1986). Technology and History: "Kranzberg's Laws." Technology and Culture, 27(3), 544–560.) already in 1985: Technology as such is neither good nor bad. Technology is a very human activity because it's what we do with it that makes the difference.

Since technology is usually designed, developed and distributed en masse by companies, companies need to think about how they may benefit from technological advances, but also what consequences this can have for the world around them.

Companies that successfully embed digital technologies in their products and services, as well as in their business models and internal processes, adopt a human-centric approach.

Much of today's devices, systems and processes, are technology-centered, designed around the capabilities of the technology with people being asked to fill in the parts that the technology cannot do. Human centricity means shifting focus and starting with the needs and abilities of and the impact on people. Companies increasingly recognize the need to take people's and societies' interests as a guiding principle in their digital innovation projects, to address societal expectations and concerns and to build trust among their stakeholders—they are taking on Corporate Digital Responsibility.

This article (1) highlights the development of Corporate Social Responsibility up into the digital era, (2) introduces Corporate Digital Responsibility as an emerging new field of corporate responsibility, (3) presents a framework of topics that are currently being discussed as building blocks of Corporate Digital Responsibility that aim to stimulate human-centric innovation and build trust in the digital world, and (4) provides some thoughts on how lawyers may contribute to shape corporate responsibility in the digital world.

1 From Corporate Social Responsibility to Corporate Digital Responsibility

1.1 Corporate Social Responsibility

The concept of corporate social responsibility (CSR) as it is discussed today originated in the USA, where businessmen and scholars began to deal with the social responsibility of companies in the 1950s. After the end of the Second World

War, the plight of people of the Western world was great and the economy was willing to do something to improve the general public's difficult situation. At that time, the focus was on the contribution to society's social challenges.

Since Milton Friedman's landmark essay in 1970, "The social responsibility of business is to increase its profits", the role of business in society has been discussed and expanded upon over the years. In the 1970s, because of the oil price crisis, a new awareness of the finite nature of non-renewable natural resources and raw materials emerged and brought environmental protection into the public and corporate eye. Since the mid-1990s, ecological issues have increasingly also been discussed in the context of corporate social responsibility.

Around the same time, corporate social responsibility as a systematic global concept has gained momentum due to increasing globalization and the associated negative effects and global challenges such as poverty, climate change or lack of access to health care and education. Archie Carroll's concept of the "Pyramid of Corporate Social Responsibility"[1] which suggests that a corporate must fulfil responsibility at four levels—economic, legal, ethical and philanthropic—has become one of the most accepted corporate theories of CSR since.

In 2000, the United Nations Global Compact[2] was launched, a voluntary pact to encourage businesses and firms worldwide to adopt sustainable and socially responsible policies, and to report on their implementation as a voluntary commitment.

Shortly thereafter, the EU published the EU Green Paper on CSR[3] to launch a debate about the concept of corporate social responsibility (CSR), emphasizing equal awareness of environmental protection and social concerns.

In the business world, too, the topic of corporate responsibility began to gain importance, in particular in the financial sector. Investment philosophies began to cluster around sustainability and, thereafter, socially responsible or impact investing. Early efforts focused on excluding companies from portfolios largely due to ethical concerns (e.g., screening out tobacco, controversial weapons, or adult entertainment companies from investment portfolios). This was then expanded to assessing companies for environmental, social or governance risk factors ("ESG")[4] as the basis for an investment decision to achieve better risk-adjusted returns. The ESG approach, i.e., defining metrics and ratings that help to make the sustainability of a corporation comparable, became the basis of the UN Principles of Responsible Investment (PRI)[5] in 2006 and the Sustainable Stock Exchange Initiative (SSEI) in 2007.

[1] Carroll (2016).

[2] https://www.unglobalcompact.org/.

[3] Promoting a European framework for corporate social responsibility - Green Paper - Publications Office of the EU (europa.eu).

[4] https://corpgov.law.harvard.edu/2020/08/01/introduction-to-esg/.

[5] https://www.unpri.org/pri/about-the-pri.

In 2015, the United Nations Sustainable Development Goals (SDG)[6] were adopted by all UN member states and are intended to be achieved by the year 2030. The SDGs are a collection of 17 interlinked global goals designed to be a "blueprint to achieve a better and more sustainable future for all". An increasing number of companies have begun to address SDGs explicitly and proactively through innovative offerings in areas such as poverty, hunger, health, climate change, water, energy, environment, sanitation, education, gender equality and social justice, and report on these efforts. It can be observed that the focus of investors, and not only of social impact investors, is shifting to companies that prioritize their ESG ratings and that incorporate contribution to the SDGs as core elements of strategic positioning.

When the COVID-19 virus led to a pandemic in 2020, there was concern by many that strategic sustainability and ESG issues would fall to the wayside, as governments, investors and businesses struggled to stay afloat, focusing on solving immediate problems. Yet, the opposite has proven true. The Principles of Responsible Investment initiative for example are witnessing record levels of take-up of sustainability strategies and activities in ESG investment.[7] The importance of sustainability, ESG and corporate responsibility in politics, public debate and in the corporate world has increased exponentially as a result of this crisis and is even referred to as the megatrend of this century.[8]

This brief overview of some of the cornerstones of CSR development shows how the areas of corporate responsibility have expanded over time, closely correlating with the development of business advances and their impact on people and the planet.

1.2 Era of Digital Transformation

A second megatrend of our time is digitalization.

Over the past two decades, exponentially increasing storage capacities, falling data storage and processing costs, extremely fast and ultra-broadband connectivity, as well as the proliferation of devices and cheap sensors capable of generating and transferring data have enabled the generation and storage of huge amounts of data.

With the spread of powerful sensors and microchips in everyday infrastructure, a digitally networked environment is emerging. The introduction of the 5G network standard will drive this growth massively. Soon, billions of devices, machines, and systems will be connected to the internet in real time. By 2025, forecasts suggest that there will be more than 75 billion devices in use that are connected to the internet, which form the Internet of Things (IoT). IoT takes manufacturing to another level as

[6] https://sdgs.un.org/.

[7] https://www.unpri.org/pri-blog/covid-19-accelerates-esg-trends-global-investors-confirm/6372.article.

[8] https://globalinvestmentdaily.com/esg-the-biggest-megatrend-in-a-century/.

data derived from connected devices or sensors can help to increase productivity, minimize unexpected expenses, and influence working security. IoT data creates opportunities for new situational business models, helps to improve personalized services, and may even support agriculture, e.g., smart greenhouse, crop monitoring, soil monitoring. People use smart devices for a more comfortable life, e.g., smart watches to make payments, to monitor their health or track their fitness.

To comprehend these masses of data and to turn them into valuable insights, "big data" emerged, a field that develops ways to analyze, systematically extract information from, or otherwise deal with data sets that are too large or complex to be understood by the human brain or even to be dealt with by traditional data-processing application software.

Recording and processing data on a blockchain, a shared and immutable ledger that can only be accessed by members with permission, enhances security, provides greater transparency, and eliminates any opportunity for fraud, provides instant traceability and increases efficiency and speed. In industries where consumers are concerned about environmental or human rights issues surrounding a product—or an industry troubled by counterfeiting and fraud—this helps provide the proof.

Algorithms and artificial intelligence (AI) systems can recognize patterns and draw inferences from large amounts of data on a scale that no human ever could. AI refers to systems or machines that mimic human intelligence to perform tasks and can iteratively improve themselves based on the data and information they collect. AI technology is improving enterprise performance and productivity by automating processes or tasks that once required human power. That capability can return substantial business benefits. AI has value for almost every function, business, and industry.

AI can also make human life safer, easier and better. Facial recognition technology, for instance, an area of AI, can be used as a security tool for locking homes or personal devices like mobile phones, or to make identity validation at airport border check gates faster and easier. It can even help blind people to recognize friends and describe people around them, which is a valuable gain in quality of life for people with visual impairments.

Digital technologies have such profound effects on all areas of life that the transformational changes are referred to as the fourth industrial revolution.[9]

We are indeed not living in an era of change but in a change of era.

1.3 Taking Responsibility in the Digital World

So far, corporate social responsibility and digitalization have developed in parallel and without notable touchpoints. But now these two megatrends are beginning to merge.

[9]Fourth Industrial Revolution | World Economic Forum (weforum.org).

Just as the innovation of the steam engine and the spread of electricity have changed societies of the past, so digitalization has begun to change our society of today. The significant impact of this transformation forces us to think not only about the economic benefits that we can derive from these technological advances, but also about how they affect our lives, how they impact the fundamental values that shape our society—and even what it means to be human.

Algorithms and data as "digital artifacts" represent what is now the largest part of humanity's knowledge. They are thus a resource that should be sustainably shaped and used in the interest of the common good today and in the future, just like natural resources.

The era of digital transformation is an opportunity to use data, algorithms, and technologies to create a prosperous, inclusive, human-oriented future—within the boundaries of our planet. The use cases of how digital technologies present opportunities for economic growth and the realization of the UN Sustainable Development Goals (SDGs) and thus sustainable development and prosperity are countless.[10]

But this "tech for good" is not a given, it is not an automatic process.

The use of digital technologies can also create highly unsustainable effects, risks, and challenges. In the last few years, some particularly negative examples have become public that have put a strain on trust in digital technologies, e.g.:

- Hackers stole the data of more than 300 million customers of an international hotel chain. The data included names, contact information, passport number, travel information, and other personal information as well as credit and debit card numbers, and expiration dates of more than 100 million customers.[11]
- The Facebook–Cambridge Analytica data scandal concerned the obtaining of the personal data of millions of Facebook users without their consent by the British consulting firm Cambridge Analytica, predominantly to be used for political advertising.[12]
- A flawed algorithm used by the UK Government and its 'rigid insistence' on automating welfare benefits was reported to threaten the rights of people most at risk of poverty in Britain and cause hardship among those who lack digital skills.[13]

---

[10] See for many examples: http://www3.weforum.org/docs/Unlocking_Technology_for_the_Global_Goals.pdf.

[11] Marriott Hotels fined £18.4m for data breach that hit millions—BBC News.

[12] https://www.bbc.com/news/technology-54722362.

[13] https://www.independent.co.uk/news/uk/home-news/universal-credit-algorithm-hunger-debt-human-rights-watch-dwp-b670953.html.

- A facial recognition system used by US local law enforcement could misidentify 28 sitting members of Congress as criminals -an error disproportionately affecting people of color.[14]
- A digital assistant recorded private conversations and sent them to a random contact.[15]

Three decades ago, Melvin Kranzberg, a professor of the history of technology at Georgia Institute of Technology who died in 1995, wrote six laws to summarize the impact of technology on society to help handle society's unease with the power and pervasiveness of technology.[16] The cornerstones are built by the first law "Technology is neither good nor bad; nor is it neutral" and by the sixth law "Technology is a very human activity."

Digital technology as such has no set purpose. Its effects are driven by human decisions and actions—it's what we do with it that makes all the difference.

Data generated from IoT devices, for instance, increase transparency, improve personalized services such as medical treatments, facilitate predictions, e.g., about ecological risks, and creates opportunities for new business models. But permanent monitoring and measuring also increases the risk of far-reaching surveillance and compromised system integrity due to system failure or hacking and carries the risk of privacy loss.

Or consider facial recognition software. It can be used to improve security protocols, but also for tracking and surveillance. Fed with faulty data sets, it may lead to biased or discriminatory decisions.

This is where corporate responsibility enters the scene.

A Company Acts Responsibly When It Aims to Achieve a Positive Balance Between the Risks and Opportunities of Digitalization for a Sustainable and Humane Development of Our Future

Within most companies, the sustainability aspects of digitalization have not been in focus so far. Bringing these elements together under one umbrella allows them to be addressed in a consistent and complementary manner. This new, consolidated focus is known as Corporate Digital Responsibility ("CDR").

The aim of the CDR is to systematically reconcile social, cultural, ecological, and economic as well as data-related interests as leading indicators and leading drivers of business opportunities and risks along the digital value chain.

[14] https://www.technologyreview.com/2021/05/21/1025155/amazon-face-recognition-federal-ban-police-reform/.

[15] https://www.theguardian.com/technology/2018/may/24/amazon-alexa-recorded-conversation.

[16] https://www.wsj.com/articles/the-6-laws-of-technology-everyone-should-know-1511701201.

2 CDR: A Newly Evolving/Emerging Concept

2.1 Definition & Concept

The era of digital transformation has only just begun, and so have thoughts and discussions on corporate responsibility in the digital world. There is no agreed definition of Corporate Digital Responsibility yet, nor is there a generally accepted concept or recognized approach. For corporate social responsibility the development of standards took over 10 years.

Accordingly, the development of CDR standards will take some time, too, although a faster pace is to be expected. Technology research advisory Gartner, for instance, highlighted "digital ethics and privacy" as one of the top 10 strategic technology trends changing or not yet widely recognized trends that will impact and transform industries through 2023.[17] And Accenture identified "responsible use of technology" as one out of four "forerunner" topics.[18]

The term Corporate Digital Responsibility is linked to the established term "corporate (social) responsibility" and was first used internationally in 2015.[19] CDR is about recognizing that organizations driving forward the advancement of digital technology, and those that leverage such technologies for their processes, business models, products and services, have a responsibility to do so in a manner that leads society toward a positive humane future, which puts people at its center. The issues are often also discussed under the heading of "digital ethics" or "tech for good".

2.1.1 What People Expect from Digitally Responsible Companies

Two surveys from two countries illustrate what people expect from digitally responsible companies and what concerns they have with regard to digitalization:

An opinion poll [20] of US-based respondents carried out in 2019 illustrates the perceived opportunities and threats associated by US consumers with digitalization (the order of topics corresponds to the importance attributed by respondents) (Fig. 1).

A representative survey[21] carried out in Germany in 2021 found that consumers saw as the two biggest risks of digitalization: theft and misuse of data (56%) as well as financial damage due to fraud or incorrect payment processing (38%). As possible measures to increase trust in digital, high data protection and security standards found the greatest approval of the consumers surveyed (54%), followed by the

---

[17] https://www.gartner.com/en/documents/3904420/top-10-strategic-technology-trends-for-2019-digital-ethi.

[18] https://www.accenture.com/us-en/insights/research/rise-forerunners.

[19] https://de.wikipedia.org/wiki/Corporate_Digital_Responsibility.

[20] Herden et al. (2021).

[21] https://www.bmjv.de/SharedDocs/Downloads/DE/PDF/Berichte/CDR_ConPolicy_Fact_Sheets.html.

	I think digitalization will provide benefits, such as...	I think digitalization will confront us with many challenges, such as...
1.	Better services	Cyber crime
2.	Reduction of strenous work	Threats to data security
3.	Better information dissemination and transparence	Problems with data ownership and privacy
4.	More efficient cross-border exchange and trade	Manipulation of public opinion (e.g., fake news)
5.	Increas in societal productivity	Labor market disruptions (e.g., job loss due to artificial intelligence and robotics)
6.	Reduction of transaction costs	Exclusion of certain groups in society (e.g., those with lower digital literacy)
7.	Better understanding across cultures	Discrimination through biased artificial intelligence
8.	Effective digital democracy	Unreliability of digital systems
9.	Fairness and equality	Higher environmental impact through energy consumption and digital waste

Fig. 1 Perceived opportunities and threats associated by US consumers with digitalization, author's own illustration. Source: based on data from Herden, C.J., Alliu, E., Cakici, A. et al. "Corporate Digital Responsibility" (See Fn. 14)

possibility of contacting the provider's employees directly (39%), more transparent and easier to understand contractual and data privacy terms and conditions (37%) and better protection for financial transactions (36%).

2.1.2 The Corporate and Institutional View on CDR

There are still different approaches to creating concepts for CDR, but they all revolve around similar topics. This is illustrated by the following three examples:

The **German Federal Ministry of Justice and Consumer Protection (BMJV)**, in collaboration with industry representatives, launched the "CDR Initiative" to develop key principles and priorities for Corporate Digital Responsibility. A **CDR Codex**[22] that was published in June 2021 addresses 5 areas of responsibility:

1. Data responsibility
2. Education relating to digitalization
3. Protection of climate and resources
4. Employee involvement relating to the digital transformation of work
5. Societal inclusion relating to the access to digital offerings

Corporate responsibility in the digital world is increasingly seen in the context of the **ESG criteria.** This means consideration of the social, economic, and environmental

[22]https://cdr-initiative.de/kodex.

Table 1 CDR in relation to ESG; author's own illustration

CDR in relation to ...	Means considering these key topics...
Environment & Climate	• using natural resources efficiently
	• reducing environmental damage
	• imparting knowledge about the use of resources
Society & Employees	• providing career prospects and supporting the acquisition of skills
	• enabling participation in the digital transformation
	• creating trust in change processes
Governance & Economy	• handling data related to digital products and services transparently
	• ensuring an ethical use of new technologies and innovations
	• ensuring measurability and comparability in company processes

Source: based on data from econsense—Blueprint for Implementing Digital Responsibility in Companies (See Fn. 16)

impact of digital business activities on society and the use of data and digital technologies in a sustainable and responsible manner.

Econsense, a corporate sustainability network of internationally active companies, for example, advises that corporate responsibility regarding the use of digital technologies should be regarded holistically and consider effects and consequences in the three key areas of corporate responsibility: Environment, Society and Governance (Table 1).[23]

There are also first voices in the corporate and financial world who raise the data and digital topics to an independent pillar and extend the ESG criteria by a "D"—**ESG&D:**

- Whitepaper for the World Economic Forum (WEF), Richard Samans, Managing Director, WEF, and Jane Nelson, Director, Corporate Responsibility Initiative, Harvard Kennedy School of Government, USA:

> This profound shift in the operating context of companies is rendering environmental, social, governance and data stewardship (ESG&D) considerations increasingly material to the fundamental purpose of companies – sustainable value creation.[24]

- Indian online business magazine Business World: *"Integrated corporate governance today encompasses notions of environmental, social, governance and data stewardship (ESG&D) aspects."*[25]

[23] https://econsense.de/app/uploads/2020/11/201119_econsense_Blueprint_E.pdf.

[24] https://www.weforum.org/whitepapers/integrated-corporate-governance-a-practical-guide-to-stakeholder-capitalism-for-boards-of-directors.

[25] http://www.businessworld.in/article/Case-for-Integrated-Corporate-Governance/03-11-2020-339014/.

– According to *Fidelity's*, one of the largest financial asset managers in the world, *"traditional ESG metrics are a good initial filter"*, however, *"a more insightful way to measure these companies is by assessing their 'digital ethics', or ESG&D."*[26]

2.2 Initiatives and Stakeholders Coining the Concept

Although there are no generally agreed definitions and standards for CDR yet, the question no longer arises as to whether CDR will come, but only when and with which focus areas. The relevance of CDR becomes clear when looking at the long list of actors on national and international level who are already engaged in developing, coining and driving CDR principles forward:

In Germany, for example:

- The Federal Ministry of Justice and Consumer Protection (BMJV) together with companies initiated a process to develop principles and guidelines for CDR already in 2018[27] and issued the first Corporate Digital Responsibility Codex[28] in June 2021.
- The big auditing firms as well as specialized strategy and management consulting firms offer development of CDR concepts for their clients.[29]
- Industry associations like Bitkom[30] and BVDW[31] as well as initiatives like Initiative D21,[32] work on concepts for CDR.
- And, of course, a number of companies have already engaged and developed their own criteria, which vary depending on the relevance in their field of business.

[26] https://esgclarity.com/esgd-four-core-issues-in-digital-ethics/.

[27] https://www.bmjv.de/DE/Themen/FokusThemen/CDR_Initiative/CDR_Initiative_ node.html.

[28] https://cdr-initiative.de/.

[29] https://www.pwc.de/de/digitale-transformation/corporate-digital-responsibility-cdr.html; https://www2.deloitte.com/de/de/pages/innovation/contents/redesigning-corporate-responsibility.html.

[30] https://www.bitkom.org/Bitkom/Publikationen/Empfehlungen-fuer-den-verantwortlichen-Einsatz-von-KI-und-automatisierten-Entscheidungen-Corporate-Digital-Responsibility-and-Decision-Making.html.

[31] https://corporate-digital-responsibility.de/article/verbandsperspektive-wie-der-bvdw-cdr-mitglieder-uebergreifend-thematisiert/.

[32] https://initiatived21.de/initiative-d21-launcht-weltweit-erstes-online-magazin-zur-corporate-digital-responsibility/.

Additionally, several activities can be observed internationally, for example:

- The EU Commission launched a public consultation in March 2021 on the formulation of a set of principles to promote and uphold EU values in the digital space.[33]
- The Office of the UN High Commissioner for Human Rights (OHCHR) and the Principles for Responsible Investment initiative (PRI) started discussions on the role and responsibility of institutional investors in promoting the uptake of the UN Guiding Principles on Business and Human Rights (UNGPs) among digital technology companies.[34]
- The Swiss Digital Trust Initiative, that is supported by high-ranking representatives of the global and Swiss economy, leading representatives of Swiss universities and international organizations, aims to safeguard ethical standards in the digital world through concrete projects such as a "Digital Trust Label"[35]
- And global firms in particular in the technology sector e.g., in Europe, in the USA as well as in Japan have become active.

3 Building a CDR Framework

The biggest challenge with CDR is that there are no checklists you can apply.

It is still too early for that. Digital technologies, their use cases, benefits, and risks are just evolving. At this early stage of CDR, the focus is on building a new understanding of responsibility under the dynamic conditions of digital innovation and balancing diverging interests of stakeholders.

CDR extends corporate responsibility into the digital world. Thus, it is helpful to apply well-established CSR-frameworks to identify areas in which CDR becomes relevant and how.

The ESG&D model can be used to categorize what topics may be relevant for CDR. Environment, social and governance represent the three main pillars in which a corporation can according to this model have an impact and demonstrate sustainable practices. The ESG criteria are a set of standards designed to guide a company's business activities with regard to sustainability and to make sustainability verifiable, measurable and comparable for externals, in particular investors oriented towards sustainability. The model takes into account the use of opportunities in the respective ESG areas, as well as business practices and resulting risks. As discussed above in Sect. 2.1.2, "D" as "Data Responsibility" is rising as a fourth pillar of this model.

[33] https://digital-strategy.ec.europa.eu/en/news/europes-digital-decade-commission-launches-consultation-and-discussion-eu-digital-principles.

[34] https://www.unpri.org/all-events-and-webinars/digital-technology-companies-investments-and-human-rights/7468.article.

[35] https://www.swiss-digital-initiative.org/digital-trust-label/.

Caroll's **Pyramid of CSR**[36] may be helpful as a second dimension to flesh out how corporations can and should take digital responsibility. Carroll's pyramid suggests that a corporate has to fulfil responsibility at four levels—economic, legal, ethical and philanthropic:

- **Economic Responsibility** builds the basis of the pyramid and represents a business's first responsibility, which is to be profitable. Being profitable is the only way for a company to be able to survive long term, secure jobs, and benefit society. This includes the obligation to produce goods and services that are required/desired by the customers and also want to be purchased by the customers from this company.
- **Legal Responsibility**, as the second level, is the business's legal obligation to obey the law. This is the most important responsibility out of the four levels as this will show how reliably companies conduct their business in the marketplace.
- **Ethical Responsibility**, the third layer, is about doing the right thing, acting in line with fundamental societal values, creating benefit and avoiding harm, being fair and transparent. A company should not only obey the law, but it should also do its business ethically, sustainably and in a human-centric way. Unlike the first two levels, this is something that a company is not obligated to do. It is voluntary. Customers will feel more comfortable purchasing goods/services from the company if the company is perceived as ethical. It is important to note, however, that ethical principles and societal values are not globally uniform and may vary depending on national cultures and traditions.
- **Philanthropic Responsibility,** at the top of the pyramid, occupying the smallest space is philanthropy. Businesses benefit from the communities they operate in by using resources, infrastructure, impacting the environment etc. Therefore, "giving back" to society is well perceived by the public and people would want to do business with companies that are giving back to society. Philanthropic activities include cash donations to charities, in-house projects, where companies lead their own philanthropic activities and collaboration between corporations and non-corporate partners e.g., for corporate volunteering or other initiatives.

It is beyond the scope of this article to delve into all possible fields and respective details of potential risk and opportunity. However, the article provides a systematic overview on the most addressed topics and offers some practical examples.

3.1 Data Responsibility

Data is without a doubt the basis of all digital products, services, and processes and as such at the core of corporate digital responsibility.

[36]Carroll (2016).

3.1.1 Economic Responsibility

Data is said to be the new oil, and it gushes incessantly. The total amount of data created, captured, copied and consumed in the world is predicted to reach a mind-boggling 175 zettabyte by 2025.[37] Vast streams of data generated through digital transactions, mobile phones, social media platforms, GPS or IoT devices and sensors, are technically easily accessible. In 2001, oil, energy and automobile companies dominated the list of top ten most valuable firms in the world, but in 2021, the list is dominated by data firms like Apple, Facebook, Alibaba, Amazon and Microsoft. Without access to data and the use of data, the benefits of digitalization cannot be achieved.

Companies demonstrate *economic* responsibility when making the best possible use of the data available to them for value creation and increased efficiency and effectiveness.

Identifying, linking, and protecting all these connected devices and generated data efficiently will be the central challenge of this entire new ecosystem. Companies have to maintain security for their corporate IT systems and additionally need to ensure that connected devices that operate in a decentral fashion have additional security standards in place. In the past, when IT systems were huge mainframes, information was stored on tapes, and these systems were considered to be part of a closed environment. This has changed drastically. With every new technological advance comes a new set of security considerations with various levels of vulnerabilities, threats, and risk levels. That is why data security has become a key priority for companies when handling data. Companies must protect data made available to them from loss, misuse, and destruction.

3.1.2 Legal Responsibility

Compliance with contracts and laws, in particular data privacy and data security laws, is the indispensable basis for data responsibility.

(1) **Industrial Data**, i.e., any information not relating to an identified or identifiable natural person. Whereas companies may freely use their own industrial data, they must observe relevant contractual agreements when using industrial data created or provided by third parties.

(2) **Personal Data,** i.e., any information relating to an identified or identifiable natural person. Data privacy of individuals is recognized as a human right under numerous declarations and treaties. The EU General Data Privacy Regulation (GDPR), for instance, regulates the right to the protection of personal data as a fundamental right and freedom of natural persons and accordingly limits the use of personal data. For the use of personal data, companies have to comply with the GDPR requirements, e.g., to obtain the individuals' consent to the use of their personal data for the specific purpose, or when the processing of data is necessary for the performance of a contract to which the individual is party.

[37] One zettabyte is 8,000,000,000,000,000,000,000 bits; https://www.weforum.org/agenda/2021/05/world-data-produced-stored-global-gb-tb-zb/.

When using the personal data, companies have to comply with the principles relating to processing of personal data (Art. 5 GDPR): lawfulness, fairness and transparency; purpose limitation; data minimisation; accuracy; storage limitation; integrity and confidentiality; and accountability.

Responsible companies foster trust by applying the spirit of the law, rather than stretching or bending interpretations or exploiting loopholes at the expense of the data owner.

(3) **Data Security.** Data privacy and data security go hand-in-hand and are two sides of the same coin. If either of the two is weak, it also weakens the other.

Security of data is a critical element of all privacy regulation. Since 2015, the issue of cyber security has been addressed by various legal acts in both German and European legislation. These include the German BDSG, the German IT Security Act (IT-SiG, 2015), German IT Security Act 2.0 (IT-SiG 2.0, effective since May 2021), the EU GDPR, the EU Directive on Network and Information Security (NIS Directive, 2016) and the EU Cybersecurity Regulation (June 2019).

Art. 32 GDPR, for instance, requires the implementation of appropriate technical and organizational measures to ensure a level of security appropriate to the risk, such as the pseudonymization and encryption of personal data; the ability to ensure the ongoing confidentiality, integrity, availability and resilience of processing systems and services; the ability to restore the availability and access to personal data in a timely manner in the event of a physical or technical incident; a process for regularly testing, assessing, and evaluating the effectiveness of technical and organisational measures for ensuring the security of the processing.

3.1.3 Ethical Responsibility

Ethical responsibility is demonstrated when a company not only obeys the letter of the law (possibly using loopholes or tweaking legal interpretation to its own advantage, yet possible disadvantage of the individual), but it conducts its business sustainably and in a human-centric way. This can become relevant during the whole lifecycle of data management.

To illustrate how ethical data practices help to gain and maintain user acceptance, the introduction of the electronic patient file (ePA) is a good example, since health data are among the most sensitive data. The ePA, which health insurance companies in Germany have to offer to their clients from 2021, is at the heart of all healthcare digitalization efforts. Rather than saving the patient data in a decentralized way across various doctors' offices, it is possible with the ePA to store all data related to a patient in one place managed centrally by the patient's health insurance company.

3.1.3.1 Provide Transparency

Adequate transparency regarding the handling of data is indispensable to promote and maintain trust in a corporation's data practices. Therefore, sufficient information should be provided to all relevant stakeholders to inform what data is collected, when and for what purpose, to explain how data privacy and security are safeguarded, and on the corporation's position on data responsibility in general.

Taking the example of the ePA, this means that the insurance company openly informs the insured person which data is stored, how the data is stored, what happens to the data that the insured person stores in the ePA, for what purposes the data is used and who will get access to the data. The ePA tool or app is designed in a user-friendly way and explains offered modules, options, and configurations in a simple way.

3.1.3.2 Respect Personal Choice

Ensure sovereign decision-making and informational self-determination of the individual, i.e., designing products and processes in such a way that enables people to decide themselves what services they actually use and what data they want to share—either through consent, by contract or at the push of a button. This includes ensuring that informed consent of the user can be obtained in a way that is as simple, clear and catchy as possible for the user.

For example, when designing the ePA, the guiding principle should be that the insured person alone determines everything. Does the person want to have a file at all, which documents should be on display there, and who gets to see them? The insured must have the data under their full control and can take their health management into their own hands. That sounds reasonable, but respecting personal choice also comes with a downside. Insurers and even more importantly doctors and medical staff, whose work the ePA is intended to facilitate, may not be able to rely fully on the data in the ePA as the file may not be complete due to personal choice to store only a selection of health and medical data in the file.

To further illustrate this important topic of freedom of choice with a negative example: informational self-determination is hindered if the interaction with the users is designed to manipulate the users into consenting to the use of their data e.g., by applying findings from behavioural psychology research known as "nudges". This is done, for example, by optically highlighting the OK button, which confirms all pre-filled fields, and greying out the further options, which can be often seen in cookie consent forms.

If a user interface is deliberately designed to mislead the user and—in the worst case—lead the user to take an action he or she did not want to perform, this is called a "dark pattern". For example, an e-commerce website that asks the customer three different times in three different ways to join a premium service as part of the check-out process.

3.1.3.3 Personal Benefit

When data are collected from individuals, the individuals should be offered benefits that are proportionate to the data requested from them.

In our example case of the ePA, in return for storing their health information in the insurance company's ePA file system, the insured benefit from this collection of highly sensitive personal data. Informed doctors can make better decisions, interactions between medications from different therapists can be recognized early, etc. and patients receive better treatment, more transparency and can manage themselves more effectively. This seems well balanced.

If the data would mainly be used to the benefit of the insurance company, e.g., to calculate individual risk profiles, adjust insurance premiums or to use the data as basis for commercial offerings, this would appear out of balance and thus unethical.

3.1.3.4 Data Quality

Ensure fit-for-purpose data quality. Responsible use of data includes ensuring a high level of data quality that is fit for the relevant purpose, e.g., respective data sets are relevant, not outdated, not corrupted and not selective.

For example, data bias in machine learning is a type of error in which certain elements of a dataset are more heavily weighted and/or represented than others. A biased dataset does not accurately represent a model's use case, resulting in skewed outcomes, low accuracy levels, and analytical errors. A facial recognition system, for example, that is trained primarily on images of white men fails to recognize people of color as accurately as it does Caucasians.

3.1.3.5 Ethical Use

Ensure that data is handled ethically, i.e., checking for ethical conflicts when using data, applying transparency and fairness and a human-centric approach that does no harm to the user.

Returning to our example of e-health, some health insurance companies promote digitally controlled healthy lifestyles and therefore subsidize the purchase of smart watches or fitness trackers. These grants are usually only available as part of a bonus program, i.e., the insured person must use the device to prove certain sports activities and transmit certain data, such as the number of steps walked per day, the heart rate and calorie consumption. The aim of such programs is to motivate people to engage in physical exercise that supports health and contributes to disease prevention. In some cases, participation in such programs is linked to further advantages, such as tariff rebates or paybacks.

Such programs raise a whole range of ethical questions. Is it right to motivate people to rely more and more on technology instead of listening to their own body and without being technically monitored? Which data can the health insurance company ask for and for which purpose? To what extent and for which period of time?

Another point of criticism is the fear that some health insurance companies could in the long run combine the cheapest tariffs with the demand for continuous transmission of health data. This is seen to entail that financially weaker groups may feel forced to trade privacy for insurance coverage plus the risk of discriminating individuals that suffer from chronic or genetically based physical conditions. Potential misuse and social inequalities must be considered. Ethical design of such programs has to analyse and balance the real risks and opportunities for humans and society.

3.1.3.6 Data Security

With increasing connectivity and an expanding network of connected devices, the risks of data misuse, data theft and cyberattacks are increasing, too. Companies should see themselves as trustees of the personal data in their care and make data security a central priority. Data security needs to be ensured throughout the data lifecycle, e.g.;

- **"Data during transmission"** collected from a local source (e.g. a smartphone or sensor): the local source should incorporate security by design in form of authentication, i.e. a mechanism to ensure that any data created is sent and received by authorized parties only. And data should be transmitted via a secure connection to the platform on which the data are stored, so that no attackers can intervene.
- **"Data at rest" that is stored and managed.** It should be ensured that not only the company's own data storage systems are reliable and secure, but also that their outsourced data storage systems (incl. cloud services) are selected, monitored, and managed in a way that ensures reliability and security of data. Data generated and stored (in a decentral fashion on the device) must be protected. Data are encrypted and there is access control and rights management to manage the individuals having access to data. Ensure that stored anonymized data cannot be traced back to the individuals to whom they refer.
- **"Data in use" that are being processed.** It should be ensured that activities are monitored, applications that process the data are secure, rights management is followed through, and controls are exercised. Apply technical measures for protecting the privacy of customers are appropriate and proportionate. Define clear rules regarding access to and use of stored data (who may access/use, when, under what conditions, and how access is logged or tracked).
- **When data is destroyed.** Define rules for the deletion of data with the aim of reducing the risk of damage from unauthorized access. Consider in advance what to do with the data of inactive accounts or former customers.

3.1.3.7 Ecosystem of Trust

Create an ecosystem of partners that value trust: companies need an ecosystem of partners, e.g., in their supply chain, as technology and platform providers, as well as in delivery channels. Corporations should work with partners that share their approach to data and privacy. To do this, you should find out about the partners' stance on the subject of data responsibility, e.g. how does a partner inform about their data practice on their website, in their ESG / CSR report, does the partner have certifications, etc. When data are acquired from third parties like data brokers, it should be verified that the data were collected in a legal and ethical manner and all information needed for the assessment of data use is passed on.

As organizations increasingly rely on Cloud Computing for their digital services, they will need to ensure that their cloud service provider's platform offers the five elements of trust: privacy, security, reliability, ethics, and compliance, meets the highest standards of certifications, and is designed for efficiency and availability at the same time.

3.1.4 Data Philanthropy

Data Philanthropy describes a form of collaboration in which private sector companies share data for public benefit. There are multiple uses of data philanthropy being explored from humanitarian, corporate, human rights, and academic use. Since introducing the term in 2011, the United Nations Global Pulse has advocated for a global "data philanthropy movement". There are several first initiatives:[38] French telecommunications company France Telecom-Orange, for example, has made anonymized records of five million mobile phone users in Cote d'Ivoire available to the research community as part of the Data for Development Challenge. Popular URL shortening service Bitly has launched Bitly Social Data APIs giving developers access to data collected from the billions of clicks that Bitly receives each month. And international organizations such as UNDP and the World Bank have made efforts at opening up their own internal data, allowing for applied research experiments and correlation with external data sources like social media or mobile phone data at a series of Data Dives.

The EU aims to support data donations and data sharing with its Data Governance Regulation[39] to unlock the economic and societal potential of data and technologies like artificial intelligence, while respecting EU rules and values.

3.2 Governance

Governance in the context of ESG is essentially about how well and trustworthily a company is managed. It covers topics such as board structure and diversity, executive remuneration, tax transparency, competitive behavior, legal compliance, risk management, political lobbying, transparency of reporting as well as business ethics, i.e., procedures and processes to ensure appropriate decision making and behavior.

For the "digital side" of business, this means of course that all digital products, services and business models are built in line with applicable laws and that appropriate risk management is applied. As new technologies are opening up entirely new fields of use which have not yet been regulated, ethical considerations in the development of business models and offerings are becoming noticeably more important. A special focus on digital business ethics thus becomes the basis for the building of trust. This comprises the establishment of processes that examine digital innovations for their possible positive and negative effects on the environment, human beings and society and that steer ethical decision-making.

3.2.1 Trust

The rapid advancements in new areas like artificial intelligence (AI) and the Internet of Things (IoT), and their massive utilization offer great opportunities but also risks, and they raise concerns in public discussion. These concerns are not only related to

[38] https://www.unglobalpulse.org/2013/05/data-philanthropy-where-are-we-now/.

[39] https://digital-strategy.ec.europa.eu/en/policies/data-governance.

security and data privacy, but sometimes relate to rather dystopic visions of de-humanization of society through the rise of robotics, mass surveillance and manipulation of the free human will, criminally abused IT systems, or even out-of-control autonomous systems. In order to ensure that the many opportunities presented by these new technologies continue to find a high level of user and public acceptance, the establishment of trust between all related stakeholders is fundamental.

A representative survey[40] was carried out in Germany in April 2021 to explore the attitudes and knowledge of the German population regarding "Corporate Digital Responsibility", including the question of consumers' expectations and concerns regarding the use of digital products and services. The survey results showed that **trust** in digital products and services is essential for consumers to use them. 78% of the respondents said that the trustworthiness of the providers is rather important or very important to them. Trust is essential for customer loyalty.

Trust is usually defined as the belief that someone is good and honest and will not harm you, or that something is safe and reliable.[41]

A study[42] in the German financial services sector, for instance, found a particularly strong correlation between perceptions of caring and trust. According to the study, trust in banks depends primarily on the extent to which customers perceive their bank as caring and acting in the best interest of the customer. As the second strongest factor, perceived competence is associated with trust. Together, competence and care form the core drivers of trust., i.e., the expectation that promises will be kept, and that vulnerabilities will not be exploited.

The survey results further showed that banks do fairly well on perceptions of competence, but that they are rarely seen as caring by their customers.

The claim in the study is that to increase trust, the banking industry should focus on demonstrating genuine care by looking after the financial wellbeing of the customer, in particular in the banks' digitalization efforts. Yet, the analysis found that often digital transformation focuses on automation and cost-savings. The researchers drew a notable conclusion: *"But if care is lost, then trust is lost. And without trust, banks and their technology are obsolete."*[43]

As a result, the study advocates "Trust Tech", i.e., using technology and processes that are designed to foster trust in particular by demonstrating competent care for the users' interests.

The building of digital trust is supported by four key pillars:[44]

---

[40] https://www.bmjv.de/SharedDocs/Downloads/DE/PDF/Berichte/CDR_ConPolicy_Fact_Sheets.html.

[41] https://dictionary.cambridge.org/dictionary/english/trust.

[42] https://digitalwellbeing.org/wp-content/uploads/2019/10/Trust-Tech-The-Future-of-Digital-Banking-SYZYGY-Digital-Insight-Report-2019-DE-1.pdf.

[43] https://digitalwellbeing.org/wp-content/uploads/2019/10/Trust-Tech-The-Future-of-Digital-Banking-SYZYGY-Digital-Insight-Report-2019-DE-1.pdf p.12.

[44] Also see: https://www2.deloitte.com/us/en/insights/topics/digital-transformation/building-long-term-trust-in-digital-technology.html.

- **Ethics and responsibility**—an organization's willingness to work toward the welfare of customers can generate higher levels of credibility and trust.
- **Transparency and accessibility**—transparent communication on the organization's position on and approach to ethical questions and digital business practices in general can help to build trust in the organisation's intentions and its promise to deliver quality products and services that are useful to the customer.
- **Privacy and control**—an organization that respects customer preferences regarding personal data is able to gain greater permission to handle customer information and provide personalized services.
- **Security and reliability**—by using the latest technology and security practices an organization can assure its customers to provide best protection against cyber risks and to keep products and services secure and reliable.

A company's reputation as well as its consistency of communication, policies and actually demonstrated practices are further elements that contribute to the building of trust.

3.2.2 Responsible AI

Artificial intelligence has already been mentioned several times in this article as one of the important new digital technologies that offer great opportunities, but the use of which can also entail complex and critical new risks.

So far there is no law governing the use of AI. However, the EU Commission has recently developed and proposed key principles to guide the European approach to AI that take into account the social and environmental impact of AI technologies. The "EU principles on AI" aim to turn Europe into the global hub for trustworthy artificial intelligence. The first-ever legal framework on AI shall guarantee the safety and fundamental rights of people and businesses, while strengthening AI uptake, investment, and innovation across the EU. New rules on machinery shall complement this approach by adapting safety rules to increase users' trust in the new, versatile generation of products.

The EU principles classify AI systems in four categories:[45]

(1) **Threat to safety.** AI systems considered a clear threat to the safety, livelihoods and rights of people will be banned. This includes AI systems or applications that manipulate human behavior to circumvent users' free will (e.g. toys using voice assistance encouraging dangerous behavior of minors) and systems that allow 'social scoring' by governments.

(2) **High-risk.** AI systems in this category will be subject to strict obligations before they can be put on the market. This includes for example critical infrastructures (e.g. transport), that could put the life and health of citizens at risk; educational or vocational training, that may determine the access to education and professional course of someone's life (e.g. scoring of exams); employment, workers'

[45] https://ec.europa.eu/commission/presscorner/detail/en/IP_21_1682.

management and access to self-employment (e.g. CV-sorting software for recruitment procedures); essential private and public services (e.g. credit scoring denying citizens opportunity to obtain a loan), all remote biometric identification systems.

High-risk AI systems will require adequate risk assessment and mitigation systems; high quality of the datasets feeding the system to minimize risks and discriminatory outcomes; logging of activity to ensure traceability of results, detailed documentation providing all information necessary on the system and its purpose for authorities to assess its compliance; clear and adequate information to the user; appropriate human oversight measures to minimize risk; and high level of robustness, security and accuracy.

(3) **Limited risk**, i.e., AI systems in this category will have specific transparency obligations: When using AI systems such as chatbots, users should be aware that they are interacting with a machine so they can take an informed decision to continue or step back.

(4) **Minimal risk:** The legal proposal allows the free use of applications such as AI-enabled video games or spam filters. The vast majority of AI systems fall into this category. The draft Regulation does not intervene here, as these AI systems represent only minimal or no risk for citizens' rights or safety.

Several "forerunner" companies have already voluntarily established their own ethical guidelines for their approach to and use of AI. The AI Ethics Guidelines Global Inventory,[46] a project by *AlgorithmWatch,* maps frameworks that seek to set out principles of how systems for automated decision-making can be developed and implemented ethically. The database currently includes 173 guidelines of private companies, but also of governments, industry associations and others.

3.3 Social Aspects

Social aspects in the ESG framework examine how a company manages its relationships with humans, i.e. employees, suppliers, customers and the community. Health and safety of employees, diversity, inclusion and equal opportunity, product safety and supply chain management are typically included in this pillar.

3.3.1 Digital Inclusion

Social inclusion in the digital context is the effort to ensure that everybody can contribute to and benefit from the digital economy and society. Provision of digital services should not discriminate between users or prevent marginalized or unserved/underserved users from completing basic activities. However, according to a UN report in 2019,[47] nearly half of the world's population remains offline and excluded

[46] https://algorithmwatch.org/en/ai-ethics-guidelines-global-inventory/.

[47] https://www.un.org/press/en/2019/gaef3523.doc.htm.

from the benefits of digitalization. This growing "digital divide" has a negative impact on socio-economically disadvantaged people and groups, such as low-income households, rural communities, the elderly, the illiterate, people with disabilities, and at the enterprise level of micro, small and medium-sized enterprises (SMEs). If the digital divide remains untapped, large sections of the population will miss the opportunities offered by digital technology. The consequences of neglecting digital inclusion are twofold: lower economic growth due to the immobilization of part of the workforce and user pool and the weakening of social cohesion as the digital divide grows.

Digitalization provides opportunity for new products, solutions and business models that foster social inclusion e.g., by improving people's economic and life chances, supporting health and social progress or supporting equality. For example, mobile money, such as Kenya's transfer system M-Pesa,[48] has helped boost financial inclusion for people who did not have a bank account by letting users treat their phone like a wallet and send money using a text message.

However, if the social effects of a digitalization project are not adequately taken into account, this may hinder the objectives pursued, undermine user acceptance and trust and lead to negative press and reputational issues, as the example in Sect. 1.3 above illustrates where the UK's 'rigid insistence' on automating welfare benefits was reported to threaten the rights of people most at risk of poverty.

A recent study[49] identified **4 key levers for digital inclusion:**

1. **Accessibility:** making information and communication technology (ICT) more accessible for all and fostering new methodologies for technology development (design for all).
2. **Affordability:** The financial capability/support to pay for hardware and software which is required for digital access.
3. **Ability:** Digital literacy regarding the use and knowledge of ICT as part of digital readiness. This can be fostered by active learning support to build digital literacy and skills. Supporting the development of ICT that assists people with disabilities for enabling them to perform activities that they have not been able to do before and to interact better with technologies.
4. **Attitude:** The trust and enthusiasm to harness ICT which is supported by a safe digital environment to ease security fears and by awareness and usage campaigning to enhance enthusiasm for digital.

3.3.2 Care for Employees

To fully leverage the potential of digitalization **an engaged workforce** is needed, ready and willing to embrace transformation and change. However, as a study[50]

[48] Six ways digitalization is helping Africa's environment | Environment| All topics from climate change to conservation | DW | 08.04.2019.

[49] https://www.rolandberger.com/en/Insights/Publications/Bridging-the-digital-divide.html.

[50] https://brainstation.io/blog/how-employee-training-can-help-your-digital-transformation.

found, 49% of employees fear change when digital transformation initiatives are introduced, 59% are concerned about job security where tasks are automated, and 39% feel anxious at the introduction of new technology.

To address these concerns, companies may

- Emphasize the collaborative potential of new digital technologies;
- Acknowledge the anxiety that change can cause and provide support;
- Allow people to experience new technologies themselves;
- Make it clear how new digital technologies should fit within your environment;
- Establish a forward-thinking culture of continuous improvement and innovation.

Regular digital skills training can help address each of these suggestions, demystifying new technology for employees, empowering them with skills and experience, and establishing a company mindset that is ready and willing to learn new ideas and techniques.

A second aspect is the impact of digital or remote work on **people's well-being**. This is particularly relevant for employees who had to work at home during the COVID-19 pandemic. But it is also relevant for hybrid working models, that are becoming more and more popular. Remote work offers a number of benefits: no commuting, more flexibility and freedom, better work-life balance. However, remote work in poor infrastructure (e.g. office at the kitchen table), feelings of loneliness and emotional exhaustion, challenges in managing the work-life boundary and an inability to "switch off" can negatively affect well-being and may eventually cause health problems.

3.4 Environmental Impact

Environment in the context of ESG considers how a company performs as a steward of nature. Aspects in this pillar typically address topics like climate change strategy, environmental management system, environmental impact of products and services, greenhouse gas emission, energy efficiency, waste and pollution.

Digitalization provides opportunity for new products and business models that help protect the environment. Precision farming, for instance, makes use of GPS, sensor and software-supported machines and devices to cultivate agricultural areas with high precision and thus can improve environmental protection, resource efficiency and productivity. Digitally enhanced monitoring of ecosystems and soil conditions (including forests and wildlife) strengthen the protection of terrestrial ecosystems and biodiversity. Saving energy and resources, reducing GHG emissions and air pollution through smart city mobility (traffic control and optimization), smart logistics, smart buildings etc.

Yet, the process of digitalization requires an enormous amount of ICT hardware equipment (e.g., computing devices, data centres, networks, sensors and accompanying infrastructures like cooling, uninterrupted power supply, etc.). All this equipment becomes waste at the end of its life. This type of waste contains a complex mixture of materials, some of which are hazardous. These can cause major environmental and health problems if the discarded devices are not managed properly. In addition, modern electronics contain rare and expensive resources, which can be recycled and re-used if the waste is effectively managed. Improving the collection, treatment and recycling of electrical and electronic equipment at the end of their life can improve sustainable production and consumption, increase resource efficiency and contribute to the circular economy. Therefore, the EU has introduced the **WEEE Directive** and the **RoHS Directive** to tackle the issue of the growing amount of waste from electrical and electronic equipment. The WEEE Directive for example requires producers of electronic equipment to registered on the National Register to provide regular declaration of material placed on the market, inform end-users and mark requirements, make information available to recyclers, organize the collection and recycling of the equipment, finance take-back systems, waste treatment and recycling operations and report to the national authority on a regular basis the quantities that they have collected and treated.

This ICT infrastructure demands **energy, water and resources**.

In 2016, it was reported that the world's data centers used three percent of the global electricity supply, accounted for about two percent of total greenhouse gas emissions, and thus were said to have the same carbon footprint as the aviation industry.[51]

Commissioned by the EU, Öko Institute e.V. conducted a comprehensive analysis on the "Impacts of the digital transformation on the environment and sustainability".[52] The study found several direct impacts arising from ICT final goods, data centers, data transmission networks and software as regards greenhouse gas emissions, resource depletion, water consumption, land use and biodiversity.

It is not a given that digitalization will automatically lead to resource and energy efficiency or other environmental benefits. A holistic approach needs to be taken to properly understand the impacts and to take adequate action to avoid a rebound effect.

4 The Role of Lawyers

As this article has shown, digital technologies enable a variety of new business models, products, services and process improvements.

In areas where the use of such technologies can lead to tensions, conflicts with stakeholder interests or cause harm to environment or society, legislatures have already begun to establish regulation. However, due to the enormous innovation potential and speed that digitalization offers legal regulation is not always possible in

[51] https://www.computerworld.com/article/3431148/why-data-centres-are-the-new-frontier-in-the-fight-against-climate-change.html.

[52] https://ec.europa.eu/environment/enveco/resource_efficiency/pdf/studies/ issue_paper_digital_transformation_20191220_final.pdf.

a timely manner. And even where laws already exist, they may not always provide clear answers to new ideas.

Lawyers, and in particular in-house lawyers, can actively support Corporate Digital Responsibility in several ways:

- The first and most obvious one is that lawyers know and advise on applicable laws and regulations and they observe, monitor and sometimes contribute to legislative initiatives and procedures regarding new laws relevant to their clients' business. As discussed in this article, compliance with the law is the most important responsibility, as this shows how reliably companies conduct their business in the marketplace.
- If there is no relevant law yet or if the existing laws leave room for interpretation, situations can arise in which not only the direct interest of the company may be decisive, but ethical considerations and diverging stakeholder interests need to be taken into account in responsible decision making.
- Lawyers are well equipped to advise and guide in such situations as they are trained to consider diverging interests and to establish a solid and defensible position for their clients which helps to balance sustainability risks with company interest and the corporate executives' duty of care. This becomes even more relevant as the EU Commission has recently published a Sustainable Corporate Governance Initiative,[53] which aims at an explicit obligation for boards and corporate directors to include relevant CSR/ESG issues and stakeholder interests in their decision making.
- And finally, lawyers who act as a business partner may help their clients/company to use regulation or ethical issues of the digital world as an opportunity—in B2C relationships to actively build trust in their digital offerings and in B2B relationships to develop offerings that enable their customers to digitize responsibly, trustworthy and in a human-centric manner.

We all do our part to shape the future with innovations, whether as inventors, developers, technology providers, advisors or users.

Technology is neither good nor bad—it's what **we** do with it that makes the difference.

Liquid Legal Waves to Other Chapters, Written by the Editors

> Having gained a clearer view on the inhouse role in CDR, it is fascinating to read *Ivar's* and *Michiel's* account of the responsibility of the public sector to leverage the new digital means in redefining the interface towards the citizen.

(continued)

[53] https://ec.europa.eu/info/law/better-regulation/have-your-say/initiatives/12548-Sustainable-corporate-governance_en.

In their chapter *"Digitization of government services from the citizen's perspective"*, they get to the heart of the issue: Digital public services are not about convenience—they are about regaining the trust of the citizens!

CDR is about taking people's and societies' interests as a guiding principle in digital innovation projects. *Wolfgang* and *Sebastian* build on that when they discuss *"Value Creation Through Blockchain-based Tokens: Transforming Traditional Collaboration Structures"*. Is a security token economy the *conditio sine qua non* for a Common Legal Platform to develop and thrive?

Martina makes a strong case for the opportunity for lawyers to engage in CDR. *Thomas'* chapter on *"Designing Legal Systems for an Algorithmic Society"* underpins that. While the information age fundamentally challenges the traditional legal systems, it reciprocally also demands public oversight—and lawyers have a key role to play.

References

Carroll AB (2016) Carroll's pyramid of CSR: taking another look. Int J Corp Soc Responsib 1:3. https://doi.org/10.1186/s40991-016-0004-6

Herden CJ, Alliu E, Cakici A et al (2021) Corporate digital responsibility. NachhaltigkeitsManagementForum. https://doi.org/10.1007/s00550-020-00509-x

Martina Seidl is Group Chief Legal & Compliance Officer for Giesecke+Devrient (G+D), a global security technology group which provides solutions in four major playing fields: enabling secure payment, providing trusted connectivity, safeguarding identities and protecting digital infrastructures. In her role, she oversees G+D's legal, compliance and data privacy functions. Prior to joining G+D in 2019, Martina held various legal management positions in the IT industry which included Vice President Legal & Commercial at Fujitsu Technology Solutions and Head of M&A and Corporate Law at Fujitsu Siemens Computers. Martina studied Law at Ludwig Maximilians Universität in Munich and was admitted as lawyer in 2001. Martina Seidl stands for a modern and future-oriented management of governance and support functions that act as business partners of the business units.

Designing Legal Systems for an Algorithm Society

Thomas D. Barton

Contents

Abstract

The Information Age challenges the competency and cultural acceptability of traditional legal systems. Reciprocally, some AI methods are themselves in need of public oversight and stronger social trust. Legal systems and information technology are, however, positioned to help each other; each realm has specific tools to address the problems faced by the other. If properly integrated, their partnership can enhance the law's efficacy as well as reduce AI's potential dangers.

This work reaches what may seem a paradoxical conclusion: that the strongest contribution to humanizing the law may be to *redirect some attention away from humans and their individual choices*. Doing so encourages a legal/AI framework that focuses less on individual choices or their market-place aggregation, and

Tom Barton is Professor Emeritus of law at California Western School of Law in San Diego, California.

T. D. Barton (✉)
San Diego, CA, USA
e-mail: tbarton@cwsl.edu

K. Jacob et al. (eds.), *Liquid Legal – Humanization and the Law*, Law for Professionals, https://doi.org/10.1007/978-3-031-14240-6_5

more on the environments in which people actually live, the behaviors or outcomes produced inside those settings, and the measure of those outcomes against explicitly stated justice goals. In an increasingly algorithmic society, AI tools should enable stronger legal problem-solving; but *ex ante* and *post hoc* legal oversight should also ensure algorithmic outcomes that are more just as well as more accurate.

This Chapter reflects on what the tools of AI, combined with the law, may offer: a process of understanding social environments more realistically, designing them more deliberatively, and seeking defined ends for a differently imagined humanity.

1 Introduction[1]

The intriguing concept for this book, Humanization and the Law: A Call to Action for the Digital Age, prompts a vital agenda for social governance and human self-understanding in the twenty-first century: "to . . . focus on . . . what a given innovation may mean for humanity [and] to prioritize the co-development of the framework required to humanize such innovation." (Strathausen 2020) This chapter focuses on the innovations of artificial intelligence (AI) and its fast-unfolding subsets of algorithmic pattern recognition, probabilistic prediction, and automated decision-making, especially as accelerated by machine learning. It addresses the co-development of an interactive framework between AI and legal systems, with the goal of humanizing both.

The phrase "humanization of the law" raises several connotations. First, it suggests a need to create or supply human qualities to the law now missing or inadequate. Second, the idea raises difficult questions of method, especially in an age where "internationalization increases and legal regulations become more complex, and as artificial intelligence outperforms human decision-making . . . ." (Strathausen

[1] "Algorithmic Society" is a phrase popularized by Jack M. Balkin. He writes:

> We are rapidly moving from the age of the Internet to the Algorithmic Society, and soon we will look back on the digital age as the precursor to the Algorithmic Society. What do I mean by the Algorithmic Society? I mean a society organized around social and economic decision-making by algorithms, robots, and AI agents, who not only make the decisions but also, in some cases, carry them out. (Balkin 2017).

My use of the phrase in this Chapter follows Balkin's: it references algorithms as a subset of Artificial Intelligence that mines aggregated databases according to human or machine-created algorithms to achieve predictions or patterned explanations of queried phenomena—and possibly to take self-executing actions based on the algorithmic outcomes. I focus on the potentials for expanded environmental understanding and more particularized governance based on algorithms. The broader term "Artificial Intelligence" or AI is often used interchangeably in this Chapter for convenience, often in contexts when referencing longer historical trends.

2020) Finally, the phrase speaks to the purpose of this book: "we want to understand if Humanization can help us become more humane." (Strathausen 2020)

Part of being human is the possibility of self-reflection, and this need is especially compelling as human thought begins to converge with an automated intelligence that is helpless as to purposes, finding guidance only from us. As Yuval Harari states,

> The only thing we can try to do is to influence the direction scientists are taking. But since we might soon be able to engineer our desires too, the real question facing us is not 'What do we want to become?' but 'What do we want to want?' . . .
>
> [D]espite the astonishing things that humans are capable of doing, we remain unsure of our goals and we seem to be as discontented as ever. . . . Self-made gods with only the laws of physics to keep us company, we are accountable to no one. . . . Is there anything more dangerous than dissatisfied and irresponsible gods who don't know what they want? (Harari 2015)

I claim no divinity, but welcome the opportunity afforded by the Liquid Legal Institute to explore the innovations of AI and speculate on their co-development with the law. The Chapter necessarily brings in my personal opinions and values. I hope those are realistic, but some are frankly aspirational for others' imaginations and capabilities. My goals for a humanized legal/AI framework can be stated in verbs, qualities, and language sets. *Verbs:* A legal/AI framework should listen as well as command; explain as well as direct; inspire as well as constrain. *Qualities:* It should be competent, trustworthy, and fair. *Language:* It should speak with words of humility and morality as well as authority.[2]

This chapter reaches a conclusion that will strike some as paradoxical, and perhaps troubling. Ultimately, however, I consider it optimistic: the strongest contribution to humanizing the law may now be to *redirect some attention away from humans and their individual choices*. Doing so encourages a legal/AI framework that focuses less on individual choices or their market-place aggregation, and more on a careful scrutiny of the physical, social, and technological environments in which people are embedded; the behaviors or outcomes produced inside those settings; and the measure of those outcomes against explicitly stated justice goals.

We may have reached a watershed historical moment in which the prevailing paradigm of justice and governance based on choices made by autonomous, formally equal individuals may be diverting attention from other possibilities and needs that are more urgent. This Chapter reflects on what the tools of AI, combined with the law, may offer: a process of examining and understanding environments more broadly and with an appreciation for their shaping effects; designing environments more deliberatively; and seeking defined ends for a differently imagined humanity.

---

[2] As Balkin puts it, "behind the robots, AI agents, and algorithms are social relations between human beings and groups of human beings. So the laws we need are obligations of fair dealing, nonmanipulation, and nondomination between those who make and use the algorithms and those who are governed by them." (Balkin 2017)

The Information Age—digitalization, internet interconnection, and AI—has unlocked enormous potentials for productivity gains and human problem solving. These same technologies, however, challenge the capabilities of legal systems by generating disputes that surpass the law's conventional decisional, remedial, or regulatory capabilities (Barton 2016, 2020). Further, the immediacy, self-direction capabilities, and participatory ethic of internet-based communication contrast with the law's far more traditional style of information collection, classification, and authoritative use—potentially contributing to cultural frustration with the general inaccessibility and expense of current legal systems.

Yet AI has competency and cultural acceptance needs of its own. To avert potentially serious popular backlash to its widespread use, decision-making based on algorithmic analysis must win social trust against serious-minded concerns about surveillance (Burk 2021; Froomkin 2015); opacity (Bloch-Wehba 2020); arbitrariness (Engstrom and Ho 2020); discrimination (Radavoi 2020); and loss of human control (Winfield and Jirotka 2018).

Legal systems and information technology are positioned to help each other; each realm has specific tools to address the problems faced by the other. If properly integrated, their partnership can enhance the law's efficacy as well as reduce AI's potential dangers. Both goals—respect for the soundness and authority of legal judgments and trust in the fairness of algorithmic determinations—are crucial to future social governance.[3] Ignoring the challenges to either risks a social turn toward tyranny or atavistic populist demagoguery.[4] Law and AI need one another, and society needs both to be effective and fair.

2 Humanization: Its Historic Creation, Limitations, and New Possibilities

The Enlightenment image of a human being, which still animates much civic discourse and legal decision-making, is envisioned as an atomized abstraction: formally equal beings who self-maximize in social transactions and are responsible for transcending environmental barriers. The ideas stem from Rene Descartes, who deemed each of us human purely by possession of consciousness: *cogito ergo sum*. Humans, the subjects, are radically separated from environments, which are the objects of our will. We control environments; they do not control us. Legal attention thus focuses on our choices: the products of our accountable minds and will.

[3]"The Algorithmic Society is a way of governing populations. By governance, I mean the way that people who control algorithms analyze, control, direct, order, and shape the people who are the subjects of the data." (Balkin 2017)

[4]As legal philosophy Lon Fuller wrote a generation ago, whenever the evolution of problem-solving methods cannot keep pace with the sophistication of social problems, people will turn to tyranny (Fuller 1965). In modern times, the tyrant may perhaps take the form not of a human despot, but instead a social self-blinding and abdication to unconstrained and non-accountable algorithmic decisions.

The autonomous choosing self was always a philosophical and aspirational construct, rather than an accurate portrayal of how humans come to behave as they do. Unquestionably, Enlightenment autonomy concepts represented a breathtaking advance toward according universal dignity and respect to every human. Yet much has changed in the ensuing centuries. We seem increasingly to be ossifying social strata and inequalities, and widespread use of algorithmic decision-making could make it worse. We need now to find courage in ourselves, our emerging technological tools, and our formal normative institutions of democracy and law to grope toward more realism and pragmatic human meaning. We need to connect people more deeply to social and physical environments and their outcomes, rather than hold people accountable for individual choices that are not completely free. We must recognize how social environments can channel people's behaviors. We should acknowledge the past—its injustices, lingering inequalities, and obstructions—and work toward the possibility of a different future.

The humanity envisioned here for the Information Age is not necessarily heroic, but instead rooted in the everyday material and dignity needs of diverse people embedded in powerful social or political structures that consign some to generational inequality. It is no longer sufficient in either our morality or in our legal systems to imagine autonomous humans who can simply transcend their environments through the exercise of detached, rational free will. Like it or not, people are being measured, assessed, and categorized—often unknowingly and with potentially unjust results—inside strongly channeling environments. The goal is not to eliminate those environments; that is not possible. The goal instead is to ensure that those environments operate fairly, with genuine opportunities for all to live safe and rewarding lives. Freedom and dignity, writes B.F. Skinner, should not define exclusively the meaning of humanity (Skinner 1972). We should be conscious of the limits of our freedom, and understand the origins of those limits. They come not fully from a lack of will or choice, but from environments that shape us. We should measure ourselves by the imagination and justness of what we can build rather than heroically overcome (Skinner 1972).

We need, therefore, to set heritage assumptions about humanity against social reality and make adjustments. The Enlightenment self should never be abandoned: it represents a stunning humanistic achievement. Let it not be said that we failed to protect our heritage through deference to technical expertise that most of us do not fully understand; but let it also not be said that we hid behind abstractions and historic rhetoric while failing to engage concretely with injustices unfolding before our eyes.

Three historic premises stem from the Enlightenment dualism detaching mind from object, and humans from environments: *the primacy of individual choice; the formal legal equality of all people; and the reluctance to measure outcomes by specified justice goals*. Each deserves a new examination, and I attempt to do so throughout this Chapter as I describe possibilities for a stronger partnership of AI and the law.[5] AI offers the prospect of an augmented intelligence that may come to rival the technological impact of the scientific revolution, simultaneously sparking a search for a more humanized law.

2.1 Lowered Information Costs: A Source of Disruptions and Possible Solutions

Uniting the disparate reform needs for law, Enlightenment images of humanity, and algorithms are their shared connections to the dramatic reduction in information costs accompanying the digital revolution of the past four decades.[6] Although reduced information costs have enabled enormous efficiencies throughout public and private life, the possibilities of better data and more comprehensive analysis also reveal some technical limitations and philosophical blind spots in law and its liberal underpinnings. Simultaneously, however, lowered costs of information, especially coupled with data mining and machine learning, could enable far-reaching expansions in conceptions of justice and its everyday achievement.

---

[5]These principles are associated with liberalism—the political and economic principles that grew out of Enlightenment thought and that overlap with the equality and autonomy ideas explored here. Lest it be misunderstood, I pursue the inquiry of this Chapter out of deep concern for the well-being of liberalism, if not its survival. Western heritage ideas and institutions for social governance based on atomistic individualism and invisible market hands are under serious stress. Illiberal forces undermining free expression and democracy are spreading and growing more flagrant in their disregard for Western values. *The goals here are to enhance the viability of legal institutions and community respect for the rule of law, and to offer fresh outlooks on fundamental liberal ideas that better accord with contemporary culture and standards of justice.* A true liberal, valuing the inherent dignity and rights of all human beings, need not be fiercely libertarian or disdain the distribution of outcomes. Far from it: a committed liberal can be deeply concerned for the genuineness of social opportunities and mobility, and work toward guarantees of universal minimal levels of material well-being as well as human rights. It is toward those ends that I suggest reform of liberal ideas.

[6]M. Ethan Katsh highlights crucial connections between legal systems and information:

> Law can be looked at in many ways, but in every incarnation, information is a central component. As one lawyer recently wrote, "from the moment we lawyers enter our offices, until we turn off the lights at night, we deal with information." Information is the fundamental building block that is present and is the focus of attention at almost every stage of the legal process. Legal doctrine, for example, is information that is stored, organized, processed, and transmitted. Legal judgments are actions that involve obtaining information, evaluating it, storing it, and communicating it. Lawyers have expertise in and have control over a body of legal information. . . . Indeed, one way of understanding the legal process is to view information as being at its core and to see much of the work of participants as involving communication. In this process, information is always moving—from client to lawyer, from lawyer to jury, from judge to the public, from the public to the government, and so on. (Katsh 1995).

We can identify a historical analogy to the connections between legal institutions and lowered transactional costs.[7] Technologies accompanying the nineteenth century Industrial Revolution substantially reduced costs of communication and transportation, resulting in pressure for legal systems to standardize content and methods across local political boundaries. As commerce spread outward, more transactions were completed among strangers. People needed to rely on consistent, reliable overarching authority and frameworks as substitutes for the personal trust and traditional social controls of previous smaller-scale agrarian communities.

Legal systems responded to these socio-technical changes by centralizing their authority, regularizing their procedures, and homogenizing their regulation. In Anglo-American jurisprudence, what had been separate courts of Equity dispensing particularized justice were largely abolished during this period. Their principles became integrated (and subordinated) to the Common Law in a single, amalgamated legal system. Significantly, the law's image of human beings also homogenized. Kantian views from the eighteenth and early nineteenth century were embraced, constructing a more abstracted humanity that came to be associated with liberal ideals of formally equal respect and dignity, coupled with strong notions of legal duty, individual choice, and accountability.[8] And just as industrial technology enabled a vision of more standardized, mass-produced products radiating outward in almost unlimited geographic scope toward increasingly homogeneous consumers, so also with legal systems: they centralized and standardized their techniques while homogenizing their vision of human beings.

Arguably the law conformed itself to the needs of a new era by mimicking the methods of the emergent technology. Legal systems and industrial economies co-evolved; indeed, they became vaguely isomorphic in their structures, methods of production and distribution, and even standardization of human composition and expectations (Hadfield 2017). But as Gillian Hadfield observes, that era has been eclipsed by the complexity of the Information society: legal frameworks "stagnated in the twentieth century," being "well designed for the nation-based mass-

[7] Although I develop the analogy between the Industrial Revolution and the Information Age, we might have looked to an earlier example suggested by M. Ethan Katsh. The invention of the printing press enabled a systematization of information which spawned dramatic changes in legal systems. Katsh summarizes:

> The embodiment of law in printed form did not simply replace law in [handwritten] form. Rather, it replaced a system of dispute resolution that had often involved written law and oral tradition working together. Printed law, therefore, emphasized decision making according to rules more than some previous systems because attention was focused on rules in a way that had not occurred earlier. In this respect, it is important to recognize that print also brought about a narrowing of the judge's focus. Judges in earlier periods had been able at times to escape rule-oriented decisions because their attention was not bound to a printed or even a written text. They had options that were not available to later generation of judges whose decision had to be made "by the book." (Katsh 1989)

[8] "Kant held that free will is essential; human dignity is related to human agency, the ability of humans to choose their own actions." https://en.wikipedia.org/wiki/Dignity#Kant.

manufacturing economy but badly out of step with the digitized, global environment we now inhabit. . . . [O]ur mechanisms for creating and implementing law . . . are not up to the task." (Hadfield 2017)

Nearly two hundred years following the Industrial Revolution's reductions of transportation and communication costs—thereby spawning profound structural changes in social institutions—we watch the arrival of the digital age with its powerful reductions in information costs. As developed below, this immense breakthrough in the availability and processing of data can be felt in the law through the possibilities for stronger *predictability* of future events; finer *granularity* of analysis in individual cases; more *interactional* capabilities with the users of legal rules and institutions; and broader *remedial and regulatory reach*. Just as the Industrial Revolution prompted changes in legal institutions and outlook on human beings, so also does the Information Age reveal the need for compatible reforms of legal systems and its Enlightenment construction of humanity.

First, however, we can take the historical analogy between industrial innovation and the law one step further. Recall that by the dawn of the twentieth century industrial commerce came to threaten its own viability and social acceptance through the unchecked growth of exploitative monopolies and robber-baron run "trusts." Eventually, Progressive Era antitrust regulation like the Sherman and Clayton Acts tempered these excesses, enabling a steadier, more accountable, and more trusted commercial life for everyday people. And so also now: explosive growth of largely unregulated AI—and especially algorithms propelled by machine learning—could threaten not only individuals and historically disadvantaged groups but also the social trust underpinning social acceptance of AI. If AI is to advance without potentially dramatic popular backlash, it should partner with the law to govern its own methods. And conversely, if law is to improve its problem-solving capabilities, it should embrace some of the methods of emergent technologies.

3 Tools for Mutual Support Between Law and AI

As stated in the Introduction, contemporary legal systems and algorithmic technology each face challenges of competency and cultural acceptability, although stemming from different sources. These challenges may at least partially be addressed through a judicious use of one another's tools. Through requiring thoughtfulness and experimentation, the law could tighten social confidence in AI by formalizing a combination of *ex ante* industry standards for its design and *post hoc* legal monitoring of algorithmic outcomes (Kroll 2018). Reciprocally, through its powers of pattern recognition, probabilistic assessment, and closer particularity of analysis, AI could extend the law's capabilities in preventing or resolving complex, elusive problems. I have written previously about those challenges (Barton 2016, 2020), so the issues are only briefly summarized below.

3.1 Competency and Cultural Acceptance Challenges for Law and AI

Decision-making by judges shares some qualities with decisions made algorithmically. Both are governed by rules—precedent or statutes for the law, training set algorithms for AI. Yet the two realms obviously diverge significantly in processing methods and in public interface—creating distinctive competency and cultural acceptance challenges for both law and AI.

3.1.1 Legal Systems

The competency limitations of the law stem from the slowness of its processing, the limited variables it can consider, its inability to forecast alternate scenario outcomes, and the crudeness of its remedies. Our prevailing legal methods evolved to cope with the needs of an earlier era.[9] The courts and rule structures of Western legal systems are optimized for gathering evidence, making decisions, and remedying the sorts of problems that prevail in agrarian or industrial societies (Barton 2016, 2020). These problems tend to be structurally simple: disputes emerging from simple human relationships, involving issues resolvable with a binary decision and money compensation for contested ownership of property, contractual performance, or negligent behavior. Information Age problems, in contrast, often bear attributes of intricacy, geographic reach, volatility, or speed that surpass the decisional or remedial capabilities of our conventional legal systems (Barton 2016, 2020).

Not only structures and procedures, but conventional legal thinking itself may be better suited to fast-disappearing social and technical environments. Befitting the relatively simple composition of problems that fueled the evolution of our legal systems, traditional legal analysis tends to operate through sorting—stuffing a problem into one doctrine or remedy rather than another. Separation and distinctiveness characterize our traditional legal thinking. It is largely taxonomic—an exercise in proper classification and then applying the frames surrounding the boxes.

But modern environments and problems tend to be more ecological, enmeshed in fluid connections calling for ongoing mutual adjustments rather than singular binary judgments (Barton 2016, 2020). Simply put, legal problems are increasingly relational and systemic rather than transactional. The complexity and enduring volatility characterizing modern problems is more given to approaches of understanding and resolution through trade-offs among multiple variables—almost impossible to achieve using traditional litigation—and remedies based more on the sloping curves of gradual trends and accommodation than one-time transfers of money damages.

As to cultural acceptance, the law has strengths of transparency due to the relatively open, public nature of its rules and decision-making. However, on a

[9] "The accountability mechanisms and legal standards that govern such decision processes have not kept pace with technology. The tools currently available to policymakers, legislators, and courts were developed to oversee human decisionmakers and often fail when applied to computers instead." (Kroll et al. 2017).

practical level neither the content of the law nor the operations of its procedures are easily accessed, either intellectually or financially. In realms of law that affect large populations like consumer contract-making or marital dissolution and child custody, people have little choice but to make legally binding promises without reading or understanding what they sign or click-through, or to represent themselves in court without professional counsel and without a sense of how to structure an effective legal argument—often with highly disadvantageous outcomes.

Information Age data retrieval, processing, participation, and use are far more democratically inspired and personalized than the print technology employed by conventional legal systems (Katsh 1989). In print society, information is classified and sequenced expertly—and then handed down through authored books that frequently reference established disciplines. Readers are presented with curated associations of facts and ideas arranged by chapters. By contrast, in everyday use many digital platforms permit people to stitch together information according to their personal unstructured searches. The associations they make among the data are their own. Frequently, people interact socially with the information and are invited to contribute to, or at least publicly rate, the content. Individuals may cut and paste ideas and images across sources as they choose and easily share their re-arrangements with others. It is an "open" system, inviting participation and creativity (Lessig 2001).

Legal systems, by contrast, are largely closed to non-professionals. The orientation toward information inside legal systems remains rooted in print culture, even if now usually presented in electronic formats. The ideas are strongly established in categories and rules. The vocabulary is dense and often inaccessible. Creativity and effective interaction with the material is limited for those who lack legal training. Attempts at self-interpretation or contribution invite failure in any formal encounter with legal institutions. Contrasted with the open system of the Internet, the law is an expert system that discourages participation or even social connection. In its style of public communication and imposition of hierarchical authority, the law may increasingly appear remote, elitist, or serving largely the interests of the powerful.

3.1.2 Algorithms

In contrast to conventional legal methods, AI is capable of almost unimaginable speed of processing, can correlate/optimize the interaction of hundreds of distinct variables in scenario-testing and generate iterative resolutions gradually refined by multiple ongoing feedback loops. As developed below, such strengths could naturally address some of the decisional and remedial shortcomings of conventional legal systems. Yet algorithms lack common sense, an intuitive sense of context, and self-reflectiveness on normative ends or human aspiration—all strengths of legal systems.

The competency and public acceptance challenges for AI tend to be overlapping. On the one hand the computing power and impersonality of AI can be admired; but on the other hand, many reports have now circulated referencing algorithms that produce discriminatory results, or outcomes that appear naïve in their inability to perceive factual or relational contexts that are immediately intuited by humans.

Understandably, competency criticisms as well as acceptance qualms are leveled at AI based on instances of reliance on databases infected by decades of structural racism or misogyny; lack of transparency of decisional process; perceived arbitrariness; coder bias; or the significant invasions of privacy or surveillance that could be required to improve the decisional quality of algorithmic decision-making.

3.2 Incorporating AI Tools into Law, and Vice-Versa

Incorporating some AI techniques into legal systems, and subjecting AI to a systemic mixture of *ex ante* regulation and *post hoc* accountability could potentially address many of these competency and cultural acceptability challenges. But mutual borrowing of each other's tools is not without risks. Legal systems could expand their capabilities through incorporating AI tools into some of its evidence gathering, assessment, and supervision of remedies; and yet the shortcomings of algorithmic assessments are especially sensitive when applied in governmental settings.[10] Our official public normative realm is constructed, in part, explicitly to combat some of these very issues of discrimination and unaccountable decision-making or exercises of power to which AI is vulnerable. Reciprocally, the competency of AI can be enhanced through a variety of legal oversight measures that can promote social trust in algorithmic methods—with the caveat that AI development should not be suffocated by regulatory mandates seeking total risk elimination or divulgence of trade secret detail.[11]

In looking through the suggested possibilities below, I note how each is directed either to the *environments* in which the decisional methods are formulated or applied; or to assessing or rectifying the *outcomes* of the decisions. Each also demonstrates a commensurate softening of one of more Enlightenment principles

[10]Hannah Bloch-Wehba, for example, lists a variety of current governmental uses of algorithms but adds a cautionary note:

> Government decision-making is increasingly automated. Cities use machine-learning algorithms to track gunshots, determine where to send police on patrol, and fire ineffective teachers. State agencies use algorithms to predict criminal behavior, interpret DNA evidence, and allocate Medicaid benefits. Courts decide, using "decision-support" tools, whether a suspect poses a risk, eligibility for pretrial release, and how harsh a sentence to impose. The federal government uses algorithms to put individuals on immigrant and terrorist watchlists, make policy decisions about whether and how to change Social Security, and catch tax evaders. … But increasing automation may also make government less participatory and open to public oversight and input. (Bloch-Wehba 2020) (citations omitted).

[11]"[T]ransparency may be undesirable because it defeats the legitimate protection of consumer data, commercial proprietary information, or trade secrets." (Kroll et al. 2017) Furthermore, such disclosure is not necessarily required for adequate accountability: "Disclosure of source code is often neither necessary (because of alternative techniques from computer science) nor sufficient (because of the issues analyzing code) to demonstrate the fairness of a process." Id.

regarding individual choice, formal equality, and the reluctance to articulate ultimate social ends.

3.2.1 AI Tools for Legal Systems

Legal systems could benefit from the probabilistic *predictive* powers of AI; its fine *granularity* of analysis that could apply the law more justly to individual cases; its enhanced capabilities of *informational interface* with legal users; and its *iterative* powers based on ongoing feedback or incorporation of internet data-streams.

The predictive power of AI has the potential to bring a previously uncertain future into more immediate view, like a telescope. The granularity potential works more like a microscope, bringing details invisible to the human eye into workable range. The interactional capabilities permit personalization of information through guided electronic "wizards" and hyperlinks to everyday language explanations and practical advice. And the iterative ability gives courts the option to administer and enforce long-term remedies or regulation. All four powers may work to address competency or cultural challenges to traditional legal systems.

3.2.1.1 Enhanced Predictive Capabilities: Quantifying Risks

Bringing the future into closer view through probabilistic prediction could make the law simpler and make human interactions more malleable toward preventing problems.[12] Public regulation could thereby become more targeted and effective—a topic addressed further below. Another example, however, reveals a different effect. Applied to contracting environments, AI augmentations can far better identify the probability of risks and their likely costs. Once such potential costs are identified, they can be incorporated into negotiations surrounding the contract price. Functionally, that removes these risks from the need to draft elaborate disclaimer or liquidated damages clauses surrounding those risks. The contract price simply takes the risks into account probabilistically, even if the future does not always fully unfold as expected. This permits legal simplification, and therefore also contract simplification.

Much of the complexity and obtuseness of contracting stem not from the terms of the actual economic exchange, but rather from the self-protective *legal* clauses addressing risks that have historically been difficult to quantify or monetize. Faced with ignorance about the scope of various future risks, lawyers have drafted escape and limitation clauses for their clients—which add to the length and legalese of the agreement. Where, however, the incidence and likely costs of risks are available to both contracting parties at the formation stage of contracting, they can simply adjust the contract consideration accordingly—and dispense with much of contract language that is included more to prevail in possible litigation rather than to advance the

[12] Addressing risks while environments are still shapeable—to prevent risks turning into actual injuries or other more serious problems—has long been the domain of "Preventive Law" or "Proactive Law" as it is known in Europe. *See, e.g.*, Brown (1950), Barton (2009) and Berger-Walliser (2012). AI-enabled predictions could greatly assist in discerning risks and enabling early interventions to avert problems as they become more foreseeable.

transaction. Where future environments are better understood, prospective risk mitigation is less needed.

Replacing guesswork and the need for downside insurance protection in contracting does not meaningfully reduce human choice or freedom; it simply extends the realm of potential human rationality by reducing uncertainty and the need for detail. That said, a strong caveat should be registered: we should not allow AI probabilistic predictability to lull us into normative laziness. We can analogize to autonomous self-driving vehicles for an illustration of this danger. The algorithms literally driving such cars do so by anticipating needs for steering, braking, etc. through constant environmental interaction. It brings risks forward to the present, into the realm of what can be averted automatically while the environment is still malleable. Yet such cars are also highly likely to make the human operators of such cars less attentive. They will take their eyes off the road. That will generally be fine in the largely non-normative spaces of our highways. But in the legal space especially, we should not allow AI probability to lull our normative attention. AI prediction has the potential to make more of life *seem* inevitable—painting vividly the ways things are (even though particular instances of the various phenomena have not yet occurred), and thus not the sorts of matters with which humans should tinker (Barton 2020). At its core, the law is about our normative self-governance—about what *ought* to be for ourselves and how to achieve it peaceably and fairly. We must not abdicate moral responsibility in an algorithmic society.

3.2.1.2 Enhanced Particularity: Distinguishing Risks

The AI literature is rife with instances in which the algorithms designed for the legal space have operated clumsily or discriminatorily. But with stronger self-consciousness of these problems, AI's granular analytical capabilities may find instances in which formally equal, standardized treatment of people could be *improved upon*. Hannah Bloch-Wehba offers an example, pertaining to alternatives to criminal bail system based on posting cash bonds. Even though algorithmic risk assessment about potential criminality has historically produced some discriminatory outcomes she describes such instruments as:

> [holding] substantial promise to reduce overincarceration by making more accurate decisions about who poses a potential risk to society. This need is particularly pronounced in the contexts of pretrial release and bail: many pretrial detainees are at low risk of committing violent offenses if they are released. Detaining individuals simply because they cannot afford to pay bail is unjust, unconstitutional, and expensive. (Bloch-Wehba 2020)

Enhanced granularity of data may, in other words, permit some appropriate individuation of legal treatment, just as AI-enabled personalized medicine offers the prospect of more effective health treatment. Algorithms raise the prospect for achieving better justice by understanding differences—i.e., that not all those who stand before a particular law do so equally—and then treating those persons differently. The Enlightenment principle of formal equality could thereby soften: do we secure better justice by imagining all persons to be equal and treating them (theoretically) alike? Or instead, do we act more justly by acknowledging unequals as such, and then treating them *unequally*? That question is beyond the scope of this Chapter, but it is worth noting that stronger technological capabilities not infrequently have the effect of forcing ethical decisions on issues that previously lay fallow, beyond human reach. A justice of sameness may be our heritage—even an Enlightened one—but it no longer is our inevitable future. Better data make possible a different sort of justice; we should consider its possibilities.

3.2.1.3 Enhanced Interactional Capabilities: Empowering Law's Users

Contracting can also illustrate the interactional capabilities of AI, and how the law could use them to help address the law's cultural acceptance challenge. The example below is taken from everyday consumer contracting, increasingly accomplished by "click-through" approvals to electronic contracts dozens of pages long (Kim 2019). Just as legal *procedures* evolved to deal with problems of relatively simple socio-economic structure, so also nineteenth century classical contract law *rules* were formulated by imagining two autonomous, self-maximizing individuals who were free, and authorized, to parry offers with counteroffers and who were thereby accountable for their promises.

Many contemporary consumer contracting environments, however, are hopelessly non-negotiable, with one party being presented a long, dense document with vocabulary and concepts that untrained people cannot understand. Many people do not bother to read the contractual agreements they make because they would not understand them anyway; and even if they did and objected to a clause it may well be difficult to find a person within the issuing organization with authority to change the provision. Most often, people just click-through, agreeing unwittingly to provisions like compulsory arbitration of disputes or threatened payment of punishing liquidated damages for posting criticisms of the services they receive under the agreement.

The law moves timidly in permitting people to escape such contracts, perhaps fearing the limits of its own administrative ability to oversee the content of every consumer agreement. The law typically settles instead for one-size-fits-all Enlightenment logic that upholds the agreement. Apart from some exceptional incapacity, people are deemed rational, free to bargain or walk away, and under a duty to read the documents they sign. Hence, they must honor their agreements, with the law paying homage to an ethereal ideal of individual choice.

But suppose that an AI-enabled tool was available to consumers, enabling them to review contracts instantly for any provisions that are likely significantly adverse to their interests—and suggest alternative language to force genuine negotiation or a create a forum for shared information? (Barton 2020) Contract review software exists for professionals[13] and could arrive soon for consumer use.[14] (Semmler and

[13] Examples include Law Geex (www.lawgeex.com/platform and Legal Sifter (www.legalsifter.com.

[14] Sean Semmler and Zeeve Rose describe "Beagle," one such software development effort:

Rose 2017) Used thoughtfully, AI can reshape informational environments to make individual choice more plausible as well as culturally attractive. That said, we should keep in mind that balanced contract negotiations are limited by the potential for exercises of self-interested power. Knowing what is customary or just is not enough, by itself, to ensure a fair contract for both parties. That is another reason why the emergence of AI should not lull us into normative nonchalance.

3.2.1.4 Iterative AI: Extending the Reach of Remedies and Regulation

As with much in the AI/Law interface, automated decision-making can both challenge and assist legal remedies and regulation.[15] The iterative qualities of algorithms—their capacity to self-respond through machine learning and adaptation to changing environments through ongoing internet inputs—create more moving targets and networked relationships that are difficult to bring under regulatory or injunctive control. Conversely, AI may offer legal systems better calibration or management of that same public regulation monitoring or long-term remedies. In any context in which the law needs ongoing information updates or requires ongoing remedial supervision, legal systems could be made more accurate, responsive, and efficient through partnering with AI systems. Receiving such external "advice" electronically is not a radical procedural move; courts routinely look to human special masters to gather facts and present recommendations to judges.

In transitioning to the final section below on how the law may effectively oversee and assist AI, Mark Lemley and Bryan Casey reflect nicely on the connections between AI and human remedy. Their passage echoes the broader themes of this Chapter about humanizing the law through greater realism, equality, and articulation of explicit ends:

> Beagle is an A.I. tool for contract review that is primarily targeted at non-lawyers. Beagle is designed for users who need to review and manage contracts, but lack the expertise to do it themselves or the money to hire an attorney. First, users upload their contracts to the platform. Then, the natural language processing system identifies key clauses for review. This is done by identifying which clauses are used most often (for the type of contract at hand) and analyzing how this contract deviates from the norm. It also has a built-in communication system where users can interact with each other and discuss their documents. In addition to the system's ability to learn from the individuals who use the tool, the system is able to learn the personal preferences of different users, and incorporate those preferences in future documents. (Semmler and Rose 2017)

[15]Concerning regulation, David Freeman Engstrom and Daniel E. Ho capture both the challenge and the potential:

> First, the new algorithmic enforcement tools hold important implications for the accountability of agency enforcement activities. It remains unclear whether the new tools will *degrade* or *enhance* legal and political accountability relative to the status quo. On the one hand, the technical opacity and "black box" nature of the more sophisticated AI-based tools may erode overall accountability by rendering agency enforcement decisions even more inscrutable than the human judgments of dispersed agency enforcement staff. But the opposite might also prove true: formalizing and making explicit agency priorities could render an agency's enforcement decision making relatively more tractable compared to pools of agency enforcement staff. (Engstrom and Ho 2020)

> A final lesson is that our legal system sweeps some hard problems under the rug. We don't tell the world how much a human life is worth. We make judgments on that issue every day, but we do them haphazardly and indirectly, often while denying we are doing any such thing. We make compromises and bargains in the jury room, awarding damages that don't reflect the actual injury the law is intended to redress but some other, perhaps impermissible consideration. And we make judgments about people and situations in- and outside of court without articulating a reason for it, and often in circumstances in which we either couldn't articulate that decision-making process or in which doing so would make it clear we were violating the law. We swerve our car on reflex or instinct, sometimes avoiding danger but sometimes making things worse. We don't do that because of a rational cost-benefit calculus, but in a split-second judgment based on imperfect information. Police decide whether to stop a car, and judges whether to grant bail, based on experience, instinct, and bias as much as on cold, hard data.
>
> Robots expose those hidden aspects of our legal system and our society. A robot can't make an instinctive judgment about the value of a human life, or about the safety of swerving to avoid a squirrel, or about the likelihood of female convicts reoffending compared to their male counterparts. If robots have to make those decisions--and they will, just as people do--*they will have to show their work.* And showing that work will, at times, expose the tolerances and affordances our legal system currently ignores. That might be a good thing, ferreting out our racism, unequal treatment, and sloppy economic thinking in the valuation of life and property. Or it might be a bad thing, particularly if we have to confront our failings but can't actually do away with them. It's probably both. But whatever one thinks about it, robots make explicit many decisions our legal system and our society have long decided not to think or talk about. For that, if nothing else, remedies for robots deserve serious attention (Lemley and Casey 2019).

3.2.2 Legal Tools to Improve AI

Applying traditional legal oversight or assessment tools to algorithms and their results will be difficult. The very qualities of AI that give it breakthrough effectiveness—the elusiveness of its pattern recognition process across millions of datapoints, constant iterative refinement, uneven dataset quality, and unpredictability of contextual blind-spots—all test the effectiveness of potential legal regulation.[16] As suggested above, our heritage legal procedures respond to far simpler problem structures. Further, our various traditional categories of legal thought—tools available for *ex post* oversight like tort, products liability, breach of contract, property, nuisance law—seem slightly out of fit, applicable to AI control more by analogy than directly.[17]

[16] "AI causes unpredictable injuries because of its ability to exhibit surprising behavior, also known as emergent behavior, which is itself a product of AI's aforementioned ability to learn rules from training data autonomously. . . . As AI grows even more sophisticated, it will even become difficult to fix or understand AI behavior ex post facto." (Yoshikawa 2019) (citations omitted).

[17] Jin Yoshikawa, for example, details legal clumsiness and inadequacy in addressing injuries based on doctrines of tortious design; tortious use; strict liability for design defects; and public regulation applied to specific industries or generalized AI application (the author calls for no-fault social insurance against AI injuries) (Yoshikawa 2019). Balkin, however, holds out more hope for the application by analogy of nuisance, fiduciary concepts, and pollution control (Balkin 2017).

Creative ideas for the effective regulation and oversight of algorithmic determinations are proliferating, and we should look forward to thoughtful experimentation. Rather than expand on particular proposals I offer three general parameters that might help guide fitting AI better into a Law/AI framework. First: keep the focus on the design environment (including the quality of databases) and its outcomes, rather than the actual code and opaque processing. Second: be systemic, following the vision of Joshua A. Kroll and colleagues who advocate a looping and iterative feedback between *ex ante* regulation and *ex post* impact oversight. Finally, create structural "second look" capabilities that are accessible to all persons or groups who may be affected by algorithmic decisions—even in the form of newly resurrected formal, separate Courts of AI Equity. I address each parameter in greater detail below.

3.2.2.1 Focus More on Design Environment and Outcomes, Than Code

Underpinning much of this Chapter is a premise: that the locus of social action is gradually moving outward in opposite directions from individual decision-making. Social action is moving upstream from personal choice into more strongly channeling environments, and downstream to the differential impacts of outputs. The law, I contend, can ironically become more human by paying closer attention to the entire river rather than focusing strongly on bends in the middle. In applying law to algorithmic design and application, look at the people designing the algorithmic environment and the social results of those algorithms—not just the actual code and its processing. "The simplest way to understand a piece of technology is to understand what it was designed to do, how it was designed to do that, and why it was designed in that particular way instead of some other way." (Kroll 2018)

Legal responsibility thus may be more reachable and effectively realized through considering the people at either end of design or result, than by trying to unlock the actual machine learning.

> Data-driven systems, like all human-programmed software systems, involve choices and assumptions in their creation, which circumscribe how the system's authors intend the system to function. Responsibility and ethics attach not to the specifics of a technical tool, but rather to the ways that tool is used in a sociotechnical context, which are always considered when tools are created (Kroll 2018).

3.2.2.2 Building an Integrated, Iterative System of Ex Ante and Ex Post Measures

As stated by Joshua A. Kroll and colleagues, "accountability must be part of the system's design from the start. Designers of such systems, and the nontechnical stakeholders who often oversee or control system design, must begin with oversight and accountability in mind." (Kroll et al. 2017). Their approach is certainly to employ both *ex ante* and *ex post* legal features, but not to silo each. Instead, the algorithmic design process should be systemically integrated with its intended goals through mandated feedback and testing.

For example, Kroll et al. recommend that before code-writing even begins, the software creators should devise tests which they can eventually use to measure how well their algorithm is functioning *before* release, and its performance and consequences *following* release. These tests, and the reasoning behind their creation, should be mandated and preserved for later scrutiny against a legal standard of malpractice or action as an information fiduciary (Kroll 2018; Balkin 2017).

Such tests illustrate their larger point of merging *ex ante* and *ex post* measures. They "describe how technical tools for verifying the correctness of computer systems can be used to ensure that appropriate evidence exists for later oversight," tools which include software verification, cryptographic commitments, zero-knowledge proofs, and fair random choices (Kroll et al. 2017). Another such tool, "prospective benchmarking," is described by David Freeman Engstrom and Daniel E. Ho: "By requiring agencies to reserve a random set of cases for manual decision making, benchmarking offers a concrete and accessible test of the validity and legality of machine outputs, enabling agencies, courts, and the public to learn about, validate, and correct errors in algorithmic decision making." (Engstrom and Ho 2020) Yet another tool is "near neighbor analysis"—looking humanly at the next highest-scoring outcomes of an algorithmic question to compare against the top-scoring alternative, which may reveal some important contextual feature that was missed by the top-scoring outcome and resulted in a socially naïve or obviously clumsy conclusion[18] (Lau and Biedermann 2020). As with the test used for initial algorithmic design, the effectiveness of these tools for legal accountability turns on mandating record-keeping and contemporaneous reflections as the design is created, and hopefully improved through ongoing impact assessment.

The integrated approach combining various legal doctrines addressing a range of systemic entry points—human and digital, *ex ante* and *ex* post—has been addressed by other writers. Pagallo, for example, suggests a comprehensive system that includes applying liability norms to AI producers; mandating design parameters for AI that prevents abuse by the *users* of AI; regulating recognition of the legal effectiveness of problematic AI outputs; and insertion of "normative constraints into design" of the algorithms (Pagallo 2018). Kroll concludes:

> [D]emands for transparency must cover the entire design process: how were requirements determined? By whom were requirements determined? Were alternatives considered? Which ones? Why were they rejected? Was a particular negative outcome under scrutiny a property of only some alternatives, or was it a necessary consequence of the system however it was designed? How do we know that the system in practice satisfies the requirements that were established for it? (Kroll 2018)

[18]Effective "near neighbor analysis," say Lau and Biedermann, should address two distinct algorithmic determinations: "identification," which pertains to whether the algorithm has built proper classifications; and "individuation," which pertains to whether it has fit particular data properly within those categories. They write: "Underlying identification is the assumption of likeness, meaning that objects can be categorized together based on the existence of a common set of properties. In contrast, underlying individualization is the assumption of discernible and ascertainable uniqueness." (Lau and Biedermann 2020)

3.2.2.3 Building in Second Looks to the Legal System

"Systems become trustworthy because of how they are validated and how that validation is verified either directly to end users or indirectly through governance bodies." (Kroll 2018). In the first two subsections above we considered technical aspects of validating algorithmic systems and their public verification. This final section of the Chapter suggests a highly *non*-technical tool that speaks directly to individuals or groups who allege error or grievance surrounding an automated algorithmic decision. I propose at least exploring the idea of resurrecting formal, separate courts of equity for the sole purpose of offering a judicial "second look" at algorithmic outcomes.

This may sound radical or wildly expensive, but it need not be either. First, some U.S. state-level equity courts have survived the general nineteenth century merger of the common law and equity court systems, their functions preserved by state constitutions or "statutorily-empowered masters."[19] These courts preserve the flavor and methods of historic equity or "chancery" courts, which were originally designed for cases in which applying Common Law rules would be unjust. That is precisely the argument for the resurrection of such courts, in the form of an AI Court of Equity: to review matters in which adequate justice may not be secured through an algorithm.

The following description of equity court powers and methods may be especially helpful for readers accustomed to Civil Law, rather than Common Law, traditions. Noah J. Gordon in Texas Jurisprudence, 3rd edition writes:

> [C]ourts of equity are not bound by cast-iron rules but are governed by flexible rules that adapt themselves to particular exigencies so that relief will be granted whenever, in view of all the circumstances, to deny it would permit one party to suffer a gross wrong at the hands of another. In contemplation of exercising its traditional equitable powers, a court must weigh several factors to determine whether a party's request for equitable relief should be granted, including the probability of irreparable damage to the moving party in the absence of relief, the possibility of harm to the nonmoving party if the requested relief is granted, and the public interest.
>
> Courts possess broad equitable powers and the discretion to grant relief against grave injustice in cases where no specific procedure has been provided, and the courts exercise broad discretion in balancing the equities in cases seeking equitable relief. Equitable relief is not mandatory because the expediency, necessity, or propriety of such relief is committed to the trial court's discretion, which is reviewed for an abuse of discretion. (Gordon 2021 update) (citations omitted).

An AI Court of Equity could be constructed to require threshold standards of a *prima facie* showing of likely error or harm, to avoid the court being deluged by dubious claims. It could be staffed by judges with a basic, but not necessarily expert,

[19]S.C. Code Ann. §§ 14-11-10, 14-11-15 (Law. Co-op. Supp. 1992), as amended, "Establishment of Master-in-Equity Court." Corpus Juris Secundum, CJS EQUITY § 41: "A state constitution may also be a source of a particular court's equity powers, in which case the courts' equitable authority cannot be diminished by statute."

understanding of AI operations. They would not be bound to specific rules, nor would their judgments be part of *stare decisis*. The judges would instead be alert to exceptional cases in which an AI determination has somehow overlooked important contextual issues, or employed databases foreordained to conclusions that play out historical patterns of economic, gender, or racial inequality. The judges could be empowered to render broad, flexible equitable remedies that might require a defendant to consult with court-appointed technical experts, or encourage co-operative relationships between contesting parties to improve the software.

How does a judge think or speak, if not necessarily bound to the consistency of legal rules? That idea may frighten some, but modern precedents can be found. Recent analogues are the development of problem-solving courts devoted to issues arising out of drug addition, homelessness, or return from military service (Vigil 2016). Judges of those courts—typically diversions from traditional criminal courts where the defendant has pleaded guilty—sometimes dispense with conventional courtroom trappings or protocol like raised benches that convey detached authority. They are often forthrightly humanistic. Judges in such courts may speak ongoingly and directly with defendants and outside social support professionals, toward shared goals of solving chronic, systemic problems in the defendant's life.

Rather than working toward a judgment about the defendant, the judges of problem-solving courts seek a defendant's self-understanding, commitment to change, and possible transformation. The language may include vocabularies of forgiveness, mercy, acceptance, and redemption. The approach of problem-solving courts is not for wholesale adoption throughout a legal system; it typically proceeds after a defendant has accepted accountability for the defendant's behaviors. But as a part of a larger legal system, it offers a place where compassion and empathy toward human frailty seems especially fruitful as well as needed.

Problem solving courts and the AI Court of Equity proposed here can offer what another Enlightenment thinker, Adam Smith, advocated: a look at moral sentiments. The basic rules of prudence and justice are needed for social survival, wrote Smith, but beneficent actions will allow it to flourish.[20] We should not be so timid, or so lacking in self-confidence in our liberal social engagement, that we are embarrassed by public officials using language of moral exceptionalism in considering AI outcomes that do not seem to process adequately our social context, history, or larger goals. It may well be that we are out of practice in using such concepts, and that our vocabularies and analysis are thin. But the further the penetration of algorithmic decision-making in our lives, the stronger may be the need for such human voices to assert themselves.

[20]"[Adam Smith's] Theory Of Moral Sentiments was a real scientific breakthrough. It shows that our moral ideas and actions are a product of our very nature as social creatures. It argues that this social psychology is a better guide to moral action than is reason. It identifies the basic rules of prudence and justice that are needed for society to survive, and explains the additional, beneficent, actions that enable it to flourish." https://www.adamsmith.org/the-theory-of-moral-sentiments.

4 Conclusion

I spoke in the introduction of verbs, qualities, and language sets that formed my goals for a legal/AI framework: "A humanized legal/AI framework should listen as well as command; explain as well as direct; inspire as well as constrain. It is competent, trustworthy, and fair. It speaks with words of humility and morality as well as authority." The tools of AI to augment legal systems and the reciprocal regulation and oversight by law of AI work toward qualities of competence, trustworthiness, and fairness. Creative AI-driven informational interfaces for legal users could explain and inspire, rather than merely direct and constrain. Finally, the proposed Court of AI Equity could speak in a different voice—with humility and morality.

The algorithmic society will not be turned back: it offers capabilities and efficiencies that humans will simply not refuse. The legal system cannot responsibly detach itself from this technology. To do so is to invite gradual cultural abandonment of legal methods, possibly even legal authority. The coming AI environment challenges legal systems in many ways, but its embrace offers opportunities for growth—both in the law itself and in human self-understanding. "[T]he next stage of history will include not only technological and organizational transformations, but also fundamental transformations in human consciousness and identity. And these could be so fundamental that they will call the term 'human' into question." (Harari 2015)

Even as we direct the law, it shapes us emotionally and morally as well as transactionally (White 1994). We need human environments and outputs to be evaluated against standards of justice that we specify: standards that are more realistic about history, enduring discrimination, and fair distributions of material well-being as well as opportunity. A legal/AI framework may bring the future forward for us, making it more malleable and purposeful within our conscious design.

Liquid Legal Waves to Other Chapters, Written by the Editors

Tom lays out the opportunity that comes with the integration of AI and the Law: a process of understanding social environments more realistically and designing them more deliberately. *Sven* and *Philipp* build on that and pursue the question if true digitalization will bring us closer to the vision of *"The Paradigm shift in AI: From Human Labor to Humane Creativity"*.

Tom's vision of designing social environments in a more ethical manner ties into a relationship of trust between the citizen and public authorities that *Ivar* and *Michiel* tackle in their chapter on *"Digitization of Government Services from the Citizen's Perspective - Putting Humans first"*.

In the upcoming chapter, *Wolfgang* discusses the thesis that in a digitized society, a society "imagined differently" (as *Tom* puts it), money may not be the sole medium of exchange. To truly unlock free capacity of work in society, security tokens may be the way to go: *"Value Creation Through Blockchain-based Tokens"*.

References

Balkin J (2017) 2016 Sidley Austin distinguished lecture on big data law and policy: the three laws of robotics in the age of big data. Ohio State Law J 78:1217–1214

Barton TD (2009) Preventive law and problem solving: lawyering for the future. Vandeplas, Lake Mary, Florida

Barton TD (2016) Re-designing law and lawyering for the information age. Notre Dame J Law Ethics Pub Policy 30:1–36

Barton TD (2020) Artificial intelligence: designing a legal platform to prevent and resolve legal problems. In: Jacob K, Schindler D, Strathausen R (eds) Liquid legal: toward a common platform, liquid legal institute. Springer, Switzerland

Berger-Walliser G (2012) The past and future of proactive law: an overview of the development of the proactive law movement. In: Berger-Walliser G, Ostergaard K (eds) Proactive law in a business environment. DJCF, Sweden

Bloch-Wehba (2020) Access to algorithms. Fordham Law Rev 88:1265–1314

Brown LM (1950) Preventive law. Greenwood, Westport, Conn

Burk DL (2021) Algorithmic legal metrics. Notre Dame Law Rev 90:1147–1203

Dignity. https://en.wikipedia.org/wiki/Dignity#Kant

Engstrom DF, Ho DE (2020) Algorithmic accountability in the administrative state. Yale Law J 37: 800–854

Froomkin AM (2015) Regulating mass surveillance as privacy pollution: learning from environmental impact statements. Univ Ill Law Rev 2015:1713–1790

Fuller LL (1965) Irrigation and tyranny. Stanford Law Rev 17:1021–1042

Hadfield GK (2017) Rules for a flat world: why humans invented law and how to reinvent it for a complex global economy. Oxford University Press

Harari YN (2015) Sapiens: a brief history of humankind. HarperCollins, New York

Katsh ME (1989) The electronic media and the transformation of law. Oxford University Press, Oxford

Katsh ME (1995) Law in a digital world. Oxford University Press, Oxford

Kim NS (2019) Consentability: consent and its limits. Cambridge University Press, Cambridge

Kroll J (2018) The fallacy of inscrutability. Philos Trans R Soc 376:20180084

Kroll J, Huey J, Barocas S, Felten EW, Reidenberg JR, Robinson DG, Yu H (2017) Accountable algorithms. Univ Pa Law Rev 165:633–705

Lau T, Biedermann E (2020) Assessing AI output in legal decision-making with nearest neighbors. Penn State Law Rev 124:609–653

Law Geex (www.lawgeex.com/platform

Legal Sifter (www.legalsifter.com

Lemley M, Casey B (2019) Remedies for robots. Univ Chic Law Rev 86:1311–1396

Lessig L (2001) The future of ideas: the fate of the commons in a connected world random house. New York

Pagallo U (2018) Apples, oranges, robots: four misunderstandings in today's debate on the legal status of AI systems. Philos Trans R Soc 376:20180168

Radavoi CN (2020) The impact of artificial intelligence on freedom, rationality, the rule of law and democracy: should we not be debating it? Tex J Civ Lib Civ Rights 25:107–129
Semmler S, Rose Z (2017) Artificial intelligence: application today and implications tomorrow. Duke Law Technol Rev 16:85–98
Skinner BF (1972) Beyond freedom and dignity. Bantam, New York
Strathausen (2020) Call for papers. In: Jacob K, Schindler D, Strathausen R (eds) Humanization and the law: a call to action for the digital age, liquid legal institute. Springer, Switzerland
White JB (1994) Imagining the law. In: Sarat A, Kearns TR (eds) The rhetoric of law. University of Michigan, Ann Arbor
Winfield AFT, Jirotka M (2018) Ethical governance is essential to building trust in robotics and artificial intelligence systems. Philos Trans R Soc 376:20180085
Yoshikawa J (2019) Sharing the costs of artificial intelligence: universal no-fault social insurance for personal injuries. Vanderbilt J Entertain Technol Law 21:1155–1187

Thomas D. Barton is Professor Emeritus of law at California Western School of Law in San Diego, California. He has taught Contract Law, Civil Procedure, Problem Solving and Preventive Law, Torts, and Intellectual Property and Technology. He writes and speaks broadly on topics concerning contracting, legal design, dispute prevention and resolution, and the influence of technology on legal systems. He is the author of the book PROBLEM SOLVING AND PREVENTIVE LAW: LAWYERING FOR THE FUTURE (2009).

Value Creation Through Blockchain-Based Tokens: Transforming Traditional Collaboration Structures

Wolfgang Richter and Sebastian Richter

Contents

Abstract

1. Money is viewed as a medium of exchange, a unit of account, and a store of value. This article focuses on the "store of value" and rephrases it as

Wolfgang Richter is Managing Partner of gunnercooke Germany.

Sebastian Richter is Professor for information systems at Baden-Wuerttemberg State University in Stuttgart, Germany.

W. Richter (✉)
Berlin, Germany
e-mail: wolfgang.richter@gunnercooke.de

S. Richter
Stuttgart, Germany
e-mail: sebastian.richter@dhbw-stuttgart.de

K. Jacob et al. (eds.), *Liquid Legal – Humanization and the Law*, Law for Professionals, https://doi.org/10.1007/978-3-031-14240-6_6

"representing potential futures". Assessing the buying power of one's money relies on the assumption that the person will be able to buy in the future what he or she can buy today. However, this notion does not consider the impact of an increase in buying potential (through rising productivity) or of a decrease (through external shocks and other structural changes).

2. In the case of external shocks such as the coronavirus crisis, attempts are made to mitigate the consequences by injecting liquidity into the hard-hit sectors. Yet, we are still faced with the internal devaluation dilemma: All long-term contracts, such as loans and rents, do not decrease even though the reduced payment capacity of the contractual partners requires a downward adjustment. It can take months or even years for such an adjustment to occur, at the cost of a tremendous loss of productivity, which is often accompanied by social unrest.
3. Digital units, which represent an underlying asset, share or right, the so-called "security tokens", have the same quality as a currency in regard to their immutability. Therefore, they can function like a currency in this respect. Compared to traditional legal instruments for organizing work products, a security token can very effectively and with no prohibitive contractual arrangements tie the success of a business project to the security token. This means that even an anonymous workforce can participate successfully in a business project and be remunerated by tokens. Today there are liquidity options available which give immediate liquidity to the security token. Security tokens can instigate the production of goods and services, thereby expanding the potential futures for everyone.
4. Such a (security) token economy allows for a fair platform economy as compared to traditional centralized platforms since the token governance and value distribution can be organized effectively through a token structure including all stakeholders in the process. Achieving the same result with the traditional legal and economic instruments is close to impossible.
5. Hence, such a security token economy is a valid option for implementation into the Common Legal Platform (CLP).

1 Money as a Store of Value or Representation of Potential Futures?

Any economic textbook bases money on three pillars: medium of exchange, unit of account, and store of value.[1] Medium of exchange refers to the convenience to exchange money, which is easy to transport and transfer, for goods and services.

[1] Schäfer (2013), p. 261.

Unit of account describes that money can be counted, compared and therefore reflects pricing. Store of value refers to that money received and held today will buy me goods and services tomorrow as it does today. This is also reflected in the standard description of the functions of money by any central bank. The concept is the basis for policy recommendations which obviously rest on different interpretations of those three pillars with the opposing positions of Keynesianism and monetarism[2] and all kinds of combinations thereof. Keynesianism rests on the assumption that government induced spending will trigger economic development, whereas monetarism sees the control of the supply of money as the appropriate public policy instrument. Our analysis, however, uses a different starting point and therefore gives a different perspective to policy recommendations.

At any given moment, we can find a set of goods and services to be allocated to the participants in the market, i.e. private individuals, corporations, the public sector. Allocation is a concept describing a specific set of decision-making power as to what exactly to do with the goods and services. The decision-making power is specified through the respective legal systems, depending largely on ownership structures on the one hand and decision rights of governments and administrations on the other.

In this decision-making system, money has a unique function. Everyone assumes that tomorrow my money will buy me the same as today: I pay the same for e.g. bread, a car or a trip with a taxi (if this assumption does not hold up, for instance in case of hyperinflation, the functions of money are impaired, since I might have to pay 100 EUR for my sandwich, I can buy today for 1 EUR; therefore, no store of value and no unit of account operates as the pricing system is off). Therefore, in the split-second right now, it actually does not matter what amount of money I have available, since I am simply stuck with the goods and services I have right now. Yet, in the next moment, it may matter a lot, depending on what kind of goods and services I want to acquire, and, as a reflection of this, I may have to pay others if I am indebted to them, which obviously then reduces my available cash (no bread, no car, no extra trip).

Even though this is a standard description and it easily can be subsumed under the category "store of value", our focus here is on the fact that the value of money

(a) depends on what others will actually be ready to exchange as goods or services for money (this includes concluding an agreement of receiving goods or services in the future); and
(b) what is actually available in terms of goods and services to non-prohibitive pricing, according to my own priorities.

[2] Kindleberger (2013), p. 11.

2 The Value of Money

From the perspective of everyone right now, the value of money is what we think we can buy with it in the future. Therefore, it actually represents potential futures, i.e. what we specifically can do when spending money. We think that rephrasing the term "store of value" into "representing potential futures" allows for a different view of what is actually going on since this allows a better look into what our current choices mean for our envisioned future. In fact, there are several decisions we are taking right now which are motivated by envisioning specific futures: for instance, spending quality time with friends in order to establish relationships which allow us in the future to do things we want to, calling them if we need help, going on vacation together, or simply having a good time. We all understand that money may play a role in this, such as when inviting friends to an excellent restaurant, and this may even be viewed as an investment, assuming that the favour will be returned. So, if we look at our activities throughout the day, there are usually many actions which have potential futures which are not represented by getting money in the pocket. Therefore, the question is what exactly is the role of money when we look at the decisions everyone makes throughout the day.

Obviously, each individual person will come up with a different answer, even when looking at his/her own decision-making, which is a mix of decisions about immediate consumption, saving, investing, paying into pension plans, charity, throwing parties, and so on. Here, we will only look at the decisions taken for value creation. We define value creation as any act which results in something for which somebody else is willing to pay for. This includes acts such as benefiting ourselves, which we otherwise would have to pay others to perform. However, the end result of the value creation is not necessarily something that immediately has a market value and can be monetized. For instance, if a group of software developers is working on an open-source project, there is value creation even though it may yet be unclear at which point the open-source software is workable and actually used in whatever kind of business or private process.

The link of value creation to potential futures is that the value creation is remunerated by receiving money, which therefore represents potential futures for the recipient. The work product may either be immediately consumed by the recipient, such as when cooking and serving the meal in the restaurant, or it may be a potential future for somebody else, such as growing corn on my land to sell it in autumn or producing a refrigerator ready to be sold within a month. This distinction is very important since actually the value immediately consumed does not represent any potential in the future. The money paid for it allows the recipient to enhance his or her potential futures but, all things being equal, if the meal in the restaurant would not have been served, the potential futures would be exactly the same. The only difference is that the decision-making about the future represented by the restaurant bill still rests with the guest and not with the restaurant owner.

Very often, guests will not make up for this later, since the moment of non-consumption has passed and they do not run a log taking account whether they have been to enough restaurants. In a situation like the coronavirus shutdown, it is clear that people simply will not make up for lost restaurant visits, vacation trips, etc. Therefore, all things being equal, the restaurant owner just has less potential futures, even though the capacity for the production of goods and services stays exactly the same. This means that, in competing for potential futures, the guest has the money not spent in the restaurant as an available amount. If the guest spends this amount in the future exactly like the restaurant owner would have, there would be no change in terms of the demand for goods and services and therefore no change in terms of inflationary or deflationary pressure on their pricing. Yet apparently, looking at the ongoing changes on our planet, it does make a big difference whether the guest or the restaurant owner holds the amount since this has different spending consequences in a very significant manner.

However, if we assume that suddenly nobody visits restaurants for an extended period of time and all restaurants have to shut down, then the potential future of going to restaurants has been substantially impaired. Therefore, it is clear that policy measures will be considered that would allow the restaurants to bridge the period of the shutdown and keep the restaurant future intact, as is the case with anything else that is considered a key community infrastructure to be supported by the public sector.

What this also shows is that potential futures are a fabric of the community. It is based on the assumption that, in the future, the seller of goods and services will in fact sell us the product or service that we want at a price that is acceptable to us. In turn, this clearly will only work if the seller, looking forward, also relies on others doing the same with his or her desires for the exchange of goods and services. Therefore, the entire system is based on a general assumption of the community: i.e. the community will stick to this kind of behaviour, expecting stability in exchange situations and always envisioning potential futures.

The widespread notion for guaranteeing such stability rests with the government and, even more so, with the central banks. Stability in this sense means keeping a set of circumstances which allow the community members to believe in having stabilized expectations in terms of what future exchange situations will look like. For this, the general assumption is that a mild inflation of for instance 2% per annum should be kept at any time and that, in light of external shocks such the coronavirus crisis or substantial structural issues, and presupposing a more or less Keynesian view, there should be state financed bridging and investment programs.

Given globalization, though, potential futures represented by currencies depend on the stability of exchange rates between various currencies. Their fluctuation against each other has an impact on the potential future of the participants in the respective currencies since goods and services out of trading with other currencies, i.e. other communities, will be either more expensive or cheaper. This then has an impact on the stability of expectations: for instance, what we will have to pay for electronic equipment or raw materials. The impact of this is apparent when looking at countries hit with hyperinflation, as this has an immediate cost-driving effect on all imported merchandise which, in turn, given the globalization, always represents a sizable part of individual spending in nearly any country.

In summary, it is fair to say that, within the global scientific community as well as the general public, the guardian for safekeeping the system of potential futures represented by currencies are the central banks and governments. It is an inherently public sector task with no governing or structural input by the private sector in terms of safeguarding such stability. Key to this is the notion that the public sector should control of the local currency and that no additional currency structures should be implemented.

This article has the objective to demonstrate that this commonly held notion is unfounded and limited.

3 What Is Available for Buying with Money

In our current state, we assume that in the future we can buy for our money what we could buy now. That is the only criteria that we have available, and so it seems as though we assume that in 10 years from now our money will buy us the same as today. However, we do have the actual problem that our potential future expectations will not take into account the rising productivity, external shocks such as the coronavirus crisis, external shocks through major climate changes, etc., so the potential deviation goes both ways: our money could buy us more or less in comparison to what we are expecting now. It may be less obvious to which degree the current expectations might be inaccurate in terms of how much specific products and services will cost in the future. But if we only go back 30 years and look at the costs and means of mobility and of communication, we see how both, products and services, have certainly increased tremendously in terms of quality and speed while at the same time decreasing considerably in terms of costs.[3]

In terms of building trust in our expected future options, which in turn conditions what we actually offer today, be it our workforce, merchandise, etc., the question is at what point should there be a community effort to cushion undesired effects of unexpected developments? Therefore, in terms of the restaurant example above, the question is whether there should be a community effort to support the restaurant owners by providing them at least some kind of compensation for the potential futures they have lost due to the shutdown of the business. Hence, the support could be motivated not only by criteria of social justice, but also by the desire to keep the restaurant infrastructure intact.

Obviously, the option for support is not limited to simple financing or subsidizing. It could also be a bonus program guaranteeing certain access to specific products or services in the future, tax subsidies, trade advantages, etc.

[3] Busse, Matthias (2002): *HWWA Discussion Paper Nr. 116*; Bundesverband der Deutschen Industrie (BDI); Außenwirtschafts-Report 04/2002.

4 The Internal Devaluation Dilemma

As the example of the coronavirus shutdown for restaurants shows, the crisis leads to a loss in the gross national product, not just a loss for the restaurant owner. Consequently, it also means less tax revenue for the public sector.[4] The effect to note here is that this happens although the capacity for the production of goods and services in the future is not diminished (disregarding the element of the potential restaurant infrastructure). In other words, we have the same potential futures for the community available. They are simply distributed differently between the community members. Yet the *intuitive understanding* is that there is actually a loss of potential futures because the reduced gross national product seems to indicate this result. However, it is probably fair to say that within the economist's prevailing views, this consequence is correctly described as the part that consumption plays in the gross national product, i.e. as a key driver of the economy. For instance, the gross national product in Germany depends on consumption by approximately 70%.[5]

It is naturally of prime importance to hold unemployment to a minimum. Notwithstanding the undesired results of personal hardship, social unrest, overextended states transferring payments, etc., we want to focus on the fact that unemployment actually limits the overall available potential futures. The immediate effect is that the unemployed simply do not contribute anything to the community in terms of offering services and therefore potential futures but, even more importantly, the more pressing issue is the unresolved structural challenge of moving the workforce to areas where there is a demand for their potential performance.

In this article, we define "unemployment" in a broader sense. It is not just the formally registered unemployed worker but also refers to anybody's free capacity for producing goods and services. Examples of this include programming work by a software developer in the evening after finishing the day job, local community support of by housemen/housewives or pensioners, and so on. Therefore, in the following we will also refer to "unemployment" as "free capacity".

The difficulty is that structural unemployment and unemployment as a result of external shocks are placed into a situation in which the ongoing pricing environment cannot be adjusted immediately, due to long-term contracts and obligations in place. Hence, the loans both to producers of goods and services as well as to consumers stay the same, rents are not adjusted automatically, and any long-term contractual obligations stay the same. Such external shocks therefore lead to immediate winners and losers. Basically, anybody on the receiving end of future cash flows is a winner, and the ones that have not been able to sell their performance, such as the restaurant owner, are the losers. For this analysis, we look strictly at the right to claim potential

[4] Gewerbesteuereinnahmen im Jahr 2020. Pressemitteilung (6. Oktober 2021). In: Statistisches Bundesamt (Destatis), Nr. 469.

[5] Bruttoinlandsprodukt für Deutschland. In: Statistisches Bundesamt (Destatis), Begleitmaterial zur Pressekonferenz am 14. Januar 2021 "Anteile der Wirtschaftszweige an der Bruttowertschöpfung in Deutschland im Jahr 2020.", p. 11.

futures in the future. Under the assumption that the overall potential futures are not impaired, the receivers of cash are facing less competition and will therefore have better choices. Even though the recipients of future cash flows seem to be on the winning end, it is clear that they also lose out in the long term. This is because their contractual partner might not be able to meet his or her obligations and, in any case, the next time such a contract is up for negotiation, it will have a less favourable result for the recipient.

As everyone can see, policymakers are well aware of this effect. Therefore, in order to deal with the consequences of the coronavirus shutdown, legislation has been put in place which allows borrowers and tenants to not have to meet their contractual payment obligations.[6] This is the case in Germany, for instance.

Contrary to the financial crisis of 2008, there was an almost general consensus on how to deal with the coronavirus crisis: namely, by "anaesthetising" the economy with an injection of a large amount of money (aid funds), partly in the form of non-repayable loans and partly in the form of loans to be repaid. The economic crisis caused by Corona was not a crisis of the financial system, like the one in 2008, but a sudden and extraordinary suspension of demand caused by the confinements and, later, by the restrictions imposed on mobility, social activities, etc. In any case, the injection of money will have enormous consequences for the public accounts of EU countries in the coming years. Yet, the policy options are regularly analysed as if it were a financial crisis and therefore lead to improper suggestions.

The end result, caused by market developments or parliament and/or government intervention, is what is called internal devaluation. This describes the fact that the value of goods and services expressed in prices is being reduced. The issue is discussed in relation to the exchange rate of currencies and the question whether one currency should maintain a specific exchange rate supported by government and central bank actions, with the consequences that prices have to be adjusted domestically by internal devaluation.[7] The situation has been intensely analysed by looking at policy options such as those related to Greece in the debt crisis of 2010 onwards.[8]

The difficulty with internal devaluation is that it is a slow and painful process because the pricing environment has to be adjusted contrary to ongoing contracts. Yet, socially speaking, violating ongoing contracts is not a desirable process, given all the conflict potential raised by it as well as the slowness in moving the unused resources into productive activities. Therefore, it is extremely important to employ strategies that avoid stressful internal devaluation processes. Obviously, government intervention in terms of contractual payment obligations, if at all, should be only used in extreme situations since, again, it does not stabilize expectations in terms of our contractual environment. We do not want to see the result that contractual terms

[6]Gesetz zur Abmilderung der Folgen der COVID-19-Pandemie im Zivil-, Insolvenz- und Strafverfahrensrecht vom 27. März 2020.

[7]Wasmer (2012), pp. 769–771.

[8]Theodoropoulou, Sotiria (04.02.2016) Unemployment, internal devaluation and labour market deregulation in Europe, P. 25. Available via https://www.researchgate.net/publication/292703524.

are not holding up. Therefore, we want to see which instruments are available so that the private sector itself regulates the internal devaluation issue without having to rely on the necessarily crude governmental intervention.

Still, in our analysis, we want to focus on how to actually extend potential futures overall. For this, the question is how to reach maximum productivity by taking advantage of all available resources. The problem with internal devaluation in this context is that there is either no, or not sufficient, demand available for the performance of the unemployed: i.e. free capacity will not be addressed by demand. In other words, no consensus is reached between potential demanders and free capacity since the demanders are not ready to pay the price which would be appropriate according to correct (devaluated) pricing. This is why devaluation of the currency works so well in terms of boosting employment. Since the local employers are also subject to the increase of the costs for the imported goods and services, the same as the unemployed, it is therefore much easier to meet the pricing criteria in the relation between employer and unemployed (free capacity) as they are sitting in the same boat.

The remaining question is this: Are tools available to avoid the internal devaluation scenarios not just between currencies of countries and currency zones but also within currencies?

5 Multiple Parallel Currencies

The key to a currency is that each unit just exists once. The euro in the pocket will always be just one euro, and the euros on the bank account, where they are in fact just a digital unit and otherwise not physically present, will also only be there once. This is the underlying assumption we all have regarding currencies. It is based on the trust that the bank will not tamper with that digital information and that there will be no stealing of that digital unit. In other words, we assume that the digital data is immutable—nobody can interfere with it.

However, we also know that this is not true in all potential circumstances. It could be the case that the bank is actually stealing the digital unit and we have to sue them to restore the bank account. Moreover, if the bank goes bankrupt, we may have a recovery claim against the government if there is a bank deposit guarantee. But still, the absolutely prevailing assumption certainly everybody has is that the money is safe in the bank.

The second important assumption is that the central bank and the government will make sure that there is no extensive inflationary process which, in light of our potential futures, suddenly reduces our options unexpectedly. In fact, this assumption has to be carefully measured against what actually is available for which prices in the future: i.e. what are the results of the increase in productivity on the one hand, and detrimental external shocks on the other. For the average consumer, this is rather an analysis ex posteriori since the overwhelming majority of decision-making will not be based on a careful calculation as to what their money will buy 10 years from now. However, it still does play a role when deciding about pension plans. Thus, for every mid-and long-term investor, the estimated prices of goods and services in 5, 10 or 20 years or even longer periods (e.g. for life insurers), and what kind of investment strategy is best under the respective analytical results, are extremely important evaluation aspects.

But if we look at long-term investments, there is always the trade-off between investing into a long-term project and balancing it against the liquidity shortcomings if there is an immediate cash requirement. Also, the securer the future cash flows are, the lower the upside is. In order to participate in large upsides, it may make sense to invest into higher risk projects (venture capital, hedge funds, etc.) in order to create overall higher returns. Hence, today's pricing of those assets are based on today's expectations as to how those assets will perform in the future. Therefore, the potential futures attached to those assets are not available in currency as of today but in an expected future cash flow stream. We may be able to sell the assets now, converting it immediately into usable potential futures, but then we have to accept the pricing based on the current evaluation, which leaves the potential upside on the table (or, in fact, we are curbing our downside).

Hence, what is the link of such future cash flows and, therefore, potential futures of those non-liquid assets to boosting employment? The link now available to do the trick is technology: the blockchain-based token infrastructure.

6 Blockchain-Based Tokens as Parallel Currencies

The term blockchain refers to a complex digital technology by emphasizing its data structure. The broader term distributed ledger technology (DLT) involves blockchain technology but also various implementations with the central feature of storing transaction data immutably.[9] This is the core quality from which everything derives. DLT is aimed at building a ledger which stores transactions and has the following characteristics:[10]

- the ledger is replicated on various computer server nodes and exists as long as at least one node is active,
- the acceptance of transactions (validity) is confirmed by an automated decentralised (e.g. democratic) process between the nodes,
- the sequence of transactions is unchangeable,
- transactions are protected against subsequent manipulations by cryptographic techniques.

[9] Jongerius, Silvan (13.08.2019) GDPR's Right to be Forgotten in Blockchain: it's not black and white. Available via www.techgdpr.com.

Politou, Eugenia; Casino, Fran; IEEE; Alepis, Efthimios (24.07.2019) Blockchain Mutability: Challenges and Proposed Solutions, I. Introduction.

[10] Heumüller and Richter (2018), pp. 60–65.

Although the energy consumption (waste) of blockchain solutions such as Bitcoin is immense, there are various implementations which feature low energy emissions, especially the consensus mechanism. Thus, the costs of keeping a DLT infrastructure running will be highly competitive as compared to the costs of the banking and transfer infrastructure.

Therefore, DLT transaction data can have exactly the same quality as the digital data on our bank accounts in terms of the assumed immutability. A unit of such data, comparable to a currency in terms of its storage and transferability capacity, is called a token.[11] Since a token is just a non-descript digital unit, it can have distinctive qualities. There are several valuable frameworks clustering tokens on the base of various perspectives. For our purposes here, we categorize three classes of tokens: (1) Payment tokens such as Bitcoin or Ether, which have no other function as a means of exchange and are therefore comparable so far with traditional currencies. As a consequence, most central banks worldwide are looking into options to also issue the local currency as a digital unit, i.e. as a token. These tokens are somewhat context-free as it appears possible to exchange every exchangeable unit with such tokens. (2) Utility tokens, which allow a specific usage or service promised by the issuer. (3) Security tokens, which represent a specific right of the token holder against the issuer, for instance a profit participation, a share, an asset, etc.[12] Such tokens (2 and 3) are context-specific as they serve a specific purpose, at least in the moment of issuance.

In the following, we focus primarily on security tokens, since only those have the potential for a tremendous impact in terms of multiple currencies. Although utility tokens also can have the same effect of community building and engaging free capacity, in the following we will just refer to security tokens. To explain the potential impact, we have to look at how potential futures related to the workforce are distributed as of now.

So far, our forms and structures of cooperation function according to patterns that have been tested and developed over centuries. We live in families, have associations, are organized in companies and state-run organizations. Everywhere, the common denominator is a matter of people gathering in a joint project and making arrangements about how future events will be represented. In a company, for example, employees receive a fixed remuneration for their work, perhaps with a performance-related bonus, shareholders receive profits if they are achieved, etc. There are legally binding activities in limited companies, associations, and cooperatives but also legally non-binding activities. The laws and rules are partly codified and are partly agreed upon individually, yet the framework is always defined by the legal system. This is also the case when cooperation outside of a

[11] BaFin, Merkblatt *Zweites Hinweisschreiben zum Prospekt- und Erlaubnispflichten im Zusammenhang mit der Ausgabe sogenannter Krypto-Token*, WA 51-Wp 7100-2019/0011 und IF 1-AZB 1505-2019/0003, p. 1.

[12] Fromberger/Haffke/Zimmermann (6.4.2018) *Regulierungen von Token*. In: Blockchain Bundesverband, p. 10 f., BKR 2019, 377; Zickgraf, AG 2018, 293, 295; Veil, ZHR 2019, 346, 248.

formal structure is agreed upon in groups, as in the case of a success commission for brokerage or a service provider who receives a fixed fee for catering.

Meanwhile, collaborations in our digital age have reached an enormous extent, where services of participants are provided without any direct remuneration, for example in open-source projects. What they all have in common is that they are always about the future. The legal system structures the content of future actions because it provides the basis for the parties' behaviour but also provides the legal frame to shape future processes. Contrary to the common understanding, this is the far more important function of the legal system as compared to the task of bindingly deciding on conflicts between parties.

A peculiar quality of the immutability of data is that other forms of cooperation are now possible. This follows from the amazing fact that a token, equivalent to a chip in a casino, can be linked to any agreement.[13] We can agree that this token represents a life circumstance, any life circumstance! A token can therefore represent a company share, a license right, a share of the proceeds from a concert, anything! An effective legal agreement may often not be trivial, but it is doable (short of marriage) as we can use trustee structures if token holders cannot hold the right directly, as is the case, for instance, in all passive investment structures.

This allows for innovative forms of employment since, other than up to now, as an employer, we do not need to devise an employment contract or a freelance contract in order to let the unemployed as defined above take part in our business proposal. We only have to post digitally, or through other communication channels, that contributions of free capacity to our business proposal will have the promised participation in the business success. The participation could be structured like a shareholder, an agent, a freelancer, or even an employee. The payment can be executed digitally through the issued token; however, it is also possible and technically easily executable through payments of so-called stable coins (tokens)[14] which are pegged to a central bank currency (US-dollars, Euro, Yen, i.e. any central bank issued currency, also called "FIAT"). Certainly, we are already in the early stages of the governance of such token issuances, which leads to the challenge of how to control the supply of tokens in order to control the development of the value. However, for the security tokens we are looking at right now, this will be easier than for classical currencies since the security tokens are tied to a specific underlying asset. Therefore, the supply of tokens can be synchronized with the underlying asset, and we can use governance structures, for instance, as they are in place for capital increases for stock noted companies. However, such a specific underlying asset does not mean that the future is fixed. As the tokens only represent the underlying asset or, more concisely, the kind of value the community of token holders experience in holding the representation of the underlying asset, such tokens have the quality of liquidity and thus represent potential different futures.

[13] Kaulartz, Markus / Matzke, Robin (2018) *Die Tokenisierung des Rechts*, NJW 2018, 3278.

[14] See Buterin, Vitalik (2014) *The Search for a Stable Cryptocurrency*. Available via Ethereum Blog, 11.11.2014, http://blog.ethereum.org/2014/11/11/search-stable-cryptocurrency/.

It is therefore now possible to record and process the contributions of team members for future success (and failure) via a blockchain with the help of a token structure. We no longer have to be accepted into an organization, we no longer have to conclude an individual contract, and we no longer have to perform our work as an open source participant without reward, because success is reflected in the value of the token.

The tokens are extremely easy to handle as compared to traditional bank payments, for instance. One simply enters the public key of the account of the person one wants to transfer the token to. This public key addresses the target wallet. Doing this, the token will be transferred immediately out of one's wallet wherever the target person in whatever jurisdiction is located. Admittedly, as of today, the majority of the global population still cannot handle token structures and token transfers as they do payment structures. However, we are seeing a rapid development in making digital token transfer intuitive and easy to handle for everybody and certainly, within the next five years, it will be already a widespread commonly used technology, also in the private sector.

The possibility of participating in projects allows a new quality of global interdependence in which cooperation structures directed towards the future can be formed beyond national, religious, educational, and other borders. This requires an even more far-reaching shift from a mechanical world view to the adventure of objectified collaborative structures suddenly being conceived as a social factor. Yet also for local community projects, this is an easy, inexpensive, and effective way of organizing value creation.

As an example, we can look at the LEV market in Israel: For two years, a pilot project in Israel ran with LEV coins (pre-blockchain), privately issued certificates. The humble origins were that it was supposed to be a currency for mothers trading all kinds of goods and services (babysitting, cooking for neighbours, strollers, toys, etc.). 20,000 Israeli mothers participated, and during the peak, there were 1000 transactions a day, amounting to a trade value of US $20 million over a period of two years. Without the LEV, this value creation would not have happened since there was no currency available which could incentivize a mother to do the value creation as there was no cash available to pay for it. Although the potential future in the beginning was very limited, e.g. the LEV may allow a women to get a meal next week from the mother of the child in return for babysitting services, the growing scope of services rendered and rewarded by LEV led to such an increase of options that the babysitter was certainly having a lot more of choices than just a meal.

It is difficult to predict what entrepreneurs will devise as business projects through token offerings, including the workforce. However, there is a high probability that this will be more effective than any other method. The reason is that the increase of productivity depends on entrepreneurial behaviour anyway, so anything which expands options to entrepreneurs will boost their imagination and their activities. The current environment that boosts working from home is certainly helping any digital offering, so it is a perfect moment to introduce such digital collaboration. Yet this is not just confined to anonymous or even cross-border collaboration. It can also work well in a local set-up like the LEV market, but executing on it by organizing the local contacting and payment structure effectively through a security token offering.

To summarize the notion above, a token that represents the result of a collaboration structure is also the representation of a potential future, namely the future result of the collaboration. Just like the Euro. The only difference is that the Euro has liquidity. In other words, if we have one Euro, we assume that we can buy any potential future anywhere in the Euro zone if we can pay its price. The same holds for non-Euro countries. We just have to exchange our Euros for the local currency. However, the token will only allow us credibly potential futures if there is a credible exchange mechanism for converting the token into a FIAT currency. In the end, it is the same challenge as for holding our non-liquid assets that are not noted at a stock exchange, with the risk of selling it considerably under the price that can be monetized. Also, we usually cannot compartmentalize non-liquid assets such as real estate: We either sell it in total, or we have to hold on to it.

So how can collaboration structures represented by tokens create immediate liquidity?

7 Token Economy and Liquidity

Liquidity implies unfreezing the future. In the end, we always associate liquidity with central banks and government guaranteed currency. Liquidity is if we can get FIAT into our bank accounts. We also assume now that nearly every global currency is fine as long as we can immediately exchange it into our local currency, which is the case with all the major currencies.

We feel "liquidity" when just one phone call to our broker (due to stock-noted shares and bonds) allows us to have cash in our account on the next day, at the latest. Astonishingly enough, the token economy will allow an even more effective exchange process due to the fact that those exchanges are available online and we do not even need a broker to exchange our token into FIAT.

Admittedly, after about 10 years into blockchain technology, we have not yet reached the point where this type of exchange for security tokens is conveniently available. However, all the major regulators and legislators worldwide are involved in the process of evaluating how such exchanges can be set up and regulated appropriately. Given our analysis, the importance of moving fast here is obvious.

What will such exchanges achieve? It will allow seamless liquidity to any token without regulatory and jurisdictional constraints. Effectively, this will lead to a "global asset exchange" for any tokenized asset. Since any asset actually can be represented by a token, in some cases by means of a trustee structure, we can basically have a number of such global asset exchanges for every asset worth tokenizing.

The immediate liquidity, meaning the potential exchange into FIAT, is currently the main challenge. There are already numerous platforms to tokenize any underlying asset. But what they are lacking is an effective liquidity component. However, there are now innovative structures in the making which resolve this problem. One of the solutions we want to focus on is structured around the so-called *bonding curve model*.[15] Every project starting out in the beginning will not have the market recognition in order to devise a sufficiently deep liquidity to be interesting for market makers to provide a listing on an exchange. There simply will not be the expectation of having a sufficiently sizable buyer and seller market in order for this. This circumstance is certainly different for projects such as Libra by Facebook where everybody assumes that it will have immediately tremendous market depths.

Since we are looking at projects in which employers are using token offerings in return for work performance, they usually will not be sufficiently established and calculable for being listed immediately. Yet what can be done immediately is to set up a cash/token pool, provided by the employer or a third party, which typically can amount to 5 to 10% of the equity necessary for the business project. Such a cash/token pool then serves as a counterparty to the workforce receiving tokens for the project, and they can trade their tokens against the cash component. In fact, anybody holding the token can trade against the cash component. The pricing of the cash/token pool is predefined through an algorithm which, in its simplest form, is cash in the pool divided by the number of tokens in the pool. *Therefore, in the beginning, there is a specific price for each token which then changes with every transaction according to the pricing formula.* Yet since the prize moves to infinity once the number of tokens are approaching zero, and the number of tokens move to infinity once the prices moved to zero, there will always be a range within which the tokens are exchanged against cash and vice versa since no trading will take place close to the extremes.

As a consequence, there is an immediate liquidity option available, easily manageable on digital platforms and accessible through one's smart phone. Obviously, in the beginning, there will not be a very deep liquidity situation: i.e. if somebody wants to sell off a 10% stake of a token issuance, it will not be possible since the pricing will immediately plummet. Yet this is not different as compared to a classical stock exchange share situation in which a 10% stake is offered at once. Both, with the bonding curve cash flow as well as with a traditional stock exchange, large quantities have to be transacted carefully over time, protecting the token/share price.

How are security tokens with a bonding curve cash/token pool helping using free capacity as opposed to alternative policy strategies?

[15] Alexandria "*The bonding curve is a mathematical curve that defines the relationship between token supply and asset price.* https://coinmarketcap.com/alexandria/glossary/bonding-curve. See also Riady, Yos (10.11.2018) *Bonding Curves Explained*. Available via https://yos.io/2018/11/10/bonding-curves/.

8 Battling the Internal Devaluation Dilemma with the Security Token Economy

Traditional strategies to deal with free capacity differ between the free capacities' characters. The first and most visible type of free capacity is the one that is actually completely unemployed: i.e. not having any income as a result of their work performance, no one wants to "employ" them. As a result of an external shock, shown by the coronavirus crisis, substantial unemployment looms if the problem continues. Policy remedies of current or expected unemployment focus around using subsidy payments to subsidize the unemployed or those who are on the verge of becoming unemployed. This is especially important if the beneficiary of the subsidy has no savings and is already barely holding out to the end of the month. Therefore, those measures are not geared to actually incentivizing a sensible work performance but rather just to mitigate immediate cash needs.

However, in situations of threatening long-term unemployment, government agencies tend to set up state-run employment companies for otherwise unemployed, who then embark on an activity which seems to give some added value to society, one example being low-qualified infrastructure maintenance work in cities. Again, this does not give incentives to motivate the workforce into positions of sensible productivity.

One issue that is not at all addressed by government policy is the part of unemployment which is only a fraction of the work performance of the worker, or is related to those who have other sources of income and do not have to rely on the remuneration for their unused work capacity. In other words, government policy does not address free capacity. In order to move free capacity into productivity and therefore contribute to the gross national product, this depends entirely on the private sector. Tax and other incentives for this play a negligible role.

As a result, there is no market induced competition going on for entrepreneurs to take advantage of the available free capacity. The internal devaluation dilemma blocks the massive offering to such a workforce since there is simply not enough liquidity available to the entrepreneurs to pay the workforce, given the returns that they can expect. They have to wait until the pricing level of the long-term contracts have been adjusted, a process that usually takes years, and then employ the workers with a lower remuneration.

However, if they can offer (at least partial) payment through a token structure attached to the underlying success of the business model (one possible future), they can afford the workforce now. Depending on the individual situation of the person with free capacity, there obviously has to be a larger, smaller, or even no immediate cash component to it. But let us not underestimate in terms of availability of such a workforce what scope this can have. If we look at the open source development community, every year we have billions of euros worth of performance even without any financial remuneration at all. Hence, if there is a remuneration even if it is with a token with an undefined cash value, this might be even much more enticing.

Consequently, the token represents potential futures like a FIAT currency does. However, the mechanism is different in several aspects. First, there is not the same level of certainty as to what we can buy for our token in the future. Yet this is by no means necessarily a disadvantage. In fact, by attaching ourselves to a specific token, we form part of that specific community, either local or international, and therefore we are participating in the future success of this specific community. Therefore, we do not just have to rely on our FIAT community and its inflation and deflation. With our token exposure, we actually then have diversified our potential future position which in turn makes it more stable. Second, an entrepreneur paying FIAT accumulates entrepreneurial risk, as the entrepreneur requires customers for revenue to pay the FIAT. The token, however, represents a risk-splitting scheme for the entrepreneur and the future token holder. It is like a bet for the success of the community. Thus, the token as result of the free capacity carries worth exactly when people want to have access into the community represented by the token, independent of being a customer or a rent-seeking investor. The person with free capacity accumulates risk as the entrepreneur does but participates in the future success in the same way as the entrepreneur according to the token share.

We particularly have to consider that there will be fierce competition going on between the entrepreneurs to convince our target workforce to accept their offering. This is very different from an employment program run by a government agency which necessarily does not have the flexibility to react fast and effectively to market developments.

The elegance of using a token structure for the entrepreneur's production process by making digital offerings to people they may not even know and letting them contribute without a time-consuming and often prohibitive contractual set up on its own will already have a substantial impact on employment and productivity using free capacity. This is the case even if there would be no immediate liquidity option attached to it. In principle, such a workforce could also be interested in classical contract structures. Yet compared to the token option, due to the contractual, communication and payment challenges, they will often fail.

9 Liquidity Options for Security Tokens

What truly lifts the token option to a totally different level is the liquidity element. Through the bonding curve cash/token pool, any unemployed person receiving tokens can immediately exchange those into FIAT. Obviously, this will not work if anyone receiving tokens immediately wants to exchange it against cash and nobody wants to invest in the token. Yet even in such an extreme situation, there is the government option to actually provide cash to the cash pool in order to maintain a specific pricing level that resembles a central bank's operations to influence the exchange rate of the local currency, or price management of a stock noted company for its share price. There have to be procedures in place in order to avoid frontrunning and other illegal manipulation while trading the token. In principle, the same rules and measures can apply for safeguarding as compared to stock noted share prices, for instance. The only difference is that the price discovery is run through the algorithm and needs protective structures accordingly.

As a consequence, the result will be that the government agency will hold a certain amount of the token and will therefore participate in the future of the cash flows out of the underlying asset, share or right. Economically, this can be viewed as a profit participation right for the business project by the government agency for helping to finance the project. Economically, this is comparable to many of the financing projects by state-owned banks, such as by the currently state-owned KfW bank in Germany with a multibillion euro dimension. Yet, the selection process for such financing would be different. It would actually be focused on getting free capacity used and rewarding and supporting this process as opposed to just financing companies with a much weaker link to boost employment.

Depending on the projects and the participants and the overall attractiveness of the project, there might be a much lower necessity for government funding if the workforce does not immediately cash out but if it views the project as a type of saving scheme. Moreover, if the project is sufficiently attractive, there will be private investments into the token once the token price falls under a specific threshold.

Another, and in our point of view promising variant to "finance" such communities and their intended futures is to guarantee a price of a token. Imagine any government agency wants to support the development of a community. That community might emit a token for an entrepreneurial endeavour. The token supply can be fixed with one million tokens for the endeavour. Such a token might be worth only the promise of having value in the future. If the government agency now guarantees to pay one Euro per token, for example, then the token is worth one Euro. But what happens when the agency guarantees the exchange rate in the future, perhaps in two years from now? In that case, the token is now worth more than nothing and maybe less than one Euro. However, the token is now tradable and the endeavour has financial assets. Given that the endeavour is successful, it might be that the token is worth more than one Euro after two years. This means that the government agency paid nothing to finance the endeavour. The interesting aspect of this mechanism is that it is easy to build and that the transaction costs are low.

Therefore, the government backed spending to fight unemployment under such a token economy scenario will very likely be considerably lower with better effects as compared to the current undifferentiated approach. *What governments and legislators must do is create the structural and regulatory prerequisites to execute on such an effective token economy approach.* However, looking at the latest developments in major European jurisdictions such as Germany, a viable regulatory environment is already available and the market participants are in the process of acting on it. But it clearly makes a considerable difference whether this is supported by the political establishment or whether this is seen as a non-priority issue.

In terms of FIAT money supply, there are no adverse effects to be expected, since additional inflationary pressure as compared to the current situation is highly unlikely. For one, even government provided funding to unemployed will only exert unwarranted inflationary pressure if this leads to demand competing with additional demand by citizens making up for the "restaurant bills" they were sparing in order to stay with the example above. This scenario is highly unlikely.

What cannot be helped by the token economy is the necessary downward adjustment of the pricing in long-term contracts. However, it can help substantially in reducing the necessity for such adjustments by quickly moving the unemployed into productive employment. This makes all the difference, so the political establishment should have the priority of fighting unemployment to foster the token economy.

The notion that the money supply is controlled by the central banks is a myth anyway. In fact, central banks have only very indirect measures available to control the money supply since the commercial banks, through their lending activity, are the ones which primarily impact the money supply, and their lending policies are obviously influenced by policy measures related to the prime rate, minimum reserves, etc. However, the key is still the underwriting policy of the bank for the loans, and this may only be marginally influenced by the prime rate, for example, as was shown as a consequence of the financial crisis of 2008. Therefore, even in the current situation, the private sector, through the commercial banks, are playing a decisive role for the money supply and therefore for the stability of pricing levels.[16]

What our analysis shows though is that the notion of a single local currency is suboptimal since it does not reflect the fact that a currency is nothing else than a community stabilizing expectations of potential futures represented by sums of such currency. On the basis of their immutability, security tokens issued by the private sector can have the same quality as a traditional currency, and they can represent potential futures like a traditional currency. They coexist with traditional currencies and are connected to them through exchanges similar to the manner in which global currencies are connected through Forex exchanges. The exchange rates reflect in a competitive manner based on the perceived probability of success as to how the global and local market participants view the potential futures related to the specific security tokens.

Therefore, the private sector is absolutely vital in providing a multiple currency environment that can fight unemployment.

10 Structural Challenges to Implement Security Token Programs

Free capacity very often has to be addressed at a grassroot level. This means that small initiatives start out with no substantial budgets available. As we have seen in the last decades, it is absolutely vital to have a vibrant start-up scene happy to begin on a grassroot level. Silicon Valley and the latest development of the start-up scene in Berlin are just a few examples of this. From an attorney's point of view, though, such start-ups practically always operate grossly under-lawyered, running tremendous risks in terms of their regulatory position. Moreover, they very often sub-perform grossly in terms of their contractual status. One of the key issues for

[16]Link and Omlor (2021).

them is how to come to terms with investors and other stakeholders such as major customers and major service providers. Structuring this in the traditional legal financing and collaboration structures immediately requires legal advice, which can easily cost between €10,000 and €50,000—funds that (even if theoretically available, which in practice often is not the case) are decided to be allocated according to technical, commercial or other issues.

The legal community does not provide easy-to-handle structural support for such relationships. However, the Common Legal Platform (CLP), which offers a set of security token structures, will make it possible for start-ups and all other small businesses to

(a) have a set of nationally and internationally available token structures to be quickly and nearly entirely documented right from the start without expensive legal advice (currently, the technical tokenization process is actually a commodity and available for anybody with minimal costs); and
(b) have a communication platform connecting with legal and technical service providers for such a token structure (which obviously will be necessary once the project has left the grassroot level).

Applied to itself, the Common Legal Platform can now use the particular characteristics of the token economy to provide the legal templates for a token structure on its platform. Obviously, given the complexity of globally usable security token templates taking into account the various jurisdictions, a tremendous effort has to be made by the global legal community to devise sound templates. Furthermore, these templates will require constant adaptation, given the constantly changing legal and regulatory environment.

The legal community members can be motivated to contribute to the templates by rewarding them with a token program that involves the Common Legal Platform. Such tokens will be granted to contributors based on the quality of their contribution. Measuring the contribution is a challenge, but such a challenge is one faced by all who wants to measure the reward for a contribution today when the success in the future is unclear. The situation we are facing here is this: If an attorney enters a specific template onto the platform, it is not clear what demand such a template will have and what success the users will have due to the template. But still, as in other comparable situations, there are various options available in order to tackle the uncertainty, for instance by rewarding the attorney through tokens based on the number of uses of the template and, if available, on the success of the users. Obviously, this has to be balanced by the obligation and incentive of the user and/or other participants on the platform to actually have to purchase such tokens in order to create liquidity for them.

One has also to take into account that artificial intelligence will boost the quality of such templates, including constant updates. In conjunction with available token templates, this will immediately give any start-up an accessible and low-cost option to include other stakeholders in the business model without being faced with prohibitive legal costs.

11 Revenue Distribution on the Common Legal Platform

As the name suggests, the Common Legal Platform is a platform. Platforms are socio-technical setups which support customers with core functionality. Customers in a platform setting are those formally independent, loosely coupled entities which make an offering. These customers are typically called complementors as they complement the service of the platform. Such complementors provide their services for the other class of customers called consumers. Thus, a platform enables the match of consumers and service-providing complementors via functionality of the platform. "Socio" means that the platform is typically a legal entity, legally independent from both classes of customers. The value proposition of such an entity is the match making of consumers and complementors and the creation of a transaction-friendly service environment. "Technical" means that nowadays such platforms predominantly act digitally as such digital market or innovation places rapidly scale and create network effects.[17]

For the CLP, two different business model components are probable. The first business model component is a "freemium" model. In this context, freemium means that consumers are attracted to use the platform by free-of-charge content that is valuable for the consumers. This attraction is to be expected to convince the consumers to use the platform for the premium and charged services. A well-known platform using this business model is SPOTIFY, which gives away most of its content for free but interrupts with advertising and less functionality.

One central problem for the CLP with the freemium model is how to attract complementors to contribute with giving access to high-quality content for the consumers. It seems very unlikely that SPOTIFY does not pay the artists for music that a consumer streamed in the freemium case. The token concept described above can help to solve this problem. We hypothesize that twenty percent of all premium revenue is planned to be given away for complementors who support the platform with free content. This is easy to implement via smart contracts featuring automation by using tokens. However, how is it then possible to remunerate the contributors who deliver high-quality content? It might be beneficial for the CLP for contributions to be consumed numerously. Then it is obvious to pay more tokens to the complementors whose content was downloaded in a high number by different consumers. It might also be beneficial for the platform to have consumers pay per time of use. Then it is obvious to pay more tokens for the complementors who have content that consumers consume longer (such indicators are measurable in the digital world). However, the exact remuneration mechanism depends—as always—on the objectives of the platform. Interestingly, the value of the token quantum a contributor gets as remuneration trivially depends not only on the number of tokens but also on the development of the platform endeavour in total. When the platform has success, the token exchange value will rise. Thus, the complementor directly influences the value of the platform and therefore the platform token.

[17]E.g. Parker et al. (2016).

The second business model component offers a consumer the option to request a proposal (and later the service) for a complex question of law. Further, we assume that such a question can be divided into several subtasks. Then the CLP, as a coordinator of complementors, is responsible for coordinating the request for the consumer. In this scenario such platform ecosystems face an important governance problem: fair value distribution.[18] Centrally organized platforms, such platforms which are governed by a central authority, are able to implement an unbalanced value distribution with ongoing growth. It is a typical pattern that complementors are disintermediated by the platform from their customers and, with that happening, the complementors lose prosperity. This makes it less attractive for complementors to engage in a centralized platform ecosystem.

How is the CLP able to address this concern? With the help of a token structure, it is possible to implement a simple revenue split scheme that mitigates the problem. Imagine that a consumer requests a proposal via the platform. Then, the platform divides this proposal into subtasks and makes a call for contribution to its complementors. With that act, the problem of selecting the proper contributor arises. How can this selection process be done fairly and economically?

One idea of fairness is that a contributor whose contribution is larger should be remunerated higher. One can also argue that the remuneration should be higher with a growing risk. Both can be implemented in the selection process here. The idea is that a complementor claims a ratio of the revenue that a consumer will pay for the project. This ratio is claimed before the complementors know the exact revenue stream. For example, there are three different tasks with approximately one third of volume each. Then there are three complementors that claim for the first task and offer their ratios (e.g. complementor A wants 30%, B wants 31%, and C wants 35%). The same happens with the second and the third task. Then the task of the CLP is to select an appropriate (valid) selection of complementors. All selections are valid if they have a sum of ratios below or equal to one hundred percent. One possibility is to select the lowest ratio by using an auction mechanism. In the case described here, this is complementor A for task one. The difference between one hundred and the actual sum could be the remuneration of the platform.

What happens in this scenario? First, who gets how much of the cake become transparent. The contributor who provides more output can claim a higher ratio. This means fairness according to the equity theory. Second, all contributors as well as the platform split their risk according to their claimed ratio. There is no accumulation of entrepreneurial risk along the value chain. Third, governing the platform using a consortium of key contributors instead of a central authority avoids structural power imbalances, which are often the reason for unfair value distribution.

In that scenario, tokens are relevant as reflectors of value. The advantage of the tokens is that they are accounted by the DLT and the distribution of the tokens are

[18] See Richter et al. (2020), https://aisel.aisnet.org/acis2020/39 for an analogous argumentation in a different context.

automated using smart contracts. Thus, once the platform has negotiated with the complementors the split revenue scheme and all necessary contracts, these contracts are codified in the language of the DLT and published in a smart contract for the consumer. Then the selected complementors provide their part of the project and connect it to the smart contract. If all parts of the project are completed, the smart contract awaits the payment by the consumer. After the consumer transfers the tokens to the smart contract, the tokens are split according to the split revenue scheme and the tokens are directly transferred to all complementors. There is no central authority accountable for distributing the payout.

With these mechanisms it is possible to enable a trustful cooperation initiative. Thus, small sized complementors who have innovative ideas and free capacity can engage in larger endeavours of interesting co-creation partnerships without losing their sovereignty and without fear of an overwhelmingly powerful central platform.

12 Application of a Token Structure to the Common Legal Platform

The actors on the Common Legal Platform are legal professionals such as the "complementors" for the content, on the one hand, and the customer seeking advice, the "consumer", on the other. Key to the success is that the complementors are motivated by using free capacity to enter high-quality legal content. The notion that such complementors will do so with an "open source mentality", that is, by getting nothing in return, is clearly too optimistic. A standard approach would be to look into a freemium economy here, which would mean that the complementors are ready to have their base contribution unrewarded with the expectation that further demand for their services will be rewarded. The reward in this context could then be via a platform-token depending on the number and intensity of usage of more sophisticated legal content.

This is clearly not a trivial process. However, this is exactly what a flexible token-based reward system can deliver much better as compared to traditional value distribution structures. It can allow specific expectations of the legal content providers, the complementors, of an attractive reward and also allow the customer of the legal content, the consumer, to flexibly decide what level of advice is appropriate for the situation and, therefore, what kind of payment the consumer is ready to make. Such a token economy also allows to devise realistic options for the consumer to make a request for proposal for legal advice.

Finally, it is obvious that it is key to distribute the value created on and through the Common Legal Platform fairly between the stakeholders. The split of the value created on the platform can be subject to a balanced governance structure and managed through the platform token. The added quality for a fair distribution through such a token economy has the potential to play a pivotal role in its success.

13 Token Structures to Better Humanise Society

For humans, 'taking our destiny into our own hands', is the ultimate accomplishment. The challenge is balancing personal destiny with the societal destiny of humankind. For this, token structures allow a coordinated, yet individualistic approach never available within our traditional legal and monetary system. The reason for this is that one can decide individually to which token community they want to contribute and what contribution they want to make, while no longer being boxed in by rigid currency and employment structures.

Obviously, it will take time for society to acclimate to all the repercussions that token structures can have. This will be on multiple levels, from the legal structures to government involvement to simple social interactions, the entire gamut of "life". Concomitantly, it will take time for the business world to fully embrace the opportunities related to token structures. As a result, it will lead to an accelerated empowerment of individuals and smaller organisations, and will curb the—further—monopolisation of economic power.

Therefore, we feel that it is fair to say that token structures will contribute greater balance and betterment of the world through this new paradigm.

Liquid Legal Waves to Other Chapters, Written by the Editors

Wolfgang and Sebastian illustrate their pledge for a security token system being the enabler for accessing free capacity in society with the example of the functioning of a Common Legal Platform. This connects to *Martina's* call to action for lawyers to get involved in the various aspects of *"Corporate Digital Responsibility"*—maybe not just as guides, but also as innovators, showing how collaborative ecosystems can function?

If security tokens can instigate the production of goods and services, thereby expanding the potential futures for everyone, they might be an element to transform the legal 'ego-system' into a true 'eco-system', thereby laying the foundation for *"Patagonia: Everything a law firm is not, but could be?"* that *Emma* and *Madeleine* describe.

What *Wolfgang and Sebastian* envision will surely demand a variety of skills not traditionally associated or developed by professionals in the legal field. In the upcoming chapter *"Transforming legal ecosystems"*, *Valérie* and *Filip* present the 'EASE-model', an approach directly developed in the pursuit of innovation and transformation of their teams.

References

Heumüller E, Richter S (2018) Das Blockchain-Ökosystem als Analyse-Ansatz. Wirtschaftsinformatik & Management 3:60–65

Kindleberger CP (2013) Keynesianism vs. Monetarism: and other essays in financial history. Taylor & Francis, Vereinigtes Königreich, p 11

Link M, Omlor S (2021) Kryptowährungen und Token. Fachmedien Recht und Wirtschaft, Frankfurt am Main, Deutschland: Kapitel 2, V. 63

Parker GG, Van Alstyne MW, Choudary SP (2016) Platform revolution. How networked markets are transforming the economy and how to make them work for you. W. W. Norton & Company, New York, London

Richter S, Schmidt L, Heumüller E (2020) Fair is fair: a fair value distribution mechanism for cloud manufacturing ecosystem. In: Proceedings of the ACIS 2020, https://aisel.aisnet.org/acis2020/39

Schäfer H (2013) Währungsqualität, asymmetrische Information und Transaktionskosten. Springer, Berlin, Heidelberg, p 261

Wasmer E (2012) An introduction to the special feature section: price, wage and employment adjustments in 2007-2008 and some inference for the current European crisis. Labour Econ 19: 769–771

Wolfgang Richter is a finance lawyer and economist with deep expertise across the financial industry, lately focusing on FinTech, blockchain and crypto currencies. As Managing Partner of gunner*cooke* Germany, Wolfgang is driving the expansion of the UK's fastest-growing challenger law firm in its first international venture. He has over two decades of leadership experience within major international law firms. He is an expert in digital transformation issues including regulatory set-ups in the crypto currency space, structured financing, M&A deals in the financial sector, as well as advising investors and financial institutions on product development and strategy. Wolfgang is an experienced currency expert and, having worked as an investment banker, has developed parallel currency concepts.

Sebastian Richter is professor for information systems at Baden-Wuerttemberg State University in Stuttgart, Germany. He holds a diploma and a doctorate degree in information systems research, both from the Bundeswehruniversität München. In September 2016, he was appointed as professor with the focus on information management and information systems. His main research interests cover the topics of distributed ledger technologies and its business adoption and the future development of digital transformation.

Transforming Legal Ecosystems: A Conceptual Framework Derived from Our Practice

Valérie M. Saintot and F. Lulić

Contents

Abstract

This paper is primarily aimed at legal professionals in larger in-house departments, particularly those in the position to ignite and drive change processes. Yet, the insights shared can be easily transported to a wide variety of other contexts. The authors' views on some key cognitive biases often standing in the way of meaningful and long-lasting transformation are presented. Ways to overcome them are also proposed. The main focus is placed on how people could be empowered to deliver on their tasks, together with ever developing

The publication reflects the personal views of the author(s), which do not necessarily reflect the views of the ECB. The authors wish to thank Per Nymand-Andersen, Rafael Garcia-Oliva, Tatyana Filipova and Eugenio Corallo for their most valuable suggestions as early readers of the article.

Valérie M. Saintot is Lawyer, Adjunct Professor, Author.

Filip Lulić is Legal analyst in Legal Knowledge Management team, Directorate General Legal Services at the European Central Bank.

V. M. Saintot (✉) · F. Lulić
Frankfurt am Main, Germany

K. Jacob et al. (eds.), *Liquid Legal – Humanization and the Law*, Law for Professionals, https://doi.org/10.1007/978-3-031-14240-6_7

digital technologies. At the heart lies the need to use some skills not traditionally associated or developed by professionals in the legal field. Legal design principles, knowledge visualisation techniques and proficiency in legal project management are promoted and exemplified in three case studies. The authors posit that such upskilling of legal professionals is necessary to avoid being overwhelmed by the disruptive way in which legal services are increasingly requested, consumed, and valued by clients. To structure and thematise actions that are enabling the shift to be implemented, a model is derived—named 'ease legal model' where EASE stands for Engage—Aim—See—Empower. It is completed by a concise guide for legal practitioners.

1 Introduction

One of the major defining characteristics of our times is the so-called 'digital revolution'. While many legal professionals are still catching up on this reality, a new and more powerful shift is upon us—the rise of the "artificial intelligence" algorithms, internet of things and general blurring of the lines between the physical and virtual space. And as technology is unstoppably spreading over our private and professional lives, it is crucial to develop skills to be able to surf on this wave instead of being overwhelmed by it.

First, let's define a legal ecosystem as a community or group of professionals, processes, digital tools, and interactions meant to deliver legal output. Second, we understand transformation as more than change management. We mean a mind-set shift and upskilling that has structural and sustainable impact, as a response to change trends that tend to be cosmetic and short lived. Third and final, the mention of human interactions in legal ecosystems has the ambition to cover everyone involved, beyond titles and rank. It aspires to underline that everyone in the collective is the self-responsible leader in the transformation process. Cumulating these three dimensions empowers us to own the challenges and design new solutions together, or in other words, to co-create legal platforms catering for twenty-first century needs.

So, what problem(s) are we trying to solve when we speak about transforming the legal ecosystem? What knowledge and know-how do we need to address the problem impactfully? With whom should we have conversations about the transformation? How can we transform the human interactions to ease and facilitate that transformation? How should we go from having good ideas to structurally improving the working platform in legal departments?

Starting with asking questions is at the heart of transforming human interactions. With the present article we integrate insights we gathered when customising leadership toolboxes to transform the way we practice the law in an in-house legal department. It is our belief that the practices we highlight are relevant beyond our immediate context. In the process of transforming the working platform, we began to appreciate that twenty-first century legal professionals need more than just core legal expertise to tackle the challenges in front of them. This realisation was reflected in the design of transversal capability building initiatives to grow more cross-disciplinary legal profiles. At its core, the need for in-depth legal expertise is, of course, still there, but mastering, or at least valuing, competencies and toolboxes beyond the legal field proved crucial for success. Borrowing from other industries and fields, this view of the legal professional profile is metaphorically described as evolving from 'I-shaped' lawyer competency profiles (focusing on legal expertise) to 'T-shaped' profiles (also including skills beyond legal expertise).

The overarching idea behind this article is to explain what we learned about the importance of focusing on the human part of the equation, to achieve a healthy equilibrium between the human and technological aspects. On the one hand, it is a factor of stability that professionals in the legal field seem to be escaping management and technological fads. On the other hand, this stability only adds value if it is a conscious choice versus a mere resistance to change, or worse yet, a sense of being above and outside societal trends.

While drawing on technology to augment our cognition and perception, it became clear how behavioural competencies and leadership qualities need to be mobilised to support and direct the shift. The change makes sense when the mindset and culture of the ecosystem transform to move to more advanced ways to interpret and perform professional roles, rather than just repackaging the 'safe' old ways and attitudes. As history teaches us, more of the same cannot bring the new.

What are the obstacles on that path? As usual, it is our own cognitive biases that seek to entrench the old ways. The article attempts to identify four of those biases, commonly found in legal ecosystems, that need to be debunked if the legal profession wants to retain its fundamental robustness while acquiring some new strings to its bow.

The scale and scope of the change depends on the attitude of the people experiencing it. A vision that is glossy on paper, but does not engage the heads, hearts, and hands of those concerned, will be short lived or merely a repeat of the established, and at times even counterproductive. It will likely delay the synchronisation of overdue updates and upgrades in the processes, tools, and skills of the different professionals involved.

This article uses some of the building blocks we have extracted and systematised from our practice to demonstrate how we attempted to address some of the pitfalls on the way. Knowledge visualization and design thinking are central tools in our practice, so this article follows this approach to be almost as visual as textual. Some readers may only look at the visuals; others may enjoy the combination of text and visuals.

We did not shy away from a provocative and complex write-up of our case studies. We believe that we and other legal professionals 'Know' (with a capital 'K') with more than our brains. This phenomenon is called extended cognition. We Know with our bodies where perceptions are generated, and memories stored; this is called embodied cognition. We Know in relation to others and in context, drawing on

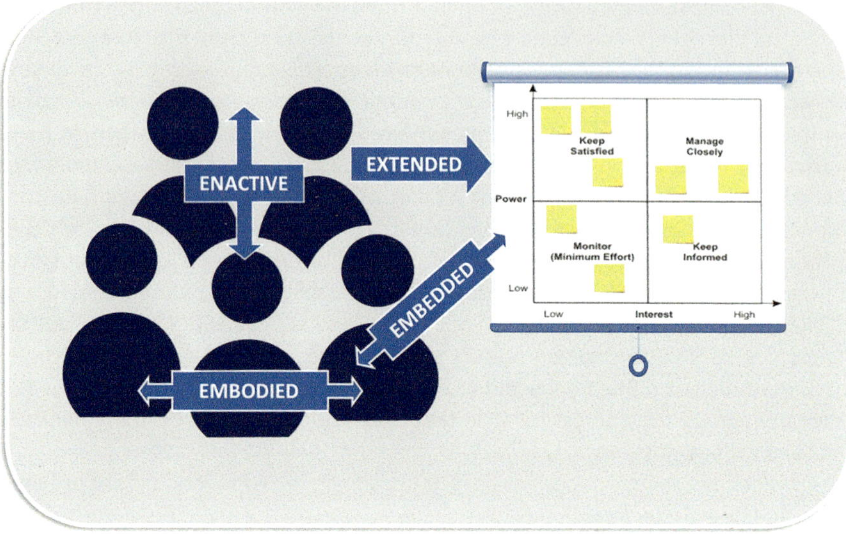

Fig. 1 4E cognition

embedded cognition. We also Know in action, where we combine thinking and making, which is called enactive cognition. When we embrace and are open to these multiple forms of cognition presented on Fig. 1, we empower ourselves to tap the full potential of our human intelligence and face with confidence the challenges and opportunities brought by the growing discussions around new technologies, in particular 'artificial intelligence'.

The article focuses on five aspects which, looking back, proved crucial on our learning journey in the legal ecosystems we have been interacting with. The five key dimensions we bring forth are summarised below before being explained in detail in the remainder of the article:

1. *The elephants in the room*: we start by pointing out four cognitive biases commonly encountered in legal ecosystems, and which need attention to avoid them having a negative effect on the evolution of the ecosystem.
2. *In the eye of the storm with ease*: looking at the constructive dimension of the cognitive biases, we offer "antidotes" that can help avoid undesirable expressions in the form of the heuristic we entitled 'EASE legal' (read: ease legal). The acronym stands for: Engage, Aim, See, Empower.
3. *A gavel is no longer enough*: the saying goes that if all you have is a hammer, then everything looks like a nail. Translated into the legal field, you need more than a gavel or else you will not be able to appropriately address the complexity of problems in front of you. Teams wanting to evolve their ecosystem need to, alongside methods, acquire the necessary set of tools and behavioural competencies. This section also highlights the influence of the way we think

and make legal ecosystems, expanding self-expression beyond the textual—to include numerical, graphical, and other signage. Such move beyond classical reliance on text exclusively, allows team members to collaborate and communicate more efficiently and to wider audiences, through use of legal design and data/ knowledge visualization techniques.

4. *The proof is in the making*: the first three sections focus on the building blocks we used. In this section, three use cases belonging to capability building, knowledge mobilisation, and navigating the law are staged to exemplify the need for T-shaped skill profiles and a holistic approach to evolve legal ecosystems.
5. *'Ease' legal smart guide*: the actionable tip of the iceberg is made available at one glance. The guide helps underpin the concepts presented in the article and highlights the essence of what we hope will be retained by the reader. It mirrors a knowledge management technique we developed as a way of aligning understanding and building capability through visual communication in the form of one-pagers summarising key take away.

2 The Elephants in the Room

Legal departments consist of different teams that are composed of a wide range of professionals. The group which captures most of the attention are the lawyers. Around them, several other professional profiles gravitate. Management functions are often performed by senior lawyers who speak and understand the way thinking and decision making is done at the very top. Other professional profiles are also part of the ecosystem: litigators, legal analysts, legal technologists, professionals without a law degree, etc.

In this context, the most influential decision-makers may fall prey to several cognitive biases in good faith. A cognitive bias can be defined as a pattern made of own thoughts, beliefs or convictions about a topic or situation, a form of subjective reality. Based on this personal understanding of how the world works, every person chooses to behave in a certain way. Such patterns save time and offer shortcuts to make decisions, which is useful in many instances.

Unfortunately, cognitive biases may also lead to misinterpretation, perceptual distortions, or inaccurate judgements. The irrational mind takes over. Cognitive biases may lead to sub-optimal decisions. Lawyers, when acting as formal managers or informal leaders, may also take decisions based on cognitive biases without even being aware of them. Some of these biases are archetypal to the legal profession and manifest themselves often enough to deserve attention and mitigation. They equally affect relations within the legal team and relations with clients.

Our attempt is to propose four biases we consider archetypal for legal ecosystems as presented in Fig. 2. Their names and definitions have been proposed by the authors. They are presented here because without articulating them explicitly, it is the authors' conviction that the transformation process will hardly be successful and risks to impede the evolution of the legal profession.

Fig. 2 Four cognitive biases commonly found in legal ecosystems

The *hierarchy bias* is rather obvious. It encompasses both the place of an individual in the organisational chart as well as the level of academic degree team members may hold. This bias not only affects those that are higher up in the organisational chart or those that hold multiple degrees. It is also present in the way other members in a given team look at those having the highest position or most advanced degrees. Too much emphasis on hierarchy can create a culture in which the best idea will not even come to the surface and be expressed and obviously won't prevail.

The *disclaimer bias* hints at the dynamic of managing legal liabilities and risks before client business needs and objectives. Lawyers, especially those working for in-house legal departments, tend to explain to their clients what is not possible, instead of designing legally sound and business-friendly legal solutions.

The *right answer bias* seems to push lawyers and legal departments to delays, in the quest for perfection and (over-)exhaustiveness. Often, lawyers do so out of good intentions, but don't consider the effects in the medium to long term. This can generate frustration and misunderstanding with the clients, which could be easily avoided.

The *status quo bias* is a complicated one, because it is both a curse and a blessing. It originates in the important legal concepts of legitimate expectations and legal certainty that lawyers naturally promote in their work. It brings stability and predictability to the playing field, yet when exacerbated, it can paralyse operations.

The next section will give some insights how we went about taking these biases into account and how the 'ease legal model' can help move beyond them.

3 In the Eye of the Storm with Ease

With the 'ease legal model', we have conceptualised the way we worked to make several processes for legal operations and legal knowledge management more effective and efficient following the model we call 'EASE legal model' (Fig. 3). Kindly note that EASE should be read as in the verb 'to ease' and not spelled out as an acronym.

The four main active verbs—Engage, Aim, See, Empower—do not express the steps of a sequential process. They describe non-linear activities which helped us make a difference in our projects. The model places its attention on engaging with stakeholders. It recommends being explicit about the aim of given efforts. It promotes the need to ensure that everyone involved sees the same problem and agrees on the solution. Those in charge need to be empowered to be change agents. It can be used both to support the transformation and the steering of day-to-day operations.

'Engage' involves the development of a culture based on open communication and dialogue focusing on members' input versus their status in the team. This is directed at mitigating risk of entrenched hierarchical biases which limit both managers and their subordinates to their rigid roles in the organisation, instead of promoting a culture in which understanding interdependence is central. We can go fast alone, but we can only go far together.

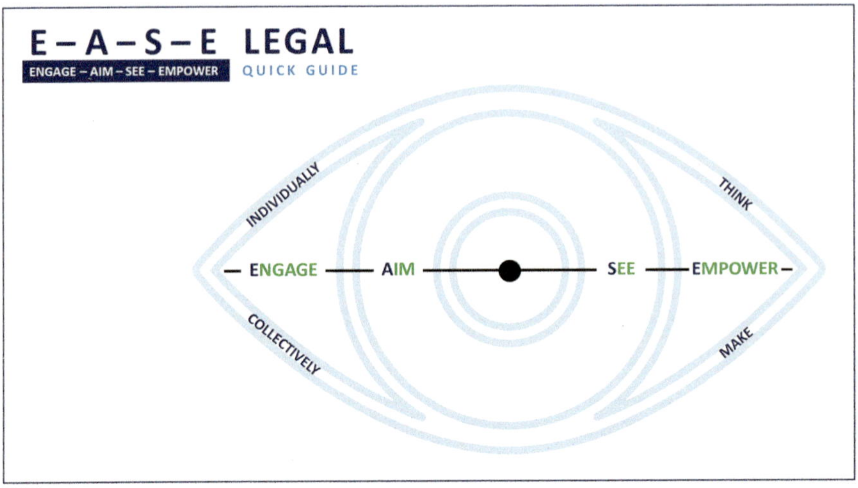

Fig. 3 Ease legal model

'*Aim'* designates the attribute of having the intention of the change clearly spelled out. The goal of being explicit is to influence the mentality from the start, so that the parties involved can move towards a culture of possibilities and away from a culture of disclaimers. It steers away from the extensive description of what is not possible or compliant towards a culture of analysing needs and giving priority to the user perspective—without compromising on legal soundness.

'*See*' encompasses a way of approaching work by giving visualization a prominent place. It is not only about presenting ideas visually, but also first and foremost to manage knowledge and know-how more effectively and efficiently. Having a common understanding which is made transparent and visualized with words, graphs, and/or numbers is transformative. It enables teams to develop a tangible sense of the problem at hand and agree on the data/facts at stake. It also proved to be useful tool that helped facilitate conversations and garner support of decision makers and senior executives. The latter often face a real lack of time and plenty of competing topics requiring their attention. Seeing what is, where to, with whom and how—all presented using visualisation methods suited for the way our brains process information—is a huge success factor in change management and innovation in the legal field.

'*Empower*' is the fourth active force at play. It points out to the need of changing the dynamics between the professional in presence. Empower hints at the need to develop a culture where a useful idea prevails irrespective of who proposes it. Empowerment also promotes the idea of placing a decision as close as possible to where such decisions have an effect versus referring to line management or to the expert in charge for every detail.

In addition, three pairs of polarities highlight the constitutive fibres of the canvas where the actions unfold:

- Pair 1: *individual-collective* refers to the human dynamics and space for interactions.
- Pair 2: *tacit-explicit* refers to knowledge sharing and know-how mobilisation.
- Pair 3: *think-make* refers to iterative process going from ideas to prototypes to implementation.

The aim in using the 'Ease legal model' as an overview is to insist on the need to have a holistic approach to change. There is only so much time available to team members driving the change, who are usually expected to deliver on their day-to-day tasks in addition to being involved in optimisation projects. Having a workable map helps to ensure that the most important aspects will be covered by the designated project managers. It prevents practitioners from getting lost in detail or getting scattered across too many items or overwhelmed by the perceived need to utilize too many toolboxes.

The key values of the 'Ease legal model' (engage, aim, see, empower) conveniently support the mitigation of the four archetypal cognitive biases often present in legal ecosystems (hierarchy, disclaimer, right answer, and status quo) as summarised in Fig. 4.

To moderate the tendency to be hierarchical beyond necessity, it is important to develop a communication culture where what matters is the act of communicating more than the status of the communicator. If encouraged and practiced diligently over time, such culture grows trust, which in turn helps develop an environment in which reporting a mistake, or a challenge encountered becomes an opportunity to outgrow past and current inefficiencies.

To outgrow the mentality of 'disclaimer first – solution if and when later', it matters that the actors of the legal ecosystems look at the needs of their clients. What problem are they trying to solve? Which objectives are they trying to meet? Clients often come with impossible requests or last-minute deadlines and are not always articulate about their problems and needs. A discussion that ensues on such unstable ground, is destined to deplete everyone's time and energy, often leading to dead ends. Legal professionals should avoid jumping to finding solutions immediately, in order to help both themselves and their clients. Before applying legal expertise, they should be focusing on the business needs and looking at things from client's perspective.

To fight the syndrome of "always wanting to get it right", it would be more effective and efficient to spend time making the tenants of the issue as explicit and visible as possible. Seeing the problem correctly means positioning yourself to solve the problem. An inquiring mindset, with ambition to unveil the interrelations at play, could help lawyers advise on more sustainable and ecosystem-oriented solutions.

To identify which change to prioritise, while being mindful of the need for stability and certainty, prototyping change and testing ideas need to be learned by practicing lawyers using design thinking and agile project management methods.

Different competencies and toolboxes have helped us anchor the vision and strategy into actions and outcomes.

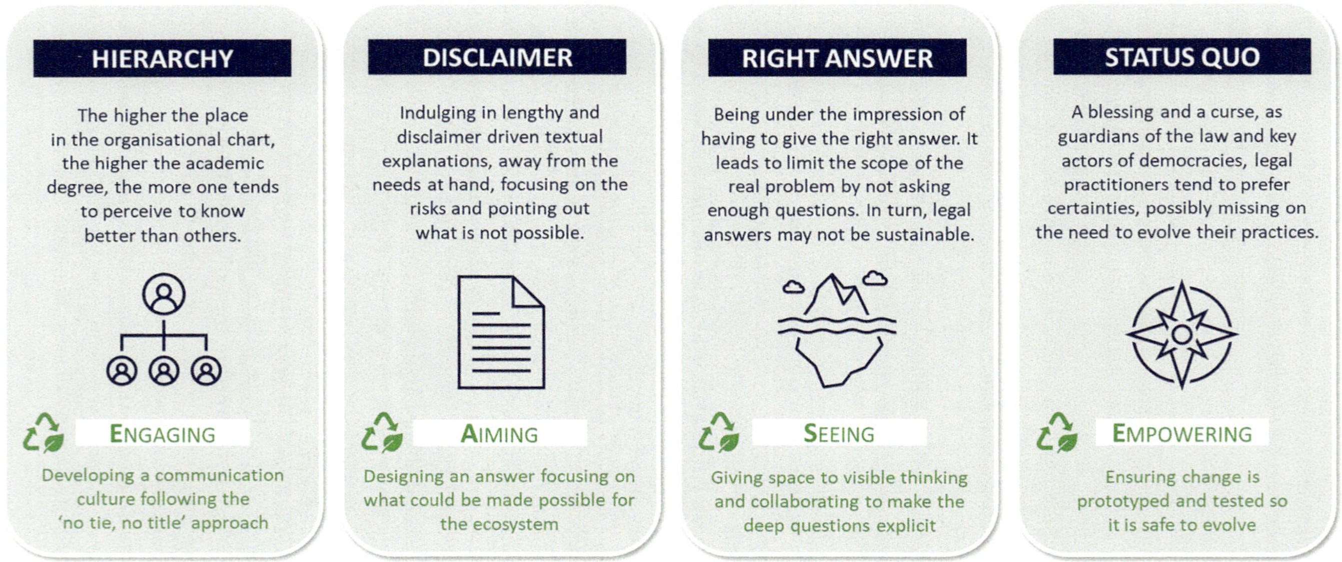

Fig. 4 Four cognitive biases common to legal ecosystems and the actions to mitigate them

4 A Gavel Is No Longer Enough

The purpose of this section is to account for the diversity of toolboxes we used. Without mobilising these various elements, it would have been more difficult to attempt a significant shift. Lawyers would be wise to learn from the fact that many other professions have also had to acquire more than their core legal qualifying skills and competencies. This trend has been especially noticeable in the last couple of decades. Viewing general management and leadership tools also relevant for lawyers is not only useful, but indispensable. It shall become a part of their continuous and life-long learning.

We have decided to highlight eight essential transversal toolboxes, clustered in two categories. These are certainly not the only ones but offer a good start.

The first category relates to vision and people and encompasses four toolboxes: (i) leadership, (ii) coaching, (iii) facilitation, (iv) communication. The second category relates to planning and implementation and encompasses four toolboxes: (i) project management, (ii) process management, (iii) design thinking, (iv) visualization, as presented in Fig. 5.

On the vision and people side, trained and matured leadership skills need to be invested in the quest to guide the evolution of legal ecosystems. Coaching is manifested as a working style focused on enabling the various stakeholders to nurture an appreciative inquiry mindset. Facilitation skills are important to activate collective intelligence. Merely sending an agenda and chairing a meeting is not what we have in mind when we speak about facilitation. Instead, it refers to a holistic approach to problem solving, ideation, advanced co-creation and solution design. When it comes to communication, lawyers often believe that this skill is already mastered, due to their frequent use of the written form and, for some, advanced oratory skills. But that potentially leaves lawyers blind to understand and develop other advanced communication skills. This is especially relevant for visual and data-driven executive communication which has become a key success factor in business. Legal ecosystems are no exception to this necessity.

Our summary of the above, set out in Fig. 6, is not an exhaustive toolbox collection, but we offer it as an example and encouragement to enable other teams to transition from a tacit toolbox which "somehow appears to work" to an explicit, thought through toolbox really showing "this is how it works". When teams move their know-how from tacit to explicit and from individual to collective, a real upskilling can take place. Structural shifts become possible, where the new is

Fig. 5 Key domain of competencies beyond legal knowledge and know-how

VISION & PEOPLE			
LEAD & MANAGE	COACH	FACILITATE	COMMUNICATE
EMBODIED	GOALS DRIVEN	HYBRID	ANALYTICAL
ENGAGED	PROCESS ORIENTED	SYSTEMIC	CREATIVE
EVIDENCE BASED	PERSON CENTRED	heART OF HOSTING	CRITICAL
SENSE MAKING		THEME CENTRED	

Fig. 6 Gist of the transversal vision and people skills put into action

PLANNING & IMPLEMENTATION			
PROJECT MANAGE	PROCESS DESIGN	DESIGN LEGAL	VISUALIZE
SCOPE	USE PILOTS	OPERATIONS	DATA
STAKEHOLDERS	DIGITALIZE	CONTRACTS	INFORMATION
COMMUNICATION	SELECT & DROP ITEMS	LEGAL DRAFTING	KNOWLEDGE
MONITORING		PUBLICATIONS	KNOW-HOW

Fig. 7 A gist of the planning and implementation skills put into action

anchored in a conscious understanding of what is at stake and what it takes to outgrow yesterday's limitations.

On the planning and implementation side (Fig. 7), skill sets stemming from project management and process management need to be much more obvious and integrated in the curricula of law schools and later in lawyers' day-to-day practice. If lawyers are well established in their topical areas, it might therefore be a good investment of their time to skip the next topical legal conference and attend, for instance, a project management course.

Similarly, the development of legal design thinking and legal knowledge visualization should not be seen as secondary for those who can draw and "use PowerPoint". No! It should rather be seen as augmenting thinking, analysing, understanding, collaborating, ideating, building complex legal arguments, designing ergonomic contracts, etc. The challenges of our times are of such magnitude that a single brain cannot do it all alone. And to truly join forces, a radical humanisation of the dialogue space is required. Orchestrating a culture of high performance based on human collaboration is the ultimate soft skill enabling teams to make best use of technological opportunities of our times.

Legal design helps lawyers with improving their working platforms, the way they present legal document or the way they collaborate within their teams or with their clients. Legal design is the one key toolbox that we want to highlight here. Our practice shows that legal design and legal knowledge visualization have been instrumental for enabling our agenda. Comparing legal design and legal knowledge visualization, we would say that they both help with democratizing the creation and access to legal deliverables. Legal design in our practice focuses more on optimization of products, processes, and user experience while legal knowledge visualization focuses more on knowledge management, know-how mobilization and overall practice sharing.

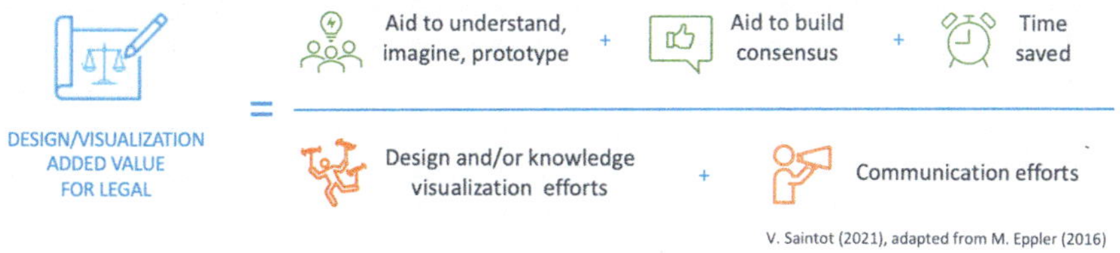

Fig. 8 The value of legal design and knowledge visualization

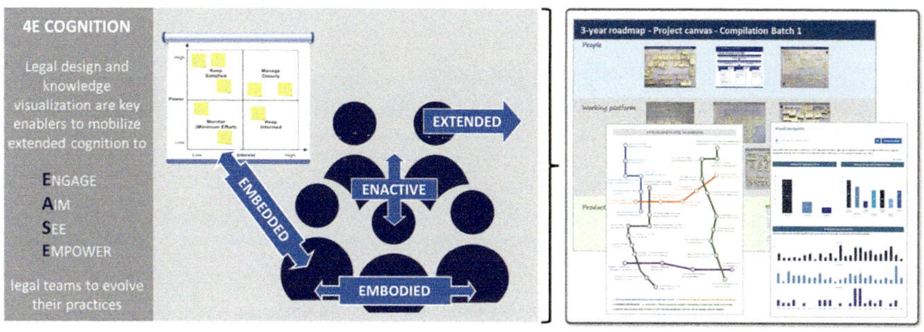

Fig. 9 Overview of the key enablers to transform the work of legal teams

We consider that reduced to its essence, legal design helps to (i) understand, imagine, and protype (ii) build consensus, and (iii) save time. Obviously, this has a cost in that it implies design and/or knowledge visualization, and communication efforts as summarised in Fig. 8. Books and trainings tailor-made to lawyers are blossoming. We cannot recommend enough that legal teams consider seriously expanding their capabilities with legal design and legal knowledge visualization.

We use legal design and legal knowledge visualization on different levels of complexity. Some use cases are central to core legal work, such as explaining a core legal problem, legal concept, or legal framework. At other times, we apply the general principles of design thinking, and knowledge and data visualizations to different operational issues. It is important to understand the role of creating the awareness, growing appetite, nurturing the momentum, and sticking with propagating the skills long enough until the breakthrough happens, and a critical mass of professionals are naturally starting to use it.

The reason we care to spell out more than the obvious tools and try and explain the underlying models and dynamics is to explain the need for a deep shift and not a short-lived one. When proceeding with the adequate depth, the conditions for a lasting upskilling, for innovation and transformation are united and can make any team successful. Figure 9 brings together the key enablers to transform the work of legal teams.

As a legal knowledge management team, we strive to embody the spirit and practices of both legal design and legal knowledge visualization in most of our products and outputs. On a consistent basis, we created a visual landscape establishing—iteration after iteration—a natural way to work. The reception of such products by both senior management and peers in the legal department was overwhelmingly positive, which in turn acted as a big accelerator on the journey to move from text dominated output to more diverse expressions, including data, graphs, and flowcharts—of course, providing that the task at hand justifies such formats.

5 The Proof Is in the Making

In this section, our purpose is to illustrate the use of the building blocks and methodological aspects presented in the previous sections. It is also intended to let the reader experience that transformation is not for the fainthearted. Transformation does not have to take long; it only needs to be intentional for both management and a critical mass of team members. Focused and deep intention, together with hard work contains the potential to bring lasting transformation.

There are a lot of fads in management and leadership. The next hype is always creeping up and at an ever-faster pace. Here, we promote evidenced-based management and leadership and draw on well researched models. Time and resources should be treated as precious and need to be invested with an eye on return on investment in the private sector and return on time in the public sector.

We have chosen three distinct use cases, as Fig. 10a–c shows. They cover a diverse set of needs addressed; they encompass significant projects; and the output delivered has contributed to a concrete transformation.

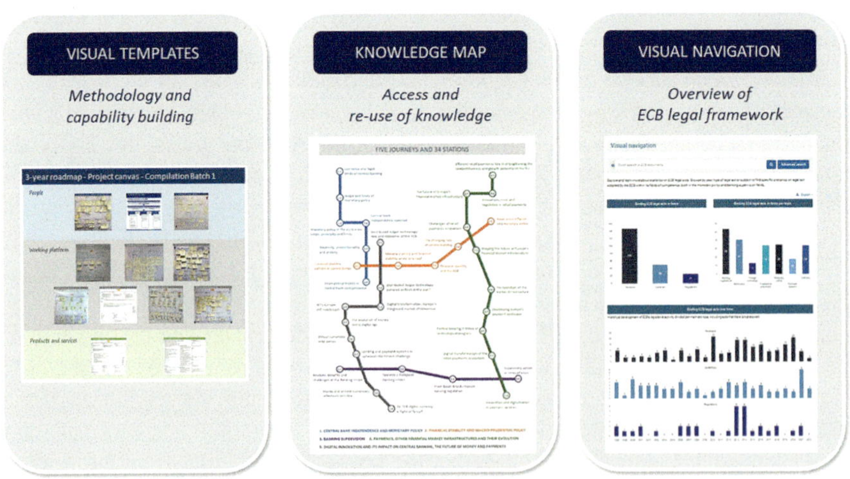

Fig. 10 **a–c** Three examples of output created by applying the EASE model

The first case study is an example of building horizontal skills to help plan and execute the transformation of a legal unit. The focus was on using visual templates, specifically a project canvas, to grow a common understanding on how to team up to meet the transformation objectives.

The second case study relates to the use of knowledge visualization to display the big picture of eight years of legal work in the form of a knowledge map.

The third case study relates to the use of data visualization to create an accessible entry point to the ECB legal framework using interactive data visualization accessible online via EUR-Lex (https://eur-lex.europa.eu).

5.1 Building 'T-shaped' Profiles with Business Templates: A Mini-MBA

We realised that a primary factor that prevents change is less the resistance to overhaul habits, than the unconscious and genuine anxiety generated by not knowing how to work differently. If one could know how to make it simpler and more efficient, one would just do it. Not seeing how things could be less transactional and more transformational paralyses the ability of teams to initiate and embrace change. How is it possible to move past these constraints? By investing in capability building, empowering, and training people, and creating a space in which it is okay to not know something—as long as it is seen as the first step on the learning journey. Instead of spending all the time managing existing knowledge, we should dare to manage ignorance. For this case study, we used visual templates. A research shows, a visual template works as a nudge, an architectural choice to help teams unfold their thinking, collaborate more efficiently, share their knowledge and know-how more explicitly. Overall a visual template is a unique supportive framework that helps to align and bring together team members wishing to ideate, mobilise knowledge, define options, make decision, plan work and report progress. By using the visual template to plan different projects, we achieved many goals in one go, while supporting individual and collective capability building. Using visual templates is worth scaling up. It could be applied very broadly to various business needs and problems as our research shows.

5.1.1 Case Study 1: Use of Visual Templates for Building Project Management Capabilities[1]

What Problem Were We Trying to Solve?

In essence, here we were trying to modernise the working platform of a team of 40 lawyers. The evolution of the working platform had to be done from within the team. Team members would have to both deliver on their main work mandate and find a system to dedicate time to help evolve their working platform.

[1] See Fig. 10a.

How Did We Engage?
The conduct of the transformation project required skills which legitimately were outside the standard skills of the team members and managers. To help team members to align, we decided to use visual templates to plan a three-year change roadmap. To support the learning and development of the team, we used an approach to collaboration based on knowledge visualization techniques developed by Professor Martin J. Eppler and his team at University of St Gallen. The purpose was to equip lawyers with a concrete set of tools they would immediately apply to the roadmap sub-task they volunteered for. Learning in the classroom in short sessions on how to use the project canvas, filled with relevant questions and perspectives created quick knowledge jump in terms of project management skills.

What Did We Aim For?
We aimed at mobilising the extensive tacit know-how present individually and collectively in the team. The vision was to create output types which showed the specificities of the function, the professional mastery involved in performing the function, the uniqueness of its added value with the overarching aim of being able to better quantify and qualify what could be delegated to computer assisted processes and what needed to remain the privilege of the people performing a highly intellectual and knowledge driven function.

How Did We Visualize the Project?
Using a project canvas, an empty template with pre-set topics, the teams defined their project: objectives, resources, stakeholders, work packages, milestones, working methods, timeline, reporting, governance, risks, etc. This created a deep dive into the basics of project management without the burden and cost of a long formal training filled with lots of theory and standards. From there, team members took the templates they worked on together and made entries in a common project management roadmap, displaying what each team had committed to do.

How Did Empowerment Manifest Itself?
Teams regularly visualized their progress and achievements. Over time, a visual collaboration culture, fostering accountability and transparency, established itself across the various project sub-teams. Over the months that followed, we could observe an increase of mastery and level of comfort with utilizing the project management, design thinking and visualization skills and tools. Initial doubt and insecurity concerning how to go about the sub-tasks and use of project canvas was gradually replaced with regular use of this visual template. It also enabled easier integration of additional templates later. As the mastery grew, team members took their project management methods and transported them organically to new activities and tasks they were handling, well beyond the overall transformation project. Newer team members were induced by others with more experience and a dynamic of peer-based learning and feedback culture was slowly put in motion. In doing so, the foundation for 'T-shaped' lawyers was laid in the team.

5.2 Knowledge Map: Helping to Navigate Complexity

Legal knowledge management is another thrilling and challenging domain. It is not just an ancillary function for depositing documents in cupboards. It is a conscious set of activities serving to extract tacit knowledge and create explicit usable output, not only limited to the moment of knowledge creation, but also at any later point in time. Finding ways to value in-house created legal knowledge assets poses challenges that usual information taxonomies and enterprise content management tools may not always address. Such approaches focus more on the "cupboards and drawers" structures than on the actual knowledge assets placed in them. Our legal knowledge management team has had solid experience with applying knowledge visualization principles to help find ways through the maze of documents created and stored.

5.2.1 Case Study 2: Use of Tube Maps to Structure Legal Knowledge and Make It Easy to Access[2]

What Problem Were We Trying to Solve?

We were tasked with finding a way to retrieve, select, structure, and make accessible some fifty pieces of legal doctrine produced in-house over a period of eight years. We realised quickly that the pieces had their own internal logic when examined individually. Yet, when brought together the lack of obvious red thread across the pieces created quite of a dissonant collection. This was when we decided to use design thinking to create a coherent overview, where the selected pieces would find their place and eloquently journal eight years of legal development and doctrine building.

How Did We Engage?

For this task, four lawyers teamed up. Two lawyers were deeply knowledgeable about the legal content at hand. A third lawyer had advanced knowledge visualization know-how and a fourth lawyer mastered knowledge visualization and possessed relevant software skills. After fully understanding the challenge (and getting enthusiastic about it), we defined the scope, ideated in a few rounds, then prototyped quickly, tested this prototype with key stakeholders and put the production of the final product (a book) in motion.

What Did We Aim For?

The goal was to find a way to organise knowledge in an effective (relevant pieces) and efficient (easily accessible) structure to account for eight years of work. Besides the conceptual complexity of the endeavour, there was the issue of forging a new path with this product and the time available was extremely limited. This would have taken too long and the topics and outputs at hand were too scattered and diverse to be able to deal with in a purely linear fashion. It took a combination of legal design thinking methods, combined with knowledge visualization principles to be able to

[2] See Fig. 10b.

deliver on this complex task. Having a clear and fast-forwarding path and method were crucial factors for success.

How Did We Visualize the Project?

A set of visuals were created in PowerPoint and knowledge assets (represented with their titles) were visualized, arranged, and re-arranged and structured. We were attempting to find a visual metaphor that would help the reader to better grasp the legal content. Following the principle of "big picture first and details on demand", we settled on the visual metaphor of a tube map to structure thirty-four legal documents finally selected along five tube lines. The idea was that each tube line would symbolise a legal topic while each station would be a particular legal advice. Conceptually, lines would cross at the same station only if the legal advice would pertain to both lines.

How Did Empowerment Manifest Itself?

From idea to print, we delivered in less than a month which set new record for creating and printing such a tangible two hundred pages' compilation. It exposed the colleagues involved to an alternative way of structuring knowledge. The produced visual was meant for a printed copy, but it would be easy to create an interactive digital version and make it accessible online. It was not the purpose of this project, but it empowered us to expand ideas in that direction for future occasions.

5.3 Legislative Data Visualization: Navigating the Law

Making a legal framework more visible is useful for both the core legal matter experts as well as the general public. Legislation, although by default made public, is still sometimes available in a space that is quite hard to navigate in a user-friendly way that most people have grown accustomed to (predominantly via the internet). When we started getting interested in that topic, we were quick to realise that it was not so easy to obtain reliable quantitative data about legislation (e.g. acts in force or historical development), due to the limitations of the platform and lack of sensitivity for the bigger picture. When an opportunity presented itself, we launched a project aimed at making a shift in the way users access the 20 years of legislative activity of the European Central Bank. The playground for this project our was the official EU law database/platform, called EUR-Lex.

5.3.1 Case Study 3: Visual Navigation of ECB Legal Framework[3]

What Problem Were We Trying to Solve?

Before this project, it was not possible to find, in real time and without significant manual efforts, the exact composition of the ECB legal framework, or query it in different ways. Besides, being knowledgeable about the details of a given legal topic

[3] See Fig. 10c.

was mostly reserved for experts working in that domain, whilst the general public would have a hard time finding their way around ECB's legislation on EUR-Lex. Hence, the problem we were trying to solve was to make the legal framework more transparent and accessible to anyone interested in its basic content and features.

How Did We Engage?

This was one of the most complex projects we took on and it also included joining forces with externals. This required adjustment of our usual working methods, to bring together different professional profiles that were bringing different knowledge and talents to the table. Before the project, understanding the legal framework was very much relying on tacit knowledge of experts. One of the main steps was to correctly identify who could be the key contributors and sponsors.

What Did We Aim For?

The goal was to create a new institutional landing page on EUR-Lex, which would be dedicated to the ECB's legislation and related case-law. It would include novel and interactive features to enter the sphere of EC- related legal documents, building on already powerful underlying database.

How Did We Visualize the Project?

Time and efforts were invested in prototyping. Starting with hand drawn mocks to own the vision, we went on to create more sophisticated concepts. We used Excel to extract and clean underlying data and loaded it in Tableau. After examining different proposals, we settled for a basic and reliable dashboard. Over time, building on the direct feedback from users and some statistics about the usage of the pages, new, possibly more diverse data visualization graphs may enrich the starter kit we created and implemented.

How Did Empowerment Manifest Itself?

The main empowerment effect manifested itself in showing that navigating the law does not need to be exclusively textual. We created a space where ECB's legislation is quantified in different, easy to grasp and visual ways (per act type, according to topic, over time or currently in force). This fosters transparency and accountability by making the content and physiognomy of the ECB's legal framework understandable. The project received positive feedback from various academics. It also inspired conversations with other EU legislators to investigate other ways to make the EU law even more easily accessible.

6 'Ease Legal' Smart Guide

Our closing words will take the form of what we call a 'smart guide'. It is a mini manifesto (Fig. 11). We created it to visually document our working principles. We believe that these principles can help transform the legal ecosystems by putting focus

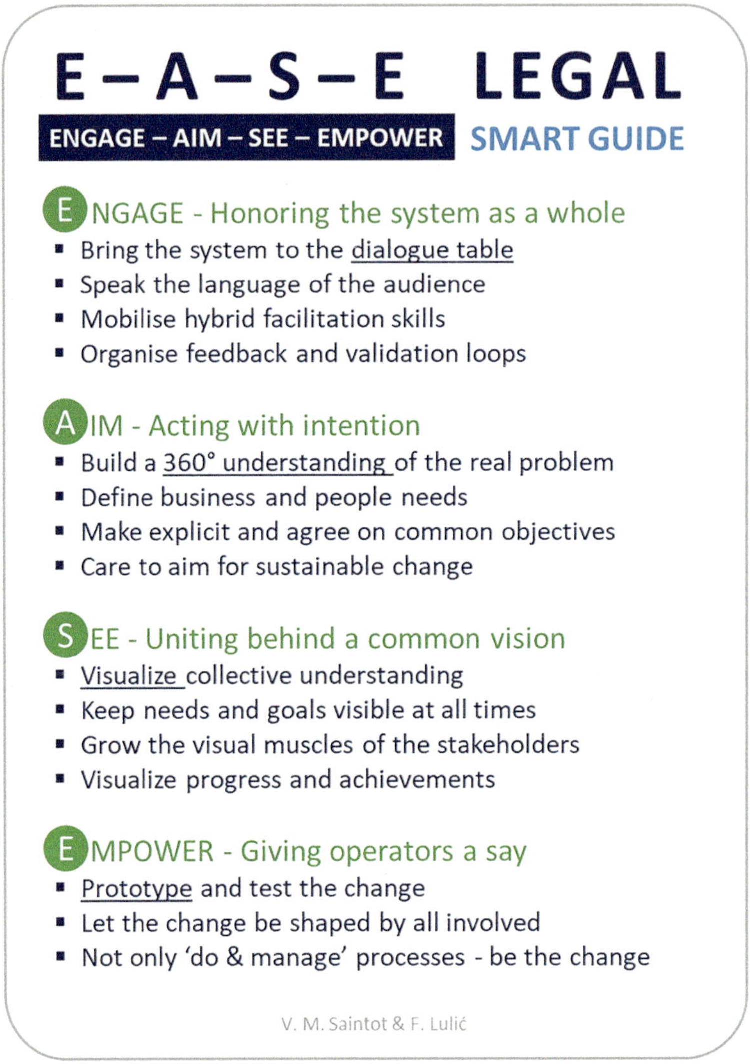

Fig. 11 EASE legal smart guide

on human aspects of the equation and in turn enable a sustainable business practice for the greater good.

Liquid Legal Waves to Other Chapters, Written by the Editors

Valérie and *Filip* put the focus on cognitive biases that can stand in the way of fundamental and long-lasting digital transformation. Their thesis complements *Dierk's* pledge for humanizing strategy and communication in change: If transformation is all about efficiency and effectiveness ('more, better, faster'), we are missing the point—we must focus on *"The missing Piece"*!

Valérie's and *Filip's* chapter introducing the EASE model is also a direct Segway to the rise of the self-aware organization that *Liam*, *John* and *Joyce* describe in *"The Elevated Workplace"*. The characteristics of the elevated workplace are safety, belonging, esteem and fulfilment motivating employees to honestly care about the organization's success.

Time to take a look at another stakeholder equally important: the client! In the following chapter on *"Elevating Customer Experience"*, *Stephen* explains how a true meeting of the minds between employees and clients will positively impact both, employee happiness and customer experience.

Recommended Reading

On Leadership, Organisational Development, and Collaboration

Laloux F (2014) Reinventing organization. A guide to creating organizations inspired by the next stage of human consciousness. Nelson Parker, Brussels

Saintot V, Friedrich K (2016) Das MeetingLAB der Europäischen Zentralbank, OranisationsEntwicklung Nr. 4, pp 6–12

Eppler M, Kernbach S, Pfister R (2016) Dynagrams Denken in Stereo: Mit dynamischen Diagrammen schärfer denken, effizienter zusammenarbeiten und klarer kommunizieren. Schäffer-Poeschel verlag, Stuttgart

Scharmer C-O (2018) The essential of Theory U. Core principles and applications. Berret-Koehler, Oakland

Eppler M, Kernbach S (2021) Meet up!: Better meetings through nudging. Cambridge University Press, Cambridge, UK

On Embodiment and Knowing More Than with Our Brains

Newen A, De Bruin L, Gallagher S (2018) The Oxford handbook of 4E cognition. Oxford University Press, New York

On Design, Data, and Visualization

Katz D, Hartung D, Bucerius Law School: Center for Legal Technology and Data Science. https://www.law-school.de/international/research-faculty/institutes-centers/center-for-legal-technology-and-data-science

Saintot V (2021) Data visualisation: developing capabilities to make decisions and communicate. In: Data science in economics and finance for decision makers. RiskBooks, London

Kohlmeier A, Klemola M (2021) The legal design book: doing law in the 21st century. Ground M, USA

Project Management

International Project Management Association (2021) The IMPA homepage. https://www.ipma.world/

On the Evolution of the Legal Profession

Smathers R-A (2015) The 21st-century T-shaped lawyer. Connecticut Lawyer

Susskind R (2017) Tomorrow's lawyers: an introduction to your future. Oxford University Press, New York

V. M. Saintot, LLM, PhD, is a lawyer with three decades of professional experience in both private and public sector. She started her career at the European Court of Justice in Luxembourg in 1994. Before focusing on lecturing, she has been the Head of Legislation Division, Directorate General Legal Services at the European Central Bank in Frankfurt where she also led a team in charge of legal knowledge management. She holds four postgraduate degrees in law, psychology, and research. She regularly speaks at events promoting knowledge visualization and is author of management articles in this domain.

Valérie is passionate about helping teams activate their full potential. To this end, she has been using for two decades knowledge visualization and (legal) design thinking. She has experienced the power of both to support collaboration, innovation, decision-making and communication. Valérie managed the team in charge of the creation of the ECB visitor centre which opened in 2017. This project gave her the opportunity to manifest in a large scale the power of visual and design thinking for outreach purposes. She is also working on developing legislative data visualization methods to help experts and citizens alike navigate online legal frameworks in a more transparent and intuitive way.

F. Lulić holds a Master of Laws degree from University of Rijeka, Croatia. After working for several companies in Croatia, he moved to Frankfurt to join the European Central Bank legal services as a lawyer linguist. Over the years, he specialised in legal tech and AI projects, and settled in the Legal Knowledge Management Team, where he works on digital agenda of the legal department. Filip manages a wide variety of legal tech projects like creation of digital workflows, legal content analytics and building taxonomies, information architecture and knowledge/legislation databases. Among his many interests, he is particularly passionate about legal design and knowledge visualisation techniques that he is not only using in his work, but also teaches to others in a community of practice that he facilitates.

Elevating the Customer Experience

Stephen Allen, Lizzie Christmas, and Rachel Barnes

Contents

Abstract

A company does not operate as an end in and of itself; its mission is to create sustainable value, and to do that, it needs to attract and retain customers. This requires more than "customer satisfaction," and it encompasses the customer experience beyond simply using the company's products and services. This paradigm—Experience-Centric Design—improves customers' satisfaction,

Stephen Allen, Vice President Get Sh*t Done, Elevate.

Lizzie Christmas, Director, Solutions and Consulting, Elevate.

Rachel Barnes, Director, Solutions and Consulting, Elevate.

S. Allen (✉) · L. Christmas · R. Barnes
Los Angeles, California, USA
e-mail: thestephenallen@icloud.com; rachel.barnes@elevateservices.com

K. Jacob et al. (eds.), *Liquid Legal – Humanization and the Law*, Law for Professionals, https://doi.org/10.1007/978-3-031-14240-6_8

enjoyment, and meaning from the work they do. Fundamentally, it makes their lives simpler and better, allowing them to worry less about the problems they entrust to the companies they use.

1 What's for Sale?

A foundational question for any organisation is, "What is the essence of our purpose?" As far as companies go, the prevailing answer—accepted too often as an "obvious truth"—is that companies exist solely to enrich their owners. This notion, that of so-called Shareholder Value, was perhaps most famously articulated by Milton Friedman in his 1970 essay in *The New York Times*, "A Friedman Doctrine: The Social Responsibility of Business is to Increase Its Profits."[1]

This doctrine is blind to a more powerful understanding of what ought to be the central motivating principle of business enterprises and their employees. Simply put, a company's *raison d'etre* should be to elevate and empower customers.[2] Only those businesses that do so will endure.

A growing body of research[3] validates this hypothesis, and the repudiation of Friedman is becoming increasingly heard. In August 2019, a meeting of the Business Round Table (BRT) generated headlines in leading publications, such as "Shareholder Value Is No Longer Everything, Top CEOs Say"[4] (*New York Times*) and "Group of US corporate leaders ditches shareholder-first mantra"[5] (*Financial Times*). Such sorts of headlines are becoming more frequent in the business press.

Of course, the phrase "elevate and empower" require some specificity. It is more than "customer satisfaction" and includes the moment-to-moment emotional experience of customers in interacting with a company and its products and services. Customers are elevated and feel empowered when they feel more capable and effective in completing the purpose of their roles (their "jobs to be done").[6] This has been covered in numerous academic studies and was heralded in a 2021 *Forbes* article, "Welcome To The Age Of Customer Empowerment."[7]

[1] *See* Friedman (1970).

[2] We use the term 'customer' rather than 'client,' with the former referring to *human* relationships—typically with numerous interconnections—between a buyer (or "user," "consumer," etc.) and individuals at a provider (or "merchant," "seller," etc.), as opposed to an *entity-to-entity* relationship (e.g., a contractual arrangement between corporations).

[3] *See, e.g.*, Berraies and Hamouda (2018).

[4] Gelles and Yaffe-Bellany (2019).

[5] Henderson and Temple-West (2019).

[6] *See* Christensen et al. (2016).

[7] Martin (2021).

Note that jobs-to-be-done are *not* the same as tasks to be accomplished. Tasks are how an individual accomplishes—or achieves—an activity.[8] A job-to-be-done concerns the outcome that an individual seeks. Addressing a job-to-be-done is not about optimising the performance of a task; it is about designing and deploying a product, process, or service (or combination thereof) to meet a customer's needs and solve that customer's problems, thus creating customer value.

A crucial but oft-overlooked point, jobs-to-be-done include an emotional and experiential component. To take an example far afield from the legal industry, we might imagine a manufacturing plant where a particular machine on the assembly line keeps breaking. Those who operate the plant feel stress and anxiety about the situation because the delays caused whenever the machine stops working result in the plant failing to produce enough widgets to fulfil the company's contractual obligations to its customers. In this case, the job-to-be-done goes beyond whatever happens with the machine in question (e.g., repairing, resetting, replacing it, etc.). The operators need more than just a machine that is up and running again; they need to feel confident that the plant will operate reliably at the capacity necessary to meet customer expectations. Ultimately, they need to feel certain that, no matter what happens, their customers will be satisfied. This is essential to build trust—thus taking the customer relationship from a contractually regulated one to, instead, a partnership.

Once we understand the full scope and purpose of a job-to-be-done, we can readily see that meeting a customer's needs relative to a job-to-be-done requires more than delivering value or increasing efficiency. First, a company must internalise customers' needs and grasp the outcome—including feeling-states—that customers experience as they contend with a given job-to-be-done. Then, the company must innovate.

Innovation means more than a company integrating new ways of accomplishing jobs-to-be-done into its offerings. In addition to doing so, the enterprise must provide a novel and improved experience. The customer must feel differently—ideally, *better*—in using your product or service than they have when using existing or competing solutions. This is not always easy to measure. Net Promoter Scores (NPS) are one way of doing this, but the true measure is the stickiness of relationships and how they increase in scale.

The need to sell an experience is readily understood in the realm of consumer products. Consider the automobile: it is more than a tool; it is an experience. To succeed commercially, a car must *elicit enjoyable emotions*. In addition to enabling an individual to achieve a physical outcome (get from point A to point B), a car must generate feelings. It must be fun to drive. Or deliver a feeling of safety or environmental responsibility. Or increase the owner's sense of being successful (e.g., a luxury vehicle), frugal (e.g., a "sensible" car), powerful (e.g., a sports car),

[8] *See* Clement A (2016) What Is Jobs to be Done (JTBD)? https://jtbd.info/2-what-is-jobs-to-be-done-jtbd-796b82081cca.

discerning (e.g., a vehicle with elegant, distinctive, or cutting-edge design), or some other feeling state.

Note that none of these outcomes has anything to do with the intrinsic functionality of a car (or, for that matter, of sunscreen, a loaf of bread, legal advice, a B2B SaaS offering, or any other product or service). Rather, those outcomes involve the emotional state of the consumer.

To summarise, an enterprise must create sustainable value, and to do so, it needs to attract and retain customers. That requires elevating and empowering customers, which involves providing them with an outcome that includes an experiential dimension. And only a company that identifies customers' feelings and then identifies *with* those feelings can succeed in delivering a compelling experience. But how can this be accomplished?

2 Do You Feel Like I Feel?

Answers begin with questions. The crucial first step in providing a compelling customer experience is to ask the right questions—ones that elicit and illuminate what a customer truly wants or needs. This can be defined as "What is the job-to-be-done confronting the customer?"

A classic take on this question is attributed to famed Harvard Business School marketing professor Theodore Levitt, who conceptualised the answer as, "People don't want to buy a quarter-inch drill. They want a quarter-inch hole." To be sure, it's a clever answer, but ultimately a shallow understanding of the situation because it stops short of getting behind the apparent customer need. Why do they want a hole? And why do they think they need a hole instead of something else?

To extend Levitt's thought, perhaps the customer claims they want a drill to make a guide hole for a screw onto which they will hang a painting. They don't want a drill, and they don't want a hole—but they don't truly (or solely) want an image on their office wall. They want an outcome that includes a specific emotional experience. This emotional dimension reflects what the customer attributes to what they *claim* they want. To return to the example of an automobile, the customer wants transportation and claims to want a car—and yet wants more than that: in addition to accomplishing something (i.e., to get from A to B), the customer wants to feel something in particular (e.g., a sense of geographic freedom, the excitement of the wind rushing through one's hair, the satisfaction of owning a coveted possession, etc.).

This more comprehensive understanding—if we exercise our curiosity—leads to more and deeper questions. Why does the customer feel a need for the feel-state they believe gazing at the painting will generate? Are they bored staring at a blank wall? Do they find their job difficult, unpleasant, or unfulfilling and believe that artwork will be a welcome distraction or a reassuring sight?

We could delve even further, but the point is that we shouldn't take a customer's understanding of a problem or need at face value. Never mistake the apparent for the truth. We must tease out a more fundamental conception of what is going on, what is

Stated Need:	What the customer believes they need → Drill
Apparent Goal:	The outcome the customer appears to seek to achieve → Hole (to hang a picture)
Actual Need:	What the customer truly wants → Comfort/Distraction/Reassurance/Motivation
Optimal Solution:	What best addresses the customer's actual Job-to-Be-Done → (varies by customer)

Fig. 1 Needs, goals, solutions, and jobs-to-be-done (Elevate)

at stake, and the emotional context at hand. Only once we have done so will we understand the job-to-be-done and work towards delivering the most appropriate solution (Fig. 1).

3 The Solution Is to Solution

The activity of empathetic listening to determine a customer's actual needs is, for most organisations, a novel approach. As such, it deserves a name that distinguishes it from existing standard approaches. The term "solutioning" fits because, ultimately, the goal is to address a customer's jobs-to-be-done. Operationalising this approach defies reduction to a rigid series of steps or a flowchart. It requires, fundamentally, caring about a customer, listening to them, and striving to grasp their fundamental needs.

It is a collaborative endeavour and an iterative one. It combines open-mindedness, paying attention, sensitivity, and alignment (that is, working together with the customer in their best interest). It is as much an art as a science—at once structured yet simultaneously allowing for improvisation. This is listening, not hearing.

This seems like a simple enough endeavour. Yet, few organisations adhere to this approach, usually for one of two reasons:

Sell What You've Got This is the all-too-common phenomenon of any organisation framing customer needs solely based on what the organisation has to offer. Typically, the practitioner diagnoses problems according to the tools at hand—as summarised by the old saw, "When all you have is a hammer, every problem appears as a nail." This is understandable; after all, how can you stay in business if you don't sell the product or service you presently offer? (Besides, the fact you have remained in business all this time presumably proves there is a thriving market for hammers.) And such an approach is all well and good. . .until you encounter a customer trying to tighten a bolt. Avoiding such an outcome begins with asking the right question. Instead of asking, "What do we have available to sell customers," the question should be, "What are potential customers' jobs-to-be-done that we – or our competitors – might address?" Done well, your people will be inspired to act as 'intrapreneurs'—motivated to create customer delight over more traditional corporate targets.

"The Eye Sees Only What the Mind Knows" Pre-existing mental schemas constrain our ability to perceive novel situations. We may not even be aware of the set of ideas and understandings upon which we rely to comprehend the world around us. Taking a wide array of assumptions as givens is often sensible; it relieves us of the overwhelming cognitive load we would face if we questioned everything we perceived and thought we knew. But this strategy generates the risk that we may fail to perceive and then consider crucial—and typically subtle—details that our mental model is not configured to notice. When something happens that seems very much like a type of event we have previously encountered, we are quick to discount the possibility that another explanation may be at work.

This phenomenon is most apparent in "edge cases" that challenge the limits of a classification system whereby things get grouped into mutually exclusive categories according to a limited set of criteria. When something has characteristics of two groups, we are befuddled. Perhaps this is something we haven't seen before?

Solutioning seeks to avoid these pitfalls by adhering to a set of understandings. These include:

- A situation can be both unique from and similar to other situations.[9]
- The problem may be exactly as it appears. Or not as it appears. Or, it may be both.
- Do not confuse certainty for accuracy.
- You may not possess (or be able to offer) the best solution to the customer's problem.

As this list suggests, to a large extent, solutioning is a gestalt rather than a methodology. Yes, there are steps that the solutioneer must take, and there is a progression of stages to solutioning. But there are moments when intuition comes into play and when a standard approach is inappropriate.

Nevertheless, the paradigm of solutioning is of little (read: no) use unless we can operationalise it. How, then, can we put solutioning into action? What must be done to "solution" a problem?

4 The Components of Solutioning

As stated above, reducing solutioning to a series of steps is a perilous endeavour because every step includes caveats. Nevertheless, as a practical matter, it is possible to describe a set of principles to follow when solutioning.[10]

[9]The so-called "Stovellian Contradiction," to use the term coined by James B. Stovell of Harvard University. *See* Stovell (1862), p. 374.

[10]This section draws on Golan and Allen (2021).

Feel Empathy The foundation of successful solutioning is sincere concern for the customer's well-being (we must never forget that we are dealing with humans, always. They think, feel and assess through that human experience and thus their 'well-being' is key). This requires understanding and sharing the customer's emotional state. It is more than lip service; it entails, for example, internalising the anxiety a customer feels about completing a particular job-to-be-done. You are more than an observer; you are a participant in the customer's experience, a travelling companion who has committed to help bear the burdens the customer is shouldering. A customer must feel something more than "you are on my side" and more akin to "you are part of my team." Many of you will think of 'Design Thinking' principles when reading this. But really, this is Experience-Centric Design.

Exhibit Curiosity and Ask Questions Another crucial activity of solutioning is demonstrating an ardent desire to know and comprehend. This can go beyond querying the customer and include interrogating data. Asking questions—including difficult ones—is the *sine qua non* of comprehending a situation. And a fulsome understanding of a situation—its causes, context, characteristics, and course—is a prerequisite to solving problems.

Clarify Desired Outcomes It is tempting to leap from diagnosing a problem to suggesting a solution. This omits the critical step of drawing out of a customer what they seek (what they are attempting to find) and want (what they crave). These may not be identical. A customer may seek "a system for categorising and tracking our contracts," yet what they want is reassurance that no hidden risks are lurking in their relationships with their vendors and customers.

Clarifying desired outcomes demands humility and a keen ear. Humility is the maintenance of a mindset of scepticism towards one's knowledge.[11] You may know far more about the type of problem that it seems a customer is facing. But the customer knows far more than you do about the actual problem they face. After all, they have lived it long before you arrived on the scene.

A keen ear involves more than hearing a customer's words. Often, what a customer does not say is as important—sometimes even more important—than what they tell you. There are many reasons for unarticulated statements. A particular fact may be embarrassing to disclose; it may seem so obvious to the customer that they think it goes without saying. Whatever the cause, one must listen for the "sound in the silence."[12]

Iterate Solutions Rarely do solutions present themselves fully formed. More often, solutions are honed through a repetitive process of testing a tentative solution against

---

[11] *See* Deikman (1983). ("Humility is the acceptance of the possibility that someone else can teach you something else you do not know already.")

[12] Wright (1994).

a desired outcome—so-called "agile design." After assessing flaws and gaps in the proposed solution, refinements occur to eliminate deficiencies in the solution.

Optimising a solution often requires accepting tradeoffs because it is impossible to craft a solution that excels in all aspects. Indeed, pursuing the "perfect" solution may be a fool's errand.[13] The alternative, to use the term coined by economist Herbert Simon, is "satisficing," whereby individuals assess iterations of a solution according to a "threshold of acceptability." Once the process has (a) produced a proposed way forward that meets some set of minimum requirements and (b) reached a point of diminishing marginal returns, it's time to stop iterating.

Meet Minds One might think that having arrived at a solution, solutioning is complete. In truth, the process has just begun because solutioning involves implementing solutions, not just creating them. However, before starting the implementation stage, those involved need to come to what the law terms "a meeting of the mind"; that is, mutual comprehension of identical understandings of the solution and its context. There must be no confusion about the fundamental problem to be solved, the jobs-to-be-done, or the terms of the proposed solution.

Achieving a meeting of the minds requires empathy. You must internalise the customer's conception of the solution—both what the customer thinks about it and how they feel about it. Doing so is a prerequisite for implementing the solution because an empathetic understanding of the customer's perspective helps to ensure that implementation accords with the customer's expectations, concerns, and constraints.

The above-described set of actions is not meant to delineate a sequence of tasks. Each activity interacts with the others. Feeling empathy must animate your curiosity and your attempt to come to a meeting of the mind. Clarifying desired outcomes and iterating solutions require that the participants come to a meeting of the minds concerning what precisely a solution entails. And so on. There is no series of steps; there are goals to achieve, with activities informed by principles.

5 Solutioning the Design

Description in the preceding section of the components of solutioning presupposes that the solutioning involves a single customer. But what about solutioning, say, software, where one anticipates multiple—hopefully, multitudes—of customers?

The fundamental principles—empathy, inquiry, listening, humility, and collaboration—remain the same, but they are translated into a different, more structured approach, often referred to as "design thinking."[14] Definitions vary, but a common

[13] Simon (1956), pp. 129–138. *See also,* Voltaire (1770) *Dictionnaire philosophique. Basic Books Inc., (Peter Gay, ed.) 1962)* ("...the perfect is the enemy of the good.").

[14] For an overview of the genesis of design thinking, *see, e.g.,* Szczepanska J (2017) Design thinking origin story plus some of the people who made it all happen. https://szczpanks.medium.com/design-thinking-where-it-came-from-and-the-type-of-people-who-made-it-all-happen-dc3a05411e53. See also Dam and Siang (2020).

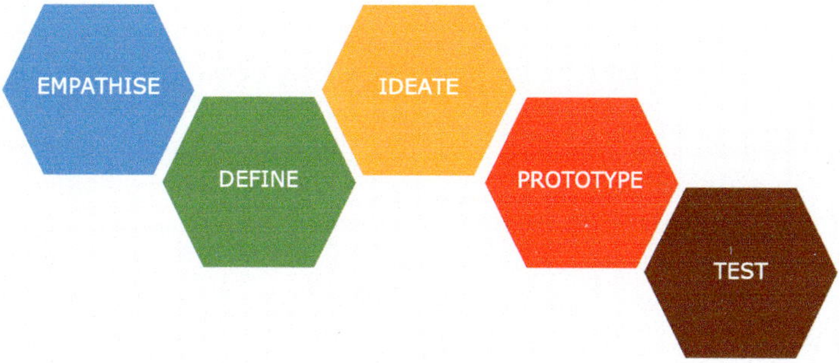

Fig. 2 Design Thinking (Stanford d.school legacy streamline design process, circa 2012 (Hasso Plattner School of Design at Stanford University)

theme is an emphasis on human-centred design. In the mid-2000s, a standard description of the Design Thinking methodology emerged, consisting of five steps: Empathise, Define, Ideate, Prototype, and Test (*see* Fig. 2).[15] These readily track to the steps described above as comprising the solutioning process.

A crucial commonality of Design Thinking and Solutioning is the centrality of a human (in design-speak, the user; in business-speak, the customer). But Experience-Centric Design focuses on human experience beyond the use of a product or service. It includes the full emotional and social results of a human's interaction with the thing in question. It is more than, "How does the user feel while using our software?" Rather, it encompasses "In what new ways does this individual conceive of themselves and view their relationships with others as a result of the range of ways they experience our software?" In other words, it involves an examination of how the offering has transformed the user.

6 Beyond the Customer's Experience

The discussion thus far has omitted any mention of a key group of participants in solutioning: your employees. What of the people sitting across from (or, ideally, alongside) the customer? Undeniably, their experience, skills, and state of mind directly impact whether Experience-Centric Design is possible.

Consider the case of an employee who feels disconnected from their work, resents their boss, is distracted by family matters, or feels disheartened by what they perceive as a stagnant career. It is doubtful this employee can rise to the challenge of solutioning. At a minimum, it seems certain that they won't be able to "bring their

[15]The five-step process is attributed to the Stanford Design School. *See* Mattson (2021). However, since pioneering this process, the school (now known as Stanford d.school) has evolved its pedagogy, with this hexagon graphic supplanted by other designs.

best" to bear. And it seems equally certain such an employee will not solution as well as an employee who feels engaged in their work, views their boss as an ally, has adequate time and mental bandwidth to attend to concerns beyond work, and has reason to believe their career is evolving as they would like.

This leads to a critical point: employees have jobs-to-be-done as much as customers do. Therefore, part of your responsibility is to enable and assist your employees in those jobs-to-be-done. As noted above, this involves more than just providing them with the means by which to perform tasks. It extends to helping them to achieve outcomes and innovate. And it encompasses attending to the full range of the experience an employee goes through. In other words, any attempt to implement Experience-Centric Design succeeds only when the employee experience is integrated into the endeavour. If we are to succeed at solutioning for customers, we must first engage in solutioning for our colleagues. Put another way—and borrowing language from the outset of this chapter—part of a company's *raison d'etre* is to elevate and empower its employees, and only those businesses that do so will endure.

7 Work as an Existential Endeavour

Assuming a 40-h workweek and 8 h of sleep per night, individuals will spend more than a third of their waking hours working. For those of us with commutes and longer hours, the figure may approach 80%. If we are sincere in our commitment to Experience-Centric Design, we must contend with the reality that employees' jobs-to-be-done are, quite literally, a central component of their existence. When solutioning for customers, we must empathise with their employees, be curious about their needs, goals, and experience of their work, assist them in determining desired outcomes, iterate solutions with them, and come to a meeting of the minds. (Indeed, this provides a definition of the concept of Humanisation—the entire focus of the book in which this chapter appears!)

Easier said than done. Perhaps the biggest barriers to solutioning with employees are the mindsets that stand in the way. A few mental traps are common to many organisations—including (and importantly) those of our customers.

The Beatings Will Continue Until Morale Improves In quite a few organisations, the powers-that-be conceive work as an unpleasant but necessary activity, and they assess employees according to productivity (however defined). A vicious feedback loop arises. Sometimes work, as the saying goes, is like a pie-eating contest where the prize is more pie.

This mindset overlooks the possibility that one's work might be simultaneously important and enjoyable and that employees might work harder and better if that were the case. The irony is that most executives readily grasp that, all things being equal, a product that is more pleasant for a customer to use compared to an incumbent product will triumph in the marketplace. Yet, many of these same executives fail to understand that employees are a type of customer—they are "buying" a product called "a job at your company." If a company is to attract top talent, it must elevate employees and provide them with a superb experience of completing their jobs-to-be-done.

As far as the customer experience goes, it is worth remembering that your customer may have to contend with a challenging (read: difficult, unpleasant, etc.) corporate culture. They may not think about their jobs-to-be-done in terms of including a positive experience; they have come to expect otherwise. But you understand that jobs-to-be-done include an emotional dimension, and you therefore solution accordingly.

Nice Guys Finish Last A related phenomenon is the belief that anything that might assist employees in accomplishing their jobs-to-be-done will undermine productivity and embolden them to ask for accommodations and perks that will further reduce output. What might seem like a nice thing to do for employees will come back to haunt the employer.

The flaw in this way of thinking is that helping employees accomplish their jobs-to-be-done is not synonymous with coddling workers or letting them do whatever they like. Employees must be held accountable and be productive. But there are better and worse ways of doing so. Work conditions that lead to employees feeling valued and that their work has meaning are not "perks"; they are a crucial component in providing an employee experience that workers will cherish. When solutioning with customers, it may be an uphill climb when trying to get customers to understand that addressing the emotional dimensions of jobs-to-be-done isn't a concession, it's a virtue.

Nothing to See Here At some companies, management believes that they do a sufficient job when it comes to employee experience. They pay well; the working conditions are good; the culture is humane. What more could someone want in a job?

A reasonable retort is, "I'm not sure what more someone might want in their job – have you asked your employees that question?" Put another way, have you tried to empathise with your employees to understand what they seek and want, and are you helping them with their jobs-to-be-done? Have you done with your employees the exact same thing you must do with your customers?

We're [Company Name]—Everything We Do Is Awesome! A more extreme version of Nothing to See Here occurs when company leaders believe that their company excels at "what matters" in a work environment. Perhaps the company has all the indicia of "a great place to work"—accolades from publications and trade organisations, low turnover, high job satisfaction ratings from employees, and so forth (Fig. 3).

If we recall the tenets of solutioning, this self-congratulatory stance ought to set alarm bells ringing. Consider the following:

Fig. 3 What could possibly be wrong? (Copyright 2013 by KC Green)

- A company may be simultaneously excellent and flawed.
- Management may be unable to perceive an organisation's deficiencies.
- Executives may confuse positive feedback with an accurate view of what is truly going on.
- An organisation may not possess the best solution for its employees' jobs-to-be-done.

Once we disabuse ourselves of our delusions, solutioning may proceed. What does solutioning look like when it comes to employees' jobs-to-be-done?

8 The Art in Solutioning[16]

At this point, you might perceive a looming paradox: Solutioning cannot be reduced to a series of operations, and each employee is unique. How then are we to arrive at a unified description of employees' jobs-to-be-done? How are we to fashion a single, "one-size-fits-all" solution?

The answer, of course, is that we cannot, any more than we can for customers. But we can look to industrial and organisational psychology, research on well-being, and other sources to provide a framework for understanding the characteristics of employees' jobs-to-be-done and the components of suitable solutions. Doing so, we obtain a framework that is equally applicable to our customers' jobs-to-be-done.

Universal Human Needs Among the most well-known frameworks that speak to the psychological aspects of any job-to-be-done is the "hierarchy of needs" formulated by American psychologist Abraham Maslow. He postulated that all humans possess similar needs, spanning more basic ones—i.e., physiological ones (nutritional, environmental, etc.) and ones relating to safety (be it physical,

[16]This section is adapted from Brown et al. (2022).

psychological, economic, social, or moral)—all the way to "higher" needs pertaining to esteem and self-actualisation.[17]

Necessary Conditions In the workplace, these needs map to certain conditions that must exist for an individual to apply their full capabilities to the work at hand. Psychological safety is paramount: the workplace must be an environment where people are not afraid to bring their views to the table without fear of failure, rebuke, or repercussion. This requires building trust amongst colleagues. Transparency is a must, as opaqueness (e.g., lack of openness and consistency in decision-making processes) erodes the predictability[18] that contributes to establishing and maintaining trust. Workplace conditions must also be conducive to vulnerability (a form of risk-taking in which an individual offers ideas and shares thoughts despite the possibility of rebuke or rejection) because vulnerability is a component of creativity, innovation, and hard work.[19]

The Content of Work Assuming the working environment is psychologically safe, it must address other, more complex needs related to an individual's intellectual, social, and moral experience. Ideally, the work simultaneously challenges and engages an individual.[20] It ought to also provide a sense of communal belonging and shared accomplishment. The work needs to provide positive and affirming meaning such that an individual experiences their work as fulfilling. And the work must resonate with the individual's moral precepts, such as concern about the environment and support for diversity, equitability, and inclusion.

The Trajectory of Work Another aspect of the employee experience is the extent to which conditions allow the individual to grow, deepen, and expand their competencies, and become able to take on new challenges. Obviously, fostering professional development delivers benefits to the organisation itself. But from the standpoint of the employee experience, opportunities for professional development must dovetail with employees' jobs-to-be-done. Providing professional development opportunities goes beyond instruction in technical skills. For instance, it also encompasses helping employees attain and hone "soft skills" that positively impact interpersonal relationships—whether with colleagues, customers, or individuals outside of work.

A crucial point in this discussion is that meeting our employees' needs is a critical aspect of being effective solutioneers. By solutioning the "product" you are always "selling" to your employees—that is, the act of joining your organisation and continuing to work for it—you develop and retain employees with the skills and

[17] *See* Maslow (1943), pp. 370–396.

[18] *See, e.g.*, Stevenson and Moldoveanu (1995).

[19] *See, e.g.*, Brown (2018).

[20] *See* Csikszentmihalyi (1990).

Empathy for Employee ↔ Empathy for Customer

Input and Feedback from Employee ↔ Input and Feedback from Customer

Collaboration with Employee ↔ Collaboration with Customer

Fig. 4 Some commonalities between solutioning for employees and customers (Elevate.)

motivation to undertake Experience-Centric Design with your prospective and existing customers. As we shall see in the next section, solutioning the workplace provides a template for solutioning for your customers.

9 Coming Full Circle

It goes without saying that, in many respects, the needs of your customers parallel those of your employees. It follows that an organisation built to continuously elevate the employee experience can readily leverage its tools and techniques to continuously elevate how it assists customers with their jobs-to-be-done. The same principles, techniques, and processes you bring to bear in optimising the employment experience apply to optimising the product/service experience. A modified version of the Golden Rule applies: Treat those to whom you sell as you treat those whom you employ (and vice-versa) (see Fig. 4).

Another point bears emphasis: ultimately, enabling customers to complete their jobs-to-be-done is a shared experience whereby rigid distinctions between your employees and customers begin to blur. Your customer and your employees—and you—are engaged in a common endeavour. Your employees find their work meaningful, and therefore they value customers because helping and working with customers is a central component of your employees' jobs. You and your colleagues model for one another the act of listening; therefore, you and they are able to—and, indeed, all of you do—listen well to customers. Members of a company develop an understanding that the same things each member wants and needs from their situation—whether professional or personal—are things customers want from their situation. Everyone within the organisation develops an awareness that each person in the enterprise is either assisting or detracting from colleagues' and customers' efforts to fulfil their wants and needs.

10 Conclusion

If we accept the maxim proposed above, we begin to understand that, at a certain level of abstraction, the distinction between customers and employees is beside the point. The crucial insight is two-fold: everyone has a job-to-be-done, and solutioning anyone's job-to-be-done rests on Experience-Centric Design. The only uncertainty for you and those you lead is, given those twinned truths, how will you proceed?

Liquid Legal Waves to Other Chapters, Written by the Editors

Stephen, Lizzie, and Rachel introduce the vision of a very different workplace that demands not only new skills, but also a new mindset from its employees. Adding in technology, the question arises: How does young talent enter such a transformed workplace?—*Matthias* tackles that in his chapter on *"Entry-Level Professionals and the Digital Transformation of Legal Services"*.

So, how can we best develop existing talent in times of disruptive digital transformation? What is the combination of human skills and machine muscle that will distinguish individual talent? *Duc* provides the answer in his chapter on *"Injecting Humanity (Back) Into Talent Development"* and points out the highly valued skill of complex problem-solving.

As we get a clearer picture on the importance of the soft skills, of the principles and values that drive customer experience and employee happiness, we must ask ourselves: How does that affect the interaction between citizens and the government in times of waning trust into government authorities? By putting humans first, argue *Michiel* and *Ivar* in the upcoming chapter on *"Digitization of Government Services from the Citizen's Perspective"*.

References

Berraies S, Hamouda M (2018) Customer empowerment and firms' performance: the mediating effects of innovation and customer satisfaction. Int J Bank Market 36

Brown B (2018) Dare to lead. Random House, New York

Brown L et al (2022) The elevated workplace. in: Jacob K et al (eds) Humanisation and the law, Chap. 15. Springer Nature, Basel

Christensen C, Hall T et al (2016) Know your customers' 'jobs to be done. Harvard Bus. Rev. https://hbr.org/2016/09/know-your-customers-jobs-to-be-done

Csikszentmihalyi M (1990) Flow: the psychology of optimal experience. Harper & Row, New York

Dam RF, Siang TY (2020) Design thinking: get a quick overview of the history. Interaction Design Foundation. https://www.interaction-design.org/literature/article/design-thinking-get-a-quick-overview-of-the-history

Deikman A (1983) The observing self. Beacon Press, Boston

Friedman M (1970) A Friedman doctrine: the social responsibility of business is to increase its profits. NY Times: SM 17

Gelles D, Yaffe-Bellany D (2019) Shareholder value is no longer everything, top CEOs say. NY Times. https://www.nytimes.com/2019/08/19/business/business-roundtable-ceos-corporations.html
Golan N, Allen S (2021) Forget consulting. Find solutioning. Elevate. Expertise. Blog. https://expertise.elevateservices.com/post/102gwjy/forget-consulting-find-solutioning
Henderson R, Temple-West P (2019) Group of US corporate leaders ditches shareholder-first mantra. Financial Times. https://www.ft.com/content/e21a9fac-c1f5-11e9-a8e9-296ca66511c9
Martin C (2021) Welcome to the age of customer empowerment. Forbes. https://www.forbes.com/sites/forbesagencycouncil/2021/11/04/welcome-to-the-age-of-customer-empowerment/
Maslow A (1943) A theory of human motivation. Psychol Rev 50(4):370–396
Mattson C (2021) Design thinking Part 2: design thinking as a step-by-step process. In: The BYU Design Review. https://www.designreview.byu.edu/collections/design-thinking-part-2-design-thinking-as-a-step-by-step-process
Simon H (1956) Rational choice and the structure of the environment. Psychol Rev 63(2):129–138
Stevenson HH, Moldoveanu M (1995) The power of predictability. Harvard Business Review, Jul.–Aug. 1995, available at https://hbr.org/1995/07/the-power-of-predictability
Stovell J (1862) Harvard Magazine VIII: 374
Wright J (1994) The moving image. In: Collected poems. Angus and Robertson, Sydney

Stephen Allen's career in legal industry transformation includes as VP Get Sh*t Done at Elevate, leading Elevate's work solving business-of-law problems faced by law departments and law firms, and at Hogan Lovells, where he was responsible for innovation, data science, legal tech (AI, Machine Learning, Automation), digitalization, legal operations, and disruption. Earlier in his career, he worked as a lawyer both in private practice and in-house, subsequently becoming Managing Director of two divisions of Orange-France Télécom in the UK and Continental Europe. A Fellow of the College of Law Practice Management, Stephen's achievements as a leader in legal services transformation include architecting and implementing the multi-award winning Managed Legal Service^{SM} BLP contract for Thames Water, the first-ever multi-year, fixed-price law firm deal for legal services. In 2019, *Financial Times* named him the inaugural recipient of Legal Entrepreneur of the Year in the 2019 Innovative Lawyers Awards.

Lizzie Christmas's, experience includes her work as a Director in the Solutions and Consulting team at Elevate, leading consulting engagements. She takes a holistic approach to solutioning the innovative use of people, processes, data, and technology to optimise how law organisations accomplish critical operational activities. Lizzie's work as an Innovation Consultant followed her graduation from Cornell Tech's Master of Laws, Technology, and Entrepreneurship program. Before that, she worked as a Corporate Finance Solicitor at leading New Zealand law firm Chapman Tripp, where she helped launch Zeren, the firm's technology and innovation business. In parallel, Lizzie co-founded and launched a small-scale start-up focused on social enterprise and impact. Lizzie received her Bachelor of Arts (majoring in Politics) and Bachelor of Laws with Honours from the University of Otago in Dunedin, New Zealand. She is also a Fulbright Scholar.

Rachel Barnes, Director, Solutions and Consulting, Elevate, Elevate. In her role leading consulting engagements, she works with customers to optimise their use of people, processes, data, and technology solutions to meet the full spectrum of their needs. Rachel joined Elevate in September 2021, having previously worked in Innovation and Transformation at Ashurst and Herbert Smith Freehills. Prior to that, Rachel spent 11 years in Investment Banking, leading Transformation, Change and Innovation initiatives in London, Paris and New York. Rachel received her Bachelor of Arts (majoring in International Business) from the University of Northumbria, UK. Rachel is an APMG Change Management Practitioner.

Putting Humans First

Digitisation of Government Services from the Citizen's Perspective

Michiel Scheltema and Ivar Timmer

Contents

Michiel Scheltema is Professor emeritus Administrative Law at Groningen University, former government commissioner for the General Administrative Law Act, and co-founder of the Hague institute for innovation of Law.

Ivar Timmer is lecturer Legal management & Technology at Amsterdam University of Applied Sciences.

This chapter is an adaptation of an article written by Michiel Scheltema for the *Nederlands Tijdschrift voor Bestuursrecht* (Dutch Journal for Administrative Law), supplemented with several other topics, new experiences and insights.

M. Scheltema
Den Haag, Netherlands

I. Timmer (✉)
Amsterdam, Netherlands
e-mail: i.timmer@hva.nl

K. Jacob et al. (eds.), *Liquid Legal – Humanization and the Law*, Law for Professionals, https://doi.org/10.1007/978-3-031-14240-6_9

Abstract

Many countries experience waning public trust in government, while digitisation of society is on the rise and public authorities continue to further digitise their services. If governments do not pay enough attention to the perspective of citizens and adopt a citizen-centric approach while designing digital services, accessibility of government services may decrease and further erode public trust. Against this background, this chapter explores the digitisation of government services from a citizen's perspective, with a special focus on the role of the law and legal professionals. The chapter is based on the experiences of the authors over the past years with using digitisation to enhance citizens' access to the law and to improve the way in which (internal and external) processes of public legal departments work.

In current practice, the logic of the law often requires that citizens split up their problems or requests for help and approach different government bodies for different aspects of their problem. Well-designed digital government services put real-life problems that citizens experience first and combine all regulations that offer possible solutions, thus reducing complexity for the citizen and increasing their capacity to act. The limited capacity for personal contact can then be reserved for those citizens that need it. From a legal perspective, it is essential that government services are based on a traceable and transparent connection to the underlying regulations, using external knowledge models. Current government practices leave a lot to be desired in this respect. Methodologies are available to create these connections and are an important element for designing legally sound and citizen-centric government services.

1 Introduction

Trust is a core component of human relations. Over the past years, there have been several major scandals in the Netherlands that have hurt the citizens' trust in the authorities. In the northern province of Groningen, for instance, the authorities were slow to pay compensation for the damage caused by earthquakes to the homes of thousands of residents. The earthquakes had been brought on by the sinking ground following decades of gas extraction. Possibly even more damaging was the so-called *childcare benefits scandal*. Due to a combination of rigid regulations, the use of defective algorithms and data for detecting fraud—wrongly accusing no less than 26,000 families of fraud—and the distrustful attitude of the implementing officials, several thousands of families were required to pay back large amounts, which drove some of them in financial hardship. Moreover, the families received inadequate protection from the judiciary. The scandal led to the resignation of the third Rutte cabinet. In November 2021, the highest administrative court apologised to the affected families: a first in Dutch legal history.

Waning trust in the government is a common occurrence in many countries.[1] This became blatantly clear during the Covid-19 pandemic when certain groups in society, supported by social media, proved extremely distrustful of the government. It is against this background of eroding trust in the government and a state under the rule of law that we write this chapter on the digitisation of government services, with a special focus on the role of the law and legal professionals. A highly topical issue. The digitisation of society is on the rise and public authorities will continue to further digitise their services. If, however, they fail to consider the citizen's perspective—a people-oriented approach -, or fail to do justice to legal principles, the faith of citizens in the government is at risk of being eroded even further.[2] Lower trust in government will have negative effects on the public's willingness to comply with regulations and the overall functioning of the rule of law. Conversely, a well-wrought citizen-centric approach in organizing government services will have positive effects.[3]

Based on Dutch practice, this chapter makes connections to theoretical insights on several points. It is a record of our experiences over the past years with using digitisation to enhance citizens' access to the law and to improve the way in which (internal and external) processes of public legal departments work. Although interest is on the up, we feel that legal professionals do not pay enough attention yet to this topic, while it is of major importance to a well-functioning state under the rule of law. For today's citizens, after all, contact with the authorities is mostly digital. In almost all procedures digital aspects play a role. Such—partially—digital processes and procedures should be designed with an eye to legal principles (such as careful consideration and transparent and well-founded decision-making) and *procedural justice.* This latter concept refers to how citizens experience procedures and is affected, among other things, by the extent to which citizens feel they can present their position *(voice),* receive clarification *(explanation)* and how they are treated *(respect).* Achieving an appropriate level of procedural justice is not only intrinsically valuable, but also has a favourable effect on the valuation of outcomes and interactions with the authorities.[4] From a more practical perspective, we also believe that designing (the digital implementation of) regulation from the citizen's perspective might require more effort upfront, but will prove to be more cost-effective in the long run, by increasing the overall ability of citizens to manage their own affairs, while preventing errors and unnecessary procedures.

In the wake of the childcare benefits scandal, Dutch parliament asked the Council of Europe's Venice Commission for an opinion on the rule of law in the

[1] See generally, https://www.oecd.org/gov/trust-in-government.htm.

[2] See generally Coglianese (2021), p. 3 on the increasing use of algorithms in administrative law and the challenge to ensure that an automated state is also an *empathic* one.

[3] Dudly et al. (2015).

[4] See generally Tyler and Lind (1988).

Netherlands.[5] The Commission concluded that the Netherlands, 'in general, is a well-functioning state with strong democratic institutions and safeguards for the rule of law.' The Commission, however, listed several points for improvement in, among other things, workable regulations and supervision of implementation. Elements that did not work well in the childcare benefits scandal. Here, the following recommendation of the Commission is particularly relevant:

> For individuals, access to relevant information should be made easier, complaint procedures should be made simple and informal and help should be offered on how to complain under a duty of neutrality.[6]

This chapter explores how digitisation can contribute to realising this recommendation.

2 Structure

The chapter is structured as follows. We will first advocate the importance of the citizen's perspective as a starting point in government services. That is important because digitisation is often shaped from the government's perspective, while this is not the best starting point for helping citizens. We will then go on to outline the opportunities digitisation offers to support citizens in government processes containing major legal aspects.[7] We will use simple examples from our own experience—also outside the public domain—and repeatedly refer to the *administrative appeal* (in Dutch: *bezwaarprocedure*). This is a core procedure in Dutch administrative law that enables citizens to officially object to government decisions that affect their legal position. By that procedure citizens can express their content-specific objections, expand on the consequences of the decision for them personally, and supplement any missing facts. The procedure is settled within the same government organisation, but at a different level than where the primary decision was made. In practice, legal professionals within the government organisation handle the procedure. The rationale behind the administrative appeal is that it allows the authorities to reconsider decisions and remedy any errors or incorrect interpretations in the primary process. The procedure is the mandatory gateway to the administrative court. Every year, government agencies in the Netherlands handle over 2.5 million administrative appeals, which makes it the primary 'complaint procedure', as referred to in the Venice Commission's recommendation, in Dutch administrative law. Citizen-friendly digitisation that supports citizens better and prevents unnecessary administrative appeals could thus have a major impact and, as mentioned above,

[5] European Commission for democracy through law/Venice Commission (2021). *Opinion on the legal protection of citizens. Adopted by the Venice Commission at its 128th Plenary Session*, p. 26. url: https://www.venice.coe.int/webforms/documents/?pdf=CDL-AD(2021)031-e.

[6] Ibid., p. 28.

[7] A general discussion of the possibilities of digital procedures can be found in Susskind (2019).

contribute to overall trust in government and cost-effectiveness of governments services.

Lastly, we will go into safeguarding the link between digital systems and regulations. Responsible and effective digitisation from the citizen's perspective demands offering transparency to users about the regulations on which the systems are based and the exact functioning of systems. Legal rules can never be converted directly to a digital system. This requires many choices and interpretations on how to 'translate' the rules to a digital system. Offering transparency therefore requires a methodology that includes some form of knowledge models that document—in a very detailed manner—how rules are translated to a system.[8] A sound methodology, however, is regularly missing in practice. Our experience is that legal professionals, for lack of knowledge, are often not aware of the importance of a methodology, nor is this fully on the radar of many ICT professionals. Fortunately, practitioners and researchers increasingly have honed in on this subject over the past years.[9] In a recent opinion, the Dutch Council of State stressed the importance of using a methodology in preparing and designing the digital implementation of regulations.[10] We will highlight some key elements of the methods that could be used and in closing will present an overarching conclusion.

3 Government Perspective Dominant in Digitisation

Digitisation in public administration commonly starts from how authorities are organised. Various processes that must be completed within government bodies are very suitable for forms of automation and digitisation. Especially where large numbers of decisions must be made, fixed routines are established. They offer a good starting point for digitisation, and this is what frequently happens. It is the government body that primarily benefits. Even though citizens are meant to benefit from better government services—and this usually holds true for simpler services—citizens often suffer from adverse consequences of this modernisation: authorities appear to become (even more) inaccessible. Often, it is not easy to speak to an actual member of staff, and the routes of decision-making are often untraceable for citizens.

In the current situation, procedures for applying for benefits, allowances and licences usually focus on the question that is crucial to the authorities: What is the right decision to be taken by a specific government body based on a particular law? In the authorities' way of thinking, the implementing of rules might call for a different organisation for every rule. If there are ten laws to be implemented, it could be efficient to engage ten organisations: one organisation for each law.

[8] Instead of this knowledge 'being locked up in the system', see Lokin (2018) (see p. 297 of the English summary).

[9] The research of Lokin (2018) in the previous note is a good example.

[10] In today's practice, most regulations require some form of digital execution, albeit partially, making these methodologies important for virtually all new regulations. Council of State (2021).

Sometimes, these are different departments within one organisation, such as departments of a municipal authority. Sometimes, these are organisations that work independently of each other. The citizen's role is often bent to fit that mould. Citizens must split up their problems or requests for help into parts in accordance with the logic of the government body. With every part, the government body is interested only in those particulars that are relevant to the regulations on that part. The ability of citizens to play their role well in this landscape is generally overestimated. The division of citizens' problems into different parts pushes citizens as a whole out of the picture. Citizens can also get into a Kafkaesque fix if somewhere within the government organisation information is administered incorrectly and is then accepted as correct by other institutions.[11]

4 The Citizen's Perspective Is Different

The world of citizens is not made up of laws but of life events or problems that are relevant to them and often bring them into contact with government bodies. For instance, income, birth, divorce, and work are subjects that require every citizen to get involved with the government. This applies even more for citizens who have financial problems. Citizens who are in financial dire straits will find that the Dutch government has designed all kinds of rules to help them, each with its own portal: Social assistance, special assistance, other individual allowances, unemployment benefits, and several other portals. In Covid-19 times, the number of portals has become even higher. From the citizen's perspective, just one subject or question is relevant: How can the government help me to keep my head above water? A question that is not split up in the myriad questions that are dominant in the government's perspective: Does this citizen qualify for *social assistance,* for a *municipal allowance, unemployment benefit*, or *Covid-19 financial support*? Part of the joint project of Amsterdam University of Applied Sciences and various government bodies (see footnote 1) is an experiment with a large Dutch municipality in which the first steps are being taken towards a *Virtual Income Portal* that applies an approach from the citizen's perspective to provisions in which the municipal authority is involved.[12] The ultimate goal is to assess all different income schemes via one application, which is made as simple as possible.

The government's perspective is dominant also in the administrative appeals mentioned earlier. They follow the government's mould: The central question for the authorities is whether a specific decision is correct or not. Usually, this does not align with the citizen's intentions. That citizen simply follows the route of filing appeal because the problem for which the application was filed has not yet been resolved, and the letter or email they received from the authorities mentioned the

[11] See generally, Van Eck (2018) (p. 440 for a summary in English).

[12] The experiment is led bij ICTU: the Dutch centre of expertise for government ICT. See https://www.ictu.nl/about-us.

possibility of appeal. More and clearer explanations, applying to a different portal, filing a new and improved application, a good conversation or aid are often alternatives to resolve the citizen's problem that are more likely to succeed. After all, as a rule, citizens do not wish to litigate against the authorities. They want a solution to their problem or at least a better explanation to help them understand why the authorities cannot offer a solution.

If authorities would offer digital support from the citizen's perspective, there is a change in perspective of the design of application procedures and decision-making. In our opinion, administrative law professionals should have an important say in this, together with communication professionals and other experts. Whenever ICT professionals are in the lead, as they often are in practice, they tend to seek a link with existing work processes and procedures. Innovative design is possible only if administrative law insights are combined with the leeway provided by regulations, principles of service design—which always revolves around the user: citizens in this case—[13] and the possibilities offered by ICT. The criteria of people-centred justice set by the Organisation for Economic Co-operation and Development (OECD) also offer useful points of reference.[14]

A basic principle in designing from the citizen's perspective is that we cannot expect citizens to understand all the rules. This causes friction with the adage applied in legal practice that citizens are *presumed* to know the law. Although at times it should be possible to remind citizens that ignorance is not an excuse, it is a welcome development that administrative law gradually applies a more realistic viewpoint. In the Netherlands, the 2017 report of the Scientific Council for Government Policy, *'Why knowing what to do is not enough. A realistic perspective on self-reliance'*[15] played a major role. In summary, the report analyses behavioural insights, concluding that the *capacity to act* (a citizen's actual ability to act in concrete situations) is less than a citizen's *capacity to think* (the ability to theoretically know how they should act). The government's actions are often wrongly based on the assumption that offering information (so that citizens *know* what is expected of them) is enough to make citizens *do* what is expected of them. For most citizens, this assumption is not realistic. That knowing what to do is not enough holds even more true for citizens who are in vulnerable positions, permanently or temporarily. Examples include (temporary) poverty, or having to cope with death, divorce, or other life-changing events. These behavioural insights require that digital government services are designed as citizen-friendly as possible to enable even citizens with a limited ability to act to digitally get their affairs in order.[16]

[13]See e.g. Downe (2020). This book formulates principles of service design and, based on, among other things, work on redesigning services for the UK government.

[14]https://www.oecd.org/governance/global-roundtables-access-to-justice/oecd-criteria-for-people-centred-design-and-delivery-of-legal-and-justice-services.pdf.

[15]Scientific Council for Government Policy (2017). English summary via: https://english.wrr.nl/publications/reports/2019/10/14/why-knowing-what-to-do-is-not-enough.

[16]See also, Ranchordas (2022, forthcoming).

It is important to stress that digitisation should never be the only possible route. Some citizens cannot use even the most user-friendly digital tools. Personal contact should always remain possible, therefore.[17] Our view is that personnel capacity at government bodies always has its limits. Well-designed and user-friendly digital tools are valuable in making optimal use of this available personnel capacity. They allow a large majority of citizens to independently settle their business with the authorities digitally, and to offer personal support to those citizens who need that support, because their capacity to act is limited, permanently or temporarily, or who are subject to special circumstances.

5 Possibilities of Digitisation from the Citizen's Perspective

Below we will outline some simple examples and subjects where digitisation can support public legal services. Our sources of inspiration include our experience with the digital design of divorce procedures at Uitelkaar.nl and collaborations with a variety of government institutions, where we trained a great deal of legal professionals in the basic principles of service design and the possibilities offered by digitisation. These legal professionals then built prototypes for digital decision-support tools for processes from their own practices. Subsequently, promising prototypes were further developed. The first prototypes have been implemented, with more to follow.

The digital services[18] provided by Uitelkaar.nl aim at supporting partners who want to realise their divorce amicably and wish to avoid a nasty divorce. The services are based on the partners' perspective: What is the best way to help them getting divorced by mutual agreement? Once they have made arrangements for the children, the division of their assets and so on, the court can pronounce divorce in a simple procedure. Providing information, setting up a well-supported dialogue between the partners, and helping them draft the relevant legal documents required for the divorce are all part of the system. The underlying idea is that the system supports understanding for the partner, cooperation, and de-escalation of points of dispute. Here, too, digitisation is not an isolated tool; the partners are also supported by a case manager offering human contact where necessary. A solidly designed digital system, however, considerably increases a citizen's self-reliance. The experiences of the case managers and the on-going analysis of the questions that users pose help to improve the digital system continuously and to respond to user needs even better. Ultimately, this method will ensure that limited human capacity will be employed as effectively as possible: when really necessary. At Uitelkaar.nl, partners achieve a high degree of self-reliance in complex divorce proceedings. This shows the potential for increasing that self-reliance also in government procedures.

---

[17] Also see footnote 5, p. 27.

[18] Initially developed by the Hague Institute for the Innovation of Law (see footnote 1), currently implemented independently by Justice42, under the name Uitelkaar.nl.

5.1 Increasing the Citizen's Capacity to Act

Digitisation from the citizen's perspective can first of all help citizens to effectively find their way through the red tape. Information could be offered in a form that meets the citizen's needs. Meaning not the full text of a law, or long pieces of legalese on websites, but information that focuses on the information citizens want to know. By asking some simple questions, it is possible to offer more specific information without a citizen having to decide which bits apply. This is the practical application of a service design principle that information should be offered in an understandable, task-oriented and layered way, when it is relevant for users. Uitelkaar.nl implements this principle by providing information in doses, at a point in time when they need it to make the arrangements that the partners work on. For instance, when the partners are ready to make living arrangements, the information that is offered is confined to what is relevant to them. That means no information on owner-occupied properties, if they live in a rental. Precisely because the users have access to the information anytime when it suits them, this method of providing information is usually more effective than providing more general information or information provided by a portal, as it gets lost more easily.

Of course, authorities sometimes already provide simple diagnostic tools for citizens to offer them more specific information on their particular situation. However, most authorities still apply the traditional government perspective that revolves around separate laws. That means that information is provided on the question whether a citizen is eligible for a specific decision, or specific benefit, or subsidy from a specific government body. This is not always the question asked by the citizen, who has just been fired or gotten a divorce and wishes to know what this means in relation to the government. Or a citizen has fallen into debt and is looking for a way out. In those cases, it is not about whether a specific administrative body could help that citizen with a specific decision, but about what *all* administrative bodies and *all* relevant regulations combined could mean to that citizen. With that as starting point, a digital system could offer support that goes beyond the demarcated competences of authorities. An example from Uitelkaar.nl's practice is that in settling a divorce the income position of one or both partners can present a problem. Often, they are not aware of the problem because other aspects of the divorce claim their attention, and they have no insight yet into their finances after the divorce. The digital system identifies the problem well in time and can help to get the partners' finances in order or grant access to useful facilities.

Of course, a citizen's ability to act does not relate only to finding the right information, but also to how that information could be used best in the given situation, e.g. filing an application or objection, or appealing to a court of law. Those actions call for the drafting of a document which for many people presents a high threshold. Most people are not well-versed in drafting such documents and are afraid to make mistakes that will come back to bite them. Here, digital support could really help, both in drafting the document and in supplying data.

At Uitelkaar.nl, partners wishing to divorce draw up a covenant that should address many of the issues that should be resolved. 'Ordinary' citizens, not skilled in the subject matter, appear perfectly capable if further to a diagnosis sound information and possible solutions are provided as well as relevant sample texts. Fun fact: The texts produced are often much less complicated than if they had been drawn up by a lawyer, while legally adequate to determine the claims. This is a step forward: Ultimately, the citizens concerned are the ones who should understand what has been put down in writing.

For now, digital support that goes beyond providing information by the authorities is not very common or advanced. In the research project mentioned earlier, several municipal authorities work on developing a system that supports requests under the Government Information (Public Access) Act. The system covers internal aspects (supporting the public officials who have to handle requests correctly and in doing so have to weigh up the interests at stake). But the subsequent objective is to serve citizens better and to provide targeted information in a user-friendly manner about their rights in relation to access to government information. The ultimate objective of digital support is to help citizens shape their requests in a well-informed and structured manner, thus increasing their *capacity to act*. Requests under the Government Information (Public Access) Act, incidentally, often show that citizens are not so much interested in obtaining information as in presenting an underlying complaint or question that could be resolved by means of a conversation or explanation. A digital system could continue to ask questions, identify the issue, and suggest a more appropriate route, if necessary.

Sometimes citizens are convinced that a government body has taken a wrong or unreasonable decision. As part of the project of Amsterdam University of Applied Sciences (see footnote 1), Amsterdam municipality has developed a system for objections to decisions about the removal of wrongly parked bicycles (for instance, because they hinder traffic, or were parked outside designated areas). A very common occurrence in Amsterdam, the self-declared ‘bicycle capital of the world’. Citizens receive these decisions when they come to the pound to collect their towed bicycles and have to pay the costs of towing and of storage. Many citizens file appeal, often using arguments that cannot lead to another decision. A user-friendly digital diagnosis was designed, informing citizens about the municipality’s policy and a realistic assessment of an appeal’s chances of success. Extensive tests with citizens showed that they appreciated this way of being informed, avoiding unnecessary appeals. Digital support, of course, should not stop citizens from exercising their legal rights, and thus not wrongly discourage appeals. Citizens, however, appear to have a need for information that helps them decide whether filing appeal is useful. Providing realistic information is in the interest of both citizens and the authorities.

5.2 Customised Services

The discussion about digitisation from the citizen’s perspective can be set against the broader debate in the Netherlands about transitioning towards a so-called more *responsive* government as compared to a *bureaucratic* government. A responsive government starts from the citizen's perspective and is realistic about citizens' *capacity to act*.[19] An important point under discussion is the wish to provide customised services in the implementation of regulations. Citizens should receive a bespoke treatment when their special circumstances require this. Some people think that digitisation and customisation are incompatible. In our opinion, however, this is a matter of good system design. If the system incorporates flexibility, digitisation can foster customisation by the authorities. In procedures, for instance, citizens could be given a choice between an informal conversation instead of an immediate formal hearing of a committee (an option in Dutch administrative appeal proceedings) or between a video hearing and a live hearing. All these options are easily realised in a digital system.

A digital system designed to provide customised services could show citizens, clearly and comprehensibly, the data underlying a proposed decision, and invite citizens to report special circumstances, if any. The system could include examples as well. This approach could be more effective than organising an expansive flow of data exchanges among authorities to determine whether or not there are special circumstances Not only could this be technically vulnerable, it also has disadvantages in terms of privacy: Government bodies would exchange many more data than necessary for most citizens. Letting citizens themselves provide the information through a user-friendly system significantly reduces these disadvantages. In the future, developments in self-sovereign identity (with citizens, in summary, being even more in control of their digital identities and data) might offer even more exciting possibilities.

A criticism we hear sometimes is that if a digital system gives examples of special circumstances that could lead to customisation, it would encourage calculating behaviour. Citizens could phrase their applications such that they would be considered a special case. We think this is a minor risk. Several studies show that just a very small percentage of citizens tends to commit fraud intentionally.[20] The bulk, therefore, deserves to be trusted. Moreover, applications in which special circumstances play a role, will have to be handled *outside* the digital system to appraise whether the facts presented are plausible and to ask for further evidence if necessary.

The upside of digitisation of course is that it can improve the consistency of decisions where desired. Behavioural insights teach us that professionals often appraise similar situations differently although not justified by objective facts.[21] If properly designed, algorithmic digital support could counter such adverse effects. Moreover, digital systems often make continuous and systematic quality control

[19]This concept has been derived, in part, from the literature on *responsive law*, a term coined by Philip Nonett and Philip Selznick. See generally Nonett and Selznick (1978).

[20]See e.g. report from the Dutch Ombudsman on the Dutch National Fraud Law, https://www.nationaleombudsman.nl/system/files/bijlage/Rapport%202014-159%20Geen%20fraudeur%2C%20toch%20boete%20%28printversie%29_0.pdf.

[21]See generally, Kahneman et al. (2021).

easier than it is in analogue practice. Good system design should seek to make optimum use of the strong points of both digitisation and human decision-making.

5.3 Encouraging De-Escalation and Solution-Oriented Approach

As mentioned earlier, citizens are usually more interested in solutions than in conflicts. In practice, legal proceedings are designed such that they reinforce or even incite conflicts. To stick with the example of the Dutch administrative appeal: Traditionally, that procedure is directed at determining whether or not the decision is right or wrong. Almost naturally, that leads to two opposite positions: The party filing appeal thinks the decision is wrong, while the government body believes it is right. Both sides present arguments to support their position and empathise with that position—a risk that occurs in citizens in particular, as non-professionals. Due to the procedure's structure, solutions that are acceptable to both sides receive less attention. A simple example is the refusal of a licence for simple alterations to a home. Experience shows that minor changes in design, materials, or colour sometimes are enough to make the alterations compliant with regulations or to overcome a neighbour's objections. In that case, the decision whether or not the primary decision was right is irrelevant to the solution of the citizen's problem.

When digitising the administrative appeal, it is possible to design diagnosis and communication such that they are directed towards reaching a solution. A solid diagnosis and a demarcation of the limits of what is possible will increase citizens' awareness of the fact that filing appeal is not always the only or most likely way to resolve their problems. This could clear the way to reach a solution in other ways, for instance by discussing alternatives. Behavioural insights could contribute here. Uitelkaar.nl's system uses those insights to encourage de-escalation, which in the divorce process is of major importance, obviously. Forms of nudging,[22] too, could play a role in arriving at a good solution.

It is important to realise that citizens often have no clue what to expect of the authorities. They do not know what benefits are available or which allowances they could claim. This means that they do not know whether or not to be happy with what they get. A citizen applies for a benefit and gets a letter saying that a certain amount will be received every month. The letter also mentions that an appeal can be filed. Why would the citizen appeal? Is the amount perhaps too low? How is one to know? Or a licence is granted, with an annex listing several conditions. Is it now possible to go forward with the plans the citizen has? Should an appeal be filed? Is there a point? If authorities provide inadequate information, are hard to reach, or take decisions routinely, discontentment is just around the corner, and could take the form of unnecessary litigation and conflicts.

Of course, communication between administrative bodies and citizens quite often proceeds smoothly. As mentioned earlier, however, the problem is rather that this

[22] See generally, Thaler and Sunstein (2009).

communication only concerns the task executed by the body in question, while the citizen's question goes beyond that body's field of activity.

5.4 Integration of the Chain or of Facilities from the Citizen's Perspective; the Digital File

The way in which government bodies are organised is decisive for how citizens are treated. Every decision, every department and every law has its own entry point. In the current situation, citizens' questions must be split into just as many parts to get access to all those entry points. And within procedures, the different phases are often also split unnecessarily. A simple example is when citizens ask for a specific decision. If their application is not honoured, it is possible in the Netherlands to file appeal with the same body, followed by appeal to the court. The problem remains the same for citizens, but at different stages. As practice stands today, citizens get three different files from different government bodies. Digitisation offers the possibility to offer all different stages on one platform. The digital file created at one stage can be used at subsequent stages by making it accessible also to new members of staff, other departments and ultimately to the administrative court.

Obviously, this is just a simple example to realise cohesion for citizens through digitisation, which will become necessary in practice because the authorities cut up the citizen's problems in bits and pieces. A next step would be to let the needs or problems of citizens take pride of place and not a decision or the field of activity of a government department. We are happy to note that many government bodies increasingly consider thinking in *life events* an important principle:[23] Which rules are triggered when citizens get children, lose their jobs, move house, start their own businesses or lose loved ones? The citizen's perspective requires citizens to get support for such life events as a whole: 'the one-portal idea'. Digital systems built by collaborating government bodies from the citizen's perspective could offer life event-based systems. The practical advantage of digitisation thus structured would be that in principle authorities need not change the way in which they are organised, and that procedures could be followed step-by-step and not by means of risky, large scale ICT operations. The methods discussed in the next paragraphs could be helpful.

[23] The Dutch government program 'Mens centraal' (or: 'putting humans first') is a good example of this 'thinking in life events'. It uses, among other things, the insights of the WRR-report and 'no wrong door-principles' in exploring how to redesign procedures related to unemployment benefits and governmental services for unemployed citizens. See (in Dutch): https://www.programmamenscentraal.nl/levensgebeurtenissen/werkloos/werkwijze-en-betrokken-organisaties/er-ontstaat-ruimte-voor-echte-verbeteringen.

6 From Rules to Digital Systems

The preceding paragraphs did not go into *how* legal rules are converted into digital systems. Every legal professional will understand that one-on-one conversions are usually not possible. Rules of law often contain standards with a more or less open character that require interpretation. Sometimes this is the—in terms of legal quality—undesirable consequence of political compromise, but more often it is a deliberate choice to ensure that regulations remain flexible to do justice to complex realities. Digital systems work with exact instructions and there is no room for open standards. In designing and structuring systems that support the implementation of regulations, many choices must be made about which rules can and which rules cannot be digitised, which interpretations are necessary, and at which point the system should refer to professionals for further assessment. In practice, this presents several problems in the design and development process of digital systems. First, the choices made about the explanation and interpretation of legal standards are not always well-documented, in part because time-pressure can be high. For that reason, it happens regularly that the exact policy can be found only in the specifications or computer code of the system. The interpretations are then 'locked in the system'.[24] Should the regulations change later, it will, without the help of an external knowledge model, be a struggle to determine how the system is affected *exactly*. This has extremely adverse consequences for the *maintainability* of systems. Moreover, this is an undesirable situation because individual citizens, with or without legal aid, and the public in general should be able to check policy and rules without having to decipher computer codes.

An associated problem is that in today's government practice the conversion of rules of law to systems is often—at least partially—done by software suppliers. The over 350 municipalities in the Netherlands, for example, have responsibilities in implementing social regulations. The market for software supporting that implementation is controlled by just a couple of software suppliers. Together with government professionals, these suppliers work on designing and updating these systems, but frequently the intellectual property rights in the systems' specifications in fact vest in the suppliers. This, too, is a problem that from the viewpoint of democratic checks and transparency is nothing less than unacceptable. Moreover, this situation causes major dependency on these suppliers (*vendor lock-in*).

Remarkably, various studies about digitisation within the Dutch government show that legal professionals are usually only marginally involved in designing and structuring systems for implementing regulations. They advise indirectly about content-specific subjects, or are consulted about privacy aspects, but as a rule legal professionals are not involved from start to finish. Based on our experience, the situation in other countries will not be much different. It is our impression that legal professionals are insufficiently aware that their involvement at this stage is a prerequisite for the legal quality of government services. If the connection between

[24] See note 5.

steps in the digital system and regulations receives insufficient consideration, it has an adverse effect on the explainability and justification of decisions. If, however, those connections are based on a clear and external knowledge model, every step in the system can be explained, and the system will be transparent from a legal perspective. This is important from the legal quality perspective and the justification of how systems work to citizens. After all, they should not have the feeling that these systems are a black box. Citizens or their legal assistance providers who feel the need for an exact justification should be able to easily trace the underlying functioning. In our opinion, this will enhance trust in these systems. The right to know how systems work has meanwhile been anchored in Dutch case law. When a decision that is (partly) based on a the outcome of a digital system is challenged by a citizen, governmental bodies should disclose all relevant assumptions, choices and interpretations that have been made in designing and developing the system, if necessary for the protection of their rights.[25]

Thankfully, several organisations in the Netherlands increasingly recognise the importance of a good methodology and documentation of the conversion of legal rules to systems, in part owing to the above case law. Several municipalities, for instance, develop an algorithm register, explaining and accounting for how the algorithms work that are used for decision-making or enforcement.[26]

It is no coincidence that major initiatives originate with the Tax and Customs Administration. This body is entrusted with implementing tax regulations which are complex and subject to frequent changes. The problems caused by the lack of a sound methodology have led to the methodology of *agile implementation of legislation.*[27] This method focuses on the importance of traceable, transparent, and explainable conversion of regulations to digital systems.[28] It would go too far here to discuss this method in greater detail, but the gist is that this method systematically dissects rules of law, creating elements that can be used to formulate detailed specifications for digital systems in a natural language. The software (*agile law execution factory* or ALEF) translates those specifications into computer code. During the process, scenarios are tested on an ongoing basis to ensure that the system generates the outcomes as foreseen when designing the system. All interpretations of the required standards are carefully documented in external knowledge models. Almost all steps in this process are supported by open-source software.[29] This working method guarantees transparency. Other government bodies and organisations, too, are

[25] An important case in this respect was the so-called AERIUS-case; a verdict by the Administrative Jurisdiction Division of the Council of State, the country's highest general administrative court. AERIUS is a digital system to determine nitrogen depositions. It is used by governmental bodies when issuing permits in the field of environmental law, see https://www.raadvanstate.nl/uitspraken/@107500/201600614-1-r2/.

[26] See e.g. https://algoritmeregister.amsterdam.nl/en/ai-register/.

[27] In Dutch: *Wendbare wetsuitvoering*.

[28] Also see footnote 4.

[29] The ambition is to support all steps with open source software in the near future. Currently, some steps still use software that requires licences.

working on similar methodologies. The main advantage of those working methods is that the organisation itself designs the specifications for a digital system. This reduces the dependency on external suppliers as the intellectual property remains in the public domain. While those suppliers can still provide supportive services, they now do so based on the specifications that vest in the government body. The use of open-source software for (parts of) the process can reduce the dependency on external suppliers even further.

The project in which Amsterdam University for Applied Sciences works with six municipal and provincial authorities on digital decision support for the practice of legal departments uses the core elements of these methods to guarantee the transparency of systems and their outcomes. Testing legal scenarios on an ongoing basis is a first, important, ingredient. Next are frequent and solid user tests to ensure a good user experience. This intensive procedure is necessary to create legally sound, effective, maintainable and at the same time user-friendly systems. The involvement of other professionals (communication, ICT, policy) is essential. Ideally, systems supporting the implementation of regulations are designed and structured by a multidisciplinary team guided by the citizen's perspective in every phase of the process. In our opinion, any extra efforts made in advance will pay off later. Moreover, experience shows that the very detailed analysis of regulations will expose any inconsistencies and ambiguities and that this working method will thus—ultimately—contribute to better regulations. We are well aware that the daily practice of government bodies and the political reality of legislation processes often leave little room and time for the thorough approach that we advocate. The situation is complicated by the different execution layers within government bodies, and the rift that often exists between policy and execution. Sometimes, there is a huge gap between how regulations are designed and what works in reality. Only by recognising this gap, will there be room for real improvement. Despite this complex situation, it appears that the political climate in the Netherlands is favourable in 2022. The feasibility of execution of regulations by the different layers of government bodies are high on the agenda, also due to the childcare benefits scandal. We believe attention to the citizen's perspective and the elements set out in this paragraph are indispensable in realising more workable regulations. Politics and government bodies together will have to find a way to make this working method the standard.

7 Conclusion

This chapter highlighted several aspects of digitisation from the citizen's perspective. In the current situation, the government's perspective dominates the execution of regulations and the accompanying digital systems. This perspective views the reality of citizens through the lens of legal regulations. The citizen's perspective is different. Citizens' thinking does not start from legal regulations, but from actual events that happen to them. Authorities that design digital systems from the citizen's perspective put themselves in the citizen's position and thus choose an essentially different, more humane, starting point.

Well-designed digital systems have major advantages, both for citizens and for the authorities. They can increase the citizens' *capacity to act* and allows employment of the always limited personnel capacity of the government in places and at times where it is most valuable and most needed. If executed on a large scale, the standardisation of regulations is inevitable and effective. However, there are always special cases that could require customisation. If systems are well-designed, customisation and digitisation need not be at odds. Digital systems can feature several ways to filter out special cases in time, for instance by inviting citizens to actively report when special circumstances could apply to them. Lastly, digitisation from the citizen's perspective could make sure that citizens have to go to just one portal and avoid unnecessary division of their files.

The last key element is that in designing and structuring systems a traceable and transparent connection should be made to the underlying regulations through external knowledge models. Current government practice in the Netherlands leaves a lot to be desired in this respect, as is the case in many other countries. It is a huge challenge to transition to citizen-friendly digital systems. Although in our view some main elements are undeniable, government practice is too diverse and too complex to allow for an all-encompassing blueprint for citizen-friendly digitisation. A better alternative appears to be phasing-in the citizen's perspective and sound digitisation in a way that complements and ties in with current government processes. We are convinced that we will stand a chance of success only if numerous legal government professionals and policy makers will seriously look into the importance of the citizen's perspective, the possibilities offered by technology, and the conditions for the sound digitisation of government services that citizens can trust.

Liquid Legal Waves to Other Chapters, Written by the Editors

Trust is the core component of human relations. The government must meet the citizens where they are in their lives, when they turn to public authorities. But trust also rests firmly on respect, i.e. accepting the individuality and diversity of each person and life situation, as *Roger* beautifully underlines in *"Who are you…? - A Story About a Gay Humanist Working at a Law Firm"*.

Michiel and Ivar caution that if public authorities fail to consider the citizen's perspective, people's faith in the government will be eroded even further. The same is true for contracts and contracting in the private sector, as Rob, Helena and Stefania remind us in their chapter on "Layered Contracts: Both Legally Functional and Human-friendly". Lack of accessibility to content of contracts and lawyers writing just for lawyers will erode trust in the rule of law.

Accessibility of the law and its representatives (e.g. lawyers or public authorities) and derivates (e.g. contracts) is of paramount importance to maintain trust in the rule of law. In the following chapter on *"Helping Lawyers to Better Visualize their Knowledge"*, *Valérie* and *Gabriele* will introduce a concept of how visualization can increase readability and understanding of law.

References

Coglianese C (2021) Administrative law in the automated state. Daedalus 150:3

Council of State (2021) Digitalisering wetgeving en bestuursrechtspraak. Raad van State, Den Haag. https://www.raadvanstate.nl/@125918/publicatie-digitalisering/

Downe L (2020) How to design services that work. BIS Publishers, Amsterdam

Dudly E, Yi Lin D, Mancini M, Ng J (2015) Implementing a citizen-centric approach to delivering government services. McKinsey Center for Government. https://www.mckinsey.com/industries/public-and-social-sector/our-insights/implementing-a-citizen-centric-approach-to-delivering-government-services

Kahneman D, Sibony O, Sunstein CR (2021) Noise: a flaw in human judgment. Little Brown Spark, New York

Lokin MHAF (2018) Wendbaar wetgeven, De wetgever als systeembeheerder, 'NILG serie: Governance & Recht'. Boom Juridisch, Den Haag

Nonett P, Selznick P (1978) Law and society in transition: toward responsive law. Harper & Row, New York

Ranchordas S (2022, forthcoming) Empathy in the digital administrative state. Duke Law J 72

Scientific Council for Government Policy (2017) Weten is nog geen doen. Een realistisch perspectief op redzaamheid. WRR, Den Haag

Susskind R (2019) Online courts and the future of justice. Oxford University Press, Oxford

Thaler RH, Sunstein CR (2009) Nudge. Penguin, New York

Tyler TR, Lind EA (1988) The social psychology of procedural justice. Springer Science, New York

Van Eck M (2018) Geautomatiseerde ketenbesluiten & rechtsbescherming: Een onderzoek naar de praktijk van geautomatiseerde ketenbesluiten over een financieel belang in relatie tot rechtsbescherming. Tilburg University, Tilburg

Michiel Scheltema has been professor of administrative law at the universities of Groningen and Utrecht. He is co-founder of the Hague institute for innovation of Law (HiiL, an internationally operating institute that aims at improving access to the law, www.hiil.org). As a co-founder and advisor, he is also associated with Justice42, which aims at promoting a better access to the law with help op digitalisation. It offers a procedure for divorce since 2018 (www.uitelkaar.nl), and received a subsidy to develop a platform for supporting administrative appeals.

Michiel was (junior) minister of justice (cabinet Van Agt II and III) and afterwards government commissioner for the General Administrative Law Act (1983–2019). In that capacity he was chairman of the commission for the drafting of the act, and defended the bills in parliament. Also he was chairman of the Scientific Council for Government Policy.

Michiel studied law at the University of Leyden (LL.M) and the Harvard Law School (LL.M.) and received a Dr. h.c. from Leyden University.

Ivar Timmer is a professor of Legal management & Technology at the Amsterdam University of Applied Sciences (AUAS). In his research, he focuses on how legal tech can improve legal quality, user experience and efficiency within organizations in legal practice, both in the private and public sector. He holds a Phd in Legal risk management and has (co-) authored several books and articles on topics related to legal tech and legal management. He was one of the founders of the Dutch Legal Tech Alliance, a collaboration between 12 Dutch UAS that exchange knowledge and experiences on legal tech education. In 2018, he received a grant from the Royal Netherlands Academy of Arts and Sciences for the innovation of education in legal tech. He is the research coordinator of the Legal Tech Lab, that connects legal tech research, legal tech education and more than a dozen organizations from legal practice. The lab is part of the AUAS Centre of Expertise of Applied Artificial Intelligence.

Helping Lawyers to Better Visualize Their Knowledge: A Formula and Four Scenarios

Valérie M. Saintot and Gabriele Di Matteo

Contents

Abstract

With this article, we aim to bring our voice as practitioners and knowledge management (KM) lawyers to the innovation table. To facilitate the retrieval of legal knowledge and its mapping, we have tested different forms of visualization of law and we have been exploring how, in our context, technology could be used or has already been used to support the work of lawyers. We have summarised our insights to foster further conversations on this key topic. We wish to steer the conversation towards what its practitioners need and how data scientists and technology experts can cater better for these needs.

The publication reflects the personal views of the author(s), which do not necessarily reflect the views of the ECB.

Valérie M. Saintot, LLM, PhD is Lawyer, Adjunct Professor, Author.

Gabriele Di Matteo is Legal analyst at the European Central Bank.

V. M. Saintot (✉) · G. Di Matteo
Frankfurt am Main, Germany

K. Jacob et al. (eds.), *Liquid Legal – Humanization and the Law*, Law for Professionals, https://doi.org/10.1007/978-3-031-14240-6_10

In a two-step approach we present our angle as KM lawyers. First, we explain what we call the 'Knowledge Formula', showing four scenarios in which varying degrees of technological support were deployed and, as a result, the access to legal knowledge differed. Second, we provide two examples as to how knowledge visualization can be applied to support legal KM.

We employ a mathematical formula to describe our understanding of the current opportunities and limitations and to draw some of the boundaries of the map of legal knowledge visualization. Then, we provide an analysis of two specific visualization case studies. The results of this conceptual and practical exercise stress the essential role visualization plays in increasing the readability and understanding of law. Furthermore, we formulate some of the needs practitioners may have. We show potential solutions for the issues encountered during the process of visualizing law, with a particular focus on the challenges and limitations.

Visualizing the knowledge encapsulated in law brings us closer to the objective of assisting better drafting. Better drafting will translate into more effective legal interpretation, more efficient production and increased impact on the practitioner's day-to-day business. In addition, it will facilitate any sharing of knowledge and its understanding, improve collaboration among key stakeholders and nurture legal work to make it fit for the third decade of the twenty-first century.

1 Introduction

While the approach applicable to KM has evolved over the last 30 years, in particular thanks to technology, the definition by Tom Davenport of '*Knowledge Management [as] the process of capturing, distributing, and effectively using knowledge*' (Davenport 1994) still captures the gist of how we understand KM today and still practice it. Visualization, taxonomies and knowledge graphs should not remain empty terms/phraseology coined to sell KM as a valuable function. These terms should be filled with life, made operational and support the day-to-day business of societal actors. We work in a knowledge economy in which entities increasingly have to make it part of their core business to manage intangible knowledge and the data it is based on as their core business. Such entities that live up to that challenge will see a higher stock exchange value than that of traditional listed companies. [Therefore, it is paramount to turn knowledge into an ever better sellable good. An area in which the legal industry is well advised to invest in view of the restructuring of tasks between human and AI which is already ongoing.]

In the recent years of our field practice, coding KM deliverables into an easy and readily accessible visual format has played a growing role—providing insights, facilitating collaboration and problem-solving aids. Legal experts are on a daily basis confronted with the challenge the inherent complexity of the legal frameworks poses, and the task of regulating it within the different areas of law they practice. This is particularly true for teams dealing with multiple legal knowledge frameworks relating to varied legal topics (Monteguado 2019). Such complexity is often experienced as a maze, an intricate knot which is hard to untie and to explain without instruments capable of retaining a significant number of relevant legal acts, case-law and doctrinal articles in the human mind (Katz et al. 2020). The law is made for the many and mastered in practice by the few. This is where the visualization of law comes into play to guide, as a modern version of Ariadne's thread, lawyers in their exploration and understanding of even the most intricate legal frameworks.

Visualizing law is not an easy task: a visualization, indeed, can be valuable only as far as it respects the integrity of the legal knowledge and does not trivialize reality, whilst still focusing on reducing complexity (Berger-Walliser et al. 2017). Moreover, multiple factors may influence the ability of KM lawyers to visualize law: the presence or absence of a well-structured database of the relevant legal knowledge assets, the role of readily available automated tools, technological literacy, the availability of digital analytical tools. All these factors impact some of the most critical parts of a KM lawyer's work, i.e. the research, extraction and analysis of legal sources. The possibility of having smart, AI-driven tools capable of immediately extracting meaningful knowledge into a visualization could really represent a game changer for the legal practice.

Such progress could also play an important role in the public discourse, especially with regards to the "accessibility of law" which could be brought to a whole new level. It could extend access to complex legal frameworks to a new audience that has previously been excluded by a lack of visual maps which are easily understood to navigate the territory. Apart from the clear and practical benefits in terms of time and economic resources, these new forms of visualizations (e.g. knowledge graphs as the one developed by LeReTo[1]) could help live up to the objective included in the second paragraph of Article 1 of the Treaty on European Union, whereby the Treaty '*marks a new stage in the process of creating an even closer union among the peoples of Europe, in which decisions are taken as openly and as closely as possible to the citizens*'.

We start by explaining our thinking around the challenges of being able to better tap into legal data and describe our experience in what we call our '*Knowledge Formula*', which uses the visual language of mathematics to explain why and how we believe visualization has the potential to influence KM for legal work and increase the retrievability of knowledge and its transference (1).

We then provide two case studies in which we explore two topics of relevance: One case study relates to the interpretation of a legal provision; the other case study focuses on a case-law related question. These two different forms of visualization open the spectrum in which visualization is possible (2).

[1] See LeReto, https://lereto.com/.

To conclude, we summarise our vision and expectations in relation to future developments.

2 Legal Knowledge Visualization Scenarios

Over the last two decades, the strong relationship which connects visualization and knowledge management has been established (Sparrow 1998). One of the first theoretical frameworks for knowledge visualization dates back to the early 2000s and lays out how knowledge visualization can help in multiple ways (Eppler and Burkhard 2007).

In the Big Data era, when human brains are challenged with an incredible amount of data (isolated facts) and information (facts in context) to be processed (Agrawal et al. 2015), the role of visualization in transferring and conveying knowledge (insights about those same facts) has gained considerable importance. To give a concrete example, one could think of the increasing role that graphs have been playing all around the globe in the Covid-19 pandemic: corona virus monitoring tools, such as the one developed by the Johns Hopkins University to keep track of the spread of the disease,[2] or the Italian portal which provides daily data about the level of vaccines administered,[3] entered our daily lives, empowering any citizen in the understanding of both quantitative and qualitative data, information and even knowledge, i.e. covering all those three dimensions of visualization (Tergan and Keller 2005).

The law, even if developing at a slower pace than other fields, is not extraneous to the increasing role of visualization. One example of this is the Legislative Explorer developed by the University of Washington,[4] which provides great insights on the overall legislative process at the US Congress.

Nevertheless, textuality continues to play a primary role in the law: after all, before the advent of written law, the law was mainly situational and customary (Cyras et al. 2018), while the reception of Roman law, the cornerstone of any European civil law system, was possible only through textualization since the appearance of the *duodecim tabularum leges*. However, the increasing complexity of legal systems (Katz et al. 2020) and the increase in legislative production strictly related to the fast-paced advancement of technology (Feigenson et al. 2006) put into question the way in which lawyers have been interacting with the law so far.

Without undermining the central and indispensable role of textuality, our plea is to augment legal cognition when working with legal frameworks through visible thinking. This will support legal operations and legal deliverables alike.

[2] See John Hopkins University, https://coronavirus.jhu.edu/map.html.

[3] See il Sole 24 ore, https://lab24.ilsole24ore.com/numeri-vaccini-italia-mondo/.

[4] See Legal Explore, http://www.legex.org/.

2.1 Our 'Knowledge Formula'

There are some basic questions lawyers could ask: what can I expect from legal knowledge visualization? How much can I use it myself and how much will I depend on someone else to access it? Can it be automated? To theoretically cover some elements of the answers to these questions, we decided to experiment: borrowing the format of a mathematical formula to explain our field experience and make explicit the patterns of the daily challenges we face as KM lawyers. Thus, the 'Knowledge Formula' is our way of rendering our tacit knowledge explicit and creating a conversation around our experience, being aware that in the real practice these factors may differ or carry a different weight. Our intention is to take stock and help develop the vision we have and would like to see manifested. Despite the complexity and acknowledged limitations of the formula, we believe the starting point must be to articulate and name the factors capable of influencing the present and the next future of KM. The formula represents a true conceptual and intellectual experiment; it has no claim of being 100% mathematically correct nor accurate. Borrowing Penrose fourfold classification of theories, we could define the knowledge formula a "tentative class" (Penrose 2016): the formula is imperfect yet tangible. It helps with manifesting some of the challenges faced when pondering about the future of legal knowledge management and possibly to sit at the innovation table and to enable a dialogue with various stakeholders.

Knowledge visualization facilitates the capability of functioning as a '*conceptual bridge to increase the speed and the quality of knowledge transfer among and between individuals, groups or even whole organization*' (Meyer 2009, p. 2).

Law students and professionals are likely to have experienced the need to produce arguments in the form of mind-maps or to have doodled the relationship between different legal acts and concepts on a piece of paper in order to understand and to clarify their thinking. Neuroergonomic measures of information visualization based on the *Cognitive Load Theory* (Chandler and Sweller 1991) show that good forms of visualizations can improve the performance of the human brain in capturing information (which can become knowledge) and reducing at the same time the mental effort (and time) needed to understand that same information (Nuamah and Mehta 2020).

We have summarised in our 'Knowledge Formula' different enablers that may play a role in the usability of legal knowledge visualization. The main aim of this theoretical formula is to be able to visually grasp the sources of knowledge used and the **level of knowledge (K)** which is expected, embracing both the opportunities and constraints we face. The formula represents a conceptual experiment: the sources of knowledge, indeed, may vary and depend both on the tacit expertise of the analyst/practitioner visualizing the law and on the explicit legal knowledge available in different formats (e.g. analogical or digital) and/or types (e.g. textual, numerical). The formula has not been tested quantitatively and therefore needs to be understood as a mean to visualise our thinking. Displaying the formula "will cut down the general readership by half" (Penrose 2016). We decided to stick with it because we believe its visual character helps with understanding the tenants of the conversations.

More work would be needed to embody it into a quantitative calculation and demonstration. This is not its initial intent and this is why the **level of knowledge (K)** we refer to should be seen as an absolute value which may vary according to the interplay of the different factors hereby presented.

As a matter of background, the concept of knowledge referred to at this juncture of our discourse is inspired by the SECI (Socialization, Externalization, Combination and Internalization) theory of knowledge management by Nonaka and Takeuchi (1995), since it considers both the tacit dimensions of knowledge (more subjective and related to the bodily experience of the lawyer) and the explicit dimension of knowledge (more objective and related to the mind). The Knowledge Formula is comprised of six different elements and we define them as follows:

K stands for **knowledge** and indicates the concrete output resulting from the interaction of the factors which may influence it in the process of knowledge visualization. Being aware of the multiple epistemological and philosophical facets of knowledge, **K** should be seen as the ideal combination of the quantitative and qualitative nature of knowledge potentially obtainable and transferable via the use of visualization (**V**).

D refers to the quality of the **available** digital database. Clearly, quality is a multidimensional concept and can be influenced by many factors. For the sake of our plea, we consider the quality of a database to be 'good' if it is capable of effectively transforming data and the information therein into concrete knowledge (Piattini et al. 2002).

A relates to the quantity and quality of automation which is involved, with specific reference to AI. Automation may refer to an incredible variety of technologies, but we adhere to the definition given by the IEEE, i.e. the field of "*research [that] emphasizes efficiency, productivity, quality, and reliability, focusing on systems that operate autonomously, often in structured environments over extended periods, and on the explicit structuring of such environments*" (IEEE Robotics & Automation Society 2021).

V covers the quantity and quality of visualization which is involved, i.e. on the efficiency of the utilization of visualization used (Nuamah and Mehta 2020), which is based on the factors of mental effort (e.g. the cognitive load, represented by the physical level of concentration of oxygenated haemoglobin needed to process the visual) and performance (e.g. accuracy and response time in the understanding and processing of the visual).

T represents the time involved to produce knowledge. In the Knowledge Formula, T is inversely proportional to V, building on the working hypothesis and neuroergonomic findings that effective forms of visuals are capable to substantially reduce the time needed by our brain to capture information (and consequently knowledge) (Nuamah and Mehta 2020).

tl brings in the technological literacy of the stakeholders, i.e. the effective legal knowledge visualisers. This concept aims at capturing the intrinsic understanding of the digital and technological tools (Davies 2011) lawyers interact with. In our framework, the higher the levels of the D and A are, the lower tl needs to be, since good databases and more user-oriented analytical tools may substantially decrease the barriers for using technology. At the same time, in our thinking, tl and T are directly proportional, since the higher the tl needed (i.e. the concrete mastery of tools used to visualize), the higher the T (time) which is needed to produce those visuals.

h = constant of proportionality. In our case, our constant of proportionality will be represented by the constant ratio between the result of D (database) multiplied by A (automation), divided by tl (technology literacy). More specifically, the result of D × A is directly proportional to V (visualisation), since good databases and automated analytical tools would improve drastically the quality of visualization, reducing at the same time the tl needed, as well as T (time).

Additionally, the following dimensions are included as well:

- ε = refers to an arbitrarily small quantity
- n = refers to an exponentially big quantity
- $D > D\,\varepsilon$
- $A > A\,\varepsilon$

Considering all of the above and remembering that our purpose here is to map the space for future conversations and pilots, our Knowledge Formula reads as follows:

$$\boldsymbol{K} = \boldsymbol{h} \times \frac{\boldsymbol{V}}{\boldsymbol{T}} \text{ where} \rightarrow \boldsymbol{h} = \frac{\boldsymbol{D} \times \boldsymbol{A}}{\boldsymbol{tl}}$$

To articulate and thematise our learnings and findings further, we present four different scenarios in which the concrete interplay of the aforementioned variables illustrates how the knowledge obtainable and visualized could vary. As a matter of fact, the quantitative and qualitative increase of specific factors (as the automation, the quality and quantity of the database, the technology literacy of the practitioner) may result in better forms of visualizations produced in a shorter period of time and enabling a faster and more significant knowledge transfer.

2.1.1 Scenario 1: Mobilizing Tacit Legal Knowledge

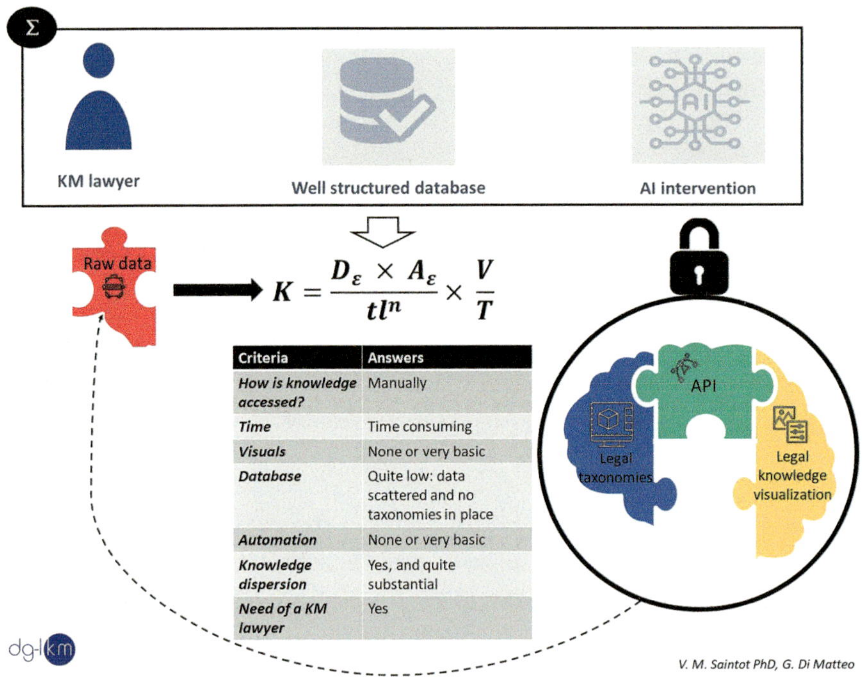

Criteria	Answers
How is knowledge accessed?	Manually
Time	Time consuming
Visuals	None or very basic
Database	Quite low: data scattered and no taxonomies in place
Automation	None or very basic
Knowledge dispersion	Yes, and quite substantial
Need of a KM lawyer	Yes

The first scenario envisions the presence of a KM lawyer who does not have a database (D_ε) nor a lot of automation involved (A_ε) to create visuals.

These two factors exponentially influence the level of technology literacy (tl^n) needed to produce knowledge (K): the KM lawyer, indeed, needs to master the (scarce) resources at his/her disposal to produce quite limited forms of legal knowledge visualizations, relying mostly on raw data, such as simple laws or case-law collections, with no or very basic visuals involved.

The time (T) needed to produce easy to use legal output formats is high, too.

2.1.2 Scenario 2: Combining Tacit and Explicit Legal Knowledge

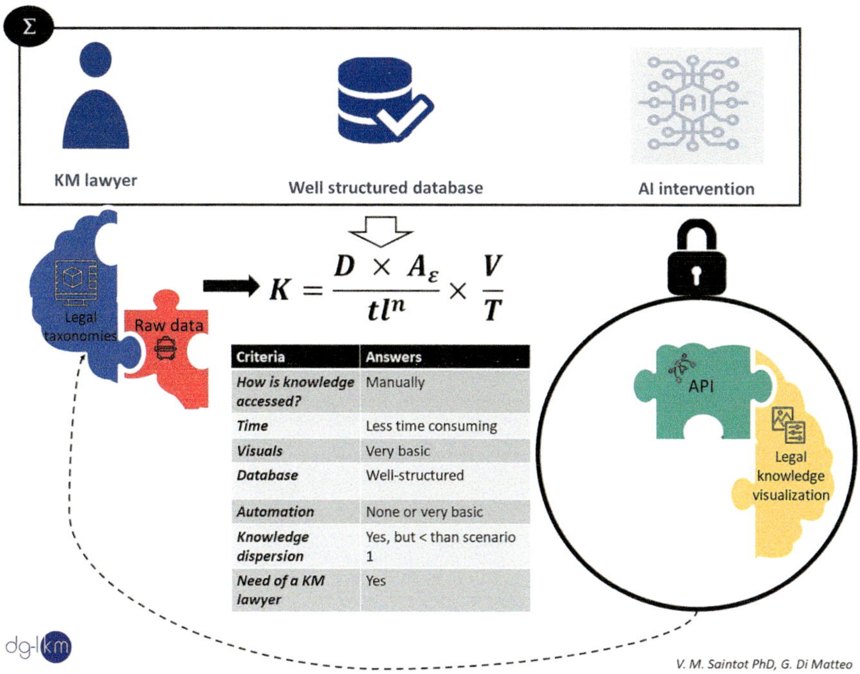

Criteria	Answers
How is knowledge accessed?	Manually
Time	Less time consuming
Visuals	Very basic
Database	Well-structured
Automation	None or very basic
Knowledge dispersion	Yes, but < than scenario 1
Need of a KM lawyer	Yes

The second scenario envisions the presence of a KM lawyer who this time can rely on a well-structured database (***D***), still missing however a sufficient level of automation (A_ε), and therefore without analytical tools capable of producing meaningful visuals of the law.

Thus, the level of technological literacy (tl^n) needed remains quite high, since a KM lawyer skilled in the tools at his/her disposal is still needed to produce meaningful visuals.

Nevertheless, we can already see an improvement in the quantity and quality of knowledge (***K***) obtainable: a good database could, indeed, serve as the essential basis for a proper legal taxonomy and eventually an ontology, capable of describing the relationships between the different legal documents (Ajani et al. 2016).

The same existence of such a taxonomy, accompanied by a strong set of metadata, would speed up the KM lawyer's time (***T***) needed to obtain access to meaningful data and information in order to produce visuals.

2.1.3 Scenario 3: Scaling Up Legal Knowledge Mobilization

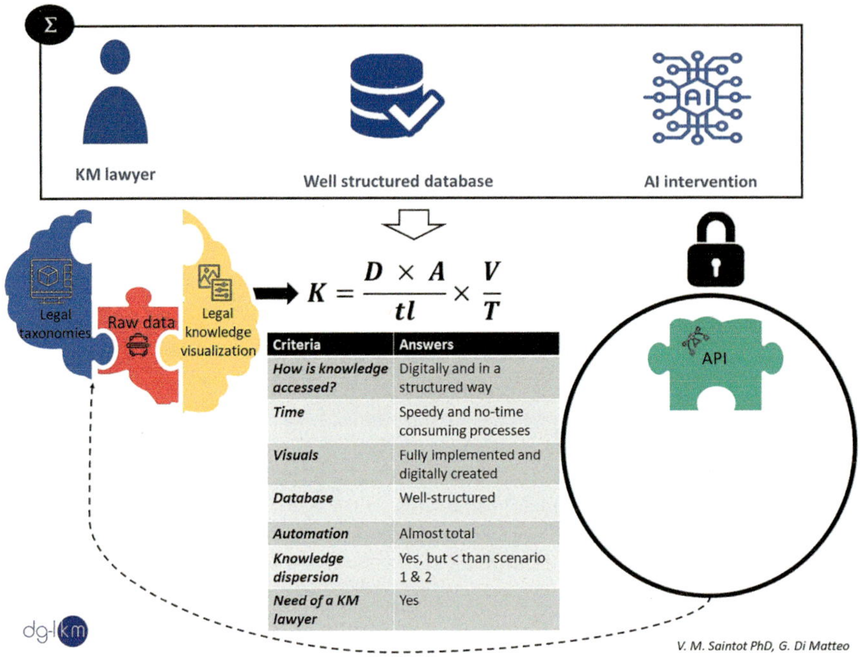

$$K = \frac{D \times A}{tl} \times \frac{V}{T}$$

Criteria	Answers
How is knowledge accessed?	Digitally and in a structured way
Time	Speedy and no-time consuming processes
Visuals	Fully implemented and digitally created
Database	Well-structured
Automation	Almost total
Knowledge dispersion	Yes, but < than scenario 1 & 2
Need of a KM lawyer	Yes

The third scenario represents an optimal situation for the KM lawyer producing visuals: thanks to a well-structured database (***D***), a significant level of automation (***A***) involved in the retrieval of legal data and information, as well as in the concrete production of visuals, the amount of knowledge (***K***) accessible and transferable via visualization (***V***) increases significantly, reducing drastically the time (***T***) needed to produce them.

Even though in such scenario a skilled KM lawyer with a good understanding of specific tools is still needed to produce visuals, the factor of the technological literacy has decreased substantially (***tl***): thanks to good databases and automated tools, indeed, the KM lawyer would not need to master and rely on several tech tools to produce the same visual.

Although legal knowledge mobilization is scaling up when compared to scenarios 1 and 2, thanks to better databases (***D***) and additional automated tools (***A***), there is still a risk of having knowledge scattered, i.e. the likelihood of missing relevant legal information. Such a phenomenon is the result of a fairly common tendency amongst the relevant actors (e.g. providers of databases, technologists, legal practitioners) and which is to work in silos (Tett 2016), something which could be mitigated by API (*Application Programming Interface*) connecting the different sources of knowledge the KM lawyer draws upon on to produce visual output.

2.1.4 Scenario 4: Augmenting and Automating Legal Knowledge Mobilization

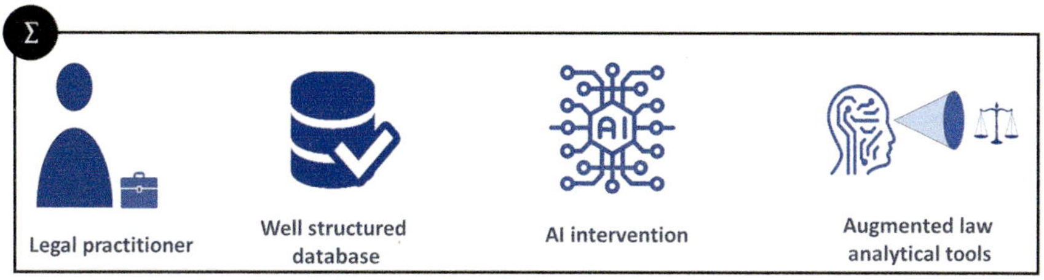

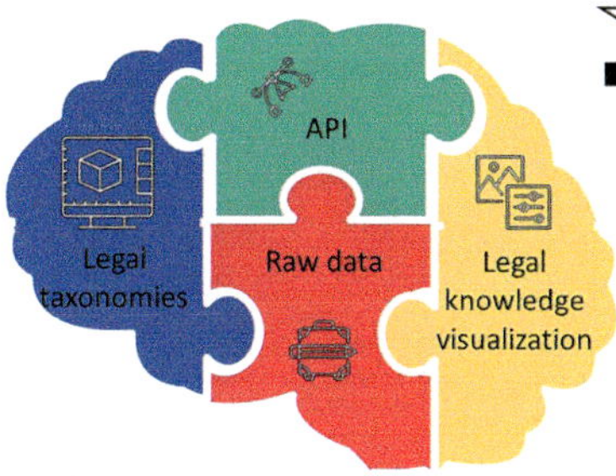

$$K = \frac{D \times A^n}{tl_\varepsilon} \times \frac{V}{T}$$

Criteria	Answers
How is knowledge accessed?	Digitally and in a structured way
Time aspects	Speedy and no-time consuming processes
Visuals	Fully implemented and digitally created
Database	Well-structured
Automation	Almost total and > than scenario 3
Knowledge dispersion	Minimal
Need of a KM lawyer	No, thanks to augmented law analytical tools, which reduce technological barriers (**tl**)

V. M. Saintot PhD, G. Di Matteo

The last scenario represents the way in which we see the future of legal knowledge visualization: thanks to well-structured databases (***D***), an exponential level of AI intervention and augmented analytical tools in law (A^n), the quantity and quality of knowledge (***K***) accessible via visualization (***V***) would simply be of a different scale.

The augmented analytical tools in law we are referring to could take different forms, but the primary tool we have in mind is based on a combination of ML (*Machine Learning*), knowledge graphs and API (see chapter 4).

Thanks to the combination of these three elements, the "*Third generation of knowledge management*" (Tuomi 2002), which was envisaged by Ikka Tuomi almost 20 years ago, would become reality, allowing for flexible, inter-linked, multi-dimensional and interactive forms of knowledge visualization. In this way, the general lawyer would not only transfer knowledge, but even generate insights, opening the door to a new era of interactivity for the practitioners with the law.

This also explains why the KM lawyer, previously essential in the concrete creation of visuals, has disappeared from the equation, due to the increasing role of automation and AI in the process of legal knowledge visualization, which drastically reduces the technological literacy required (tl^ε), therefore 'democratising' the process of legal knowledge visualization and allowing the KM lawyer to dedicate time to new challenges.

We want to stress that in all four scenarios, human interventions are not substituted but augmented. Indeed, the goal pursued is augmenting analytical skills to increase quality, speed, depth of the analytical capability available (Rouse 2018).

However, with the increasing improvement of **(a) database capabilities**, **(b) the level of AI intervention** and **(c) the use of augmented analytical tools in law**, the level of knowledge which becomes obtainable (using well defined meta-data and taxonomies and ontologies) both from a quantitative and qualitative perspective grows exponentially: while in the first scenario only raw data is available, in the last scenario even APIs come into play, opening the door to knowledge-linking in one of the most sophisticated ways possible (e.g. ML-based knowledge graphs).

Moreover, in the last scenario, the technological barriers originally preventing many legal practitioners from accessing incredibly useful knowledge have almost disappeared, substantially democratizing the legal knowledge visualization (and creation) process.

The above is a plea not to further delay the use of legal knowledge visualization for the exploration of the law: thanks to analytical tools augmenting the highly conceptual and knowledge driven analytical skills of lawyers, any legal practitioner (and not only KM lawyers) could tap into the whole spectrum of legal knowledge. Actors across silos, industries and expertise alike would benefit from establishing a structured conversation to have a useful map of the territory. It would enable the design of an innovative and result-oriented agenda. We believe that users need to be less passive about articulating the limitations they encounter, and also be more vocal at explaining what their needs are: in this way, database owners as well as app and platform developers would have a clearer understanding about the readiness, for instance of KM lawyers, to support their internal stakeholders with making better use of legal knowledge visualization, not as a 'nice to have', but as a fast-forward and 'must-have' in terms of collective legal cognition to address and tackle ever more complex issues.

3 Legal Knowledge Visualization Examples

Having articulated what may influence the visualization of legal knowledge, we will discuss two case studies in which the situation was comparable to those depicted in scenarios 1 and 2 above.

Important disclaimer: for the sake of focusing on the theme of this article, the content relating to the legal issues analysed are not presented at length. The case studies are solely used to illustrate the challenges faced and the need for future developments. They are the outcome of a legal KM process and are not to be taken as eliciting a public policy stance. The case studies are used for the reader to learn from, and not to induce the reader in the substantive legal questions they raise. Their obvious imperfections and shortcomings merely serve to focus the authors of this article on discussions concerning the need to automate the production of such visuals in the future and make them digital and interactive over time.

For each case study, four dimensions are presented:

- Which **knowledge related issue** did we tackle?
- Why did we choose a particular **visual representation**?
- What was the **impact** observed?
- Which **opportunities for development and further exploration** presented themselves in the process?

3.1 Case Study 1: Visualization of Competing Factors

In the area of public policy making, legal frameworks are often discussed from multiple angles, not only from a legal perspective. The legal considerations are obviously essential as the rule of law is the ultimate argument in such discussions. Yet discussions around possible competing interpretations of a given set of duties or a mandate can be facilitated by predominantly graphical rather than solely textual representations.

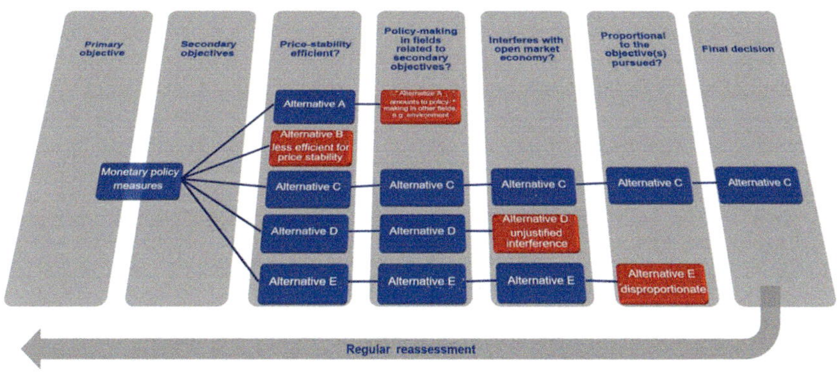

Knowledge Problem Explored

The issue in terms of knowledge was to find a way to render more visually explicit the competing and/or successive parameters helping to interpret the legal provision under review and, in doing so, offer an alternative to the strictly textual version of the provision. A small group of lawyers specialized in the relevant topic and sharing a comparable analytical mindset may already need a significant amount of time to bring their positions together through oral and written argumentation. If lawyers and non-lawyers, who are not experts in this specific domain, join the discussion, the situation becomes even more challenging. When experts from other disciplines bring their take, it often becomes difficult to reach a consensus. This is where visualization, even if it can obviously not replace the textual analysis, can help map the territory of the parameters, bottlenecks, as well as the clear and less clear aspects of the legal issue at hand.

Visual Representation Chosen

The choice was to use a horizontal decision tree. The logic of the choice was to be able to have a sequential step-by-step wise analysis of the legal provision and be in a position to work with competing alternatives for each step. The reason for using the 'box style' version decision-tree diagram is tactical more than conceptual: it is, indeed, closer to a textual take of the provision then and if/then more process description type. The reader's need to feel at ease with the visual rendering has been experienced as a key lever to increase the acceptance of visible thinking in the legal community.

Impact of Visual Representation

The value of the legal knowledge visualized resided in the visual deconstruction of the elements to be considered for the benefit of the discussion. It helped structure the conversation and progress it through the exploration of the various parameters. The visual was effective in making explicit the different steps and options for the interpretation. This helped building bridges to create dialogues with those holding different viewpoints. Legal knowledge visualization strengthens lateral thinking for lawyers and also enables a discussion to take the full complexity of a matter into account in a shorter time. Literally, the big picture makes tangible the terms of the discussion and makes them accessible to all discussants on an ongoing basis as the discussion unfolds. Besides, the visual can be enriched and adjusted allowing to fine-tune, improve, focus and iterate the alignment of agreements and disagreements or any new understanding.

Opportunities for Developments

Beyond data, semantics, AI and before investing efforts in advanced technological developments, a visual grammar and a certain set of principles supporting a more visual approach to eliciting legal interpretation challenges are needed. The aim is not to have a machine substituting the human mind behind the decision, but a "visual guide" to augment the cognition of those having to solve a given problem. Thanks to the computational and analytical processing offered by AI, the humans behind the decision (Jarray 2018) should be able to weigh and process the inherent complexity of the legal framework regulating a complicated interpretation and/or decision.

3.2 Case Study 2: Relative Weight of Legal Criteria

It is a common challenge to come with the explicit criteria to be applied to solve a particular legal question. At times, these criteria are scattered across several legal acts. In addition, the reasoning by analogy employed when an answer may not be found directly in the legal act of immediate relevance also requires an appreciation and consideration of the impact of comparable criteria. A further aspect is that relevant case-law may also play a role in refining the relative weighing of the said criteria.

The kind of context described above is rather common. Below, we present one case study of how we used knowledge visualization to help make sense of the process and supported a process by which the bigger picture emerged. In particular, the case study is aimed at providing, in a compact and accessible way, an overview on the main concepts behind a given methodology. This overview did not solve the problem in place of the legal counsels, yet it provided useful insights that would not have been as explicit as this at a glance.

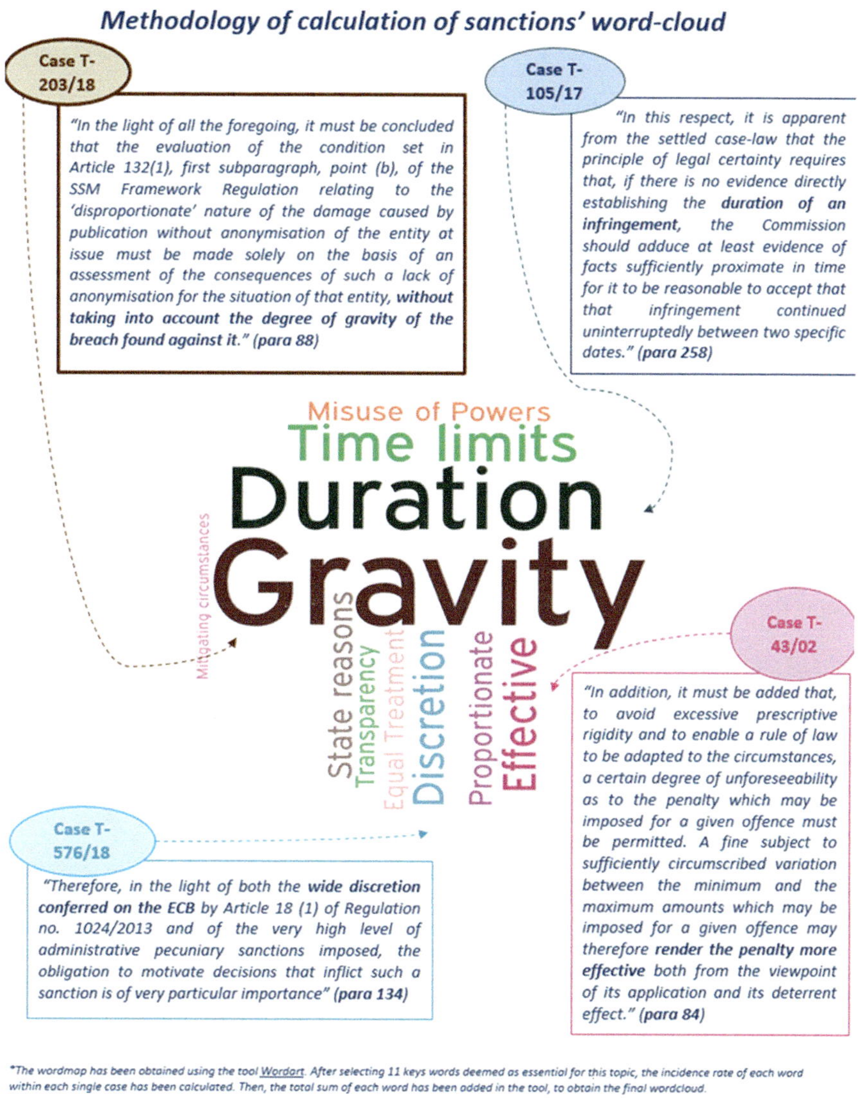

Knowledge Problem Explored

The challenge, a rather typical one by the way, was the fact that the relevant legal information was scattered across several legal fields and had been referred to in different judgments. The goal was not to generate legal advice, but to find a way to give an overview of the elements of information that needed to be considered. Another aspect was to create a sense of relative weight of the different key aspects influencing the analysis.

Visual Representation Chosen

To generate a rough overview, extracts relating to the question under review were compiled from the most relevant judgements. The process consisted of research, dialogue, analysis, and design. The KM lawyer also chose the visual representation to meet the need to understand the relative weight of the different aspects influencing the question under examination. It was decided that the visual weighing appearing on a word cloud would make a decent contribution to enable the list of key aspects to be considered at a glance. The difference in the font size of the words in the cloud would then take care of displaying the relative weight of each word in the matter analysed.

In the absence of adequate technology, the production of this visual required a substantial amount of manual work by the KM lawyer, including: **(i)** reading different judgments; **(ii)** identifying the relevant paragraphs mentioning the specific concept of methodology, relying on the Ctrl+F command; **(iii)** selecting the main recurrent concepts according to the case law and the doctrine; and **(iv)** finally, visualizing everything by relying on a word-cloud tool and on PowerPoint.

Impact of the Visual Representation

As part of a broader set of analytical input, it was perceived as useful to have a word cloud designed on the basis of the relevant quotes in case. It helped give a single overview on the aspects that needed to be discussed and further explored as the legal counsels developed their analysis and arguments for the new challenges they were facing in this area. It facilitated the discussions and growth a shared understanding of current and future developments in the area. Last but not least, it was also considered to be of help when discussing the developments in the relevant policy areas with non-lawyers.

Opportunities for Development

The above case study indicates that there is room for automation. Specific ML-based knowledge discovering tools have been quite successful in providing useful insights for the practitioners in other jurisdictions (Grajzl and Murrel 2021). EU case-law provides a good testing environment for an ML-based tool identifying relevant parts of each case containing a specific key word(s). Thereafter, the machine would be able to link that case to other cases containing the same key word(s), which are often quoted within the same case. With this raw data, the machine could then produce a similar if not better word-cloud, but with a great addition: interactivity. By clicking on each word, direct access to relevant case law could be enabled, including relevant quotes containing the specific 'hits' (keywords).

4 Conclusion and Outlook

We have no doubt there is a long way to go to make law and case law much more visually accessible and interactive. Our experience shows that the challenge might be less the technology than the leadership and the ability of different stakeholders to accept that leaving their comfort zone is necessary to venture into a world of pluri-disciplinarity. The conversation is about the interoperability between human and machine, it is about augmentation versus substitution. The highly conceptual and knowledge-driven profile of lawyers make them sound partners to fast forward the conversation. Better legal knowledge visualization is not a 'nice to have', it is a necessity in the light of the extraordinary complexity and cumulation of todays' issues we seem to be facing in all walks of society.

In this strive for improvement, an AI-based legal knowledge tool relying on efficient and interconnected databases via API and knowledge graphs will play a central role. The combination of these three elements, indeed, could make it possible to realize a sort of 'pooled system of available knowledge', allowing the whole spectrum of legal knowledge in combination with analytical tools to augment (and not substitute) the analytical skills of lawyers in their exploration of law.

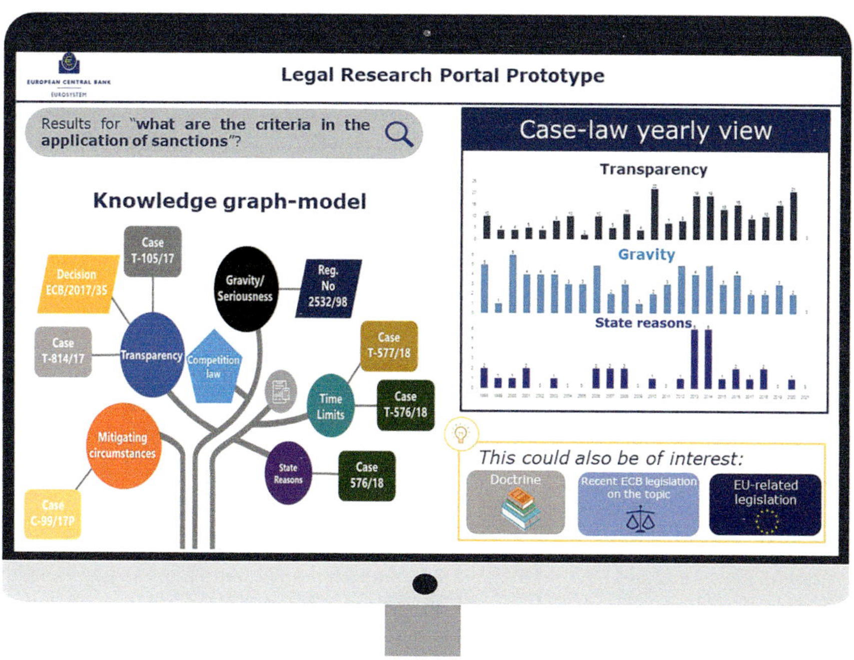

Prototype of a Visual and Interactive Dashboard

To move from announcements such as "*AI will transform the field of law*" (Toews 2019) to effective benefits for the day-to-day activity of any legal practitioner, it is time to leave behind this tendency to work in silos. Legal practitioners, data scientists and technology developers need to draw a common map of the challenges and define a common language to venture into mobilising more modern ways of generating insights and reducing complexity. From this perspective, we should not save on our efforts to foster the conversation between '*two sides of the same coin*' (Linna 2019): the synergy of machine and humans. To outgrow current limitations, lawyers and technologists need to be able to connect users' needs and technological opportunities more proactively.

Liquid Legal Waves to Other Chapters, Written by the Editors

This chapter on the power of visualization for better drafting, more effective legal interpretation and a higher degree of knowledge sharing directly builds on the earlier chapter of *Valérie* and *Filip* on *"Transforming legal ecosystems"* in which they share the 'EASE-model'—a practical concept of changing the mindset by involving all cross-functional stakeholders.

The knowledge management technique *Valérie* and *Gabriele* developed as a way of aligning understanding and building capability through visual communication creates an immediate link on how to direct that outcome into contract drafting and contract design, as presented by *Rob*, *Helena*, and *Stefania* in *"Layered Contracts: Both Legally Functional and Human-friendly"*.

Valérie and *Gabriele* make the strong point that, as lawyers, we 'know' with more than our brains, referring to embedded (in context) and enacted (in action) cognition. In the upcoming chapter *Sven* and *Philipp* extend that line of thought towards *"The Paradigm shift in AI: From human labor to humane creativity"*.

References

Agrawal R, Andres F, Kadadi A, Dai X (2015) Challenges and opportunities with Big Data Visualization. In: Paper presented at the 7th International Conference on Management of computational and collective Intelligence in Digital EcoSystems (MEDES), Caraguatatuba, Brazil, 15 October 2015

Ajani G, Boella G, Di Caro L, Humphreys L, Praduroux S, Rossi P, Violato A (2016) The European taxonomy syllabus: a multi-lingual, multi-level ontology framework to untangle the web of European legal terminology. Appl Ontol 11:325–375. https://doi.org/10.3233/AO-170174

Berger-Walliser G, Barton T-D, Haapio H (2017) From visualization to legal design: a collaborative and creative process. Am Bus Law J 54(2):347–392. https://doi.org/10.1111/ablj.12101

Chandler P, Sweller J (1991) Cognitive load theory and the format of instruction. Cogn Instr 8(4): 293–332. https://doi.org/10.1207/s1532690xci0804_2. https://www.researchgate.net/publication/48828982_Cognitive_Load_Theory_and_the_Format_of_Instruction

Cyras V, Lachmayer F, Hoffman H, Wenig Y-H (2018) Introduction to legal visualization. In: Schweighofer E et al (eds) Data Protection/LegalTech: Proceedings of the 21st International Legal Informatics Symposium. Weblaw, Vienna, pp 437–444

Davenport T (1994) Saving IT's soul: human centred information management. Harv Bus Rev 72(2):119–131. https://hbr.org/1994/03/saving-its-sou-human-centered-information-management [The actual quote was pronounced for the first time at the Boston Conference of '93]

Davies R-S (2011) Understanding technology literacy: a framework for evaluating educational technology integration. Tech Trends 55(5):45–52. https://doi.org/10.1007/s11528-011-0527-3

Eppler M, Burkhard R (2007) Visual representations in knowledge management: framework and cases. J Knowl Manag 11(4):112–122. https://doi.org/10.1108/13673270710762756. https://www.uky.edu/~gmswan3/575/Eppler_and_Burkhard_2007.PDF

Feigenson N, Sherwin R, Spiesel C-O (2006) Law in the digital age: how visual communication technologies are transforming practice, theory, and teaching of law. NYLS Legal Studies Research Paper No. 05/06-6. https://doi.org/10.2139/ssrn.804424

Grajzl P, Murrel P (2021) A machine-learning history of English caselaw and legal ideas prior to the Industrial Revolution I: generating and interpreting the estimates. J Inst Econ 17(1):1–19. https://doi.org/10.1017/S1744137420000326

IEEE Robotics &Automation Society (2021) Governance. https://www.ieee-ras.org/about-ras/governance

Jarray M-H (2018) Artificial intelligence and the future of work: human-AI symbiosis in organizational decision making. Bus Horiz 61(4):577–586. https://doi.org/10.1016/j.bushor.2018.03.007

Katz D, Coupette C, Beckedorf J, Hartung D (2020) Complex societies and the growth of the law. Sci Rep 10(1). https://doi.org/10.1038/s41598-020-73623-x

Linna D-W Jr (2019) The future of law and computational technologies: two sides of the same coin. In: MIT computational law report. Available via SSRN: https://papers.ssrn.com/sol3/papers.cfm?abstract_id=3554591

Meyer R (2009) Knowledge visualization. In: LFE Medieninformatik. Available via Semantic Scholar: https://www.semanticscholar.org/paper/Knowledge-Visualization-Meyer-Medieninformatik/d84e9b0aef14c348e9eede8a23fc69afb7a3a289#paper-header

Monteguado M (2019) Central banks and ethics: the virtual paradox of transparency and confidentiality mandates. In: Russo C et al (eds) Research handbook on law and ethics in banking and finance. Edward Elgar, Cheltenham, pp 351–367. https://doi.org/10.4337/9781784716547). Elgar, https://www.elgaronline.com/view/edcoll/9781784716530/9781784716530.00028.xml

Nonaka I, Takeuchi H (1995) The knowledge creating company: how Japanese companies create the dynamics of innovation. Oxford University Press, New York

Nuamah J-K, Mehta R-K (2020) Neuroergonomic applications in information visualization. In: Nam C-S (ed) Neuroergonomics: principles and practice. Springer, Switzerland, pp 437–444

Penrose R (2016) The emperor's new mind. Oxford University Press, New York

Piattini M-G, Calero C, Genero M-F (2002) Information and database quality. Springer Science +Business Media, New York

Rouse W-B (2018) Automating versus augmenting intelligence. J Enterp Transformation 8(1-2): 1–21. https://doi.org/10.1080/19488289.2018.1424059

Sparrow J (1998) Knowledge in organization: access to thinking at work. Sage Publications, London

Tergan S-O, Keller T (2005) Knowledge and information visualization. Searching for synergies. In: Tergan S-O, Keller T (eds) Lectures notes in computer science, vol 3426. Springer, Tübingen, p 3

Tett G (2016) The Silo effect: the peril of expertise and the promise of breaking down barriers. Simon & Schuster, United States

Toews R (2019) AI will transform the field of law. Available via Forbes. https://www.forbes.com/sites/robtoews/2019/12/19/ai-will-transform-the-field-of-law/. https://www.forbes.com/sites/robtoews/2019/12/19/ai-will-transform-the-field-of-law/?sh=66cef44c7f01

Tuomi I (2002) The future of knowledge management. Lifelong Learn Europe 7(2):69–79

Valérie M. Saintot, LLM, PhD, is a lawyer with three decades of professional experience in both private and public sector. She started her career at the European Court of Justice in Luxembourg in 1994. Before focusing on lecturing, she has been the Head of Legislation Division, Directorate General Legal Services at the European Central Bank in Frankfurt where she also led a team in charge of legal knowledge management. She holds four postgraduate degrees in law, psychology, and research. She regularly speaks at events promoting visualization and is author of management articles in this domain.

Valérie is passionate about helping teams activate their full potential. To this end, she has been using for two decades knowledge visualization and (legal) design thinking. She has experienced the power of both to support collaboration, innovation, decision-making and communication. Valérie managed the team in charge of the creation of the ECB visitor centre which opened in 2017. This project gave her the opportunity to manifest in a large scale the power of visual and design thinking for outreach purposes. She is also working on developing legislative data visualization methods to help experts and citizens alike navigate online legal frameworks in a more transparent and intuitive way.

Gabriele Di Matteo is currently a legal analyst at the European Central Bank. After graduating in law with summa cum laude at the University of Bologna, he specialized in the interrelation between Law & Technology. He completed an LLM in Law & Technology at the University of Tilburg, where he graduated with distinction discussing a thesis on Public ODR and Access to Justice. After a brief parenthesis as a research assistant at the University of Tilburg, during which he explored the challenges and the issues related to data-driven technologies in the humanitarian sector, he was offered the opportunity to join the Knowledge Management Team of the European Central Bank. During this experience, he took part to different legal tech-projects aiming at improving the efficiency and the productivity of the ECB legal teams, as the ECB—Eur-lex project which culminated in the creation of a corner in Eur-lex wherein all the ECB legislative production is now publicly available. His current interests cover a variety of legal fields: privacy and data protection; access to justice; access to law and transparency principle; algorithmic discriminations; knowledge management and visualization.

The Paradigm Shift in AI: From Human Labor to Humane Creativity

Philipp Glock and Sven von Alemann

Contents

Philipp Glock is Partner at KPMG Law, Head of Legal Corporate Services as well as Head of Innovation, Co-Head of Legal Operations & Technology Services and Head of the KPMG Law office in Leipzig.

Sven von Alemann is Senior Manager at KPMG Law in the Legal Operations & Technology Services team.

The male pronouns are meant to be inclusive.

P. Glock · S. von Alemann (✉)
KPMG Law, Legal Operations & Technology Services, Berlin, Germany
e-mail: pglock@kpmg-law.com; svonalemann@kpmg-law.com

K. Jacob et al. (eds.), *Liquid Legal – Humanization and the Law*, Law for Professionals, https://doi.org/10.1007/978-3-031-14240-6_11

Abstract

Digitization is already here. By today's standards, every legal professional possesses his personal computer and smartphone and utilizes standard software. But is this already a digital transformation? Digital transformation, i.e. *digitalization*, does not only mean converting analog into digital information, but rather the integration of digital technology into all areas of business in the form of a fundamental transformation of how businesses operate. Therefore, it has the potential to include a positive paradigm shift towards a smart and technological world that emphasizes the creative input of human work. The resulting gains in efficiency were, however, accompanied by a change in expectations of employers, clients and business partners. The workload of (legal) professionals has increased even further because the possibility of automation raises expectations and the need for automation. The hope that *digitization* would enable humans to work differently with a shift from fast-paced mundane to creative and quality work has so far been proven wrong. Will a true *digitalization* in the sense of a paradigm shift and digital transformation bring us closer to turning that vision into reality?

Digitization has led to an abundance of information. This poses the difficult problem of information overload. The distinction between relevant and irrelevant data has become one of the main challenges of our informational age. Artificial Intelligence (AI) offers the possibility to cause a paradigm shift, freeing humans from simple and repetitive tasks by automation and informational analysis.

Automation is already in widespread use. For example, legal documents can be created automatically, eliminating common human mistakes such as misjudgments, omissions, missing references or even simple typos. Or document-intake including understanding its content and automated triage can be carried out by bots without much human contribution. This enables humans to channel their energy into more creative and complex tasks like designing legal processes or complex negotiations.

Informational analysis, however, is still a bottleneck. AI can already process millions of datasets. However, humans have a hard time using the information an AI system processes efficiently as they often lack a clear understanding of the results of the analysis and how it was calculated. AI and human intelligence "perceive" our reality differently. AI "thinks" in correlations, whereas humans mainly use causality to link data (*Leetaru*, A Reminder That Machine Learning Is About Correlations Not Causation, https://www.forbes.com/sites/kalevleetaru/2019/01/15/a-reminder-that-machine-learning-is-about-correlations-not-causation/?sh=535c6fc96161). We can overcome this hurdle by using visualization of the results and well-designed processes. Visualization can make it easier for humans to use the information provided by AI-processing and thus bridge the gap between the difference in AI's and human's perception of data.

In summary, digitalization, in particular technologies such as AI, have the potential to bring a paradigm shift upon human work. Humans may be relieved from repetitive work, allowing them to be more creative, and therefore more humane. What will be most important is to be innovative instead of productive.

1 Current State of Digitalization

To assess the possibility of a paradigm shift for the application of technology, AI and automation, it is necessary to first describe the current state of digitalization and determine if there is still untapped potential for how digital means can transform the industry.[1]

Lawyers have already begun to regularly use digital means and devices in their work and for their services, e.g. digital databases or smart contract tools, even though their field of work is, in general, more akin to tradition than innovation. With digitization having arrived in the generally tradition-based legal industry, it can be assumed that in other industries it is even more commonly applied. It also means that the old days, when lawyer's cases were still stored away in filing cabinets, will not return, even if this was only 10 years ago. In the same way that those files are now stored completely digitally, digital work tools have already become the norm in today's legal profession. But is this already digital transformation?

One aspect of digitalization is automation. Many simple tasks can be automated due to the higher efficiency and efficacy of (*inter alia*) AI and other technologies today.[2] It starts with optical character recognition (OCR) as a basic prerequisite for further digitalization of previously analogous documents, which also acts as a bridge between the classic working means using paper documents and more advanced digital methods. It continues with data extraction, pattern recognition and predictive analysis as more advanced processes made possible by the application of AI.

Besides these technological advances, digitalization also provides opportunities for new services in the legal market. (Alternative) legal service providers are using new technologies to compete with established law firms.[3] By utilizing automation and AI, these service providers can work more efficiently, leading to lower cost and a higher quantitative output.

However, it seems that the amount of work has generally increased, but our use of technology to help manage this workload has not. Is this due to a lack of potential on

---

[1] The authors would like to thank Tom Lüxmann, research associate at KPMG Law, for the valuable contribution and support in creating this article.

[2] Semmler and Rose (2017), pp. 85, 86 et seq. Also, the area of credit scoring is widely automated nowadays, compare Burell (2016), p. 2; Binns (2018), pp. 31, 543, 545.

[3] Smaller firms can suddenly compete with big law firms utilizing technology instead of manpower, compare Semmler and Rose (2017), pp. 85, 90. Also, by using such innovative means new law firms can quickly establish a competitive market position, which is illustrated by the Big Four's emergence as market competitors.

the side of digitalization or have we not seized the chance that digitalization holds just yet?

Let us take a look at the discrepancy between expectations and current reality of digitalization, especially with regards to the application of AI in the legal industry. We will also elaborate on the reason for the current shortcomings of the digitalization in our work. At least in the legal profession, a shift from a high workload of (partly) rather simple and repetitive tasks to a new way of working using digital means is an exception. Despite advancements in AI-driven contract analysis and other automation technologies, humans still carry out almost the full range of tasks from simple to high-end.[4] So why have automation and AI not yet had a major impact on the way we are working?

An example of automation enhancing current business models is the emergence of (alternative) legal service providers. There is a pressing need for this. "More for Less" as famously coined by Richard Susskind has become the motive of the early twenty-first century digitalization. This has been visible in legal departments in the past few years and is a challenge for many GCs: more regulation and topics like Compliance, ESG and financial regulation require more and specialized work while, at the same time, budgets for internal and external resources are under pressure. If the only concern is reducing the workload and coping with this "More for Less" dilemma, automation can help a great deal. Contract automation, decision automation or assisted intake processes are examples for reducing manual work. Decision automation solutions, for example, usually use decision trees to give answers to recurring requests. These systems ask users for input at every step or parameter of a decision and can give a result for the request after collecting all necessary information. That way, there is no need to manually answer standard requests, except in exceptional cases.

However, "More for Less" cannot be the sole reason why the workload in the industry seems to increase constantly.[5] Why do the automation efforts have such a limited effect? The reason could be that pure digitization of processes is not enough if it is not a digitalization in the sense of a transformation effort. We will describe several reasons why the legal market is still largely defined by a high manual effort, the opposite of a humanized working environment.

While legal services can be performed more effectively with the use of digital processes, legal risks remain out of scope.[6] A contract automation software for instance can produce a huge number of contracts in a shorter timespan than a lawyer could manually. However, while the use of software will reduce common human error, other risks arise with automation. For this reason, there need to be safeguards to make sure it creates no additional legal risks. Such risks may be caused by generalization, change of law or facts, or errors in the software or its use. The more intensively automation is used, the higher the legal risks of errors or omissions will be.

---

[4] Chang (2021).

[5] Norton Rose Fulbright, 2020 Annual Litigation Trends Survey.

[6] Semmler and Rose (2017), pp. 85, 88 et seq.

The possibility of efficiency creates the necessity of efficiency. Coincidently, necessity is the mother of invention, and therefore also the mother of innovation. Innovation in this sense is to put an invention (an idea or method) to (commercially successful) use. So, the good news is, competition between legal service providers and established law firms accelerates legal innovation and the transformation of the industry.

We are moving towards a digitally transformed industry. While some established law firms still cling to the old way of working, new business models flourish due to their innovation and creativity in challenging traditional processes in the legal space. This has led to an interesting landscape where new business models compete with other more traditional business models. Still, both models have some unique advantages. While the traditional legal branch is a highly specialized stronghold of human creativity and high-end legal work, new business models excel at efficiently handle massive amounts of data, repetitive tasks and processes. Therefore, a combination of the two models will be a perfect synergy of the respective advantages and potential. This will create digitalization in its true sense: a transformation of the industry.

2 Challenges of the Digital Landscape

Although digitization is fully on its way into the legal industry and legal technologies are being adopted more and more, digital transformation and digitalization still face several challenges. Among those, but not limited to, are the mastering of technology and combatting informational overload that pose a critical threat to the successful adoption of legal technology.

2.1 Mastering Technology

The legal profession is in the process of adopting legal technologies and also mastering the technology that is theoretically ready to be utilized. This will require an understanding of the technologies, its underlying processes, requirements and possibilities. It is an ongoing process and requires openness and willingness to learn and change from all stakeholders in the legal industry, from the General Counsel and legal departments to law firms and their partners, as well as in the public sector and the judiciary.

The digital transformation of the legal landscape is taking its toll on lawyers, paralegals and support staff. Especially during the process of adopting technology, of learning the ins and outs of the tools and sources of possible errors, digitalization may sometimes seem to be more of a burden than a blessing. It is therefore important to communicate the potential and benefits that come with such technology and to further maximize gains while reducing the necessary input of time and maintenance. As soon as a certain technology is used intensively on a day-to-day basis, the positive change this technology has on the everyday (working) life will be realized.

Furthermore, automation will only be adopted and used successfully if it is reliable. Otherwise, if automatically generated results need to be manually checked in detail, the work carried out by the machine is no real reduction of workload. In this case, it may create more work than it was meant to take away.

This can happen because of the use of deficient technology[7] or deficient use of that technology: Even the best software will not run properly if the user does not execute it correctly or is not properly trained for it. On the other hand, a technically poor software might not run properly, even if the user follows all instructions in the documentation.

Therefore, the concept of digital literacy is an essential prerequisite for successful digitalization. While literacy in general refers to being able to read and write, hence to make sense of the world and express oneself, digital literacy can be defined as the ability to make sense of the *digital* world. This includes an understanding of how to use IT and digital technology; find, research and evaluate information; adapt new technology as well as communicate and explain technology. To what extent users must show an aptitude in utilizing programs will vary depending on position and industry. For example, an employee in industrial manufacturing will need more in-depth digital literacy than a person working in delivery. However, with digitalization touching almost every aspect of working life, it is a prerequisite for successfully preparing for the future.

2.2 Informational Overload

Advancing digitalization comes with a variety of informational advantages. Just by storing contracts digitally, for example, there is data readily available, just waiting to be accessed and transformed into insights. Different drafts of a contract can be analyzed to find out which clauses were quickly amended and what positions were heavily contested in negotiations. Also, huge amounts of data can be analyzed and a variety of metadata, patterns and deviations be extracted automatically.

This may bring about challenges. They can be summarized by the term informational overload.[8] This term refers to a volume of data too large for humans to effectively process. This informational overload is caused by the same reason that led to the recent rise of AI: the ever-increasing amount of data.[9] Generally, AI and ML models can produce more accurate predictions and learn more effectively if they are provided with more data. More data generally is not a challenge but, on the contrary, a benefit for AI algorithms that use machine learning. Humans, on the other hand, are quickly overwhelmed by too much data.

[7] Compare technical measures to test software Kroll et al. (2017), pp. 633, 643 et seq.

[8] See on that Koltay (2017), pp. 197, 198 et seq.

[9] Burell (2016), p. 2; Pagallo (2018), pp. 507, 511; Earnshaw et al. (2019), p. 14.

For humans, it is difficult to differentiate between relevant and irrelevant data when facing large amounts of it.[10] They will quickly lose themselves in a sea of data and may falsely focus on data that does not allow accurate deductions, but instead obscure the actual patterns that would lead to insight. It is an overload of information.

In contrast, AI can quickly discard specific datapoints as anomalies, or focus on those data points, depending on what it is trained to identify.[11] An AI system may take mere seconds to identify an anomaly in a dataset, regardless of whether it has to take 1000, 100,000 or 1,000,000 data entries into account.[12] Artificial intelligence and big data systems are more scalable than human intelligence.[13] This is one of its unique advantages over human intelligence.

2.3 Lack of Processes

Finally, a barrier to digitalization is the sometimes-severe lack of optimized processes for digital working methods.[14] It is a similar topic as mentioned before: Even if automation is performed efficiently and effectively in 95% of the cases, there are still 5% left which do not work. Particularly in the legal service market, these 5% of cases cannot be discarded as irrelevant. Therefore, there must be processes in place to cover this 5% because a major risk may be realized in these very cases.

If such processes are missing, even the 95% of theoretically correctly automated results can be corrupted by only 5% falsely generated results if there is no mechanism to distinguish the false results afterwards. To avoid such corruption, processes must be defined to account for possible failures in automation. These processes must identify and remedy possible errors, or check and ensure that these are cases with only minor risks.

While some tasks can be performed effectively using automation, adequate processes in the organization are needed to maximize its potential. In the worst-case scenario, every result has to be checked after the automated processing to avoid any risk. In the best-case scenario, only those results with errors need to be checked because processes were established that ensure a certain quality for the rest. The difference between these scenarios might be 95% or an addition to one's workload. This shows that a lack of processes to address potential mistakes might corrupt the complete automation effort altogether.

---

[10] Koltay (2017), pp. 197, 200 et seq.

[11] For instance, in the field of IT-security it is much more important to identify statistical outliers like dubious lump sum payments to single bank accounts, that are not usually payees. In contrast to that, predictive analytics usually focus on certain reoccurring patterns within person's decisions to identify a certain modus operandi that can be relied upon as a general rule. Cf. Ahmed and Najmul Islam (2020), pp. 427, 430.

[12] Burell (2016), p. 5.

[13] Earnshaw et al. (2019), p. 20.

[14] Cf. in regard to Legal Departments Bosse and Schulz (2020), pp. 441, 445

3 The New Age of AI

How can these challenges be tackled in the new age of AI and digitalization?

3.1 Automation

Automation is a good start. It can be assumed that digital literacy of users, as defined above, will rise at the same time as technology is generally adopted, also in their private life. If technology gets more widespread and commonly used, organizations will have no choice but to use such technology to stay competitive and attract talent.

Simultaneously, by broadening the adoption of legal technology and therefore increasing the number of users, (legal) tech companies will improve their understanding of what their users need in terms of functionalities and usability. It should not be underestimated how intuitive navigation and easy usability of tools drive adoption for customers and developers.[15] An example for this can be seen with the release of Apple's iPod. While there were many other MP3 players on the market at the time, many of them technologically advanced, Apple designed its iPod for simple use and with an ecosystem to support the customer's needs.[16] This dramatically drove adoption of MP3 technology.

Organizations will have to make the difficult decision to adopt new technologies and processes even though a return on their investment may take some time. The first steps are the most difficult ones. After that, there will be an increase in knowledge and data, and the digitalization process could be right on its way. In the legal profession, we are still in the process of establishing automation in our field of work. Therefore, errors might occur, and growing pains will be had. This should not prevent us from starting to experiment with automation. However, it cannot stop at simple automation. Digitized processes will create large volumes of data. Without an analysis of that data, it remains untapped potential. For the potential of digitalization to be completely realized, informational analysis is needed.

3.2 Informational Analysis

Data is not the same as information. The difference between data and information is the contextual embedding within reality. If we take the example of contract clauses, the pure amount of amendments or annotations to a clause is just a datapoint. Only by contextualizing it do we understand that the clause may have been heavily contested in contract negotiations, and with that additional insight we have

[15] Semmler and Rose (2017), pp. 85, 89.

[16] *Sousa*, What The iPod Teaches Us About Workforce Adoption, https://www.forbes.com/sites/forbestechcouncil/2018/12/04/what-the-ipod-teaches-us-about-workforce-adoption/?sh=332693226d15.

information and not just data.[17] However, the reason for a high number of annotations may also be a sign of a poorly drafted clause that needs to be cleared and corrected in the form of amendments and annotations. We get the correct information by the context of the contract negotiations. Such contextualization that is not limited to a given framework, however, is currently still a hallmark of human intelligence. Artificial Intelligence may help to give indications for such informational insights by identifying the patterns and anomalies in specific datasets.[18]

Another important insight about informational analysis by AI models, or more precisely Machine Learning models, is their statistical approach. By finding correlations and patterns in huge datasets, AI can uncover correlations that were previously undetected by humans. AI can take into account more data than human intelligence ever could within a much shorter period of time. However, an AI system is limited by the data input and respective training. Its insights are construed within the boundaries of the information that is included in the training and productive data. AI may find new patterns but cannot take external information into account. This is a limiting factor of AI.

3.3 Overfitting and Underfitting

A major challenge in AI models is described as overfitting[19] and underfitting. AI models are trained on training data. It uses the data to identify patterns that can be generalized as a rule. The objective of an AI model is to transfer these rules to other datasets different from the training data. It is a balancing act between identifying specific patterns and simultaneously keeping the model applicable to new datasets. If the model cannot be applied to different data, because it is trained in a way to identify specifically those patterns lying within the training data, it is described as overfitting.[20] If, on the other hand, it is not applicable to new datasets, because it has not identified any patterns within the training data and can therefore not see any patterns within new data concurrently, this is described as underfitting.[21] The optimal state of learning of an AI-model lies in between these two states. One might also say, the AI model must fit.

---

[17] This might be done by the computer system automatically, which does not stipulate an act of original artificial intelligence though, because it will most likely be implemented as a guideline to the computer system by a human programmer. This is then an element of the in comparison to machine learning much older form of symbolic artificial intelligence, for it represents a relation that can easily be articulated with symbolic language.

[18] LawGeex for instance analyses contracts and suggests possible edits, Semmler and Rose (2017), pp. 85, 88.

[19] Webb (2011). https://doi.org/10.1007/978-0-387-30164-8_623.

[20] Kroll et al. (2017), pp. 633, 684. Instructive albeit in German on that matter also Hermstrüwer (2020), p. 488.

[21] In video-game AI's it might for instance cause a trained AI-model to fail, just because a graphical element in the game has changed after the training process, Garnelo and Shanahan (2019), p. 17.

It means that there is a high error-potential and an inherent risk of over- or underfitting when training an AI model. It also shows that AI models must be built and trained for specific use cases. There is no magic one-size-fits-all model. Also, testing models is crucial in every step. Effective tests can be done when the results and underlying functioning of the AI model are understandable for humans. Otherwise, biases might not even be noticed in the application of the model.

In the end, correct results are often not a matter of technical errors. An AI model might function correctly and as it was designed to—and still produce biased or incorrect results. The reason normally is not a malfunctioning technology but rather a 'malfunctioning' database[22] an error which is much harder to uncover and assess.

A way to tackle biased results from AI models is a better understanding of *why* results are generated. Users and lawyers need to build up AI literacy. Effective visualization of results and its correlations with the underlying database can support this.

3.4 The Problem of Interpretability

Often, it is difficult for people to understand how AI models produced their results, with the exception of highly trained specialists. This is a result of the opacity of AI.[23] Considering the impact of AI-analysis on human decision making, this leads to the question: how should such results be interpreted?

We have seen that the nature of AI processing relies on mathematical probability evaluation. This, however, is different from the human way of thinking. While AI mostly takes correlations and deduced probabilities into account, humans usually establish causality by linking cause and effect.[24] This is a significant difference in the way conclusions are reached. Humans generally tend to mistake the way AI models generate its results to be similar to their own way of thinking if they are not aware of the difference. This creates confusion about causality and correlation and therefore the way the results can be used in reality.

This, in turn, creates the necessity to contextualize the results of AI models critically.[25] In order to achieve that, users have to either understand the database and its inherent patterns or the reasons that have led to the result of the AI model. The first will often be ineffective, as it takes too much time to assess the database oneself and reducing time and effort is the reason why AI is being used in the first place. To understand why the AI model predicted or identified certain patterns, the concrete

[22] Sometimes called "dirty data", Won Kim et al. (2003), p. 81. Even official data, like police data, can often not be relied upon, compare Richardson et al. (2019), pp. 192, 197 et seq.

[23] For that reason AI-systems based on machine learning (especially deep neural networks) are often labeled as a blackbox in today's AI-discourse, cf. Wischmeyer (2020), p. 75, passim; Garnelo and Shanahan (2019), pp. 29, 17; Ferguson (2017), pp. 1109, 1165.

[24] Burell (2016), pp. 1 et seq.

[25] Wischmeyer (2020), pp. 75, 87.

datasets that were most important to the AI-decision need to be assessed. This is the aim of Explainable AI, which is still a huge challenge for Machine Learning and software engineers.[26]

Visualization could be a key concept in reaching explainable AI for humans.[27]

3.5 Visualization to Enable the Uniqueness of the Human Mind

The human mind processes visualizations differently than rows of data entries.[28] This is anecdotally proven by the fact that presentation of data often relies on visualization like charts and graphs. These visualizations allow for the intuitive understanding of complex matters. This intuitive understanding is unique to human intelligence. AI, on the other hand, identifies existing patterns and takes those as the basis of its results, be it the prediction of behavior or extracting data or identifying patterns or deviations. It lacks creativity, which remains a hallmark of human intelligence.[29]

If visualization is done right, human intuitive intelligence and creativity will be based upon deep insights into data. This combines the advantages of both human and artificial intelligence. It is the human's decision to use the informational analysis that was presented by the AI model. The human decision is based upon the data curated by AI into informational analysis. In this scenario, humans are truly autonomous because they are not constrained by their limit to process only a limited amount of data anymore. The AI system functions as a tool to enhance human decision making, effectively an augmented intelligence.

It is clear that in isolation, both, human intelligence without the foundation of (visualized) data, and artificial intelligence without further contextualization, are not as effective as a combined approach. Human minds are overwhelmed by the high volume of data and burdened by information overload. AI on the other hand cannot contextualize the data in a creative way but it can only perpetuate[30] what is already there and not induce a creative new way of thinking.[31] The synergy between the two is what generates true value.

By visualizing the results of AI-assessments, they become more understandable and predictable for humans - which will be the basic prerequisites for higher trust in AI, as it will not appear like an ominous oracle but a reasonable tool to assess high

[26] See inter alia Wischmeyer (2020), p. 75, passim.

[27] Cf. Kirste (2019), pp. 58, 61.

[28] Earnshaw et al. (2019), pp. 40 et seq.

[29] Therefore, in the field of design and marketing, AI-technologies might be utilized, but never replace human intelligence altogether, see Liikkanen (2019), pp. 600–604, 603.

[30] Cf. on that matter the interesting discussion of computing as a diagnostic and formalizing measure in effectuating social changes, Abebe et al. (2020), pp. 252–260, 253 et seq.

[31] Cf. the attempt of creative artificial intelligence discussed by Stubbe et al. (2019), pp. 255, 259 et seq.

volumes of data.[32] Visualization can be done in different ways: while tables, pie charts or graphs used to be the most common formats, additional techniques became popular such as infographics, heat maps, scatter charts or tree maps. It emerged recently as its own software category and specialization area for experts.

3.6 Processes to Enable Substantial Progress

As shown above, without any processes to ensure well-designed interfaces between human work and AI, the true potential of digital work means cannot unfold.

An important aspect of combining AI and human intelligence are adequate workflows. Implementation of technology must be a holistic approach that also includes those processes within which the technology will be implemented.

Processes will need to ensure that the output of AI and automation is understood and that its potential shortcomings and pitfalls are identified. There should also be put more emphasis on the training aspect. The "human-in-the-loop" principle should be built into every step, i.e. the implemented technologies need to request human feedback and interaction to avoid errors and improve the overall results. Specifically, the digital solution can display results with a low confidentiality and notify users to get feedback for these results. The solution should be designed in a way that human strengths, contextualization and creativity, as mentioned above, are taken into account.

Such a process might heavily utilize visualization to effectively make AI technologies more operable for legal experts.[33]

A separate aspect, however connected to it, is an increased *AI* literacy, which will enable lawyers to better understand which and how much data will be needed to train a model for a specific use case. In line with the definition of digital literacy, AI literacy means making sense of AI technology, its use cases, results and processes. There should also be a better mix of competencies in organizations—be it law firms, corporates, or public service. Legal professionals can work effectively together with data scientists, engineers, and business analysts.

4 The Paradigm Shift to a New Age of Creativity

The example of legal service providers shows one important aspect of digital technologies: competition via innovation. It is not about working the longest hours and manually doing tasks with a strong human workforce anymore but concentrating on working effectively and using the resources in a smart way. Technology can be

[32] Kirste (2019), pp. 58, 67. As studies show this is also an important factor in the effectiveness of AI-suggestions, see inter alia Grgić-Hlača et al. (2019), pp. 1, 10 et seq.

[33] Cf on that Barton (2020), pp. 61, 69 who could only touch upon that point though.

used in an innovative way to support human labor. The paradigm shift is in how human resources are being used.

Everything that can be automated will (and should) be automated. Simple and repetitive tasks will be carried out by software and bots instead of humans. What cannot be automated or sourced out to machines is creativity and a holistic perspective. This will remain the distinguishing factor of the human workforce. The ongoing automation of processes that were previously performed by humans is a real blessing in disguise. What appears to be lost work for humans that is taken over by machines at first is, in fact, the digital transformation we were hoping for. Why? Because the type of work that is automated often adds little value or requires little expert knowledge and creative thinking. It will be crucial to make sure that the gained time is used for valuable and creative work. This requires a clear strategy and decision in organizations on how to deal with technology and automation. If such a strategy is not defined at the beginning of the digital transformation journey, it will be difficult to ensure that this time will be used in a meaningful way to add value to the organization.

A key aspect for this paradigm shift in digitalization is to overcome the informational overload. As we have described, visualization and proper processes are key concepts in order to achieve a better synergy between humans and AI systems. Visualization can function as a bridge between the data-focused analysis of AI models and human creative and innovative thinking. Processes need to ensure that the distribution of tasks between software and humans is correct and in line with their respective strengths. For this, there needs to be a proper implementation of the technology and an intuitive usability.

By overcoming the problem of informational overload, we can reach a new age of creativity. In this new age, it will not be important how many hours were spent on a contract draft; the quality, simplicity, and creativeness of the contract draft will become the most important aspects of the work completed. Simple and repetitive tasks will be automated and therefore do not give a competitive advantage anymore if performed cheaply and quickly. Legal service providers and many legal tech services already showcase the strength of innovation. Even established law firms are implementing these technologies more and more, often driven by competition or pushed by clients. As creativity and innovation will remain the human area of expertise, those will excel who concentrate on this and outsource the trivial tasks to AI and other automation software.

This creativity will lead to more innovative and better technology, to prevailing business models or better legal advice. To differentiate relevant from irrelevant information, lawyers can use AI results augmented by visualization and process the presented data intuitively instead of mathematically, and processes to ensure the best distribution of work. This ought to be our ideal of digitalization and the benefit of using AI.

Liquid Legal Waves to Other Chapters, Written by the Editors

Sven and *Philipp* make the case for visualization being the bridge to connect causal thinking of humans with the functioning in correlations of AI.—What if visualization and content design were already built into contracts directly, as *Rob*, *Helena* and *Stefania* propose in *"Layered Contracts: Both Legally Functional and Human-friendly"*?

AI-based legal tech already processes an avalanche of data. Informational analysis, however, is still a bottleneck. Humans have a hard time efficiently using the information an AI system processes, and sometimes there is even a lack of annotated data that would allow for meaningful analysis. Could *"Value Creation Through Blockchain-based Tokens: Transforming Tradi-tional Collaboration Structures"* be a solution, as *Wolfgang* and *Sebastian* propose?

Sven and *Philipp* end their chapter on a high note: Digitalization and AI have the potential to bring a paradigm shift upon human work, freeing humans from repetitive work to be more creative, and therefore more humane.—In the upcoming chapter, *Matthias* looks at the flipside of this, as traditional entry-level work vanishes that today represents a big portion of the experiential basis of learning for young talent.

References

Abebe R, Barocas S, Kleinberg J et al (2020) Roles for computing in social change. In: Hildebrandt M, Castillo C (eds) FAT* '20: Proceedings of the 2020 conference on fairness, accountability, and transparency, Barcelona, January 27–30, 2020, pp 252–260. https://doi.org/10.1145/3351095.3372871

Ahmed M, Najmul Islam AKM (2020) Deep learning: hope or hype. Annals Data Sci 7(3):427–432

Barton TD (2020) Artificial intelligence: designing a legal platform to prevent and resolve legal problems. In: Jacob K, Schindler D, Strathausen R (eds) Liquid legal – towards a common legal platform. Springer, pp 61–83

Binns R (2018) Algorithmic accountability and public reason. Philos Technol 31(4):543–556. https://doi.org/10.1007/s13347-017-0263-5

Bosse C, Schulz J (2020) Legal department 4.0: operating model of the future. In: Jacob K, Schindler D, Strathausen R (eds) Liquid legal – towards a common legal platform. Springer, pp 441–457

Burell J (2016) How the machine 'thinks': understanding opacity in machine learning algorithms. Big Data Soc. https://doi.org/10.1177/2053951715622512

Chang O (2021) Forbes 3/2021, Maschinen, die (nicht) denken, https://www.forbes.at/artikel/maschinen-die-nicht-denken.html

Earnshaw R, Dill J, Kasik D (2019) Data science and visual computing. Springer, Cham
Ferguson AG (2017) Policing predictive policing. Wash Univ Law Rev 94(5):1109–1189
Garnelo M, Shanahan M (2019) Reconciling deep learning with symbolic artificial intelligence: representing objects and relations. Curr Opin Behav Sci 29:17–23. https://doi.org/10.1016/j.cobeha.2018.12.010
Grgić-Hlača N, Engel C, Gummadi KP (2019) Human decision making with machine assistance: an experiment on bailing and jailing. Proc ACM Hum-Comput Interact 3(CSCW):1–25. https://doi.org/10.1145/3359280
Hermstrüwer Y (2020) Fairnessprinzipien der algorithmischen Verwaltung. AöR 145(3):479–521. https://doi.org/10.1628/aoer-2020-0013
Kim WY, Choi BJ, Hong EK et al (2003) A taxonomy of dirty data. Data Mining Knowl Disc 7(1): 81–99. https://doi.org/10.1023/A:1021564703268
Kirste M (2019) Augmented Intelligence. In: Wittpahl V (ed) Künstliche Intelligenz, pp 58–71. https://doi.org/10.1007/978-3-662-58042-4_4
Koltay T (2017) Information overload in a data-intensive world. In: Schuster AJ (ed) Understanding information. Springer, Cham, pp 197–217. https://doi.org/10.1007/978-3-319-59090-5
Kroll JA, Huey J, Barocas S et al (2017) Accountable algorithms. Univ PA Law Rev 165:633–705
Leetaru K (2019) A reminder that machine learning is about correlations not causation. https://www.forbes.com/sites/kalevleetaru/2019/01/15/a-reminder-that-machine-learning-is-about-correlations-not-causation/?sh=535c6fc96161
Liikkanen LA (2019) It ain't nuttin' new. In: Lamas D, Loizides F, Nacke L et al (eds) INTERACT 2019. 17th IFIP TC 13 International Conference, Paphos, Cyprus September 2–6 2019. pp 600–604
Pagallo U (2018) Algo-rhythm and the beat of the legal drum. Philos Technol 31(4):507–524. https://doi.org/10.1007/s13347-017-0277-z
Richardson R, Schultz JM, Crawford K (2019) Dirty data, bad predictions. N Y Univ Law Rev 94: 192–233
Semmler S, Rose Z (2017) Artificial intelligence: application today and implications tomorrow. Duke Law Technol Rev 16(1):85–99
Sousa B (2018) What the iPod Teaches Us About Workforce Adoption. https://www.forbes.com/sites/forbestechcouncil/2018/12/04/what-the-ipod-teaches-us-about-workforce-adoption/?sh=332693226d15
Stubbe J, Lutze M, Ferdinand JP (2019) Kreative Algorithmen für kreative Arbeit? In: Wittpahl V (ed) Künstliche Intelligenz, pp 255–272. https://doi.org/10.1007/978-3-662-58042-4_16
Webb GI (2011) Overfitting. In: Sammut C, Webb GI (eds) Encyclopedia of machine learning. Springer, Boston. https://doi.org/10.1007/978-0-387-30164-8_623
Wischmeyer T (2020) Artificial intelligence and transparency: opening the black box. In: Wischmeyer T, Rademacher T (eds) Regulating artificial intelligence. Springer, Cham, pp 75–102

Philipp Glock is a lawyer and partner at KPMG Law. He is Head of Legal Corporate Services as well as Head of Innovation, Co-Head of Legal Operations & Technology Services and Head of the KPMG Law office in Leipzig. He is an expert regarding the latest digital solutions for companies of all sizes. Philipp regularly supports companies and their legal departments in analyzing and adapting their business processes and advises with the selection and implementation of appropriate legal tech solutions. Additional areas of focus are the design of legal managed services and the management of legal projects, including large-scale mass projects. Philipp's legal background is in corporate law.

Sven von Alemann is an entrepreneur and attorney with 13+ years of experience in IT and technology law. He practiced for McDermott Will & Emery in TMT law. He also worked in the legal departments of technology companies and start-ups, including as Legal Counsel at Fujitsu and Senior Legal Counsel at SAP Hybris. In 2017, Sven co-founded rfrnz, a contract intelligence platform that automated contract analysis with artificial intelligence (AI) and served as its CEO. In 2021, Sven joined KPMG Law as Senior Manager in the Legal Operations & Technology Services team. Sven holds a PhD from the University of Hanover, an LL.M. from the University of Canterbury (NZ) and an Executive MBA from the Technical University Munich.

How Will People Enter the Legal Job Market in Ten Years' Time?

Entry-Level Professionals and the Digital Transformation of Legal Services

Matthias Bosbach

Contents

Abstract

When it comes to the Humanization of the Law, I cannot help but think of my first few years as a junior associate in legal services. My work was often about browsing through documents and data in order to find keywords, numbers or other pieces of information. Although it was all available in a digital format, I

Matthias Bosbach is Generalist at Ebner Stolz.

M. Bosbach (✉)
Kirchheim, Germany
e-mail: matthias.bosbach@ebnerstolz.de

K. Jacob et al. (eds.), *Liquid Legal – Humanization and the Law*, Law for Professionals, https://doi.org/10.1007/978-3-031-14240-6_12

preferred to work with printouts and my multi-colour set of highlighters (I still do).

I often wonder if future junior associates will still have to do this sort of work. For it seems all but certain that such repetitive tasks will increasingly be delegated to technology.

At first glance, the idea of ever-increasing automation seems like something to look forward to. Who wouldn't want to trade grinding monotony for stimulating think-pieces and substantial contributions to cases?

But entry-level tasks are traditionally used to make sure graduates integrate into the workplace well. Since there is only so much a formal education can teach, the rookie stage is typically needed before more demanding work can be mastered. What may seem like a waste of time at first ideally offers the required skill-building and earning. After all, there is a salary payment to be justified.

So, the result of the digital transformation we can see today may well be the following question: assuming traditional rookie services will be less and less required, how can entry-level professionals continue to earn a salary and progress on the learning curve?

It is presently impossible to answer this question with any degree of certainty, of course.

One way to approach it, however, might be to remain optimistic and expect legal services to change rather than to disappear. Many industries have undergone considerable transformation only to find that modified products and services were even more in demand than the traditional kind. IBM's transition from mainframe producer to a software and service provider is a classic example. While the challenges the legal services industry currently faces shouldn't be downplayed, there is no reason to believe such a transition is out of reach.

While much is still unknown, it is obvious that the future tasks of junior associates will depend on how the legal consulting industry develops.

In particular, they will require a different skill set due to the changing nature of legal services and how they are delivered. If the past few years are any indication, these requirements will not replace the traditional skills necessary for a legal career but come on top. This is to say that entry-level professionals will have to be accomplished lawyers and something else as well.

Given the time and financial investment a legal education requires even in its classic form, prospective law students have a right to understand what is expected of them and to know how to successfully prepare for the altered service landscape. So, the various stakeholders currently engaged in the digital transformation of legal services should get involved and describe their own key take-aways from the changes they witness: what may be currently missing from educational curricula, what can be said about training on the job, which sort of skills should become more and more important?

Against this background, the idea for this article grew around my work in and with IT platforms for specific and well-known workflows—or rather the pain points businesses typically identify therein. Users can log in through a web page and find specific products or processes ready for use. At first glance, this does not seem to affect legal services since it concentrates on the underlying business matter.

Nothing could be further from the truth! In fact, the business model is nothing short of a revolution on a scale not seen in legal consulting since the middle ages.

Like any other member of the liberal professions, legal advisors make a living by providing access to specialist knowledge. Short of studying the matter themselves, clients traditionally have no choice but to retain the services of one such person or another.

The three software solutions selected for this contribution, however, provide platforms with standardized knowledge for typical cases—material which would otherwise have to be sourced from human specialists.

Such classic input is typically bespoke and valid only at a certain point in time for one particular set of facts. The platforms, on the other hand, provide standardized value for typical cases embedded in typical workflows. They are continuously updated and expanded as time goes on.

So, the software solutions presented here address a specific matter by dividing the related caseload into standard and non-standard cases before human advisors have any say about it.

Standard cases are supposed to function automatically without further assistance, just as if they had been assessed on a bespoke basis in times of old. This is not about simply pre-processing data so the advisors can have a look at it. The platforms propose to automate the very procedure of consulting standard cases by providing the solution upfront, in a scalable format and for a fraction of the fee.

Non-standard cases still do provide opportunities for classic consulting to human advisors, provided they find themselves highlighted, recommended, or better yet selected by the platform.

The best strategy to reach this position on the platform is to provide the standardized value users are looking for. This will not immediately result in payouts, but rather require a substantial investment.

What a fundamental change! Being used to a monopoly on specialist knowledge clients simply cannot source otherwise, most legal advisors would much rather ask clients to pay the time they spend analyzing the specific case at hand—again, again and again, until they retire. They now have to rationalize themselves out of the bulk of cases by providing free input they may well be held liable for given the masses of cases it should be applied to. Since all they get in exchange is a rather vague promise of billable hours distributed through the platform, most are somewhat underwhelmed.

These underlying thoughts are anything but new, of course, and have been highlighted by thought leaders for years (See for example Suesskind, Patrick, 2010, The end of lawyers, 2nd edition, Oxford.).

What is interesting in the current phase is that platform models show a progression. They started out from well-defined bases in subject matters of no major significance to legal consulting but have been steadily increasing in relevance and value provided. Once users make the conversion to platform use, they typically are not coming back, but ask for more. Indeed, the three solutions selected show that core areas of legal consulting are no longer off-limits.

This is even more relevant to future junior associates. The work they have traditionally been assigned is primarily about understanding and mastering standard cases, a necessary step if they want to make an impact in non-standard constellations.

In order to provide some insight of value to future graduates in this and related developments, three questions need to be answered:

1. What do providers of platform solutions have to say to prospective legal graduates?
2. What does this specific change have to teach us in terms of necessary skills and how they are put to use as part of a career?
3. What new roles and positions are currently being created on the basis of these skills?

To answer these questions, this paper will first analyse use cases of tools and/or IT solutions which are already in the market, affecting rookie services. In a second part, it will show what can be inferred in terms of on-top skills from these examples. Finally, it will look to new job roles currently emerging.

Each of these topics is built around a series of interviews with professionals from the field, sharing their experiences and views. While most of the questions asked will be identical in each respective section, some have been modified to better express what the interviewee wanted to communicate.

Interviewees

- Dr. Julius Heintz, CEO and Founder of DVKG Deutsche Visa und Konsular Gesellschaft mbH (DVKG)—www.dvkg.de
- Jan Baksa Lesjak, managing director of 42DBS GmbH, a subsidiary of Zejn Group—www.42dbs.com/de/wer-wir-sind/
- Andrew Klein, Founder and CEO at legal tech platform Reynen Court—www.reynencourt.com/about/history
- Dr. Martin Allmendinger, co-founder and managing director of OMM Solutions GmbH—www.omm-solutions.de/home/
- Johannes Maurer, Head of Solutions Engineering at BRYTER—www.bryter.com/blog/hogan-lovells-banking-and-finance-lawyer-to-lead-bryters-content-strategy/?utm_source=google&utm_medium=organic
- Dr. Bernhard Waltl, Legal Operations Officer at BMW Group—www.ml-tech.org/blog/get-to-know-dr-bernhard-waltl/
- Lisa Waizenhöfer, Legal Project Manager Digitalisation at Siemens Healthineers
- Nina Stoeckel, Head of the Group Legal and Compliance Operations team at Merck KGaA—www.breakingthrough.de/portraet-nina-stoeckel
- Madeleine Werner, Digitalisierungsmanagerin Recht at Ebner Stolz
- Astrid Kohlmeier, legal design expert—www.astridkohlmeier.de/about/

1 An Emerging Solutions Landscape

It is particularly important to note what three providers of platform solutions have to say to prospective legal graduates.

The interviews are designed around a set of specific questions centered around the following topics:

- What does the solution offer?
- Why do the interviewees expect digital change to continue?
- What does this mean for future graduates?

1.1 Deutsche Visa and Konsular Gesellschaft

Where Do You Work and What Do You Do?
I am Dr. Julius Heintz, CEO and Founder of DVKG Deutsche Visa und Konsular Gesellschaft mbH (DVKG), available at www.dvkg.de. DVKG offers a web-based software solution for all application processes (e.g. EU-Notification, A1 Certificate, Visa, Employment contract).

What Tool/What Solution Do You Offer?
Key features of the DVKG solution are:

- dynamic and web-based application forms
- self-learning software, reducing any redundancies (e.g. filling in information, uploading documents)
- customizing possible depending on client needs

What Value Proposition Do You Have?
The Deutsche Visa und Konsular Gesellschaft has improved the quality and cost-efficiency of the application processes (e.g. for visas/A1 certificates and EU notifications) for the benefit of its customers through technologically modern solutions. The DVKG is an expert in taking over your administrative processes in the field of consular services.

Why Do You Expect the Digital Transformation to Continue?
Digitization is a key to the success of law firms, especially and because of the increasing dynamics of action, the reduction of time, resources and cost pressure. Clients' needs will expect self-explanatory, solution-oriented options for action that can be accessed online/on the spot. Companies and law firms will have to be measured against the degree of networking and automation.

How Does This Impact the Classic Rookie Stage in Legal Services?
Law firms are facing a digital transformation. The individual consultant will have to leave siloed thinking and action. In the future, information will be shared without relinquishing the driver seat. This mindset will accelerate digitization. The result will be a further focusing of consulting on legally complex cases, while structured recurring cases will be handled via digital solutions and controlled with the help of algorithms.

Could You Please Rank (i) Three Hard Skills and (ii) Three Soft Skills Junior Legal Professionals Are Currently Lacking?
Junior legal professionals might be quite digital in their private life. They will know how to manage the amount of different digital devices. The challenge might be to transfer the knowledge into the daily work and to recognize 360-degree opportunities. Their lacking skills might be driven by the traditional education, the role model of the senior legal professionals and traditional industry/company culture. With today's solutions, data security and data protection should not be an obstacle.

Do You Have Any Other Advice for Prospective Legal Graduates?
Have the big picture in mind and work on small steps of digitalization. Share your idea and win over your internal community. Involve internal specialists and do not hesitate to include experts from outside. Convince your stakeholders. Again, focus on small steps to deliver quick wins.

1.2 ShakeSpeare® Software

Where Do You Work and What Do You Do?
I am Jan Baksa Lesjak, I manage a software company headquartered in Munich, named 42DBS GmbH, which is responsible for development and sales of the ShakeSpeare® Software platform in the DACH region. 42DBS is a subsidiary of Zejn Group headquartered in Ljubljana, Slovenia.

In addition to that my mandate is to prepare a stable and strong foundation in terms of in-house knowledge and product capability for globalisation of the business (focus other markets in Europe and N. America). We are very active in the compliance and legal-tech segments where we automate and develop many applications related to the use-cases fitting into that category.

What Tool/What Solution Do You Offer?
We provide solutions built on the ShakeSpeare® Software platform. Our focus is in legal, compliance, healthcare, finance, insurance and general back-office process automation.

Flagship products are invoice processing, validation and management solution, S-Invoice, solution for Purchase to pay (combination of S-Order and S-Invoice), contract management (S-Contract) and many custom applications or off-the shelf products for legal and compliance (i.e. case-management, document automation, mass litigation applications, traffic violations—OWI, Labour law litigation automation, etc.).

What Value Proposition Do You Have?
We reduce the burden of administration, reduce internal costs and most of all transfer inter-organization know-how into a digital platform to provide automated, partially automated, or digital service delivery to end clients or internally in organizations.

In legal, we reduce processing costs, risk of error and capability to manage large amounts of standardised litigation cases. By reducing costs, we allow new business models to be developed and we are happy to think that with that we also help democratizing access to legal representation for the general public and smaller companies.

Why Do You Expect the Digital Transformation to Continue?
There is no other option open. The lack of people with appropriate skills is evident and since the risks are high that organizations will not be able to deliver services internally or externally due to key personnel leaving, retiring, or other reasons is high. Market pressure on pricing and digital service delivery is increasing as traditional industries are scrutinised by clients because of slow communication and delivery processes as well as high processing cost.

With competition investing in digital tools (similar as what happened in processing and manufacturing industry), winners will be those who are able to keep rich know-how in house and provide an efficient and effective service delivery on demand.

How Does This Impact the Classic Rookie Stage in Legal Services?
The requirement to be aware of technical and tool options on the market will become more relevant and will provide a competitive advantage when starting a career path. Having an adequate if not good understanding of what is possible and how it works is mandatory in order to have the capacity to use such technology and tools or apply them.

Same as a driver's license, you will need technical understanding to be able to do your job with the efficiency that will be required.

Could You Please Rank (i) Three Hard Skills and (ii) Three Soft Skills Junior Legal Professionals Are Currently Lacking?
Hard:

- Understanding of technical tools that improve office and legal work
- Use of basic computer devices and optimal use of standard office tools and applications for lawyers/legal professionals
- Application of logical thinking on work processes with the involvement of technical tools/software available on market

Soft:

- Team-work skillset—communication and how to work in teams
- Business development approaches to work and change management frameworks
- Understanding business processes and economical thinking (how can I deliver same value with less effort or more value with same effort—the min/max principle)

Do You Have Any Other Advice for Prospective Legal Graduates?
Work on skills that you are not learning at the university. We use modern technology in every step of our daily life—from payment solutions, to mobility, communication, etc. Knowing and understanding the possibilities will allow you to develop into a valued legal professional that will also be able to deliver value for less effort if you do so.

As a legal professional you can still think critically about the work processes and how it can be easier. One of our clients (one of the managing partners in a law firm) nicely said: "I am learning and investing in technology because I want to make myself obsolete. I do not want to work 10 hours every day for the rest of my life. If I can be responsible for the know-how and the process and someone else can take off most of my work after that, I would much prefer to spend more time with my family and friends than in the office." We should not be afraid of what technology can bring us, we should embrace it and apply it in our everyday work.

1.3 Reynen Court

Where Do You Work and What Do You Do?
I am Andrew Klein, Founder and CEO at legal tech platform Reynen Court.

What Tool/What Solution Do You Offer?
We provide an app store for legal technology. A platform designed to make it fast and easy for law firms and law departments to find, test and adopt new cloud-based technologies.

What Value Proposition Do You Have?
We save legal organizations time and money and help them avoid risk by keeping control over their data. Through our platform, buyers of legal technology can bring third-party applications to run in their own private clouds.

Why Do You Expect the Digital Transformation to Continue?
Software is taking costs and time out of business processes everywhere and will continue to do so. AI and other highly advanced automation tools will clearly redefine how legal work is accomplished.

How Does This Impact the Classic Rookie Stage in Legal Services?
There will always be opportunities for talented lawyers. But there are increasingly opportunities for professionals who can marry traditional skills with knowledge and understanding of what automation and new technologies can contribute to in the transformation of how work gets done. Computer skills—or more importantly—a high level understanding of what AI and modern technology can offer will no doubt be in great demand far into the next period.

Could You Please Rank (i) Three Hard Skills and (ii) Three Soft Skills Junior Legal Professionals Are Currently Lacking?
Very few seem to know much about software in general or AI specifically. Basic programming skills would be very useful, if just to give one with a confidence they can relate to engineers and understand what could be accomplished. Process engineering is just as important. Soft skills could include a curiosity about innovation.

Do You Have Any Other Advice for Prospective Legal Graduates?
Learn something about software development and keep an open mind to becoming a force for innovation.

1.4 Key Take-Aways

The first batch of three interviews shows that the providers of platform solutions encourage prospective graduates to be open to the change that is coming. In part, this refers to the necessary skills needed to run and operate such platforms, e.g. process engineering.

But more broadly, they take note that young people already live with and use technology more than any other generation before them. This should give them an edge in a professional sector only now beginning to show the same level of digital integration.

2 An Emerging Skill Set

Platform solutions and the change they bring are a specific sector, however. So, the next question of relevance for prospective graduates is what this has to teach us in terms of necessary skills and how they are put to use as part of a career.

Answering this should start by noting that the solutions all stress the importance of "knowing your way around anything tech/digital".

While that is accurate in itself, a further challenge lies in the fact that this individual know-how needs to be successfully combined with legal skills, company culture, mindset, etc. to meet client needs and generate a salary.

The world the legal industry operates in is changing. This does not just concern law firms themselves, but also their clients. If it is true that law firms rise and fall with the clients they advise, it follows that the advisors will want to acquire those clients which stand survive their own digital disruption, indeed thrive on it. Digital change is not limited to the legal services industry. Indeed, in many ways it is much more advanced outside of it.

At the moment, there is no established schedule, plan or training to meet this challenge. All which can be said is that advisors will need innovation skills and adapt their value to client needs.

When choosing employers, prospective future graduates should concentrate on two aspects to make sure they themselves are best equipped for an age of digital transformation:

- choose companies with an outstanding track record at digital innovation
- make sure this structure allows them to develop their own career, up to and including building a profile entirely off the traditional paths

The following two interviews aim to give prospective graduates a first glance of what this represents in practice:

- what do they need to know about innovation skills in the specific context of adapting entire business models to digital change? What is this discipline that the firms themselves are currently trying to master?
- what does it mean to develop your own digital career in structures still very much oriented towards a time-tested model?

2.1 Innovation Skills as Key Components of Future Careers

Where Do You Work and What Do You Do?
I am Dr. Martin Allmendinger, co-founder and managing director of OMM Solutions GmbH. I am responsible for the Innovation as a Service unit and Legal Ai Network lead at OMM.

What Is Your Connection to the Digital Transformation?
At OMM Solutions, we support organisations from the upper SME sector along their digital transformation journey. Therefore we offer customer-centric solutions in our three competence areas: Automation, Technology and Innovation. The Innovation as a Service unit that I am responsible for deals with three business pillars: the enablement of firms, the creation for firms and cocreation between firms.

The companies we advise range from the financial, industrial, automotive, social, educational and textile sectors, as well as from the professional service firms sector in particular.

For instance, we organise the Legal Innovation Challenge (https://legal.inno-challenge.eu/), one of the largest legal innovation hackathons in the DACH region. At this hackathon, law firms, legal departments, student legal tech associations and further players from the legal sector are participating.

How Did You Come to Be in This Position?
Having a genuine interest for digital technologies and innovation I founded OMM Solutions together with Malte and Olaf Horstmann about 10 years ago. Prior to that, I gained professional experience in professional services firms (e.g. KPMG, Deloitte, Baker Tilly) as well as in other companies with digital core competencies such as Diconium and United Internet. We also published the HAUFE pocket guide "Digitale Innovation entwickeln" in 2020. Next to that I received a Ph.D. from the University of Hohenheim, where I worked as a Researcher at the department for Entrepreneurship (Thesis: Towards asymmetric partnership management against the background of corporate entrepreneurship and open innovation literature).

Why Do You Expect the Digital Transformation to Continue?
Technological progress has always existed in mankind. The entry of new competitors, increasing regulatory requirements, accelerating globalisation and changing customer expectations and behaviour will continue to radically change why, how and where organisations are going to create value in the forthcoming years.

Under these intensified competitive conditions, law firms must find innovative ways to promptly place and further develop data-driven business models in their quest to solve pertinent customer pains with the help of agile frameworks and methods.

What Are Crucial Skills Necessary for the Digital Transformation of Legal Consulting Services?
We attach crucial importance to the following skills or better competences in the context of the advancing digitalisation. Incidentally, many skills are not exclusive to the legal industry, but affect most companies in various industries.

Innovation Competence
Anchoring a problem-first mindset and systematically transforming client pain into validatable concepts and business models and adopting them continuously.

Entrepreneurship/Intrapreneurship Competence
Thinking and acting proactively and consciously making quick decisions under uncertainty.

Cooperation Competence
The competence to create value for clients with different partners in different ecosystems and concrete cooperation models based on trust.

Process Competence
The competence to think in processes, to model them and then to optimise or automate them.

Technology Competence
Understanding current technologies and being able to evaluate sensible fields of application for digital services/business models.

Methodological Competence
Establishing a skills-based methodological toolbox (e.g. Agile Project Management, Legal Design Thinking, Lean Startup) that enables to think and act in a well-structured, iterative and systematic way.

Data Competence
The competence to structure data, to relate it to each other and to draw meaningful conclusions.

Personal Marketing Competence
Using the "Reputation Economy" to generate visibility for its individual skills and competencies "Personal branding".

Why Are These Really Innovation Skills?
These skills are innovation skills since they enable organisations and their employees to discover and define relevant (internal) customer (aka client) pains and develop as well as deliver value-based and business-oriented solutions.

What Is the Difference Between Radical and Incremental Innovation?
The difference between radical and incremental innovation can be found in the degree of innovation along the dimensions of market and product.

Incremental innovation consists of either using existing services in new markets or bringing new or further developed solutions to existing markets. In contrast, radical innovation represent a stronger departure from previous business models. Here, organisations bring completely new solutions to new markets in order to satisfy new customer groups.

Hence, radical innovations require organisations to have radically new skills and toolsets. Furthermore, these kinds of innovations demand more time and an increased willingness to take risks compared to incremental innovations. The art and mastery to simultaneously not neglect the existing core business on the one hand and develop and market such radical innovations on the other hand is also referred to as "ambidexterity". A term which illustrates the strategic, operational and cultural challenge that radical innovations embody.

What Are Three Key Components for Successful Innovation Prospective Legal Graduates Should Look Out for?
The three key components for successful innovation prospective legal graduates should look out for are:

- Firstly, an open mindset, especially a propensity towards lifelong learning when it comes to new technologies and innovative business models but also to other business sectors except legal.
- Secondly, a grasp of customer centric methods that enable to think outside the box and systematically right at the heart of customer pains as well as to develop tech-enabled solutions that are desirable to customers.
- Thirdly, first hands-on experience with digital tools to collaborate (i.e. G-Suite for presentations/calculations, MS Teams for meetings) and deal with specific legal tasks (i.e. Contract Analysis, E-Discovery) as well as first insights into tools for automating processes (solutions like Legal RPA, No-/Low-Code platforms).

Which Three Factors Typically Need to Be Overcome by Law Firms and Legal Departments to Become Effective Innovation Agents?
Three factors that typically need to be overcome by law firms and legal departments are:

Firstly, internal cultural obstacles towards new business models since the established business logic (still) works and the corporate culture under which lawyers normally operate is highly risk-averse which is incommensurable with the risks associated with innovation.

Secondly, missing the right skill- and toolset to systematically identify, develop, test, and implement new business models and offer digital products and services.

Thirdly, an inadequate incentive structure for innovation. The predominant business logic in law firms is the billable hour which devalues ex-ante to work on anything outside this business framework (like innovation projects whose return on investment is from a monetary point of view unpredictable. That's why we believe that the business return on innovation is the learning outcome.) Hence, if success is measured exclusively by the amount of billable hours and not other metrics more suited for innovation (i.e., identification of relevant customer pains, share of revenue of solutions developed in the past 3/5 years compared to the entire portfolio) there is no resilient basis incentivizing lawyers to deal with innovation.

What Is the Best Preparation for This Environment—In Terms of Practical Experience?
To get ready for the digital transformation prospective lawyers could do internships in companies that are data-driven and tech savvy. This can be a legal internship where lawyers are part of interdisciplinary teams working on the development of digital solutions. There are also different legal tech associations where law students can engage in open discussions, participate in workshops or develop digital solutions (i.e. Legal Hackers Chapters or student associations like Cologne Legal Tech Lab, eLegal, Tübingen Legal Tech, i.e.). Furthermore, there are hackathons where you can learn and apply hands-on digital tools supervised by experienced innovation practitioners, law firms and coaches of legal departments (i.e. https://legal.inno-challenge.eu/).

What Is the Best Preparation for This Environment—In Terms of Education? Please Detail the Following Options: (a) Classic Legal Education/State Examination, (b) LL.B./LL.M. Plus Extra Components or (c) Bachelor/Master Other Than Legal Plus Legal Components
There is no best preparation for this environment, instead there are different paths prospective lawyers can choose to follow depending on their career ambitions and personal preferences.

a) A classic legal education which culminates in the successful passing of the State Examination gives you a comprehensive and extensive foundation for mastering legal issues. This can be enriched by internships in established organisations or start-ups with a digital mindset—within or outside the legal industry.
b) An LL.B/LL.M. is a versatile and powerful instrument since it consists of a comparable small time span (1 year in most cases) and there are already a couple of programs dealing with legal and economic issues at the intersection of the ongoing digital transformation. Hence it can be helpful to deepen your knowledge in a specific (digital) related area.
c) A Bachelor or Master program in a field outside of a classical legal education (State examination) preferably related to digital business/innovation or technology/data science plus additional legal components is highly recommendable for people seeking to work in an interdisciplinary environment, especially focusing on the development of digital legal products addressing clients' needs.

How Does This Innovation Setting Impact the Classic Rookie Stage in Legal Services?
The classic rookie stage in legal services is impacted by the ongoing providing of digital tools and service especially when it comes to:

- highly repetitive tasks that do not require empathy or creativity and are vulnerable to mistakes due to their monotonous nature (i.e. cross-checking of tax forms, copy pasting entries from excel sheets into other digital tools).
- tasks dealing with the identification of anomalies or anti-patterns amidst lots of information (i.e. Due Diligence in M&A transactions).

These kinds of tasks are typically assigned to lawyers entering legal service firms after finishing their education and passing the bar exam. On the one hand these tasks notwithstanding their potential for frustration offer the opportunity to become familiar with routines and juridical pitfalls and increasing the competency from a legal point of view. Hence this begs the question what kind of legal challenges replace this kind of practical rookie education. On the other hand, the saved time can be invested into assigning rookies tasks that deal with the discovery, development and validation of promising digital products and services outside of the classical billable hour business model helping law firms and corporate legal departments finding new values outside their core business. Hence, truly mastering the challenges of ambidexterity in a rapidly changing legal industry.

Do You Have Any Other Advice for Prospective Legal Graduates?
Trial and error: when you are a prospective legal graduate, chances are higher (than later as a professional) that mistakes are acceptable. So, try different approaches, investigate different industries, and advance by erroring, learning, and adjusting. This can help you shaping your mindset, making your career path more anti-fragile and providing you with insights you can't find in a textbook.

2.2 Crafting a Digital Career Using Digital Skills

Where Do You Work and What Do You Do?
I am Johannes Maurer, I work at BRYTER GmbH as Head of Solutions Engineering.

How Did You Come to Be in This Position?
I started with legal studies at Heidelberg and spent a year in London during this phase. Right up to the first state exam, I had much of the same tech skills as everybody else. This is to say I could format a Word document and had some experience with PowerPoint.

A classic legal education in Germany takes (much) longer than studies in comparable disciplines, e.g., economics. So, it wasn't before long that my friends from these fields had completed their B.Sc. and were off to start their careers while I had years of training still ahead of me.

What startled me then was how much more emphasis they put on gaining actual experience doing something. By comparison, a classic legal education prioritizes formal qualifications, notably the two state exams, the grades obtained therein as well as a PhD and an LL.M. Not only are these theoretical exercises, they also take at least one year in preparation each.

While I have only the highest respect for anyone with a full track record of these achievements, I soon realized that my case was different.

Since I wanted to become a lawyer, I decided to complete both state exams. I opted against both the PhD and the LL.M. since I wanted to dedicate my time to more practical occupations. So, while preparing for the second state exam, I took up coding. At about the same time, a fellow student of mine and myself set out to program an app (which turned out to become gesetze.io).

This was a real stroke of luck since it allowed me to really go into coding—not for some abstract idea of value to my future career, but because we were trying to make something work.

By mid-2018, I had completed my legal education by passing the second state exam and started working at the Frankfurt office of an international law firm. I did enjoy the work there, all the more so since LegalTech was already on everyone's radar.

But in the end, I realized that in order to work at the intersection of law and coding, I had to move on. So, I joined BRYTER.

What Is Solutions Engineering About?

BRYTER is a software company. Its product is a no-code enterprise software centred on displaying processes based on an "if, then" logic. Its current primary use is in regulated matters and/or industries, such as compliance, tax or legal applications in tax firms, law firms or companies.

While this is the most common use made of it, it is only the entry product in terms of complexity. Clients often proceed to higher levels after having mastered the first stage and find that the software is so much more capable in terms of diverse use cases.

At this point, they typically go beyond the principle of no code which stipulates that even without coding skills, users can create software. More demanding work focused on specific features or integrating other data/software will require coding know-how, however.

By way of example, a typical starter set is the process to draft and finalize an employment agreement. This contains all current steps of the process, up to and including legal department review. Going beyond this entry stage, some users opt to include existing HR software or to embed the solution with their clients.

This requires work on subjects such as data flows, workflows, or automated analysis of thousands of documents, all combined and organized to fit into a holistic project management approach—a core activity of solutions engineering.

Another part of solutions engineering is to make use of the know-how acquired in such customizing projects and devise pre-fabricated solutions on the basis of assumptions about future demand for e.g. Contract Lifecycle Management. This work much resembles model semi-detached houses built in industrial areas: this is not for the purposes of living, but so that prospective buyers may get a look and feel. While the precise details such as the children's room or the kitchen may vary, the set-up as such would remain unchanged.

What Options Do Digitally-minded Legal Graduates Have in Consulting?

One option is to be "the LegalTech person" of the firm. This describes someone with a classic background (two state exams and possibly a PhD and LL.M.) engaged in consulting with a lead role in shaping their firm's digital transformation footprint.

This role is a good fit since for now at least, there are few clients/assignments composed only of LegalTech work. A good part of legal advice centred on a specific practice area is always required.

The question to address is whether this role is sufficient to make partner since digital transformation work requires time that would otherwise be invested into e.g., classic billable hours. This measure of success very much remains the industry standard and continues to govern career paths. In case the answer to the question is no, the remaining options would typically be the counsel track or the business support lawyer track.

Another possibility is to leave the classic advisor role behind and concentrate specifically on LegalTech projects/use cases. While full legal regalia are not required, a sound awareness of legal issues and processes is certainly necessary, along with a deep understanding of LegalTech and project management. Practical experience in such an environment is the key.

Such roles are emerging in a back-office setting across the board, e.g., in IT departments. Front-end positions of this kind in the sense of digital consulting services in areas previously reserved for classic consulting exist mostly at start-up level or in the bigger firms. In the latter case, these units are sometimes grouped into a separate legal entity. This stand-alone structure typically does not (yet) have nowhere near the same size as the "mothership".

This should change over time, however, if the example of more advanced countries such as the US or the UK is any guide.

Finally, a position entirely off the trodden paths may be interesting, such as the solutions engineer for candidates with a passion for coding and solid skills therein.

The challenge to meet here is that the profile of legal advisor and developer, while providing value to projects, very often needs to craft its own job first: law firms do not need the tech depth such a person provides, while software companies typically require tech skills at a level which is very difficult to achieve for lawyers whose legal education is already one of the most challenging ones.

This is not to say that finding such a job is impossible. As with many rare profiles meeting specific needs spot-on, such positions will simply be less likely to be openly advertised. An extensive network as well as a talent for selling positions not yet created will certainly help.

How Can Prospective Legal Graduates Prepare for Such an Environment?
It is essential to know where you want to go and why since there are so many roles to be filled, many of which have not yet been invented.

In any case, some legal component will be required. While the German system now has options aside from the classic state exams in the form of LL.B.s and LL.M.s, we are still a far cry from more flexible countries such as the UK.

Unfortunately, the same very much goes for the combination of legal and tech elements where neither the state exams nor its more recent alternatives offer much substance.

This is relevant since in Legal Tech and actual coding more than anywhere else, practical experience on the job is crucial, slowly but steadily acquired over years and on many occasions.

Again, this is not about repeating a tutorial, but best acquired when taking care of a well-limited project. The app I was trying to set up involved lots of learnings acquired the hard way, typically by realizing at the end of an entire weekend that we had failed to spot the most basic and rather obvious of mistakes at the very beginning of our code the whole time.

For prospective legal graduates looking to combine the law with the skills likely required due to digital change, this translates into the need to set up their own path, combining projects and stints wherever possible as they go along what they have chosen as their main course (be it the law, computer science or something else). For this path will have its own waymarks, e.g., the state exams, that are each unlikely to afford many diversions.

In the beginning, possibly the best way to meet this challenge is to concentrate on one main subject at a time, while deepening tech skills in periods of substantial occupation in-between, such as a gap year. This can typically be prepared along e.g., studying for the main objective.

A little further down the line and after the very basics have been mastered in each discipline, the two could be pursued in parallel, as many legal graduates do when writing a PhD next to their job.

In order to get to this stage, a period of uncertainty needs to be overcome since the time invest to be undertaken cannot yet be matched with much in the way of results.

During this phase, mentoring and networking is crucial to make sure that the areas of concentration and learning are meaningful, and the effort is not wasted on what may turn out to be an irrelevant topic. This will almost certainly comprise failure and the need to re-adjust, making timely contact with LegalTech providers successfully in the market a crucial factor.

Do You Have Any Other Advice for Prospective Legal Graduates?
The classic legal education in Germany was and still is highly driven by the grades in both state exams. There are good reasons for this.

Still, no one I know in the digital transformation scene put these grades above everything else. We all followed our passion, even though this did feel very uncertain at times—especially when compared to the relative safety of concentrating exclusively on the exams.

As legal consulting moves through the cycles of digital transformation, I expect the importance of these grades to decrease if only because legal teams should have a more diverse background. This is to say that they will require input from disciplines not covered by the exams and therefore, their grades. What should evolve as the main distinction is the ability to deliver as a team in practice.

2.3 Key Take-Aways

The main take-away for what the rise of platform solutions has to teach in terms of necessary skills and how they are put to good use is that this is no secondary matter. The two interviews show that both candidates and companies fail if they assume digital change can be addressed "next" to what people are "actually" supposed to accomplish.

A truly innovative company has a dedicated team and full-time positions charged with taking digital change forward, enabling the rest of their colleagues to thrive in a new setting.

3 An Emerging Job Market

In the end, there is only so much insight to be gained from extrapolation. What should matter in the years to come is the on-hand experience gained by various pioneers in their respective roles.

This is why the final section of this article is dedicated to new roles and positions currently emerging on the basis of these skills and in such dedicated teams.

3.1 Legal Operations Officer

Where Do You Work and What Do You Do?
I am Dr. Bernhard Waltl, Legal Operations Officer, BMW Group

What Is Your Connection to the Digital Transformation?
Within my role I am—together with my team—identifying, evaluating, and implementing innovative (digital) methods, tools, and services contributing to a digital legal department. Our mission is to provide state-of-the-art tools so that we can leverage the potential of the digital-first mindset.

How Did You Come to Be in This Position?
I did my PhD in computer science at the Technical University of Munich in 2017. Afterwards, I joined the department of emerging technologies of the BMW Group IT and worked there for two years. In 2020 I switched my position and became the first Legal Operations Officer of BMW Group.

Why Do You Expect the Digital Transformation to Continue?
Many processes and tasks are still performed manually or without (or insufficient) support by digital methods. This doesn't only mean tools and software applications but also other great achievements from tech, such as Agile Working, Collaboration, Open-Source, etc. With a digital mindset many more opportunities can be leveraged—to the best of all employees and the whole organization. Therefore, I firmly believe that the journey towards a fully digitalized working environment has just yet started.

What Is the New Role Called?
Legal Operations Officer

How Does a Typical Working Day Look Like in This Role?
My main three areas of work are

1. Communicating: I am in constant exchange with my team and other colleagues of my legal department. We are supporting during the roll-out of new technologies and methods, but also listening and supporting in creation of new ideas. We try to

be as transparent as possible and regularly report to management or other departments.
2. Implementing: Based on the feedback we receive we update existing structures or introduce new tools. Ideally, we could get to a stage in which we provide self-service platforms (no-code/low-code) are available and could be used by non-tech people, such that they are enabled to develop new ideas by themselves (or at least prototype them).
3. Evaluating: We need to be honest to ourselves and critically reflect whether a digital-first solution really solves a problem we have. We constantly see that some problems cannot solved with IT or tech but require something different. The role of legal operations is not to throw IT on everything but to thoroughly understand an issue openly evaluate how a solution could look like.

What Need Does This Role Address, What Kind of Value Does It Bring?
From my perspective, Legal Operations is a primary contact and advice service for internal requests to support the digital transformation, which focusses on problems and their solutions end-to-end. The added value is having a dedicated and highly specialized team providing solutions for non-legal work within a legal department.

Why Was the Role Created, What Was the Situation Like Before?
Before Legal Operations was established, the IT demands were met by our internal IT department. This was working well for many years, but due to increased demand of digitalization skills, the legal department needed to react by setting up a Legal Operations Office.

Could You Name Three Hard/Soft Skills Essential for This Role?
1. Tech savviness
2. Digital-first mindset
3. Communication

In addition, a strong background in legal and/or IT is a strong plus.

Who Is the Ideal Candidate for This Role?
In my opinion it is not about the candidate but about the team that needs to be comprehensive regarding their skills, open in the way they communicate (internally/externally) and driven by passion to change the status-quo.

What Is the Best Preparation for This Role—In Terms of Practical Experience?
I lack experience to fully answer this question, but I guess that there is no single path to prepare for this role. To me, my PhD work was helpful because I really went deep into one very specific topic between Legal and IT. However, other preparations might be helpful as well.

What Is the Best Preparation for This Role—In Terms of Education? Please Detail the Following Options: (a) Classic Legal Education/State Examination, (b) LL.B./LL.M. Plus Extra Components or (c) Bachelor/Master Other Than Legal Plus Legal Components
I always benefited from my PhD thesis and my research visit at the Stanford Law School (as a computer scientist!). However, I guess every education that provides deep insights into IT and how technology works prepares well for Legal Operations. In addition, having a background and a strong interest in legal topics is a strong plus. I guess the emerging classes at universities will contribute to professionalize the education.

Do You Have Any Other Advice for Prospective Legal Graduates?
Be open to interdisciplinary work. Go for the opportunities whenever you can work or exchange with an expert outside of the legal area, be it tech, IT, or other areas such as automotive, pharmacy, medicine, etc. Legal Operations benefits from understanding and speaking the language of someone else. This requires time and openness.

3.2 Project Manager Digitalisation

Where Do You Work and What Do You Do?
I am Lisa Waizenhöfer, I currently work as Legal Project Manager Digitalisation in the Legal and Compliance department of Siemens Healthineers. Previously, I worked several years as AI Manager for Linklaters LLP. As both roles relate to the digital transformation of the legal industry, I will touch upon both roles in the following.

In my current role as Legal Project Manager Digitalisation, I accompany, coordinate, and manage several digitalisation projects like automated contract approval processes and contract lifecycle management using agile project management methods like Scrum.

As AI Manager I was responsible for the selection, implementation, and training of AI tools for transactional teams globally.

What Is Your Connection to the Digital Transformation?
My day-to-day work is all about the digital transformation in the legal industry. In the law firm, I acted as ambassador for artificial intelligence (AI) by either calming lawyers that AI is not their enemy but friend or disillusioning them by explaining that no AI tool can think and act like a human being within a second, not yet at least.

Because of this role I wanted to tackle a very common challenge of the digital transformation, the quality of documents, at its source. In the law firm, you take a very narrow look at the documents/contracts during a specific event like a transaction. However, contracts originate in the companies, so why not transforming contracts and ancillary documents into the twenty-first century at its source? This was a huge motivator for me to move in-house.

Both law firm and in-house lawyers have one thing in common: they often still work like in the 1980s, and the digital transformation is still only at the beginning in the legal industry compared to other professional groups. My mission is to make the lawyer's life easier and convince them that the digital transformation is a big chance with a lot of wonderful possibilities.

To sum it up the digital transformation is my bread and butter.

How Did You Come to Be in This Position?
I started my professional life as Transaction Lawyer in the law firms Linklaters and DLA Piper. As a Corporate and Real Estate Transactional Lawyer, one is usually given the honour of reading, or shall I better say, digging through huge piles of documents in virtual data rooms to identify transactional relevant items. Additionally, as Real Estate Transaction Lawyer I could even experience physical data rooms. At the latest when I was navigating my way through two floors of dusty lease agreements and building permits for several days and nights, I thought there must be a modern, different way. This was when I stumbled over Legal Tech or better AI hit me. I soon realised I must learn many things in my free time and, at least in 2015, contrary to what some tech providers claimed legal AI tools were at the very beginning. Then one thing led to another, and I soon found myself working with lawyers all over the world on finding solutions how tech can help them and not the other way around.

Why Do You Expect the Digital Transformation to Continue?
In my opinion, there are two major challenges the world is facing in the coming years and decades the climate change and digitalisation. There is simply no way that lawyers can suspend this.

What Is the New Role Called?
The roles I worked in are called AI Manager and Project Manager Digitalisation. However, these titles are not set in stone and are often only an attempt to give new tasks a title. One could perform the same work at three different companies with three different titles. Hence, there is no such thing as the new role or specific new role names. We are still at a stage where there is a lot of room for manoeuvre.

However, I do believe that all new roles require allrounders that like to build bridges. Bridges must be created between the core "law" and other specialists and their specialised disciplines like:

- IT, both internal IT departments as well as external software providers,
- business development,
- resource management,
- pricing and budgeting.

What Does a Typical Working Day Look Like in This Role?
I believe there is no such thing as a typical working day in the whole legal industry, every day is different. However, a typical day as AI Manager consisted of several

meetings with teams across the globe to train AI regarding the specific local law either during a live transaction or based on historic data, before jumping on a call regarding the AI quality control workstream for an urgent Due Diligence, followed by a review meeting with a software provider, ending the working day with a price calculation for a pitch.

As Legal Project Manager my working day consists of a lot of meetings with both internal and external stakeholders, testing and looking into new technology, kind emails and calls to make sure that deadlines are met and finally, documenting project status.

What Need Does This Role Address, What Kind of Value Does It Bring?
All kind of needs and values are needed, which is why Allrounders that like to build bridges are required: Importantly, at the end of the day, the crucial core was, is and will remain legal advice. Why should a General Counsel or Partner acquire in-depth IT knowledge? In my opinion, also the associate does not have to have a basic knowledge of programming, but at least be prepared not to have to print out every document with three sentences to be able to edit it. They rather need experts at their side to support them and build bridges to other necessary disciplines. That is what these new roles are all about.

As an AI manager, this meant for me to be able to talk to the software provider at eye level so as not to be taken to the cleaners and, what is often even more important, to be able to translate between the language of lawyers and that of computer scientists, to set up a business plan for the acquisition of a new tool, to provide the Partner with the right information regarding costs and functionality of the Legal Tech application for communication with the client and even to advise on an efficient resourcing meaning who should best work with the Legal Tech application and at what stage.

Also, the Legal and Compliance Process and Technology Management team (short PTE team) at Siemens Healthineers is building bridges every day. As Legal Project Manager, I belong to the PTE team. In brief, our tasks include the optimisation of processes within the legal and compliance department as well as innovation. The centrepiece is of course the implementation of new technology. This requires the involvement and consideration of the complete ecosystem of a legal and compliance department and, probably most importantly, careful and understanding change management regarding the change of lawyer's working methods. The interdisciplinary team consists of employees that have classic/established education backgrounds (law, business studies, computer science) but none of us is working in his/her respective classic discipline. Everyone builds bridges every day, and although they can't be given a fixed job title for it, we do a colourful bouquet of new professions. For me, the key to success is thereby clearly the interdisciplinary set-up of the team and the agile working methods.

Why Was the Role Created, What Was the Situation Like Before?
There is probably rarely a conscious decision that a new role with a specific title and a clearly defined set of tasks and skill set is required. Often these are gradual

processes where further tasks are required and suddenly those new tasks require a 100% attention. Taking the PTE team as an example once again:

The team set-up allows us to realise large-scale projects with external software providers but also to create quick and innovative solutions with no external involvement. Low and no code applications create wonderful possibilities. Amongst others, the PTE team has built an App based on Microsoft PowerApps that successfully replaces repetitive manual processes by bundling the request, approval and archiving process of a time intensive contract type for users from 30 countries in one App. This required one computer scientist, one expert from the business, one legal operations specialist and one project manager.

Could You Please Rank (i) Three Hard Skills and (ii) Three Soft Skills Essential for This Role?
Hard skills: the core/heart is and should stay law, plus business skills (like drafting a business plan, pricing, marketing) and basic knowledge in computer science (I do not believe that lawyers need to know how to code).

Soft skills: good listener, communicator, and motivator.

Who Is the Ideal Candidate for This Role?
The basis should always be law plus additional basic knowledge in computer science and business. To sum it up, an Allrounder that understands itself as lawyer with an open mind and great interest in computer science and business.

What Is the Best Preparation for This Role—In Terms of Practical Experience?
Learning by doing. Unfortunately, classic law studies (*Rechtswissenschaften auf Staatsexamen* and *Wirtschaftsrecht*) do not include preparation regarding legal technology so far. Practical experience in law firms, in-house legal department and legal tech providers can help a lot. However, it is difficult to distinguish who is successfully using legal tech as nearly everybody is claiming to do so these days despite the majority using it very rudimentary. Hopefully, books like *Humanization of the Law* and initiatives like the LLI can help to navigate in the future.

What Is the Best Preparation for This Role—In Terms of Education? Please Detail the Following Options: (a) Classic Legal Education/State Examination, (b) LL.B./LL.M. Plus Extra Components or (c) Bachelor/Master Other Than Legal Plus Legal Components
A Legal Tech LL.B. would be great. But in-depth lectures (*Schwerpunkt*) of the above listed classic legal education options is desirable. If none of these options exists, LL.B./LL.M. (Wirtschaftsrecht) has the greatest common denominator with the skill set required for these new roles.

How Does This Impact the Classic Rookie Stage in Legal Services?
The classic rookie stage is impacted in two ways. First, the classic rookie receives help in the form of new roles to navigate through this brave new world as described in detail above. The rookie can therefore concentrate on the law. Secondly, it is true

that Legal Tech can replace repetitive tasks that would have classically been covered by the rookie but there are a lot of things that still need to be covered by a human being and Legal Tech can help to structure and streamline this practical training and dissolve disadvantages that can be created by bad trainers/mentors. For example, the formal education does not teach a M&A rookie lawyer how to spot transaction relevant items that need to be flagged and raised with the client. The learning curve of a M&A rookie lawyer classically often depends on a good trainer/mentor. However, an AI based contract extraction tool can, if well taught, point the lawyer to respective clauses in a contract which needs to be quality checked and then of course analysed by the M&A lawyer. As AI Manager, I have seen that this process of pointing, quality check and legal analysis structures, streamlines and harmonizes the training process immensely.

Do You Have Any Other Advice for Prospective Legal Graduates?
Don't hate maths. I remember that I have been told at my first day at university that good lawyers have most likely been great in German and Maths in school. Thus, I do not understand why many lawyers are still so afraid of maths. If you are open minded towards maths you benefit from clear rules and structures to navigate through the business and computer science world.

AND please be open minded towards new technology and continuous review of your working methods. Technology is not your enemy but your friend.

3.3 Legal Process Owner

Where Do You Work and What Do You Do?
I am Nina Stoeckel, I work at Merck KGaA, Darmstadt heading the Group Legal and Compliance Operations team.

What Is Your Connection to the Digital Transformation?
One of our key objectives is to drive innovation and digitalization for the Merck Legal and Compliance organization.

How Did You Come to Be in This Position?
I have been the co-head leading the development of the Group Legal and Compliance Strategy in 2018–2019. The Group Legal and Compliance Operations team has been one of the suggested initiatives and in July 2019 I have been appointed as Head of the newly created department.

Why Do You Expect the Digital Transformation to Continue?
Many processes in the legal and compliance department are still manual and/or not streamlined. To me, first step is getting the processes right and then starting to digitize. The legal and compliance teams are part of a corporate ecosystem and need to develop in line with the company digitalization strategy. Especially for Legal I see a way to go there.

What Is the New Role Called?
Legal Process Owner

What Does a Typical Working Day Look Like in This Role?
Usually, the Legal Process Owner has a split role with a day-to-day job as Lawyer or Paralegal in a Legal Team. The Legal Process Owner part comes into play whenever requirements resulting from current or future processes in the respective legal teams needs to be transferred to requirements for a new tool/tool upgrade or new process or change in process. So currently, the Process owner role is not a full-time job at Merck.

Examples:

- Definition of templates eligible for self-service in the global Contract Life Cycle System
- Gathering of requirements for a Legal/Litigation Hold process
- Redesign/streamlining of the CDA contracting process

What Need Does This Role Address, What Kind of Value Does It Bring?
The Legal Process Owner understands the processes and requirements in the specific legal team and can link/translate them to the design of new tools and processes or process improvements. This understanding is usually not present in a typical lawyer role in a legal department. The Legal Process Owner should have also a good understanding of the interaction Legal—Business as the involvement of the business also needs to be reflected in the processes.

Why Was the Role Created, What Was the Situation Like Before?
With the increased focus on processes and process improvements/digitalization of the legal department the respective input from the legal teams increased. To have a dedicated person/colleagues with the capabilities within the legal teams has increased the quality and the efficiency of information/requirement gathering. In defining one go-to-person the ad hoc requests to the teams could be bundled and over time the experience of the Legal Process Owner increased. This provides also great development opportunities as this person drives topics across one team with visibility within but also outside the team.

Could You Please Rank (i) Three Hard Skills and (ii) Three Soft Skills Essential for This Role?

- Project Management Capabilities
- Excellent English skills (when working in an international environment)
- Good PPT and Excel skills

- Leading (a project) in a matrix organization
- Process oriented thinking
- Inclusive and target group oriented communication
- Holistic thinking

Who Is the Ideal Candidate for This Role?
A colleague with passion for improvements and able to challenge the status quo. Being able to think outside the box, having no issues to connect with colleagues across and outside the team and very good in communication.

What Is the Best Preparation for This Role—In Terms of Practical Experience?
Participation in a project, on the job experience

What Is the Best Preparation for This Role—In Terms of Education? Please Detail the Following Options: (a) Classic Legal Education/State Examination, (b) LL.B./LL.M. Plus Extra Components or (c) Bachelor/Master Other Than Legal Plus Legal Components
No formal education needed, more important is the process understanding. A certain seniority (lawyer vs. paralegal) might be helpful, especially to discuss on-eye-level with colleagues across the department.

How Does This Impact the Classic Rookie Stage in Legal Services?
It's never too early to start gaining experience beyond the traditional legal tasks.

Do You Have Any Other Advice for Prospective Legal Graduates?
Join digitalization/innovation projects within your legal department whenever an opportunity comes up.

3.4 Change Champion

Where Do You Work and What Do You Do?
I am Nina Stoeckel, I work at Merck KGaA, Darmstadt heading the Group Legal and Compliance Operations team.

What Is Your Connection to the Digital Transformation?
One of our key objectives is to drive innovation and digitalization for the Merck Legal and Compliance organization.

How Did You Come to Be in This Position?
I have been the co-head leading the development of the Group Legal and Compliance Strategy in 2018–2019. The Group Legal and Compliance Operations team has been one of the suggested initiatives and in July 2019 I have been appointed as Head of the newly created department.

Why Do You Expect the Digital Transformation to Continue?
Many processes in the legal and compliance department are still manual and/or not streamlined. To me, first step is getting the processes right and then starting to digitize. The legal and compliance teams are part of a corporate ecosystem and need

to develop in line with the company digitalization strategy. Especially for Legal I see a way to go there.

What Is the New Role Called?
Change Champion

What Does a Typical Working Day Look Like in This Role?
A Change Champion would have this role in addition to a day-to-day job as lawyer or paralegal in a legal department. Managing change does include communication about activities from a project that need to be implemented in a legal team. Setting up training sessions, scheduling feedback and Q&A sessions, being in meetings with the core project team to catch up with the latest updates, answering tickets (related to "how-to" questions re a new system or process).

What Need Does This Role Address, What Kind of Value Does It Bring?
With the usual lean project setup, a comprehensive change and training concept cannot be managed with centrally available resources. Often there is a train-the-trainer approach that builds on colleagues in the different teams to educate about a new tool or process, comparable to Concur or SAP Key users.

Why Was the Role Created, What Was the Situation Like Before?
In preparing the roll-out of a global Contract Management Tool a concept for the communication and training had to be provided. As the project budget and scope did not include fully staffed training and coms resources, the Change Champion Role has been created. But this is not a one-off activity, the Change Champions will take over Key user tasks after the initial roll-out and implementation phase. This role is a permanent activity.

Could You Please Rank (i) Three Hard Skills and (ii) Three Soft Skills Essential for This Role?

- Project Management Capabilities
- Communication Skills
- Running presentations and trainings

- Willingness to take over tasks on top of the day-to-day job
- Being a person that likes to connect with others

Who Is the Ideal Candidate for This Role?
A person that has strong communication skills and is a very good presenter/can conduct training sessions.

What Is the Best Preparation for This Role—In Terms of Practical Experience?
On the job experience by joining projects and supporting Change and Communication, training and roll-out activities.

What Is the Best Preparation for This Role—In Terms of Education? Please Detail the Following Options: (a) Classic Legal Education/State Examination, (b) LL.B./LL.M. Plus Extra Components or (c) Bachelor/Master Other Than Legal Plus Legal Components
Change and Communication background, potentially as part of bachelor or master studies. Coaching experience/education

How Does This Impact the Classic Rookie Stage in Legal Services?
A rookie should see this as in interesting role to gain visibility within the team, to gain additional skills and to broaden the skill set.

Do You Have Any Other Advice for Prospective Legal Graduates?
I would focus also on communication and change skills and capabilities as this is a skillset that is not only needed when supporting the roll-out of a new tool or process but also very helpful in the daily client interaction.

3.5 Digitalisierungsmanagerin Recht[1]

Where Do You Work and What Do You Do?
I am Madeleine Werner, Digitalisierungsmanagerin Recht at Ebner Stolz in Stuttgart. In the organization chart, I am part of the IT department, but work at the intersection of IT and law.

For example, I am responsible for the project management of IT projects and of those relating to the processes of our legal department.

What Is Your Connection to the Digital Transformation?
Primarily, I document and optimize internal processes. Inserting IT modules into these as new/alternative components comes only second.

How Did You Come to Be in This Position?
I came to be in my position due to my professional experience. Rather than going to college, I trained as an office clerk. That gives me a broad economic and commercial knowledge which has allowed me to start work supporting legal consultants.

This means I know the operations and procedures of legal teams and departments. It is crucial to bring this experience in order to perform in my role.

Although I do not have a technical background, I managed to acquire a broad technical understanding which now proves essential: what is an interconnection, what does it do? What constitutes a piece of data and what role could it play?

Looking back, I think the combination of all these elements made the difference.

My role is less about the full depth of all these disciplines. That is left to my contacts in the various departments concerned, i.e., the specialists.

[1] This roughly translates to Digital Change Manager (Legal).

What I bring to them is an overview, an anticipation of potential conflicts and possible ways of resolving them together.

Why Do You Expect the Digital Transformation to Continue?
... because it is a human thing to try out new ways and improve upon what is there. This character trait has been given an enormous playground with digital change. There will always be people willing to use the possibilities this affords them.

Both in our professional and private lives, we are slowly growing into fundamentally different ways and hitherto unimaginable possibilities, perhaps without realizing it all that much. Just imagine what did change in the last 20 years since I started working in 2002, e.g. by realizing how outlandish the paperless office seemed, let alone home office for significant portions of the national workforce.

What Is the New Role Called?
Digitalisierungsmanagerin Recht (manager legal digitalization)

What Does a Typical Working Day Look Like in This Role?
My days are mostly filled with appointments and calls to coordinate various topics with colleagues and service providers.

In between, I document processes so we can optimize them and manage projects.

By way of example, I conceive new features to software we are already using or looking to source, define deliverability and cost with software providers, go through proposals, manage the various requirements of the departments involved, analyze them, etc.

It is very important to me to deliver, so there is always some fine tuning and that last bit of work to be done; my projects are mostly work in progress and have a chance to succeed only if the departments' feedback is considered and processed in a timely manner.

What Need Does This Role Address, What Kind of Value Does It Bring?
Digital change concerns a range of topics which continues to expand and grow, both in number and in complexity. This means one person must have an overview both over the number and kind of projects as well as over how they are being pushed and completed.

It is also necessary to build an excellent relationship with IT. Digital change in legal consulting cannot succeed unless topics such as IT infrastructure, data protection and IT safety are correctly handled—from the point of view and as per the criteria of the IT department, not that of a typical lawyer.

On the plus side, IT departments already have the necessary skills and capacity to do so, embedded into project management processes. This is to say that other departments (such as legal) do not need to create these from scratch.

The IT's value proposition must be completed by a legal component, however, so that the legal teams can use as planned whatever is created.

So, for example, it is my role to document and to standardize regional know-how pools. These have so far existed apart from one another and can now be accessed by the entire firm through IT components/tools. A firm such as ours with many offices, teams and practice areas has a great opportunity in digital change to go beyond the office grapevine when it comes to providing standard consulting modules faster and better than the competition.

Why Was the Role Created, What Was the Situation Like Before?
The role was created for me at the occasion of my joining Ebner Stolz. It is part of that firm's digitalization roadmap.

I understand my activities did not previously exist as a full-time occupation but were distributed among different people and teams.

Could You Please Rank (i) Three Hard Skills and (ii) Three Soft Skills Essential for This Role?
Hard Skills

- Commercial and legal operational awareness as well as a good understanding of IT subjects (both operational and administrative)
- Project management
- Data and process administration

Soft Skills

- personal: initiative and independence in how to drive and prioritize issues
- methodical: analytical mind, holistic approach regarding the whole range of disciplines covered
- social: interpersonal skills allowing you to communicate with e.g. IT partners and colleagues, team playing abilities

Who Is the Ideal Candidate for This Role?
A person who unlike much of the competition combines conceptional thinking with a sound awareness of what all departments involved want and do, namely IT and legal.

What Is the Best Preparation for This Role—In Terms of Practical Experience?
There is no theoretical training as of today, so the best preparation is experience on the job, ideally through a posting in all the aspects involved (organizational, administrative, technical).

What Is the Best Preparation for This Role—In Terms of Education? Please Detail the Following Options: (a) Classic Legal Education/State Examination, (b) LL.B./LL.M. Plus Extra Components or (c) Bachelor/Master Other Than Legal Plus Legal Components
Either (b) or (c).

How Does This Impact the Classic Rookie Stage in Legal Services?
Keeping to the categories (a) to (c) above, we are likely to see (much) more of (b) and (c) than we are used to, although the switch should be gradual and take (many) years.

Do You Have Any Other Advice for Prospective Legal Graduates?
It is understandable and of course recommendable for legal graduates to seek employment in a law firm. It must be honestly said, however, that the legal profession has not yet embraced digital change the way other sectors have.

This statement of facts is entirely neutral since digital change is not a goal as such. One piece of advice for prospective graduates derives from it, however: a stint in the businesses to be consulted might allow them to realize what a higher degree/pace of digital transformation is capable of. This should be beneficial since the assumption is that the legal industry can also expect this development.

3.6 Legal Designer

What Do You Do?
I am Astrid Kohlmeier, a lawyer and internationally renowned legal design pioneer and have been combining law and design for more than 15 years, with senior roles in the insurance-, litigation finance- and service design industries. As a legal design expert I advise legal inhouse departments and law firms such as Clifford Chance, Linklaters, Airbus, SAP, SIEMENS, Implenia AG and many more. My work led to winning several design awards (e.g. IF Design award) and I was honoured as "woman of legal tech". In my consultancy business I develop user-centric legal solutions with a focus on innovation and digital transformation. Besides I am a member and lecturer of the Executive Faculty at the Bucerius Center on the Legal Profession, co-founder of the non-profit organization "Liquid Legal Institute e.V.", speaker at relevant conferences worldwide and work with a global network of legal designers. I am actively engaged at the intersection of education and method development to establish the profession of "legal designers" worldwide.

What Is Your Connection to the Digital Transformation?
Legal Design is an innovation method and almost every client of mine is facing the need to innovate their legal business. One crucial aspect in becoming more innovative in the legal field is to streamline workflows and processes to make them fit for digitalization. A major part of my work is about to analyse the existing workflows in enterprises and find, together with the inhouse team, the right strategy how and where to digitalize and turn analogue workstreams into automated processes.

How Did You Come to Be in This Position?
I have an educational Background in Law and Mediadesign and combine these two professions for almost 20 Years. During my studies of Mediadesign I also immersed myself into coding to learn about the fundamental principles of data architecture and

coding in order to apply it to design intuitive user interfaces. To develop delightful user experiences, I focused also on experience and interaction design.

In my career I always worked at the intersection of law and design and gained a multi-perspective on the legal market by the help of different professional positions: I started as a student in the advertising industry, then worked as a Lawyer for IP in a law firm, afterwards I focused on the litigation industry where I helped to build a litigation funding company as a subsidiary of ERGO/Munich Re. As part of the management team, I had the role of director for marketing and communications and realized that the way how lawyers work and express their deliverables does often not meet the clients' needs. As a first step into innovation, I then combined my design knowledge with the challenges in law and began intuitively to improve the communication between lawyers and clients. This work not only was awarded with several design prices but happened to lead to one of the first legal tech applications in Germany: a website to match lawyers and clients based on their personal needs. Later I took a position as co-entrepreneur at the service design company IXDS (now belonging to PwC) where I connected services design and Law and deepen my knowledge about Design Thinking and the development of delightful user experiences through user centric interaction design of services and products.

Why Do You Expect the Digital Transformation to Continue?

Because the expectation and behaviour of us all as we are humans and citizens are changing toward digital services and products, no matter if one like it or not. Almost everything we desire nowadays has a digital component. And this changing behaviour influences the legal services market tremendously. We also see with events like the pandemic that many systems are not fit yet for remote work and total digital accessibility. Events like this drives the industry towards a fully digital environment to make seamless work possible, not matter where legal teams are physically working.

What Is the New Role Called?

Legal Designer

What Does a Typical Working Day Look Like in This Role?

Depending on the projects you are working on the typical day includes

- research (desk research and 1:1 interviews with different stakeholders),
- creating and writing concepts for projects,
- collaborate with clients and work on specific challenges in interactive workshops,
- prepare workshops,
- write workshop concepts,
- moderate and lead workshops,
- summarize the insights in collaboration with team members and work on research insights.
- extract the main problem of challenges and transform the problems into open questions to prepare them for creating many solutions.

- design new solutions in teamwork or alone,
- create prototypes like wireframes or click dummies,
- discuss prototypes with clients and work on iterations
- work on legal content and make it easy to understand which means to re-write e.g. a whole contract in a more simple wording without losing the legal necessities based on the intention of a company or client,
- work on visualizations for a variety of results,
- communicate with IT personnel if a solution is placed in a digital environment and work together on a detail briefing for coding a solution.
- lead an manage projects to make solutions finally implementable
- write articles about Legal Design
- etc. so much more to do ☺

What Need Does This Role Address, What Kind of Value Does It Bring?
It addresses the need for innovation and how to find the relevant innovation path depending on the companies' goals.

The value is to make sure that a legal organisation invests only in solutions that are viable, useful, and intuitive.

With the research of the individual human needs in any ecosystem you ensure to understand what the challenges for every participant of an ecosystems are, make them visible AND create a solution that is tested and iterated as often as necessary in order to really solve the existing problems.

Legal Design helps to decide where to invest in innovation and digitalisation. When working with a legal designer, everyone participating in a project learn new skills and how to solve problem in a creative way. This leads to incremental innovation but can also lead to develop disruptive elements that can set an organization at the top of market and set new industry standards.

Why Was the Role Created, What Was the Situation Like Before?
The Law and how it is delivered by lawyers often lack the awareness of the real needs of the different addressees. Traditional legal services and systems usually do not consider different backgrounds and perspectives of legal knowledge and consists of too much legalese. Legal Design is helping to find better solutions that fit exactly the need of humans with a need for legal information or to manage crucial legal requirements in business or private tasks. By adding the users' perspective on law legal design make sure, that the relevant legal content still stays, but consider the expectation and background of the people the legal interaction or service is relevant for. Legal design helps to find the right balance of what is legally necessary and what is possible by using design elements and processes.

Could You Please Rank (i) Three Hard Skills and (ii) Three Soft Skills Essential for This Role?
Legal Knowledge and practical legal experience

Design knowledge and practical experience

Strong business understanding and business skills

Empathy
Strong facilitation abilities
Communicational abilities
See also: Floating model | "The legal design book" by Astrid Kohlmeier and Meera Klemola

Who Is the Ideal Candidate for This Role?

The skills of a legal designer

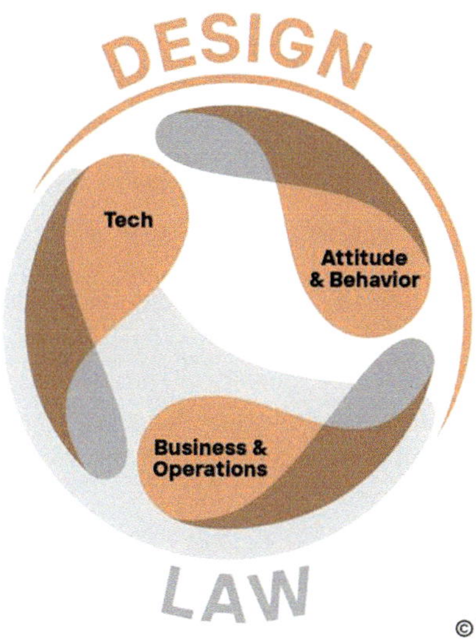

© The Floating Model
by Klemola & Kohlmeier

A legal designer has to bring a variety of skills and education to the table that enable them to perform legal design work. We have created the Floating Model to express the various capabilities that are needed. The capabilities that legal designers require can be grouped into what we call five areas of expertise:Law

- Design
- Technology
- Business and operations
- Attitudes and behavior

What Is the Best Preparation for This Role—In Terms of Practical Experience? The best preparation is to immerse yourself into legal innovation and begin to challenge the status quo of legal work. Gain practical experience in a law firm or legal department and look out for people working on innovative topics. Join an innovation team and learn from others. Keep your eyes open for new developments in the tech industry and try to make connections to the legal industry. Build analogies with existing services in other industries such as health care or finance.

What Is the Best Preparation for This Role—In Terms of Education? Please Detail the Following Options: (a) Classic Legal Education/State Examination, (b) LL.B./LL.M. Plus Extra Components or (c) Bachelor/Master Other Than Legal Plus Legal Components

At the moment, there is no established educational path for legal designers. Some universities such as Helsinki implement legal design courses in the legal curriculum, but we are far away from a standardised educational framework to become a legal designer.

I recommend in the first place a broad personal interest in the topic, in best case based in a classical legal education or classical design education in universities. Helpful is also to study Design Thinking in a serious institution (not only taking a one-day workshop).

Read the legal design book and other literature about Legal Design, Educate yourself in Design (e.g. Bucerius Executive Faculty, Legal Design Lab Stanford) and Design Thinking (e.g. HPI, Hasso Plattner Institute).

How Does This Impact the Classic Rookie Stage in Legal Services?

Legal design will help to transform the legal industry and bring it to another level that is more human centric, less complicated and includes tech where it makes sense. Legal Services become better, more useful and less costive. Legal Design is the answer of HOW to transform legal services and bring them into a digital age.

Do You Have Any Other Advice for Prospective Legal Graduates?

Be open to find new ways and don't stick too much to traditions. Start asking questions without forgetting about the purpose of law the legal basics—Legal Design is NOT about reducing legal position and rights. It's all about making law better accessible, transparent and user centric. It's a booster for every service or product development.

3.7 Key Take-Aways

The interviewees in this section are trailblazers who succeeded in creating job roles and pioneer entire concepts.

As a key take-away, this points to a time of great opportunity. It is currently possible to develop into new roles and grow while doing so because the people needed for future tasks and roles simply do not exist in the market. They have to be developed and employers know it.

4 Summary

It is on this note that I think this article should end. If readers retain only one idea from it, it should be this:

No-one can tell how the legal services industry will develop in the years to come. There simply is no plan and no amount of practical insight will change this. Prospective graduates should note, however, that this uncertainty affects clients, firms and the workforce alike.

Faced with this, the people I interviewed for this article all decided at some point to just get up and do: acquire new skills, create a role, set up a company, own a practice area, call for change.

While they all made (horrific) mistakes along the way and have not always seen things turn out the way they expected, not one of them would dream of reverting to what they did before.

For they are now with people who, just like themselves, are where they are because this is where they want to be. And that is an encouraging thought!

Liquid Legal Waves to Other Chapters, Written by the Editors

Matthias describes the changing nature of legal services and how it poses new demands on young legal talent, demands that come on top of the traditional legal hard skills. Entry-level professionals will have to be accomplished lawyers and something else as well. This calls for diversity—which is a challenge for traditional legal environments, as *Roger* tells us in *"Who are you...? - A Story About a Gay Humanist Working at a Law Firm"*.

As traditional tasks of lawyers get cannibalized by legal tech, creating opportunities as well as challenges to the human lawyer, *Barbara* in her chapter *"Of Mice and Lawyers. Learning From Calhoun's Rodent Utopia"* takes a completely different angle to that phenomenon: Hell is 'just' lawyers. If we invite new skills and collaborate with other functions, we might be able to create heaven.

A precondition for cross functional collaboration is breaking the silo (or ivory tower) that we as lawyers have created for ourselves, and that starts with our communication. In the next chapter *Rob*, *Helena* and *Stefania* remind us that, long ago, lawyers have started to write for lawyers—even in contract drafting—thereby ignoring all other stakeholders. Time to consider *"Layered Contracts: Both Legally Functional and Human-friendly"*.

Matthias Bosbach is a generalist at Ebner Stolz with over ten years of experience in helping companies navigate cross-border legal and tax issues. Deeply involved in the digital transformation of this field, he enables companies and consultants to build solutions and processes that combine both human and tech modules.

As an active contributor to the Liquid Legal Institute e.V., Matthias is part of the team that secured the GAIA-X prize with the DIKE project.

On top of law degrees obtained in Germany and France, Matthias joined the 2.5% of German lawyers to also have qualified as tax consultant. He started his career at Bird&Bird in Brussels and is an active volunteer in his community.

Layered Contracts: Both Legally Functional and Human-Friendly

Robert Waller, Stefania Passera, and Helena Haapio

Contents

Abstract

This paper addresses a debate that frequently arises when contract simplification is discussed. For business users, a clear contract is one that helps them understand

Robert Waller is President of the International Institute for Information Design.

Stefania Passera is CEO and Contract Designer at Passera Design, and Contract Designer in Residence at World Commerce & Contracting.

Helena Haapio is Associate Professor of Business Law at the University of Vaasa, Finland, an Adjunct Professor of Proactive Law and Contract Design at the University of Lapland and a Contract Strategist at Lexpert Ltd.

R. Waller (✉)
Frome, UK

S. Passera
Espoo, Finland

H. Haapio
Helsinki, Finland
e-mail: helena.haapio@lexpert.com

K. Jacob et al. (eds.), *Liquid Legal – Humanization and the Law*, Law for Professionals, https://doi.org/10.1007/978-3-031-14240-6_13

the deal, implement its terms and encourages a productive business relationship. Legal teams, on the other hand, often worry about their responsibility to protect their client against excessive risk and potential litigation. For them, a clear document is unambiguous and legally watertight, resulting in complex documents that can be hard for non-lawyers to use. In this paper we discuss a layered approach that can reconcile competing definitions of clarity, functionality and user needs, and we speculate about the role of information design and emerging technologies in the development of human-centred layers to traditional contract wording.

1 Introduction

Traditionally, the focus of contract drafters and doctrine has been predominantly on the needs of the legal community. Much of the discussion about using contracts has been about applying them reactively, *ex post*, after a conflict or dispute has arisen (Haapio 2013). Even management scholars and economists have treated contracts mainly as devices to safeguard the parties' interests (Williamson 1979; Verbeke and Greidanus 2009; Wathne and Heide 2000). While important for commercial contracts, a focus on this role alone has obscured other important roles for contracts, such as facilitating communication and coordination between people, clarifying expectations, guiding behavior, and fostering shared understanding (e.g. Hurmerinta-Haanpää 2021; IACCM 2017; Haapio 2013).

While some contracts may need to work as evidence in court, most contracts do not. Instead, they need to work as business tools for the parties so they get the results they want to accomplish. But still today, most contracts seem to be written *by* lawyers *for* lawyers, the goal being water-tight, legally functional contracts.

Over the last ten years or so, there has been increasing interest in a different, modern kind of contract design, which focuses on the needs of the business community: the contracting organizations and the people who work with contracts. On this idea, information designers and proactive legal practitioners have built fruitful collaborations to innovate contract practices. Contract design has become a major focus of a new specialism, legal information design or, at a more general level, legal design (which applies design to wider issues of law and justice) (Legal Design Manifesto n.d.; Hagan n.d.; Corrales Compagnucci et al. 2021). The authors of this chapter have been closely involved with this development, and in this chapter we propose a new layered approach to contract design which aims to reconcile competing definitions of clarity, functionality and user needs. Our approach strives for balance and inclusion, reserving space for both business and legal users, readers and writers, to be an empowered participant of the conversation mediated by contracts. While taking stock of progress so far, we also speculate on how emerging technologies could be deployed not only to increase efficiency and scalability, but also human-centeredness.

2 Revolution or Evolution?

Haapio (2013) described a paradigm shift in contracting, characterised by the entrance of information design and a new mindset based on proactive law, with the goal of enabling contracts to be used proactively, *ex ante*, so that the parties achieve the objectives of their collaboration, balance risk with reward, and prevent problems and disputes. A paradigm shift (Kuhn 1962) is a fundamental change in the way we understand a particular field. Paradigm shifts classically involve significant, and even angry, misunderstandings between those who represent the old and those who represent the new.

As contract designers, we have sometimes experienced negative and dismissive attitudes from what we might term old-school legal drafters. For example, we have heard transactional lawyers explicitly state that they are not concerned whether their contracts can be understood, since their sole duty is to protect their client from risk.

But we have also encountered many realistic and sympathetic legal teams who understand that the organisation they serve is trying to build relationships with customers, suppliers, employees, and others. They may see the need to innovate contract practices, and they work with us to achieve this, but they are genuinely concerned about abandoning precedent and potentially entering unknown legal territories if problems arise.

So the model we present in this chapter makes it clear that old and new approaches need to co-exist—it can be an evolution, not a revolution.

Projects we have been involved with (e.g., Waller et al. 2016; Passera et al. 2016; Doyle and Passera 2021) allow traditional legal drafting to sit alongside clearly presented information about operational matters aimed at business readers. Operational clauses might be about ordering, payment and delivery, while legal matters include such things as applicable law and dispute resolution, along with wording dealing with exclusion or limitation of liability. Visualizations are used to explain particularly complex processes and mechanisms, but text is still predominant (Fig. 1).

Some well-publicised modern contract projects have used radical visual design, including comic book formats (Vitasek 2017; Pitkäsalo and Kalliomaa-Puha 2019; Baasch Andersen and de Rooy 2022), and some opposition voices may assume that this is where all contract modernisers are heading. But these formats are relative outliers, designed for very specific purposes in situations where readers typically have poor levels of literacy.

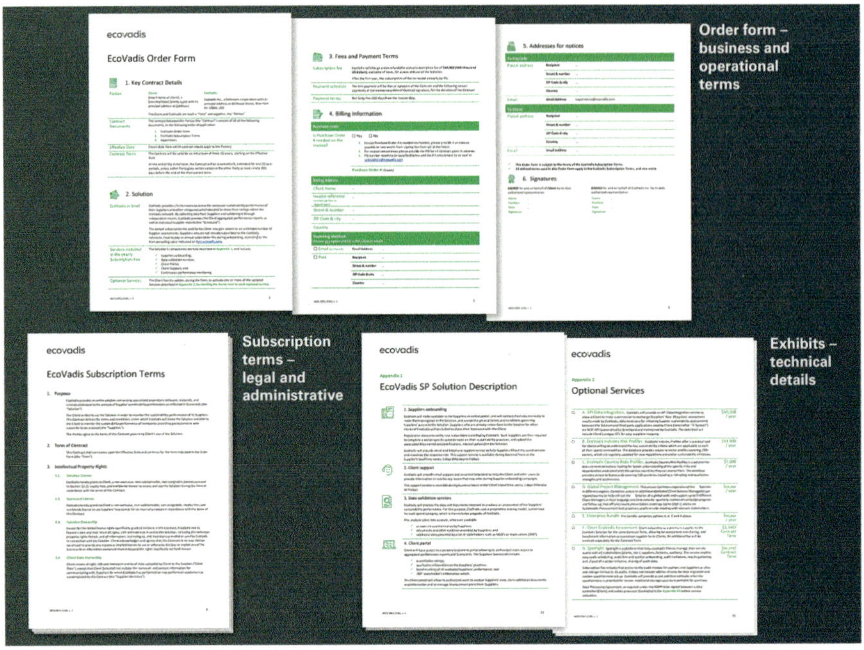

Fig. 1 Example of redesigned contract, by Stefania Passera/World Commerce & Contracting for EcoVadis. The document presents upfront the operational terms, then introduces the legal and administrative issues, and lastly introduces technical details in exhibits. ©2020 EcoVadis. Used with permission

3 What Do We Mean by Clear? Simplifiers vs Completists

In a contract simplification project, we often find ourselves managing a debate between *simplifiers* who prioritise a quick and practical user experience, and *completists* who prioritise legal integrity and seek above all to defend the organisation from excessive risk.

Most information designers are simplifiers by instinct. They strip out unnecessary words, use clearer sentence structures supported by helps such as diagrams or notes, and present the content in a legible layout that helps users read and search information effectively.

But traditional contract drafters have their own concept of clarity which is more to do with ensuring accuracy, precision and completeness. A short and simple contract, they might say, is by its nature imprecise and therefore unclear, even dangerous. It may fail to adequately provide a plan for performance and risk, and it may leave room for undesirable or unrecognized default rules, trade usages or interpretations if conflicts arise, especially when dealing across borders and industries. The detail that is characteristic of traditional legal language arises from the wish to avoid negative surprise and button down every contingency.

Organisations attempting to simplify often end up with awkward juxtapositions of style—friendly headings sit next to dense legal text in a way that calls to mind the good cop/bad cop trope of crime dramas. As an example, let us take a few sentences from the Terms of Service offered by Medium (2020), the publishing and blogging platform. The most recent version incorporates informal introductions to the terms themselves[1] and each section—the good cop voice of the marketing team. For example:

> Medium aims to give you great Services but there are some things we can't guarantee.

A non-lawyer simplifier might leave the matter there (perhaps editing out the phrase 'some things' as it implies there are some things which *can* be guaranteed).

But the clause[2] goes on, showing that a traditional legal drafter has taken over:

> Your use of our Services is at your sole risk. You understand that our Services and any content posted or shared by users on the Services are provided 'as is' and 'as available' without warranties of any kind, either express or implied, including implied warranties of merchantability, fitness for a particular purpose, title, and non-infringement. In addition, Medium doesn't represent or warrant that our Services are accurate, complete, reliable, current or error-free. No advice or information obtained from Medium or through the Services will create any warranty or representation not expressly made in this paragraph.

This legal drafter might be just as interested in clarity but defines it differently. In their view, a text is clear when it leaves no room for doubt about the meaning and no room for unwanted warranties or obligations. So potential claims are foreseen and headed off with complicated constructions such as:

> without warranties of any kind, either express or implied, including implied warranties of merchantability. . . .

To most other writers the phrase "of any kind" sounds completely inclusive. But for the legal drafter this does not suffice. To effectively exclude warranties, the drafter has clarified that this includes both "express and implied", and has further clarified what "implied" includes. Why? We expect the reason to be that in the legal drafter's jurisdiction, a seller who wishes to effectively exclude or limit the implied warranty of merchantability must mention the word "merchantability"; general language such as "no implied warranties are made" is not sufficient.[3] Here the audience in the mind

[1] Unlike the previous version of the Terms (effective date March 7, 2016), the new Terms begin with "Thanks for using Medium. Our mission is to deepen people's understanding of the world and spread ideas that matter."

[2] See bolded section under the heading Disclaimers—Service is "As Is".

[3] For US law, see, e.g., American Bar Association, Business Law Section, Warranties and Online Sales https://www.americanbar.org/groups/business_law/safeselling/warranties/.

of the drafter comprises opposing counsel and a judge. Traditional legal drafters also seek to close off all possible misinterpretations through lists of synonyms ("accurate, complete, reliable, current or error-free"), embedded definitions, and complex sentences that avoid the use of punctuation (Tiersma 2005).

In contrast to this completist approach, simplifiers focus on the everyday user, and their limited ability to attend to and comprehend complex information—particularly in the case of contracts aimed at consumers or SMEs (small to medium-sized businesses). The approach is highly pragmatic: if users can't pay attention to every detail, why not ensure that at least the most important points are understood? If users misunderstand the words, why not add examples or visual explainers to increase their chance of understanding it correctly? If users do not understand what they need to do in practice to comply with the agreement, why not redraft and redesign it to be more similar to user guides or instructions?

When viewing a short, visualised contract, simplifiers see a glass that is half full—a clear communication that represents a healthy and cooperative business relationship.

Completists, on the other hand, see a glass that is half empty. As we saw in the example from Medium, they worry that a failure to button down the detail, disclaim all unwanted warranties and anticipate every possible breach, will expose their client to risk. And further, they worry that departing from conventional wordings means that they are not protecting their client to the fullest and not relying on the collective experience and judgement of their peers.

4 Towards a Layered Model

One way to resolve the debate is through layout and layering.

Layering is an age-old design pattern which has its origins in ancient religious texts.[4] In this traditional form, a central sacred message, which cannot be changed, is layered with headings, commentary, cross-references, reader's helps, and even commentary on the commentary. It is a classic solution to the design of any text where different users are to be addressed, and different voices present in the conversation.

Applying layering to the Medium example (Fig. 2), the larger, bolder text on the left makes the top level information available at a glance for "everyday" readers, while the rest is in smaller type on the right for expert legal readers—actually discouraging the business readers from engaging with it.

Repeated across the whole document, we would have a format in which the user can skim down the left-hand side to get the gist of the content, and be alerted to important issues. In effect, we could describe this left-side column as the user's territory. The writer needs to make an effort so the reader doesn't have to. The headings and summaries need to work as a set and form a coherent sequence that can

[4] See e.g. Kwakkel (2018a, b) for examples.

Medium aims to give you great Services but there are some things we can't guarantee.	Your use of our Services is at your sole risk. You understand that our Services and any content posted or shared by users on the Services are provided 'as is' and 'as available' without warranties of any kind, either express or implied, including implied warranties of merchantability, fitness for a particular purpose, title, and non-infringement. In addition, Medium doesn't represent or warrant that our Services are accurate, complete, reliable, current or error-free. No advice or information obtained from Medium or through the Services will create any warranty or representation not expressly made in this paragraph.

Fig. 2 Simple example of layering, applied to an excerpt of Medium's terms. Layout © 2021 Waller, Passera and Haapio. Used with permission

be easily skimmed. Information and content design provide tools to help the writer determine exactly what the reader needs, such as audience analysis (Schriver 1997, pp. 151–164), customer journey mapping (Stickdorn and Schneider 2010, pp. 158–161), user-testing (Pontis 2018), and pattern libraries (World Commerce & Contracting, Passera and Haapio n.d.).

The right-hand column, on the other hand, is the writer's territory and serves their essential purposes. If the user is to read this, it is they that need to make the effort.

As well as providing an easy route through the contract for the user, a two-column layout of this kind reveals flaws and gaps in the sequencing of clauses. The left-hand column creates a narrative flow through the contract, and so demands some logical basis. For example, we might find a clause covering late payment has been placed ahead of a clause outlining payment terms. This is quickly revealed when the left-hand column is drafted.

In practice, we've found that most projects benefit from a three-layers approach, rather than just the two (Waller 2022). We call the for-the-user layer (the left-hand column above) the Action layer, and the right-hand expert layer the Reference or Full Text layer. Between the two we add the Explanation layer. The Explanation layer requires effort from both the reader and the writer in the contract conversation. When writing, the expert needs to take the time to express their knowledge in a form the user can understand and relate to, such as examples or explanatory diagrams.

In fact, the Medium terms do include some explanatory text (for example the clause showed in Fig. 3), although it is not graphically signalled.

5 Layered Information Architectures: Drill-down and Filtered

In our work, we observed how layering approaches can be roughly distinguished into *drill-down* and *filtered* information architectures. Drill-down architectures feature the progressive elaboration of the same content through different layers. In filtered architectures, predominantly legal clauses in the Reference layer are filtered out of the users' attention to a separate section, or even a separate document. Some

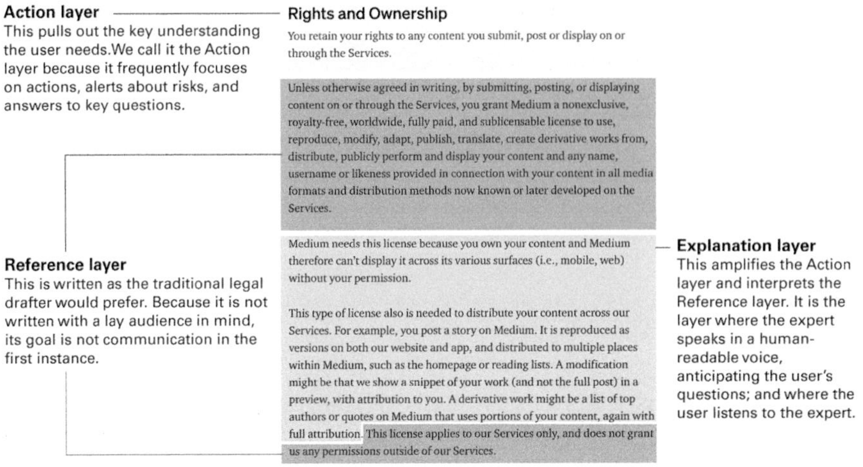

Fig. 3 The terms may already include Action and Explanatory content, although it is not graphically signalled. This interpretation © 2021 Waller, Passera and Haapio. Used with permission

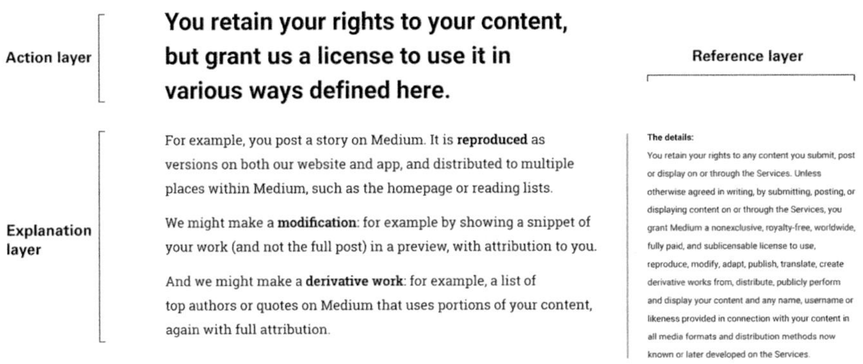

Fig. 4 Example of drill-down information architecture applied to an excerpt of Medium's terms. This interpretation © 2021 Waller, Passera and Haapio. Used with permission

documents combine these two approaches, with only some of the full text separated out.

Let's go back to the Medium example. On a large screen or page, we could use a layout with multiple columns to implement a drill-down information architecture (Fig. 4). On smaller screens, we may need to introduce interactive elements, such as accordions, links, and panels to achieve the same goal (Fig. 5): users can open and collapse the information layers on demand, depending on their task and needs at hand, as well as their preference. In a way, these interactive elements exist in between drill-down and filtered approaches, depending on whether the user is interacting with them or not. When opened, the content of a pop-up note or an

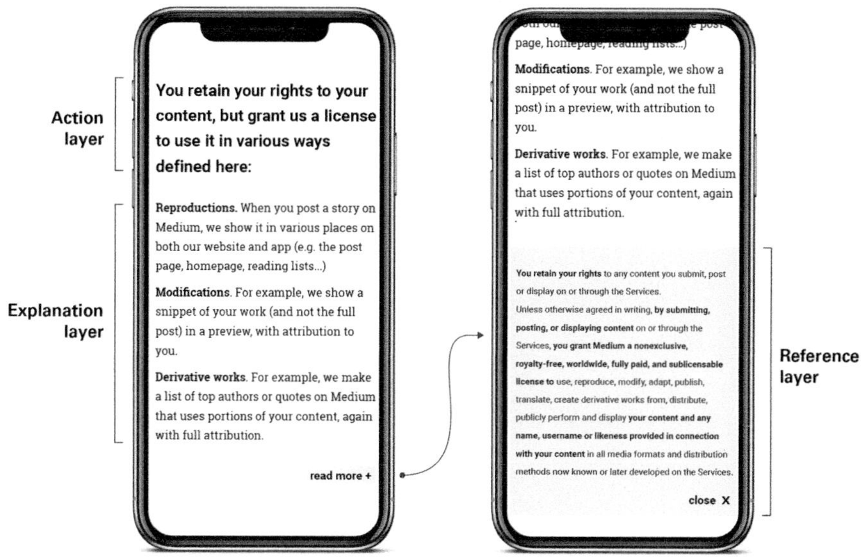

Fig. 5 Interactive elements, such as accordions, are necessary for implementing effective layering strategies on small screens. This interpretation © 2021 Waller, Passera and Haapio. Used with permission

accordion tab coexists on the same plane of the main text; when closed, their content is fully filtered out of the perception of the user.

Creative Commons (n.d.-c) has used a layered approach for a number of years, and is a good example of a filtered-out architecture. A system of simple icons is used on licensed materials to indicate that they are covered by a Creative Commons license (Action layer). Clicking on the icons, the user is brought to a so-called "human-readable summary" of the license, which employs plain language and icons to explain what one can or cannot do with the licensed material and under what conditions (Explanation layer).[5] By clicking on a link, the user can read the full license text (lawyer-readable "legal code", which we call Reference (or Full Text) layer).

This example also shows how a drill-down approach can be nested within a single, separated layer of a filtered-out information architecture. Consider the human-readable summary: within this section, the blue icons, the prominent headings, and the concepts set in bold work as an Action layer, giving visual prominence and attracting attention to the key information. Consider also the full

[5] The text on the top of this layer makes it clear that this is not the full license, by stating: "This is a human-readable summary of (and not a substitute for) the license." Clicking on the word "Disclaimer" reveals more: "This deed highlights only some of the key features and terms of the actual license. It is not a license and has no legal value. You should carefully review all of the terms and conditions of the actual license before using the licensed material."

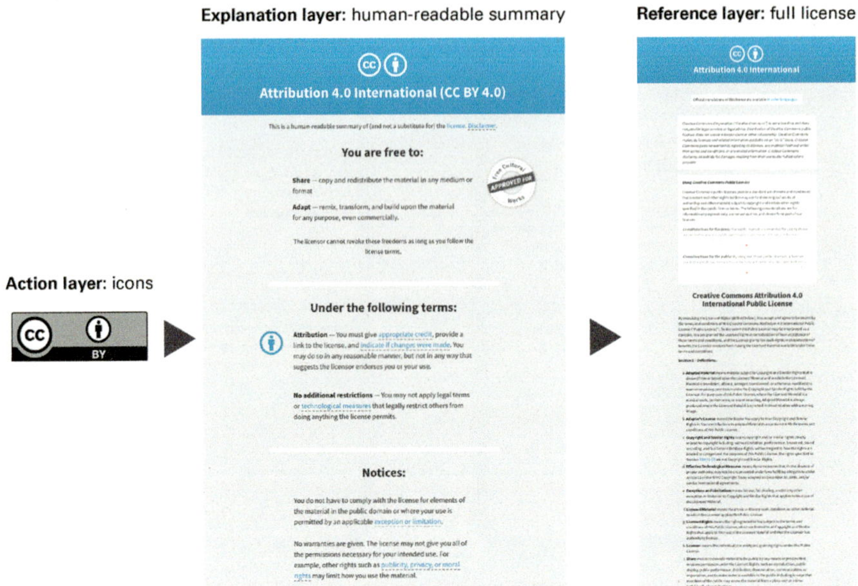

Fig. 6 The filtered-out architecture of a CreativeCommons licence (Creative Commons n.d.-a, n.d.-b and n.d.-d). Licensed under CC BY 4.0, https://creativecommons.org/licenses/by/4.0/

license: just before the full body of the license deed, the authors added a white, expandable panel that explains what Creative Commons are and lists considerations for licensors and the public alike—effectively working as an Explanation layer (Fig. 6).

Lastly, we can see how different types of visuals can be effectively used in all layers. Icons can act as visual cues to attract attention, signal topics, or aid memorization on the Action layer (as seen in the Creative Commons example); diagrams such as timelines and flowcharts are ideal elements to elaborate and expand meaning on the Explanation layer (Fig. 7); in the Reference layer, we can use bulleted and numbered lists (Fig. 7), indentation, highlights (such as the bolded words in Fig. 5) and other typographical interventions can improve the legibility and usability.[6]

6 Cooperative Channels and Contracts-as-Conversations

In explaining the layered model, we've talked about the different levels of attention paid to each column by different readers in the business and the legal expert community. Layered designs make it possible to address different audiences within

[6]What is and is not part of the contract and what role each layer should play in contract interpretation in our examples is beyond the scope of this brief chapter. For making the interpretation of images in contracts more predictable, see Haapio et al. (2020). See also Annola et al. (2022).

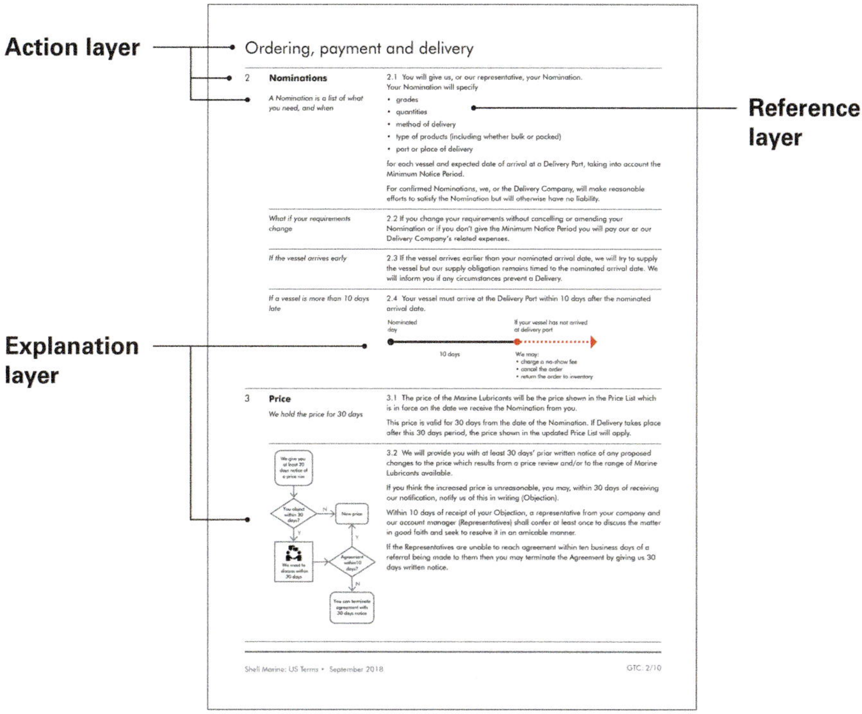

Ordering, payment and delivery

2	**Nominations** *A Nomination is a list of what you need, and when*	2.1 You will give us, or our representative, your Nomination. Your Nomination will specify • grades • quantities • method of delivery • type of products (including whether bulk or packed) • port or place of delivery for each vessel and expected date of arrival at a Delivery Port, taking into account the Minimum Notice Period. For confirmed Nominations, we, or the Delivery Company, will make reasonable efforts to satisfy the Nomination but will otherwise have no liability.
	What if your requirements change	2.2 If you change your requirements without cancelling or amending your Nomination or if you don't give the Minimum Notice Period you will pay our or our Delivery Company's related expenses.
	If the vessel arrives early	2.3 If the vessel arrives earlier than your nominated arrival date, we will try to supply the vessel but our supply obligation remains timed to the nominated arrival date. We will inform you if any circumstances prevent a Delivery.
	If a vessel is more than 10 days late	2.4 Your vessel must arrive at the Delivery Port within 10 days after the nominated arrival date.
3	**Price** *We hold the price for 30 days*	3.1 The price of the Marine Lubricants will be the price shown in the Price List which is in force on the date we receive the Nomination from you. This price is valid for 30 days from the date of the Nomination. If Delivery takes place after this 30 days period, the price shown in the updated Price List will apply.
		3.2 We will provide you with at least 30 days' prior written notice of any proposed changes to the price which results from a price review and/or to the range of Marine Lubricants available. If you think the increased price is unreasonable, you may, within 30 days of receiving our notification, notify us of this in writing (Objection). Within 10 days of receipt of your Objection, a representative from your company and our account manager (Representatives) shall confer at least once to discuss the matter in good faith and seek to resolve it in an amicable manner. If the Representatives are unable to reach agreement within ten business days of a referral being made to them then you may terminate the Agreement by giving us 30 days written notice.

Shell Marine: US Terms • September 2018 GTC: 2/10

Fig. 7 Excerpt from the Shell Marine (2018) General Terms and Conditions of Sale (US). Highly visible and skimmable headings on the left side of the document are used in the Action layer; diagrams are used in the Explanation layer; bulleted lists are used in the Reference layer. Used with permission

a single document. The document has moved from an unyielding monologue into something more like a dialogue or conversation.

In a normal spoken conversation, all the parties involved make a conscious effort to communicate. The speaker makes an effort to use language and arguments which are meaningful to the hearer and will look out for signs that they are not being understood, or that they are being misunderstood. For their part, the hearer makes an effort to understand what is being said, to place the speaker's words in context and to understand their intent as well as their literal meaning—the context being one of mutual cooperation to exchange information, to agree the facts, to complete a transaction or whatever it might be. And using turn-taking cues (Sacks et al. 1974), the two parties switch between roles—questioning, explaining, reiterating and confirming understanding.

While this is obvious in a spoken conversation between equals, texts can also be seen as conversational to a degree. The writer has the most control over the conversation, so for it to be successful they need to make an effort to understand their readers—their motives, their understanding of words, and their specific literacies (for example, their financial literacy, their legal literacy or their industry-specific literacy).

Turn-taking in text is achieved through a clear rhetorical structure at the paragraph level and a clear access structure (headings, layout, and the like) at the page level. This allows the reader to break free of the linear string of text in order to discern higher level structures and to search for answers to their questions. So, in an ideal textual conversation, a reader is led through the content in a logical manner, offered choices of route through, and offered ways to resolve their questions.

Waller and Delin (2003) described the concept of cooperative channels:

> A cooperative channel is one that allows participants in a conversation to respond to each other. In an ideal world, for example, bank customers could visit a branch, pick up a phone, or log on to the Web, and get answers to all their questions, conduct any transactions they want, and perhaps even be presented proactively with ideas for new products that fit their needs perfectly. So long as the process is collaborative and cooperative, it is not important whether it is achieved through a human being or a machine. And if a paper document allows the customer to achieve as much, because it has perfectly anticipated the order in which he or she wants to receive information and has provided answers to all his or her questions, then it too can be considered a cooperative channel.

Contracts are a special form of conversational text, since in many cases there is an imbalance of power and expertise. Moreover, as traditional drafters are aware, they may need to anticipate an uncooperative reader, or even a hostile one who actively searches for loopholes. In the words of Mellinkoff (1982, p. 15): 'Some day someone will read what you have written, trying to find something wrong with it. This is the special burden of legal writing, and the special incentive to be as precise as you can'.

A B2C (business to consumer) contract for a product such as a bank loan tends to be an unbalanced conversation between a legally naïve customer, optimistically aware of the brand's marketing promises, and the bank's legal team which has high expertise. Since these terms are non-negotiable, it is often a rational choice for the consumer to tune out of the monologue and decide not to read—although the consumer does need to understand any aspects of the contract that could punish them if they transgress (e.g. late payments, early cancellation, etc.). Smaller B2B (business to business) contracts may also be similarly non-negotiable.

In contrast to this, a large bespoke B2B contract—when being negotiated—can become a conversation between two sets of legal teams, each with high levels of interest and expertise. Every aspect of the contract is negotiated, and at this stage it is a conversation between equals. Once signed, however, the large B2B contract has to be implemented by a new set of people who enter the conversation post-signature—those responsible for acting on the contract, delivering the solution or monitoring performance. They are in a similar position to the consumer or small business: they need to understand what the contract expects of them, and act on it accordingly.

Our layered approach recognises the realities of contract conversations—the potential imbalance of motivation and expertise, and the need for each party to have a measure of control over the communication process. The concept of turn-taking is served by the layers—each party (including their business stakeholders) has their voice in the contract, where the focus is on their needs and where the other party needs to make the greater effort to make communication happen.

7 Looking at the Future: Beyond Human Designers and Readers

Humans are not the only ones taking part in conversations through and about contracts: contracts are increasingly machine-readable, digital, even to some extent self-executable entities. New emerging technologies may soon offer a precious tool to both writers and readers, especially when contract drafters may be unwilling to make a communication effort or simply lack the skills, time, or budget to redesign their contracts in a human-centered, layered manner.

The opportunities offered by web translators such as Google Translate and DeepL Translator[7] are already widely used when translating between languages. DeepL has recently added glossary support to translating contracts and other documents with legal terminology (sometimes even in Latin), and more language combinations are in the works.[8] Open AI's GPT-3, Generative Pre-trained Transformer 3 (Brown et al. 2020), is already able to translate legalese into plain language (and vice versa). AI-powered translation of legalese into ordinary language could be leveraged by contract drafters to populate the Action and Explanation layers at a fraction of the time and effort currently required. The DALL-E neural network,[9] also built on top of GPT-3, is a program that is able to generate images from textual descriptions. While currently the output of DALL-E is mostly in the form of photo renderings or illustrations in various degrees of sleekness, we envision that the technology could be trained to generate diagrams, flowcharts, swimlanes and other typical visual design patterns employed as explanations in contracts (Haapio and Passera 2021).

What is perhaps even more promising for our purposes is the ability of GPT-3 and other language models[10] to move from text to code, creating functional code from ordinary language.[11] Researchers have already started to study the possibilities, costs, and risks relating to the use of computable language models in the context of contracts (Arbel and Becher 2022; Kolt forthcoming). Corrales Compagnucci et al. (2022) focus on the need of contracts to be both legally functional and comprehensible for their users (whether people or machines), envisioning the

[7] https://translate.google.com/; https://www.deepl.com/translator.

[8] https://www.deepl.com/en/blog/announcing-glossary-support-for-deepl-api.

[9] https://openai.com/blog/dall-e/.

[10] Apart from GPT-3, there are many other promising language models. See, e.g., 10 Leading Language Models For NLP In 2021, https://www.topbots.com/leading-nlp-language-models-2020/.

[11] For OpenAI Codex, an AI system that translates natural language to code, see https://openai.com/blog/openai-codex/.

computable contract designer of the future employing no- or low-code software solutions and libraries to design and build customized digital contracts; the authors show a sample three-layered contract clause for buying a car 'as is' where the explanation layer has been generated by GPT-3. Maybe in a few years' time we can just write a short description of what we want, for example skimmable headings, diagrams, and a three-layered layout to a to-do list, and submit the list to GPT-3 (or GPT-4 or higher) which then generates the code which generates what we want. We could also add a fourth layer, code, for smart or computable contracts—something similar to what is already happening in the context of Creative Commons licenses, whose machine-readable layer enables search engines, filters and tools to find and sort CC licensed content (Creative Commons n.d.-e).

On the other hand, should contract drafters be unwilling or unable to leverage GPT-3 to design better contracts, the same technologies could be used by readers to break through the impenetrable fog of legalese. A "smart reader" app running on GPT-3 could offer plain language translations from legalese and bureaucratese, empowering readers with a fuller understanding of their rights and obligations (Arbel and Becher 2022; Kolt forthcoming).

8 A New Understanding of "I Have Read and Understood..."

Despite their differences, simplifiers often share an underlying assumption with completists: that people should read contracts in their entirety—that's why they try to make them shorter and easier. But this is still an unrealistic expectation.

As a consumer or a business reader, you seldom feel the need to read every word of a contract any more than you need to read every word on a grocery pack or every sign you pass in the street. Even in bespoke B2B deals, business users should be able to read only what they need, when they need it, and not necessarily everything. And many consumer contracts or simple contracts like the non-disclosure agreement could be commoditized along the lines of industry standards, regulations, and common sense[12]—you should be able not to read and rely instead on heuristics such as trusting that a reputable organization will adhere to recognized standards and laws.

It is an explicit aim of the layered model that users should not be required to read every word of the contract, if they do not want to. Research shows that almost no one does this, yet life goes on. As Ben-Shahar (2009, p. 5) puts it,

> ... there is nothing wrong with one's autonomous choice to enter a contract not knowing the legal terms, not even caring about the opportunity to read. For those who (smartly) prefer not to know, it is utterly irrelevant whether the terms-they-don't-know are available before or after the deal, inside or outside the shrink-wrap, in small or large print ... in legal or laymen's language...

[12] See e.g. the OneNDA initiative, https://onenda.org/.

But of course, the classic declaration which we are asked to sign or click our assent to is "I have read and understood" the terms. This phrase is much mocked as "the greatest lie on the internet" (Lannerö 2013; Obar and Oeldorf-Hirsch 2020), and journalists can get an easy story from counting the words and pretending to be shocked (e.g. Hern 2015). But actually this takes an unrealistic and unnecessarily strict view of what it means to read and understand.

It's unrealistic because no one in their right mind would read thousands of words before completing every transaction in their daily life. And if they did, we can be pretty certain the "understand" part of the declaration would remain a lie.

And it's unnecessary because the definition of "reading" need not mean reading every word you see. Wright (1988) used the term NOT-reading to describe the process of deliberate and strategic skipping. In literacy assessment, higher scores mean you can read selectively, in a self-directed way, to solve problems. The layered model is designed to encourage and enable this type of reading, and to ensure it is focused rather than random. Layering offers the foundation on which the needs and interests of readers and writers can be balanced so that contracts can genuinely serve both the contracting organisations and the people (and, increasingly, machines) working with contracts. Yes, with the help of layering, we can indeed make contracts both legally functional and human-friendly.

Liquid Legal Waves to Other Chapters, Written by the Editors

"I have read and understood"—this cynical web box we click almost every day is a symbol for how regulators and practicing lawyers ignore the citizen, the client, and the lawyer's broader role in the legal system. This ignorance has even worse effects when it happens not just in civil law, but in public law where citizens face the power of the state, as Ivar and Michiel explain in their chapter on *"Digitization of Government Services from the Citizen's Perspective - Putting Humans First"*.

The concept of private autonomy forms a central link between contracts as a legal instrument and humanity as an ethical principle. Private autonomy and freedom of contract are both primarily expressions of human freedom and human dignity. Whatever gets in the way, be it bad drafting, the downside of automation, or the shift in power towards large platform players, needs to be mitigated, argue Carl and Michael in their chapter on *"Contracts and Humanity – How Freedom and Fairness of Contract can be secured in the Digital Age"*.

Beyond the legal hard skills, we must focus on and prioritize *"Injecting Humanity (Back) Into Talent Development"*, says Duc in the upcoming chapter. He lays out a heuristic framework to illustrate how training lawyers at the intersection of law, business and interpersonal relationships will enable lawyers to provide legal services that are not only correct, but *useful* to clients.

References

Annola V, Haapio H, Koskela M (2022) Interpreting images in contracts. In: Corrales Compagnucci M, Haapio H, Fenwick M (eds) Research handbook on contract design. Edward Elgar

Arbel YA, Becher S (2022) Contracts in the age of smart readers. George Wash Law Rev 90(1): 83–146

Baasch Andersen C, de Rooy R (2022) Employment agreements in comic book form – what a difference cartoons make. In: Corrales Compagnucci M, Haapio H, Fenwick M (eds) Research handbook on contract design. Edward Elgar

Ben-Shahar O (2009) The myth of the "opportunity to read" in contract law. Eur Rev Contract Law 5(1):1–28. https://doi.org/10.1515/ERCL.2009.1

Brown TB et al (2020) Language models are few-shot learners. https://arxiv.org/pdf/2005.14165.pdf

Corrales Compagnucci M, Haapio H, Hagan M, Doherty M (eds) (2021) Legal design: integrating business, design and legal thinking with technology. Edward Elgar

Corrales Compagnucci M, Fenwick M, Haapio H (2022) Digital technology, future lawyers and the computable contract designer of tomorrow. In: Corrales Compagnucci M, Haapio H, Fenwick M (eds) Research handbook on contract design. Edward Elgar

Creative Commons (n.d.-a) Attribution 4.0 International. https://creativecommons.org/licenses/by/4.0/legalcode

Creative Commons (n.d.-b) Attribution 4.0 International (CC BY 4.0). https://creativecommons.org/licenses/by/4.0/

Creative Commons (n.d.-c) Attribution-NonCommercial 4.0 International (CC BY-NC 4.0). https://creativecommons.org/licenses/by-nc/4.0/

Creative Commons (n.d.-d) Choose a License. https://creativecommons.org/choose/results-one?license_code=by&jurisdiction=&version=4.0&lang=en

Creative Commons (n.d.-e) Frequently asked questions: what does it mean that Creative Commons licenses are "machine-readable"? https://creativecommons.org/faq/#what-does-it-mean-that-creative-commons-licenses-are-machine-readable

Doyle P, Passera S (2021) Contract design and simplification – is this now a must-do? Int In-house Counsel J 14(56):1. https://www.iicj.net/subscribersonly/21july/iicjjuly5-contracts-pauladoyle-worldcc-usa.pdf

Haapio H (2013) Next generation contracts: a paradigm shift. Lexpert, Helsinki

Haapio H, Passera S (2021) Contracts as interfaces: visual representation patterns in contract design. In: Katz DM, Dolin R, Bommarito MJ (eds) Legal informatics. Cambridge University Press, Cambridge, pp 213–238

Haapio H, Annola V, Koskela M (2020) Ten ways to make the interpretation of images more predictable. Contracting Excellence Journal, 5 November. https://journal.iaccm.com/contracting-excellence-journal/calculating-cost-recovery-in-commercial-item-contracts-significance-of-present-value-part-2-0

Hagan MD (n.d.) Law by design. https://lawbydesign.co/legal-design/

Hern A (2015) I read all the small print on the internet and it made me want to die. The Guardian, 15 June. http://www.theguardian.com/technology/2015/jun/15/i-read-all-the-small-print-on-the-internet
Hurmerinta-Haanpää A (2021) The many functions of contracts. Doctoral Dissertation. University of Turku. http://urn.fi/URN:ISBN:978-951-29-8433-6
International Association for Contract and Commercial Management IACCM (2017) The purpose of a contract - an IACCM research report. https://www.worldcc.com/Portals/IACCM/resources/files/9876_j18069-iaccm-purpose-of-contract-a4-2017-11-14-v1-webready.pdf
Kolt N (forthcoming) Predicting consumer contracts. Berkeley Technol Law J 37
Kuhn TS (1962) The structure of scientific revolutions. University of Chicago Press, Chicago
Kwakkel E (2018a) Books before print. ARC Humanities Press, Amsterdam
Kwakkel E (2018b) The architecture of the medieval page. https://medievalbooks.nl/2018/09/07/the-architecture-of-the-medieval-page/
Lannerö P (2013) Fighting the biggest lie on the internet: common terms beta proposal. Metamatrix. http://commonterms.org/commonterms_beta_proposal.pdf
Legal Design Manifesto (n.d.). https://www.legaldesignalliance.org/
Medium (2020) Medium terms of service, effective September 1, 2020. 2 September. https://policy.medium.com/medium-terms-of-service-9db0094a1e0f
Mellinkoff D (1982) Legal writing: sense & nonsense. West Publishing, St. Paul, MN
Obar JA, Oeldorf-Hirsch A (2020) The biggest lie on the internet: ignoring the privacy policies and terms of service policies of social networking services. Inf Commun Soc 23(1):128–147. https://doi.org/10.1080/1369118X.2018.1486870
Passera S, Smedlund A, Liinasuo M (2016) Exploring contract visualization: clarification and framing strategies to shape collaborative business relationships. J Strateg Contract Negot 2(1–2):69–100. https://doi.org/10.1177/2055563616669739
Pitkäsalo E, Kalliomaa-Puha L (2019) Democratizing access to justice. Translation Matters 1(2): 30–42. https://doi.org/10.21747/21844585/tm1_2a2
Pontis S (2018) Making sense of field research a practical guide for information designers. Routledge, London
Sacks H, Schegloff EA, Jefferson G (1974) A simplest systematics for the organisation of turn-taking in conversations. Language 50(4):696–735. https://doi.org/10.1353/lan.1974.0010
Schriver KA (1997) Dynamics in document design. Wiley & Sons, New York
Shell Marine (2018) General terms and conditions of sale (US). https://www.shell.com/business-customers/marine/contact-shell-marine/lubricants/_jcr_content/par/toptasks.stream/1591106590441/f44886f744b4779df44d5e83f42926d5cd03b9e7/shell-marine-gtc-lubes-and-shipcare-us-law-final.pdf
Stickdorn M, Schneider J (2010) This is service design thinking. Basics – tools – cases. BIS Publishers, Amsterdam
Tiersma P (2005) Some myths about legal language. Loyola-LA Legal Studies Paper No 2005-26. https://ssrn.com/abstract=845928
Verbeke A, Greidanus NS (2009) The end of the opportunism vs trust debate: bounded reliability as a new envelope concept in research on MNE governance. J Int Bus Stud 40(9):1471–1495. https://doi.org/10.1057/jibs.2009.44
Vitasek K (2017) Comic contracts: a novel approach to contract clarity and accessibility. Forbes, 14 February. https://www.forbes.com/sites/katevitasek/2017/02/14/comic-contracts-a-novel-approach-to-contract-clarity-and-accessibility/?sh=10ec6af77635
Waller R (2022) Designing contracts for human readers. In: Corrales Compagnucci M, Haapio H, Fenwick M (eds) Research handbook on contract design. Edward Elgar
Waller R, Delin J (2003) Cooperative brands: the importance of customer information for service brands. Des Manag J 14(4):63–69. https://doi.org/10.1111/j.1948-7169.2003.tb00353.x
Waller R, Waller J, Haapio H, Crag G, Morrisseau S (2016) Cooperation through clarity: designing simplified contracts. J Strateg Contract Negot 2(1–2):48–68. https://doi.org/10.1177/2055563616668893

Wathne KH, Heide JB (2000) Opportunism in interfirm relationships: forms, outcomes, and solutions. J Market 64(4):36–51. https://doi.org/10.1509/jmkg.64.4.36.18070

Williamson OE (1979) Transaction-cost economics: the governance of contractual relations. J Law Econ 22(2):233–261. https://doi.org/10.1086/466942

World Commerce & Contracting, Passera S, Haapio H (n.d.) Contract design pattern library. https://contract-design.worldcc.com

Wright P (1988) The need for theories of NOT reading: some psychological aspects of the human-computer interface. In: Elsendoorn BAG, Bouma H (eds) Working models of human perception. Academic Press, London, pp 319–340

Robert Waller is an information designer with a wide experience of practice, research, writing and teaching. He has been associated with the development of information design as a specialism, founding Information Design Journal in 1979 and organising a series of Information Design Conferences starting in 1982. He is the current President of the International Institute for Information Design and runs the non-profit Simplification Centre. Rob was formerly Professor of Information Design at the University of Reading, UK, where he originally studied, with a doctorate exploring the relationship between language and typography. He has since published many papers developing this theme, and lately on its application to legal information design. Rob's design agency, eventually acquired by the global marketing group WPP, developed communications for many well-known brands including Vodafone, Barclays, AXA, Aegon, and his projects have been as diverse as gas bills, flight information displays, dictionaries, museum signing, tax forms, lottery tickets and board games. He has consulted on innovative clear contracts with organisations including Accenture, Airbus Defence & Space, Nexen/CNOOC, and Shell.

Stefania Passera is CEO and Contract Designer at Passera Design, and Contract Designer in Residence at World Commerce & Contracting. After completing her studies in graphic design at Politecnico di Milano, Italy, and Aalto University, Finland, Stefania obtained a Doctorate of Science in Organizational Studies at Aalto University, Finland, writing her empirical dissertation on how visualizations can enhance the comprehension and user experience of contracts and foster better business relationships. She has served as Assistant Professor of Business Law at the Univrsity of Vaasa, Finland, and guest lectured at prestigious institutions such as Stanford University, Bucerius Center on the Legal Profession, KU Leuven, UC Louvain, European University Institute, ESADE Law School, and California Western School of Law. Her research on contract design and visualization has been published in international journals and edited books. A pioneer in contract design and legal design, Stefania is a co-founder of the Legal Design Alliance, a co-author of the Legal Design Manifesto, and the creator of Legal Design Jam. She has received the European Women of Legal Tech Award in 2020, and has been a WorldCC Fellow since 2018.

Helena Haapio is an Associate Professor of Business Law at the University of Vaasa, Finland, an Adjunct Professor of Proactive Law and Contract Design at the University of Lapland and a Contract Strategist at Lexpert Ltd. After completing legal studies at the University of Turku, Finland, and Cambridge University, England, she served for several years as in-house Legal Counsel in Europe and the USA. A pioneer of the Proactive Law approach, she has for many years promoted the use of simplification and visualization in commercial contracting. Her multidisciplinary research focuses on ways to enhance the functionality and usability of contracts through design. Her recent books include Research Handbook on Contract Design (Edward Elgar 2022), Legal Design (Edward Elgar 2021), Legal Tech, Smart Contracts and Blockchain (Springer 2019); Next Generation Contracts: A Paradigm Shift (Lexpert 2013), and two titles co-authored with Professor George Siedel, A Short Guide to Contract Risk (Gower 2013) and Proactive Law for Managers: A Hidden Source of Competitive Advantage (Gower 2011). She is also a co-founder of the Legal Design Alliance and a co-author of its Legal Design Manifesto.

Injecting Humanity (Back) into Talent Development

Duc V. Trang

Contents

Abstract

Many clients buy legal expertise, but often they demand more. Clients want their lawyer, in providing legal services, to understand their broader personal or business issues, of which legal issues constitute only one part. Some of these attributes fall under the general rubric of complex *problem-solving*, such as problem-assessment, strategic/systemic thinking, judgment, commercial/business acumen, judgment, etc. These skills are critical to enable lawyers to understand the context of their clients' broader problems, in order to supply not just correct, but *useful,* advice. It is not coincidental that many of these described skills are

Duc Vinh Trang is Managing Director, Global Advisory Services, Major, Lindsey & Africa.

D. V. Trang (✉)
London, UK
e-mail: dtrang@mlaglobal.com

K. Jacob et al. (eds.), *Liquid Legal – Humanization and the Law*, Law for Professionals, https://doi.org/10.1007/978-3-031-14240-6_14

similar or the same as those identified in multiple studies about future workforce skills that will both be in demand *and* less subject to automation.

Anecdotes and surveys, however, suggest that surprisingly few lawyers have these skills associated with complex problem-solving (beyond legal problem-solving). At the same time, law firms and corporate legal departments continue to spend significant amounts on talent development, with limited returns on those investments.

This chapter explores why current approaches in legal training and education, focused primarily on developing technical expertise, is incomplete, inefficient or ineffective in developing complex problem-solving skills. To help re-examine traditional legal training and education, the author articulates two different problem-solving schemas. The first correlates to the legal training or specialist training currently dominant in law schools pedagogy and in professional training. The second problem-solving schema examines "wicked" problems—the more complex problems that clients and lawyers face in real life, and one that is not taught systematically in the legal profession.

By deconstructing the elements of "wicked" problems and associated problem-solving skills, the profession and legal industry can be more intentional in developing new training tools and methodologies for those skills and mindsets that clients demand. The author offers an example of such approach in transactional lawyering, to illustrate how complex problem-solving skills can be incorporated into traditional pedagogy. Doing so enables lawyers to better understand and assess of the root causes of a problem before applying legal expertise and delivering legal services—which goes to the heart of the humanization of law—to deliver services grounded in deeper understanding of the clients and their problems.

1 Introduction

Talent consistently is raised as a key concern or strategic priority for leaders of legal services organisations (e.g., general counsel, law firm partners, etc.). This is not surprising, given that the legal industry remains predominantly a professional "services" industry. What is surprising, however, is the prominence of this concern given how much the industry invests in talent development.

Concurrently, many industry pundits peddle the narrative that technology or machine learning soon will displace (or replace) large swathes of lawyers.[1] There's no question that technology will be increasingly incorporated into the legal profession and the delivery of legal services. The question is not whether technology will become more pervasive. It will. The question is—what exactly will machines be

[1] There are too many examples to list here, but see generally Susskind (2009).

doing and what will people be doing? How do you couple "human" capabilities with machine-learning capabilities to drive better outcomes? What is the combination of human skills and machine muscle that will distinguish individual talent? Getting this right will translate into organisational results—creating competitive advantage or strategic value.

Predicting the interplay between humans and machines in the legal industry leads us to the ongoing, often murky, challenge of how the legal profession approaches education and talent development. Indeed, clients expect lawyers to know the law and advise on legal issues. That is table stakes. What one hears from clients and consumers of legal services about what lawyers do to "add value", however, goes *beyond* legal expertise.

We will explore and disaggregate what clients consider "value"—specifically, the highly-valued skill of complex problem-solving, and associated competencies. We then examine how current approaches to legal education and training supply only half of the puzzle. Doctrinal and technical legal training remain the predominant focus of law schools and at law firms, where many lawyers are trained. That is good, but *incomplete*. We observe that much talent development is left to *unstructured* "experiential training", which is inefficient and leaves key gaps.

We then offer an example of a heuristic framework to illustrate how legal education and training can fuse doctrinal training and relationship and contextual understanding that are critical to the highly valued skill of complex problem-solving. We describe how such holistic approach to training will accelerate the development of higher cognitive problem-solving skills that clients demand today (and in the future) of lawyers.

The suggested approach illustrates how training lawyers at the *intersection* of law, business and interpersonal relationships will enable lawyers to provide legal services that are not only correct, but *useful* to clients or end users of legal services. This is what we often mean when we urge lawyers to be "client-centric". This "humanisation" of legal talent development is not just desirable; it's required for the effectiveness of lawyering at scale.

2 What Do Lawyers "Do"?

As Ronald Gilson once posed—what do lawyers "do"?[2] What he was really asking is what do lawyers do that is valued by clients.

Clients expect that lawyers are capable of doing what is traditionally expected of lawyers—identifying legal issues, applying the applicable law to the facts, evaluating arguments, assessing the legal risks, and advising clients on courses of actions. These traditional tasks relate primarily to *legal* issues.

Clients, however, have a broader view of what their "problems" are. Whether in family law, the law of obligations, or transactional law, the clients' problems contain

[2]Gilson (1984), p. 241.

many different constituent parts of which legal is only one. A lawyer providing legal advice that may be "correct", may not necessarily be *useful* to the clients if such advice disregards the other components (e.g. financial, interpersonal, reputational, etc.) of the problem; and in fact, may create unintended, unfavorable consequences for clients.

What clients expect and value *today* are certain attributes, many of which I call higher cognitive traits underlying the broad notion of *problem-solving*: problem-assessment; strategic thinking; judgment, strategic/systemic thinking (e.g., understanding the big picture); commercial/business acumen, etc.

Interestingly, this list correlates with the results of studies about *future* workforce skills. The World Economic Forum in its *Future of Jobs Report* (2020)[3] sets out the top 10 skills in demand for jobs in 2025—these include (1) complex problem-solving skills and (2) critical/analytical thinking and analysis among the top skills group. These skills have remained at the top of the list with *year-on-year* consistency.[4] This finding found further support in various studies by the McKinsey Institute. "Demand for higher cognitive skills, such as creativity, critical thinking, decision making, and complex information processing, will grow through 2030, by 19 percent in the United States and by 14 percent in Europe, from sizable bases today."[5]

While technology slowly and surely will pervade the legal industry, there's nothing that would suggest that the higher cognitive functions will be less in demand. In fact, if anything, these traits will not only be the distinguishing factors of humans, but become even more valuable.

3 Problem-Solving

We now explore in detail the area of effective lawyering that is emphasised strongly by clients, and those in both the practising profession and in academia—helping clients solve problems and make decisions.

This skill can be reframed as follows: "[p]roblem solving is decision making when there is complexity and uncertainty that rules out obvious answers" or "where a method of solution is not immediately obvious".[6] Whether characterized as *problem-solving* or *decision-making*, the task fundamentally involves: (1) accurately

[3] World Economic Forum, Future of Jobs Report 2020 (https://www.weforum.org/reports/the-future-of-jobs-report-2020).

[4] See, e.g., World Economic Forum, The Future of Jobs Report 2018 (https://www3.weforum.org/docs/WEF_Future_of_Jobs_2018.pdf); The Future of Jobs Report (2016) (https://reports.weforum.org/future-of-jobs-2016/).

[5] McKinsey Institute, Defining the skills citizens will need in the future world of work (2021) (https://www.mckinsey.com/industries/public-and-social-sector/our-insights/defining-the-skills-citizens-will-need-in-the-future-world-of-work?cid=always-pso-twi-mip-mck-tsp-2108-i1a&sid=6111db6c5195cb3119992032).

[6] Conn and Mclean (2018), p. xvii.

framing the problem or outcome; (2) identifying the problem's root causes; (3) developing possible solutions; and (4) where relevant, prioritizing the solutions by degree of impact and trade-offs.

In a world that is getting more complex, and where technology is becoming a greater force, more and more people, especially in senior positions, "require . . . more independent judgment and better problem-solving skills".[7] In other words, learning "how to define a problem, creatively break into manageable parts, and systematically work toward a solution has become *the* core skill for the twenty-first century workforce . . . ."[8]

The essential role of lawyers helping clients solve more than just legal issues has long been recognized in the profession. The American Bar Association (ABA) first articulated this concept in its MacCrate Report—a comprehensive study of lawyers' education and professional development needs—in which the ABA identified problem-solving as a "fundamental lawyering skill".

It describes what problem-solving entails, which is *not* limited to solving legal issues:

> In order to develop and evaluate strategies for solving a problem or accomplishing an objective a lawyer should be familiar with the skills and concepts involved in:
>
> (a) Identifying and Diagnosing the Problem;
> (b) Generating Alternative Solutions and Strategies
> (c) Developing a Plan of Action
> (d) Implementing the Plan
> (e) Keeping the Planning Process Open to New Information and New Ideas.[9]

More recently, the UK Solicitors Regulation Authority (SRA) promulgated the revised Statement of Solicitor Competence, which articulates similar expectations about broader problem-solving skills:[10]

> B3. Develop and advise on relevant options, strategies and solutions, including:
>
> a. Understanding and assessing a client's *commercial and personal* circumstances, their *needs, objectives, priorities and constraints*
> b. Ensuring that advice is informed by appropriate legal and factual analysis and identifies the consequences of different options
>
> B6. Negotiate solutions to clients' issues, including

[7] Ewenstein et al. (2016).

[8] Conn and Mclean (2018), p. xiii.

[9] (Report of the Task Force on Law Schools and the Profession: Narrowing the Gap): (Illinois: American Bar Association, 1992).

[10] SRA, Statement of solicitor competence (2019) (emphasis added) (https://www.sra.org.uk/solicitors/resources/continuing-competence/cpd/competence-statement/#:~:text=This%20document%20takes%20a%20broad,%26%20du%20Boulay%2C%202001).

a. Identifying all parties' *interests, objectives and limits*
b. Developing and formulating best options for meeting parties' *objectives*
c. Presenting options for compromise persuasively
d. Responding to options presented by the other side
e. Developing compromises between options or parties

The SRA's expectations of "competence" is clear—lawyers are expected to not resolve solely legal issues, but help clients solve problems with respect to a client's "commercial and personal" circumstances, and their "interests, objectives, and priorities". Again, such problem-solving requirements are not limited to legal issues.

Similarly, a common observation (or complaint) of clients of private practice lawyers is that the lawyers demonstrate weak commercial acumen—they do not know the clients' business or do not entirely understand the underlying commercial issues in a transaction in order to solve the client's problem. Recent market data confirms that clients value a lawyer's problem-solving skills beyond legal expertise; a survey by ALM Intelligence of corporate counsel indicates that one of the top two frustrations clients have with even their most valued firms is the inability to consider business objectives in providing legal advice.[11]

More revealing is the recent survey "GC Thought Leaders Experiment" by AdvanceLaw, an organisation consisting of 200 general counsel. The study specifically examined the correlation of certain performance indicators of law firms and the general counsel's willingness to recommend or refer the law firm to another general counsel. The data contained the key finding that the skills to find a solution—an ability and willingness of lawyers to offer different assessment paths forward to solve a business problem—was the primary indicator for general counsel to refer a firm to another peer. The general counsel value the ability to demonstrate "creativity" or "strategic thinking" in solving their problems more than, while still important, the quality of legal advice. In other words, the clients' view of "value" is reaching a resolution of a problem as a whole, of which legal is only one of many components; there are no parallel universes of "legal" problems and "non-legal" problems. As a general counsel of a Fortune 100 company observed—all problems are business problems.[12]

In other words, what effective lawyers do essentially is problem-solving *applied* to a specific business or personal context. "But no matter who the client, what the substantive legal issues or whether the situation involves litigation or planning, your principal role as lawyer will almost always be the same – to help clients achieve effective solutions to their problems."[13] It's a misconception to see this strategic adviser role as a newfound phenomenon. That is what clients expect *now*, as

[11] "ALM Corporate Counsel 2018 Agenda" (31 May 2018), https://www.law.com/2018/05/31/filling-the-gaps-for-corporate-counsel/.

[12] "Cisco's Mark Chandler on How Lawyers Should Become Disruptors" https://www.dlapipertechsummit.com/blog/2016/ciscos-mark-chandler-on-how-lawyers-should-become-disruptors.html (30 September 2016).

[13] Binder et al. (1991), p. 3.

problems are becoming increasingly multidisciplinary, involving more than just legal issues.

Unfortunately, problem-solving, remains a *buzzword* in the profession. The ABA or the SRA's articulation of the concept for example is at a level of abstraction that do not offer any constructive guidance to help a lawyer develop skills and tools to "generate alternative solutions and strategies". Further, our research of literature reveals that commentators, professional and academic, struggle to provide meaningful guidance on how lawyers can play that role, other than banal encouragements for lawyers to "educate" themselves about "new areas of law or other subject matter".[14] This general exhortation often is conveyed without offering lawyers any tools to help them to do it; pedagogically, it is of limited utility.

4 "Kind" and "Wicked" Problems: Different Problem-Solving Paradigms

To provide further insight on how we can resolve the lack of useful guidance, we address the "describability" problem—"how to describe what [experts] are doing in a way that allows other people also to learn".[15] Unless we delineate what effective problem-solving lawyers do, it will be difficult to be intentional in teaching it—that is, understanding both *what* and *how* to teach.

There are two different types of problem-solving skills that professionals, such as lawyers, exercise. These can be described problem-solving of "kind" and "wicked" problems *or* environments.[16] While both involve problem-solving and decision-making, they are fundamentally different.

"Kind" problems or environments have the following characteristics:[17]

- Rules are clear
- Patterns repeat; and
- Feedback is accurate and usually rapid

In a kind learning environment, one can excel simply by undertaking the activity, repeating the activity, and trying to improve. Examples include chess and golf—the ball or piece is moved according to clear rules and boundaries; the consequence of an

[14]Kosuri (2015), p. 480. See also Neumann (2013), p. 55. (Lawyers should "[c]reate options that wouldn't be there except for your insights and problem-solving skills. And the options should go beyond law: They should be practical solutions that will work in the real world where the client lives, and not just in law books".)

[15]Schön (1995), p. 247.

[16]This taxonomy was initially identified for different learning environments, in Hogarth (2001). Indeed, one may draw a distinction between "problems" and "environments". For purposes of this discussion, we use the two terms *interchangeably* to illustrate the difference that are relevant to the issue of talent development.

[17]Epstein (2019), p. 21.

action or decision is clear and quick; and challenges, albeit slightly different, occur repeatedly. In these activities, the participant takes action, observes what happens, responds and attempts to correct the error (if any), and tries again and again (perhaps over years) to get better. Because reactions and responses are known, patterns can be developed or refined over time.

There are analogous examples in law. Let's consider a lawyer analyzing a limitation of liability clause and advising a client how to negotiate such a clause and what the client may consider before agreeing with the other contractual party. That lawyer will (hopefully) have studied how such clauses are interpreted or applied in that jurisdiction and will have a view on how drafting changes or certain wording in the clause will impact how a third-party adjudicator will apply and rule on such wording. And, if that lawyer has years of experience negotiating hundreds (or thousands?) of limitation of liability clauses, that person will develop deep expertise and judgment in advising a client on the risks of different formulations of a limitation of liability clauses.

One can see similarities in other "legal" problems on which lawyers advise or help solve: the risks to the borrowers under the "material adverse clause"; the implied obligation to act in "good faith" in a contractual relationship; what constitutes "consideration" for an enforceable contract; the legal duties of members of a board of directors; etc.

"Wicked" problems or environment, in contrast, have characteristics that are diametrical to those of "kind" problems:[18]

1. Rules may be unclear or incomplete
2. There may not be repetitive patterns, or the patterns may not be obvious
3. Feedback is often delayed, inaccurate or both.

I would add a few more:

1. There are interdependencies, many of which extend across potentially different subject matter areas
2. The causal relationships of certain decisions or events are not clear
3. There may be multiple unintended consequences when seeking to solve the problem
4. Value disagreements among the stakeholders

For a simplistic comparison, to follow on earlier sports examples, it's as if you were playing a game of "golf", and (1) it's unclear how many players there are; (2) players are communicated and playing under different "rules", etc.; the ball rolls in different directions from hole to hole, even though the plane of the green may be the same, etc.

But back to a real world "wicked" problem or decision. A company runs a successful business in North America selling headphones through a broad

[18] Id.; see also generally Conn and Mclean (2018), p. xx.

distribution network, which then sells to end users. The company has preliminarily decided to enter the China market, and is now faced with the decision whether to (1) establish a wholly-owned subsidiary in China to operate the business or (2) enter into a joint venture with an established Chinese company. That decision necessarily involves legal issues (e.g., JV licensing, business license, human resources requirements, intellectual property ownership rights, etc.), but much more. There will be a broad array of business and operational issues that will differ between the two decisions: financial models, profitability models, size of market, marketing strategies (e.g., branding, business development, etc.), operational issues, trust issues between the joint venture parties, the ability to establish a distribution network, etc. Further, it may not be possible to gauge the impact of some of these choices until later in the future—e.g., how the joint venture parties work together, the effectiveness of the branding and marketing programs, the demand for the products, etc. More importantly, for a lawyer advising the senior management team, the legal issues are connected to other issues. For example, in the joint venture, the creation and protection of each JV partner's intellectual property ownership rights conceivably will be impacted by the legal rules in that jurisdiction, but also by the operational processes (e.g., tracking the respective party's contribution) as well as the trust level between the two parties. So, if the intellectual property rules are not entirely clear in that jurisdiction, as is often the case, how will the lawyer advise the company on whether to proceed with the decision on whether to enter into the joint venture.

What can we take away from these two problem environment paradigms?

"Kind" problems, such as a negotiation on a limitation of liability clause, may indeed be "complicated" and even thorny. But it is not "complex", like wicked problems, which are comparatively more *unstructured*.

Research offers a number of insights into the differences for kind and wicked problems:[19]

- For kind domains, deliberate and extended practice can be effective—often called "specialization";
- Experience does not necessarily lead to expertise in problem-solving of wicked problems. Deep experience in a domain for which there is predictable response to patterns work well for chess (kind), but is not a better predictor for political or financial trends, or of how employees or patients would behave (wicked);
- For wicked problems, reliance on experience or patterns based on experience may lead to bad and even disastrous events;
- Being a good problem-solver of wicked problems is analogous to the observation that someone is "strategic" or employs strategic thinking; both involve a similar process: extracting clarity about the problem, deconstructing or disaggregating the problem, and setting directions or priorities.

[19] Jones (1995), Epstein (2019) and Conn and Mclean (2018).

Not surprisingly, because kind problems or environments have more easily defined patterns arising from quick feedback, problem-solving skills for kind problems are more likely to be displaced by technology. Pattern recognition that is inherent in artificial intelligence, for example, is easily adaptable to the tasks associated with kind problems.

Conversely, because wicked problems, by definition, cannot be captured by clear or consistent patterns, it is less subject to machine learning. Further, recognizing where humans excel—wicked problem-solving—provides insight on how better to pair human capabilities and machine learning capability. The machine and technology can enable the cognitive problem-solving skills by providing more information/data and faster. In many cases, technology will force humans to be better problem solvers because technology will perform much of the tasks today that is occupying human brain power. This strategic adviser role is even more important (and valuable) as technology gets embedded in the profession and takes over the less complex legal tasks, including subject matter knowledge.

Let's take a legal example: a contract dispute involving the meaning of the limitation of liability clause. The client is weighing the merits of the decision whether to proceed to trial. It is imminently plausible to imagine technology/software will be able to review hundreds/thousands of previous cases in that jurisdiction to extract patterns based upon the facts of the case, previous case law, and the judge allocated to hear the case, and then predict the probability of what that judge will ultimately decide. And that technology will likely perform that task both more accurately (i.e., canvassing a larger number of data sets, e.g., cases) and more quickly than a human lawyer. Machine learning conceivably may be able to predict, for example, an exact percentage of success (e.g., 68%).

However, the likelihood of success at trial may *not* be the main problem or decision facing a client; instead, the broader decision facing the client is whether to proceed to trial at all, or to try to negotiate a settlement. Such a consideration may involve a number of other interests or concerns the client may have associated with the trial: the ongoing legal costs; the adverse publicity and reputational impact; the impact on key relationships; the diversion of attention of key executives, etc. In advising a client, the skill that will less likely be displaced by machine learning is how a lawyer may help the client navigate how those various concerns should be assessed in totality. Helping the client explore the multiple facets of that decision requires the lawyer not only to know the legal impact of litigation, but how the decision to litigate or not litigate will impact the other interests of the client.

In this example, one can see the interplay of *both* kind and wicked environments. The kind environment involves the *legal* analysis of the scope of the limitation liability clause. The wicked problem is whether the client should proceed to trial to fully adjudicate the dispute. In other words, if lawyers are keen being effective (and also not be replaced by technology), they should have a plan to cultivate problem-solving skills for *both* kind and wicked problems.

5 What Problem-Solving Skills Are We Trying to Teach?

Given that the characteristics of each of kind and wicked environments or problems are fundamentally different, are the skills and competencies required to solve each problem archetype also fundamentally different?

5.1 "Kind" Problem-Solving

Kind problems or environments often involve *discrete* issues. For example, a lawyer may be asked to opine on the scope of an indemnity clause, whether the contemplated activity is permitted under the law, the enforceability of a clause, *etc.*

Those questions require a lawyer to understand the applicable law; to apply the law to the facts at hand; to assess legal implications and risks to her client; and, then, to formulate recommendations of alternatives to her clients to mitigate or eliminate those *legal* risks.

Experts in this decision-making paradigm make good decisions if they are able to recognise in the problem a pattern of a certain kind and to "retrieve" a solution from a stored repertoire of solutions to similar problems. Such expertise can be based on a sufficiently *large* number of data sets or situations that the practitioner has observed or experienced, which she then organises in a structured manner to enable her to retrieve potential solutions when faced with a *similar* problem.

We referenced earlier the example of a lawyer analyzing a limitation of liability clause. A lawyer who has studied how such clauses are interpreted or applied in that jurisdiction, and has years of experience negotiating hundreds (or thousands?) of limitation of liability clauses, that person will develop deep expertise and judgment in advising a client on the risks of different formulations of a limitation of liability clauses. This example applies to any other legal issues that require analysis and repeated practice for improvement.

In this discrete decision-making paradigm, when comparing an expert with a novice, the difference is two-fold. First, the expert is able to come to a decision more quickly through having access to a larger volume of data of potential solutions. The *quality* of the expert's decision is likely to be higher, given the richness of the data from which she extracts potential solutions. Let us take the example of chess. For a novice chess player looking at a chess board, the novice observes a large number of potential moves that may materialise over the course of the game. In contrast, an expert chess player relies on a greater set of data and experience from which to form richer situation analyses; she is therefore able to see a *smaller* number of potential paths and patterns—made up of many individual moves—of the game. As a result, the expert is able both to make better individual chess moves, and to do so much more quickly than a novice.

One can see analogous situations in the practice of law. Let us take a simple example of a client who is considering appealing against a lower court decision finding that there was no enforceable contract between the client and the counter-party. The commercial litigation partner at the law firm representing the client asks a junior associate to do legal research and provide an assessment of the likelihood that the appeal would be successful. The junior associate, who is assumed to be diligent, will try her best to review the relevant legislation on enforceable obligations (if any) and numerous written or documented cases on what constitutes an enforceable contract. Based on that review, the junior associate will make an assessment, based on the facts of the current case, of the chances that an appeal will be successful, by arguing whether the facts of the current case are similar to other previously decided cases that suggest a certain outcome.

The partner, in contrast, presumably will have a much large reservoir of data to make her assessment. The partner will have been familiar with a larger number of contract cases—those that have gone to court and those that have settled before trial. She will be familiar with the argument that opposing counsel make in these cases. She will be more familiar with the court or judge who will hear the appeal and have a better assessment of how the arguments she can make on behalf of her client will fare in front of that court or judge. Or, she may ask the client to provide certain additional evidence to confirm certain facts that may strengthen the arguments she may make on behalf of the client. Based on the partner's comparative larger set of data than that of the junior associate, the confidence level in the accuracy of the partner's assessment will likely be higher.

Although the legal analysis involved in this example of kind problem may be complicated, the problem-solving skill may be developed by *repeated* practice and knowledge of, in this case, a larger number of contract dispute cases over time—based heavily on experience.

There are key drawbacks, however, to relying primarily on individualised decision-making expertise in environments that become more "wicked". The pattern of thinking that underlies the strength of this approach will underperform if the problem itself has unkind elements. Such risks include:

- When expertise—accuracy, speed and reasoning—is based on *previously* observed and stored patterns of similar problems, there is an automatic response which may result in reliance on the *wrong* pattern. Or, in other words, there is a risk of jumping to conclusions before all the facts are gathered, or an over-reliance on patterns of knowledge that may not apply in that context;
- Some problems are simply too complex (aka, "wicked") to rely on the process of problem recognition and solution retrieval as a path to problem-solving. Such complex problems may involve a number of micro issues to which the problem-solver has had little or no exposure to form any useful schema or structured knowledge. The complexity may also come from the situation or environment changing over time or as a result of the choices or actions taken; and
- When faced with *new or different* facts or assumptions that diverge from the facts or assumption underlying the initial schema formed during the lawyer's expertise creation stage, the practitioner may not have sufficient patterns of solutions in the database to analyse and assess the new scenario.

Excessive reliance on experiential learning may result in inferior cognitive agility in wicked environments or problems—one that is changing quickly or is different from previously seen patterns—simply because the person has *not* observed or experienced the new or different problem. In other words, over-reliance on problem-solving techniques based on repeated practice may result in "cognitive entrenchment"[20] and may prevent a lawyer from being adaptable to change and formulating solutions to novel or ambiguous problems.

In summary, lawyers behaving as legal technical experts may have depth in their functional wheelhouse, but they often run into trouble when they come across a problem that exceeds the traditional or doctrinal taxonomies in which they were trained. This is more true as one becomes more senior in an organization and is likely to face more complex and wicked problems that don't neatly fit into nice categories.

5.2 "Wicked" Problem-Solving

As we have seen, the legal issues that lawyers analyse and advise on, while important in and of themselves, do not necessarily solve the clients' underlying problem.

The client has a desired outcome but may face certain constraints blocking the path to such outcome. While some of those impediments may be legal in nature (*e.g.*, is the transaction permitted under applicable law, what risks does the liability clause pose, *etc.*), often there are many *non-legal issues* that must be considered. In a transaction, for example, these issues may include the counterparty having a different risk assessment or valuation, each party having a budget constraint, conditions that are unknown to the parties as of the proposed date of the contract, *etc*. In this example, the lawyer must design and implement a strategy that will achieve the client's ultimate objective—completing the transaction—within the constraints of that problem.

This problem-solving or decision-making paradigm in wicked or complex environments is not unique to the legal profession. You can see similar examples in business, architecture, medicine, etc. Problem-solving in wicked environments can be described as follows:

- The problem involves a *larger* objective that will need to be broken down into discrete issues or problems that involve individual or micro decisions to be made by the parties. One can define the larger objective to be achieved as a situation where the desired status differs from the current status, and there is no clear path to reach the desired status.
- The facts with which to design a solution may either not be available or not entirely known, the ambiguity of which may be exacerbated by the fact that certain individual decisions under consideration have not yet been made. In fact, even the goals of the stakeholders in that problem may change over time, as the parties are being continuously advised on and considering numerous micro decisions to be made.

---

[20]Dane (2010), pp. 579–603.

- Unlike kind problems, unkind or "wicked" problems entail issues that require a solution to address issues that may emerge over days, months or even longer.

Problem-solving in unkind environments therefore is a construct of a series of *interdependent* decisions, within which no single decision (i.e., legal) is necessarily—and, in fact, highly unlikely—determinative of the ultimate solution. The exercise therefore requires the holistic consideration of the linkages between the various discrete decisions—legal or non-legal—to be made. Rather than focusing on any individual or small group of decisions, the lawyer must consider and formulate a *menu* of possible paths to the desired destination. As such, these problems do not necessarily have right answers, only better or worse ones.

The "expertise" involved therefore is the ability to understand which decisions are relevant, the interdependencies and implications among the various decision points, including the sequencing of those decisions, and then help the client make the best choices in order to achieve the desired end goal.

This *systemic* approach to problem-solving therefore entails a potentially complex *matrix* of micro decisions, some of which are contingent on the continuously evolving contours of the final solution as a result of the outcomes of such micro decisions themselves. The scope of uncertainty and complexity of the wicked problem-solving process can dwarf that of those involved for "kind" problems or environments.

Let us return to the original query of what lawyers "do". We have so far examined developing expertise in problem-solving in two different constructs—the "kind" and "wicked" problem-solving models.

Deep knowledge about a legal subject matter—the core competency of a lawyer—generally aligns under the "kind" micro problem-solving paradigm. This is consistent, as examined in the next section, with the traditional training that law students and lawyers receive: using deductive and analogical reasoning to analyse and make recommendations on discrete legal issues.

In contrast, in the model of unkind problem-solving, the lawyer may be asked, based upon a series of inter-related micro issues (only some of which have strong legal elements), to analyse and design potential solutions to a larger problem.

The lawyer's approach in solving kind or discrete problems may well be sufficient or adequate for dealing with a high percentage of the issues on which lawyers are asked to advise. It's the other 10%—the wicked problems—that create more strategic value for clients, and where the normal problem-solving approach are unlikely to provide better answers or better decisions. As noted, lawyers who have deep expertise in legal "specialisation" often are at a loss when facing a problem that doesn't neatly fit into one of the patterns they've learned from kind environments.

In the realm of problem-solving or decision-making, educators often confuse the types of *critical thinking* involved. Effective critical thinking includes both *structuring* and *analysis*. Problem-solving of wicked problem requires the ability to structure the problem *before* analyzing the incumbent parts of the problem. Structuring essentially is a holistic or overall roadmap of what components of the complex problem requires further analysis. In doing so, structuring accomplishes two critical tasks: (1) first, it separates the multiple constituent elements of a problem in an *organized* way and (2) second, it provides high-level guidance of alternative solutions.

Analysis then is the deconstructing of the components of a problem into further constituent elements, which also provides guidance on how the components are related to each other. How one structures the problem—both identification and assessment—can therefore guide (or misguide) the analysis of the micro issues.

Complex problem-solving therefore requires the ability to identify key components of a problem. Jumping directly to analyzing individual constituent elements of a complex problem without going through the cognitive process of identifying relevant patterns has the following analytic "sins":

- Weak problem statements
- Asserting the answer
- Failure to disaggregate the problem
- Incomplete analytic tool set
- Failure to link conclusions with the storyline for action
- Failure to see the connections or interdependencies among the relevant parts of a problem
- Risk of being subject to cognitive biases, such as confirmation bias
- Failure to pay attention to alternative solutions to consider trade-off decisions
- Risk of applying more obvious solutions when they don't necessarily apply
- Viewing the problem in a haphazard or random way

We now transition to the question of how effective are law schools and the practising profession in educating and training transactional lawyers in the problem-solving paradigms of kind and wicked environments.

6 How Do the Academy or Law Firms Teach and Train Lawyers?

A review of how lawyers currently are trained provides a consistent view—there is little systemic effort to understand the higher cognitive problem-solving skills in which effective lawyers engage. As a result, the efforts of higher education (the Academy) and the profession to equip lawyers with wicked problem-solving skills have been haphazard at best.

6.1 Law Schools/Academy

While it is clear that not all law schools teach the same way, strong traditional and historical bases of the teaching of law influence thinking across law schools and even jurisdictions. While we address here educational practices in common law jurisdictions, many of the pedagogical themes can be found in non-common law systems. Doctrinal training in common law jurisdictions, for example, often involves applying statutory sources of law, given the expansion of the regulatory state in these countries. Conversely, law students in civil law countries employ a similar methodology as their common law counterparts—analysing how judges apply the law to a set of facts to understand how legal principles work in practice.

The initial phase of legal education follows a familiar path in most jurisdictions. In the first year or two, students spend significant time studying statutes, cases, and other sources of law and how they are applied and resolved under different sets of facts. Students study judicial decisions and other commentaries with the goal of distilling from such cases a set of doctrines. This act of comparing and contrasting appellate cases and legal sources creates a deeper understanding of legal concepts while embedding a set of foundational analytical skills—it trains students to identify and formulate issues, distinguish legally relevant facts, understand how the facts apply and for what purposes, think critically about language in both statutes and opinions, assess arguments, and adopt methods of interpretation. Students learn how to think about and advocate for certain legal results by applying the jurisprudential theory and sources of law in the legal field of study—the elements of a contract, of other obligations, etc. The learning outcome associated with this method is to instill certain "habits of mind that characterize a distinctively lawyer-like mode of analysis and reasoning".[21]

The pedagogy in upper-level law courses is not dissimilar, and continues to examine primarily *legal* issues. Let's take transactional lawyering. One finds limited coverage of how parties, beyond legal requirements, go about structuring their commercial relationships, or what Gilson calls private orderings. As a result, the teaching often devolves to studying how public regulatory frameworks and case law apply to private arrangements. The study of these *public orderings* is the principal teaching focus of traditional, upper-level business courses. And, how is this taught? Often, it involves studying cases about how the courts apply and interpret the regulatory requirements that apply to particular transactions. In a Finance course, for example, the class may study cases about the registration requirements of public securities. Or, in a mergers and acquisitions ("M&A") course, students may analyse cases about the obligations and duties of boards of directors in connection with an offer to buy the assets of a company. In other words, the education in upper-level business law courses effectively is the study of "the output of government involvement in private arrangements",[22] and often does not cover how private parties go about arranging their affairs—an essential component of transactional lawyering.

The subject matter or sector-based training found in the Academy facilitates learning of doctrinal or "black-letter law". Despite the fact that the core assumptions underlying a doctrinal knowledge-focused education have been heavily criticised, the pedagogy continues to thrive precisely because it does impart a set of foundational lawyering skills of legal argumentation and analysis. By thinking critically about legal principles, facts, language, argumentation principles and interpretation

[21] Kruse (2013), p. 10.

[22] Gilson (1984), pp. 304–305.

skills, and crafting persuasive arguments in support of one party or the other, students undergoing this doctrinal training ostensibly learn how to "think like a lawyer".

The current and dominant pedagogy of doctrinal training is consistent with the problem-solving paradigm for "kind" problems—analyzing and solving individualised, and sometimes complex, *legal* problems. This provides the foundational path for legal "specialisation"—an in-depth study of discrete areas of law.

In contrast, there is limited effort in the Academy to impart the tools of systemic or "wicked" problem-solving skills. Indeed, a doctrine-focused approach to education and training can hinder a lawyer's ability to develop broad problem-solving skills. These include: a heavy emphasis on issue and problem-spotting; the analytic tools to spot problems, but not necessarily the skills to solve them; and a "negative" mindset—what went wrong, rather than navigating a set of alternative outcomes.

Returning to our transactional lawyering example. We are not arguing that transactional lawyers do not benefit from doctrinal training. Far from it. The foundational habits of thinking engendered by doctrinal training are part of the core skills of transactional lawyers. Transactional lawyers need those skills, for example, in order to spot the specific legal issues in the deal, draft effective contracts, and assist in the assessment of contractual interpretation in a manner that would minimise future disputes. Skills gained from doctrinal training allow transactional lawyers to craft the relevant language with the appropriate level of nuance and specificity to accomplish the goals of the parties, while minimising potential conflicts or disputes in the future.

If, however, one views transactional lawyering as problem-solving in a broader set of activities within a more complex environment from an *ex-ante* perspective, *more* is required. The expertise creation methodology behind doctrinal training is perfectly adequate if the ultimate goal is to train litigators, advocates and judges, and for developing individualised, or "kind", problem-solving skills. Yet, the same methodology has been used to educate *all* types of lawyers, even though the patterns of learning offered by doctrinal training do not, as discussed earlier, entirely fit the tasks and activities of a transactional lawyer. Doctrinal training, gained within more established parameters and facts from an *ex-post* perspective, provides the "kind" problem-solving expertise that, while essential, is *incomplete* for transactional lawyers and for "wicked" problems.

Law school graduates therefore leave school with limited capacity or foundation to learn how to think strategically and holistically about a problem—precisely the kind of skill that clients demand. Unfortunately, we find the same result in the other dominant forum for training of new lawyers—law firms.

6.2 Law Firms

As with Academy, law firms generally do not have structured programs to develop complex problem-solving skills. Instead, the focus is to inculcate deep legal expertise and specialisation, while the development of higher cognitive skills that clients consistently convey as important—problem solving, commercial acumen, judgment, strategic thinking, etc.—are left to general exhortations and *unstructured* experiential training.

Training at law firms follows a familiar path across jurisdictions. The primary method is experiential training to reinforce doctrinal education, with the *hope* that this eventually develops into complex and broader problem-solving skills. This long-standing apprenticeship model aims to provide young lawyers exposure to as many matters or transactions as possible under the supervision, instruction and guidance of more experienced and presumably more qualified senior lawyers (senior associates and partners).

The second defining characteristic of law firm training for transactional lawyers is that it is sector- (*e.g.*, oil and gas, technology, *etc.*) or practice area- (*e.g.*, intellectual property) based. Most new lawyers are assigned to a specific practice group, and their mentors or supervising lawyers often have deep experience primarily in that industry. Additionally, there is heavy reliance during training on contractual templates that have been in use for a long time. While these templates often were crafted by experienced practitioners, many lawyers often do not fully understand the rationale behind many of the contractual clauses or the overall structure of the document.

That subject matter or practice area focus of expertise is reflected in the formal and informal training programmes at law firms. The foundational level of training at law firms is designed to promote subject matter expertise—training on substantive law in the lawyer's assigned practice area, and associated "practice skills", such and drafting and negotiating skills.

Fundamentally, the approach in training transactional lawyers at law firms is this: teach young lawyers the "law", have them work on many matters, and then keep the ones who demonstrate commercial, strategic and problem-solving skills after eight to ten years of practice. This methodology produces a small number of lawyers who thrive in such a learning environment, who are promoted and eventually made partner. These lawyers are credited with the right natural abilities: they "have it" or just "get it". A much larger proportion of the law firm population do not.

The consequences of law firms' experience-based training approach are predictable. One can easily observe expertise creation in problem-solving skills in "kind" environments. The repetitive practice of seeing how the law is applied to a certain group of issues in a familiar (same) business context or industry triggers analogical and deductive learning processes. For example, many lawyers negotiating information technology contracts will have ample experience negotiating intellectual property indemnity clauses, which set out the obligations of the service provider to the customer in the event of a third-party intellectual property infringement claim. Service providers wish to limit the scope of these clauses while their customers often negotiate to expand such scope. After negotiating tens or hundreds of these clauses, these lawyers can easily visualise and implement the various negotiating positions and arguments that both sides make, and the various options in resolving successfully these negotiations. The same can be said of banking lawyers who negotiate financial covenants or a material adverse change clause in loan agreements.

After working on multiple transactions using similar templates, advising on, negotiating and drafting these clauses become almost second nature.

That the law firm and its apprentice or experience-based mode is generally successful at developing lawyers' problem-solving ability of discrete legal issues is expected. However, how does this square with the current perception of clients about the value that lawyers add—the skills to solve complex problems? Despite the focus and increased investment in training at law firms, recent market surveys of clients confirm a common theme: even after a significant tenure of practice, many lawyers (even at the senior levels) may be considered good legal experts, but most are not considered strong problem-solvers when faced with non-legal complexity.[23] These lawyers are capable or even very good at identifying legal risks and proposing solutions to those legal risks, but often have difficulty understanding the entire transaction or contributing to the resolution of the overall business problem.

The shortcomings in this apprentice-type pedagogy based on experience and observation of experts are predictable. First, it is *inefficient*. It takes a significant amount of time and number of transactions or matters to provide that repetition-based type of expertise. Law firms spend enormous amounts (significantly funded by clients) to train their lawyers, with the result that only a few eventually develop those systemic or "wicked" problem-solving skills that clients so value. Indeed, it is precisely because of such inefficiency that some clients are no longer willing to pay for junior associates to accumulate such experience.

Second, even if lawyers are exposed to a sufficiently large number of transactions and matters, it is not clear whether the apprenticeship model is that effective in developing the sought-after complex problem-solving expertise. Cognitive psychologists have explored why it is difficult for expert practitioners to convert their expertise into what Llewellyn has called "teachable experience and competence".[24] In fact, many expert practitioners themselves may not be able to *explain* what they do—tacit knowledge—and are therefore unable to properly teach it. Expert problem-solvers have over time developed internal schemas of structured knowledge on which they rely when faced with a new problem, to distil the relevant facts, analyse the problem, and craft possible solutions based on previous experience or knowledge of "structurally similar problems". Although it may appear to an outsider that there are multiple, complex steps in the process, an expert problem-solver often will move seamlessly through the process as though it were second nature. Unfortunately, most senior lawyers, whether in law firms or in house, do not have the tools to explain what they do; they are not able to deconstruct their expertise into discrete steps, and therefore would have difficulty teaching those complex problem-solving skills to junior lawyers, thus limiting the likelihood that an apprentice-type arrangement would be successful.

[23] See note 12 and associated discussion.

[24] Karl L Llewellyn's views shaped the 1944 report of the Committee on Curriculum of the Association of American Law Schools, published as "The Place of Skills in Legal Education" (1945) 45 Colum L Rev 345. See also Krieger (2004), p. 167.

Finally, in addition to these limitations of experiential learning, a young lawyer's training is dependent on the kind of transactions or matter that she is exposed to, and the quality of the mentorship or instructions. The process is highly *ad hoc* and arbitrary, thereby creating gaps in learning.

To generalise, law firms train lawyers to have a detailed look at a few (legal) trees, but no view of the forest (the client's overall problem). The training is structured around a select set of issues in often a singular industry, with only secondary comprehension of the client's overall business or concern. It is therefore difficult for lawyers to distinguish what is more or less important, particularly when faced with a problem (or client) *different* from what they are used to seeing or have seen. As a result, many lawyers approach legal issues and risks based on what they know—as a legal expert and risk manager—rather than a problem-solver in the broader context of a specific matter or deal.

Law firm training of junior and mid-level associate levels therefore is akin to the expertise creation observed in "kind" problem-solving. The emphasis on the training of core legal skills based on experiential training results in lawyers who are proficient or very good at advising or managing specific or individualised *legal* problems. The skills involved in complex or "wicked" problem-solving are *not* part of the foundational training in law firms, but left essentially to chance and to a combination of each lawyer's natural abilities and quality of training.

7 Modeling Complex Problem-Solving

We now explore *one example* of how lawyers can develop problem-solving skills of wicked problems in one key area of law—*transactional lawyering*. A modern society and economy are based on a wide range of contractual arrangements. Most if not all lawyers deal with or advise on transactions and contracts at some point in time. Given the broad scope of transactions and exchanges in modern societies, and the significant role of lawyers advising on them, transactional lawyering is a good *proxy* if one is interested in assessing the education and training of lawyers.

The range of complexity in transactions will vary, which drives different problem-solving paradigms for transactional lawyers. On one end of the spectrum, there are "kind" or discrete transactions where the nature of exchange effectively requires little or no input from professional advisers, such as lawyers, on the structure of the deal. More complex transactions present a different problem-solving challenge for lawyers advising clients on what is required to achieve the goal of completing the transaction. What makes these transactions "complex" or, in our vernacular, "wicked"?

A specific legal issue may be complex in nature (*e.g.*, is the proposed activity permitted by applicable rules and regulations?) and may in fact require deep legal skills to solve. But legal complexity is different from *transactional complexity*. For many transactions, even if the parties have come to an agreement in principle on a handful of key terms (*e.g.*, what is to be exchanged, the compensation amount, etc.), there often are multiple issues or challenges—both legal and non-legal—that may prevent the parties from coming to final agreement. The facts, conditions or parties' expectations surrounding the exchange may not be available, determinable or aligned *at the time* of contract design.

From the clients' perspective, there may be gaps or misalignments that may act to prevent the parties from concluding the transaction. These gaps collectively create a "wicked" environment or problem for clients to come to a transactional structure that is acceptable to all contractual parties. These gaps may include:

(a) relevant facts or information that may not be entirely known or are ambiguous at the time of contracting;
(b) issues of lack of trust and co-operation, or fear of strategic and opportunistic behaviour, between the parties, which may affect requirements (including risk assessments) on how parties will work together in the future;
(c) the parties having different expectations about risk, valuation and compensation in the transaction;
(d) anticipated contingent events or dependencies that will affect the parties' assessment of risk and pricing that, by definition, have not materialised at the time of contracting;
(e) unanticipated contingent events or dependencies over which the parties have no control after the signing of a contract, which would affect the parties' overall assessment of the value and risk profile of a transaction; and
(f) issues with a more "legal" flavour than the other elements, which arise from, for example, regulatory requirements or disagreements between the parties about how clauses are drafted or interpreted, and the risk allocation arising from the drafting itself.

These factors or constraints, which for each transaction are a unique mix of legal and non-legal components, contribute to the complexity of what the final structure or design of the transaction may look like. We call this scenario a *complex transactional* environment.

The key challenge for clients is that each of these issues or constraints does not exist in isolation. How one party assesses the meaning (or risk profile) of a specific constraint, and the decisions made to manage such constraints, will affect or be linked to how one or other issues constraints are resolved or decided. As a simple illustration, the allocation of the risk of a contingent event to one party may change the counterparty's valuation of the transaction. This may then change the other party's assessment of how other rights or risks in the transaction are allocated. We call each of these individual issues a "micro" decision to be made by the client. However, a client's choice on a micro decision—perhaps based on advice and recommendations of her lawyer—may or will affect other elements or constraints in the transaction.

First, the choice made in resolving one micro decision (*e.g.*, the scope of a party's right to exit the contractual relationship) affects how the parties view a number of other elements or micro decisions in the transaction. It is therefore difficult for the parties to resolve the exit right issue in isolation; the parties will need to confront a number of other issue and risks that the exit right triggers.

Second, it is difficult to separate "legal" and "business" issues; business decisions have legal consequences and legal decisions have business consequences. The client's interests and concerns are therefore inter-linked and multi-dimensional. Let's take an example of a prospective investment by an investor in a start-up company, and they are negotiating the terms of the investment. The investor is requesting certain input into the management decisions of the company, of which the entrepreneur is resistant. The interpersonal or "trust" challenge in the parties' relationship casts a different risk assessment of the exit right issue (and, therefore, pricing) for the entrepreneur. The design of the contract will need to address that interpersonal risk for the entrepreneur. The client therefore would need assistance in assessing and responding to legal issues that are intertwined with multiple non-legal concerns or, *vice versa*, to non-legal issues that may prompt certain legal concerns. In this hypothetical example, there is a combination of issues and concerns for the parties, such as exit strategies, pricing and payment, interpersonal concerns, corporate management rights, implications for future fundraising activities, *etc*.

For a client in a transaction, therefore, the "problem" to be solved is how to get the deal done; it is not necessarily get the "best" deal, but a transaction design that achieves the client's commercial goals, *and* is good enough or sufficiently attractive to induce the counter-parties to agree. There are often multiple and interdependent issues involved, and a transactional lawyer providing recommendations on solving just the legal issues at the expense of, or little or no consideration of how such recommendations affect, the other deal issues adds little "value" to clients. Crafting an iron-clad contractual document, but which fails to achieve agreement of the contractual parties, does not add benefit to clients. Lawyers who merely identify—and even manage—legal risks without regard to the other, non-legal elements in a transaction are sometimes considered "deal killers".

As far as we are aware, to date, there is to date no conceptual framework about problem-solving *in a transactional context* offered by either law schools or practitioners. To create or *accelerate* expertise development for problem-solving in complex transactional environments, lawyers would need to create or borrow models. But from what and from where would that theory come from?

That theory would look something like the Framework for Transactional Lawyering (**Framework**), which is built upon the initial work by transactional economists.[25] The Framework is a set of heuristic tools to understand and assess the positions and interests of contractual parties in a transaction. The Framework consists of ten elements, and guides the transactional lawyer to explore possible methodologies and general schemas for analysing and making more informed contractual *design choices*. The intention here is not to explore in detail the different elements of the Framework, but to illustrate how a tool to train lawyers in problem-solving skills for "wicked" problems can be *constructed*.

[25] See generally Trang (2019).

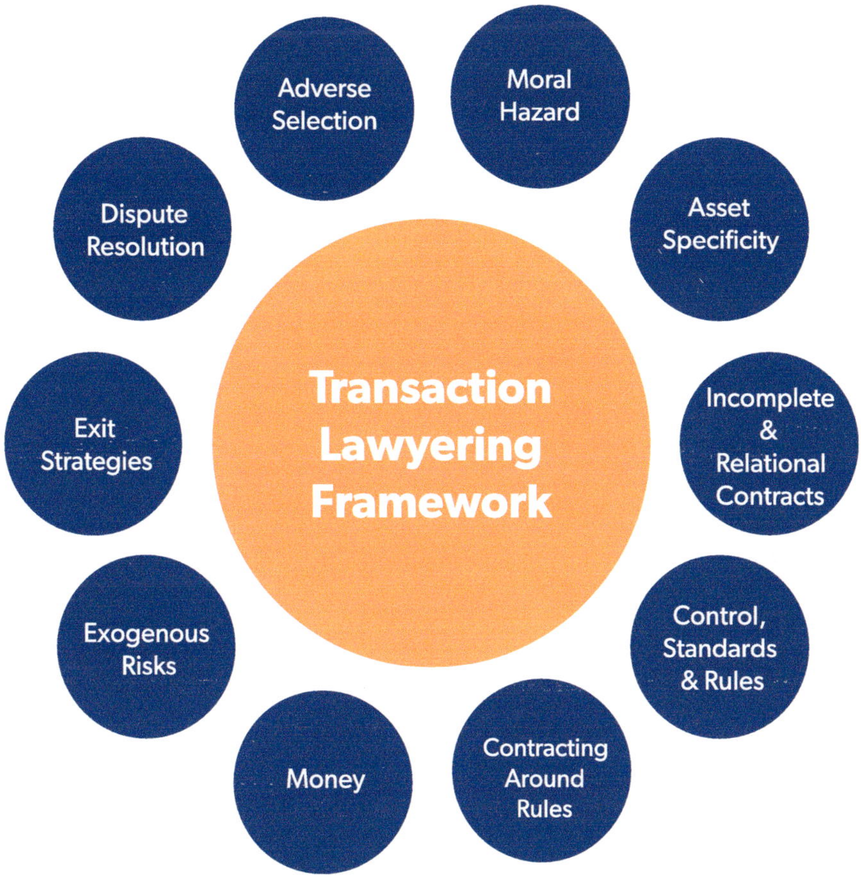

Mechanically, the Framework leverages principles of law, transactional economics, and commercial principles. Under its ten elements, the Framework translates legal, business and interpersonal issues into the domains of economics and, at times, psychology, and maps the likely results and consequences in those domains. This then enables the transactional lawyer to assess the connections among a set of issues *and* potential combinations of such decisions to be made by the client. The Framework provides the structure to examine a series of decisions on a systemic or interconnected basis. Based on that assessment, the lawyer translates the resulting conclusions back to the world of law in order to advise the client on possible contractual designs for the transaction.

The Framework essentially operates as a *simulation model* from which a transactional lawyer derives and extracts insight or judgment on relevant commercial *and* legal issues. The transactional lawyer can collect the relevant "data" or information on each of the relevant components in the deal—*e.g.*, the nature of the adverse selection problem, the scope of the moral hazard problem, the economics of the asset specificity issue (if any), the client's wishes on exit strategies, which areas of the contractual arrangements are "incomplete", the level of trust among the parties, *etc*. She can then feed that data through the Framework to understand the scope of the areas of concerns and gaps that act as key barriers to the deal, as well as how those areas are interlinked. The model then generates an initial view of possible responses by her client to those gaps, as well as potential responses from the counterparty to those initial responses. Finally, the lawyer will incorporate all of that data to construct various potential options of deal architecture with which to consult with and advise her client.

The Framework does not stop at providing a structure for lawyers to navigate the analysis of how various deal elements are linked together; it also offers a set of possible design responses to address those elements, which are designed to minimise gaps and align incentives among contractual parties. The Framework supplies an architecture of possible solution patterns to each of those problems or gaps, and maps how those patterns are related to other problem schemas in that transactional environment.

Framed differently, the Framework operates as a set of "shorthand algorithms" to guide lawyers in decision-making or help their clients make better decisions in unkind environments. While seemingly formulaic, the Framework does not necessarily generate one single correct answer. Instead, the Framework helps the transactional lawyer navigate and parse the decisions that may be made by the client and the counterparties, by setting out a matrix of possibilities and providing a more accurate assessment of the consequences of those decisions. The Framework, in short, provides a more informed set of choices for the contractual parties to make the final decision to complete the transaction.

The Framework does not necessarily provide definitive answers for an ideal contract structure for a particular transaction. It operates as a *roadmap* for a lawyer to navigate issues in a complex transactional environment, by providing the tools for a transactional lawyer to better understand: (a) the commercial elements unique to that deal and (b) potential pitfalls in contractual design *choices*. This pattern- or algorithm-based approach guides a lawyer to formulate a holistic or systemic view of the various issues or constraints to getting the deal done. As a result, the Framework facilitates better recommendations and ultimately more informed decision-making by clients on transactional issues, legal and non-legal.

Using the Framework does not mean that the lawyer would or should abdicate her role in providing sound legal analysis or playing a strong risk management role for her client—solving "kind" problems. A deal architect still needs to be a good legal technician in identifying and managing legal risks, or eventually translating or drafting the commercial agreements into written documents. Those are important skills, but only a portion of the set of skills that the lawyer will need to marshal in advising her clients on how to complete a transaction. What the Framework suggests, however, is that such legal or risk management role should not be a dominant aspect of every single engagement. A transactional lawyer will exercise such legal analytical role as part of the process and will discuss the legal risks with the clients at the appropriate time, but an effective transactional lawyer does not *lead* with the legal analysis, unless the circumstances so dictate.

The Framework departs from ingrained patterns of thinking about talent development, which relies primarily on natural talent and experience; it does so through *modelling transactional complexity*. As the Framework is industry agnostic, lawyers learn the core foundations of exchanges which enables them to sidestep the "cognitive entrenchment" found in the pedagogy of training lawyers in specific verticals (e.g., licensing, M&A, lending agreements, etc.).

The Framework also allows a lawyer to leapfrog the traditional learning process by defining upfront *patterns* that can be tested and refined by the lawyer over the course of her career. Applying the Framework allows less experienced or less naturally-skilled lawyers to gain more quickly the *structured* knowledge critical to gaining expertise, by organising complex transactional environments and identifying the decisions or combinations of decisions to be made by clients. By seeing the relevant connections, lawyers will be able to more accurately assess the impact of a single position or issue against the overall architecture and strategic goals of the clients and counterparties This tool, in combination with experience, will contribute to a lawyer's development and exercise of good "judgment" when advising her client about when and what to fight for in order to close the deal at the client's acceptable level of both commercial gains and risk.

The overall impact of the Framework is that lawyers will (a) learn more quickly patterns that can be applied to different, new or "wicked" contexts and (b) make better recommendations on discrete legal, as well as overall strategic, decisions about a transaction. Ultimately, it will help lawyers deliver a service that is prized and valued highly by clients—the ability to think and act strategically in designing a successful transaction.

The Framework creates a real opportunity to teach problem-solving skills in "wicked" transactional environments to a broad swathe of law students and lawyers, not merely to those lucky enough to have access to extended and quality individual mentoring relationships. It also *complements* the current and preferred method of experiential training and learning on the job. By providing a holistic approach to dissect and understand a transaction, expertise creation will no longer depend primarily on years of observing or working on a large number of situations or deals, nor will it rely on one's natural ability to see "the big picture". The Framework will allow transactional lawyers to create and apply complex problem-solving skills earlier in their careers.

By providing a business-based baseline for analysing transactions, the emphasis of the Framework on understanding and catering for clients' business goals positions the lawyer to be perceived as "strategic", "commercial" and "knowing the business". This will enhance her reputation with clients as a "problem solver" with strong commercial acumen and strategic thinking abilities—skills that will augment the lawyer's competitiveness in the professional services market.

8 Conclusion

Lawyers ultimately provide value through problem-solving. Legal expertise is part of the confidence and comfort that clients crave, but does not necessarily drive it. And complex problem-solving requires understanding relationships and the broader context of problems that clients face. This will enable lawyers to couch and frame legal advice that takes into the broader consideration of the clients' problems, which often are not singularly legal in nature. This is true of clients who are trying of close a sales transaction, negotiate a divorce settlement agreement, or a company acquiring another company.

Effective lawyers understand how relationships *and* context (non-legal elements) drive the underlying problems, of which law and legal issues are only one part. That is the connection between law and humanity. Humanity is about *relationships*. Humanity is about *context*. Those who excel at the law understand that *effective* legal services is about deploying legal expertise and advice to help clients "solve" their problems, within each client's unique context and *beyond* the attendant legal issues.

The profession has long understood that lawyers need to develop the higher cognitive skills examined here, including problem-solving skills in complex and unkind environments. Indeed, developing such skills is even more critical today as technology and machine learning threaten to take over more repeatable, even if complicated, tasks performed by lawyers.

Unfortunately, the Academy and practicing profession have not demonstrated rigor in deconstructing those skills necessary to create a *blueprint* of the content and pedagogy to help lawyers develop those skills. To begin crafting that blueprint, I've offered a set of lenses first to understand the two key problem-solving paradigms that lawyers face—"kind" and "wicked". The characteristics of each problem-solving taxonomy offer significant insight not only about potential changes to both law school and law firm training pedagogy, but a valuable tool for each lawyer to think about her own professional development.

I've also presented the Transactional Lawyering Framework as an *example* of what a set of heuristics may look like in helping lawyers develop the problem-solving skills long-identified as key requirements for effective lawyering, both by bar associations and, more importantly, by clients. I'm confident that similar frameworks can be developed for other areas of the legal practice.

The education and training in law schools and the practising profession need to go beyond developing technical legal skills and legal specialization. This is not a call to jettison traditional law school pedagogy; rather, it is a call to acknowledge and assess its *incompleteness,* and to make adjustments to fill the gaps and enhance its strengths. And that requires all of us to commit to create "sustained intellectual work at the *intersection* of theory and practice to bring to the surface the *structures* that underlie expert practice and to articulate them into frameworks that are useful for teaching".[26]

[26] Kruse (2013), p. 29 (emphasis added).

Liquid Legal Waves to Other Chapters, Written by the Editors

One complexity that comes with the disruptive change of digitalization is *speed*. *Duc* rightfully points out that we must be focused and consistent in developing existing talent to meet the new demands of the legal services market and the clients. At the same time, *Matthias* describes the need for rethinking the onboarding of *"Entry-Level Professionals and the Digital Transformation of Legal Services"*, as traditional experiential learning opportunities vanish by means of automation and legal tech.

Duc also concludes that the ability of complex problem-solving will remain the distinctly human factor in lawyering. It is fueled by human creativity. *Barbara* in her chapter *"Of Mice and Lawyers"* drastically shows that creativity might be of fundamental importance for lawyers to 'survive' (and there might be a literal meaning to this).

The humanization of legal talent development is not just desirable; it's required for the effectiveness of lawyering at scale, states *Duc*. In the following chapter, *Liam*, *John* and *Joyce* will explain the concept of *"The Elevated Workplace"*, an environment that creates a self-aware and more robust and humane organization which ultimately allows for a true meeting of the minds with the client.

References

Binder D, Bergman P, Price S (1991) Lawyers as counselors: a client-centered approach. West Pub Co, p 3

Conn C, Mclean R (2018) Bulletproof problem solving

Dane E (2010) Reconsidering the trade-off between expertise and flexibility. Acad Manag Rev 35(4):579–603

Epstein E (2019) Range: how generalists triumph in a specialized world

Ewenstein B, Hancock B, Komm A (2016) Ahead of the curve; the future of performance management

Gilson R (1984) Value creation by business lawyers: legal skills and asset pricing. Yale Law J 94: 239

Hogarth R (2001) Educating intuition. Chicago University Press

Jones M (1995) The thinker's toolkit

Kosuri P (2015) Beyond Gilson: the art of business lawyering. Lewis Clark Law Rev 19:464

Krieger SH (2004) Domain knowledge and the teaching of creative legal problem solving. Clin Law Rev 11:149

Kruse K (2013) Legal education and professional skills: myths and misconceptions about theory and practice. McGeorge Law Rev 45:7
Neumann RK Jr (2013) Transactional lawyering skills. Wolters Kluwer Law and Business, p 55
Schön DA (1995) Educating the reflective legal practitioner. Clin Law Rev 2:231
Susskind R (2009) The end of lawyers. Oxford University Press
Trang D (2019) The architecture of deals: strategies for transactional lawyering. Academy Publishing, Singapore

Duc V. Trang Splitting his time between London, Singapore, San Diego, Duc advises in-house legal departments and law firms on the design and implementation of transformation projects to achieve sustainable strategic value and profitable growth. Duc's key areas of advisory expertise include the business of law, organizational design and human capital strategy. Duc brings a unique combination of experience as general counsel, executive coach, global law firm attorney, author, business leader, educator, and consultant.

Duc also provides executive coaching to general counsel, senior counsels, and law firm partners and associates on developing leadership skills and enhancing performance.

Duc founded Landon Advisory Services, which provides transactional advisory services as well as strategy and human capital consulting. Duc has worked in the United States, Asia, Europe and the Middle East. He recently published the highly acclaimed book, *Architecture of Deals: Strategies of Transactional Lawyering*, which focuses on innovation in legal education and training.

Previously, Duc was with Motorola Solutions, Inc., where he held several senior executive positions, including general counsel for Asia Pacific & Middle East regions; global general counsel of Motorola's Solutions & Services division; and country manager for Vietnam. Before Motorola, he was a senior attorney at IBM, Inc. Prior to his in-house career, Duc was in private practice in California with DLA Piper (formerly Gray Cary), specializing in corporate finance in the technology sector. He also worked at White & Case LLP in Hanoi, Ho Chi Minh City and Bangkok. Duc started his career as the executive director of the Constitutional & Legislative Policy Institute (Soros Foundation/Open Society Institute) in Budapest, Hungary, designing law reform projects in Eastern Europe and the former Soviet Union. He also has served as an adjunct professor of law at the National University of Singapore and Central European University.

Duc is a graduate of Columbia University School of Law (J.D.) and of the University of California, Berkeley (B.A).

The Elevated Workplace

Liam Brown, John Croft, and Joyce Thorne

Contents

Abstract

Starting with the dawn of the Industrial Revolution, a series of evolutions have profoundly transformed work and the workplace over the past three centuries. Presently, yet another shift is underway: the digitalisation of work. With it, a new type of entity, *the self-aware organisation*, has come into existence. With it comes the possibility of a more humanised work environment: the elevated

Liam Brown is Founder, Chairman and CEO, Elevate.

John Croft is President and Co-Founder of Elevate.

Joyce Thorne is Vice President, People, and Co-Founder at Elevate.

L. Brown (✉) · J. Croft · J. Thorne
Los Angeles, CA, USA
e-mail: liam.brown@elevateservices.com; john.croft@elevateservices.com; joyce.thorne@elevateservices.com

K. Jacob et al. (eds.), *Liquid Legal – Humanization and the Law*, Law for Professionals, https://doi.org/10.1007/978-3-031-14240-6_15

workplace. The elevated workplace meets a broad range of human needs and, in doing so, represents the future of work.

1 Introduction: *Laboro, ergo sum*[1]

Paid work has become, for most adults, the nexus of their existence. Assuming an 8-hour workday, a five-day workweek, and eight hours of sleep per night, people would spend roughly one-third of their waking hours working. For those working in the legal sector, the portion is typically higher: longer workdays are the norm, with lawyers working an average of 53 h per week[2] (and 20% of billable-hour attorneys working up to 80 h per week.)[3] Add in a typical commute,[4] and a lawyer can easily devote 50% of their life to work.

The idea that work is life can be understood in another sense: beyond the portion of time spent working, work remains indispensable to obtaining sustenance and shelter for oneself and one's family—even in developed societies with robust social welfare programmes.[5] Simply put, the ability to find and keep a job is critical to survival.

And beyond the relationship between work and our most basic needs, work is crucial for our psychological health, providing structure and routine. For most individuals, work is a primary source of social existence. Moreover, work offers a sense of identity, perhaps more so than any other human activity. [6]

It is in this context that discussion of The Elevated Workplace occurs. Later in this chapter, we delve into detail about such a workplace and describe its components. For now, it is enough to say that an elevated workplace is one that,

---

[1] "[O]ur social structures. . .offer only one option, to find and keep a job. On this depends my dignity as an individual, my place in society and my ability to survive." Sweeney (1985), p. 201. Available at https://www.jstor.org/stable/30090650. (quoting "Unemployed Woman", *Resources* magazine, Winter 1983).

[2] *Bloomberg Law's 2021 Attorney Workload and Hours Survey*. Available at https://aboutblaw.com/Xuv?utm_source=ANT&utm_medium=ANP.

[3] *Id.*

[4] In 2019, U.S. workers reported spending an average of 49 min per workday commuting, with 33% indicating their commute exceeded one hour. *See* Work and Workplace (2019). Gallup, Inc. Available at https://news.gallup.com/poll/1720/work-work-place.aspx.

[5] *See, e.g.*, Picchi A (2019) 40% of Americans only one missed paycheck away from poverty. CBS News. Available at https://www.cbsnews.com/news/40-of-americans-one-step-from-poverty-if-they-miss-a-paycheck/.

[6] *See, e.g.*, Rohrlich (1980) ("Nothing else with which we associate ourselves can give us the sense of objective identity that work can. . .[it] organizes, routinizes and structures our lives. It allows for the appropriate outlet of competitive strivings. It keeps us sane.").

by design and in its operation, strives to meet a robust range of human needs, from basic to advanced.[7]

2 The Practical Virtues of the Elevated Workplace

The elevated workplace is not an expression of benevolence or a matter of being charitable. Rather, it is good business; it confers multiple competitive advantages for the organisation that establishes and maintains such a workplace.

Research in various sectors indicates four key areas positively impacted by improvements to workplaces and the work environment: productivity, innovation, recruiting/retention, and customer relations. For example, contrary to the belief that higher pay spurs workers become lazy,[8] it seems that increased wages prompt a rise in productivity that exceeds the raise in pay.[9] Likewise, it appears that workplaces that foster employee well-being produce greater innovation.[10] Perhaps least surprisingly, elevated workplaces lead to higher quality job applicants, a higher calibre of employees, less turnover, and lower absenteeism. Finally, an elevated workplace fosters better customer relations[11] because the internal operations of such a workplace serve as a powerful template for being responsive to and establishing strong connections with customers. All these factors are advantageous to a company's competitiveness and profitability.

[7] This draws on the paradigm originated by American psychologist Abraham Maslow, who postulated that all humans possess similar needs, spanning more basic ones—i.e., physiological ones (nutritional, environmental, etc.) and ones relating to safety (be it physical, psychological, economic, social, or moral)—all the way to "higher" needs pertaining to esteem and self-actualisation. *See* Maslow (1943), pp. 370–396.

[8] *See, e.g.*, Hegarty S (2020) The boss who put everyone on 70k. BBC News. Available at https://www.bbc.com/news/stories-51332811. ("Two senior. . .employees. . .resigned in protest [over the CEO's unilateral decision to significantly and immediately increase the] the salaries of junior staff. . .and argued that it would make them lazy, and the company uncompetitive. This hasn't happened.").

[9] *See, e.g.*, Osterman (2018), pp. 3–34. *Available at* https://journals.sagepub.com/doi/full/10.1177/0019793917738757.

[10] *See* Hamill L (2019) How Employee Well-Being Drives Innovation At Work, And How Leadership Can Foster It. Forbes. Available at https://www.forbes.com/sites/forbeshumanresourcescouncil/2019/01/16/how-employee-well-being-drives-innovation-at-work-and-how-leadership-can-foster-it/?sh=7074b7211400.

[11] For a discussion of how an elevated workplace provides a foundation for greater responsiveness to customer needs, *see* Allen et al. (2022).

3 The Moral Dimension of the Elevated Workplace

Beyond its business advantages, another dimension to the elevated workplace deserves mention: promoting moral values and ethical behaviour. In an era of socially responsible investing and management, this aspect of the elevated workplace deserves consideration. This is especially true given that no organisation—whether a business or otherwise—is or can be "morally neutral." Ethical and moral behaviour encompasses more than just the activities an organisation performs. It is important to acknowledge that the behaviours that an organisation permits, it implicitly promotes. Thus, it is not just what an organisation does that matters; what it does *not* do matters, too.

This truth has profound real-world consequences. Consider the imperative of compliance with regulations, statutes, and other legal requirements. The leaders of an organisation either permit violations of such legal strictures, or they do not; employees act accordingly. Individuals either attempt to conform to what the law demands, monitor their and their colleagues' conformance, and promote the social norm of conformance—or they do not.

The same is true for considerations like environmentalism and sustainability, economic development, diversity, equitability, and inclusion (DEI). The elevated workplace recognises that its activities have a moral and ethical dimension; moreover, it establishes processes and enforces norms that promote moral and ethical behaviour concerning such matters as human dignity and social harmony.

We will return to the moral aspects of the elevated workplace later in this chapter. Meanwhile, having outlined the business and ethical considerations in elevating the workplace, it is helpful to understand the line of developments that have precipitated the rise of the elevated workplace.

4 The Evolution of Work

It is essential to understand the elevated workplace as a result of a relentless and ongoing evolution of the workplace (Fig. 1). Over the past three centuries, several revolutions in the workplace have occurred. The most significant ones include:

(1) the shift from self-employment as the dominant paradigm of work to the industrial age paradigm of employment by large organisations
(2) the decline of manufacturing jobs and rise of service-oriented industries
(3) the advent of the information age, and
(4) the transition to globalisation.

Each of these shifts has had a profound impact on work—both workplace conditions and the human experience (physical, social, economic, psychological, and otherwise) of work. For the most part, work has become safer and more lucrative.

Perhaps most profoundly, the evolution of the work paradigm has advanced (and, at times, obstructed) values related to human dignity. Consider, for example, the rise

Paradigm/Period	Human Scale	Driving Mechanism	Key Concept
Pre-industrial (prior to 18th century)	Solitary	Hand tools	Individual activity
Industrial (18th–20th centuries)	Massive	Capital intensive-machinery Urbanisation	Economies of scale
Service Economy (mid-20th century)	Localised	Higher education Disposable income	Direct customer contact
Information Age (late 20th century)	Individual	Digital machines	Interaction with data
Globalisation (end of 20th century)	Global	Transportation	Integrated supply-chain
Digital Work (21st C. onward)	Distributed	Networked digital tools	Self-aware organisation

Fig. 1 Workplace paradigms (Source: Elevate)

of labour unions, the implementation of workplace safety regulations and prohibitions on child labour. (One might well also include employer amenability to the entry of women into the workplace *en masse* and racial integration of trades and professions.) Each of these developments reflected a particular conception of what workers (that is, human beings) are entitled to and deserve.

Within the legal sector, the past century has seen a profound transformation in work,[12] particularly in private practice. For decades, the apprenticeship model reigned supreme. There was lockstep career progression, career-long affiliation with a single firm, and firms generating income through retainer agreements. Within the past two generations or so—that is, a span of four or perhaps five decades—a new model of legal work emerged. Thanks to combination of developments—such as the increase in the number of licensed attorneys, the erosion of the industry's taboo against price competition, growing client dissatisfaction with the retainer paradigm— the focus shifted from stability, loyalty, and talent development to economics. Maximising revenue and profits became the goal; productivity (as measured by billable hours) was paramount. Lateral moves—once almost unheard of—became commonplace. Junior lawyers laboured under the pressure of the "up or out" model, with the path to partnership open to only those attorneys able

[12] *See* Coleman I (2021) Is the Legal Profession Experiencing an Existential Crisis? McDermott Chairman Thinks There's a Better Way (Interview of McDermott Will & Emery chairman Ira Coleman). LegalSpeak (podcast). Available at https://www.law.com/2021/08/20/is-the-legal-profession-experiencing-an-existential-crisis-mcdermott-chairman-thinks-theres-a-better-way/.

to generate substantial revenue. The characteristics, for the most part, still describe the industry today.

This paradigm has made many lawyers miserable.[13] Increasingly, law firm leaders are voicing discomfort with the dominant BigLaw workplace paradigm. There is an emerging consciousness among those who lead law organisations that the dominant paradigm is profoundly flawed. This dawning mindset is starting to transform what work looks like within the legal ecosystem.

5 The Rise of the Self-Aware Organisation

In law and beyond, a further evolution of the workplace is underway: the rise of the self-aware organisation. This refers to an organisation in which a wide group of its members (rather than the select few at the top) actively monitor, assess, and share information concerning the organisation's "state"—not merely in terms of productivity, profit and loss, or other traditional "hard" business metrics, but also the organisation's impact on its employees, customers, the community in which it operates, and the greater society in which it exists. The self-aware organisation integrates consideration of the human impact into its analysis of further evolution of the organisation. When considering whether to make changes—deploy new technology, establish new processes, undertake a reorganisation, etc.—those who control and direct the organisation attempt to think through all the ramifications of such changes, including the psychological impact on members of the organisation. Indeed, an entire field—change management—now exists to optimise any attempt to modify how work is done (tools, staffing, processes, etc.) at an organisation.

It is no surprise that the dawn of the self-aware organisation's age coincides with the start, roughly six decades ago, of the era of digitalisation of work (especially in the legal field). There are three components of this era: digital tools (AI, collaboration tools, the cloud, etc.); digital working (including distributed organisations and 24 × 7 operations, along with a focus on the use of information); and digital workers (individuals with knowledge and proficiency across multiple disciplines). In combination, these three components facilitate and create a demand for a new type of organisation: one that, on an ongoing basis, attempts to optimise its operations not solely in terms of business performance but also worker experience. The digitalisation of work has provided the means (e.g., collaborative technologies, video conferencing, etc.) for the self-aware organisation to exist and operate. At the same time, the advent of digital work has generated demands from digital

[13] *See, e.g.*, 2021 Q1 Attorney Workload & Hours Survey. Available at https://aboutblaw.com/Ynv (reporting that 42.2% of lawyers surveyed were "unsatisfied" or "neutral" with respect to job satisfaction); Strathausen et al. (2020). Available at https://www.liquid-legal-institute.com/wp-content/uploads/2021/01/LLI-LawyerWellBeing-Survey-Findings-1.pdf. Krill et al. (2016), p. 46 (finding nearly 25% of lawyers at private firms surveyed reported problems with alcohol use and that "attorneys working in private firms experience some of the highest levels of problematic alcohol use compared with other work environments.").

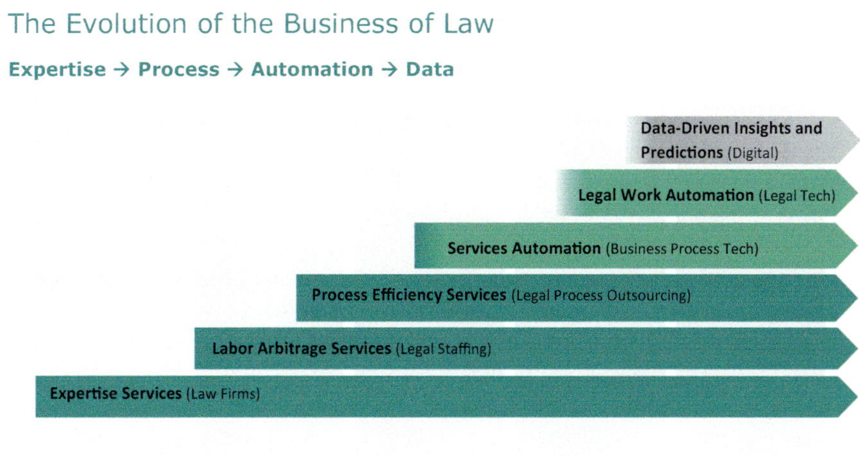

Fig. 2 The impact of digitisation on the business of law (Source: Elevate)

workers, among them legal professionals, that their employers take a holistic approach to employees' needs.

Those demands are certain to intensify in the legal sector as digitisation continues to drive profound change in the legal ecosystem. Even before the COVID-19 pandemic, digital communications technology spurred the widespread use of remote labour. Other technology has facilitated a revolution in legal operations. The digital automation of services and legal work is upon us, and artificial intelligence, machine learning, natural language processing, and other advanced technologies will further evolve the industry (Fig. 2).

A paradox emerges. Presumably, the leaders of every organisation seek for it to be as good (however defined) as possible. Moreover, increasing numbers of workers are articulating the deficiencies of the organisations at which they work. And the tools now exist to radically improve the operations of and experience at modern organisations. Yet, the overwhelming majority of organisations are not "elevated"—that is, they are neither organised (nor do they operate) so as to meet a robust range of critical human needs, from basic to advanced.

If self-awareness is a necessary precursor to improvement, how can we explain why so many leaders of organisations seemingly fail to perceive that there is room for further improvement? What blocks them from developing the necessary self-awareness to transform the organisations they lead?

6 Impediments to Progress

The most consequential barrier to an organisation becoming self-aware is its culture. If, in the words attributed to management expert Peter Drucker, "culture eats strategy for breakfast,"[14] it comes as no surprise that culture can constrain leaders at all levels of an organisations. Perhaps most significantly, culture may limit a leader's imagination as to the possibility of an elevated workplace. Moreover, culture may leave a leader unable to accurately assess the need for improvement in their organisation.

For example, some leaders view work as inevitably involving unappealing aspects. According to this school of thought, life is hard, and work is part of life; *ergo*, work is hard. Any reform of the workplace to make it more hospitable or humane flies in the face of the foundational tenet of this worldview that work is inherently disagreeable. Certain that work is inescapably arduous, management becomes indifferent to the shortcomings of the workplace experience and dismissive of calls to reimagine the workplace.

Of course, such a stance ignores the fact that toil and enjoyment are not mutually exclusive. It also wholly discounts the growing evidence, referenced at the outset of this chapter, that improvements to the working environment confer several significant benefits to the organisation that makes those improvements.

A related viewpoint, decidedly more cynical, is that because work is inescapably irritating, workers seek to avoid its demands. Under this view, whatever heightens worker satisfaction is suspect. A job is to be endured, not enjoyed, and therefore the workplace must be demanding, lest workers slack off. This sort of "spare the rod, spoil the child" ideology conceives of work environments as inherently zero-sum: whatever improves working conditions must detract from the organisation's effectiveness (productivity, profitability, etc.). Management becomes actively hostile not merely to any workplace reform but any criticism of the status quo. Sadly, this approach remains entrenched in many industries, a tragic situation given all that we know about the merits of an elevated workplace.

The third cultural constraint arises in organisations that, ironically, have a degree of self-awareness. Leadership learns of worker discontent and works to address it. Workers respond favourably, and leadership pats itself on the back. Complacency ensues, and whatever problems that remain go unaddressed.

An extreme version of this situation occurs in organisations that pride themselves on the superiority of their work environment and workplace culture. Loyalty and conformity become unstated virtues; management views those who raise concerns or have grievances as malcontents rather than messengers communicating that there is room for further improvement. Worker cynicism and resentment grow as the gap widens between the reality of the work environment and management's

---

[14]It appears unlikely that Drucker coined the phrase. *See* Culture Eats Strategy for Breakfast (documenting the use in print of the phrase by other individuals well before the earliest attribution of the phrase to Drucker). Quote Investigator. Available at https://quoteinvestigator.com/2017/05/23/culture-eats/.

self-congratulatory perceptions. Typically, this trajectory continues until a crisis exposes the discrepancy between the actual situation and management's rosy-eyed view of things.

The self-aware organisation succeeds in avoiding these pitfalls because it establishes and continually works to maintain a culture of introspection, humility, and accountability. Leadership understands that although perfection is unattainable, there is always room for improvement. Moreover, the organisation's leaders understand that work and human satisfaction are not mutually exclusive. Put another way, these leaders are capable of imagining a workplace that better meets human needs. What, then, are those needs?

7 Characteristics of an Elevated Workplace

Worker needs are, simply put, human needs. That leads us to perhaps the most well-known attempt at a comprehensive catalogue of human needs, undertaken by American psychologist Abraham Maslow in his landmark 1943 article, "A theory of human motivation." In the piece, Maslow described a "hierarchy of needs" ranging from basic psychological needs to complex ones related to self-esteem and self-actualisation.[15] Maslow's Hierarchy of Needs has since been subject to a range of criticisms.[16] Yet, it remains a fixture in discussions about universal human needs[17] and continues to serve a practical purpose as a framework for discussing them.[18]

Safety Drawing on Maslow, the most basic needs relevant to the workplace are the same as those that are most important outside of it: the need for safety. COVID-19 has underscored the degree to which physical safety is a crucial requirement for any humane workplace. At a minimum, a worker ought to expect to return home from work alive, physically intact, and uninjured.

But the workplace must provide psychological safety as well. An exhaustive discussion of the elements constituting psychological safety is beyond the scope of this chapter. However, several of its components are readily identifiable. Psychological safety entails more than just being free from fear; it also involves a sense of reassurance. Accordingly, in the elevated workplace, psychological safety goes

[15] *See* Maslow (1943), pp. 370–396.

[16] *See, e.g.*, Symposium: Revisiting Maslow: Human Needs in the 21st Century. Society 6/2017 (articles by Greenfeld L, Etzioni A, and Kenrick D).

[17] Abulof U (2017) Why We Need Maslow in the Twenty-First Century. Society. Available at https://link.springer.com/article/10.1007%2Fs12115-017-0198-6.

[18] Villarica H (2011) Maslow 2.0: A New and Improved Recipe for Happiness. The Atlantic. Available at https://www.theatlantic.com/health/archive/2011/08/maslow-20-a-new-and-improved-recipe-for-happiness/243486/.

Fig. 3 The foundations of psychological reassurance (Source: Elevate)

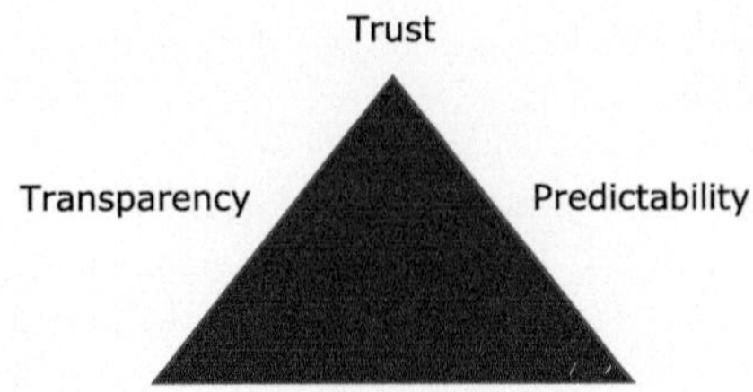

beyond preventing humiliation or retaliation; it also includes nurturing and encouraging workers.

This requires establishing trust, maintaining transparency, and ensuring predictability. Building trust requires a range of actions and norms that instil in employees a belief that an organisation is reliably unthreatening.[19] Transparency means sharing information and demonstrating openness and consistency in decision-making processes. Predictability entails acting the same in similar situations, consistent with well-understood principles of behaviour.[20]

The trust-transparency-predictability triad (Fig. 3) is a prerequisite for members of a workplace to be willing to make themselves vulnerable—that is, to take risks in sharing thoughts and ideas in the face of the possibility of rebuke or rejection.[21] To some, the idea of encouraging employees to be vulnerable may seem weird, foolish, or self-indulgent, or at least irrelevant to improving an organisation's performance. Yet, innovation requires vulnerability and being willing to risk failure; "playing it safe" precludes achieving impactful advances, whatever the field.[22] Moreover, supporting vulnerability reduces organisational risk because it gives room for members of an organisation to voice concerns or bring up "uncomfortable truths" that, left unarticulated, may come to haunt the organisation. Finally, allowing for vulnerability reinforces employees' sense of safety, spurring them to commit to an organisation's mission and goals more fully.

Belonging Once a workplace adequately addresses safety considerations, other, more complex needs come to the fore. Among them is the need to experience a sense of connectedness with colleagues. A shared sense of belonging is the basis of social cohesion that enables collaboration and effective teamwork.[23] Thus, the

[19] O'Hara C (2014) Proven Ways to Earn Your Employees' Trust. Harvard Bus. Rev. *Available at* https://hbr.org/2014/06/proven-ways-to-earn-your-employees-trust.

[20] *See, e.g.,* Stevenson HH, Moldoveanu M (2005) The Power of Predictability. Harvard Bus. Rev. Available at https://hbr.org/1995/07/the-power-of-predictability.

[21] *See, e.g.,* Brown (2018).

[22] "If you're always playing it safe and you're not failing there's a very high probability you are not doing anything particularly important." Scully J (2018) *quoted in* General Magic: The Movie. Available at https://subslikescript.com/movie/General_Magic-6849786.

[23] Carr E et al. (2019) The Value of Belonging at Work. Harvard Bus. Rev. Available at https://hbr.org/2019/12/the-value-of-belonging-at-work.

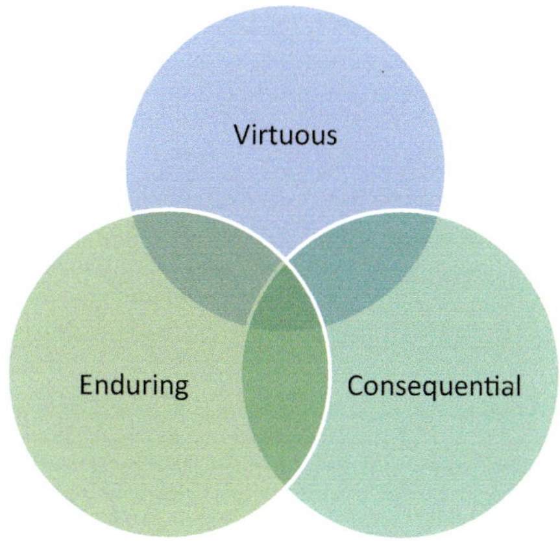

Fig. 4 The components of fulfilling work (Source: Elevate)

elevated workplace is one in which the leadership models collegiality and fosters a sense of community.

Esteem Beyond social needs, humans aspire to feel competent, creative, and accomplished. Fostering an employee's esteem needs means more than providing the opportunity for that employee to complete work. The nature of the work is crucial. It must not be menial; instead, it must engage an individual's skills and intellect. It should be challenging yet achievable.[24] It should contribute to an individual further enhancing their abilities or developing new ones. And it should allow an individual to bring their creativity to bear and offer them the chance to innovate. Accordingly, the elevated workplace operates to create situations in which individuals use their highest faculties to engage with the task at hand.

Fulfilment In addition to needing to feel self-confident and capable, humans seek a sense of purpose and meaning. Ideally, our work resonates with our moral precepts and sense of ethics, such as respect for human dignity, environmental concern, and support for diversity, equitability, and inclusion. The elevated workplace offers individuals the opportunity to believe in what they are doing, which is to say, to think and feel that they are engaged with their colleagues in something virtuous, enduring, and consequential (Fig. 4).

8 The Four Pillars of the Elevated Workplace

Having identified the needs an elevated workplace must meet, the question becomes, how to meet those needs? Answering that question begins with examining four critical aspects of organisations: vision, mission, values, and principles (Fig. 5). In the elevated workplace, each of these will have to align with human needs.

[24] *See* Csikszentmihalyi (1990).

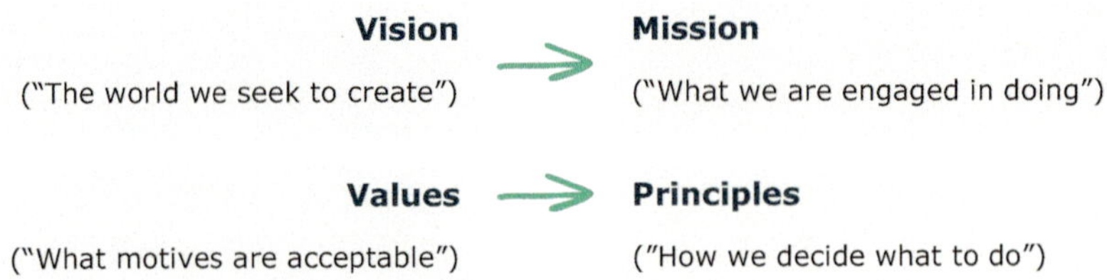

Fig. 5 The four pillars of the elevated workplace (Source: Elevate)

Vision The notion that an organisation must have a "vision" has become a cliché. Nevertheless, whether articulated or not, every organisation has some sort of end-state it seeks to achieve. By clarifying an organisation's fundamental goal, its leaders provide colleagues with a way to understand the purpose of the work they are engaged in and give them a guide for assessing the utility of a given task or project.

Mission If an organisational vision describes the destination that the organisation seeks to reach, the mission defines the work that the organisation must do to get to that destination. The terms of a given corporate mission—typically expressed in the oft-derided "mission statement"—clarify what those within the organisation ought to be doing. Well-defined missions breed teamwork and social cohesion because they specify the sorts of activities that people within the organisation ought to be doing (and, by extension, what sort of activity is secondary, tangential, or irrelevant).

Values As members of an organisation execute its mission (to realise the organisation's vision), values serve to focus and direct their activity. Values specify what sorts of motives and outcomes are sought and which ones are objectionable or unacceptable. Values help to guide individuals in formulating goals and plans.

Principles Principles are behavioural norms that serve as heuristics that help individuals choose between competing courses of action. Principles operationalise an organisation's values, directing individuals in the absence of explicit instructions from managers.

9 Elements of the Elevated Workplace

An elevated workplace must address a wide range of human needs. At the same time, as laid out in the preceding section, every organisation has—whether explicitly stated or not—a vision, mission, values, and principles. What, then, are the implications for the vision, mission, values, and principles of an organisation if it seeks to elevate its workplace? And what are the characteristics of that workplace?

Empathy In the elevated workplace, psychological well-being—including the needs for safety, esteem, and fulfilment—dictate certain values and norms of behaviour. Foremost of these is empathy, the act of identifying with and internalising another person's emotional state.[25] Empathy is the foundation of the elevated workplace because it is the basis for assessing whether efforts to craft a humane work environment are succeeding. The empathetic leader is concerned with understanding what colleagues are going through relative to the full range of needs.

Psychological Safety The elevated workplace is a psychically safe one. The participants in the elevated workplace must do more than demonstrate empathy. They must also show, through word and deed, their commitment to the psychological safety of their colleagues. There are limits on acceptable behaviour and the content and style of communication within the elevated workplace. And there are programs and policies to protect and nurture the psychic safety of those within the organisation. As discussed above, trust, transparency and predictability are paramount. Moreover, as issues related to diversity, equitability, and inclusion increasingly come to the fore, psychological safety requires an awareness of and sensitivity to the experience and perceptions of individuals across considerations such as cultural background, nationality, ethnicity, race, religion, sex, gender, sexual identity, and disability status.

Community The elevated workplace fosters a sense of authentic connection amongst its members. It provides opportunities for its members to connect personally with coworkers, whether through in-person or virtual social events, internal affinity groups, all-hands meetings, or other means. More importantly, leaders enforce a norm of involvement, teamwork, and shared responsibility. They participate in company initiatives. They collaborate with their peers, customers, vendors, those they oversee, and those by whom they are overseen. The elevated leader shares credit for success and in bearing whatever burdens circumstances impose.

Humane Expectations The elevated workplace reflects a realistic set of understandings about the quality and quantity of work its members will perform. This realism is not antithetical to setting ambitious goals and holding individuals responsible for meeting them. Indeed, humans are engaged and energised when presented with challenging work that provides a sense of meaning. But managers must set clear expectations and then assess performance relative to a standard that takes into account the limits of stamina, the demands of family life and personal needs, and the capabilities of a given individual. Indeed, doing so is more critical than ever as the era of the digitisation of work begins to unfold, with its combination

[25] It is important to emphasise the difference between empathy and sympathy. Empathy is a matter of *comprehending and sharing in* the feelings of another person, whereas sympathy concerns *feeling pity* for the circumstances confronting another person. Empathy involves an authentic and sincere effort to grasp another person's emotional experience, rather than an attempt to show compassion.

of always-on communications, globally distributed organisations, work-from-home arrangements, and digital workers increasingly unwilling to tolerate unreasonable employer demands. The leaders of the elevated workplace understand the perils of opaque and unrealistic expectations that breed resentment and unhappiness, thereby precipitating attrition, stifling innovation, and lowering productivity.

Ethical and Moral Standards The elevated workplace integrates moral and ethical considerations into its corporate vision, mission, values, and principles. This does not mean that an organisation must abandon commercial objectives if it is to elevate its workplace. Rather, its leaders must acknowledge that a company's business activities have moral and ethical implications and impacts, and they must then decide which outcomes they consider worthwhile and which ones they deem intolerable. For example, a business may decide that it values diversity, equitability, and inclusion and institute standards, processes, and procedures to advance DEI. Even in matters where existing laws and regulations outlaw particular activity—for example, human trafficking, the use of conflict minerals, and slave and child labour—companies may choose to go further in instituting policies and procedures to combat such ills. Those who lead an elevated workplace are conscious of the moral and ethical dimensions of their organisation's activity and spearhead efforts to demonstrate a meaningful commitment to defending and advancing a set of values.

10 Specific Initiatives

The elements of the elevated workplace are operationalised through various programs and initiatives. It is impossible to formulate a definitive list of such projects; each organisation must fashion its own set, tailored to its history, mission, and circumstances. However, such efforts would likely include:

Structured Development The elevated workplace provides its members with opportunities to grow personally and professionally. It does so based on the belief that individuals seek to hone their skills and acquire new ones. Up-skilling employees benefits an organisation to the extent that, as they develop professionally, those employees do better work. But the concept of the elevated workplace is predicated on a deeper conception of corporate self-interest. Providing training and opportunities for professional development benefit the organisation not merely by increasing the proficiency of employees. Offering those sorts of options enhances an individual's sense of mastery, purpose, growth, and autonomy.

To that end, the elevated workplace puts the ongoing development of its members at the centre of its operations. This is especially appropriate in legal organisations, given the necessity of developing "T-shaped" or "O-shaped" lawyers. The former term refers to a conceptualisation of the legal professional introduced by Amani

Smathers in 2014[26] and which defines the lawyer of the twenty-first century as one with

> deep legal expertise (long vertical bar of the T) but also. . .enough knowledge of and appreciation for other disciplines (shallower horizontal bar of the T) such as technology, business, analytics, and data security to better problem solve and collaborate with professionals with expertise in those areas.[27]

The concept of the O-shaped lawyer originated in 2019 centers on legal professionals developing a blend of mindsets, knowledge and skills, rather than devoting themselves to technical expertise in a particular aspect of the law.[28]

Whatever the industry it is in, an elevated organisation provides a robust range of means for its members to acquire relevant knowledge and new skills. This may include formal mentoring programs, web-based training resources, secondment to other areas of the organisation's operations, and even tuition and paid time-off to complete outside professional education and accreditation programs.

Flexible Work Hours To those with an un-elevated workplace mindset, providing employees flexibility in working hours risks decreased productivity. As a practical matter, of course, this is not necessarily the case. But hesitancy to permit employees latitude in deciding when to start and finish their work reveals a lack of imagination about the workplace. If a company succeeds in inspiring and motivating its employees, strict enforcement of starting and finishing times is beside the point. Workers empowered to modify their work schedules feel respected and are more motivated to work hard.

Expanded Opportunities for Remote Work The COVID-19 pandemic has demonstrated to many organisations the feasibility of remote work arrangements. Consequentially, even as companies reopen centralised workplaces, many workers will seek to continue working remotely. For some, it is a matter of convenience; for others, it may be reassuring to delay returning to an office until a greater level of safety exists. Whatever the case, providing the opportunity for ongoing remote work responds to deeply-felt needs. As discussed previously, the elevated workplace draws strength from its responsiveness to workers' needs.

---

[26] Smathers A (2014) The 21st-Century T-Shaped Lawyer. Law Practice. Available at http://dashboard.mazsystems.com/webreader/31892?page=35.

[27] Smathers A (2014) The T-Shaped Lawyer. Available at http://www.amanismathers.com/technolawgic/2014/2/21/t-shaped-lawyer.

[28] *See* The O Shaped Lawyer Working Group (2020) Transforming the Training & Development of Lawyers. Available at https://static1.squarespace.com/static/5e73266f0be3ab3148757f25/t/5e736114824c026bd67da1e1/1584619820423/O+Shaped+Lawyer+-+In-House+Report+%28February+2020%29.pdf.

Extended Paid Leave for Family or Personal Illness; Greater Disability Pay A profound sense of insecurity arises when an individual lacks confidence that they can meet both work and family obligations. This feeling was especially acute and widespread as COVID took hold. The elevated workplace recognises that work demands may collide with needs related to relationships outside of work. It also seeks to demonstrate leadership's sincere concern with the entirety of each worker's existence. To that end, it provides extended paid leave to enable individuals to maintain and enhance the most vital relationships in their lives. Similarly, the elevated workplace takes into account the vicissitudes of life and provides a level of disability pay sufficient to help ease anxiety over the possibility of becoming unable to work.

360-Degree Feedback In the elevated workplace, there is an ongoing dialogue about optimising the organisation's performance. Unsurprisingly, a component of this is a system of managers regularly reviewing, evaluating, and reporting employee performance (with regular and formal recognition and rewards for exemplary performance and superior achievements). However, the process works both ways in the elevated workplace, with individual employees providing feedback on their managers.

In many organisations, workers, fearing retaliation and retribution, refrain from criticising their boss, however diplomatically. In "performance-centric" organisations, managers bristle at feedback from their reports that casts them in an unfavourable light. In the elevated workplace, things are different. There is a shared belief in the organisation's vision and mission, and mutual respect undergirds interactions among colleagues. In this context, managers welcome feedback because it helps them to optimise their performance in pursuit of a mission and vision in which they ardently believe. And the psychological safety individuals feel in the elevated workplace emboldens them to make themselves vulnerable in providing such feedback. When failures occur—as they inevitably will—after-action assessments focus on remedying processes rather than assigning blame.

Diversity, Equitability and Inclusion Those who create, lead, and direct the elevated workplace recognise that diversity, equitability, and inclusion (DEI) is simultaneously a business, social, and moral imperative. A variety of efforts support that end, including:

- Recruiting individuals from under-represented groups
- Providing diverse individuals with equitable opportunities to secure employment
- Educating individuals throughout the organisation about the need for and benefits of diversity
- Re-engineering existing processes to eliminate the effects of unconscious bias
- Ensuring equal pay for equal work
- Creating affinity groups for members of under-represented groups

- Identifying and accommodating the needs of members of diverse and underrepresented groups
- Instituting anti-bias and anti-sexual harassment training
- Sponsoring organisations that advance DEI

Also, consistent with the value of transparency and demonstrating leadership of DEI issues, the elevated organisation is upfront with its members and the public about its progress on achieving diversity, equitability, and inclusion.

Sustainability As investors increasingly take into account environmental, social, and governance (ESG) in their decision-making, a growing number of individuals conceive of the work environment as including an organisation's interaction with nature. Attempting to slow global warming has become imperative. Accordingly, many people—workers and investors alike—want a workplace that minimises its environmental impact. What that entails varies from industry to industry. At a minimum, it is reasonable to expect that an elevated organisation will take meaningful steps to reduce its production of greenhouse gas, reduce, reuse, and recycle whatever materials it uses in its operations, and responsibly handle whatever waste it produces in its operations.

11 Conclusion: The Humanisation of the Workplace

The reigning workplace paradigm will not predominate forever. Already, in the legal sector, the forces of digitisation are remaking the legal profession. The legal workplace is ripe for transformation. Indeed, to remain competitive—that is, to survive—all law organisations must ultimately adapt to the new era of digital work.

Transformation of organisations within the legal ecosystem requires thoughtfulness, sensitivity, and an expansive understanding of what prompts humans to strive in a common endeavour. Leaders must appreciate that they are responsible for establishing and evolving a social entity whose productivity depends on the degree to which it supports and meets human needs. They must seek to create and operate an elevated workplace.

No two organisations are identical; accordingly, there is no one-size-fits-all approach to building and sustaining an elevated workplace. But all elevated workplaces share the same norms of empathy, safety, community, and humane expectations. Through fidelity to these values and norms, organisations can thrive, simultaneously optimising themselves and providing their members with work that sustains, uplifts, and fulfils them.

Liquid Legal Waves to Other Chapters, Written by the Editors

Liam, *John*, and *Joyce* describe the elements of a work environment that is humane and thereby allows for high performance and meaningful client outcomes through empathy, psychological safety, community, human experience, and ethical and moral standards. This directly ties into what *Dierk* has reminded us in *"The Missing Piece"*: If all we do as leaders in law is talk about effectiveness, efficiency, technology, and ROI, we leave a massive gap in our vision, mission and strategy. Humanism must dominate our transformation.

So, what exactly are we after, then? Is it *"Patagonia: Everything a law firm is not, but could be?"*, following *Emma's* and *Madeleine's* line of thought? Connecting *"The Elevated Workplace"* with their analysis of what might be one of the most humanized corporations is 'out-of-the-box' and thought-provoking, inspiring and edgy.

Beyond improving the workplace, it is contracts that enable us to shape our living conditions and determine legal consequences. And our private autonomy, reflected in the principle of freedom of contract, allows us to do that largely independently of the state. Include digital contracting reality and platform giants, and we face *Carl* and *Michael's* question on *"Contracts and Humanity – How Freedom and Fairness of Contract can be secured in the Digital Age"*.

References

Allen S et al (2022) Elevating the customer experience. In: Humanisation and the law. Springer Nature, Basel, Switzerland

Brown B (2018) Dare to lead. Random House, New York

Csikszentmihalyi M (1990) Flow: the psychology of optimal experience. Harper & Row, New York

Krill PR, Johnson R, Albert L (2016) The prevalence of substance use and other mental health concerns among American attorneys. J Addict Med 10:46

Maslow A (1943) A theory of human motivation. Psychol Rev 50(4):370–396

Osterman P (2018) In search of the high road: meaning and evidence. ILR Rev 71(1):3–34

Rohrlich J (1980) Work and love: the crucial balance. Summit Books, New York

Strathausen R, Schindler D et al (2020) Survey findings on well-being and personal health of legal professionals in times of digital transformation and social change. Liquid Legal Institute

Sweeney J (1985) I work, therefore I am. An Irish Q Rev 74(294):201

Liam Brown Elevate Founder, Chairman and CEO.

Liam helps general counsel and law firm leaders improve effectiveness and efficiency. In 2011 he launched Elevate as a law company to provide consulting, technology, and services to law departments and law firms. Liam was previously the Founder, President, and CEO of Integreon, a global LPO, which he led from a startup in 2001 to annual sales of $150 million by 2011 before selling it to private equity investors. Before Integreon, he was the Founder, President, and COO of a pioneering VC-backed Web 1.0 virtual data room legal tech company, which he sold to a public company in 2001. Liam is a frequent speaker at legal conferences and regularly publishes articles about trends in the legal sector. He is also an active investor in emerging legal technologies and an executive coach for founders of startups.

John Croft is President and Co-Founder of Elevate and one of the leading innovators in the legal services industry, having spent the last 30 years helping law departments and law firms improve their efficiency, quality, and outcomes. In addition to his extensive work with our customers, John is also acutely focused on the law company's culture and diversity and is a frequent speaker and author on the topic. Before co-founding Elevate, John served as President at Integreon, leading business development efforts, managing global client relationships, and growing revenue from $12 million to $150 million in six years. Previously, he was CEO of the financial and legal outsourcing division of ADP Inc. and, before that, European Sales Director for the financial and legal division of St. Ives Plc.

Joyce Thorne is Vice President, People, and Co-Founder at Elevate. A passionate believer in the power that can be unleashed through the engagement and development of professionals, Joyce is dedicated to providing initiatives purpose-built to suit the needs of Elevate's globally dispersed, multi-cultural, hybrid workforce. Joyce leads a global team of HR professionals on five continents who support the "Elevater" (employees and contractors) experience every step of the journey from the first meeting with a recruiter through individual career development, and finally, the positive export of talent to new opportunities.

Before co-founding Elevate in 2011, Joyce worked at Integreon, where she built the company's global learning and development function across multiple solutions and locations. Joyce was based in Mumbai, India, from 2003 until 2007, where she was a member of the global executive management team that grew Integreon from 100 to over 2000 employees.

Contracts and Humanity: How Freedom and Fairness of Contract Can Be Secured in the Digital Age

Carl Renner and Michael Zollner

Contents

Abstract

The beginnings of modern thinking about the function and meaning of contracts for society date back to the sixteenth and seventeenth centuries. For the supporters of capitalism, contracts and private autonomy are primarily an

Carl Renner is Co-Head of Pinsent Masons Vario in Germany, the Flexible Legal Services and Managed Legal Services practice of international law firm Pinsent Masons.

Michael Zollner is Co-Head of Pinsent Masons Vario in Germany, the Flexible Legal Services and Managed Legal Services practice of international law firm Pinsent Masons.

C. Renner
Tutzing, Germany
e-mail: carl.renner@pinsentmasons.com

M. Zollner (✉)
München, Germany
e-mail: michael.zollner@pinsentmasons.com

K. Jacob et al. (eds.), *Liquid Legal – Humanization and the Law*, Law for Professionals, https://doi.org/10.1007/978-3-031-14240-6_16

expression of individual freedom, namely the freedom to be able to regulate things between two private parties without the influence and tutelage of the authorities. Others argue that the ideal of two equally opposing contracting parties is in most cases a pure fiction, with the result that contracts and private autonomy were and are primarily an instrument to reinforce inequality and injustice in capitalist society and thus an instrument of bondage. The question of the meaning and function of contracts arises more than ever in the modern digitized world. Globalization and digitization have led to an exponential increase of the number of contracts concluded every day between consumers and/or private businesses. Similarly, the complexity of most contracts increased significantly.

From a legal sociological and legal ethical point of view, all of this calls for a review of the general status of freedom and fairness of contract in modern society. This article is devoted to this question by examining the priniciples of freedom and fairness of contract as traditional link between contracts as legal instrument and humanity, and by asking how these principles and humanity can be promoted and secured in the digital age.

1 Introduction

As the most important instrument for legal transactions, contracts enable us to shape our living conditions and determine legal consequences in principle independently of the state and public authorities.[1] The role and function of contracts is thereby closely linked to the idea of freedom of contract. Contracts, as voluntary agreements between two or more legal subjects, require a social and political environment that allows individuals to generally decide and act freely in their interest without political or ideological restrictions. Not only free will as an ethical axiom, but the political freedom of the individual are thereby the foundations of private autonomy and freedom of contract.[2] The concept of private autonomy forms, at the same time, one of the central links between contracts as a legal instrument and humanity as an ethical principle. Private autonomy and freedom of contract are both primarily expressions of human freedom and human dignity.[3]

In addition to the principle of freedom of contract, there is a second legal concept that links the idea of humanity with contracts: the principle of fairness of contracts.[4]

[1] Raiser (2015), p. 906.

[2] MüKoBGB/Busche (2018), p. 1729, mn 25.

[3] Wendland (2019), p. 21.

[4] *Ibid.*, p. 105 et seqq.

Freedom of contract and fairness of contract traditionally have an opposing but also complementary relationship.[5] Both principles have a long tradition in European legal systems that goes well beyond the eighteenth and nineteenth centuries, i.e. they arose in times that were radically different from our present times. The speed of technical progress and the fundamental change in economic and social life in the past decades has had a decisive impact on the role and function of contracts for the economy and our private lives. Digitization and globalization have obviously not only resulted in an exponential increase in the number of contracts concluded every day, but also the way most contracts are concluded has changed radically. All this calls for a review of the general status of freedom and fairness of contract, and how humanity in contracting can be promoted and secured in the digital age.

2 The Link Between Humanity and Contracts: Freedom and Fairness of Contract

The principles of freedom and of fairness of contract are two of the most fundamental concepts of modern legal systems, including all continental European legal systems.[6] While both concepts are closely related to the ideas of the Enlightenment and humanism—namely reason, equality, and freedom—as legal concepts, they are at the same time in a certain tension, not least because every form of legislative intervention in favor of contractual justice is at the same time an intervention in contractual freedom.

2.1 Freedom of Contract

Freedom of contract means the right of individuals and organizations to freely define and establish a legal framework between them and determine the contract provisions without (unreasonable) legal restrictions. As a legal principle, freedom of contract has a long tradition that goes back to classical Roman law.[7] However, most recognizably, the age of contractual freedom began in the second half of the nineteenth century when the bourgeoisie, hindered in its commercial development by various kinds of state regulation, demanded that the state should withdraw from the control of the economy.[8] Right from the beginning, the concept of freedom of contract had two different purposes: on the one hand, from a liberalist economic view it fulfilled the prerequisite of guaranteeing an unrestricted exchange of goods, and on the other hand, it offered individual freedom to the people to economically act in their

[5] Wendland describes this relationship as unity in complementarity, *ibid.*, p. 163.

[6] Wendland (2019), p. 3.

[7] MüKoBGB/Busche (2018), p. 1717, mn 5.

[8] *Ibid.*; Wesel (1997), p. 437, mn 282.

personal interests.[9] Today, in most legal systems, including all continental European jurisdictions, freedom of contract is not primarily justified with the economic benefits, but rather the right of the individual to free expression of their personality.[10] In this respect, freedom of contract is first and foremost seen as an expression of private autonomy, i.e. the freedom to be able to constitute and shape private legal relationships according to one's own will, without having to justify personal preferences and motivations.[11]

As important expression of private autonomy, freedom of contract is directly linked to the ideas of human freedom and human dignity.[12] As Wendland points out,[13] due to its roots in the idea of human self-determination, private autonomy, just as human freedom and dignity, does not need any additional justification to be valid. In this sense, private freedom and autonomy can be seen as *children of the Enlightenment*,[14] being based on a very general understanding of freedom and emancipation that encompassed economic, but also political and cultural freedoms in a universal meaning. With the right to conclude contracts independently and freely, individuals are at the same time not only subject to the law, but they also have the opportunity to

---

[9] MüKoBGB/Busche (2018), p. 1718, mn 5; cf. Knieper (2019), p. 195:

> Eine Auffassung betont die "gesellschaftlichen Funktionen der 'Institution' Privatautonomie. (...) Dieser Auffassung, die auf die Funktionalität und Effizienz des Marktes und der Privatautonomie orientiert ist, wird von einer anderen Schule aus der Perspektive des Freiheitsgedankens widersprochen. Nicht auf die Effizienz komme es an, sondern auf die 'Selbstherrlichkeit' des Einzelnen in der 'schöpferischen Gestaltung der Rechtsverhältnisse'. Wer die Funktionalität der Faktor-Allokation in den Vordergrund der Betrachtung der Privatautonomie stellt, habe auf den 'subjektiven Freiheitsgedanken keinen besonderen Wert gelegt', ja er trage dazu bei, 'ein System zu konstruieren, in dem jeder Einzelne in einer Art von sozialem Determinismus der ihm zugewiesenen Rolle entsprechend fungiert – oder richtiger: funktioniert'. In dieser Sicht ist Privatautonomie Ausdruck der Freiheit jedes/jeder Einzelnen, die sie/ihn legitimiert, einem subjektiv bestimmten Willen entsprechend Rechtsgeschäfte zu schließen. Subjektivität lasse sich nicht auf ökonomisches Kalkül reduzieren, sondern umfasse die 'Vielfalt der Affekte, der ästhetischen, ökonomischen, emotionalitätsbezogenen etc. Interessen'. Auf eine Vernunft des Marktes komme es nicht an: "stat pro ratione voluntas".

[10] Schäfer et al. (2020), p. 471; cf. Wendland (2019), p. 20:

> (...) selbstverständlich trägt die privatautonome Gestaltung der Lebensverhältnisse durch die Ausübung der Vertragsfreiheit ganz wesentlich zur freien Entfaltung der Produktivkräfte als Grundbedingung jeder Marktwirtschaft und damit zum ökonomischen und gesellschaftlichen Fortschritt bei. Darin erschöpft sich die Bedeutung der Privatautonomie jedoch nicht. Zweckmäßigkeit und ökonomische Erwägungen sind positive Wirkungen, nicht jedoch Geltungsgrund privatautonomen Handelns. Sie sind die Frucht der freien Entfaltung der Person. In ihr allein findet die Privatautonomie ihre Rechtfertigung (...).

[11] Neuner (2020), p. 9.

[12] Wendland (2019), p. 14.

[13] *Ibid.*, p. 20.

[14] Knieper (2019), p. 194.

actively influence it by shaping legal situations within their subjective powers.[15] However, this can only happen if some general requirements and conditions are fulfilled:

- *Free Will and Self-Determination*: The concept of freedom of contract, as correlated to the recognition of human freedom,[16] presupposes the existence of *freedom* of the acting parties, more precisely: freedom of will and self-determination. In the interests of brevity, discussion as to whether humans can have free will at all (the so-called *determinism* debate[17]) is avoided for the purposes of this analysis. Assuming we can possess something like free will, there is agreement in current legal doctrine that it is this will which is the dominant force for bringing about legal consequences through contracts.[18] In this context, free will is to be distinguished from self-determination.[19] If a party acts with free will which has been influenced, for instance, by threat or coercion, freedom of contract can be regarded as not applying either.[20] That is why most jurisdictions treat contracts made under threat or coercion as voidable or void. By doing so, the legislator links the principle of freedom of contract directly with the principle of fairness of contract.
- *Freedom from state rule and protection through state rule*: A legal system which offers individuals the possibility of regulating legal relationships independently and based on self-determination[21] is thereby at the same time creating an area free from state rule.[22] In a legal system, on the other hand, which does not limit its power to respect the freedom of the individual or leave room for their own will, but which tries to enforce a total coercive order, there is no room for truly private contracts.[23] Insofar, contracts take to a certain extent the place of the law, as already constituted in the French Code Civil of 1804 in Article 1134:

> Les conventions légalement formées tiennent lieu de loi à ceux qui les ont faites.[24]

---

[15] Kunz et al. (2006), p. 2, mn 16.

[16] Wendland (2019), p. 17.

[17] https://de.wikipedia.org/wiki/Determinismus.

[18] Wendland (2019), p. 21.

[19] *Ibid.*, p. 29.

[20] *Ibid.*

[21] Bork (2020), mn 5.

[22] Wendland (2019), p. 14.

[23] Cf Raiser (2015), p. 908

> In einem Herrschaftssystem dagegen, das seine Macht nicht beschränkt, um die Freiheit der Person zu achten und ihr Raum für eigenen Gestaltung zu lassen, sondern dass eine totale Zwangsordnung durchzusetzen versucht, ist kein Platz für Verträge.

[24] Unofficial translation: "Legally formed agreements take the place of law for those who made them."

While the state must give up power in favor of freedom of contract, at the same time it is necessary that the state uses its power to secure the ability of enforcing the individual rights set out in a contract. A legal system based on the concept of freedom of contract must ensure that the individual subjects can make use of the freedom of contract in a substantive sense, i.e., are put in a position to assert their interests in the contract process.[25] Here, as Wendland emphasizes, is the second link between the principle of freedom of contract and fairness of contract. If the parties subordinate their agreement to the law and want to use the authority of law and the enforcement instruments provided by it, private contracts leave the area of the private and enter the normative sphere of law.[26] Consequently, the contracting parties must also accept the framework conditions set by the law, as well as the evaluations implicit in the legal system, as applicable to them.[27]

- *Equality:* For staunch advocates of freedom of contract, it might seem questionable whether equality in the meaning of *equality of arms and power* is to be considered as a basis for freedom of contract. One could argue that in a free society there is hardly ever any actual equality of power, so that the principle of freedom of contract would come to nothing if one were to regard equality of power as a hard criterion for its validity. In fact, there are usually great differences between contracting parties, for instance regarding their economic power, their knowledge, or merely their negotiation skills. Not everyone has equal economic and social power and opportunities. However, since free will and self-determination are the basis for any form of contractual freedom, an imbalance of power might at least lead to a restriction of contractual freedom in situations where the self-determination of one party is significantly affected by the power of the other party. For this reason, at least a certain degree of equality of power is regarded as a prerequisite for freedom of contract in legal doctrine.[28]

[25] MüKoBGB/Busche (2018), p. 1720, mn 7:

> *Eine am Leitbild der Vertragsfreiheit orientierte Rechtsordnung muss mit anderen Worten dafür Sorge tragen, dass die einzelnen Privatrechtssubjekte im materiellen Sinne von der Vertragsfreiheit Gebrauch machen können, also* in die Lage versetzt werden, ihre Interessen im Vertragsprozess zur Geltung zu bringen.

[26] Wendland (2019), p. 27.

[27] The requirement to notarize specific types of contracts (e.g. land purchase agreements), for instance, restricts the freedom of contract in order to protect the contracting parties from themselves; cf. Singer (1995), p. 1134.

[28] Bartholomeyczik (1966), pp. 67, 68:

> Vertragsfreiheit setzt ein gewisses Machtgleichgewicht der Vertragsparteien voraus. (...) Wird die Vertragsfreiheit als Freiheit zur autonomen Gestaltung privater Rechtsverhältnisse, als rechtliche Institution, bejaht, so mißbraucht sie jeder, der mit ihr die Freiheit anderer zur freien Gestaltung ihrer wirtschaftlichen Verhältnisse antastet. Lebt das Institut des Vertrages von der Vertragsfreiheit, so verliert es mit ihr seinen Sinn, so ist jeder Vertrag institutions- und institutswidrig und damit mißbräulich geschlossen, der diesen Sinnzusammenhang aufhebt, weil den Vertragspartnern die Waffengleichheit fehlt.

2.2 Fairness of Contracts

Historically, there have been two different perspectives on the question of what the fairness of contract means. According to a liberal view that emerged in the nineteenth century, the principle of fairness of contract is simply to be equated with the principle of freedom of contract, pointedly summarized by the Latin expression: *"Volenti non fit iniuria"*—no injustice is done to the one who consents.[29]

Today, the prevailing view in most legal systems is that the principle of fairness of contract rather refers to the *content* of a (freely concluded) contract and asks whether it has a sufficient level of fairness, or, more precisely, does not fall under a certain level of unfairness. This does not mean that there is a general right to fair contracts in modern jurisdictions, or that contracts which are unfair are per se be withdrawn from the protection of the legal order. The unjust, unfair contract is generally also protected by our legal systems. Each contracting party always bears the risk of an unfavorable contract. That is the price for the recognition of the legal will of individuals by the legal order. As Busche[30] points out, the contract, as an act of arbitrariness on the part of the parties, does not derive its binding force from the implementation of a supra-individual standard of justice. Self-determined realization of interests always takes place under the influence of motivations, errors, and misjudgments. However, in all modern jurisdictions the legislature intervenes in freely concluded contracts, through supplementary or overriding provisions, if certain deficits in justice or fairness exist that justify protection of one of the contracting parties (or third parties, or the public). The principle of fairness of contracts is expressed in these legislative interventions.

All modern legal system have instruments of substantive content control of contracts based on contractual fairness.[31] In German private law, for instance, Sections 134, 138 and 242 of the German Civil Code (BGB) as well as all consumer protection regulations that are incorporated into the BGB, can be seen as expressions of the principle of fairness of contracts.[32] In addition, there are restrictions on private autonomy in favor of contractual fairness by means of the German regulations on general terms and conditions or social tenancy law, to name just a few further examples.

The main purpose of the principle of fairness of contracts is arguably its function in promoting a peaceful existence.[33] Justice and fairness can be considered the central and fundamental ordering principles of human coexistence.[34] As with

[29]Wendland (2019), p, 1.

[30]MüKoBGB/Busche (2018), p. 1719 et seqq.

[31]Wendland (2019), p. 140.

[32]MüKoBGB/Busche (2018), p. 1719 et seqq.

[33]Wendland (2019), p. 141.

[34]*Ibid.*, p 105:

> Aus rechtsgeschichtlicher und rechtsvergleichende Perspektive gehört es heute zum Gemeingut, dass die Frage nach der Gerechtigkeit zu den Grundfragen des Rechts schlechthin gehört, letztlich die eine Kernfrage des Rechts überhaupt betrifft.

freedom of contract, in addition to the direct relationship of fairness of contracts to human dignity, there is also a justification for fairness of contracts which relates to economic advantages. Schäfer, for example, stresses that it is essential for fair contracts to be concluded without deception, threats, price dictation, monopoly power etc. as they increase the benefit of both parties if the contracting parties act rationally, i.e., contracts are not a zero-sum game in which the advantage of one is always exactly the same as the disadvantage of the other. Rather, in contrast to unproductive zero-sum games, they represent productive games with an added benefit greater than zero and the expectation of a positive benefit for each contracting party upon conclusion of the contract.[35]

The above-mentioned basic requirements for the development of contractual freedom—free will and self-determination, freedom from and protection by state-rule and equality—also play a role in relation to the principle of contractual justice, albeit only indirectly. Contracts that are concluded without free will or under duress naturally have an inherent risk of containing unfair provisions.

3 Freedom and Fairness of Contract in the Digital Age

The function and role of the contract as a *humane* legal instrument are closely linked to social and political developments in the past centuries. These developments include the Enlightenment and liberalization, the various social movements which took place worldwide, as well as globalization and major technological change. Looking at the role and function of contracts from this point of view, the question arises whether the principles of freedom and fairness of contract can still be sufficiently reflected in today's times of digital standard—and mass—contracts, of global tech giants who significantly influence our behavior and who primarily see the individual as influenceable consumer, and in a spiral of economic and social complexity. As much as globalization and the digital economy have brought about radical changes for most industries and the economy in general, digitalization also has a disruptive effect on contracts as legal instrument.

---

[35] Cf Schäfer et al. (2020), p. 472:

> Wesentlich an fairen Verträgen (Täuschung, Drohung, Preisdiktat, Monopolmacht sind ausgeschlossen) ist zunächst einmal, dass sie bei rationalem Verhalten der Vertragsparteien den Nutzen beider Parteien erhöhen. Verträge sind also kein Nullsummenspiel, bei dem der Vorteil des einen immer genau gleich dem Nachteil des anderen ist. Vielmehr stellen sie im Gegensatz zu den unproduktiven Nullsummenspielen produktive Spiele mit einem aufaddierten Nutzen von größer als null sowie der Erwartung eines positiven Nutzens für jede Vertragspartei bei Vertragsabschluss dar. Natürlich kann ein fairer Vertrag sich im Nachhinein als nachteilig für eine oder beide Seiten herausstellen. Das gilt aber deshalb, weil zum Zeitpunkt des Vertragsabschlusses bestimmte Informationen nicht verfügbar und bestimmte Entwicklungen nicht voraussehbar waren, oder weil die Zuweisung bestimmter Risiken Vertragsgegenstand wurde (z. B. beim Aktienkauf oder bei nachhaltiger Unmöglichkeit der Leistung.

3.1 Contracts: An Antiquated Instrument in Modern Society?

One could argue that contracts as legal instruments are facing a kind of crisis in modern society. While on one hand they are arguably more important than ever for a functioning and flowing economy, on the other hand they appear in many ways as an antiquated instrument in the globalized information society, no longer completely suitable for the speed and complexity of modern private and commercial life. To be more precise, it is not so much the contract as an instrument, but rather the technique and methodology of the conclusion of contracts which in many cases appear to be outdated. In the modern business world, individually negotiated written contracts are very often a brake and stumbling block for fast and efficient transactions. They are laboriously negotiated, without effective technological support, only to end up largely disregarded in the contract manager's drawer. Besides, contracts are often concluded without any prior negotiation at all, merely because one of the parties has such superior negotiating power that the other party is simply faced with the choice: Take it or leave it. Finally, a type of contract has established itself, especially in the context of end consumer agreements, that are not read at all by one of the contracting parties. This applies in particular to the millions of purchase-, service- and data protection agreements that are entered into by consumers online every day. These contracts usually involve general terms and conditions, often in small print or otherwise inconveniently presented, generally either never noticed or considered by the contractual partners.

In view of these observations, the question arises to what extent freedom and fairness of contract are accordingly at risk in our modern globalized digital society.

3.2 Major Threats to Freedom of and Fairness of Contract in the Digital Age

As outlined above, freedom and fairness of contract need certain basic conditions to apply, namely (i) a minimum degree of free will and self-determination of the acting parties, (ii) an area free from state rule as well as the guarantee of enforceability of the contract with state help, and (iii) at least a reasonable degree of balance of power between the parties.

There have, of course, always been dangers and limitations to both freedom and fairness of contract, not least due to the tension between these two principles. However, in the age of globalization and digitization, the role and importance of contracts as a legal instrument has in many respects increased and, at the same time, new challenges and threats to contractual freedom and fairness have arisen.

It would go beyond the scope of this article to illuminate all these challenges and threats in detail. However, the following aspects appear to be of relevance:

- *The tendency of the digital economy to monopolies and imbalance of power*: A frequent characteristic of the digital market is that "the winner takes it all", prominently illustrated by the big five tech giants Alphabet (Google), Amazon,

Apple, Meta (Facebook) and Microsoft. According to economists, the main reason for this monopolization tendency is that digital products often have high fixed costs but almost zero marginal costs. This results in increasing economies of scale.[36] A second reason for the monopoly tendency of the modern economy can be seen in globalization. Coming back to the topic of humanity and contracts, the obvious problem is that monopolies are by nature a threat to both freedom and fairness of contract, if and to the extent providers dominating a market use their power to enforce contractual provisions to their unilateral advantage. The legislature has a long history of seeking, through competition law and consumer protection regulations, to prevent monopolists from abusing their economic power. However, given the power of modern international and national tech giants, it is becoming more and more difficult, at least on a national level, to limit their contractual power. Data protection law is a good example of the challenges that international technology companies and their practices pose for contractual justice in the form of consumer protection. Hardly anyone reads the terms of use of social media platforms or mobile providers they are using, let alone understands the details of the terms they have accepted. At the same time, it is often impossible for individual consumers as well as local authorities to check compliance (e.g., where data is actually stored) or to effectively punish violations.

- *Standardization and Contract-Automation:* Linked to the problem of the increasing imbalance of power between contracting parties in the digital society is another phenomenon—namely the tendency towards standardized mass contracts and contract automation. While general terms and conditions and the mass conclusion of contracts in business are not an invention of the digital economy, digitalization has accelerated exponentially the trend towards standardized, non-negotiable contracts and full automation of the contract conclusion process. In most cases, concluding a contract has become a mechanical, algorithmic process in which only a button needs be clicked for the confirmation that a contract text has been read and accepted (albeit it was likely never taken note of by the consenting party). As Busche notes, these developments pose a serious threat to freedom of contract,[37] and consequently also to fairness of contracts. Busche argues that in an economic environment that is increasingly geared

[36] Jung et al. (2016), p. 373:

> Die Digitalisierung begünstigt Szenarien, die zu einer Monopolisierung führen. Hintergrund sind aus ökonomischer Sicht die gegen null tendierenden Grenzkosten digitaler Produkte in Verbindung mit hohen Fixkosten. Es ergeben sich damit steigende Skalenerträge. Die so genannten Big Five des Internets (Apple, Microsoft, Google, Amazon und Facebook) haben sich in den letzten Jahren von produktorientierten Unternehmen zu digitalen Plattform-Unternehmen entwickelt, die in ihren jeweiligen Kompetenzbereichen deutliche Marktführer sind. Die Plattformfunktion selbst ist ebenfalls weitgehend digital und da liegt daher denselben Gesetzen der Skalierbarkeit. Die so entstehenden natürlichen Monopole werden zusätzlich durch Netzwerkeffekte und Standards verstärkt.

[37] MüKoBGB/Busche (2018), p. 1720.

towards the conclusion of standardized contracts, freedom of contract would be threatened with marginalization, and it is questionable whether contract law would in future even be able to perform its intended function under these circumstances. While freedom of contract includes the right to conclude contracts the content of which is unknown, the authors agree with Busche that the mass phenomenon of concluding contracts without reading them renders the idea of freedom of contract as absurd.[38] Even more so since standardization and automation of contracts are only just beginning. Smart contracts and computable contracts are, relatively speaking, still in the starting blocks. In the most extreme form, contracts will in future be concluded without any human involvement in contract negotiation and conclusion. Proponents of such new technologies point to radical savings in transaction costs and corresponding increases in efficiency. However, such developments will inevitably also drive the trend towards the de-humanization of contracts.[39]

- *Manipulation and Behavioral Economics*: Another phenomenon that is indirectly linked to the problem of increasing power imbalance in modern societies is the so-called behavioral economy. There are today increasingly sophisticated ways in which providers tend to influence user and customer decisions. In 2017, the Nobel Prize for Economics was won by one of the most prominent representatives of behavioral economics, Richard Thaler. This is no coincidence, as Knieper notes,[40] pointing out that advertising, influencing and social control have always existed, but have reached an unparalleled level of inescapability today in the digital economy. Given the scientifically sophisticated mechanisms of influencing now being deployed, the question arises whether consumers manipulated by advertising and invisible persuasion still have enough free will for contractual freedom and fairness of contract to apply.
- *The Complexity Challenge of Modern Society*: A further major threat for freedom and fairness of contract in modern society can be seen in the increasing complexity and dynamics of economic and social life. It is a scientifically proven fact that the world is becoming more and more complex,[41] and almost all areas of life are affected by the "spiral of complexity" in which the world finds itself in modern society.[42] In other words: Complexity is our "postmodern destiny".[43] The increasing complexity of everyday life often makes it difficult for consumers, as well as enterprises, to sufficiently assess all circumstances that are of relevance for a contract. In addition, the increasing sophistication of the subjects of contracts has inevitably led to mounting complexity of contract wording itself, as well as of the relevant statutory provisions. These phenomena make it more

[38] *Ibid.*

[39] Knieper (2019), p. 200.

[40] *Ibid.*, p. 199 et seqq.

[41] Davies (1990), p. 37.

[42] Ahlemeyer et al. (1997), p. 8.

[43] *Ibid.*, p. 383.

and more difficult for individuals to keep track of and process all information and criteria of relevance for a contract.

- *Bureaucracy and Over-Regulation*: The above-mentioned challenges and threats justify increased intervention by the legislator in contractual freedom in favor of fairness of contracts. However, there is at the same time the risk that the pendulum swings too far and freedom of contract is overly restricted. This leads back to the classic discussion concerning the necessary degree of regulation by and freedom from state-rule in a society, a topic that would go beyond the scope of this article. However, just as complexity in modern societies increases, so it appears does the problem of over-regulation and bureaucracy in almost all modern jurisdictions - with seemingly naturally more and more cases in which freedom of contract is restricted by superfluous or too far-reaching regulations. It can be assumed that this problem will rather increase in the future.

4 How Freedom and Fairness of Contract Can Be Secured in the Digital Age

Given the above outlined threats and challenges to freedom and fairness of contract in modern society, the question arises whether the instrument of text-based contracts which was developed in the analog era is reaching its limits in today's world, and if so, how contracts as legal instruments can be made future-proof.

As outlined earlier, the central problems with freedom and fairness of contract in modern jurisdictions are that contracts are often concluded (i) in a very standardized way without the contracting party knowing their content at all, and (ii) with a considerable imbalance of power between the parties. If freedom and fairness of contract are to be secured in the future, these aspects must be addressed. The key will be to find ways to compensate for the growing information deficits and arms imbalances between contracting parties and to enable consumers to make informed decisions about the content and conclusion of contracts, even in times of largely automated contract conclusion. Here are some thoughts on how contracts can be made future-proof against this background:

4.1 Rethinking the Technique and Methodology of Contracts

So far, the legislature has tried to meet the challenges outlined above with conventional means and instruments that were largely developed in the analog, pre-digital era, accompanied by legal interventions in the freedom of contract where this appeared necessary (from the legislator's perspective) to secure fairness of contracts. However, as with other social or economic concerns, it is questionable whether we should reply to the challenges of our time by simply sticking to instruments and methods that were developed in the pre-digital world.

What we need is a rethinking of the technology and methodology of contracts and contract law, more adequately considering the ideals of freedom and fairness of contract. Again, it would go beyond the scope of this article to develop and outline a new comprehensive technique and methodology of contracting in the digital age in full detail. However, we suggest that the following two aspects should be considered:

- *Contract Law should be adapted to the Digital Age, with Standard Contract Templates to be developed by the Legislator:* In most modern jurisdictions, contract law is largely based on regulations that were drafted many decades or even centuries ago, far back in the analog world. While these rules have been periodically adapted to new circumstances, they are in most cases still based on essentially pre-digital laws. With a view to the topic of this article, the question arises whether contract law should not be rethought more comprehensively to meet the challenges outlined above. A new comprehensive *contract law for the digital age* should, accordingly, also take up a concept from the German Civil Code and other European Civil Codes that is more than a hundred years old but seem to have been pushed back by the Anglo-American approaches to contract law in the recent decades: The concept of the legislature specifying essential terms of frequently occurring standard contracts abstractly as a standard regulation which can be incorporated, supplemented, or modified by individual contracts. In the German Civil Code, the second book contains provisions on traditional types of contracts such as purchase or rental contracts, but not yet on modern types of contracts such as web-shop terms and conditions, social media terms of use, software license agreements, IT project contracts or—in the B2B world very practice-relevant types of contracts such as—non-disclosure agreements. However, the concept of abstract rules that are pre-formulated for many cases, namely in the form of standard terms applying to the most relevant contract types, has many advantages. If these standard terms—or contract templates—would be freely accessible, they could be assessed and commented by experts and the public independently and serve as orientation and benchmark for fair, transparent agreements and, thereby, at the same time counter existing information deficits and power inequalities. Whilst it was argued above that the use of standard contracts in the form of general terms and conditions often leads to restriction of freedom and fairness of contract, the opposite would arguably be the case if they were drafted and proposed by the legislature, or, alternatively, by non-profit industry organizations. Practical examples such as the recommendations of the German Association of the Automotive Industry (VDA) for purchasing conditions served the goal of balancing out an existing power imbalance between contracting parties (here: suppliers and OEMs or manufacturers in the automotive industry) by means of a largely balanced and fair contractual basis. Legislators should, therefore, consider developing comparable standard contract conditions for the most relevant contract types in the digital age, accompanied by corresponding legal regulations and guidelines.
- *We need to develop Contracts that are both Human- and Machine-Readable:* For the most important contract types, we see great potential with regard to freedom and fairness of contract in the further development of better technologies for the

representation and management of contracts. While in most other disciplines and industries the processing of complex information is largely supported by technology, contracts are generally still concluded today as thousands of years ago, namely as unsorted text, only being fully understandable by (expert) human beings, but not machines. Contract intelligence tools available on the market which are trained based on natural language are reliable to a far lesser degree when it comes to legal language (legalese).[44] Other approaches to achieve machine readability of contracts which rely on so-called formal contract languages never caught on.[45] What is needed, from our perspective, are contract languages that can be read by both humans and machines. A promising approach to achieve this could be the development of so-called *controlled natural contract languages*. The concept of *controlled natural languages* comes from the technical field where it is used to minimize ambiguities and room for interpretation in the documentation of technical processes by specifying certain terms and syntax rules.[46] Controlled natural contract languages would offer a wide range of options (e.g., automatic, cost-effective evaluations of contracts in real time, automated contract negotiation tools) directly or indirectly supporting freedom and fairness of contract. Just the possibility of being able to easily gain transparency about the content of a contract during the entire contract life cycle would be a great benefit in relation to the above-mentioned prerequisites for freedom of contract and contractual fairness.

4.2 Adoption of Concepts for Reducing Complexity from Other Disciplines

In addition to information processing technologies, a look at other disciplines and industries offers further potential for learning how to reduce complexity in contracting. Here are some ideas:

- *Better Contracts with the Help of Linguists and Visualization:* The complexity and relative incomprehensibility of many contracts is largely due to them being linguistically poorly drafted and, for example, containing an unnecessarily large number of redundancies, nesting, long sentences, or references. This topic offers

[44] The reason for this is that there is no uniform, universally valid or standardized contract language, i.e. inaccuracies in the contract language lead to room for interpretation which, according to the current state of the art, requires legal expert knowledge that such tools generally do not have. On the other hand, these tools often lack enough data to optimize their capabilities, since the content of contracts is usually confidential and is, therefore, not available to an unlimited extent for evaluations and machine learning.

[45] In the Anglo-American area in particular, legal tech experts are working for more than two decades on the development of contractual languages which, comparable to a programming language, reproduce contractual rules in a form that is clear and legible for computer programs.

[46] See https://en.wikipedia.org/wiki/Controlled_natural_language.

great potential. Comparatively little scientific work has been conducted on good style in contracts. How can contractual regulations be presented as simply and briefly as possible? How can unnecessary ambiguities be avoided? How can the content of contracts be better visualized? There are experts in this area, such as linguists or maybe even computer linguists, with whom criteria for good contract language and the reduction or measurement of complexity in contracts could be developed.

- *Contract-Fairness-Scores:* Nutri-Scores in the form of traffic light systems for food are used in many countries to show consumers, in an easily understandable way, the content of health-relevant nutrients (such as fats, saturated fatty acids, sugar and salt[47]) in food products. The situation of a consumer who buys food without knowing the exact ingredients of the product is in many aspects comparable to that of an internet-user who concludes a contract online without knowing the exact content of the contract terms. In both cases, the aim is to reduce the complexity of the information into an easily understandable form for the benefit of the consumer, enabling them to make an informed decision. In the case of such a system for contracts, further aspects would of course have to be considered that, due to practical scope limits, will not be discussed here (e.g., the question of what the standard for such a traffic light system could be). However, there seems to be potential in respective *Contract-Fairness-Scores* for consumer contracts developed by consumer organizations or authorities. Apart from the fairness of a contract, as outlined above, the complexity of contracts as quality criteria could potentially also be assessed in a comparable way.
- *Instruction Leaflets and Further Warning Obligations for General Terms & Conditions:* Medicines usually come with an instruction leaflet, goods with dangerous contents indicators or cigarette packs with clear health warnings etc. Purchasing medicines without such guiding information would in certain key respects be comparable with consumers (or enterprises) concluding contracts whose disadvantageous terms they are not aware of or cannot envisage. In some jurisdictions, there are already comprehensive transparency and notification obligations with regard to specific types of contracts (e.g., data protection agreements) or contract terms (e.g., standard terms and conditions). However, it is certainly worth considering whether an expansion of these obligations, comparable to the measures mentioned with respect to medicines, could be appropriate in favor of contractual fairness and contractual freedom. For example, providers could be obliged to give clear warnings outside of the usual small print in the form of videos in which the use of their personal data is explained to consumers in a straightforward manner. In return, the better and more transparent explanations of "small print" in contracts could become something that sets providers apart from other companies (incentivizing such measures to drive sales).
- *Standardization and Benchmarking:* A look at other disciplines and industries shows that one of the best ways to reduce complexity is standardization. It has

[47] See https://de.wikipedia.org/wiki/Lebensmittelampel.

already been suggested above that the legislator shall develop and provide standard contract templates for the most important types of contracts. The more the legislature creates or incentivizes the overarching standardization of contract content, the easier it will be for the contracting parties in practice to assess (or have assessed via technology or otherwise) to what extent the content of a contract is fair and/or corresponds to the norm (including whether it deviates to its disadvantage or advantage).

The above ideas are only examples of possible starting points for making contracts better and consequently more humane by using concepts and ideas from other disciplines.

4.3 Rebalancing Contractual Fairness Against Contractual Freedom

In addition, a third way to secure humanity in contracts is to constantly rebalance the principles of fairness and freedom of contract.

Due to their connection to the central values of freedom and justice, the struggle for the right balance between freedom of contract and fairness of contract touches on one of the central fundamental questions of contract law and our understanding of what law is and what law should be.[48] Each society must decide on an ongoing basis on the right relationship between the creative powers of freedom and fairness, which is linked to the question of the necessary and permissible degrees of capitalism and materialism.[49]

However, freedom of contract traditionally plays a much more prominent role in legal doctrine than the principle of contractual justice,[50] even though fairness of contracts is undoubtedly one of the central and most recognized principles of

[48] Raiser (2015), p. 908.

[49] *Ibid.*, p. 5.

[50] Wendland (2019), p. 105; *ibid.*, p. 149:

> Der Gedanke der Vertragsgerechtigkeit - wenn gleich in Rechtsprechung und Gesetzgebung faktisch unangefochten - hat es in weiten Teilen der zivilistischen Diskussion indes nicht leicht. Seit dem Ende des 19. Jh., dem großen Zeitalter des Liberalismus, der Industrialisierung, des wirtschaftlichen Aufbaus und der politischen Emanzipation, steht die Gerechtigkeit im Schatten der Privatautonomie. Die Behandlung beider Rechtsgrundsätze in der Privatrechtsdogmatik könnte ungleicher nicht sein: wird die Vertragsgerechtigkeit überhaupt behandelt, beschränkt sich die Darstellung - von einigen wenigen Ausnahmen abgesehen - regelmäßig auf grobe Grundzüge (...). Eine nähere Auseinandersetzung mit der klassischen aristotelisch-thomistischen Gerechtigkeitslehre, die etwa mit Blick auf das Äquivalenzprinzip zahlreichen Regelungen des bürgerlichen Rechts implizit zu Grunde liegt, findet in der Regel nicht statt, ihre Anwendung auf das Privatrecht ist erstaunlicherweise kein Thema.

European private law.[51] While freedom of contract is generally recognized as a universal principle, it also seems to be self-evident and widely accepted that there is no general right to fair contracts.

The developments outlined above, in particular the trend towards digitization and automation of the contract conclusion process and the tendency of the digital economy towards monopolies, suggest that it seems necessary to give greater weight to contractual justice on the expense of contractual freedom in future. As considered in this article, contractual freedom is in many cases only an apparent freedom in the digital age. The more automatized and complex the world becomes, the more difficult it will become for contracting parties to sufficiently appreciate the relevant circumstances and content of the contracts they conclude. The legislature will, therefore, in all likelihood be asked more and more in the future to ensure contractual fairness by intervening in cases where the content of a contract concluded under such circumstances violates central legal principles and the idea of justice. In other words: contractual justice gained and will continue to gain in importance in favor of (in practice often already limited) freedom of contract. In order to also sufficiently facilitate freedom of contract, the legislator is asked to support the improvement and development of techniques and methodologies through which contractual fairness can be achieved even without the intervention of the legislature in the content of the contract, e.g., by means of development of fair standard contract templates or computable contract technology.

Liquid Legal Waves to Other Chapters, Written by the Editors

Carl and *Michael* put a spotlight on the ambiguity of the digital age: the ease of access to digital services via click-through contracts, versus the massive imbalance of power between contractual parties that undermines our freedom of contract and ultimately our private autonomy. Their suggested solutions around clear language, visualization and even warning obligations link back to the concepts *Rob*, *Helena* and *Stefania* propose in *"Layered Contracts: Both Legally Functional and Human-friendly"*.

While *Carl* and *Michael* hone in on the challenges between private parties and the risk of eroding fundamental principles of humanity in the interaction of legal subjects, *Ivar* and *Michiel* in their chapter on *"Digitization of Government Services from the Citizen's Perspective - Putting Humans First"* add the risk of eroding trust between the citizen and the state in the digital age.

[51] *Ibid.*, p. 138 et seqq.

As the digital age puts both, our private autonomy as well as our relationship as citizens to the state under pressure, do we need to ask more fundamental questions? Do we need to apply headstand thinking and ask for *"Patagonia: Everything a law firm is not, but could be?"*, as *Emma* and *Madeleine* do in their upcoming chapter.

References

Ahlemeyer H et al (1997) Komplexität managen – Strategien, Konzepte und Fallbeispiele, Dr. Th. Gabler Verlag, Wiesbaden

Bartholomeyczik H (1966) Äquivalenzprinzip, Waffengleichheit und Gegengewichtsprinzip in der modernen Rechtsentwicklung. In: Archiv für die civilistische Praxis, 1966, vol 166 1/2 (1966), Mohr Siebeck GmbH & Co. KG, Tübingen, pp 30–75

Bork R (2020) Vorbem zu §§ 145 ff. In: von Staudingers Kommentar zum Bürgerlichen Gesetzbuch mit Einführungsgesetz und Nebengesetz, Buch 1, Allgemeiner Teil

Busche J (2018) in Münchner Kommentar BGB, 8th edn., C.H. Beck Verlag, München, Vor § 145

Davies P (1990) Prinzip Chaos: Die neue Ordnung des Kosmos. Goldmann Verlag, München

Jung H et al (ed) (2016) Digital vernetzt. Transformation der Wertschöpfung: Szenarien, Optionen und Erfolgsmodelle für smarte Geschäftsmodelle, Produkte und Services Gebundene, Carl Hanser Verlag GmbH & Co. KG, München

Knieper R (2019) Von der Vertragsfreiheit zum smart contract. Kritische Jahresschrift 52(2): 193–202

Kunz K-L et al (2006) Rechtsphilosophie, Rechtstheorie, Rechtssoziologie, Haupt Verlag, Bern

Neuner J (2020) Allgemeiner Teil des Bürgerlichen Rechts, 12th edn. C.H. Beck Verlag, München

Raiser L (2015) Vertragsfunktion und Vertragsfreiheit. In: Grundmann, S et al (ed) Privatrechtstheorie, Band I, Verlag Mohr Siebeck, Tübingen, pp 903–932

Schäfer H-B et al (2020) Lehrbuch der ökonomischen Analyse des Zivilrechts, 6th edn. Springer Gabler, Berlin

Singer R (1995) Vertragsfreiheit, Grundrechte und der Schutz des Menschen vor sich selbst. Juristen Zeitung 23:1133–1188

Wendland M (2019) Vertragsfreiheit und Vertragsgerechtigkeit. Mohr Siebeck, Tübingen

Wesel U (1997) Geschichte des Rechts, C.H. Beck, München

Dr. Carl Renner is Co-Head of Pinsent Masons Vario in Germany, the Flexible Legal Services and Managed Legal Services practice of international law firm Pinsent Masons. Before joining Vario, Carl worked for several years for an international law firm as lawyer in the field of TMT. He then successfully founded, together with Michael Zollner, a law firm specializing in the provision of flexible legal services and set up the German branch of alternative legal service provider Lawyers on Demand. Carl is particularly interested in innovative legal services, Legal Tech and NewLaw. Outside of the office, Carl enjoys spending time with his wife and his three children, fly-fishing and playing golf.

Dr. Michael Zollner, LL.M. is Co-Head of Pinsent Masons Vario in Germany, the Flexible Legal Services and Managed Legal Services practice of international law firm Pinsent Masons. Michael started his career as in-house lawyer for an international semiconductor company. He then worked for several years as a lawyer in a leading international law firm in the field of TMT and as head of legal of a German software company. After successfully founding a law firm specializing in flexible legal services together with Carl Renner, he built up the German office of Lawyers on Demand with Carl. Since end of 2020, Michael is responsible for Pinsent Masons Vario's Flexible Services and Managed Legal Services business in Germany. He is interested in interdisciplinary legal topics, the innovation of the legal market and legal tech. In his free-time, Michael spends most of his time with his family, on the tennis or hockey court or hiking in the mountains.

Patagonia: Everything a Law Firm Is Not, But Could Be?

Emma Ziercke and Madeleine Bernhardt

Contents

Abstract

Patagonia is perhaps the ultimate example of a humanized company: Its approach to human resource management is characterized by its flexible working policy known as "Let My People Go Surfing"; its founder, Yvon Chouinard, was known

Emma Ziercke is Senior Fellow at the Bucerius Center on the Legal Profession at the Bucerius Law School, Hamburg and Legal Counsel at Sunfire GmbH.

Madeleine Bernhardt is Director Strategic Leadership Development and member of the Executive Faculty of the Bucerius Center on the Legal Profession, Hamburg.

E. Ziercke (✉) · M. Bernhardt
Hamburg, Germany
e-mail: emma.ziercke@law-school.de; madeleine.bernhardt@law-school.de

K. Jacob et al. (eds.), *Liquid Legal – Humanization and the Law*, Law for Professionals, https://doi.org/10.1007/978-3-031-14240-6_17

for his "MBA" (Management-By-Absence) style of bottom-up leadership; it features in the Fortune 100 Best Workplaces for Diversity with 50% women in the workforce and 50% women executives; its declared primary purpose is not the generation of wealth for its owners and investors, but to "build the best product, and not only to do less harm but more good"; and its unconventional marketing strategy tells customers, "Don't buy this jacket" (Chouinard Y, Let my people go surfing. Penguin Books, New York, 2016).

Is the traditional law firm the antithesis of Patagonia? Although the pandemic forced the hand of law firms, suddenly making flexible working acceptable, many have returned to business-as-usual, literally driving their workers back into the office [Hyde J (2021) Law firm workers say they are being forced into the office, Law Society Gazette. Available via https://www.lawgazette.co.uk/news/law-firm-workers-say-they-are-being-forced-into-the-office/5107050.article.]. Partner leadership style is persistently top-down with key decisions being made behind closed doors. In Germany, women make up only 35% of all lawyers (According to the statistics available from the Bundesrechtsanwaltskammer, as of 1 January 2021. Available via https://www.brak.de/fuer-journalisten/zahlen-zur-anwaltschaft/.), and the percentage of female partners is around 14% (Authors' own calculation based on a review of the websites of the top 10 law firms in Germany, as ranked by Juve.). Even as the world continues to reel from the financial hardship caused by the pandemic, the AmLaw Top50 US law firms reported nearly 15% growth in profits per equity partner [Strom R (2021) The Richest Law Firms Are Hiring More Partners After Record 2020, Bloomberg Law. Available via https://news.bloomberglaw.com/business-and-practice/the-richest-law-firms-are-hiring-more-partners-after-record-2020.]. And can you imagine a law firm telling a client, "don't buy this service"?

Can law firms learn from Patagonia? In this chapter, we will consider whether the philosophies and values of the ultimate humanized company, Patagonia, can be transferred to the business of law: In particular with regard to (1) law firm culture, diversity, and values; (2) leadership and change; (3) finance and purpose; and (4) sustainability. Can law firms, in the words of Patagonia, "save our home planet"?

1 To Know and Not to Do Is Not to Know[1]

Many of the things that you can count don't count; many of the things that you can't count really count—Albert Einstein

[1] Wang Yang Ming as cited by Yvon Chouinard in Chouinard (2016), p. xii.

It feels incongruous to be writing about the *humanization* of law firms at a time when humankind is destroying the planet. It is the summer of 2021, and the world has experienced some of the highest temperatures ever recorded. Wildfires blaze in America and in many European countries, whilst other countries experience once-in-a-generation floods, landslides, and earthquakes. Political unrest and war are pervasive, and the world is still in the grip of the COVID-19 pandemic. Humanization denotes environmental destruction and war. Despite this bleak observation, the Cambridge Online Dictionary defines humanization as "*the process of making something less unpleasant and more suitable for people*".[2] Indeed, corporations are being called upon to adopt a more *humanistic* approach to business:[3] Following "*decades of corporate scandals, financial meltdowns and growing inequality*", management thought-leaders have been calling for the "*humanization of leadership*",[4] and legal scholars have been seeking to "*humanize legal education*".[5] To better understand this seemingly paradoxical concept, we investigated the ultimate example of a "*humanized*" company: Patagonia.

Patagonia is synonymous with sustainability, social and environmental activism, and of course, outdoor clothing. Constantly demonstrating the extent to which it recognises its responsibilities to its people, society, and the environment, it has a long history of achievements: It has distributed US$ 79 million in cash and in-kind donations since 1985 to grassroots conservation activists;[6] it has been listed in Fortune magazine's "*100 Best Companies to work for*"; in Working Mother magazine as one of "*100 Best Companies for Working Mothers*" and has been ranked 14th in the "*Top 25 Medium Sized Businesses*" by the Great Place to Work Institute and Society for Human Resource Management.[7] It features in Fortune magazine's "*100 Best Workplaces for Diversity*" with 50% women in the workforce and 50% women executives.[8] It is regarded as the most reputable company in the U.S.[9] and is most recognized for its sustainability leadership.[10] Its declared primary purpose is not the generation of wealth for its owners and investors, instead, for over 45 years, its mission statement has been to "*build the best product, cause no unnecessary harm, use business insights to inspire and implement solutions to the environmental crisis.*" In 2019, Patagonia changed its mission statement to "*We're in business to*

[2] https://dictionary.cambridge.org/dictionary/english/humanization.

[3] See, for example, The Boston Consulting Group, The Humanization of the Corporation, https://www.bcg.com/publications/2018/humanization-corporation.

[4] Petriglieri and Petriglieri (2015), pp. 625–647 at p 625.

[5] See for example, Glesner Fines (2008), pp. 313–326, or Hunter Schwartz (2008), pp. 235–246.

[6] Chouinard (2016), p. 70.

[7] Chouinard (2016), p. 69.

[8] Chouinard (2016), p. 159.

[9] According to the consumer Poll Axios, available at https://www.outsidebusinessjournal.com/brands/camping-and-hiking/patagonia-rated-most-reputable-company-in-the-u-s/.

[10] Globescan Sustainability Survey 2021 https://globescan.com/insight-of-the-week-unilever-patagonia-natura-ikea-most-recognized-corporate-sustainability-leaders/.

save our home planet: We aim to use the resources we have – our voice, our business and our community – to do something about our climate crisis." A dramatic statement, but not untimely.

What has this got to do with law firms? Law firms are in the business of providing legal solutions, not environmental solutions. Whilst the majority of top law firms publicize their environmental, social and governance credentials ("**ESG**") on their websites, their rationale for carrying out such activities varies significantly,[11] and as some legal market commentators assert "*the first truly green law firm is non-existent*".[12] Whilst real GDP growth in the United States fell during the second quarter of 2020 by 31.40% (numbers not seen since the Great Depression),[13] the AmLaw Top 50 U.S. law firms were not shy to award record bonuses to fee-earners and reported nearly 15% growth in profits per equity partner.[14] According to a major research project carried out by *The Lawyer* magazine into family-friendliness in the UK Top 50 law firms and their US counterparts in London, some law firms are "*institutionally sexist*".[15] In Germany, women make up only 35% of all lawyers,[16] and the percentage of female partners is around 14%.[17] According to some research,[18] lawyers are so unhappy that there is an entire industry devoted to helping them quit their jobs.[19] Are law firms the antithesis of Patagonia?

The purpose of this chapter is partly to provoke and partly to inspire law firms into taking a more pro-active and systematic approach to their environmental, social and people responsibilities. We will consider whether the philosophies and values of the ultimate humanized company can be transferred to the business of law. According to Yvon Chouinard, founder and CEO of Patagonia, "*the message is clear: if you are*

---

[11] Vaughan et al. (2015), pp. 138–163.

[12] Headline in a subscriber newsletter sent by The Lawyer magazine on 23 June 2021.

[13] Patton M (2020) The Impact of Covid-19 On U.S. Economy and Financial Markets, Forbes, October 12 2020 https://www.forbes.com/sites/mikepatton/2020/10/12/the-impact-of-covid-19-on-us-economy-and-financial-markets/?sh=1f02f58e2d20.

[14] Strom R (2021) The Richest Law Firms Are Hiring More Partners After Record 2020, Bloomberg Law. Available via https://news.bloomberglaw.com/business-and-practice/the-richest-law-firms-are-hiring-more-partners-after-record-2020.

[15] According to a summary of The Parental Fog Index 2021 Law Firm Report (available at https://executive-coaching.co.uk/latest-thinking/the-parental-fog-index-2021-law-firm-report/) provided in a subscriber newsletter sent by The Lawyer magazine on 23rd July 2021.

[16] According to the statistics available from the Bundesrechtsanwaltskammer, as of 1 January 2021. Available via https://www.brak.de/fuer-journalisten/zahlen-zur-anwaltschaft/.

[17] Authors' own calculation of the Top 10 Law Firms in Juve, February 2021.

[18] CV-Library research on over 1000 employees in the UK, of which around 100 were legal professionals. Reported in Legal Cheek, 20th November 2018 https://www.legalcheek.com/2018/11/research-50-of-lawyers-hate-their-job/.

[19] McMullan Abramson L (2014) The Only Job With an Industry Devoted to Helping People Quit, in The Atlantic, July 29th 2014 available at https://www.theatlantic.com/business/archive/2014/07/the-only-job-with-an-industry-devoted-to-helping-people-quit/375199/.

not part of the answer, you're part of the problem."[20] Where is the need for change greatest? Can law firms "*save our home planet*"?

2 Let My People Go Surfing

> Leaders of the most remarkable companies are willing to put their people first and the work second—Susan Packard, Fully Human[21]

Patagonia began as a small company designing and making climbing equipment for its employees and their friends. The employees therefore saw themselves as the ultimate customer, and work was regarded as play. Patagonia's original customer base regarded corporate life as inauthentic, illegitimate, and toxic.[22] Whilst most of the people who now work for Patagonia may no longer be their customers, they continue to be drawn to Patagonia's values: an aversion to unnecessary hierarchy and unconscious material consumption, and a passive approach to life.[23] According to Yvon Chouinard, the company has strived to maintain these values by carefully selecting new employees, treating them right, and "*training them to treat other people right*".[24] Patagonia's mission to treat its employees right is exemplified by its human resources ("HR") philosophy, "*let my people go surfing*". Patagonia has always allowed employees to work flexible hours, as long as the work gets done without any negative impact on others, but their HR philosophy takes the meaning of flexible hours to the extreme:

> A serious surfer doesn't plan to go surfing next Tuesday at two o'clock. You go surfing when there are waves and the tide and wind are right. And you go ski powder when there's powder snow.[25]

This degree of flexibility allowed Patagonia to keep valuable employees, and employees reciprocated. Rarely did an employee abuse his or her privilege. Few of us, however, can envisage asking a client to just "*hold that deal*" while we engage in a day sailing on the Alster because the conditions are "*just right*",[26] so how can Patagonia's philosophy be applied to law firms?

[20] Praise for Let My People Go Surfing, Santa Barbara News-Press in Chouinard (2016).
[21] Packard (2019), p. 5.
[22] Chouinard (2016), p. 158.
[23] Chouinard (2016), p. 158.
[24] Chouinard (2016), p. 158.
[25] Chouinard (2016), p. 162.
[26] The Alster refers to two large lakes in the centre of Hamburg, not far from Bucerius Law School. When the wind conditions are right, you will find many sailing boats on the "Außenalster".

2.1 Overworked Insecure Overachievers

In the legal world where long hours are the norm, and lawyers are considered "*insecure overachievers*",[27] it is difficult to imagine an environment in which work is regarded as play, people come first, and lawyers go surfing. Delve deeper, and recent academic and institutional research paints an even more troubling picture.[28] According to the Bellwether Report from 2019, over 66% of solicitors in the legal profession in the UK experience high levels of stress in a job they otherwise love.[29] Whilst the pandemic might have exacerbated the trend, lawyer wellbeing is on the decline.[30] One of the most poignant descriptions of lawyer wellbeing comes from a qualitative study[31] by Professor Richard Collier, of Newcastle University, in which he supplements the findings of the 2017–2019 annual Junior Lawyers Division (JLD) Resilience and Wellbeing Surveys carried out by the Law Society of England and Wales.[32] Several key themes emerging from Collier's study, combined with our own observations and research, depict a disturbing phenomenon.

2.1.1 Stress Is a Normal, Not Abnormal, Working Practice in the Legal Profession[33]

Participants in Collier's study described law as an "*anxiety-inducing*" profession: Not only is legal education, training and practice characterized by a highly competitive culture, but as a lawyer one feels a constant need to "*prove oneself*"; anxiety is a "*personality attribute*" of those working in the profession. Echoing Laura Empson's assertion that professionals regard themselves as "*insecure overachievers*":[34]

[27] Empson (2017).

[28] For example: The Liquid Legal Institute initiated a Call for Action in 2020 "The Silent Epidemic: Well- Being and Personal Health of Legal Professionals in Times of Digital Transformation and Social Change"; The Junior Lawyer Division of the Law Society of England and Wales annual surveys 2016–2019 available here https://www.lawsociety.org.uk/en/campaigns/junior-lawyers-division-campaigns/wellbeing; The International Bar Association Wellbeing Surveys available here https://www.ibanet.org/Mental-wellbeing-in-the-legal-profession, Collier (2016), pp. 41–60.

[29] Bellwether Report 2019 on Stress in the Legal Profession available at https://www.lexisnexis.co.uk/pdf/lexisnexis-bellwether-2019-stress-in-the-legal-profession.pdf. The report was compiled using data from eight in-depth interviews with lawyers in small firms and small offices of larger firms, as well as online surveys completed by 176 solicitors in England and Wales.

[30] See the IBA interim survey results on wellbeing in the legal profession https://www.ibanet.org/Mental-wellbeing-in-the-legal-profession..

[31] In-depth interviews with 11 junior lawyers.

[32] Copies of the reports can be downloaded here: https://www.lawsociety.org.uk/en/campaigns/junior-lawyers-division-campaigns/wellbeing. An executive summary of Collier's report, Anxiety and Wellbeing Amongst Junior Lawyers: A Research Study, has been provided by Anxiety UK: https://www.anxietyuk.org.uk/wp-content/uploads/2020/06/Exec-summary-report-final-June-2019.pdf.

[33] Bellwether Report 2019.

[34] "*An insecure over achiever perpetually doubts what they know, yet is compulsively driven to succeed*" in Empson (2017), p. 30 referring to Michel (2007), pp. 507–557.

> The insecure overachiever is attracted by the high status and financial rewards which professional organizations offer. At the same time, the intensively competitive and insecure working environment prevalent in many professional organisations fuels their sense of insecurity and drives them to ever more intensive patterns of work.[35]

Whilst concerns over long hours and poor work-life balance are common, they are also seen as part and parcel of the job,[36] a belief we have seen evidenced in our Next Generation Study.[37] Whilst future lawyers aspire to work for organizations that have a collegial environment, interesting work, flexible working, and career development opportunities, they believe that large international law firms cannot fulfil these aspirations.[38] In fact, when participants were asked to select words which they associated with such law firms, they chose words such as "*workhouse*", "*competitive working environment*", "*hierarchical,*" and "*in-transparent leadership*".[39] Paradoxically, despite being considered the antithesis of their dream employer, large international law firms were the preferred employer of the next generation of lawyer.[40]

2.1.2 Lawyers Are Bullet-Proof

Despite the increasing visibility of wellbeing agendas in the legal profession, Collier found a pervasive cultural stigma around disclosing mental health problems in the legal community.[41] In many German law firms, even discussing mental wellbeing is still a taboo topic.[42] The pressure to conform to the cultural norm, which can be described as "*keep calm and carry on*", only exacerbates the "*hero syndrome*": Lawyers are infallible and there is no place for emotions in a law firm.[43] In our study, "*Excellence Under Pressure*",[44] in which we explored the emotional strategies employed by some of Germany's top lawyers to navigate the pandemic, we found law firm leaders who did just this: "*I don't speak about my emotions at work: My*

---

[35] Empson (2017), p. 30.

[36] Collier R (2020) Anxiety and Wellbeing Amongst Junior Lawyers: A Research Study, an executive summary provided by Anxiety UK, available at https://www.anxietyuk.org.uk/wp-content/uploads/2020/06/Exec-summary-report-final-June-2019.pdf, p. 5.

[37] Ziercke E, Knipping C (2019) Next Generation Study, Bucerius Center on the Legal Profession, available at https://www.law-school.de/forschung-fakultaet/institute-und-zentren/center-on-the-legal-profession/studien-analysen-veroeffentlichungen.

[38] Ziercke and Knipping (2019), p. 1.

[39] Ziercke and Knipping (2019), pp. 3–4.

[40] Ziercke and Knipping (2019), pp. 3–5.

[41] Collier (2020), p. 3.

[42] See Forst M (2021) Mental Health: Immer mehr Kanzleien stellen Programme zur Gesundheitsförderung auf in Azur 11th February 2021 available at https://www.azur-online.de/artikel/mental-health-immer-mehr-kanzleien-stellen-programme-zur-gesundheitsfoerderung-auf/.

[43] See for example, Muir (2017); or Nelken (1996), pp. 420–429.

[44] Bernhardt M, Ziercke E (2021) Excellence under pressure – exploring the emotional strategies employed by some of Germany's top lawyers to navigate the pandemic, Legal Business World, available at https://excellence.legalbusinesslibrary.com/index-h5.html?page=1#page=1.

colleagues expect security, stability, clear leadership".[45] The cultural norm which dictates that lawyers should suppress or ignore emotions begins with legal education.[46] Students are conditioned to prize reason and rationality over emotions.[47] Coupled with the dominant "*employability*" narrative,[48] and intense competition, students already enter the profession with low levels of emotional wellbeing.

2.1.3 Lawyer Wellbeing Is Up to the Individual

On entering profession, the situation does not improve. Concerningly, the results of Collier's research indicates that the legal profession is "*seen to be encouraging individual lawyers to do something about their own wellbeing whilst not addressing the broader causes of their distress.*"[49] We note that lawyer wellbeing has gained significantly more visibility in the UK, from mental health and wellbeing apps (Linklaters) to video campaigns (CMS), and in Germany it is slowly gaining traction with some firms developing wellbeing programmes (DLA Piper's "MyCare", Dentons' "NextMind") or offering workshops (Heuking) and stress mentors (Freshfields Bruckhaus Deringer). However, our *Excellence under Pressure* study revealed that the strategic importance of emotional intelligence and resilience is not fully realized in law firms.[50] Some participants felt that resilience was something one acquired through experience. A focus on fixing the person, rather than the firm, legitimizes a tick-the-box approach to wellbeing, reinforcing the idea that lawyers should simply "*become resilient, rather than seeking to bring about more substantive change in the profession*".[51]

Stress and poor mental wellbeing of lawyers cannot be exonerated on account of personality attributes. As Empson explains, "*a symbiotic relationship between insecure overachieving individuals and elite professional organisations exists*".[52] The organization itself is both a product and a producer of culture.[53] Thus, law firm structure, working practices, and systems foster certain feelings in relation to work and what it means to be successful. Competition and tendencies to overachieve are bound up with a sense of living up to what was expected by others.[54] Although participants in Collier's study were aware of self-care strategies and institutions to

[45] Bernhardt M, Ziercke E (2021) Excellence under pressure – exploring the emotional strategies employed by some of Germany's top lawyers to navigate the pandemic, Legal Business World, p. 27.

[46] Jones (2020).

[47] Jones (2020).

[48] Collier (2020), p. 4.

[49] Collier (2020), p. 7.

[50] Bernhardt M, Ziercke E (2021) Excellence under pressure – exploring the emotional strategies employed by some of Germany's top lawyers to navigate the pandemic, Legal Business World, p. 30.

[51] Collier (2020), p. 7.

[52] Empson (2017), p. 126.

[53] Linstead et al. (2009), p. 157.

[54] Collier (2020), p. 5.

help lawyers with stress (for example, Anxiety UK and Lawcare), none of the participants had come across "*wellbeing objectives*" as an embedded part of performance reviews.

2.2 Can the Pandemic Reset Law Firm Culture?

For many organizations, the pandemic was the "*call to arms*" to reset how we deal with emotions at work. In fact, one of the participants in our *Excellence Under Pressure* study summarized:

> I see it as extremely positive that people are able to talk about their mental health... It was the first time that people said to me, 'I had a bad day.' That is something positive to come out of the crisis, that one can suddenly talk about things like resilience and openly discuss them.[55]

In fact, the results of our study showed that during the outset of the pandemic, law firm leaders took a more rounded view of their leadership role with an enhanced focus on caring for their people.[56] Many invested a significant amount of effort into understanding their colleagues' personal situations and communicating regularly in teams, as well as one to one and even delivering care packages to colleagues.

However, it is easy to slip back into business-as-usual. Whilst the top performers in our study demonstrated high levels of empathy and worked extremely hard to take care of their people at the outset, there was an indication that these relationships were becoming less pressing as the pandemic became our "everyday normal". Although the pandemic forced the hand of law firms, suddenly making remote working acceptable, many have returned to business-as-usual with a vengeance, literally driving their workers back into the office.[57] Even some clients have been interpreted as demanding that their external counsel should return to the office to "*avoid a decline in client service*".[58]

Law firms face a double-edge sword. The pandemic has shown that lawyers are more profitable when they work from home.[59] Not only due to the reduced

[55] Bernhardt M, Ziercke E (2021) Excellence under pressure – exploring the emotional strategies employed by some of Germany's top lawyers to navigate the pandemic, Legal Business World, p. 27.

[56] Bernhardt M, Ziercke E (2021) Excellence under pressure – exploring the emotional strategies employed by some of Germany's top lawyers to navigate the pandemic, Legal Business World, p. 27.

[57] Hyde J (2021) Law firm workers say they are being forced into the office, Law Society Gazette. Available via https://www.lawgazette.co.uk/news/law-firm-workers-say-they-are-being-forced-into-the-office/5107050.article.

[58] See for example Law.Com (2021) 'Our Profession Cannot Long Endure a Remote Work Model,' Morgan Stanley CLO Tells Law Firms, 16th July 2021 available at https://www.law.com/2021/07/16/our-profession-cannot-long-endure-a-remote-work-model-morgan-stanley-clo-tells-law-firms/.

[59] Griffiths A (2021) General-Überholung, Juve Rechtsmarkt, August 2021, p. 30.

commuting time, but because they tend to start work earlier and finish work later. This intrusion of work into lawyers' private spheres has led to increased burn-out amongst lawyers (and many other remote workers). Whilst the pandemic persuaded many law firm partners that remote working can be successful (at least from a profitability perspective), and a vast majority of top law firms have reset their flexible working policies to allow lawyers to work from home up to 50% of the time,[60] the individual pressure to come back into the office is also strong. In fact, more than half of the participants in our *Excellence Under Pressure* study continued to work from the office during the first lockdown, as one participant described "*I wanted to show the team that there was someone onboard…who stands at the helm…and watches out that the ship doesn't sink*".[61] This pressure may be understandable at the leadership level, but even associates felt this pressure to get back into the office, as part of the intensive competition for the partners' attention.[62]

The debate around hybrid working merely highlights the dynamic relationship between the long-hours culture, and lawyers' propensity to over-achieve. Patagonia's philosophy of "*let my people go surfing*" is successful as it conveys some key messages: First, it indicates that Patagonia *cares* about its people and their wellbeing. Second, it shows that Patagonia bestows *autonomy* on its people. Thirdly, this autonomy crystallises into *trust.* Managing a workforce of insecure overachievers who are predisposed to stress requires a strong focus on lawyer mental health and wellbeing, as well as the structures and processes that influence that wellbeing: In this way, law firm leaders can create a culture of caring, autonomy, and trust.

3 MBA-Style Leadership

> I go back to my three heroes [Mahatma Gandhi, Nelson Mandela, Martin Luther King]. I don't think they did anything. Instead, they enabled people to do what these people thought, in their hearts, was the right thing to do. That is the future of leadership.—Vineet Nayar, then CEO, HCL Technologies[63]

[60] See for example, Slaughter and May's "Switch On/Switch Off" policy reported on in The Financial Times: Beioley K (2021) https://www.ft.com/content/f8caa0be-e9b6-495c-b4b3-f2ccfd572f58, 14th July 2021, or Tillay M and Lock S (2021) Legal Week, Flexible Working Policies: The Latest Firm-By-Firm Guide, June 8th 2021 available at https://www.law.com/international-edition/2021/06/08/flexible-working-policies-a-firm-by-firm-guide as well as LTO (2021) Home Office darf zum Standard werden https://www.lto.de/recht/kanzleien-unternehmen/k/poellath-gsk-stockmann-corona-pandemie-homeoffice-flexibles-arbeiten/.

[61] Bernhardt M, Ziercke E (2021) Excellence under pressure – exploring the emotional strategies employed by some of Germany's top lawyers to navigate the pandemic, Legal Business World, p. 27.

[62] Griffiths, A. "General-Überholung", Juve Rechtsmarkt, August 2021, p. 30.

[63] Hill et al. (2014), p. 63.

In a time of constant and radical change, the question of how to lead effectively is more important than ever. But what kind of leadership is required? At Patagonia, Chouinard uses an "*MBA*" style of leadership. Only Chouinard is not referring to a top-down, Jack Welch style of leadership, he means "*Management By Absence*" style.[64] In other words, he trusts his people to work diligently, without him constantly breathing down their necks, and he leads by example. The "*MBA*" style is particularly challenging as it requires leaders to *trust* that their people act responsibly, that their people *want to develop and grow* and *do their best*. This combination of trust, independence, and diligence is evident at Patagonia, as Chouinard deliberately seeks out independent-minded and highly individualistic people. However, this does not result in an individualistic organizational culture. On the contrary, by placing a strong emphasis on purpose, Chouinard creates a workforce that also functions well as a team.

Adaptive organizations need leaders who create and sustain an environment "*that unlocks the slice of genius in each of their people and then combines them into collective genius.*"[65] Chouinard creates that environment by enabling his people to stay curious, to explore options, to collaborate, to make informed consensus-driven decisions and to reflect on their experiences, successes, and failures, and relentlessly learn. At Patagonia, leaders are expected to have a mindset and skillset that allow them to unceasingly adapt and grow with the job.[66] This includes the capacity to reflect on, adjust and change their behavior. By doing this, they serve as an example to their employees. Patagonia emphasizes for a good reason: "*The best leadership is by example*".[67]

3.1 Independent, Curious, Highly Individualistic People

As a leader, you cannot solve the problems that are thrown at you and your organization at a blistering pace all by yourself. You need people who think for themselves, who are willing and capable to challenge the status-quo and question decisions they regard as unwise. Thus, Patagonia deliberately hires people who are independent-minded and highly individualistic. Patagonia's founder reports that, due to this characteristic, he was told that his employees would be considered unemployable in "*typical*" companies.[68]

The art then is to align these highly individualistic people to a common cause. This common cause will help people to persistently focus on achieving the highest quality possible in whatever they do—as soon as they buy into a decision. For Patagonia, one way to gain that alignment is to form consensus-driven decisions

[64] Chouinard (2016), p. 168.

[65] Hill et al. (2014), p. 43.

[66] Chouinard (2016), p. 172.

[67] Chouinard (2016), p. 168.

[68] Chouinard (2016), p. 167.

whenever possible, rather than compromises, which often lead to those involved feeling dissatisfied with the outcome. These decision-making processes require constant, transparent communication. Office structures such as open spaces can support that idea of constant communication. At Patagonia, no one has a private office and Chouinard states: "*What we lose in "quiet thinking space" is more than made up for with better communication and an egalitarian atmosphere.*"[69]

If you want to be a creative problem-solver, you need to be curious, you need to want to explore, and learn, and understand. As Patagonia's founder states: "*Uncurious people do not lead examined lives; they cannot see causes that lie deeper than the surface.*"[70] The key to solving problems is to not stop asking the right questions to get beyond the symptoms and to the problem's root cause. In this respect, Patagonia sets an example for its employees: "*One of the most difficult things for a business to do is to investigate the environmental effects of its most successful product and, if it's bad, to change it or pull it off the shelves.*" In 1991, Patagonia began an environmental assessment programme to examine its own products. Whilst it was aware that everything that is made pollutes, it was surprised at how bad it was:

> Most organizations do not want to ask the Toyota "Five Whys" for fear of revealing the real cause of their problems, which would force them to make a change, or be left with a feeling of guilt.[71]

A business that thrives on being different requires different types of people. One core element is the strong emphasis Patagonia places on hiring people with diverse backgrounds. This brings in an immensely valuable flexibility of thought, and an openness to new ways of approaching things.[72] At Patagonia, not only are people with diverse backgrounds and thinking styles the key to success, but it is also expected that people have a life beyond work: That they have hobbies, interests, and passions that may or may not be closely linked to the company's core. Patagonia's rationale is that the more "*whole*" people feel because they fully live, the more engaged they will be at work.

3.2 Managing Lawyers Patagonia-Style?

At first glance, there seems to be a parallel between Patagonia's highly independent individuals and the typical lawyer personality, described in Larry Richard's famous article "*Herding Cats: The Lawyer Personality Revealed*" as "*highly*

[69] Chouinard (2016), p. 168.

[70] Chouinard (2016), p. 188.

[71] See for example, Ely RJ and Padavic I (2020) What's Really Holding Women Back? Harvard Business Review, March–April, in which Harvard Business School researchers were sacked by the company that engaged them after uncovering some uncomfortable truths about why women did not progress in that company.

[72] Chouinard (2016), p. 159.

autonomous".[73] Whilst autonomy is a key motivational factor, especially amongst knowledge workers,[74] the curtailment of this autonomy leads to stress in the profession. Collier's study cited "lack of autonomy" as a key stress factor,[75] Empson too, recognizes the paradox entailed in the assertion that autonomous professionals

> not only conform to, but actively co-create and celebrate, strong social controls. In the process, they develop a powerful sense of identification which anchors their potentially insecure identities.[76]

Furthermore, many law firms harbour the idea that you can postpone living until your work is done, which will of course never be the case.[77] Work is supposed to be the number one priority at all times, and it is expected that everyone misses out on important opportunities to live life to the fullest (e.g. important family gatherings) because *"clients expect it" / "this is what we are paid to do" / "if we don't do it, the client will move to the competition" / "we have no choice"* _____________ (fill in the blank with whichever explanation you use or hear most often). In contrast, research shows the tremendous positive effects of "unproductive" time. In fact, the best ideas are often generated when you (seemingly) do nothing, and let your mind wander, or when you do something that is not related to the current problem you are trying to solve.[78]

Law firm leaders should actively encourage their employees to have a life outside the firm, a life with playfulness, adventures, courageous experiments, and learning journeys. This will tremendously boost their creativity, joy, and capacity to innovate, and we all know that the more positive emotions people experience at work, the more productive they are.[79] Or as Chouinard wisely puts it: *"Work has to be fun. We value employees who live rich and rounded lives."*[80] As a law firm, are you looking for curious people who love to explore? For diversity in thinking-styles? For

[73]Richard, L. (2002). Herding Cats: The Lawyer Personality Revealed. Altman Weil Report to Legal Management, Volume 29, 11 (August) now available at https://www.lawyerbrain.com/sites/default/files/caliper_herding_cats.pdf.

[74]See for example, Birkinshaw J, Cohen J and Stach P (2020) Knowledge Workers are More Productive from Home, Harvard Business Review, August.

[75]Collier (2020), p. 5.

[76]Richard, L. (2002). Herding Cats: The Lawyer Personality Revealed. Altman Weil Report to Legal Management, Volume 29, 11 (August) now available at https://www.lawyerbrain.com/sites/default/files/caliper_herding_cats.pdf.

[77]See for example, this quote from an accountant in Empson (2017), p. 125, which expressively summarizes the system of over-work: "*I really became a robot. I thought it was normal. It shocked me when everyone around me, my husband, my parents, and friends asked me, 'Are you crazy?' I replied, 'No it's normal.' It's like brainwashing. You are in a kind of mental system where you are under increasing demands, and you say to yourself that it doesn't matter, that you will rest afterwards, but that moment never comes.*"

[78]Hussy (1998).

[79]Fredrickson (2013).

[80]Chouinard (2016), p. 162.

diversity in problem-solving styles? In hobbies and passions? Or are you looking for clones instead? A glance at law firm career websites reveals that most are still looking for conformity instead of diversity: fantastic grades in your exams, language skills and an LLM. If law firms wanted to fully leverage the potential of diversity in every sense, this would mean a very different hiring process, and subsequently a systematic learning journey for everyone in the law firm. This would be a journey that includes, and focuses on, *mindsets* rather than *skillsets*, as skills without the appropriate mindsets are superficial. As Chouinard points out, Patagonia takes the time to train its people in this regard, *"as though our future depended on it"*.[81]

It seems that law firms could use a healthy dose of the "MBA" style leadership. In this same vein, law firm leaders would need to develop their growth mindset.[82] This mindset includes the firm belief that people want to learn, grow, and develop, and are inherently motivated to do their best, provided they feel their actions have a clear purpose. It also entails the belief that neither intelligence nor personality are fixed traits but can develop and change over time. Mistakes and failures are seen as learning opportunities, and they are used as such; challenges are perceived as options to grow and learn professionally, and personally. Law firm leaders risk being caught in a vicious circle to the extent that a fixed-mindset reduces the scope for lasting change. As our *Future of Leadership* study[83] highlighted, law firms leaders need to escape their bubble and gain new perspectives in order to develop themselves and equip their people for the future.

What prevents law firm leaders from living a rounded life themselves, and what prevents them from encouraging their people to live a whole life? Is it the fear of losing control? Of declining performance? Is it a lack of awareness? Our *Excellence Under Pressure* Study revealed that although during times of stress, like the pandemic, top performers engaged in activities such as sport, being in the nature or spending time with family, they did so "*unconsciously*",[84] and therefore a more strategic and cognitive awareness of the benefits of leading a rounded life is needed. More and more people feel the desire to live and work with joy, and not to sacrifice one part of life for another, thus the pressure on law firms to provide these opportunities will grow. Those law firms which understand the enormous potential that lies in enabling people to live fully will probably win the war for talent, money won't do it in the long run.

---

[81] Chouinard (2016), p. 162.

[82] Dweck (2017).

[83] Bucerius Center on the Legal Profession in Co-operation with Egon Zehnder. The Future of Leadership available at https://www.law-school.de/fileadmin/content/law-school.de/de/units/abt_education/pdf/Studien/CLPStudie_Future_Leadership.pdf.

[84] Bernhardt M, Ziercke E (2021) Excellence under pressure – exploring the emotional strategies employed by some of Germany's top lawyers to navigate the pandemic, Legal Business World, p. 34.

4 Can Profit Happen If You Do Everything Else Right?

> Anyone who thinks you can have infinite growth on a finite planet is either a madman or an economist.—Kenneth Boulding[85]

The first part of Patagonia's original mission statement was to "*make the best product*", but what does "*the best*" mean? Yvon Chouinard uses an interesting example: His chief designer, Kate Larramendy, argued that Patagonia did not make "*the best*" clothing in the world:

> The best shirt in the world is Italian. It's made from handwoven fabric, with hand-sewn buttons and buttonholes, and impeccably finished.
>
> "But you can't throw it into the washer dryer," argued Chouinard, "it would shrink."[86]

For Chouinard, a shirt which must be treated so delicately has diminished value and is therefore not "*the best*". However, not content to settle for the observation that quality is subjective, Patagonia created criteria that made quality *objective* and *definable*. Here are some of the questions a Patagonia designer must ask about each product to see if it meets Patagonia's standards: Is it functional? Is it multi-functional? Is it durable? Can it be repaired? Does it fit our customer? Is it as simple as possible? Is the product line simple? Does it have any added value? Are we just chasing fashion? Does it cause any unnecessary harm?

In 1990, the USA entered a recession, and Patagonia's growth stopped quite suddenly. The company had to let go of 20% of the workforce, and its founder realized that the economic activity had resulted in a "*spread of deserts, acidification of lakes and forests, and the build-up of greenhouse gases.*"[87] Chouinard reflects:

> Our own company had exceeded its resources and limitations; we had become dependent, like the world economy, on growth we could not sustain.[88]

Together with several top managers, Chouinard went through a process that entailed asking themselves why they were in business and what kind of business they wanted Patagonia to be. The shift toward a long-term perspective was radical: "*We had to begin to make all our decisions as though we would be in business for a hundred years.*"[89] Chouinard, together with the top leadership team, developed a mission statement,[90] put their values into words, and led employee seminars in these newly

---

[85] Cited by Yvon Chouinard in Chouinard (2016), p. 175.

[86] Chouinard (2016), p. 77.

[87] Chouinard (2016), p. 61.

[88] Chouinard (2016), p. 61.

[89] Chouinard (2016), p. 66.

[90] Mission statement: "Make the best product, cause no unnecessary harm, and use business to inspire and implement solutions to the environmental crisis"; Chouinard (2016), p. 70.

written philosophies to ensure that everyone understood and lived these values through every decision that was made. In this way, the philosophies became an integral part of the culture.[91] The list of values emphasized the importance of taking company decisions in the context of the environmental crisis.

At Patagonia, there is a firm conviction that the focus should be on producing the highest quality product possible, but also on employees and customers, and on responsibility toward the environment, including product design, the materials used, and the production and distribution process. Profit is a welcome result of these efforts, but it is not the linchpin. This last point is the quintessence of Patagonia's strategy. By combining more than one "purpose" in its design, it ensures that more than one goal is achieved. Does Patagonia want to make profit? Yes, of course:

> Without giving its achievement primacy, we seek to profit on our activities. However, growth and expansion are values not basic to this corporation.[92]

The essence of work at Patagonia is a strong belief in a joint *purpose* which is so important to all employees that all other aspects seem secondary.[93] Purpose, or, as Rosemary Kanter calls it "institutional values", "*can evoke positive emotions, stimulate motivation, and propel self-regulation or peer regulation.*"[94]

Now, law firms are not in the business of making shirts, nor (some will say) *products*, law firms are service providers, whose owners require a return on investment, measured in profit per partner.[95] And here the analogy to Patagonia ends. Or does it? What does "*the best*" legal service look like? Can law firms be both profit and purpose orientated?

4.1 Simply the Best?

Law firm websites often push the "*best legal work product possible*" credo, but what does the best legal service look like? In his recent book chapter "*Evaluating Legal Services: The Need for a Quality Movement and Standard Measures of Quality and Value*",[96] Daniel W. Linna Jr. highlights the lack of evidenced-based, data-driven standards. Not only does the absence of objective and definable standards pose a risk for the buyers of legal services, but as Linna points out,

---

[91] Chouinard (2016), p. 66.

[92] Chouinard (2016), p. 64.

[93] https://corporate-rebels.com/patagonia/.

[94] Kanter RM (2011) How Great Companies Think Differently, Harvard Business Review, November.

[95] Note that this chapter does not address the question of whether all of Patagonia's achievements would have been possible, had it been a publicly listed company.

[96] Vogl (2021), pp. 404–431.

> The absence of a quality culture in law contributes to other pernicious problems. For example, how do our chaotic legal industry work environments - largely devoid of quality, process improvement, and project management initiatives - contribute to job dissatisfaction, work-life imbalance, depression, alcoholism, suicide, bias and the lack of diversity across the legal industry?[97]

Whilst a handful of organizations have initiated mechanisms to measure certain aspects of legal-service quality or value, Linna advocates for a quality movement, focussed on standard work, error detection, peer review, performance measurement and continuous improvement, as well as external standards for legal-services quality and value. Furthermore, to achieve "the best" anything, an organization needs to not only set objective standards, but to design the process for the production, or delivery of service, to meet those standards. Applied to legal services, *legal* design is aptly defined as "*the application of human-centered design to the world of law, to make legal systems and services more human-centered, useable and satisfying.*"[98]

The call for a more "*customer centric*" approach to legal services is also getting louder.[99] Jack Newton advocates for a focus on the client experience. In other words, the legal deliverable, and the legal experience is one product.[100] It is in the sphere of the legal experience where he sees the most opportunity for differentiation. Perhaps law firms can ask themselves the same questions as Patagonia when designing the client experience:

- Is it functional? Did the legal advice answer the client's question, did it do the job the client needed doing?
- Is it multi-functional? Can the advice be shared with other stakeholders in the client's organization?
- Is it durable? Can the law firm provide an updated version of the advice if the law changes?
- Is it as simple as possible? Did we write a lengthy memo when an e-mail would have sufficed?
- Is the product line simple? Do we need three agreements, when one would do?
- Does it have any added value? Must we carry out a full due diligence?
- Are we just chasing fashion? Does the client really want an app, or would an e-mail be better?
- Does it cause any unnecessary harm? Should I be representing an environmental polluter?[101]

---

[97] Vogl (2021), pp. 404–431.

[98] Vogl (2021), pp. 404–431.

[99] See for example, Cohen M (2020) When Will The Legal Industry Become Customer-Centric? Forbes, October 27th 2020, or Newton (2020).

[100] Newton (2020), p. 83.

[101] This is of course the most difficult question to answer. Everyone has a right to legal representation, but what would Patagonia do? See "Don't Buy This Jacket" for an idea...

4.2 Many Law Firms Are Experiencing a Purpose Crisis

What could law firms learn from Patagonia's strong emphasis on purpose? Currently, many law firms are asking themselves, at least secretly, what their purpose actually is, beyond generating wealth or allowing partners to gain a return on investment. And many struggle to come up with satisfying answers. Yes, of course, every law firm wants to provide the best service to their clients. This aspect focuses more on the "*what*" and "*how*" of doing business, but it is insufficient in answering the core question: "*Why do we as a firm exist?*"

Recent decisions of some law firms regarding salaries seem to underscore the belief of law firm leaders that, for lack of a compelling purpose, you must pay insane amounts of money so that people are willing to start working for you. And although everyone knows that people typically do not stay for a very long time when the only reward they get is money, law firms still act as if they had never heard about the research that clearly shows: the more money you pay someone, the more the internal motivation of that person drops.[102] Working, then, is largely devoid of any deeper purpose, it is simply a career step, and loyalty cannot be expected in the long run. As this path is highly unsustainable, law firms urgently need to find better solutions to the fundamental decline in the attractiveness of law firms for young lawyers. What if law firms stopped paying big bonuses and fighting salary wars, and instead focused on finding out what else they have to offer to employees, clients, and society at large, or at least on what they possibly could offer in the future? What if, instead of money as a compensation for personal suffering, they could offer more respect, appreciation, purpose, work-life balance, belonging, and joy?

And to take that thought experiment one step further: What if law firms were to finally jump off the cliff and offer fixed fees instead of relying on the billable hour? Research clearly shows that the predominance of billable hours negatively affects intrinsic motivation and causes stress.[103] Furthermore, the alleged importance of the professional relationship with clients is undermined as soon as you have to ask yourself, mid-conversation: "*Do I have to / Can I invoice this 3-minute small talk?*" There are several positive examples of firms that have carried out pilot projects to

[102] See for example, Krieger L.S, Sheldon K.M (2015) What makes lawyers happy?: A Data-Driven Prescription to Redefine Professional Success, Florida State University College of Law available at https://www.law.berkeley.edu/wp-content/uploads/2015/04/Krieger-and-Sheldon_excerpt1.pdf, or, on motivation of employees generally https://hbr.org/2003/01/one-more-time-how-do-you-motivate-employees. Davis P (2020), or Money doesn't lead to happiness in law – here is what does Forbes, October 8 2020 available at https://www.forbes.com/sites/pauladavislaack/2020/10/08/money-doesnt-lead-to-happiness-in-law%2D%2Dhere-is-what-does/?sh=1df48c2a4c81.

[103] See for example, the 2015 Study "What Makes Lawyers Happy?", The Billable Hour and its Impact on Lawyer Subjective Wellbeing and Burnout (Thesis University of Calgary) https://prism.ucalgary.ca/bitstream/handle/1880/110875/ucalgary_2019_pasyk_victoria.pdf?sequence=2&isAllowed=y and the recent results from the Liquid Legal Institute's research, "The Silent Epidemic: Well-being and Personal Health of Legal Professionals in Times of Digital Transformation and Change". https://www.liquid-legal-institute.com/wp-content/uploads/2021/01/LLI-LawyerWellBeing-Survey-Findings-1.pdf.

eradicate the billable hour, or who offer fixed fees.[104] However, whilst law firm culture, structures and processes remain in place, it will remain the dominant charging method with all its negative consequences.[105]

There is reason to believe that the answer to the question of *purpose* will become much more important for most companies in the near future. The Purpose Power Index™ is *"the first empirical measure of companies that activate purpose at the core of their business: among both employees and consumers"*.[106] The 2021 "Purpose Power Index" is the world's largest empirical study measuring perceptions of brand purpose. It shows that purpose-driven brands are increasingly being rewarded by consumers. The study assumes that companies that have learned to activate purpose are not only thriving right now, but that they will continue to do so well into the future.[107] This is echoed by Deloitte's insights into brand:

> Purpose-driven companies witness higher market share gains and grow three times faster on average than their competitors, all while achieving higher workforce and customer satisfaction.[108]

In his extensive research into progressive law firms, Mitch Kowalski concludes that,

> human behaviour and human well-being are functions of the structure of the work environment. New structures and new work processes create different behaviours, and when behaviours change, clients receive a very different experience.... 'performance and engagement are driven by people understanding purpose, and feeling they are able to influence both the purpose, and their ability to achieve that purpose.' It made me wonder if more legal services providers took this approach to their human resources, would mental wellness vastly improve among lawyers?[109]

How many more arguments do law firms need for them to learn the lessons from purpose-driven companies?

---

[104] For example, Stephenson Harwood is working with the University of Essex to develop an in-house pricing tool to price legal work, https://www.shlegal.com/news/stephenson-harwood-launches-pricing-tool-project, and new tools such as Busylamp are available to firms.

[105] See for example, Hartung/Ziercke (2018) What will replace the billable hour and how will we measure employee output without time recording? in the Minutes of the Conference on the Future of Legal Services 2018 in St. Gallen.

[106] https://www.purposepowerindex.com/.

[107] https://www.thedrum.com/profile/strawberryfrog/news/purpose-power-summit-2021-to-reveal-the-purpose-power-index.

[108] Deloitte Insights (2019). Purpose is everything: How brands that authentically lead with purpose are changing the nature of business today. URL: https://www2.deloitte.com/us/en/insights/topics/marketing-and-sales-operations/global-marketing-trends/2020/purpose-driven-companies.html.

[109] Kowalski (2017), p. 163.

5 Don't Buy This Jacket

The more you know, the less you need.—Yvon Chouinard[110]

In 2012, Patagonia ran an advertisement in The New York Times on Black Friday with a picture of a Patagonia fleece jacket and the caption, "*Don't Buy This Jacket*". Every business depends on people buying its products, so why ask people to buy less? Patagonia wanted to address the issue of consumerism. Every clothing manufacturer, whether organic, recycled or "*carbon neutral*", uses resources, and generates waste. To reduce our environmental impact, businesses need to produce less, and consumers need to consume less. According to Patagonia, "*it would be hypocritical for us to work for environmental change without encouraging customers to think before they buy*".[111] It seems that Patagonia walks the walk with regard to the proclaimed values and purpose.

The word "*sustainable*" has been "*so overused and misused as to become meaningless*", in fact "*sustainable manufacturing*" is an oxymoron.[112] By promising to "*save our planet*", Patagonia has set itself an ambitious target. It formulated six guidelines to move forward with its goal: (1) Lead an examined life, (2) clean up our own act, (3) do our penance, (4) support civil democracy, (5) do good, and (6) influence other companies.

In order to clean up its own act, Patagonia embarked on an environmental assessment programme, and acted positively to solve problems, rather than ignoring them, or trying to find a way around them. By accepting responsibility for its products, it followed the environmental footprint of every component through the production chain. The deeper you get into the supply chain, the darker it gets. However, Chouinard decided that no matter how diligent Patagonia was, everything causes some waste or pollution, and the next step was to "*pay for our sins until such a time that we hope we can stop sinning*".[113] In this way, Patagonia decided to help grassroot activists, donate to worthy causes and influence other companies, including its legal counsel, to do the same.[114]

[110]Chouinard (2016), p. 80.

[111]https://www.patagonia.com/stories/dont-buy-this-jacket-black-friday-and-the-new-york-times/story-18615.html.

[112]Chouinard (2016), pp. 178 and 190.

[113]Chouinard (2016), p. 204.

[114]Patagonia's general legal counsel in the USA prioritizes external counsel who are benefit corporations or members of "1% For the Planet", or who have made a firm commitment to advance women, see https://www.thomsonreuters.com/en-us/posts/legal/upfront-personal-hilary-dessouky-patagonia/ and https://www.onepercentfortheplanet.org/hilary-dessouky.

5.1 From Ego-System Economy to Eco-System Economy

We live in an age of disruption. Dr. C. Otto Scharmer, senior lecturer at the Massachusetts Institute of Technology (MIT), claims that due to a mindset of maximum material consumption, "*bigger is better*" thinking, and a "*profit as the benchmark*" perspective, we currently live in a state of organized irresponsibility, "*collectively creating results that nobody wants.*"[115] He dedicates his research and practice to helping leaders to "*lead from the emerging future*".

What does he mean by this? Scharmer suggests that,

> the future .... requires us to tap into a deeper level of our humanity, of who we really are and who we want to be as a society. It is a future that we can sense, feel, and actualize by shifting the inner place from which we operate. This inner shift, from fighting the old to sensing and presencing an emerging future possibility, is at the core of all deep leadership work today... It is a shift from an ego-system awareness that cares about the well-being of oneself to an eco-system awareness that cares about the well-being of all, including oneself.[116]

The imperative to shift from ego-system economy to eco-system economy points exactly in the direction that Patagonia has taken, to the extent that it asks its customers to buy less. Will law firms be able to do the same? And will they see the value in doing so?

5.2 Are Law Firms Sufficiently Educated to Lead by Example?

To make the move from ego to eco system, law firms must first and foremost lead an examined life. Whilst numerous awards are handed out for "*the best*" corporate social responsibility programmes, objective rankings for law firms are in their infancy.[117] Furthermore, very few law firms can provide reliable data on many aspects of their Environmental Social Governance. In 2015, Birmingham University reviewed the websites of the UK's top 100 law firms for public disclosures about corporate social responsibility practices, but the researchers were hampered by the poor quality of the available data.[118] Whilst some firms gather and publish wide-ranging diversity statistics, this is by no means "*standard*". In the UK, this is encouraged as the Law Society regularly publishes statistics on all aspects of diversity on the legal profession (not just gender), and campaigned, under the presidency of Christina Blacklaws, for improved diversity in the profession as

---

[115] Scharmer and Kaufer (2013), pp. 1–2.

[116] Scharmer and Kaufer (2013), pp. 1–2.

[117] See student-led organisations, such as Law Students for Climate Accountability in the United States: https://www.ls4ca.org. Only one law firm, Mishcon de Reya in the UK, has a BCorp Certificate: https://bcorporation.net/directory/mishcon-de-reya-l-l-p.

[118] For a summary of the 2015 report see https://www.birmingham.ac.uk/documents/college-artslaw/law/research/bham-law-spotlight-corporate-social-responsibility.pdf.

whole.[119] Gender pay gap reporting is also a legal requirement for law firms in the UK, and those who are unable to provide satisfactory explanations are brought before Parliament.[120] By contrast, in Germany, there is little or no statistical research or public reporting into the "*diversity deficit*"[121] or the gender pay gap in the legal profession.

Although it may appear that law firms are "*doing penance*" with pro bono initiatives, civil democracy projects, charitable donations and involvement in local communities, headline-making transgressions, such as the Presidents' Club and cum-ex scandals, suggest that law firms need to clean up their own act first.[122] According to one General Counsel "*you can't say, 'look at our ESG work' and then advise clients who destroy the environment. That's counterintuitive*".[123] It seems that law firms have yet to realize that they must lead by example. Patagonia takes a "*zero sum*" approach to environmental damage, as everything causes some waste or pollution. Law firms too, can take a deeper look into their supply chain, which is characteristically people-driven. Integrated financial reporting models, such as sustainability accounting,[124] can help law firms review and report on their ESG aspects, including employee well-being and diversity in a more comprehensive and transparent way. In this case, what gets measured has more chance of getting managed.[125] Furthermore, clients are beginning to ask for this data: According to *The Lawyer*, General Counsel are having

> serious conversations about the kind of questions we should ask firms, as a minimum we want to see how they are cutting their carbon footprint.[126]

6 There's No Business If There Is No Planet

> We are the people we have been waiting for—Navajo Medicine Man[127]

---

[119] See the Law Society for England and Wales website https://www.lawsociety.org.uk/topics/diversity-and-inclusion.

[120] In 2018 Allen & Overy came under fire from the chair of a parliamentary select committee because the firm had not given full disclosure of their partner gender pay https://www.globallegalpost.com/news/allen-amp-overy-under-fire-over-gender-pay-gap-89484815.

[121] Grünberger et al. (2021).

[122] See for example, the report in Legal Week from February 2018 https://www.law.com/international-edition/2018/02/01/male-partners-question-hypocritical-backlash-over-men-only-events-as-women-set-out-grim-reality-of-city-networking/ or the report in Legal 500 from September 2020 https://www.legal500.com/gc-magazine/special-feature/der-freshfields-skandal/.

[123] Reported on by The Lawyer in a subscriber newsletter on 23rd June 2021.

[124] See for example the Global Reporting Initiative https://www.globalreporting.org.

[125] https://hbr.org/2020/12/the-future-of-esg-is-accounting.

[126] Reported on by The Lawyer in a subscriber newsletter on 23rd June 2021.

[127] Cited by Yvon Chouinard, Chouinard (2016), p. 194.

Law firms are beginning to put their ESG credentials under the spotlight, partly driven by the need to attract and retain next generation lawyers, but also partly driven by client demand. According to the General Counsel for a major energy company in the UK

> it is no longer enough [. . .] to work with firms that focus on providing technical expertise at the right price. We want to work with firms that also share the same ethos, principles and outlook when it comes to their employees and other stakeholders. In this respect, we need to be honest and recognise that the legal profession has not changed as much as we would wish in the past two decades. Specifically, I believe that the willingness of all of us to embrace diversity and inclusion in our working practices and a fundamentally different approach to the training of lawyers, in the way advocated by the cross-industry O-Shaped Lawyer initiative, are central to the modernisation and development of the legal profession.[128]

In fact, according to research carried out by *The Lawyer*, poor cultural alignment (including ESG matters) is a key reason clients break away from their advisors. More than half of the respondents in the survey said they would switch counsel if it was not aligned with its values.[129] This resonates with research by Deloitte in which they discovered that:

> Many consumers today make decisions based on how brands treat their people, how they treat the environment, and how they support the communities in which they operate.[130]

6.1 Could Law Firms Be Like Patagonia?

Yvon Chouinard declared one of his biggest challenges to be combating complacency,[131] which is why the declared purpose of this chapter was to provoke and inspire law firms to be more "*human*". Whilst we welcome the fact that there are pockets of good examples in legal practice: firms with improving diversity statistics, mental health and wellbeing programmes, hybrid working models, and more client-centric firms, we cannot be complacent. How can law firms be more like Patagonia? The secret lies in alignment: Patagonia has eight key philosophies[132] from product design through to environment, each aligned to its then mission statement to

---

[128] https://www.thelawyer.com/dear-law-firms-seven-pandemic-love-letters-from-your-clients/ More about the O-shaped lawyer can be found here: https://www.oshapedlawyer.com.

[129] Lawyer katy Dowell June 2021 Lawyer's Inhouse Sentiment Survey.

[130] Deloitte Insights (2019). Purpose is everything: How brands that authentically lead with purpose are changing the nature of business today. URL: https://www2.deloitte.com/us/en/insights/topics/marketing-and-sales-operations/global-marketing-trends/2020/purpose-driven-companies.html.

[131] Chouinard (2016), p. 228.

[132] Product design, production, distribution, marketing, financial, human resource, management, and environmental.

> build the best product, cause no unnecessary harm, use business insights to inspire and implement solutions to the environmental crisis.

Could law firms align some of the philosophies we described with providing legal services?

- What if pro bono activities were integrated into the litigation practice, rather than being hived off into a committee?
- What if team wellbeing objectives were part of partner performance reviews? Or if partners led by example?
- What if diversity targets were part of practice group performance measurements?
- Could firms adopt Sustainable Human Resource Management policies?[133]
- What if law firms integrated environmental, social and governance metrics into their business plan?
- Or measured the carbon footprint of their work back through the whole value chain? What if law firms were required by law to produce audited reports on their ESG performance?

It is clear that, while some law firms are adopting ESG principles, these principles remain merely "*additional facts*" when considering the proclaimed purpose of law firms, mirrored in the somewhat homogenous vision, to "*provide excellent legal services*". Based on field research on admired and financially successful companies in more than 20 countries Rosemary Kanter concludes that:

> a social or institutional logic. . .lies behind the practices of many widely admired, high-performing, and enduring companies. In those firms, society and people are not afterthoughts or inputs to be used and discarded but are core to their purpose.[134]

Law firms are in a unique position to contribute to ESG in a way which compliments their goal to provide excellent legal services *and* make profit: Prioritizing diversity can lead to better financial performance, and enables firms to better respond to client needs; reducing their use of resources such as travel, paper and energy will enable firms to simultaneously reduce their costs; lawyers' pivotal role in providing access to justice can be enhanced through more pro bono and human rights work—and these are just some examples. Finally, in the words of Mahatma Gandhi, "*we mirror the world. . . If we could change ourselves, the tendencies in the world would also change.*"[135] In this way, perhaps law firms can save our home planet?

[133] See for example some simple guidelines on Sustainable HR Management: https://www.shrm.org/hr-today/trends-and-forecasting/special-reports-and-expert-views/Documents/Corporate-Social-Environmental-Sustainability.pdf.

[134] Kanter RM (2011) How Great Companies Think Differently, Harvard Business Review, November: The key ways in which great companies use institutional logic are reported to be: A common purpose, a long-term focus, emotional engagement, partnering with the public, innovation, and self-organization.

[135] Mahatma Gandhi.

Liquid Legal Waves to Other Chapters, Written by the Editors

What if we create law firms (or legal inhouse teams) that move from an 'ego-system' to a prospering 'eco-system'? What if we broke free from pure profit and growth-orientation—a state of *organized irresponsibility*, as *Emma* and *Madeleine* state? Would that be the "*Elevated Workplace*" that *Liam*, *John* and *Joyce* have described?

Valérie and *Filip* address the need to overcome our cognitive biases as a foundational step for "*Transforming Legal Ecosystems*", arguing that the scale and scope of the change depends on the attitude of the people experiencing it. Are they bridging the gap between Patagonia and today's reality of legal teams and law firms?

Patagonia is about company culture and company values. Human interaction is about culture and values, as well. In a globalized society and in globalized corporations, cultural awareness is key to a truly inclusive and thereby humanized environment. Understanding the impact culture has on human behavior allows us to factor human behavior into business and to take informed decisions, explains *Tatiana* in the next chapter on "*International Business Etiquette For Legal (IBEL)*".

References

Chouinard Y (2016) Let my people go surfing. Penguin Books, New York

Collier R (2016) Wellbeing in the legal profession: reflections on recent developments (or, what we talk about, when we talk about wellbeing?). Int J Leg Prof 23:41–60. https://doi.org/10.1080/09695958.2015.1113970

Collier R (2020) Anxiety and wellbeing amongst junior lawyers: a research study, an executive summary provided by Anxiety UK

Dweck C (2017) Mindset: changing the way you think to fulfill your potential. Robinson, London

Empson L (2017) Leading professionals – power, politics, and prima donnas. Oxford University Press, Oxford. Chapters 2 and 6

Fredrickson BL (2013) Love 2.0: how our supreme emotion affects everything we feel, think, do, and become. Penguin, London

Glesner Fines B (2008) Fundamental principles and challenges of humanizing legal education. Washburn Law J 47:313–326

Grünberger M, Mangold AK, Markard N, Payandeh M, Towfigh EV (2021) Diversität in Rechtswissenschaft und Rechtspraxis. Nomos. https://doi.org/10.5771/9783748927617

Hill LA, Brandeau G, Truelove E, Lineback K (2014) Collective genius. Harvard Business Review Press, Boston, p 63

Hunter Schwartz M (2008) Humanizing legal education: an introduction to a symposium whose time came. Washburn Law J 47:235–246. Available at https://www.washburnlaw.edu/profiles/faculty/activity/_fulltext/schwartz-michael-2008-47washburnlawjournal235.pdf
Hussy W (1998) Denken und Problemlösen. Kohlhammer, Stuttgart
Jones E (2020) Emotions in the law school. Routledge, Oxon
Kowalski M (2017) The great legal reformation, Bloomington
Linstead S et al (2009) Management and organization, a critical text, 2nd edn. Palgrave Macmillan
Michel A (2007) A distributed cognitive perspective on newcomers' change processes: the management of cognitive uncertainty in two investment banks. Adm Sci Q 52:507–557
Muir R (2017) Beyond smart: lawyering with emotional intelligence. American Bar Association
Nelken M (1996) Negotiation and psychoanalysis: if I'd wanted to learn about feelings, i wouldn't have gone to law school. J Leg Educ 46(3):420–429. http://www.jstor.org/stable/42893459
Newton J (2020) The client centered law firm. Blue Check Publishing, p 83
Packard, S (2019) Fully human: 3 steps to grow your emotional fitness in work, leadership and life. Penguin Random House LLC, New York, p 5
Petriglieri G, Petriglieri JL (2015) Can business schools humanize leadership? Acad Manag Learn Educ 14(4):625–647 at p 625. https://doi.org/10.5465/amle.2014.0201
Scharmer O, Kaufer K (2013) Leading from the emerging future: from ego-system to eco-system economies. Berrett-Koehler, San Francisco
Vaughan S, Thomas L, Young A (2015) Symbolism over substance? Large law firms and corporate social responsibility. Leg Ethics 18(2):138–163
Vogl R (2021) Research handbook on big data law. Edward Elgar, pp 404–431
Ziercke E, Knipping C (2019) Next generation study. Bucerius Center on the Legal Profession

Emma Ziercke is a solicitor (England & Wales), Senior Research Fellow at the Bucerius Center on the Legal Profession, and guest lecturer at the Bucerius Law School, Hamburg. After working as a corporate lawyer (Managing Associate) for Linklaters in London from 2002 until 2009, she moved to Hamburg, and completed a part-time Executive MBA at Nottingham University Business School, focussing on law firm management and organisational behaviour. From 2016 to 2022 she worked as a researcher at the Bucerius Center on the Legal Profession, focussing on the organisational behaviour of law firms, including gender and generational diversity, leadership and innovation, as well as law firm management. Emma is currently Legal Counsel for Commercial and Legal Operations at Sunfire GmbH.

Prof. Dr. jur. Madeleine Bernhardt, LL.M. is a lawyer, psychologist and certified Business Coach (European Coaching Association). She is Director Strategic Leadership Development and member of the Executive Faculty of the Bucerius Center on the Legal Profession, Hamburg. She regularly conducts leadership development programs for professional service firms and consults to international law firm partners on the strategic development of leadership. She is the founder of Deep Human Science (www.deephumanscience.de), a consultancy that focuses on taking leadership in professional service firms to the next level.

International Business Etiquette For Legal (IBEL)

Tatiana Caldas-Löttiger

Contents

Abstract

In today's corporate world, Diversity & Inclusion policies are at the top of the agenda in every organization—particularly, large corporations and multinationals are required to comply and people are expected to work harmoniously. However, cultural differences have been proven to be an underestimated factor in international business and often Legal departments are the ones to blame if a business deal fails. For example, when a lawyer (from Spain) could not agree on the terms of a contract because the other party (from Sweden) did not bring enough documentation to prove their argument, concluding that the uncertainty was too risky. Or, when a lawyer felt that the solution the other party was suggesting was

Tatiana Caldas-Löttiger is an Interim Senior Legal Counsel, and entrepreneur, founding president of the International Women In Business Group (IWIB), a think-tank with offices in Brussels and Stockholm, and co-founder of The Foreign Lawyers Network (FLN) based in Stockholm.

T. Caldas-Löttiger (✉)
Stockholm, Sweden
e-mail: t.caldas-lottiger@liquid-legal-institute.org

K. Jacob et al. (eds.), *Liquid Legal – Humanization and the Law*, Law for Professionals, https://doi.org/10.1007/978-3-031-14240-6_18

unethical. How do we know who was right or wrong? Maybe both lawyers were right in their assumptions—and, the human factor was at fault.

The article analyses how empathy can be developed with cultural awareness and showcases the author's personal journey into cultural awareness from living in countries with very different cultures (Colombia, Sweden, and United States). It also explains how these dilemmas have been the subject of research by the World Values Survey (WVS), the European Social Survey (ESS), and the Geert Hofstede Analysis. The article ends by explaining how Legal should implement a program that could facilitate working more efficiently with different cultures. This program has been titled by the author as **International Business Etiquette for Legal (IBEL).** According to the author IBEL could be used as a tool to improve human interactions, concluding that it could help minimize misunderstandings during negotiations, and help people to actually work harmoniously.

The pacta sunt servanda fundamental principle of law is the base of the main legal systems in the world, but not for everyone, not everywhere and not always.[1]

1 Introduction

Lawyers are expected to act in the most ethical way possible and to observe the law. But what happens when due to cultural differences what is considered morally and ethically acceptable for one legal counsel is not acceptable for the opposing counsel representing a potential client? One party might say no deal, and that would be the end of it. Another approach could be using persuasion based on empathy. Learning about cultural differences beforehand to avoid cultural clashes, helps us better prepare before a business meeting with people from other cultures. Understanding the impact that **culture** has on **human behavior** would allow us to factor human behavior into business and take informed decisions, then to act or change strategies accordingly.[2]

[1]Quote from credit expert Krum Berovski. IWIB Series on Payments. August 2020. According to Mr. Berovski, the pandemic made it clear that even though pacta sunt servanda is a fundamental principle of law that means agreements must be kept, and is the base of the main legal systems in the world. In some countries people who can, but don't want to pay their obligations forces businesses to find creative ways to secure payments.

[2]**Culture:** In simple terms, culture is the people's 'way of life', meaning the way groups do things. Different groups of people may have different cultures. For the purpose of this article, we will focus on human and organizational culture. **Human culture** is learned at home, differs mainly in values, cannot be changed but can be self managed and belong to anthropology. Whereas **organizational**

Cultural consideration would increase awareness of identifying and reading non-verbal codes which are not regulated by law such as assumptions, the feeling of fear, doubt, trust, manipulation, or emotions like the sense of inclusiveness and belonging, resentment and anger. By reading non-verbal codes lawyers can better 'read the air' during negotiations.

In this chapter, we will introduce the concept of International Business Etiquette (IBE as framework or guide that could help Legal align with the Humanization of Business.

It is important to highlight that this article is written from the perspective of an In-House Counsel working for a Legal department at a multinational corporation referred to as "Legal".[3] And, it is not about legal ethics, which are the principles of conduct that members of the legal profession are expected to observe in their practice, nor about comparative law among different legal systems.

2 The Hofstede Analysis[4] Applied to International Business Etiquette (IBE)

In the corporate world, it is widely acknowledged that culture has been identified as an often-overlooked barrier. For instance, a business meeting can jeopardize a deal if we are not familiar with the country-specific business customs and etiquette,[5] i.e., appropriate business dress codes, communication styles, social structures, gift-giving policies, and much more. Thus, IBE instructs on how to present yourself professionally in the different cultures you will be exposed to when doing businesses overseas.[6]

---

culture is learned when joining a company (Code of Conduct), can be changed or dealt with, belong to sociology. Corporate Culture is everyone's responsability despite their own. See Company Culture Is Everyone's Responsibility by Denise Lee John. Harvard Business Review, 2021. Available at: https://hbr.org/2021/02/company-culture-is-everyones-responsibility.

[3] The type of lawyer that carries out legal work directly for their employer, as opposed to a law firm or private practice lawyers who work on behalf of multiple clients.

[4] **Geert Hofstede** (1928–2020) was a Dutch Professor of Organizational Anthropology and International Management, and social psychologist who in 1971 he founded the Personnel Research Department at IBM Europe, which inspired many of todays training programs based on his book 'Culture and Organizations' on corporate international relations. See also Hofstede's best seller book is 'Cultures and Organizations: Software of the Mind'. Revised and expanded 3rd Edition. New York: McGraw-Hill USA, 2010. Available at: https://geerthofstede.com.

[5] The **word etiquette** is originally a French word that was historically used to refer to the cards that were distributed to guests of Royal French palaces and extended to include courts, official ceremonies and banquets. The cards had instructions to comply with, when meeting the King and other key figures of the government such as presidents, diplomats and ministers.

[6] See: **Passport to Trade 2.0**—a project funded with support from the European Commission to improve existing professional training materials in business culture and to incorporate materials from across the whole European Union. The project creates e-learning facilities, supporting and offering additional training materials for SMEs to improve the skills base required to trade across 25 EU countries. Available at: https://businessculture.org/business-culture/business-etiquette/.

Basic aspects related to IBE are:

- Dressing appropriately and conducting meetings according to your audience.
- Awareness of body language and communication style.
- Greeting properly and presenting business cards.
- Preliminary conversations, verbal communication and non-verbal communication.
- Learning about gift giving policies, restaurants and other types of invitations.
- Knowing what is expected in meetings and negotiations: time wise, how specific, how direct, expected end-result, negotiation style, and who has the last word or decision-making power.

In this chapter, we will focus on how cultural differences can break a deal. As legal professionals, we mostly anticipate and reduce risk to protect the business and handle conflict, but usually cultural differences are not in our list of priorities. One clear example of this is when companies are merged or acquired by another company. It is widely known that one of the main reasons all mergers and acquisitions (M&A's) fail is due to cultural preferences—human and organizational cultures.[7]

Another example is reflected in this quote extracted from a presentation on International Payments, where credit expert Krum Berovski, sums it all up:

> The pacta sunt servanda fundamental principle of law might be the base of the main legal systems in the world, but not for everyone, not everywhere and not always.

What he meant by this, is that in a global market, cultures and customs will challenge even the most universal principle in business law: ***pacta sunt servanda***, which means agreements must be kept. He stated that depending on the culture, his department could predict how people in some countries, despite the fact that they were able to pay their obligations, would not do so as agreed, due to cultural differences.

As an example he mentioned that in some countries, customers request an extension to pay just to test the seller. If granted an extension to the payment terms or allowed to pay in installments (not initially agreed), they would become the most loyal customers and long time partners, or they will offer to use unorthodox methods of payments, depending on a crisis, like the current pandemic. In order for his department to negotiate new terms in the agreements to secure payment, they needed a Legal team who was versed in international transactions in those regions and could explore other legal options to secure such payments.

Even though The Hofstede model was not originally intended specifically for the legal profession, it gives a global perspective on how cultures influence the behavior of business people across countries. The first time I heard about the Hosftede

[7] See **Cultural Issues in M&As.** The Financier World Wide Magazine (December 2019) Available at: https://www.financierworldwide.com/cultural-issues-in-ma#.Yeq6JNlKhAY.

Dimensions was at a workshop on Anti-corruption in the Netherlands in 2014, and ever since, I have made it part of my presentations at The Global Legal Skills Conference where I am a regular keynote speaker.[8] At my last keynote in 2019, I talked about Cultural & Ethical Dilemmas in Artificial Intelligence (AI) where I referred to Hofstede's link between culture and ethics, and tried conciliating the fact that AI has no borders and should be as bias-free as possible.

The Geert Hofstede Dimensions

Hofstede identified six dimensions to aid in anticipating and reducing culture clashes that are statistically correlated with a multitude of other data already collected about several countries. For example, **power distance** is correlated with the use of violence in domestic politics and with income inequality in certain countries; **uncertainty avoidance** is associated with Roman Catholicism and with legal obligation in developed countries; **individualism** is correlated with national wealth and with mobility between social classes from one generation to the next; **masculinity** is correlated negatively with the percent of women in democratically elected governments; **long-term orientation** is correlated with school results in international comparisons and **indulgence** is correlated with sexual freedom and a call for Human Rights like free expression of opinions.[9] Even though these dimensions were meant to help businesses anticipate and reduce culture clashes, for the purpose of this article, we will focus on the two dimensions that impact Legal when doing business deals and negotiations, which are usually handled by Legal: The **Power Distance & Uncertainty Avoidance** Dimensions.

2.1 Power Distance Dimension

This dimension helps understand how the decision-making process and delegation of authority function, and it gives us a good idea of who has the final say during business negotiations, in other words, who holds the decision power.

The following are some examples to illustrate how to navigate the dimension of Power Distance. As an example, we will use two regions with similar cultures: Latin American and Nordic countries.

---

[8] The **Global Legal Skills Conference** was founded by Professor Mark E. Wojcik of The John Marshall Law School as a resource for law professors, ESL professionals, and other who teach international legal skills to those who speak English as a second language. The GLS Conference Series also includes award presentations to recognize outstanding contributions to the field of international legal skills education, ***Available at:*** https://en.wikipedia.org/wiki/Global_Legal_Skills_Conference.

[9] Available at: Hofstede's website. https://geerthofstede.com.

Hierarchy and Status Egalitarianism[10] is the most dominant social value in the Nordic countries; consensus and compromise are ingrained in business and social life. In Sweden, there is a lack of outward signs of hierarchy and status, as oppose to other cultures, like in Latin-America, for example, where hierarchy and status are very prevalent. Most of the Latin societies are highly structured, and pay great attention to professional degrees, occupation, and social status, which may well also be a reflection of their need for **certainty** rather than **power distance**.

Powerful Assistants and Secretaries In Latin America, usually, the agenda of business people and executives is handled by private assistants or secretaries. Usually, they make the first 'screening', and serve as a filter between you and the client. They are very loyal and protective of their bosses, which means that secretaries have tremendous power to help or hinder your personal and professional relationship with their boss. If they like you and you gain their trust, they may even help you to schedule the meeting at a time when their boss is in high spirits in order to facilitate the business meeting's atmosphere. Thus, it would be wise to arrive 15 min early and introduce yourself to them and have a small chat. One could ask about the things they have on display on their desk, like family photos, and say something nice and wholehearted about them. And, right after you are done with your business meetings, it is more than appropriate to leave a small token of appreciation, like a box of chocolates. From my experience, this could come across as intrusive and seen as harassment in Sweden.

Communication Styles During Meetings The communication style in some countries is direct and open. Swedes, for example, tend to keep their distance when conversing and in general think that small talk is unnecessary and awkward, so they avoid engaging in conversations with strangers or acquaintances; being able to manage on your own is looked upon with both deep respect and admiration. Even before the pandemic, social distancing was the norm in the Swedish society, so there was no need to reinforce it during Covid-19. That is the reason why it is common for Swedes to avoid noisy surroundings and seek silence in nature.[11]

In contrast, this could come across as abrupt in Latin America; for example, jumping right into a meeting without any small talk can be seen as rude. Long handshakes and embracing, is also quite common, and normally, at each negotiation,

[10] In an egalitarian society, all are considered equal, regardless of gender, race, religion, or age. There is not a class system like in Latin America but relatively equal access to income and wealth. Some societies are more egalitarian than others, and some areas of egalitarianism are part of economies, politics, and laws. There isn't data for "the most egalitarian society" in the world, but in terms of economic and gender equality, Nordic countries like Sweden and Norway rank high for economic and gender equality. Available at: https://worldhappiness.report/ed/2020/the-nordic-exceptionalism-what-explains-why-the-nordic-countries-are-constantly-among-the-happiest-in-the-world/.

[11] Study from GlobalSmart. Available at: https://www.globesmart.com/blog/cultural-etiquette-and-social-distancing-around-the-world/.

friendships are established. While in the Nordics, it is customary to address a person by the first name, the opposite happens in Latin American countries, where calling someone by their first name (unless invited to do so) is considered a lack of good manners; it could create confusion and can lead to misrepresentations, if by chance two people have the same name but hold different positions. Thus, courtesy titles and full names and last names are the norm.

Dress Etiquette Like in many countries, when doing business in Latin American countries, the dress code can be more conservative. This is important because during meetings and negotiations, anyone wearing something not formal might be seen as someone who does not take business very seriously, or who has too little respect for the people they are meeting.

2.2 Uncertainty Avoidance Dimension, Refers to High Uncertainty Avoidance vs. Low Uncertainty Avoidance

The Hofstede analysis suggests that the Latin Europe and Latin American legal systems are a typical case of "**high uncertainty avoidance**", where people prefer explicit rules (e.g., about law and religion) and formally structured activities, and employees tend to remain longer with their employers.[12]

Most of these countries have a legal system based on Civil law, also known as Continental law, which is in turn based on Roman tradition, and is the predominant system of law in the world. Latin America has one of the most unified legal systems in the world, where legal and academic opinions are very important sources in the making and interpretation of the laws, but are not of obligatory observance. Instead, several codes of law set out the main principles that guide the law. One could say that, when negotiating with lawyers and clients from Latin America, one would have to prepare much documentation to increase their trust. And since their legal system is codified, one should also make references to their codes of law and be mindful that providing only jurisprudence and academic opinions might increase their uncertainty and delay the process, as these are not of obligatory observance.

In summary, it is best to provide specific rules and structures, recognize their need for information and provide lots of supporting data. Also, if appropriate, provide examples of others who have used the approach successfully, and focus on compliance with procedures and policies.

On the contrary, cultures with "**low uncertainty avoidance**" like the Swedish culture, people have trust on the regulatory systems and prefer consensus over confrontation. Swedes also prefer implicit or flexible rules or guidelines (like with the handling of Covid-19). However, the global digital economy is affecting this dimension. On March of 2019, Swedbank, one of the largest banks in Sweden was

[12]To see Hosftede-insights comparing tool results for Colombia, Spain and Sweden follow this link. Available at: https://www.hofstede-insights.com/country-comparison/colombia,spain,sweden/.

fined by the Sweden's Financial Supervisory Authority (FSA) with a record 386 million dollars over the Baltic money-laundering breaches from mostly Russian non-residents through Estonia from 2010 to 2016. According to the FSA; "The bank's awareness of the risk of money laundering and its processes, routines and control systems were insufficient". Many critics have said that personal trust was a gross breach of the bank's Know-Your-Customer (KYC) procedures.[13]

Nonetheless, besides the Hofstede Analysis, there are many more studies and sources one could use to create an International Business Etiquette framework for Legal. For example, **The World Values Survey (WVS)** argues that people's beliefs play a crucial role in their country's economic development, gender equality, and effective governments.[14]

3 Case-Study: From Colombia to Sweden & Lessons Learned

3.1 From Colombia to Sweden

Because many of the findings in The Hofstede analysis are reflected in my own personal and professional life, I find it relevant to use my own story as a case-study to showcase not only personal cultural clashes but organizational cultural clashes.

Starting with the culture where my identity and behavior stems from, I was born in Cali, Colombia,[15] a multi-cultural country with various ethnic groups. Despite this variety, the majority of people identify as being of either European or mixed European and American Indian ancestry. I personally, identify as Judeo-Christian from European ancestry but strongly embraced the Colombian Latin culture. And, as it happens in the case of many Latino families, I spent a lot of time at my grandparents' home while my parents worked. My mother worked as an anti-drug

[13] To learn more see the Sweden's Financial Supervisory Authority (FSA) /Finansinspektionen (FI) motivation to sancion. It concluded that Swedbank demonstrated major deficiencies in its work to combat money laundering in its Baltic operations. The bank's Swedish operations have not lived up to the requirements in the anti-money laundering regulations. Available at: https://www.fi.se/en/published/sanctions/financial-firms/2020/swedbank-receives-a-warning-and-an-administrative-fine-of-sek-four-billion/.

[14] The **World Values Survey (WVS)** The project's goal is to assess which impact values stability or change over time has on the social, political and economic development of countries and societies. The project grew out of the European Values Study and was started in 1981 by its Founder and first President (1981–2013) Professor Ronald Inglehart from the University of Michigan (USA) and his team, and since then has been operating in more than 120 world societies. Available at: https://www.worldvaluessurvey.org/WVSContents.jsp.

[15] The ethnic diversity of Colombia is a blend between indigenous people, Spanish colonizers, and African slaves. Thus even though Colombia has around 85 different ethnic groups and people may identify with the various ethnicities on the basis of skin color, ancestry or social status. Available at: https://www.worldatlas.com/articles/ethnic-groups-of-colombia.html.

prosecutor and my father as a tax lawyer. High integrity, moral and ethical values were core values in my family, especially during my teens in the 90s, in a time when money could corrupt anyone, so much so, that my mother was rewarded by the American government for being an incorruptible figure during the fight against the Cali Cartel.[16] I am so grateful for the way my parents raised me. They really "walked the walk".

However, the one person with the greatest influence on me was my grandfather Caldas. He, too, was a lawyer, a politician well versed in international relations and a polyglot who knew how to navigate the diplomatic world. He worked as a political advisor to various European and American ambassadors in Colombia. Sadly, due to his political support to a leader of the Democratic Party who was assassinated in 1943, he had to flee the violence that subsequently erupted in Colombia.[17] He first relocated to the USA and after the Second World War ended, he moved to Scotland where my father grew-up. His life fascinated me. Upon their return to Colombia in the late 60s is when my parents met. I was amazed by all his stories and from watching him hosting meetings at his Bogotá home and accompanying him to social gatherings from an early age. Because he expected my older siblings and I to socialize and represent the family well, we had to learn table manners and etiquette lessons and even had private English tutors at home so we would know how to interact with the diplomats who attended social and political events; I remember him saying how important it was to be cosmopolitan, so we could fit in anywhere in the world when we traveled.

3.2 Lessons Learned

Law School: From my Hometown Cali to the Capital City of Bogotá D.C. During my first year of law school, I realized I lived in a bubble and I was disconnected. I felt somewhat entitled, not only due to my upbringing, but because my last name Caldas is well-known to most people, and I thought people would like to be my friends; oh, boy was I wrong! My law school classmates could not care less about my surname or how good manners were; it was all about being a good student and showing up on time. My classmates became some of my best friends today; they

[16]The Cali Cartel (Spanish: Cartel de Cali) was a drug cartel based in southern Colombia, around my hometown, the city of Cali. At the height of the Cali Cartel's reign from 1993–1995, they were cited as having control over 90% of the world's cocaine market and for being directly responsible for the growth of the cocaine market in Europe, By the mid-1990s, the trafficking empire of the Cali Cartel was a multibillion-dollar enterprise. In 2002, was estimated that it had $30 billion in profits. Source Wikipedia. Available at: https://en.wikipedia.org/wiki/Cali_Cartel.

[17]My grandfather was a political advisor to Jorge Gaitan, a presidential candidate who was killed on April 1948, which unleashed a wave of urban violence in the wake of his assassination. A 3-day uprising, called *El Bogotazo*, left Bogotá in ruins, and forced my grandfather to leave the country as the death of Gaitán marked the beginning of an undeclared civil war with an estimated 43,557 deaths in that year. Available at: https://sites.tufts.edu/atrocityendings/2016/12/14/colombia-la-violencia-2/.

made me humble and still they make fun of me. **Lesson:** Be humble, how you see yourself is not how others see you.

As an International Law Student in Chicago, USA Back home I was not exposed to a very diverse group of people besides Colombians, Americans and Europeans, and I did not interact with other cultures, which led me to my first cultural shock with a classmate from Japan. The last day of class, I hugged her tightly, and kissed her and her boyfriend goodbye on their cheeks! They left in horror and I never heard from them again. **Lesson:** Be observant and curious. Proactively show interest about other cultures and ask questions. This was when my cultural awareness kicked-off.

The second lesson was an eye opener. I grew up thinking that my ethnicity was White-Caucasian while I was living in Colombia, but it was not until I had to fill-out a form at the University in Chicago that I was asked about my ethnicity. When I marked "White", the lady at the Admissions Office, told me I was wrong and that I should mark "Hispanic Non-Caucasian" instead. **Lesson:** Identity is not only what you identify as but also how others see you. My years in the USA helped shape my identity.

Professional Life in Sweden So far, the biggest cultural shock. It was in Sweden where that feeling of otherness became real and my sense of belonging vanished. For the first time in my life I felt like I did not belong at all. Unless Swedes around me were highly educated, well- travelled or working internationally, I was excluded and felt discriminated against. The experience that shocked me to the core happened right after I graduated from my Masters program in EU law at Stockholm University, just over a year of living in Sweden.

Because I wanted to find a job as soon as possible, and to get into the Swedish labor market against my husband's advice, I made an appointment at the Swedish Employment Office and met with a public officer/*handledare* who after reading my CV said these exact words:

> being a lawyer from Colombia means nothing in Sweden, but because you have a Masters in European law in English, I can offer you a job as a cashier at WesternUnion.

Shocking! No lesson was learned there. I just had to put on my cosmopolitan hat and turned to my international peers to be able to navigate the Swedish labour market. I kept that visit a secret and never told anyone, not even my husband. Some 12 years later, after working as a legal consultant associate for a large law firm and managing my consultancy firm, I went to work in-house for a client. Right from the beginning I realized my only colleague in Legal was not happy with me being from Colombia. For the sake of clarity, we will call her Maria. So, Maria would say things like: "she is from Colombia but lives in a very nice area", or "you make me look bad because you work after 5 pm" and "why do you wear suits, heels and red lipstick in a tech-company?". I tried to take the high road by being empathetic and attributed her insensitivity to a lack of cultural awareness. I explained to her that it was common for

Latin women to wear high-heels and red lipstick at work, and for Latinos to work after 5 pm. I even shared with her my presentation on International Business Etiquette. Nothing worked.

However, it was not until later that another employee warned me that Maria was suspicious of me being corrupt and felt unsafe around me because I was Colombian. I felt that this was jeopardizing my professional reputation and I decided to leave the company. As they say: people leave people not companies. **Lessons for the organization**: Diversity, Belonging & Inclusion training programs are useless if employees are not willing to actively listen and learn to improve how to interact with colleagues from other cultures. Organizational culture is everyone's responsibility.

After that experience, I became an advocate for Cultural Intelligence and Female Empowerment. And, in 2019 with the support of The Stockholm Chamber of Commerce, I founded **International Women In Business (IWIB)** to foster a sense of belonging and sisterhood between Swedish businesswomen, expats and international women in business.[18]

If I look back, out of the 22 years I have been interacting with different cultures, I would say that my 16 years of working and living in Sweden (since 2006) have been the most enriching. **My biggest lesson in and out of the workplace:** Do not make assumptions. At the end of the day, we are people working with people. When we interact and communicate, we will always have biases, and the environment in which we work is both personal and professional (Human Culture intertwined in the Organizational Culture). Being aware that that exists is the first step, then it will be easier for you to spot biased behaviors, and as soon as you catch it in the interaction, you can call it out.

4 What Could Legal Do to Implement International Business Etiquette?

Legal could implement the following:

A) **Debate Club.**[19] I would propose that Legal create a debate club—the International Business Etiquette Debate Club for Legal (IBEL). The IBEL Debate Club could be formed by diverse teams across functions who can bring up current, past or imaginary legal issues to create fictional scenarios, where team members,

[18] International Women In Business (IWIB) is the fastest growing business network, operating under the umbrella of The Stockholm Chamber of Commerce, growing from seven (7) members in 2018 to 370 by the end of 2021. Available at: www.iwib.online.

[19] Debate clubs encourage students to become more informed about political and global affairs, or provide a venue for students to train for debate competitions at a national and international level. Like the Model United Nations (MUN) debate club, also adopted by Stockholm's University (SMUN) in cooperation with the Department of Economic History and International Relations at Stockholm University, to help students acquire the skills and knowledge about global issues as well as practical experience that can help them in their future careers. Available at: https://www.sus.su.se/studentfreningar-p-su/stockholm-model-united-nations.

ideally from different cultures, can discuss ethical dilemmas. These dilemmas can be related to cultural differences, past situations that may have caused frustration or the loss of a deal because the way Legal handled a meeting. For example, things that could potentially happen in the middle of a negotiation of a business deal. One can even include regulatory topics where Legal gets a fictional request from R&D department about an Artificial Intelligence-driven product that gives rise to ethical concerns. This IBEL Debate Club could have a powerful effect on employees that were never heard before, as it will empower diverse voices and drive inclusivity. Furthermore, with the data collected from the IBEL Debate Club, an AI-driven prediction tool could be created in the future. Debates clubs are very common in law schools and even global corporations already use these types of clubs, like the Ethical AI Debate Club created by the AI & Data Team at H&M Group.[20]

B) **Cooperate with Human Resources (HR)**. HR is the starting point for a company's culture, as they often establish and enforce rules not only related to the Code of Conduct but influence how welcomed employees feel.[21] This is particularly important as more companies are interested in establishing diversity, equity and inclusivity initiatives. Fostering a close cooperation with HR could help Legal to have first-hand information to create surveys that could facilitate collecting anonymized and relevant data from the surveys responses. Responders could also opt for participating in the IBEL Debate Club. Based on the data collected, HR could also create a **human-centered** handbook that serves as an accessible reference guide; this guide would standardize expectations across the organization to ultimately deploy a corporate International Business Etiquette Framework based on those surveys.
   Furthermore, the surveys should include specific consent from all the participants as GDPR will require HR professionals to use the data for the specific purpose for which it was given.[22] Also, HR is often responsible for ensuring that companies comply with national and international laws (e.g., completing paperwork to verify an employee's citizenship or visa status, especially if they operate in an industry that the government regulates, or reviewing employment laws to confirm compliance).

C) **Include IBEL as part of the organization's Human-centered Foresight Strategy**.[23] Technology has opened the door for more mobility and flexibility, craving for another dimension for employee satisfaction and growth. Legal could

[20] H&M's Ethical AI Debate Club. Available at: H&M https://hmgroup.com/our-stories/responsible-ai-is-better-ai/.

[21] See the role of HR. Available at: https://www.indeed.com/career-advice/career-development/why-are-human-resources-important?from=careeradvice-US.

[22] See Art. 6 of the EU General Data Protection Regulation (GDPR) Consent Requirements. Available at: https://gdpr.eu/gdpr-consent-requirements/?cn-reloaded=1.

[23] Strategic foresight is a discipline that enables us to understand how issues unfolding today could affect our organizations tomorrow. By researching existing trends, imagining future possibilities, and implementing strategies that account for these possibilities, organizations can ensure that they

implement new guidelines that provide avenues to include IBEL in their Code of Conduct and Compliance training programs. Now, imagine that it's 2032; what has changed? A new gadget has revolutionized how we communicate; automation has supplanted millions of jobs, and climate change has transformed how we travel and where we live. Now bring yourself back to the present day and imagine you are given the task to prepare your Legal department for that future. How do you start? How to prepare for rapid change and an uncertain future? Methods like the foresight strategy in organizations are used to improve interactions with the customer of the future, and because Legal is primarily a customer-facing function, adding IBEL into the strategy could ensure that the outputs of the strategic foresight process are grounded in a human-centered customer view of the future.[24]

If none of the above is feasible for your organization, there is plenty of literature, models and training programs. One of my favorite authors is Kyle Nel, CEO & Co-founder of Uncommon Partners, whose book and training methods are very innovative. Back in 2018, he already stated that

> corporations face an opportunity for a behavioral revolution in innovation and transformation by understanding and addressing the human roadblocks to transformational change.[25]

Also, as shown on Fig. 1**, The Iceberg Model of Behavior & Culture—originally** developed by Anthropologist Edward T. Hall, is now used by many business strategists and organizations. This model combines cultural understanding and behavioral competence while working alongside people of different cultures and beliefs.[26]

---

are equipped to perform and succeed in a wide variety of uncertain future scenarios. Available at: https://www.bridgeable.com/.

[24]See: The Future of Work- How Corporations Can create human-centered transformations. Deloitte/2021. Available at: https://www2.deloitte.com/us/en/blog/human-capital-blog/2021/the-future-of-work-how-corporations-can-create-human-centered-transformations.html.

[25]In this book, Kyle et al., introduce an innovative process for creating breakthrough change, using tools such as science fiction, cartoons, rap music, and neuroprototypes to overcome people's inability to imagine or react to what doesn't yet exist, override stubborn habits and routines that prevent them from changing. The book show-cases how these tools have been used successfully by companies such as Walmart, Pepsi, IKEA, Google, Microsoft, and others, giving guidance on how to transcend the human barriers that block change in organizations. See page 168. *Leading Transformation: How To Take Charge of Your Company's Future. Nathan Furr, Kyle Nel, Thomas Zoega Ramsoy. Harvard Business Review Press. (2018).*

[26]Anthropologist Edward T. Hall developed the Cultural Iceberg Model in the 1970s as an analogy for the cultural codes that prevail in any society. Available at: https://harappa.education/harappa-diaries/iceberg-model-of-culture-and-behavior/.

Fig. 1 Version of the Iceberg Model of Behavior & Culture by Torben Rick. Available at: https://www.torbenrick.eu/blog/culture/organizational-culture-is-like-an-iceberg/

5 Conclusion

Being aware of our own identity is vital to understanding **WHY** we behave **HOW** we behave and identifying **WHAT** triggers us. We might have wrong ideas about our own identity, and it is not until we are exposed to other cultures that we discover who we are. Our identity includes how we see and define ourselves and how others define us. To succeed in the digital economy it is vital to uncover **WHY** customers prefer one product over other, make certain decisions or demand certain services.

There is no better time than now for Legal to adopt a program based on **International Business Etiquette**. In the times we live, it is essential to create new norms for **HOW** people work together going forward and post-pandemic. As an integral part of business, Legal will be increasingly pressured to align with the company's business strategy on implementing a human-centered approach across all business functions.

IBEL could hold the key for Legal to pivot on multi-cultural competency using it as a guide to reduce conflict, identify risks and better communicate and interact across business functions, which will improve results inside and outside the company when dealing with stakeholders, third-parties and international opposing counsels. However, to adopt International Business Etiquette, it is not enough to have training programs and onboarding sessions in place, like the IBEL Debate Club suggested. **WHAT** is needed is commitment from each individual.

One of the key messages from the ***pacta sunt servanda*** example[27] is that we should see people as people, and really understand that everything about their lives is intimately connected with their decisions in business, in finances, in how they perform and execute at work. As stated by American lawyer Mark A. Cohen, a noted global legal leader and member of the Liquid Legal Institute: "Legal talent requires an evolved human being" and "valuing humanity may be the greatest transformation hurdle legal culture must clear."[28]

Liquid Legal Waves to Other Chapters, Written by the Editors

ESG and CDR are top of the agenda for corporations. As lawyers get engaged and play a more active role in *"Corporate Digital Responsibility – Stimulating Human-Centric Innovation and Building Trust in the Digital World"*, as *Martina* describes it, our awareness of differing cultural norms is critical for connecting cultural diversity with the consistency required for implementing such programs successfully.

---

[27] Berovski, *supra* note 1.

[28] See Forbes article 'What is Digital Legal Talent?' by Mark A. Cohen (Oct. 2021) Available at: https://www.forbes.com/sites/markcohen1/2021/10/19/what-is-digital-legal-talent/?sh=7873d11b3af8.

While *Tatiana* rightfully reminds us of the need for cultural sensitivity and inter-cultural etiquette, *Tom* provides an interesting perspective on the role of AI in this context: The tools of AI, combined with the law, may offer the opportunity of understanding social environments more realistically, designing them more deliberatively, and seeking defined ends for a differently imagined humanity. Will *"Designing Legal Systems for an Algorithm Society"* build cross-cultural bridges?

Sometimes we don't have to look far to be challenged by cultural norms. Specifically in the more traditional settings lawyers often work in, shifts in cultural norms might still pose a challenge. This constitutes as much a gap in offering a humanized workplace as it is an impediment to the development and long-term success of the firm, as *Roger's* closing chapter *"Who are you…? - A Story About a Gay Humanist Working at a Law Firm"* suggests. *Rainer, Tanja,* and *Patryk* provide the perfect bridge in the next chapter in which they boldly rethink the traditional settings and mechanisms in law firms—*"About lawyers and Humans"*.

Tatiana Caldas-Löttiger is an international business lawyer with more than 15 years of international legal experience in the telecommunications sector who is legally trained in Colombia, USA & Sweden. She holds a Master degree in European Law and another Masters in International Business & Trade Law. A futurist lawyer passionate about Artificial Intelligence (AI), who after 20 years of living and working abroad, became an advocate for Cultural Intelligence (CQ). A topic she has been covering for the past 10 years in her keynote speeches at The Annual Legal Skills Conference in countries like USA, Italy, Austria, and Sweden. After working as a legal advisor for the Minister of Foreign Affairs in Colombia, and as a visiting attorney in United States, Tatiana worked as a legal consultant for several years at Eversheds-Sutherland Law Firm and was an in-house legal counsel at SAP Sweden in 2018. Currently, she lives in Sweden where she works as the Global Managing Partner of Executive HUB. During her spare time, she mentors young lawyers and entrepreneurs under The American-Swedish Chamber of Commerce Mentorship Program. And, is the founder and leader of International Women In Business (IWIB), and co-founder of The Foreign Lawyers Network (FLN) in Stockholm.

About Lawyers and Humans

Rainer Markfort, Tanja Podinic, and Patrycjusz Zamorski

Contents

Rainer Markfort is Corporate partner of Dentons Europe LLP.

Tanja Podinic is Global Director of Innovation Programs at Dentons Global Services UK.

Patrycjusz Zamorski is Europe Director of Talent Development at Dentons Business Services EMEA sp.zo.o.

R. Markfort (✉)
Berlin, Germany
e-mail: rainer.markfort@dentons.com

T. Podinic
London, UK
e-mail: tanja.podinic@dentons.com

P. Zamorski
Warsaw, Poland
e-mail: patrycjusz.zamorski@dentons.com

K. Jacob et al. (eds.), *Liquid Legal – Humanization and the Law*, Law for Professionals, https://doi.org/10.1007/978-3-031-14240-6_19

Abstract

The rule of law helped to humanize societies. Over ages statutes were written in plain language and meant to be read (or heard) and understood by the people. Over time, our societies, our economies, and our interactions have become increasingly complex, and so have the rules and regulations that govern them. Modern companies' legal and compliance departments play an increasingly significant role in mitigating risks associated with new projects and products. They, in turn, rely on external legal advice when specialized expertise is required. This is the playing field of international law firms. For many years the total turnover has increased well above the market. Profit per partner has increased even more. However, over time both the lawyer-client relationship as well as the working conditions of lawyers and staff have suffered from increasing economic pressures. Lawyering mutated from a profession into a profit driven business. This comes with a cost: a dehumanized working environment, huge pressure on law firm partners, regarding both qualities of work and economics. Partners push it down to associates and staff which leads to high numbers of psychological diseases, drug abuse, and suicide, or people trying to escape, which then again results in high fluctuation and a 'war for talent' (euphemism). Do we want to continue down this path? Imagine a future where law firms focused on being more "human" for both, individuals working within and for our clients. Can we imagine a law firm where the primary focus is on helping our clients understand rules and regulations to guide the way, translating the secret legal code into business language, thus granting them access to law? Can we imagine a competitive environment where client satisfaction counts more than profit per partner? Can we create an operating model providing funds for investments in the future, thus unlocking new sources of revenue that are built on value add rather than the billable hour? Can we create a less hierarchical working environment nourishing the expectations of young lawyers, valuing the contribution of professional staff and overall making law firms a place where people love to work?

> Wer will dass die Welt so bleibt wie sie ist der will nicht, dass sie bleibt (Status quo, Erich Fried)[1]

The rule of law helped to humanize societies. Over ages statutes were written in plain language and meant to be read (or heard) and understood by the people. The Codex Hammurabi, the Code Napoleon or the German Civil Code have all been drafted so that ordinary people could know their rights without the help of lawyers. They granted access to law and justice.

Over time, our societies, our economies, and our interactions have become increasingly complex, and so have the rules and regulations that govern them. It takes years of university studies to understand the basics, and there is hardly any area in modern economies where businesspersons find their way without the help of legally educated advisors. Another level of complexity is added when transactions cross borders and involve multiple jurisdictions. In a globalized economy, this is day-to-day business.

Modern companies' legal and compliance departments play an increasingly significant role in mitigating risks associated with new projects and products. They, in turn, rely on external legal advice when specialized expertise is required. This is the playing field of international law firms, an ever-growing industry since the nineteenth century.[2] For many years until the Financial Crisis in 2008 the total turnover has increased year-over-year to double digits and well above the market.[3] Profit per partner has increased even more.[4]

However, over time both the lawyer-client relationship as well as the working conditions of lawyers and staff have suffered from increasing economic pressures. Lawyering mutated from a profession into a profit driven business. This comes with a cost: a dehumanized working environment, huge pressure on law firm partners, regarding both qualities of work and economics. Partners push it down to associates and staff which leads to high numbers of psychological diseases, drug abuse, and suicide, or people trying to escape,[5] which then again results in high fluctuation and a 'war for talent' (euphemism).

Do we want to continue down this path? Imagine a future where law firms focused on being more "human" for both, individuals working within (partners, associates, and professional staff) and for our clients. Can we imagine a law firm where the primary focus is on helping our clients understand rules and regulations to

---

[1] "Who wants / that the world remains as it is / does not want it to remain". The poem of Erich Fried "status quo" describes in a few words what it is all about: If we don't change the world, it will cease to exist. And this is our mission. Changing the way how the legal profession operates in order to make it more human and thus guide the way to a (better) future.

[2] Replogle (2017), pp. 292–293. https://repository.law.umich.edu/cgi/viewcontent.cgi?article=1062&context=mbelr.

[3] Yoon (2014), pp. 697–719.

[4] https://en.wikipedia.org/wiki/List_of_largest_law_firms_by_profits_per_partner.

[5] Strathausen, Roger et al. "Lawyer Well-Being - the Silent Pandemic." Liquid Legal Institute e.V., March 23, 2022. https://www.liquid-legal-institute.com/workinggroups/lawyer-wellbeing/.

guide the way, translating the secret legal code into business language, thus granting them access to law? Can we imagine a competitive environment where client satisfaction counts more than profit per partner? Can we create an operating model providing funds for investments in the future (product development, human capital), thus unlocking new sources of revenue that are built on value add rather than the billable hour? Can we create a less hierarchical working environment nourishing the expectations of young lawyers, valuing the contribution of professional staff and overall making law firms a place where people love to work? There are some law firm leaders trying to make this become reality.

We will start with the 'unpleasant now' and analyze the current situation within law firms (1) and then look to the lawyer-client relationship (2). We will take a closer look at initiatives within law firms to support both their lawyers and professionals in developing better working habits, offering support and other means to make a law firm a better place to work (3). We will cover one of the big questions of our days—whether technology will help to humanize the way we work, or to the contrary, worsen the state (4). Finally, we turn to the current operating model of law firms and the mechanics on the legal market, we touch upon the crucial point for any change for the better: there will be no change against 'cash all out' and 'profit per partner', thus a new financial model for law firm operations is required (5).

However, we see change on the rise all over the place, in all sectors, markets, and societies. There is no reason to believe that the legal profession is exempt. We still have it in our hands to drive this change and determine the direction. If we do not, others will.

1 Profession Under Scrutiny

Law firms mean tough atmospheres, surrounded by stress, focusing on transaction and output rather than personal relationships. A place where collaboration is a key factor, where there is strong competition across all levels of professional fee earners, where the only thing they have in common is practicing in a law firm. No doubt, it is a traditional industry, or should we say 'artisanry' as it is more an accumulation of individual craftsperson rather than a strong workforce creating and selling comprehensive products or services. The profession lags behind the general business in terms of technology, efficiency, transparency, and many other aspects with one exception—quality. Quality is always close to a hundred percent.

The business model of law firms serving business clients has always been profitable and has become even more profitable over the past years.[6] This has the potential to be the poison of success. Competition is all around: legal tech startups, the Big4 and other advisory companies that offer services which lawyers

[6]Cohen, Mark A. "Are Law Firms Sustainable? It's The Model That Matters." Forbes. Forbes Magazine, August 19, 2019. https://www.forbes.com/sites/markcohen1/2019/08/19/are-law-firms-sustainable-its-the-model-that-matters/?sh=21a7cf8f628f.

traditionally provide; and they do it in a more efficient manner. Meanwhile, the only protection law firms have is professional regulation, but even this is eroding. The business environment for law firms is changing rapidly. It is unpredictable and unstable. However, people and businesses still rely on lawyers and law firms.

Overall, this seems like a grim picture, and a view that may not be shared by all in the industry. High salaries even for beginners[7] and astronomical drawings for partners—at least from the perspective of an average citizen—may be the recompense for burnout and inhuman working conditions. While our business is still profitable, we should think about how to hold our ground, to retain our talent, and transform our profession. Develop a balanced, skillful way of using artificial intelligence and technology, and free up space and time to focus on relationships. We advocate for a transformation of the law firm operating model.[8] This will enhance how law firms interact with clients and how they treat their personnel.

2 Reflections on 'Clients First'

Thirty years ago, law firms in continental European countries were small partnerships. There was no technology at all apart from a telephone and a telex. At that time, lawyers worked within small teams in a very personal setting, and the client-lawyer relationship was a very personal one as well. The first wave of technology (email communication), the growth of small to larger partnerships and then international mergers, has led to the internal law firm structure becoming more complex. Some administrative tasks were taken away from lawyers, and business processes started to be organized like in any other businesses. However, the teams within law firms remained the same; a partner, a few associates and just a secretary, this is the structure even within big law firms.

What has changed, however, is the client-lawyer relationship. Formerly a relationship with a general counsel was a lifetime affair, meaning that lawyers grew with their client contacts who typically also stayed with their companies for a lifetime. Law firm partners could even sell their book of relationships to a younger lawyer in the partnership, and professional firms helped to value the client base to establish the price. Today, all lawyers are moving around, both in-house counsel and law firm partners. There is much less loyalty and stability in the client-lawyer relationship which leads to lawyers spending much time on pitches for new projects and panel processes. We see much more rotation of our contacts within the clients' companies, and also from one company to the other. So, it has become less personal, but in a way more competitive (and more transparent).

[7] Roberts, Hannah. "Clifford Chance Bumps Germany Associate Salaries by €20K." *Law.com* International, October 11, 2021. https://www.law.com/international-edition/2021/10/11/clifford-chance-bumps-germany-associate-salariesby-e20k/?slreturn=20220121160740.

[8] See Sect. 5 below.

There is a variety of factors influencing the way law firms and their clients work together, creating a backlash on the human relations within a law firm: partner's business case, client relationship, economic pressure, client listening, invoicing by time spent, and beauty contests. Thus, it is worthwhile being conscious of these (Sect. 2.1–2.6) before having a closer look inside law firms (Sect. 3).

2.1 Center of Gravity

A law firm partner's personal relationship with their client is the center of professional work. Therefore, the business case of a partner today is still built on these relationships. It is widespread practice for law firms to test the validity of these relationships in a lateral hire process and reach out to the partners' clients to get confirmation that they would follow him or her to the new firm. It seems as if individual relationships built on personal trust count more than accolades and law firm brands.

Law firms try to institutionalize these relationships. They are willing to invest time and money in building a strong firm-to-firm relationship to benefit both the client and the law firm. Understanding the specific client's business, endeavors and challenges, enables the law firm to offer the full scale of expertise and global coverage. Clients value this approach by reducing the number of law firms they retain. More and more corporates in the past years established panels of law firms they selected to work with exclusively and thus limited the influence of a personal relationship between an outside lawyer and the general counsel or other members of the in-house team. But personal relationships still are the center of gravity in the Legal Industry.[9]

2.2 Caring

Average law firm partners are not good at taking care of their clients. What they are good at is selling themselves, their own expertise. They are good at identifying client needs if they can serve them. What partners are not good at (with some exceptions) is selling other partners' expertise. This is because they do not prioritize listening to what the clients really need beyond what they are personally able to deliver.

There is an extraordinarily strong focus on partners making the best use of their own time driven by the prevailing operating model of law firms.[10] If they were to really listen to their clients, and remain open-minded, they may realize that while they may not be able to deliver on certain client needs, there is someone else in their firm who may be able to help. Alternatively, there could be something else that they

[9] It is misleading to speak of the legal "industry" as it is much more performed as a "craft". Markfort and Zamorski (2020).

[10] See Sect. 5 below.

could offer; or even beyond what a lawyer could provide, perhaps someone in the firm's network. There are certainly some partners who really develop good and deep client relationships, but in general, partners are not always good at taking care of clients.

2.3 End-User Experience

The legal industry is one of the few businesses where customer experience is, to a significant extent, still disregarded. What do people feel when reading a contract, a policy, or a legal memorandum? Legal documents usually come across as coded language, which has been drafted by technical experts for technical experts. Lawyers often fail to consider that the ultimate end user of a work product is a businessperson, i.e., someone who is not fluent in legal coded language.

Instead of making people's lives easier, lawyers are often perceived as making things more complicated. This is true for both external and in-house lawyers. Who needs legal advice? Hardly anyone. What people are looking for is a solution to their problem, mitigating risks coming along with their endeavors and ensuring that their projects will be successful. While in-house lawyers have learnt their lesson, external lawyers are catching up.

2.4 More With Less

The 'more-for-less' challenge that law firms face these days translates to the 'more-with-less' challenge for in-house legal teams.[11] The two key drivers behind "the more" are the increased complexity and unpredictability of the world in which global corporations operate[12] and the growing number of rules and regulations they need to abide by. This drives a continuously increasing workload on in-house legal teams. In-house lawyers must constantly monitor new risks and design or adjust risk management systems.

At the same time, they need to support numerous new business initiatives that are part of the company's strategy to respond to growing complexity. The "less" results from a seismic shift that occurred after the 2008 financial crisis. For the first time in recent history, many legal departments, like any other corporate functions, had to deliver meaningful cost savings. The most recent surveys confirm this ongoing trend.[13]

[11] Markfort and Ragueneau (2022).

[12] The Biology of Corporate Survival, Harvard Business Review, January 2016, Martin Reeves, Simon Levin and Daichi Ueda ("companies operate in an increasingly complex world: Business environments are more diverse, dynamic and interconnected than ever- and far less predictable").

[13] 2020 State of Corporate Law Departments: Effectiveness, Efficiency & Expanding the Guardian Role, Thomson Reuters Acritas 2020. 90% of surveyed participants indicated that controlling outside legal costs was a high priority and 41% of this group said that bringing more work in-house was a specific focus.

Law firms need to respond to their clients' pains and adapt their way of service delivery. They should start by questioning the value that their services add to their clients' businesses. Questioning means asking questions. As simple as it may sound, in law firms' reality, client listening remains a rare art. Once lawyers understand what their clients really need, they will start rethinking their service offerings—and innovate.

2.5 Value of Time Spent

Law firms are traditionally selling legal advice by the hour, not by any quality terms or product specifics, but really by the hour. The only quality check is on the law firm itself and the specific lawyers and partners. Law firms deliver as much and as long as the client is willing to pay, not questioning whether the value-added for the client is equivalent to the amount on the invoice. Law firms leave it to the client to decide how much legal advice they want (or need), and they cannot be blamed for this.

For several years, clients have requested so called alternative fee agreements to get away from this billable hour approach. However, whenever a law firm partner comes up with a fixed fee proposal, with budgets for certain pieces of work, clients usually get back to him or her and ask for the internal calculation. They want to know the internal costs based on hourly fees because they fear that they may pay too much, i.e., more than they might have paid if they had simply agreed to pay by the hour. That is where clients are forcing lawyers and law firms to stick to the billable hour.

Also, in a larger panel selection process, the first thing that clients usually request is a list of specialties the law firm covers, and the hourly rates (by seniority). Clients may assume that quality is good overall. (There is not a real check on that, other than rankings, accolades, and other clients' references.) We see sometimes a reverse auction where all law firms in the final round compete against each other, where the client is trying to bring down timekeeper fees. Those firms who make it on the panel accept that this is then the basis for any future work.

2.6 Procurement Process

Law firms become more part of the ecosystem called business. Some years ago, the first clients made their law firms go through a procurement process, like any other supplier of goods or services. The idea behind this is that legal services are foremost services and can be measured and compared to others. Personal relationships are no longer the only means to get retained. The times when the GC alone decided on hiring a law firm, because he or she wanted this specific lawyer or firm, are gone. Procurement officers check figures and compare them with data from the competitors. These are: hourly rates, and budgets based on hourly rates. What else should they compare? How should they measure the value that a specific lawyer or law firm could add to a project? It is the clients who dictate the rules and thereby co-shape the traditional business model of law firms.

3 Inside Law Firms

Law firms are partnerships, and such partnerships often attract very specific types of individuals: ambitious, highly driven professionals who often have huge egos, engage in frightening power struggles, and can be sociopathic. This is combined, in the legal environment, with intense stress levels, chronic fatigue, burnout and depression.[14] In 2018, the American Bar Association launched efforts to address the alarming rates of alcohol use, substance abuse and other health issues among lawyers. Twenty-one percent of American lawyers have a drinking problem—more than triple the rate among the general population. Twenty-eight percent struggle with depression, and 19% suffer from severe anxiety.

It has never really been part of the paradigm at law firms to take care of people's physical, mental or emotional needs, and this applies to partners, non-partner lawyers, and business support professionals and staff (who constitute up to half of the total headcount). Is this a paradox in a profession that depends almost entirely on interpersonal relationships?

3.1 People and Profit

Law firms are partnerships, and changes must be consulted and decided upon within the partnership. Since every partner is an owner, there is only a loosely defined hierarchy, and making a final decision can be a painfully slow affair.

In most commercial law firms, partners are evaluated by financial performance and their ability to bring in business. While law firms propagate other priorities, such as client satisfaction and the ability to motivate, engage and lead their teams, these in reality are secondary. Partners tend to replace people[15] instead of going the extra mile and taking the time to work with their people on their deficiencies and their potential. Why is this so? One reason might be that time spent on human resources issues is non-billable, and is, therefore, from the partner's perspective, "time wasted". Thus, partners have no time to invest long-term in human relationships. No time to spend with the team, give feedback to individuals, or really take an interest in making people grow. Law firm partners are not bad people *per se* but suffering themselves from the intense economic pressure in the current business model. And yet, we know that partners are capable of long-lasting relationships. Wherever possible, when they leave a firm, they take their clients with them!

When organizations behave in this way, treating their people as commodities, those same people feel unappreciated and undervalued. This dissatisfaction is proved

---

[14]Tarascio, B. (n.d.). Depression among lawyers: The Statistics. Retrieved July 30, 2020, from https://www.modernlawpractice.com/depression-among-lawyers-the-statistics/; Strathausen, Roger et al. "Lawyer Well-Being - the Silent Pandemic." Liquid Legal Institute e.V., March 23, 2022. https://www.liquid-legal-institute.com/workinggroups/lawyer-wellbeing/.

[15]Ibid.

by the increase that can be seen in the number of lateral hires.[16] Thirty years ago, joining a law firm was often a lifetime decision. Today, people move around in their careers, usually by switching from one law firm to another. The firm left behind loses the talent they had invested in, and so, to fill the gap, they make lateral hires—and pay for them by offering new-joiner premiums, guaranteed draws and bonuses. This is counterproductive, but the legal profession is too slow to respond to the feedback it is getting from its own feedback processes.

Our hypothesis is that there is a better and healthier way of dealing with 'human capital'. In fact, research has been showing for decades that this is the case. What if your main focus and responsibility were on making people in your organization and your clients happy and engaged? What if you created an environment where people can thrive because they feel inspired to be at work? The evidence shows that putting people at the center of an organization translates not just into fewer days taken as sick leave, but also into a better bottom line.[17]

The recipe is not complicated. Leaders of law firms need to be genuinely interested in and accountable for their employees' happiness. To make sure they feel psychologically safe, have autonomy, and are part of a great team where they can grow and learn. To allow them to be themselves, to express themselves and their emotions freely. To make their people the focus of their activities. The rest will follow. Of course, this dramatically changes the role of the leaders of a firm. For some, it means developing completely new skills and competencies.

3.2 Covid Clarity

It could be argued that, if not for Covid-19, progress in the legal profession would have continued at a snail's pace. While the adverse effects of Covid have in many cases been catastrophic, there has been a silver lining in that the pandemic has accelerated everything. It has accelerated all the negative processes that have been eating up the legal profession for years and is forcing law firms to yield to the pressure to change. This has been termed 'Covid Clarity'. Essentially, it is a powerful moment of reflection. Covid Clarity is an opportunity for us to stop and ask ourselves, "Is what we thought was important really important?"

While certain freedoms have been lost, others have been created by the need to work remotely. Some people began working remotely in nice places they would

[16] James Carstensen, "'Everybody Is Moving Everywhere': Germany's Once-Quiet Lateral Market Heats Up," *Law.com International*, June 17, 2021, https://www.law.com/international-edition/2021/06/17/everybody-is-moving-everywhere-germanys-once-quiet-lateral-market-heats-up/.

[17] Emma Seppälä and Kim Cameron, "Proof That Positive Work Cultures Are More Productive," *Harvard Business Review*, December 01, 2015, https://hbr.org/2015/12/proof-that-positive-work-cultures-are-more-productive.

never have gone to otherwise, while others suffered from isolation and working in a small, confined space. Everyone has their own story to tell, but there has certainly been a strong emphasis on people during the crisis, evident in about every conversation. Paradoxically, then, Covid has brought people together; also paradoxically, there has been a rise in productivity, something that most experts did not anticipate.[18]

Indeed, the Covid pandemic has allowed us to take stock of what really matters. And what really matters is people. We believe it is possible to achieve a healthy balance between the pursuit of profit and the pursuit of happiness (including by using artificial intelligence to free people up so they can listen to each other, improve communication, and build relationships), and, to ultimately humanize the legal sector. One long-known dysfunction of law firms — the chasm between fee earners and business support teams (sometimes referred to by lawyers as "fee eaters" or "fee burners") — is changing, also because of the pandemic. Without the expertise of IT teams, we would not be able to work remotely in a safe way. The virtually overnight switch to work-from-home was a timely reminder of how heavily law firms depend on the work of their IT people.

Working from home mercilessly reminded us of what we were increasingly missing, things we had previously been able to take for granted, such as **the social connect**. Water cooler conversations, coffee with colleagues, the short chat about nothing at all with the guy sitting next door. These things are important, and the human connection (including another person's physical presence) is vital to how we function as human beings.[19] Take that away and we suffer. Some people found the boundary between work and private life becoming blurred, others began taking less care of themselves. The experience left many feeling naked and at rock bottom.

Yet there has been a positive side. In a way, people communicating through Zoom calls invited others into their homes, with sometimes comic results, as strange people, kids, dogs and cats appeared in the background (or foreground!). This brought us closer to each other. Some masks dropped. The pandemic forced us to just be ourselves and appreciate the human side of everything. We could no longer maintain the pretense of a wall between the private and professional worlds, because these two worlds are in fact one world. Things that were not commonly talked about or accepted at work are now becoming more common, more accepted, and we believe this is furthering the shift towards the legal profession becoming more human.

[18] Law firms of varied sizes saw revenue and demand increase in the first 9 months of this year, with the largest players seeing the biggest gains, according to a Wells Fargo survey. Law Firm Revenue Shoots Up in Booming First Nine Months of 2021 (bloomberglaw.com).

[19] Neal Stanton, "The Impact Of Remote Work On Productivity And Creativity," *Forbes*, January 14, 2022. https://www.forbes.com/sites/forbestechcouncil/2022/01/14/the-impact-of-remote-work-on-productivity-and-creativity/?sh=a3bb4cd3957b.

3.3 The Dentons Example

Dentons Europe is an example of some of the kinds of things that are taking place in many law firms. We believe that at Dentons, the emphasis has shifted in the right direction. We now know that taking care of people's mental and physical health is not just a private matter, especially in a business whose success is based on people and their performance. Nor is it an HR matter—it is a strategic issue for the whole firm. Dentons has a number of programs in place for humanizing the organization; in Europe, they are offered to all of the region's 3000+ employees.

Our **Employee Assistance Program** is a very robust initiative that offers confidential support on issues ranging from depression to personal finances to parental advice to health. Like any good EAP program, it is offered by an external provider so that all conversations are confidential. People can call a special helpline and ask for assistance in different languages. If someone needs help and wants to contact a specialist, it can be arranged.

Our **Healthy Challenge** encourages people to develop healthy habits regarding sleep, exercise, positive thinking, mindfulness and diet, using a combination of competition and fun. During the lockdown last year, for 6 months, Dentons offered all staff daily video workout sessions with top-quality trainers. We also provide ongoing coaching and mentoring assistance, including through a **Speed Coaching** program which tested the idea that 15–20 min is all it takes a coach to re-direct your mindset towards far more positive vistas. At our Shared Services Center, we run a health initiative in cooperation with a partner, Virgin Pulse Go.

Next Talent is a global initiative open to lawyers and business support professionals in which people talk to colleagues from other offices and attend short lectures on topics such as resilience, sleep and physical health. We also run Zoom workouts, yoga sessions, mindfulness sessions and coaching sessions. In fact, Dentons has introduced mindfulness into all branches and programs of the organization and was the first law firm to appoint a **Mindfulness Officer**. This effort, which has been running for 4 years now, is considered an investment rather than an expense.

Many large corporations have announced that their employees can now work from the location of their choice. Mastercard, Hitachi, and Amazon look at remote work as part of their long-term business plan. The 385,000 employees of Siemens can work from wherever they like, two or three days a week. In a similar vein, Dentons has introduced **Agile Working**, an informal arrangement that provides a high degree of autonomy (within an approved framework). In a June 2021 "return to the office" survey, 85% of Dentons' employees responded that they were equally if not more productive working from home than in the office. Agile working shifts the focus from 'where and for how long' to overall performance and what can be achieved. It also encourages a high-trust work environment. And trust ultimately humanizes the firm.

Apart from their intrinsic worth, these initiatives have also gone a long way to break down some of the barriers between fee earners and non-fee earners or business support professionals. These two major groups in the firm, traditionally perceived as being quite distinct from each other, have become one team who now focus on each other's well-being. Taking part in these initiatives together has certainly helped bring us closer together, and thereby to humanize the law.

3.4 A New Paradigm

During the pandemic, one of the Dentons Europe leaders chose to handle his stress load by walking through the woods near his home when taking part in conference calls. He found that being on the move and outdoors freed up his mind in ways that were highly beneficial. It also gave us a different view of him, and we're sure many people have had similar experiences of seeing their 'higher ups' in unconventional situations where they are perhaps more vulnerable... simply being human. Little insights into private lives. Conversations about "How are you?" and "How are you feeling?" rather than the standard business agenda.

So, the new thing is we can have feelings at work, we can confide in our feelings, value relationships, prioritize relationships, do all the things we need to do to thrive as humans—and this can be done in the corporate environment! If managed well, traumatic experiences—such as the pandemic—can result in a positive growth outcome. Recent events have made what some have known for years blindingly obvious: people have to become the center of this business again. What was a *nice-to-have* in the past is now a *must.*

4 New Entrants and Technology

As noted above, law firms of 30 years ago looked very different to law firms of today. They employ more lawyers, are in more jurisdictions and cover more practice groups than ever before. Take the largest law firm in the world for example; in 1986, the largest law firm was Baker & McKenzie with 31 offices on six continents and 800 lawyers.[20] Today, the largest law firm in the world is Dentons with over 10,000 lawyers in 190 locations.[21] How has this scale affected the people working in law firms and their clients? To answer that question, let us look at what prompted the drive to scale over the last 30 years.

Since the 1960s, legal cases have grown in complexity, corporations have become international in scope and thereby required legal services throughout the

[20] Ruth Marcus, "Nation's Large Law Offices Thrive in Age of the Megafirm," The Washington Post (WP Company, September 15, 1986), https://www.washingtonpost.com/archive/politics/1986/09/15/nations-large-law-offices-thrive-in-age-of-the-megafirm/52b6eb2c-598a-476a-bf45-43c8381f50b7/.

[21] Dentons, https://www.dentons.com/en.

world.[22] Then in 2008, the legal industry, like many others, suffered, and law firms started to merge as a way to cut costs and leverage economies of scale in back-office operations such as IT, finance and human resources.[23]

Over the last decade, clients themselves have faced tough competition in their respective markets and have been forced to cut operating costs (including legal spending) to remain competitive. [24] Large corporate clients announced a tender process for legal work in an attempt to consolidate the number of law firms used and create 'panel firms'. [25] The pharmaceutical and real estate industries were the first to start this trend, but other industries followed suit. In 2019, Teva Pharmaceutical Industries announced that their entire $330 million legal spend could go to one firm.[26] David Stark, chief legal officer at Teva Pharmaceutical Industries, explains "*Revenue growth at Teva is flat. Law firms' rates are going up. We have to do something different – that is it in a nutshell.*"[27]

This naturally increased competition amongst legal providers and spurred them to deliver 'more for less' to secure the lucrative cross continental work.[28] However, in order to compete, they needed to drive down their own costs. Within law firms, the easiest way to drive down costs is to reduce business services headcount, which appear as a large 'debt' on the balance sheet. Law firms took to restructuring back-end operations to remain profitable, and this led to leaner teams and for those who were left, longer hours.

So, we went from large legal teams in small law firms who advised local clients on relatively simple matters, to small legal teams in global law firms advising clients across multiple jurisdictions on complex matters. All while with little progress in terms of use of technology and improvement of internal processes, meaning an increased workload between less employees.

---

[22] Ruth Marcus, "Nation's Large Law Offices Thrive in Age of the Megafirm," The Washington Post (WP Company, September 15, 1986), https://www.washingtonpost.com/archive/politics/1986/09/15/nations-large-law-offices-thrive-in-age-of-the-megafirm/52b6eb2c-598a-476a-bf45-43c8381f50b7/.

[23] Sophia Gonella, "Mergers: A History and a Future," The Student Lawyer, July 31, 2020, https://thestudentlawyer.com/2020/07/31/mergers-a-history-and-a-future/.

[24] "On Notice: Teva's Entire $330M Legal Spend Could Go To One Law Firm," Perma.cc (The Legal 500, November 22, 2019), https://perma.cc/JNN3-QELY.

[25] Dan Packel, "'The Wave of the Future': Law Firm Panels Are Creating a New in-Crowd," The American Lawyer, July 29, 2018, https://www.law.com/americanlawyer/2018/07/29/the-wave-of-the-future-law-firm-panels-are-creating-a-new-in-crowd/.

[26] "On Notice: Teva's Entire $330M Legal Spend Could Go To One Law Firm," Perma.cc (The Legal 500, November 22, 2019), https://perma.cc/JNN3-QELY.

[27] Ibid.

[28] Ruth Marcus, "Nation's Large Law Offices Thrive in Age of the Megafirm," The Washington Post (WP Company, September 15, 1986), https://www.washingtonpost.com/archive/politics/1986/09/15/nations-large-law-offices-thrive-in-age-of-the-megafirm/52b6eb2c-598a-476a-bf45-43c8381f50b7/.

Yet the legal industry continued to grow, universities churned out more lawyers year on year and the number of legal sector vacancies could not keep up. In 2017, UK universities produced 21,000 new law graduates, while only 733 legal sector vacancies were recorded in the same year. That is over 28 graduates to each job. [29] It is no wonder that law firms have started to deprioritize the human factor, there is little reason to change—if one graduate says no, there are 27 behind them, who are likely begging for the job. But for how long?

4.1 The Accounting Giants

In the 1990s, the major accounting firms, then known as the Big 5[30] mounted a campaign to capture a significant part of the legal services market around the world [31] by being "*just like law firms but bigger*". [32] Unlike law firms at the time, the Big 4 had a truly global presence and were, therefore, able to service international clients with ease. However, the 2001 accounting scandals resulted in tough regulation prohibiting auditors from providing legal and other non-audit services to their audit clients. [33] The Big5 became the Big4 [34] and law firms breathed a sigh of relief as their market was safe once more.

In the decade that followed, legal regulation softened, most notably in the UK, allowing non-legal businesses to offer services under alternative business structures (ABS), which gave non-lawyers the ability to own and invest in law firms.[35] In 2014, PwC, Ernst & Young (EY) and KPMG secured ABS licences. Deloitte followed in 2018. The Big4 were back. . .except this time their strategy was not to be like law firms, but to move from a fee-for-service model to an integrated solutions model, where they 'run-the client's company'.[36]

[29] "Ratio of 28:1 for Law Graduates to Available Legal Sector Vacancies," mmadigital, April 8, 2019, https://www.mmadigital.co.uk/ratio-of-281-for-law-graduates-to-available-legal-sector-vacancies/.

[30] Arthur Andersen, KPMG, Ernst & Young, PriceWaterhouseCoopers, and Deloitte.

[31] David Wilkins and Maria Esteban, "The Reemergence of the Big Four in Law," The Practice, June 11, 2018, https://thepractice.law.harvard.edu/article/the-reemergence-of-the-big-four-in-law/.

[32] Neil Rose, "Big Four 'Cornering the Market for Legal Solutions, Not Advice,'" Legal Futures, September 2, 2021, https://www.legalfutures.co.uk/latest-news/big-four-cornering-the-market-for-legal-solutions-not-advice.

[33] David Wilkins and Maria Esteban, "The Re-emergence of the Big Four in Law," The Practice, June 11, 2018, https://thepractice.law.harvard.edu/article/the-reemergence-of-the-big-four-in-law/.

[34] Arthur Andersen was criminally indicted and declared bankruptcy—David Wilkins and Maria Esteban, "The Re-emergence of the Big Four in Law," The Practice, June 11, 2018, https://thepractice.law.harvard.edu/article/the-reemergence-of-the-big-four-in-law/.

[35] "Legal Services Act 2007", Legislation.gov.uk, Statute Law Database, 2007, https://www.legislation.gov.uk/ukpga/2007/29/contents.

[36] "The Big Four and Legal Services," LexisNexis, https://www.lexisnexis.co.uk/research-and-reports/big-4-report.html#read-full-report.

The Big4 not only provide legal advice, but they go one step further, they assess the client's legal function and then advise on how to manage their budget and reimagine their operating model for legal work,[37] incorporating themselves into the mix as much as possible. As so much legal work can be done in an automated way, e.g., making changes to certain contracts, or dealing with regulatory issues such as GDPR, they also advise clients on how to leverage scalable technology to develop efficient processes.[38] This inevitably takes existing work away from law firms. Deloitte, the current leader of the four, [39] in 2021, announced

> Our strategy is very much rooted in the needs of the client to be offered solutions and not just advice. The vision for Deloitte Legal has always been that you bring together high-quality legal advice with legal management consulting, legal managed services and legal technology. This way you can provide an end-to-end service to the client and achieve the outcomes they are looking for, not just give them advice on those outcomes.[40]

The key difference between law firms and the Big4 is that law firms battle with decades old institutionalised legacy processes and have 'their way of doing things' which has worked relatively well for them to date, while the Big4 are building new functions from the ground up. This enables the Big4 to utilize modern technology to develop more efficient processes rather than disrupting existing businesses. Nonetheless, over the last 4 years, law firms have started to actively adopt technology and revisit the way they deliver legal services because the competition is not only swiping their clients, but their talent too!

The questions to ask now are: do the Big4 consider the human element for those who they employ? Do they have a work-life balance? Do lawyers work fewer hours for better benefits? Unfortunately, the answers are all a resounding 'no'. [41] Many report poor work-life balance in the Big4, 70–80 hour weeks and the benefit of more work for talented employees without the increased salary.[42] What the Big4 *have* done however is humanize law for clients, working closely with them to solve their problems and integrating into their business rather than just providing legal

[37] Ibid.

[38] Ibid.

[39] Peter Bendor-Samuel, "The Big Four Accounting and Auditing Firms Are Becoming Challengers in Digital Transformation Services," Forbes (Forbes Magazine, November 14, 2018), https://www.forbes.com/sites/peterbendorsamuel/2018/11/14/big-4-becoming-formidable-challengers-in-digital-transformation-services/?sh=2f4081962a41.

[40] "The Big Four and Legal Services," LexisNexis, https://www.lexisnexis.co.uk/research-and-reports/big-4-report.html#read-full-report.

[41] Beecher Tuttle, "What's Wrong with Work-Life Balance at the Big Four Accounting Firms?," eFinancialCareers, May 5, 2018, https://www.efinancialcareers.co.uk/news/2018/04/work-life-balance-big-four.

[42] Ibid.

advice. [43] Law firms are trying to catch up, but their model is not conducive to rapid change.

4.2 Legal Technology

Legal technology, more commonly referred to as legal tech or lawtech, is a term used to describe technologies that aim to support, supplement or replace traditional methods for delivering legal services, or that improve the way the justice system operates. [44] Legal tech covers a wide range of tools and processes; document automation, advanced chatbots, practice management tools, predictive artificial intelligence and smart legal contracts.[45] In 2021, legal tech funding peaked at US $3.33 billion. There were 161 combination deals plus 223 notable fundraisings. [46] The estimated value of the legal tech market in 2021 was US$18 billion. [47]

There are many categories of legal tech, from e-Billing and e-Signatures to contract review and risk management. There are also different types of underlying technology that enable these tools to operate. The two that are dominating in the legal industry at the moment are: robotic process automation and artificial intelligence. Both can replicate specific tasks carried out by a lawyer more effectively, efficiently and, if the tool is well developed, it can complete tasks more accurately.

Robotic process automation or RPA, streamlines workflows and allows businesses to build, deploy, and manage software robots that emulate humans' actions interacting with digital systems and software.[48] RPA is designed to focus on repetitive and lower-value work, such as extracting, copying and inserting data, filling in forms, and populating routine analysis and reports. RPA can even perform cognitive processes like interpreting text, engaging in chats and conversations, understanding unstructured data, and applying advanced machine learning models to make complex decisions.[49] Deploying robots can effectively free up a person's time so that they can focus on other, more creative and collaborative tasks. Legal

---

[43] Madeleine Farman, "The in-House Lawyer: Who's Afraid of the Big Bad Four?," The In-House Lawyer | The Legal 500, 2017, https://www.inhouselawyer.co.uk/feature/whos-afraid-of-the-big-bad-four/#:~:text=PwC%20sits%20at%20a%20global,1%2C300%20lawyers%20spanning%2072%20countries.

[44] "What Is Lawtech?," The Law Society, June 5, 2019, https://www.lawsociety.org.uk/en/campaigns/lawtech/guides/what-is-lawtech.

[45] Ibid.

[46] Artificiallawyer, "Legal Tech Funding Hit £2.5 Bn in 2021 – Best Year Ever," Artificial Lawyer, March 2, 2022, https://www.artificiallawyer.com/2022/03/02/legal-tech-funding-hit-2-5-bn-in-2021-best-year-ever/.

[47] Thomas Alsop, "Legal Tech Market Revenue Worldwide 2019-2025," Statista, March 4, 2022, https://www.statista.com/statistics/1155852/legal-tech-market-revenue-worldwide/.

[48] "What Is Robotic Process Automation - RPA Software," UiPath, https://www.uipath.com/rpa/robotic-process-automation.

[49] Ibid.

operations and finance can routinely benefit from RPA, as it is bespoke and can be deployed for specific tasks within an organization. Legal tech RPA providers like UiPath have the ability to monitor system events, which means the background technology monitors a person's actions on the computer and suggests the tasks that could be automated.

Artificial intelligence has developed over the last 40 years[50] and continues to develop at a rapid speed. In its current narrow form, however, it is unlikely to replace lawyers in the short term. Instead, it increasingly supports their work. There are multiple fields of artificial intelligence applications in the legal industry which can aid lawyers and improve their work satisfaction. They include review and analysis tools, due diligence and compliance analysis tools, and smart contract tools (self-executing obligations).[51] AI applications available today can also support a lawyer's work in a variety of tasks: document creation from automated templates using ContractExpress[52] and saving hours in reproducing documents; document review to identify standard clauses, deviations and patterns in a large set of documents using Luminance;[53] due diligence offers automated extraction and analysis of contractual provisions from documents using Litera's KIRA.[54]

According to PwC's annual law firm survey,[55] the use of tech within law firms is a top priority, yet the average spends on legal tech for the top 100 UK firms, as a percentage of fee income, is 0.5–0.9%. [56] In comparison, companies in other sectors invest up to 10% of turnover in technology. [57] The legal tech market is booming with thousands of legal tech products currently on the market and law firms have cautiously adopted only a small fraction. The reasons why law firms are slow to adopt technology go beyond the usual 'lawyers are luddites' argument, there is more to technology adoption than just the promise of reduced costs.

Lawyers hesitate for a number of reasons:

---

[50] AI can be traced back to the 1950s. In 1954 Alan Turing explored the mathematical possibility of artificial intelligence, however given the limited computational power and alarming cost of computers at the time, the concept of building intelligent machines was not at all attractive.

[51] Markfort and Zamorski (2020).

[52] "Document Automation," HighQ | Canada | Thomson Reuters, https://www.thomsonreuters.ca/en/highq/document-automation.html.

[53] "AI-Powered Legal Process Automation," Luminance, http://www.luminance.com/.

[54] "Machine Learning Contract Search, Review and Analysis Software," Machine Learning Contract Search, Review and Analysis Software | Kira Systems, February 22, 2022, http://www.kirasystems.com/.

[55] It is quite ironic that law firms provide all of this information free of charge each year, to arguably their biggest competitors.

[56] PricewaterhouseCoopers, "Annual Report 2021," PwC, 2021, page 15, https://www.pwc.co.uk/who-we-are/annual-report.html.

[57] Nick Eason, "The Legal Sector Faces up to Its Digital Future," The Times & The Sunday Times, December 6, 2021, https://www.thetimes.co.uk/static/digital-data-tech-legal-sector-law-firms-automation-ai/.

1. Lawyers feel threatened that their existing, currently profitable practice will be **cannibalised by legal technology**. The obvious reason is that law firms have enjoyed consistent growth over decades, earning more money than ever before. Legal tech usually replaces tasks currently carried out by lawyers, which would ultimately reduce their fees in the short to medium run.
2. Lawyers lack **understanding of the technology**, its risks, and benefits. Traditionally, those working in law firms do not have a science or technology background, making it more difficult to understand the technology, how it works and how it would integrate/improve into their daily work. Further, as their days are measured in 6-min chargeable increments, there is little incentive to explore and assess legal tech solutions.
3. Available legal tech solutions often miss **quality standards**. There are thousands of tech tools out there, however few of them are of the high standard that law firms require. Many of them fail to demonstrate that they can provide consistent and reliable results.
4. Law firms are **ultimately liable** and carry all the risks; regardless of whether they have used legal tech to assist in delivering legal services or not, they are liable for the advice they provide to clients. This is especially true for tools that boast an 'artificial intelligence' element, which often lacks transparency and explainability (no-one knows how the result was produced).
5. **Change is difficult** for law firms. Most partners have been in law firms their entire careers and they are used to doing business a certain way. The model has virtually been unchanged for 50 years, so getting into the change mindset, especially if they do not believe law firms need to change, at least in their careers, is a challenge.
6. **Clients oppose** the use of legal tech. In some, albeit limited, instances law firms do not have a choice as their clients oppose the use of legal tech. This is mostly due to where their data is stored when the tool is in use. Most legal tech providers host data in the cloud and not on premise which increases the risk of a potential breach, so for government organisations, this is a non-starter.
7. Lack of **investment in technology** is a result and a hurdle. Many law firms do not invest in technology or effective training, for all of the reasons above, and thus make it difficult for lawyers to overcome their opposing attitude.

Older and larger companies are also more hesitant to adopt technology because they are often constrained by the presence of legacy systems and legacy approaches to innovation. Nevertheless, despite the various reasons to hesitate, law firms are not standing still, they are investing in technology.[58] In 2021, the top three priority areas for technology investment within law firms were: matter management, document

[58] Frank-Jürgen Richter and Gunjan Sinha, "Why Do Your Employees Resist New Tech?," Harvard Business Review, August 21, 2020, https://hbr.org/2020/08/why-do-your-employees-resist-new-tech.

automation and collaboration tools.[59] It is also important to note that the COVID-19 pandemic made it crucial for firms to start investing and adopting technology if they wanted to safely resume work. [60]

Law firms also prioritize technology for the tasks clients increasingly refuse to pay for, such as, research, document review, and document discovery. The benefit to lawyers here is that those tasks are generally very tedious, repetitive and unfulfilling. There was not much to be gained from sitting in a room for hours filtering through dozens of dusty boxes as part of a discovery process. Adoption of this technology is of great benefit to a lawyer's development, allowing them to spend more time on creative and collaborative tasks—tasks that make the legal industry more human. However, while technology has improved the quality of work, it has not done much for work-life balance as firms simply reallocated the lawyer's saved hours to other client work, continuing the long, arduous hours.

An interesting insight over the last few years is that legal tech is slowly becoming an alternative employment route for lawyers looking to leave the traditional career path. It promises work-life balance, a fast-paced environment and the ability to earn a substantial amount via commissions and referrals. In this sense, legal tech has been a game changer for lawyers who do not see law firm partnership as their ultimate career goal.

5 Key to Solution: A New Operating Model

> No need to believe that any player at FC Bayern is not valued or cuddled. Appreciation is a unit called euros - nothing else. (Karl-Heinz Rummenigge)[61]

Law firm partners and football/soccer stars have two things in common: high pressure to deliver excellent results and no-one to say, 'thank you'. The currency for expressing valuation and appraisal is money. When clients pay their lawyers' invoices based on high hourly rates, they may deem this being enough of laud. Law firms express esteem for their partners by the compensation committees' decisions on annual drawings.

[59] PricewaterhouseCoopers, "Annual Report 2021," PwC, 2021, page 15, https://www.pwc.co.uk/who-we-are/annual-report.html.

[60] Mark A. Cohen, "Getting beyond the Tech in Legal Tech," Forbes (Forbes Magazine, May 4, 2019), https://www.forbes.com/sites/markcohen1/2019/05/03/getting-beyond-the-tech-in-legal-tech/?sh=5b65e11716fc.

[61] Karl-Heinz Rummenigge: "Wertschätzung wird eigentlich nur noch in Euros gerechnet und in nichts anderem. Man braucht nicht zu glauben, dass beim FC Bayern irgendein Spieler nicht wertgeschätzt oder gekuschelt wird. Wertschätzung ist eine Einheit namens Euro - sonst gar nichts." (Kicker online, 31.01.2022 – 14:13: https://www.kicker.de/rummenigge-was-sich-suele-vielleicht-auch-mal-ueberlegen-sollte-888267/artikel).

5.1 Preventing Transformation: Profit per Partner

There is one fundamental hurdle for law firms that prevent them from investing, meaning real, sustainable and mid-term investments that will require funding and thus be 'cost' in the first years, but will pay out later. This fundamental hurdle is the 'profit per partner mantra'. Profit per partner is the KPI measuring profitability, and profitability is traditionally considered a measure of quality. The profit per partner, however, is the total net profit divided by all equity partners of a law firm being cashed out to them at the end of each (fiscal) year. Every cent that is held back and spent on future investments diminishes the profit per partner.

Why is the profit per partner dogma preventing transformation? Humanizing the law requires human resources, time, and investment in technology. These investments usually do not pay out in the first year. Some of the ideas and projects may even fail and create a loss. All this would have a negative impact on the profit per partner, as it is accounted for as cost in law firm bookkeeping, thus reducing the profit for the respective year.

According to the logic of this old-fashioned business model, any future investment is detrimental to the present. Law firms follow a strict 'shareholder value' approach which has proven to be destructive to other industries. There is no reason to believe that law firms should be exempt from this experience.

Profit per partner has two simple factors. One is revenue (Sect. 5.2). One is cost (Sect. 5.3). All of that measured annually is provoking short-term thinking, preventing law firms to invest in the future. Thus, we need to rethink existing incentive systems (Sect. 5.4).

5.2 Profitability at Its Limits

Revenue is cash income from lawyers' hours worked times the billable hourly rate. Over the past 20 years, law firms constantly increased their revenue, despite the economic and financial crisis, by three means. One is increasing the hourly rates. Second is increasing productivity, which is the time that each lawyer works on client matters per day. Third is leverage, which is the number of employee lawyers per equity partner. None of these are in the interest of clients once they have reached a certain level.

High hourly rates deprive clients of hiring lawyers within their limited budget for legal spending. Their decision will be increasingly one of 'make or buy'. The hourly cost of an in-house lawyer is roughly 1/3 of the average standard billing rate of an external lawyer's hour. Hence, the value add that the work of an external lawyer should bring to the client should at least amount to three times of what colleagues in the legal department could deliver. Today, in-house counsels usually have the same elevated level of education and qualification, and quite often they have spent some years at law firms. Thus, the traditional business model of law firms will come under pressure as in-house legal departments will turn away and either rely on their own resources and capabilities or outsource parts of their work to legal managed service providers.

However, it is not the law firms alone who stick to the billable hour system. It is also their clients.[62] Often, law firm panel selection processes start with an inverse auction on standard hourly rates. Most attempts for alternative fee arrangements end with a discussion by clients wanting to understand the internal cost calculation of the law firm, instead of accepting a fixed fee for a certain promised work delivery. The understanding of clients and law firm partners usually is that all the knowledge that a law firm has accumulated is available for free, or, to put it in other words, embedded in the hourly rates. Still, the only indicator of the value of legal work is the time that a lawyer spends. This must change.

For certain, quality has its price and highly educated and specialized lawyers ask for high salaries. However, today law firms may not win the battle for talent simply by paying high salaries. Young lawyers are no longer prepared to sell their soul for money. They select law firms as employers for other criteria: interesting work, ongoing education, good atmosphere, and enough time for family or other endeavors.

They are right: scientific studies show that high value work can only be done for a limited amount of time per day. Nobody is able to deliver 10 or 12 or even 14 hours of high-quality work daily. However, in the traditional law firm model, the billable hour is the decisive factor, no matter whether the work performed during this time is of high quality or not. Thus, there is an incentive for law firms to have routine work done by their associates.

Partner-associate leverage is a factor that is usually not in the interest of a client. Clients hire law firms for their specific expertise and experience. The more associates work in one partner's team (leverage), the more this partner will have to spend time on team management and matter administration and the less he or she can spend on client matters. Over decades, law firms educated their young lawyers on client matters. Clients no longer tolerate this 'learning-by-earning' model.

5.3 Cost and Value of Partners' Time

Turning to cost: From a pure bookkeeping standpoint, in law firms' cash-in/out accounting systems, a partner's hour comes at no cost. Consequently, every minute a partner can turn into a billable hour being paid by a client adds to the overall profit. It is the profit per partner-mantra combined with widely used merit-based incentive systems that prevent partners spending their time on work that would add real value to clients in the long term and thus be valuable for the firm's future, too.

Certainly, the 'clients first-attitude' is crucial to successful legal advisory. It is a people's business that requires commitment and dedication. However, we see cases where this is turned into the opposite. If a partner does legal work that could also be

---

[62] See Sect. 2.5 above.

done by a junior associate at lower cost for the client, simply because this partner has not yet enough billable hours on his timesheet for the day, then this attitude turns into the contrary of what it means. Instead, law firms should value their partners' time spent in a collaborative effort to develop future ready solutions that will serve clients and the firm in the mid and long term.

5.4 New Incentive Systems

If law firms want to get ready for the future, they will need to overcome their traditional annual revenue sharing model. They need to find incentive and remuneration systems that promote long-term investments and that make it beneficial for partners to spend their time on creating new products and services, rather than being driven to turn every working hour into a chargeable hour. They need to find incentive systems where research and development, product and service creation and innovative work is more attractive, or at least as attractive, as traditional billable work.

Instead of increasing billing rates and working hours, and trying to leverage headcount, law firms should thrive on leveraging their expertise by productizing their knowledge and services. Containing their lawyers' expertise by means of technology and combining with intelligent automation they create legal advice that is concise, consistent, and comprehensible and thus ready for use by their clients' businesspeople.[63] This would benefit clients by lower prices for standardized offerings, and simultaneously free funds for specialized individual legal advice where needed. Law firms would benefit from a higher margin on time (and money) they invest in creating these offerings resulting over time in a higher profitability—and let their lawyers focus on the interesting work for their clients.

6 Conclusion

The world of law is dehumanized. This presumption sounds familiar to people in legal circles and to the general public, whose views are formed by media and entertainment. Transactional in mentality, driven by money, status and ego. John Grisham's books; Harvey Specter in 'Suits'. This impression, though brutal and not entirely accurate, is widespread for a good reason. Law firms never stood for taking care of the human side, the needs of people whether at partner level or for associates and professional staff, their comfort needs, their health. A paradox for a people's business as it relies on personal relationships to deliver service to clients.

Can we make law at corporate law firms more human? Yes! Recent trends focus more on people, health and relationship, depth and purpose at work. Covid as a change accelerator has potentiated the dysfunctions, turning up the volume on the wake-up call and turning down the temperature on the cold shower that hits us. The

[63] Markfort and Ragueneau (2022).

pandemic has created fertile ground for some much-needed changes. It's good to focus on the rare positives of this global catastrophe. The pandemic accelerated change, imposing a thorough rethink about how we conduct business and making us understand that the time to humanize the legal profession is now.

Leaders are increasingly viewing people as humans, not merely as a means to get work done. The goal is to have a highly creative team that can deliver top quality work. One long-known dysfunction of law firms—the chasm between lawyers as fee earners and business support teams—is changing too, in moves accelerated by the pandemic. Without the expertise of IT teams, we would not be able to work remotely. The virtually overnight switch to work-from-home was a timely reminder of how much law firms depend on the work of IT teams. Much the same could be said about all business support teams in fact.

Our experiences in the pandemic are akin to post-traumatic stress disorder. There is a phenomenon of post-traumatic growth, where traumatic experience if managed well may result in a positive growth outcome. It is becoming clear that people have to be the center of business, which means switching the focus from transactions to people and relationships. Leaders need to understand that in the past "connecting" was a nice-to-have but that now it is simply a must. Connecting with people more often than before, having deeper conversations, active listening, being truly present, connecting authentically and humanly, perhaps more "being" than "doing", and connecting with emotions and feelings. It requires developing new skills and competencies. These competencies, as pandemic era research shows, are the key to motivating and engaging with people. This will lead to higher performance and will eventually translate into the bottom line, which is higher profits.

Technology and AI are major forces in the shift to humanizing the profession. Why not free up the precious billable hours and invest this time into a long-term policy of promoting humans and their wellbeing? The most important currency that can bring truly long lasting and sustainable profits. For a few years now, Dentons has been running programs to help their people as humans, to deal with stress, loss, grief, pain, and help connect in a meaningful way. Embracing AI forms part of the secret formula for success and profitability and for becoming more human. Technology, if managed well and introduced properly, can free up time that we can use to build relationships, be more human and create a better environment where people want to work, attracting the best talents, and at the same time invest in our relationships with clients. Technology can be a catalyst for legal services transformation and a foundational element for new delivery models, but tech tools alone will not disrupt the industry.[64]

A prerequisite, however, is changing our business model. In our current economics, investing funds in developing technology to the effect that we "sell" less time goes against the economic interests of law firms and their partners. Invested money

[64] Mark A. Cohen, "Getting Beyond The Tech in Legal Tech," *Forbes*, May 3, 2019, https://www.forbes.com/sites/markcohen1/2019/05/03/getting-beyond-the-tech-in-legal-tech/?sh=7d7b4dde16fc.

will be lacking in their pockets at the end of the fiscal year and so will the money on billable hours that have not been sold to clients. Why should lawyers go this way? Simply to make clients and their people feel better?

The general ecosystem of international law firms, how they interact with clients, their internal dynamics, the false mantra of obsessing over billable hours and, above all, the antediluvian concept of profit per partner—all these factors hold back progress. Law firms deliver quick but short-sighted returns, not long-term, stable welfare to the partnership and their people.

A sustainable business model for law firms would incentivize partners to invest their time and money in mid and long-term initiatives. A partner's stake in a law firm partnership should be re-designed along with the principles of a shareholding in a company. Accruing dividends would elevate the share value and allow the firm to invest. At the same time, it would strengthen the partner's loyalty to the firm and long-term interest in its economic welfare. Partner's time whether spent on billable client work or on innovative endeavors or on personal relationship building should be valued and accounted for. Professional staff's time should be equally valued as productive when related to client work or investment when related to productizing legal services or innovation. No doubt, this would challenge the fundamental economics of our industry.

At Dentons, we believe that profit-per-partner is not a suitable indicator to the overall success of a polycentric firm operating in multiple jurisdictions and a variety of areas of law. In 2015, the magazine The American Lawyer ranked Dentons based on estimates as Dentons did not publish profit per partner figures for their operations. Dentons challenged the publication and The American Lawyer hat to publicly admit that they were wrong. [65] Dentons' chairman Joe Andrew has told the press that the figure is "meaningless" because Dentons is a global firm, and its offices have drastically varying profitability depending on the market.[66]

Even the foundation of Dentons in 2013 was a challenge to the established industry. No-one at the time thought there was space for another global law firm in a saturated market. Dentons today is by far the largest law firm in the world and one of the leading brands in the industry.[67] This example may encourage us to challenge the traditional business model of law firms. Taking care of people's mental and physical health needs to be part of a corporate strategy in a business whose success is based on people and their performance.

While we are still earning our salaries with our traditional work, we change our business model. This requires investments in technology and innovation, but foremost in people and their competences. Finally, it requires reinventing the business

[65] Casey Sullivan, "After Clash, American Lawyer Posts Higher Profits for Dentons," Bloomberg Law, August 27, 2015, https://news.bloomberglaw.com/business-and-practice/after-clash-american-lawyer-posts-higher-profits-for-dentons.

[66] Ibid.

[67] https://www.dentons.com/en/about-dentons/news-events-and-awards/news/2021/january/dentons-is-now-the-second-best-known-law-firm-in-the-world-according-to-acritas.

model for law firms to allow for investments that merit the labelling "investment". To meet the future head-on, our profession needs a major strategy shift: away from a preoccupation with billable time towards value delivered to the client. This value orientation is the core principle of innovative thinking, and embraces modern technologies, agile working methods, and a very human—humanizing—approach.

Liquid Legal Waves to Other Chapters, Written by the Editors

If you have left *Emma's* and *Madeleine's* chapter "*Patagonia: Everything a law firm is not, but could be?*" with hesitation, whether this can become reality, *Rainer* and *Patryk* have made it real—and they have pointed out the win-win-opportunity in this: it is good for people (i.e. humans) and for business!

Reading *Rainer's* and *Patryk's* article in context with "*The Elevated Workplace*" by *Liam, John* and *Joyce*, it is noteworthy how similar the vision of a lawyer's workplace including the working environment of the future might look like, be it inhouse, at a legal service provider, or at a law-firm. The consistency is rooted in the common concept of putting the human being and the human interaction into the center.

Now—lean back and enjoy the final chapter! A literary story by Roger on what humanization & the law may soon look & feel like in a fictitious law firm! And before that, as an introduction to the fiction, from the same author, a short real-life biographical account of how the disregard of human needs in our working habits can lead to burn-out—and to FIRING-UP again!

References

Markfort R, Ragueneau A (2022) Anwaltskanzlei der Zukunft. In: Breidenbach S et al (eds) Handbuch Digitale Rechtsabteilung

Markfort R, Zamorski P (2020) AI+EI=Future. In: Jacob K et al (eds) Liquid legal - towards a common legal platform

Replogle T (2017) The business of law: evolution of the legal services market. Mich Bus Entrep Law Rev 6(2):292–293

Yoon A (2014) Competition and the evolution of large law firms. DePaul Law Rev 63(2):697–719

Rainer Markfort is a corporate partner in the Berlin office of Dentons. He focuses on advising corporations in critical situations. He supports companies' management in internal investigations and in setting up compliance management systems. Rainer has years of experience in advising on the restructuring and refinancing of companies, including insolvency advice to creditors, shareholders and management and advising on distressed M&A transactions.

Rainer joined Dentons in 2015 and co-lead the initiative to form a firmwide compliance and investigation group. In 2019 he accepted to become a global Director of Client Solutions Innovation in the global innovation team at Dentons. His focus is to leverage and connect the talent across the firm and support creating client facing solutions. In line with Dentons vision of always building the law firm of the future, he helps to accelerate innovation and disrupt the status quo both for Dentons and for its clients.

Rainer is a member of the board of DICO—Deutsches Institut für Compliance e.V. (German Institute for Compliance) and headed for many years the working committee on Business Partner Compliance at DICO. He is a lecturer at the University of Saarbrücken, the Frankfurt School for Management and Finance and the German Lawyer Academy.

Rainer studied law at the University of Münster (Germany) and Université Paris II (Paris; Maitrise en droit) and received his PhD in law from the University of Münster in 1993.

Tanja Podinic is the Global Director of Innovation Programs at Dentons, based in the London office. She focusses on operationalising innovation across the global law firm and working with colleagues around the world to develop and scale client facing solutions across multiple countries.

Tanja started as a construction litigator in Sydney, Australia and worked for a not-for-profit organisation before she moved into the legal tech scene to build and manage a start up for a Sydney university. Following the success of this project, she pivoted into big law, moving to an in-house role to advise on risk and compliance issues across several jurisdictions. Over the years innovation and legal technology became Tanja's niche and she regularly advises law firms on the benefits and risks of legal technology.

Tanja also sits on the Law and Technology Committee for the England and Wales Law Society, where her expert focus is on artificial intelligence and its impact on the legal profession.

Tanja studied at Western Sydney University in Australia, completing a Bachelor of Laws combined with a Bachelor of Business (majoring in both Economics and Finance), she also completed her Master in Law at the Australian National University in 2013.

Patrycjusz Zamorski is Europe Director of Talent Development at Dentons.

He has more than 20 years of experience coaching, training, mentoring and inspiring leaders in the professional services sector and is an accredited coach and mentor (EMCC) with a degree in Consulting and Coaching for Change from INSEAD.

He has worked for Andersen, EY, Deloitte, and for the past 14 years, Dentons, where he built the regional Talent and Learning & Development functions.

In his current role, he helps general counsel and their teams, legal departments and law firms develop, inspire and engage talent, create high-performing teams and manage the people side of transformation.

Based on the principles of neuroscience and behavioral science, he has developed numerous award-winning talent programs to help lawyers develop leadership skills and emotional intelligence. Patryk's proudest moments are winning the prestigious People's Choice Award twice—the first time at Deloitte in 2008 and again at Dentons in 2018.

His passion is nurturing talent and helping individuals, teams and organizations thrive and realise their full potential through better engagement, motivation, performance and job satisfaction.

How to FIRE-UP After Burn-Out

A Personal Story

Roger Strathausen

Abstract

This is a personal account of a professional burn-out I experienced and how I managed to overcome it and get back on track.

We burn out slowly. It takes time, it doesn't happen overnight. How could it? After all, our professional work life spans 30, 40, sometimes 50 years.

Burn-Out creeps into us like the cold in the evening desert. The sun has set, temperature is dropping fast. The first chills we simply ignore. They keep coming, though, more frequently, more intense. We put on an extra shirt; we take a blanket. Still, it's getting worse. The cold begins biting into us like mosquitos. We are freezing. And the night has just begun...

For some, it may only take a couple of months to feel burned out at work. Maybe they have a bad boss. Or are in the wrong job. Or simply are prone to mental illness to begin with. For most of us, burning out takes years. For some, it can take decades. But at some point, it happens. We all experience it sooner or later, no one is immune.

People around us realize the symptoms before we do. Colleagues worry about our job performance. Friends tell us we don't look good. Families complain we seem stressed all the time.

We respond the only way we know: *by doing more of the same*. We work longer hours. We force ourselves to be more social. We try harder to enjoy time at home.

It doesn't help. We get more tired every day. We don't sleep well, drink too much alcohol, take too many pills. Each according to our personal playbook, we

Roger Strathausen is Co-founder of the Liquid Legal Institute and serves as vice chair of the supervisory board.

R. Strathausen (✉)
Málaga, Spain
e-mail: r.strathausen@liquid-legal-institute.org

K. Jacob et al. (eds.), *Liquid Legal – Humanization and the Law*, Law for Professionals, https://doi.org/10.1007/978-3-031-14240-6_20

progress downward, until finally, we all feel the same again: *empty*. We are in the void. No desires, no motivation to do anything.

We go to doctors. Diagnosis: Burn-out. Maybe only beginning stage, fatigue. Sometimes paired with depression, or anxiety. Hard to tell, these things overlap, they don't really know. They prescribe more pills, recommend therapy. *Try to relax,* they say, *smell the roses.*

To us, all their recommendations sound equally bad, like they have been designed for losers.

We do not see ourselves as losers. Life sucks for losers. We want to win again, like we used to! We want to go back to the way things were: when we were young and strong, when we got up in the morning feeling full of energy and ready to change the world.

And so, we start hiding our emptiness first from others, and then from ourselves. Yet the more we hide, the lonelier we feel, and the more we suffer. It's a vicious circle. No energy, no success. No success, no energy.

By now, it's night in the desert. The moon is up, a sky full of shining stars. Beautiful – and cold. We feel frozen inside, every breath hurts. Will the sun ever rise again? Will we live to see it and feel its warmth on our skins?

Not all of us manage to overcome a burn-out. Some quit their dream job and do easy work to survive. Some become mentally ill and cannot work at all anymore. Some kill themselves.

Yet most of us survive! We bounce back from the burn-out—and *FIRE-UP* again. And each of us has his/her personal *FIRE-UP* story to tell.

This is mine.

I have been self-employed as a management consultant since 2007 and had a golden time in the first half of the 2010s. I was working for large companies, and orders kept coming in without me having to do anything. No marketing or sales, just doing what I loved doing: analyzing problems and designing solutions, making slides, writing texts, moderating workshops, managing projects. Clients called me and ordered services, I delivered results and wrote invoices. Done, next project. In some months, I earned 40,000–50,000 €—for me as a trained Germanist, that was a gigantic amount of money! I really thought: *You are Superman!*

But slowly, fewer orders came in. Customer contacts went into early retirement or changed jobs and had no more budget or no more need for consulting. But what was worse: I suddenly realized how tired I was. It was no normal tiredness, the kind that goes away with a good night's sleep. No, it was a much deeper, fundamental feeling of exhaustion. I started shaking when the phone rang, or when I received e-mails from clients—because I was afraid I wouldn't be able to get the work done. *I was burned out.*

I remember sitting in my reading chair at home one Sunday afternoon and thinking: *You'll never get up from here again. You're going to stay in this chair forever.* I just didn't see any reason to do anything anymore. I felt completely empty, and emptiness was all around me. Why should I move? It was all pointless anyway.

A thought came to me which deeply frustrated me and marked a turning point in my professional career: *You worked so hard for years and earned a lot of money*

- and now you must use that money just to get healthy again. In the end, you're right back where you started. You have achieved nothing. For years, you lectured clients about strategic and sustainable business development - but in your own business, you just let yourself be carried from job to job and didn't build anything sustainable at all.

I then took some time off, talked a lot with family and friends, did a therapy, and most importantly: in 2017, together with friends and colleagues, we founded the *Liquid Legal Institute*.

The LLI literally saved my life. *IT FIRED ME UP!*

How? *Because it gave me a new purpose.* Something meaningful to do with others, but in my own way and at my own pace. At the LLI, I can do the things I want to do and the way I want to do them. And as a team, all of us together, we pursue social goals much bigger than each of us could achieve alone.

We humans are social beings. It is scientifically proven that humans can only find meaning in life through others, by pursuing goals that go beyond ourselves and our own immediate needs. People who focus only on personal interests cannot not lead happy and fulfilled lives.

So, my advice to you: Should you ever experience a burn-out, or find yourself on the slippery slope towards it, first take some time off—and then FIRE-Up again! Find your tribe, do things that carry meaning for you, and work at your own pace.

It's only a glimmer at first, faint, far away on the black horizon. We are totally stiff, frozen to the bone, cannot move our heads. This light, it might just be a hallucination, conjured up by battered brains. But no, it is getting stronger, expanding to all sides, moving up! Like the headlight of an unstoppable train, it keeps coming towards us, illuminating the darkness. AND THERE SHE IS! Majestically rising, the sun appears, and with her, a new day, and the hope for a better future.

Roger Strathausen is a business consultant, author, and lecturer with expertise in legal operations, learning, and leadership whose clients are chiefly multinational companies. He took his Ph.D. from Stanford University in 1996 and was an employee at SAP and an executive at Accenture. In 2015, he published his book "Leading When You Are Not the Boss" (Apress, New York), and in 2017 and 2020, he co-edited two contributed volumes on the digital transformation of the legal industry, called "Liquid Legal" and "Towards a Common Legal Platform" (Springer, Heidelberg). He is a co-founder of the Liquid Legal Institute and serves as vice chair of the supervisory board. r.strathausen@liquid-legal-institute.org.

"Who are you. . .?"

A Story About a Gay Humanist Working at a Law Firm

Roger Strathausen

Abstract

This is a fictitious story about a gay humanist starting to work at a law firm. The story is intended to illustrate aspects of humanization in the legal industry in an aesthetic fashion which may be more immediate and leave a stronger emotional imprint on the reader than what can be achieved through academic discourse. All resemblance with real people and events is contingent and unintentional.

I'll be damned. . ., thought Rutger Hammer, looking at the printed CV on his desk, and then up again at the young guy named Keno Singer sitting in front of him.

Hammer was the office head here in Berlin, the latest location of the *Lakefield & Lakefield* law firm, and one of his tasks was to welcome new employees and show them the ropes. He was used to seeing different kinds of people, and not all of them were lawyers. Some came with background in IT or business and, given the LegalTech trend and the increasing expectations of clients to 'run legal as a business', that was okay for Hammer and made sense, as long as there were not too many exotic birds and lawyers could still be lawyers.

But this. . . Hammer had never read such a CV before, for sure not from any applicant and not even from an intern, let alone of a newly hired associate who started out with 100.000 Euro base plus bonus, a high annual salary for Berlin.

Roger Strathausen is Co-founder of the Liquid Legal Institute and serves as vice chair of the supervisory board.

This is a fictitious story; all resemblance with real people and events is contingent and unintentional.

R. Strathausen (✉)
Málaga, Spain
e-mail: r.strathausen@liquid-legal-institute.org

K. Jacob et al. (eds.), *Liquid Legal – Humanization and the Law*, Law for Professionals, https://doi.org/10.1007/978-3-031-14240-6_21

"O-kay..." he said slowly, fixating his counterpart, "you studied German language and literature... So, what does that make you?"

"It makes *me*," answered Keno, now also looking at him, while before his view had wandered around in Hammer's office and had lingered a while at the shelves with the big college football trophies.

"Well, yeah, sure Keno" continued Hammer, thinking *what a strange name, Keno,* "but what's your degree, your professional title?"—"I hold a Ph.D. in Humanities, so I guess you could say I am a Humanist," said Keno. "A *Humanist*, aha," said Hammer. *I'll be damned,* he thought again, and after one more glance at the CV, he finally looked up with a doubtful expression on his face.

"So," he continued, "Harvard... you know, we do have some graduates working here from Harvard Law School. Smart people, and good lawyers, but no one from the Humanities, no Humanist, so far... You are the first..."

Keno nodded his head and said nothing.

"How did you pass the entry test? I mean, who hired you?"

"Mr. George D. Lakefield."

The old hawk himself, thought Hammer. Going towards 80, and still kicking. Rumor had it that, while his brother Floyd, the other Lakefield in *Lakefield & Lakefield,* was the better lawyer, George possessed an infallible business sense, and with his ability to predict new trends, he was the driving force behind the firm's continued growth, including the opening of the Berlin office last year.

"And... how exactly did that happen?" Hammer continued asking. He was genuinely curious.

"Well, Mr. Lakefield and his team were looking for staff for the new Berlin office, and they came to campus and invited German speaking graduates for dinner, graduates from all departments, not only from law school. At dinner, I only spoke to Mr. Lakefield briefly, but he asked me to meet with him a couple of days later for a longer conversation, and then, I was invited to an assessment center in Manhattan. After that, I received an employment offer which I accepted. And now, I am here."

Keno thought back to the assessment center. It had started with an online personality test from *Hogan Assessment*—dozens of questions about performance, capacity for teamwork, leadership, creative motivation, and ability to execute. Some of the questions were about the same topic and contained similar statements but were worded a little differently to check the consistency of an applicant's answers. The aim was to prevent people from only checking off what they think is socially desirable, and with several dozens questions, pretending became almost impossible.

After the online test, there had been a physical meeting with all eight shortlisted applicants, five males and three females, most directly from graduate school with passed bar exams. Keno was one of two non-lawyers, the other one was a business graduate who also held a degree in computer science. They had gathered at the Hyatt conference room, and at the beginning, each applicant was asked to stand up and introduce him or herself. To determine the order of introductions, the external psychologist who was supporting the *Lakefield & Lakefield* senior partner in running the assessment center had told them to 'just go straight down the line', and Keno's neighbor tried making a joke at the end of his introduction by saying "Oh, and yeah, *I am straight.*" Some guys laughed, but neither the senior partner nor the psychologist frowned, and when it was Keno's turn, he ended his presentation by saying "..., and I am gay." There was a brief uncomfortable silence, before the psychologist said, "Hi Keno, great to have you!", and "Next, please."

When the introductions were over, the senior partner gave a little speech. He introduced *Lakefield & Lakefield* as a large multinational law firms covering all areas of law, with headquarters in New York, additional offices in Los Angeles, London, and now Berlin, and almost 100 lawyers working for them. He then spoke briefly about the two founders, George and Floyd, stressing that *Lakefield & Lakefield* combined legal excellence with a strong sense of social responsibility. While most clients were large business corporations, the founders also regularly engaged in low fee or even pro bono work for those in social need, and even for smaller businesses and start-ups. "Access to justice is important to us," the senior partner explained. "Also," he continued, "*innovation* has always been a key characteristic of our firm, both regarding our service portfolio and our company culture. The very fact that we are using assessment centers like this one as a recruitment method may attest to that, and so does the task I will give you now. We are asking you to work on a legal case and to present your results to the group. But you shall do so with a partner, instead of working on it alone, as is normally the case in law firms. The law is about community, and employees at *Lakefield & Lakefield* form a community as well, one which very much believes in the power of collaboration."

The applicants were then paired in groups of two, and each group was given a different legal case to work on. Keno was paired with Brenda from California and they were handed a case about an alleged AI patent infringement against which they had to defend their client, a global software company. While Brenda proposed to study the details of patent law and look for precedents, Keno suggested to *be innovative* and think about coopetition.

"Coope-what?" asked Brenda.

"Coopetition," repeated Keno, "a term combining the words *cooperation* and *competition*. Sometimes, it makes sense to partner with competitors to expand the market, and both sides can win. In our case, the plaintiff is a boutique firm, and our client is a large corporation. Instead of fighting over patent rights, we could design a joint solution in which they license out their patent to us and we run the software on our cloud servers. That will reduce total cost of ownership for the client, and both companies can use the client data to analyze market trends and improve their product offerings."

"That sounds great, Keno," said Brenda, "but we are a law firm and you are now turning the legal issue into a business issue..."

"Exactly!" exclaimed Keno.

Brenda looked confused. "But... We, well, sorry, at least *I* am a lawyer. And our task here is to assess the case from a legal perspective, not from a business perspective."

"Okay," Keno continued, "let us be business-minded legal practitioners and do both: analyze the case from a legal *and* a business perspective. You present your legal assessment, maybe outlining two or three scenarios of how the case could go if we indeed must go to court, and I will use your analysis to make a business argument for why and how we could avoid litigation altogether – and help our client to avoid costs and earn more money instead! Remember: Lakefield & Lakefield is all about innovation and collaboration," he added with a smile.

Brenda thought about it for a moment. Then she said: "Fine. Innovation and collaboration it is."

They each worked on their respective parts and finally created a joint PowerPoint presentation which they both delivered together. Keno's coopetition idea met with a lot of skepticism from the other applicants. But he also caught a glimpse of the senior partner's face, and from that he got the distinct impression that, in the senior partner's eyes, Brenda and he had done well.

At the end of the day, Brenda and Keno exchanged contact info, and a week later, it was official: *Lakefield & Lakefield* had made them both an offer to work in their Berlin office.

Hammer's voice brought Keno back to the presence.

"You grew up bi-lingually?" Hammer asked in German, with a strong American accent. He had learned some German at college, a time that felt like centuries ago, and had never used it again until he took over the Berlin office a year ago. He did not really need it here, either, because all his German clients spoke good English and seemed appreciative of each and any opportunity to show it. And if documents had to be created in German, it was done by his team. Luckily, *Lakefield & Lakefield* had not opened an office in Paris, because he did not speak a word of French, and in France you simply could not do any business without being fluent in French. Europe seemed altogether complicated to Hammer, so many small countries, and each one with its own language and culture. . .

"Yes," Keno replied in native German, "my mother is American, and my father is German. I was born in Berlin, and we lived here until I was ten, and then my mother took a job at an American corporation, and we moved to New York. After high school, I went to Boston and got my Ph.D."

"I see," said Hammer, switching back to English. "It says in your CV that, during your undergraduate studies, you did an internship at McKinsey, and later, as a graduate student, you founded a business consultancy with some fellow students. . . And your dissertation was about. . . the influence of French Post-Structuralism on contemporary German literature. . .?! Interesting. . . So, why do you want to work in a law firm, instead of becoming a writer, or a Humanities professor, or a business consultant?"

"I believe in justice. And it seems to me I can have a greater impact on the world working in the legal field, as opposed to working at the university or in a normal business."

"I get it," Hammer said smilingly. "You are in it for the greater good!"

"Yes," Keno replied, looking at him sternly. "Actually, I am."

"Great, great. . .", said Hammer, alternating his gaze between Keno and his CV. "Can you name three personal competencies that you developed during your studies and that qualify you for working in a law firm?"

"Of course," Keno replied confidently. "I can listen. I have learned to think abstractly, being able to look at any concrete issue from different angles and relating it to an underlying principle. And I have ideas about the future, about how things should be, as opposed to how they currently are."

"I see," Hammer said, "interesting..."

Oh, what the hell, he thought, *no use beating around the bush. Best to go straight at it and address the elephant in the room.*

"Forgive me for being blunt," he continued, "but I am not sure what to do with you... I mean, you are not a lawyer or a paralegal, so I cannot assign client cases to you. And with your background in... Humanities... and, frankly, your salary... It's all just a little strange, you know?!"

"Sure," Keno said, "I understand. What Mr. Lakefield and I had discussed before my coming here..."

O-kay, Hammer thought, *playing the hierarchy card, that part of the job he already knows...*

"... were two main tasks. For one, he thought I could go over all our text and documents, not only the Webpage and marketing material, but also client work before it is sent out and make sure that texts and documents are well written, in clear and understandable language, and not in Legalese."

"And how will you do that if you do not understand the legal issue itself?" Hammer asked.

"By understanding what the author wants to say and expressing it in the best possible way," Keno answered. "Mr. Lakefield said we have great lawyers and legal subject matter experts, but he also stated his belief that we need to bring our services closer to the business of the clients, show confidence through clear communication, instead of hiding behind complicated language. Addressing this should also include setting up some training courses on the general importance of transparency in the way we work."

"Well, most of our clients are lawyers themselves," Hammer responded, ignoring Keno's last statement about transparent work processes, "and they do understand our language... But alright, avoiding Legalese and bringing us closer to the client's business, I can get behind that. And what should be your second task?"

"Mr. Lakefield asked me to put together a service offering on sustainability," Keno said.

"A service offering on sustainability from a law firm?" Hammer looked puzzled. "So, what does that mean?"

"Well, that's for all of us to decide. The first step obviously is to think about ways to become more sustainable ourselves. That may include simple things like reducing paper printing and unnecessary air travel, but also aspects like lean operations, creating organizational structures that can adapt to changes and thus be more stable in the long run. Sustainability is also about physical and mental well-being, reducing absenteeism and turnover amongst employees by providing a healthy work climate, reducing stress and mental illnesses."

"I see," Hammer said. He wondered how much the old Lakefield had told Keno about the Berlin office. It was true that there had been quite some turmoil in the first year, with people complaining about the high workload and some new hires leaving again only after a couple of months. On the other hand, long work hours were normal in every law firm, and establishing a new office was especially hard, like with any start-up, and some churn was to be expected. *Anyway, best not to get defensive,* he thought to himself, *just go with the flow…*

"I would like to invite everyone in the office to participate in the development and implementation of our sustainability agenda," Keno continued. "Once we have achieved that, we can think about how to turn it into an offering for the clients."

"Sustainability, really, of all things?" Hammer mobilized his last argument. "Isn't that a bit too esoteric for us? I mean, we are a law firm, nobody expects us to be tree-hugging environmentalists…"

"Sustainability is not only about the environment," Keno repeated. "It includes economic and social aspects as well. It is an important political idea and has gained traction in many industries, like agriculture, manufacturing, and even in the financial industry. There is no reason why thinking more long term should not become an important principle in the legal industry as well. ESG has already become a criterion for how clients select their panels. And, by the way, Mr. Lakefield agrees with me. In fact, he said he would send you an e-mail and announce my arrival and the ideas we discussed…"

"Yes, yes, that's right… He actually did," Hammer confirmed. "O-kay then."

He got up, smiled at Keno, and walked around the desk to shake his hand.

"I was going to say *Welcome to Berlin*, but given you were born and partly grew up here, I probably should say *Welcome home!*"

"Thank you," Keno said, his slender boyish figure almost disappearing next to Hammer's massive body.

Hammer went back to his chair and looked at Keno as he walked out the door. *I'll be damned…*, he thought.

Outside Hammer's office, Keno ran into Brenda, and the two went to the kitchen for some coffee. They had already become friends and had explored the city together. Brenda, like Keno, had grown up bi-lingually with a German mother. She had never been to Berlin, though, and Keno had enjoyed showing her around, taking her to art galleries and dance clubs, noticing with a mixture of excitement and wonder how much the city had changed since his childhood.

"So, I have a question for you," Brenda said as they were sitting together. "At the assessment center…" She looked at him.

"Yes?" asked Keno.

"Why did you say that you are gay?"

"Because I am."

"Okay, *but why say it?* I mean, it does not matter for the job, so you could have just kept quiet about it."

"Well, it *does* matter for the job if I have colleagues who think homosexuality is something to make fun of. I want to help build a more diverse and tolerant society; I want to increase people's awareness of individual differences. Nothing will change if gays, lesbians, and other minorities keep hiding instead of standing up for who they are."

"But why are you working in a commercial law office, then?" Brenda interjected. "If you want to change society, you should become a politician, or a judge, or even a journalist, for that matter."

"I might actually do that at some point," Keno smiled at her. "But I think it can't hurt to gain some experience in the business world, first. Besides, social change can happen anytime and anywhere."

"Just do not get your hopes up too high when it comes to *this* place," Brenda said. "The Lakefield brothers might be very open and forward-thinking, despite their high age, but this is still a law firm, and many of the partners are traditionalists, like most lawyers. It seems like you just met with Hammer?"

"Indeed, I had the pleasure. . ."

"Well, then you know what I am talking about," Brenda added.

During the next weeks, Keno got to work. Together with the marketing department, he improved the texts on the company website and simplified and streamlined document templates. He took care only to address linguistic and formal aspects for now, in order not to step on anyone's toes, but he also made a list of subject matter and structural issues for later.

In parallel, he started on the sustainability topic by researching what other law firms were doing. He was looking for *easy wins*—ideas that could have a noticeable impact yet were easy to implement. He had meant what he had said to Hammer about involving everyone, but he also knew that he needed a conceptual framework from the start to convince people that participating in this project was worth their time.

For his internal colleagues, he set a formal project charter in Powerpoint, outlined possible activities and deliverables, and planned a town hall meeting as the official project kick-off. To promote his activities externally, he used social media channels, and especially his LinkedIn account which he had started already as a graduate student and which, by now, had several thousand followers. He announced his new position at *Lakefield & Lakefield*, and, without going into details, mentioned that he was going to lead the firm's new sustainability initiative.

While he was planning the town hall meeting on sustainability, it occurred to him that it might be good to encourage collaboration amongst the staff in general. He created another PowerPoint presentation in which he explained the principles of *Working Out Loud* (relationships, generosity, visible work, purposeful discovery, and growth mindset) and suggested one meeting every month for everyone interested.

The WOL principle of 'visible work', in turn, triggered yet another idea. He knew that Agile methodologies had outgrown their original domain of software development and were increasingly being deployed in all lines of business, including legal departments of large companies. Why not use SCRUM, Kanban, DevOps and the like in a law firm to make workloads more transparent and distribute them more evenly among the team?

He read a couple of Agile articles published by the *Liquid Legal Institute* and created a third PowerPoint presentation with an Agile blueprint for *Lakefield & Lakefield*, legitimizing his dealing with the topic by presenting it as part of his overarching sustainability initiative.

Finally, one morning, he drafted an e-mail with all his ideas in it and all documents attached, and sent it to Hammer, requesting that he as office head forward it to all employees, officially welcoming Keno to the team and asking them to support the new projects.

No sooner had he sent the draft mail to Hammer than he received a reply from him. "Please come to my office!"

When he got there, Hammer was sitting at his desk. "You said you were given two tasks by Mr. Lakefield," he started before Keno had even had a chance to sit down, "and in this e-mail, there are already four."

"Well, they are all connected…" Keno started explaining but Hammer interrupted him right away.

"Sure, everything is connected to everything," he said. "Look, Keno, I appreciate your enthusiasm, and I am as open to new ideas as the next guy, but let's take it one step at a time. You want to improve our marketing material and the legibility of our written client communication, great! You want the colleagues to collaborate more by offering these… *Working Out Loud* sessions… fine. It's voluntary, and if our lawyers see a value in it, they will come, it is up to them. And the sustainability initiative, okay, you have been asked to do that by Mr. Lakefield, so go ahead and let's see what you come up with and how people react."

Hammer made a pause.

"But this Agile thing, changing the way we work, setting up SCRUM meetings and Kanban boards, that really interferes with our business! You may not be aware of this, but this office is already profitable, after only one year of operations, and that is an achievement of which we are damned proud, of which *I* am proud. That shows me we are doing the right things in the right way. We are a law firm, we are selling legal services to our clients, and that must have priority over all internal stuff."

"Of course," Keno replied.

"Don't forget that it is us lawyers, the colleagues with client mandates and client cases, who are bringing in the money, and given that you do not do any direct client work, it is the money we earn that pays your salary."

"I know."

"Now," Hammer continued, "I asked around, and it seems none of the principals and senior associate sees a need to change the way we work, so I will delete that Agile passage from the mail which I am going to send on your behalf, alright?"

"Alright", Keno nodded, knowing that Hammer did not want to hear anything else from him.

"Okay. I guess that's all," Hammer said and began studying the papers on his desk.

"Thank you for sending the e-mail," Keno said before leaving the office, but Hammer did not look up again.

Brenda had been waiting for Keno outside.

"Rough meeting?" she asked.

Keno sighed. "As the saying goes: You can't win them all… He will delete the Agile passage from the e-mail, but at least he will send it."

"That's great!" said Brenda. "Frankly, more than I expected. It looks like you are going to shake things up around here. Good luck!"

The following days, Keno was extremely busy. After Hammer had sent the e-mail, many colleagues, lawyers, paralegals, and staff, started messaging him, introducing themselves and suggesting a plethora of ideas around sustainability.

Keno met with each person separately, integrated him or her into his project and refined his presentation for the town hall meeting and the official kick-off. He was very pleased with himself and the status of his activities. So far, his courage had paid off, and he felt the desire to be even more daring.

One evening, following an impulse, he went to his computer and started designing a flyer. "LGBT Meeting," it said in large letters. "This Friday 5 pm, in the kitchen." He printed it and put it on the kitchen black board, together with other flyers and post-it notes of people looking for an apartment or wanting to sell something.

The next morning, after he had just arrived in the office, Brenda came to his place.

"I saw your LGBT posting. Are you sure this is a good idea?" she asked.

"Well, we will find out, won't we?" Keno replied. "Maybe there are other gays or lesbians working in this office, and maybe they need a little help to come out of the closet. After all, we are in Berlin, and..."

He could not finish his sentence, because from the other side of the hall, he heard Hammer shouting his name.

"Keno, in my office. NOW!"

Keno excused himself to Brenda and walked over to Hammer's office. The door was open, and Hammer stood in the middle of the room with his back towards him.

"Close the door," he said when Keno arrived. Then he turned around, holding the flyer in his hand, and looking at Keno with a red face.

"What is this? You want to turn this office into a damn community center? We have clients coming here, senior executives from huge global corporations, what will they think when they see such controversial stuff hanging on the walls? Did it occur to you to ask my permission before putting this up? Or are you the new office head now?"

"Well, Sir, I can explain..."

"I don't want to hear any more explanations," Hammer interrupted him, increasingly losing his temper. "I have had it with you, your crazy ideas, your arrogance and your insubordination! *WHO DO YOU THINK YOU ARE?*" he yelled.

But before Keno could say anything, there was a knock at the door.

"WHAT IS IT?" Hammer barked.

His secretary slowly opened the door and put her head through.

"Mrs. Bündner called, from Glocor," she said timidly.

Glocor was Hammer's biggest client, and Mrs. Bündner was their General Counsel.

"She read something about our new sustainability initiative and requests a call back to talk about it. And..."

The secretary first looked at Keno, then at Hammer.

"... she explicitly asked for Keno to participate in the call as well... Should I set up a meeting with both of you?"

Roger Strathausen is a business consultant, author, and lecturer with expertise in legal operations, learning, and leadership whose clients are chiefly multinational companies. He took his Ph.D. from Stanford University in 1996 and was an employee at SAP and an executive at Accenture. In 2015, he published his book "Leading When You Are Not the Boss" (Apress, New York), and in 2017 and 2020, he co-edited two contributed volumes on the digital transformation of the legal industry, called "Liquid Legal" and "Towards a Common Legal Platform" (Springer, Heidelberg). He is a co-founder of the Liquid Legal Institute and serves as vice chair of the supervisory board. r.strathausen@liquid-legal-institute.org.

Printed by Printforce, United Kingdom